S0-DFI-149

THE COURT THAT
TAMED THE WEST

THE COURT THAT TAMED THE WEST

FROM THE GOLD RUSH TO THE TECH BOOM

Richard Cahan, Pia Hinckle,
and Jessica Royer Ocken

Foreword by Judge William Alsup

HEYDAY, BERKELEY, CALIFORNIA

Library of Congress Cataloging-in-Publication Data

Cahan, Richard.
 The court that tamed the West : from the gold rush to the tech boom / Richard Cahan, Pia Hinckle, and Jessica Royer Ocken, Foreword by Judge William Alsup.
     pages cm
 Includes index.
 ISBN 978-1-59714-246-5 (hardcover : alk. paper)
 1. United States. District Court (California : Northern District)--History. I. Hinckle, Pia, 1965- II. Ocken, Jessica Royer, 1974- III. Title.
 KF8755.C35C34 2013
 347.73›2209794--dc23
                     2013022066

Cover Design: The Book Designers
Interior Design/Typesetting: Nancy Austin Design
Printed in Canada by Friesens

Orders, inquiries, and correspondence should be addressed to:
        Heyday
        P.O. Box 9145, Berkeley, CA 94709
        (510) 549-3564, Fax (510) 549-1889
        www.heydaybooks.com

10 9 8 7 6 5 4 3 2 1

CONTENTS

FOREWORD

ACROSS THE LANDSCAPE of American institutions, the federal judiciary has consistently received the highest (by far) vote of confidence in public opinion polls. This has been true year after year since the Second World War. And this has been true despite the fact that federal judges serve for life—without any election whatsoever. In other words, while our federal judiciary is the least democratic of our three branches of government, it is the most trusted, a paradox for a great democracy like ours.

The trust our country places in federal judges is anchored, if you will allow an opinion, in the fact that judges rule on the merits; that is, we uphold the law and do so without regard to politics, race, gender, wealth, poverty, or any other invidious consideration. Campaign contributions and bags of money are never found in a federal courthouse. Principle prevails, popular or not. Jurors flow through our courthouses. They are part of it. They see the institution at work. Consequently, they trust it.

Yet apart from the Supreme Court, the role of our federal courts has received little attention from historians. This volume aims to correct that shortfall, at least as to one of the most colorful and productive of our nation's courts, the United States District Court for the Northern District of California.

From the beginning, every major turn in California's story has been a chapter in this federal court: freedom versus slavery, mining versus farming, valid land grants versus phony land grants, vigilantism versus order, labor versus capital, seamen versus vessels, discrimination versus freedom, internment versus freedom, the grand jury versus journalists unwilling to name sources, and marriage for some versus marriage for all, to name but a few. The story of our federal district court is the story of California.

Even California's trajectory into the Union was contentious. In rapid succession, Mexico lost California to the United States (1846–1848), gold was discovered (1848), the world poured in (1849), and California entered the Union as a free state as part of the Compromise of 1850, the price of admission being the Fugitive Slave Act. On May 19, 1851, in San Francisco, the United States District Court for the Northern District of California held its first session, the Honorable Ogden Hoffman Jr. presiding. He continued on for forty more years until his death in 1891, a longevity record that went unbroken until March 19, 2011, when our own Judge Samuel Conti broke the record (and continues to serve with vigor). Judge Hoffman served honorably through the Civil War and honorably still through a long and shameful era of virulent anti-Chinese prejudice in California. To his credit, he vindicated the immigration rights of thousands of Chinese in habeas corpus actions brought here in San Francisco, a record that presaged the later courage of federal district judges in the South who vindicated the rights of African Americans in the mid-twentieth century. The Northern District was off to a good start.

In these pages you will find some surprises. For example, while our own era has seen great strides in providing equal opportunities to women and people of color, a historic fact is that the first woman to serve as an assistant federal prosecutor in all of the United States was in San Francis-co—a century ago. She was Annette Abbott Adams and by 1918 she had risen to become our first female United States Attorney. She was in court at Seventh and Mission when two criminal defendants were shot and killed in the courtroom, on perhaps the most dramatic single day in our district court's history, April 23, 1917. Ms. Adams never quite made it to the federal bench and went on to be the presiding judge of California Court of Appeals, Division Three.

Another surprise: Did you know that Alfonso Zirpoli, one of the modern luminaries of our bench, was the young assistant US Attorney in 1942 who prosecuted Fred Korematsu and sent him into internment? Decades later, our own Marilyn Hall Patel was the one to undo this injustice. And, to take one last example, how wonderful it is to learn that our own district court was once in direct communication by telegraph with President Abraham Lincoln regarding the legal scope of his amnesty proclamation, an issue that arose in a piracy case pending before Judge Hoffman during the Civil War.

Imperfect moments, even tawdry ones, also come through in these pages, but, overwhelmingly, we should come away from this work with pride in and feeling for those judges and lawyers who pioneered the way. With skill, they rose to meet challenges and controversies of enormous consequence. Case by case, year by year, they laid the foundation for the trust and confidence placed by our public in the federal judiciary.

The Historical Society of the United States District Court for the Northern District of California commissioned Richard Cahan, Pia Hinckle, and Jessica Royer Ocken to prepare this excellent volume. Fortune smiled yet again when Heyday in Berkeley undertook to publish it. Specializing in California history, Heyday and its founder Malcolm Margolin are the gold standard in fine books and quality publishing. If there is anything unsatisfying in this work, it is only this: while the story has a beginning, it has no end. The reader will yearn for more. In another century, let the society produce a sequel.

William Alsup
United States District Judge
March 2013

CHAPTER 1

THE ADMIRALTY COURT

ON THE MORNING of May 19, 1851, Ogden Hoffman Jr. prepared to enter his courtroom for the first time. He was just twenty-nine years old and had been chosen as the first judge of the new United States District Court for the District of California. San Francisco had been a disappointment to him in terms of climate (damp, windy, and sandy, not to mention the frequent earthquakes and fires), accommodations (rustic at best), social interaction (dangerous and uncultured), and commerce (good pay, but outrageous prices). The commercial district had recently been destroyed by fire again, the third time since his arrival just a year before. The smell of smoke permeated the windows of the building that housed the offices of the city's Board of Assistant Aldermen, which had graciously allowed the court to use its rooms at the corner of Kearny and Clay Streets until a permanent location could be secured. If it wasn't for his judicial appointment by President Millard Fillmore, Hoffman would already be back in civilization in New York. Yet here he was, about to bring the unifying presence of the federal legal system to the lawless frontier state of California. He no doubt summoned the dignity of his forefathers to lend gravitas to the makeshift courtroom as he turned the doorknob and entered.

After United States Marshal David F. Douglass announced the arrival of The Honorable Judge Ogden Hoffman Jr., Hoffman presented his commission from Congress to clerk of court John A. Monroe, who read the commission and handed it to deputy clerk George Payne Johnson for filing. Hoffman's first order of business was to appoint Calhoun

FIG. 1-1 (PREVIOUS PAGE)
Following the discovery of gold in 1848, crewmen deserted their ships to join the gold seekers. Soon the waters of Yerba Buena Cove (San Francisco) became a repository for abandoned ships, as this 1850 lithograph illustrates. Courtesy of the California Historical Society Collections at the University of Southern California.

Benham, S. Chetwood, and Gregory Yale to draft procedural rules of common law; he then appointed Matthew Hall McAllister, Delos Lake, and J. McHenry to draft rules on equity. Hoffman would also rely heavily on his friend William Barbar, who had come with him from New York, to help him organize the court for business.

The first case Hoffman heard was in admiralty, the docket of the court that governed maritime disputes. The first admiralty case, *David Dowl v. Schooner JB Lipencott*, was brought over wages owed to the ship's crew. Sailors were considered wards of the admiralty court at that time, and the court was their only hope for protection from abuse, be it physical or financial. After a five-month round-trip voyage to South America, the *JB Lipencott* had returned to San Francisco in December 1850. The crew was discharged just before Christmas, but had not been paid. By the time of the hearing, the ship's captain had left California, but the *JB Lipencott* had remained anchored in San Francisco Bay. David Dowl and a half-dozen shipmates had sued the ship in rem—"against the thing"—meaning the admiralty court had the unique ability to seize and sue a ship instead of a person in order to recover damages. Hoffman ruled in favor of the sailors, and the ship was sold to pay off its debts. Dowl received $284.15.

Ships were key to the rise of both the new city and the state's economy. Until the completion of the transcontinental railroad in 1869, the surest and fastest way to get to California was by sea. San Francisco Bay, the most important harbor on the West Coast and the gateway to the goldfields, would unlock the door to development. Gold had been discovered north of San Francisco in the fall of 1848, and when President James K. Polk confirmed the "extraordinary character" of the riches, the rush was on. By the end of January 1849, the *New-York Tribune* reported that New York City was scarcely recognizable: every storefront displayed mining goods, the boarding houses and hotels were packed with people waiting for a spot on any westbound ship, newspapers were crammed with ads for sailing ships, advice on routes and necessities, and news from the hitherto little-known land of California. The state had been seized by US forces at the outbreak of the Mexican-American War in 1846, then independently organized itself as a state in 1849, skipped territorial status, and applied for admission to the Union as a free state—that is, one that did not allow slavery. After much debate, California was admitted to the Union on September 9, 1850. It took more than a month for the news to reach San Francisco.

Even before the gold rush, Congress had begun subsidizing steamships to carry mail from the east to the west coast, prompting the founding of the pioneer steamship companies that would bring rushers from the Atlantic states to California via Panama and Nicaragua. With shipping serving such a critical role in the region, admiralty would be the district court's busiest docket during Hoffman's first decade as a federal trial judge. *Dowl* would be only the first maritime case he heard. Two hundred cases were filed in 1851 alone. As Hoffman listened to the evidence in the *Dowl* case, just a few blocks away six hundred abandoned and rotting ships lay anchored in Yerba Buena Cove. Passengers were not the only newcomers heading to the mines; as soon as their anchors caught in the dark mud of San Francisco Bay, crews and captains abandoned their ships and hustled off to the mines to find El Dorado or make new lives in the mushrooming city.

California's distance from Washington, DC, in those early years—a four- to eight-month journey from the Atlantic coast—underscored the importance of the district court as the lone representative of the federal government in the new state. "The isolation of California enhanced Hoffman's understanding of the unique role his court played and the need to come up with novel solutions," wrote Christian G. Fritz in *Federal Justice in California*, his 1991 book on Hoffman's court. "The resolution of his early cases, dealing with shipboard brutality and the ill treatment of passengers, required both innovation and a strong assertion of national judicial authority." Hoffman knew that his court was the only hope for justice for most of its litigants and he took the charge very seriously.

Shipboard conditions for travelers were no abstraction for Hoffman. Like thousands of others, he had traveled from New York on a steamship via the Isthmus of Panama. Hoffman, like many other young lawyers from good New York families, caught the California fever. He had spent two years traveling in Europe after passing the bar in 1845 and was curious to see what Manifest Destiny—the dream of a continental United States from sea to shining sea—looked like. His knowledge of history must have prompted him to recognize this singular moment in US history. According to Fritz, Hoffman may have also wanted to escape the shame of a spurned romance in New York. Whatever the reason, Hoffman sailed from New York harbor in January 1850, bound for Panama. He crossed the sixty-mile isthmus by canoe and donkey through disease-ridden swamps.

On May 7, 1850, Hoffman sailed into San Francisco Bay with 230 other passengers aboard the steamship *Carolina*. After all the California hype, San Francisco must have been a dismal sight: beyond the forest of ship masts in Yerba Buena Cove there was nothing but bare hills and windswept sand dunes. The city was nearly deserted of men, who were off to the goldfields. Most of the few women were prostitutes. Just three days prior to his arrival, the city's second great fire (there would be six in all during the early years) had destroyed three important blocks of the small commercial district near the courthouse. But already a frenzied rebuilding effort had begun amid the smoldering ruins. San Francisco's citizens had just elected their first mayor since statehood, Colonel John W. Geary, and passed the first city charter, but already newspapers were accusing city officials of corruption. Crime was rampant.

Hoffman undoubtedly found rooms with friends or at one of the few reputable boarding houses. He appears in the San Francisco City Directory of 1850 as "Hoffman, Ogden Jr., lawyer, Laffan's building." Laffan's Building was located in the heart of the commercial district on the plaza of Portsmouth Square. The young lawyer was unaccustomed to the aggression and frenetic pace with which frontier business was transacted. He wrote to a friend that the press both encouraged immigration and practiced deception "to beget the most exaggerated ideas of the chances and fortunes that await the immigrant." Business in San Francisco, Hoffman wrote, was "more or less gambling," a lottery where few would win a much-advertised prize. Barely a month after his arrival, a third and larger fire swept the downtown area, causing an estimated $5 million in damages. Once again, the city rebuilt itself quickly, replacing many cheap wooden frame and canvas buildings with grander brick and iron ones.

During his first year in San Francisco, Hoffman mostly transacted maritime business for Captain Warren Delano of New York, whose son Franklin Hughes (Franklin D. Roosevelt's great-uncle) was Hoffman's childhood friend. But Hoffman needed a steady source of income. His father's political connections to the Whig Party (the precursor to the Republican Party) soon got him on the list of candidates for appointment as district judge for the new state of California. The search for a judge had begun in 1848 and intensified after California's admission to the Union. Hoffman was hardly the first choice for the job: six candidates had already turned down the commission or been rejected by the Senate.

When Congress created California's federal court system in 1850 and divided it into two districts, the annual salary offered for the Northern District judgeship was $3,500, with only $2,800 offered for the Southern District, based on the expectation of a heavier caseload in the north. In mid-1850, the cost for a modest daily board in San Francisco was about $10, so whoever took the job would barely make expenses. In contrast, California state supreme court justices were paid $10,000 a year, and some attorneys with private law firms in San Francisco made as much as $100,000 a year.

Democratic president Polk, whose administration had provoked the Mexican-American War and delivered California and the West to the Union, left office in March 1849. Whig president Zachary Taylor shepherded California's admission as a free state, but his sudden death in 1850 precluded him from appointing its judges. After Vice President Millard Fillmore succeeded to the presidency, he and Secretary of State Daniel Webster sifted through more than one hundred applications and recommendations for the Northern District judgeship. As the court's first priority would be sorting out the ownership of land grants from the Spanish and Mexican periods, they sought lawyers who were experts in commercial and property law and fluent in Spanish, and who were honest enough not to be tempted to capitalize personally on the land grant decisions they would make. Both men worried that none of the most able lawyers would consider the California appointment at such a paltry salary, and yet they needed to work fast: California was growing quickly and had become the hottest property in the Union.

On the same day that Congress admitted California, Fillmore submitted the nominations of Judah P. Benjamin, a Whig from New Orleans, for the Northern District and John Plummer Healy, Webster's Boston law partner, for the Southern District. Both men declined the positions because of the low pay and great distance. Fillmore then nominated Boston lawyer Charles B. Goodrich to the Northern District; he also turned down the offer due to the meager pay. Finally, the search was narrowed to "lawyers in California who are without families." California's first senator, Southern-leaning Democrat William M. Gwin, nominated twenty-seven-year-old James McHall Jones for the Southern District. The New Orleans native was single, fluent in Spanish and French, and had participated with Gwin in California's constitutional convention in 1849. Jones was approved by the Senate, but he suffered from chronic tuberculosis and died soon after taking the bench.

As for the northern appointment, Fillmore suddenly found himself being lobbied fiercely by the powerful William H. Aspinwell of New York. Aspinwell, president of the Pacific Mail Steamship Company, had lined up backing from the legal and business communities of New York City behind his candidate, Ogden Hoffman Jr., the son of his friend and noted lawyer J. Ogden Hoffman. Fillmore resisted and nominated John Currey, a San Francisco attorney who had support in Washington, DC, where he had clerked in New York congressman William Nelson's office. But Gwin and other Democrats didn't like Currey; the Senate rejected his nomination in early 1851. Fillmore worked to find another candidate with less political baggage. He narrowed down his choices to Hoffman, Levi Parsons, John Satterlee, and Oliver S. Halstead. Gwin and others supported Halstead, but in the end Webster convinced him to not oppose Hoffman's appointment. Hoffman, who was having a rough time in the scabrous bar of gold rush San Francisco, gratefully accepted the nomination. Hoffman "regarded the appointment not so much as recognition of his own ability [but] as a graceful compliment to his father," according to Oscar T. Shuck's 1889 history *The Bench and Bar in California*. A day after Currey's rejection, the Senate confirmed Hoffman as Northern District judge. On May 15, 1851, he took the oath of office, and four days later he opened his court.

California's Federal Courts

The federal judiciary was first created by Congress in 1789 with thirteen districts, one for each state that had ratified the Constitution. Until the end of the nineteenth century, district court judges handled admiralty cases but also served on the circuit courts that met occasionally in their district. Until 1912, circuit courts were the trial courts for most federal criminal cases, for suits between residents of different states, and for civil suits initiated by the United States. The circuit courts were also the appeals courts for all but the smallest admiralty and civil suits that originated in the district courts.

After the death of Judge Jones in 1851, Hoffman became sitting judge for the Southern District as well. California's extreme distance from Washington, DC, meant that the customary circuit court where a Supreme Court justice would visit and hear cases was impractical. Instead, California's district courts were granted the same civil jurisdiction as the circuit courts, except in appeals, which went directly to the

Supreme Court. In 1853, criminal jurisdiction was added to the Northern District's special powers.

Judge Hoffman was overwhelmed carrying out the duties for both the Northern and Southern District courts in addition to handling circuit court duties, so in 1855 Congress created a special circuit court. "The creation of the United States Circuit Court for the Districts of California was part of a two-decade effort by the United States to digest California's statehood judicially," wrote John D. Gordan III in "Authorized By No Law," his 1987 article exploring the role of the special circuit court during the 1856 San Francisco vigilance movement. Matthew Hall McAllister, a well-known lawyer and former mayor of Savannah, Georgia, who had followed his sons to San Francisco in 1850, was appointed as the lone California circuit court judge. When he resigned in 1863, Congress abolished this court and its judgeship and placed California and Oregon in the short-lived Tenth Circuit.

In 1866, the federal judiciary was reorganized into nine circuits, with California assigned to the Ninth Circuit. At this time, the state's two district courts were collapsed into one, with Hoffman now officially covering the entire state. It would be another twenty years before the state would be permanently divided into two districts, with a separate judge in the Southern District, and not until 1907 that the busy Northern District would get a second judgeship.

In 1869, Congress created a judgeship for each of the nine circuits. Lorenzo Sawyer was appointed in 1870 to the US Circuit Court for the Ninth Circuit, based in San Francisco. The circuit court was presided over by Sawyer, Hoffman, and a Supreme Court associate justice, or some combination of two of them. Sawyer and Hoffman often found themselves on the wrong side of Justice Stephen J. Field, who pointedly used his judicial superiority to overrule their decisions when they ran counter to his political aspirations. The appellate jurisdiction of the circuit courts ended in 1891 with the creation of the US Court of Appeals for the Ninth Circuit, to which Judge Sawyer was re-assigned.

A Gentleman and a Scholar

Hoffman was considered an odd choice for the federal judgeship by many California politicians. He was young, had only been in the state a year, and had little trial court experience. But he had strong backing from New York Whigs, came from a fine legal family (his father had

FIG. 1-2

This portrait of district court judge Ogden Hoffman Jr. (1822–1891) by David Neal, a Massachusetts-born artist active in California in the late nineteenth century, was presented to the district courthouse in San Francisco in 1893 and still graces its walls. General W. H. L. Barnes, a San Francisco lawyer who presided over the painting's unveiling, praised Hoffman's intellect and friendship: "That mysterious and broad growth of the mind...which we call culture—was the marked characteristic of the man....No advocate ever stood before him without comprehending that not only...his cause but also himself was being measured....I remember his annihilation of an advocate who justified questionable conduct by saying, 'I owed them nothing.' 'That may be,' replied Judge Hoffman, 'but it occurs to me that you owed something to yourself!'" Reproduced courtesy of the United States District Court for the Northern District of California.

been district attorney in New York City and served in Congress), had an excellent reputation, no family to support, and was willing to take the $3,500 annual salary.

A man who forever longed for higher office and New York, Hoffman would spend the rest of his life on the federal district court bench in San Francisco. His forty-year solo tenure, lasting until his death in August 1891, made him one of the longest-serving district court judges in US history. He frequently made unpopular rulings, opposing vigilantism and defending the constitutional rights of Chinese immigrants. Possibly unique among nineteenth-century Western judges, Hoffman was always careful to avoid the appearance of a conflict of interest in his court. He is not known to have invested in any of the popular mining and real estate speculations that made the fortune of many a California lawyer, and he had none of the usual material entanglements of powerful men in the new wide-open economy. Hoffman was a touchy person and was considered a bit of a dandy. He took himself quite seriously, could be prickly and sensitive, and maintained the dignity and distance of his judgeship, even among friends. Even so, he was respected and liked as much for his loyal friendship and intelligence as his heightened sense of personal and national honor.

Hoffman was born in Goshen, New York, in 1822. He was from a prominent but financially troubled family that was active in New York society. He was raised as a true gentleman of the era, and took great pride in his family history. His grandfather had been a well-known trial lawyer in New York City who also served as recorder and a superior court judge. In addition to his other accomplishments, his father served in the New York state assembly. Both men made fortunes and lost them, living well beyond their means all the while. Hoffman's mother died when he was a teenager, leaving Ogden, a sickly child, and his older brother Charles mainly in the care of their aunt and uncle. Og, as he was known, graduated from Columbia College in 1840 and then went to Harvard Law School. After receiving his degree in 1842, he clerked in the law offices of his father's friends in upstate New York and New York City. After passing the bar in 1845, young Hoffman took a long European tour, as was popular for a gentleman of means of his era. His father worried he wasn't serious about his career. But then Ogden went west.

In San Francisco, it appears that Hoffman continued the family tradition of living beyond his means. According to biographer Fritz, Hoffman's personal letters were full of references to shortness of funds and his frustration with his low pay and crushing caseload. Throughout his tenure, Hoffman regularly petitioned Congress for raises, finally getting his top annual salary of $6,000 in 1860. He never married, and lived the life of a bachelor gentleman. Until the early 1860s, he rented rooms near the courthouse. He was an early member of the Pacific Club and moved to its residence rooms permanently in 1868. When the club merged in 1881 with the Union Club to become the Pacific-Union Club, Hoffman moved and lived there until his death in 1891. Shortly before his death, Judge Hoffman told his friend W. H. L. Barnes that his only regret was that "he had not known the love of a good wife and had not been blessed with children who could call him father." After Hoffman's death, Barnes remarked on his years of sacrifice for the bench: "What a life of endless toil his was!...Thinking only of the right, caring for nothing but except to do justice, he lived like a philosopher and died without a dollar and without a debt."

Hoffman shied from public oration but was known as an ornate and prolific speaker both in and out of court. In *The Bench and Bar in California,* Shuck noted:

> Judge Hoffman's facility of speech has been made the excuse for any amount of wit and satire. The late Edmund Randolph regretted that the Judge did not stutter.... The Judge was once visited in his rooms by two gentlemen from the East. He was talking at the time with Richard E. Brewster. The visitors were cordially received by the Judge, who proceeded to "hold, occupy and possess" them. A half hour passed, in which they had no opportunity to open their mouths. Rising to withdraw, the judge talked them out the door, along the hall, and down the stairway. Returning to his parlor, Brewster asked, "Judge, did you get rid of those fellows?"

Poking Fun at the Judge

"The Coast Rangers," a satirical series in *Harper's Magazine* in 1861 by J. Ross Browne, recounts a hunting trip by a group of prominent San Franciscans, including Judge Hoffman. In it, Hoffman and friend Tom Fry are riding mules along a trail when Fry is thrown and lands in quicksand.

> Here Mr. Tom Fry cried out that he was about to disappear; he was already down to the pit of his stomach, and there was no hope for him whatever. He begged the Judge to inform the members of the Association of his unhappy fate, and to request them to dig for his body and give it a decent burial if they could find it.
>
> To which the Judge responded as follows: "I will certainly do so, my dear fellow, and if I can serve you in any other way, mention it while you have yet an opportunity. I don't think you will go entirely under for about ten minutes. It is even possible, calculating the rate at which you have heretofore disappeared, that you may keep your head above ground for fifteen minutes. I remember reading of a man who saved his life, under similar circumstances, by stretching himself out on the top of the sand on his belly, and working his way over the surface to the solid ground; but I

fear you are too far gone for that. It might have been done in the beginning, if one only could think of it. I have no doubt the young Lord of Ravenswood might have saved himself in the same way. You remember he was lost in the quick-sand after witnessing the insanity of his betrothed, the beautiful Lucy Ashton, the Bride of Lammermoor, who 'sat gibbering in the corner.' He rode away on his horse, and was seen to disappear in the quick-sands. There is nothing in the whole range of English literature more powerfully wrought than the closing scenes of this splendid romance; the forced marriage, the insanity of the bride, and the sad fate of the young and noble Lord of Ravenswood. I never see or hear of quick-sands that I do not think of this unfortunate youth, as he vanished from the earth almost at the threshold of life. The picture is even more impressive and affecting than the closing scene of Kenilworth, in which the unhappy heroine is suffered to fall into a deep pit, where the last that is seen of her is the fluttering of her white robes."

Here the unhappy Tom protested, with streaming eyes, that His Honor would soon see the last of him also, for he was now buried to the armpits, and was working down deeper and deeper every moment. "A very remarkable fact," said the Judge, "suggestive of the singular difference which exists between animals with warm binocular hearts and the inferior orders of creation occupying the watery elements. Even the pearl-fishers on the coast of Lower California, who are esteemed to be extraordinarily expert swimmers, and who practice diving from early childhood, cannot hold their breath under the water more than two minutes; and it is scarcely possible that the most experienced of them could exist under a deep bed of quick-sand for a much greater length of time. Of all animals with warm blood the whale possesses, perhaps, the most remarkable capacity in this respect. I have been informed that they frequently remain under the water an hour before the supply of air which they take down with them is exhausted. Indeed, it is a mooted point in the science of Cetology, whether the whale really belongs to the order of animals, or whether it is not, properly speaking, a fish. We have the authority of Scripture for it that it was a great fish that swallowed Jonah, though no mention is made of the generally received fact that the fish was a whale. Pliny refers to big fishes that were bred in the Indian Ocean, among which he mentions whales; but, on the other hand, Linntcus, in his System of Nature, undertakes to show that whales should be separated from the fish tribe on account of their warm binocular hearts, their lungs, their movable eyelids, their hollow ears, and mammiferous breasts. Hunter asserts that the blood of this order is similar to that of quadrupeds, but has an idea that the red globules are in larger proportions. Baron Cuvier describes the whale as a mammiferous animal without hind feet; and the quaint old Fuller speaks of these great leviathans as mighty animals that swim in a sea of water and have a sea of oil swimming in them. Even now, my dear fellow, we can see them sporting in the distance. These must be the California or gray whales, so abundant on this coast, and for the capture of which shore fisheries have been established at San Diego, Monterey, and Crescent City. Observe how lazily they roll about, puffing up their jets of mist as if they were enjoying the best Havana cigars. It is refreshing to see the mighty inhabitants of the deep thus disport themselves in the sheen of the blue waves, warming their glistening backs and shaking their black flippers in the sunbeams. What great, jolly fellows they are—big schoolboys of the brine at their holiday sport! It almost tempts one to turn whale-fisher, and go out and take a buffet with them—such a scene!"

Here Tom declared, in piteous tones, that he would turn whale-fisher, pearl-diver, or anything else, if it were only within the bounds of possibility to save him; but he feared he was utterly gone. At this critical juncture a voice was heard on the side of the mountain—the voice of Captain Toby, who came dashing down the cliffs on his famous Broncho, whirling his lasso round his head and singing, with stentorian lungs....By the united efforts of the Broncho, the Captain, and the Judge, Mr. Fry was safely landed on dry ground.

It was said Judge Hoffman never forgave the writer for poking fun at him. However, though he took himself quite seriously, he was not entirely without a sense of humor. One day an assistant district attorney asked the court for a venire for thirty jurors but pronounced the word *veneer*. Judge Hoffman, an able and precise linguist, retorted that he could have the veneer of black walnut or rosewood, according to his taste.

And the World Rushed In

Before the completion of the transcontinental railroad, there were two ways to get to California from the Atlantic coast: more than three thousand miles through hostile Indian country and treacherous mountain passes by wagon across the plains, or more than thirteen thousand miles by ship. Both took months and were fraught with danger and uncertainty, but ships offered greater speed and fewer physical hardships. Most

FIG. 1-3
Mail and passengers on steamship lines en route to California made the treacherous trek across the Isthmus of Panama via the Chagres River and over old Spanish trails at great risk of danger and disease. Courtesy of The Bancroft Library, University of California, Berkeley.

of the gold rush immigrants who came in 1848 and 1849 sailed from Atlantic ports all the way down the coast of South America, around Cape Horn, and back up through the Pacific Ocean, a voyage lasting three to six months. By 1850, many travelers cut that time in half by sailing to Panama and crossing the fifty-mile-wide isthmus by foot. The drawback of this fifty-two-hundred-mile route was the risk of infection and death from tropical diseases; many travelers became ill and died. But the gold rush years were all about speed, and the Panama route was the most popular in spite of the risk. By mid-1851, three out of four travelers to California went through either Panama or Nicaragua.

Ships from New York first landed at Chagres, a decrepit village with the ruins of a Spanish fort on the river of the same name. The crossing from Chagres to Panama City took about five days: three along the river in small steamers or dugout canoes poled by native guides, and the last two beating through the jungle on mule or by foot. Travelers faced unbearable heat, torrential rains, ravenous mosquitoes and other insects, venomous reptiles, and the constant dread of malaria, dysentery, cholera, and Panama, or yellow, fever. During an 1852 crossing, English travel writer Frank Marryat contracted yellow fever. In Panama City, he wrote, "I was placed in bed; the other male passengers—all of whom had arrived in good health—made themselves comfortable, and thought no more of the...rain or mud. In less than ten days they all died of yellow fever but one, and I alone of those attacked recovered."

Not until 1855, when the Panama Railway was built across the isthmus, could a person travel from steamer to steamer in relative comfort and in about three hours. The forty-seven miles of track cost a record $8 million as well as the lives of thousands of men who built it. The precursor to the Panama Canal, the railroad increased the speed and reduced the cost of the California voyage, adding to the route's popularity. Competition from the Nicaragua Railroad later brought prices down even further. All this meant that the age of passenger travel to California around Cape Horn was over—steam had replaced sail as the primary mode of marine transportation. The Panama route and canal were so crucial to joining California's economy with that of the East Coast that San Francisco celebrated its rebirth after the 1906 earthquake and fire with a world's fair dedicated to the Panama Canal—the 1915 Panama-Pacific Exposition.

Although the steamship companies naturally downplayed the health hazards of the Panama route, the dangers were significant. Initially there were not enough ships on the Pacific side to keep up with demand, so thousands of people waited weeks rather than days in Panama City for the second leg of their voyage to California. This bottleneck in a primitive setting increased the risk of infection. The steamers were far more crowded than sailing vessels, carrying up to eight hundred passengers, thus increasing the spread of disease.

"No sooner on board, my wife, worn out by fatigue and anxiety, was attacked by a violent fever. There were two young doctors on board, but both were attacked shortly after we started. Then the epidemic...broke out among the passengers, who—crowded in the hold as thick as blacks in a slaver—gave way to fear, and could not be moved from the lower deck, and so lay weltering in their filth," Marryat wrote of his 1852 voyage from Panama to San Francisco. "From the scuttlehole of our small cabin we could hear the splash of the bodies as they were tossed overboard with very little ceremony."

Passengers were understandably grateful to ship surgeons and other doctors on board. Notices of gratitude were often printed in San Francisco newspapers shortly after a ship's arrival. Judge Hoffman signed on

Yellow Eyes

You are going to have the fever,
        Yellow eyes!
In about ten days from now
Iron bands will clamp your brow;
Your tongue resemble curdled cream,
A rusty streak the centre seam;
Your mouth will taste of untold things
With claws and horns and fins and wings;
Your head will weigh a ton or more,
And forty gales within it roar!

In about ten days from now
You will feebly wonder how
All your bones can break in twain
And so quickly knit again!
You will feel a score of Jaels
In your temples driving nails!
You will wonder if you're shot
Through the liver-case, or what!
You will wonder if such heat
Isn't Hades—and repeat!
Then you'll sweat until, at length,
You—won't—have—a—kitten's—strength!

In about ten days from now
Make to health a parting bow;
For you're going to have the fever,
        Yellow eyes!

—James Stanley Gilbert, *Panama Patchwork: Poems* (1905)

Gilbert, born in Connecticut in 1855, moved to Panama in 1886, and worked for both the railroad and steamship companies. He was one of the few Americans who wrote about real life on the isthmus. He died of malaria in Colon (Aspinwell), Panama, in 1906.

to one such notice published in the May 9, 1850, edition of the *Alta California*, two days after his initial arrival in San Francisco aboard the *Carolina*. Some passengers were reportedly stricken with cholera, and an epidemic broke out in San Francisco shortly after the *Carolina*'s arrival.

Due to its popularity, the Panama route was the basis for many early lawsuits filed by passengers in the district court. One of the more tragic cases that Judge Hoffman heard in the first year of the court was Admiralty Case No. 38, *George P. Newell v. Pacific Mail Steam Ship Columbus*. Newell, his pregnant wife, Emily, and their two young daughters had traveled from New York to California in the spring of 1851. In Panama City, Newell paid $750 for staterooms that were supposed to be decent and comfortable. Instead, he told the court, they were dismal, infernally hot and noisy, and in a busy passageway right next to the ship's boiler room. Newell charged that the sweltering conditions of the room aggravated the illnesses his wife and twenty-month-old child contracted during

VIEW OF CULEBRA OR THE SUMMIT,
THE TERMINUS OF THE PANAMA RAIL ROAD IN DEC. 1854.

FIG. 1-4
A view of Culebra, or the Summit—the terminus of the Panama Railroad—in December 1854. Work on the railroad began in 1850 to improve the speed, efficiency, and safety of moving a burgeoning number of people, supplies, and mail from the eastern United States to California. Courtesy of The Bancroft Library, University of California, Berkeley.

the voyage, contributing to their deaths. He sued in rem for breach of contract and damages.

The *Columbus* had left Panama on May 1, 1851. "The [Newell] child died…on the morning of the ninth day of the voyage," said ship's surgeon James Resing in his deposition. "During the first attack (convulsions) of the infant, its mother was its nurse and attendant; upon its second attack she was herself ill and unable to attend upon her child. On the morning of the death of the child, the mother came down from the hurricane deck to the cabin to see the child and was present at its death. On the following day, we arrived in Acapulco where the child was buried. The mother, though feeble, was about the ship on the day of the child's death engaged in directing the preparations for the funeral, and on the day of the burial she was present at the service for the funeral on the deck."

About two days out from Acapulco, Dr. Resing again examined Mrs. Newell, who had suffered a renewed attack of fever. "She seemed to be much depressed about the death of her child, and despondent as to her own condition." A couple of days later, Mrs. Newell, only four months pregnant, went into labor and miscarried. Her bedclothes were soaked with blood. She died later that day.

The lawyer for the Pacific Mail Steam Ship Company asked Dr. Resing if, in his medical opinion, it was prudent for a person in the third or fourth month of pregnancy to undertake the voyage from New York to San Francisco via Panama. "Not prudent," responded Dr. Resing, "unless she were not liable to seasickness." Resing added that everything possible was done for the woman and child and that he had declined to submit a bill to Mr. Newell. The steamship lawyers argued that the district court did not have in rem jurisdiction because of the company's federal contract to deliver the mail. Hoffman disagreed and accepted the case. Ultimately, he ruled that the cabin conditions were not the cause of Mrs. Newell's death, although they might have aggravated her illness. He awarded Mr. Newell $400 plus legal costs.

Judge Hoffman took very seriously his charge to balance the interests of the shipping companies with the rights of the passengers to a safe voyage. He felt that passengers aboard a ship had entered into a special contract with the captain, crew, and owners that carried with it certain minimal expectations of safety and comfort. He did not hesitate to rule against the influential Pacific Mail Steamship Company, which was owned by William H. Aspinwall, the family friend who had supported Hoffman's judicial appointment.

Hoffman's court did not tolerate excuses given by companies for conditions that "forced 252 steerage passengers to share berths designed for 82, forced passengers to sleep on open decks or in passageways, forced 290 people to share two wash basins, or failure to provide minimal privacy and segregation of male and female passengers," wrote Norman J. Ronneberg Jr. in his 1984 article "Admiralty Law in Action." Hoffman's rulings in favor of passengers eventually compelled the shipping companies to check their greed and provide minimum standards.

In a radical departure from common law practice of the times, Hoffman allowed passengers to sue in rem rather than in personam—that is, to sue the ship rather than its captain or its owners—and allowed groups of passengers from the same ship to sue together as a sort of class action suit. Hoffman "allowed passengers to sue the ship itself for damages that were normally limited to in personam suits," wrote Fritz. "Hoffman provided an effective means of redressing passenger grievances. Even more important, such suits had the effect of forcing ship owners to settle."

"Under the circumstances of this state it is of particular importance that passengers should have a prompt and effective remedy for breaches of contract," Hoffman wrote in one of his early opinions, defending his allowance of in rem suits. "The length of the voyage, the eagerness to reach California and the large profits derived from the transportation of passengers are well calculated to beget recklessness as to the mode of fulfilling passenger contracts; and were the passenger left to seek his remedy against an owner at the distance of thousands of miles or against a master without pecuniary responsibility it might open the door to grave if not dangerous abuses."

Eugene Dupre, a passenger aboard the steamship *North America*, sued in rem in 1852 for serious injuries he received when he fell through a hatchway left open in an unlit part of the ship. Hoffman awarded him $3,000 for pain and suffering in addition to medical expenses and loss of income. In another case, Hoffman allowed a man to sue in rem the steamship *Golden Gate* for assault and battery instead of in personam against the ship's officers who beat him.

"To the passenger it affords the only substantial remedy—for a suit in personam against the master or the mates is in the most cases fruitless," wrote Hoffman, justifying his rejection of the common law notion that employers were not liable for their employees' crimes. Hoffman even held ship owners liable for maintaining minimum standards of moral decency aboard ship. Female passengers in particular deserved "civility, decency, and exemption from brutal, cruel or obscene conduct," Hoffman wrote. If a captain used foul language or behaved in a way so as to "shock the modesty and wound the susceptibilities of a virtuous woman," he and the ship owners were liable for mental distress in Hoffman's court. "It is only by the firm and constant enforcement by the courts of the rights of passengers that the repetition of abuses can be prevented," he wrote.

Sailors' Wages

A majority of the cases on the early admiralty docket were, like *Dowl*, disputes over sailors' wages. Desertion was a common cause for withholding pay. It was common during the gold rush for all hands to leave the ship when it landed in San Francisco, regardless of the ship's final destination, which the sailors had agreed to reach. California was an opportunity to strike it rich in the mines, or at least get the much higher West Coast wages if one signed on to crew a different ship. This desertion was so commonplace that it was widely assumed by sailors around the world that crews were discharged and paid off in San Francisco. The truth was that all sailors agreed to ship's articles—essentially a contract of employment—when they signed up for a voyage. The articles laid out rules of conduct ("No grog allowed!"), pay, duration of voyage, and the vessel's final destination. Each sailor signed his name, or made his mark if he couldn't write, to imply that he had understood the articles and agreed to them.

A sailor's life was a hard one: it was dangerous, poorly paid, and designed to keep most men in a poverty-ridden cycle from ship to port to boarding house to ship again. It was a tradition in maritime law that the burden of proof in these cases lay with the sailor. In 1851, Hoffman cautioned against the dishonest and collusive nature of sailors. In *Peterson v. The James C. Perkins*, he ruled that a seaman needed more than a "messmate to swear that the voyage was misrepresented to him" in order to "release himself from the obligation of the contract." But by 1860, Hoffman had found more sympathy with the sailor's plight. After hearing nearly a decade of maritime cases, he reversed himself when he re-examined the issue within the reality of California's shipping industry in the case of *Dooley v. Neptune's Car*.

"It is well known that the wages of seamen are much higher on this coast than on the Atlantic side of the continent," Hoffman wrote. "The temptation to desert and obtain greatly enhanced wages, rather than continue a voyage around the world for a period of one or more years, at the wages at which the men were shipped, is great and usually irresistible to the seamen. For a crew to continue on board the vessel at the wages mentioned in the articles is a very rare occurrence—the master knowing the men will desert usually discharges them, and for several years it has been the general [practice] not to insist upon the forfeiture of the whole wages, but merely on a deduction of a small sum to defray the expense of shipping other men, if the old crew are unwilling to remain on board at port wages."

The clipper ship *Neptune's Car* became famous in 1856 when the captain took ill and his nineteen-year-old wife, the only one on board who knew how to navigate, managed to quell a mutiny and take the ship around Cape Horn during one of the worst winters of that decade. In

FIG. 1-5
Photograph of a sailor in San Francisco in the last half of the nineteenth century. Disputes over sailors' wages constituted a majority of the cases in Judge Hoffman's admiralty court in the 1850s and 1860s. Courtesy of the Yale Collection of Western Americana, Beinecke Rare Book and Manuscript Library, Yale University.

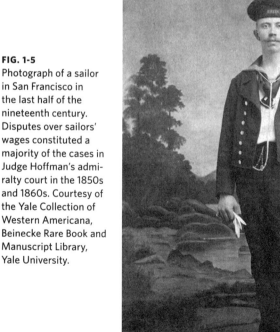

the *Dooley* case, not one of the sailors could read or write. Two of them had been pulled off the street into the shipping office in New York and asked if they wanted to sail aboard *Neptune's Car* to San Francisco. Wanting passage to California, they asked about the wages (twelve dollars a month) and signed up. A clerk wrote down their names and they touched the pen. They told Judge Hoffman that no articles were ever read to them. The ship's articles declared:

> It is agreed, between the master and seamen or mariners of the ship
> Neptune's Car of New York whereof Caleb Sprague is present master, or
> whoever shall go as master, now bound from the port of New York to
> the port of San Francisco, at and from thence, to any port or ports in the
> Pacific or Indian oceans, or China Seas, or Europe, as the master may
> direct on a general trading and freighting voyage and thence back to a
> port of discharge on the Atlantic coast in the United States for the full
> tenure of 18 calendar months. No money to be paid the crew until the
> arrival of said ship at her final port of discharge on the Atlantic coast of
> the United States.

Below each sailor's name, his age and residence were recorded along with his position on the ship, his wage, and his signature or mark.

In *Dooley*, Hoffman weighed the "notorious character of seamen" and their propensity for lying "especially if it…would secure their discharge and their wages," against the pressures to obtain a crew that "frequently lead shipping masters to misrepresent the voyage to the men." Sailors are easily made to sign a contract "which they do not understand and into which they do not mean to enter," the judge wrote.

"The facility for such practices in the case of an illiterate seaman unable to read the articles and the temptation to commit the fraud are too great," wrote Hoffman. Ship owners were moneyed, legally sophisticated, and literate, while sailors were mostly poor, ignorant, and illiterate. Sailors could be jailed for desertion in addition to losing their wages, while captains and shipping companies usually factored the cost of a new crew into their business projections. All in all, Hoffman felt that the burden of proof of a valid contract was better borne by the ship owners, and ruled in favor of sailors.

Hoffman suggested a notary system for signing up crew to avoid wage disputes. "If every crew were required to be taken before an officer of the United States appointed for the purpose, whose duty it should be to explain fully the contract to each of the men, to take his acknowledgement of its execution and to certify those facts under his seal and signature—which certificate should be final and conclusive—the seamen would obtain a protection which is often required by them and the masters would have assurances of their legal rights—which at present it is difficult to obtain," Hoffman suggested. "The courts would thus be relieved of much doubt and embarrassment and in cases of violation of the agreement, could decree a forfeiture of wages with a reasonable certainty that the contract had been fairly entered into and willfully broken."

The "Hellship" Trials

In early 1852, Hoffman was faced with his first criminal trial, and one of the most sensational of the time, which concerned the extreme clipper ship *Challenge* and its maiden voyage from New York to San Francisco.

"The *Challenge* cases were to prove, in the long run, the most important trials with which [Hoffman] was connected, in terms of the social history of the west. They were the first 'hellship' trials and, by the very fact that they did occur, they made possible, many years later, the freedom of the American merchant sailor from the brutality and tyranny of masters and mates," wrote Richard Dillon in his 1961 book *Shanghaiing Days*. "It was fortunate for all parties that Hoffman was to preside in the *Challenge* cases," Dillon wrote. "He towered over many of his colleagues of the bench....If slightly flowery and over-ornate in his language, he was still clear and strong in his arguments."

The *Challenge* cases centered on charges of murder, cruelty, and assault against Captain Robert Waterman, the most famous clipper ship captain of the day, and his first mate, James Douglass. Waterman had come out of retirement to sail the *Challenge* on her maiden voyage. Clipper-class ships were tall-masted and designed for speed, and the *Challenge* was an extreme clipper, the largest and sleekest ship built to date. Its launch was covered by newspapers in New York and Boston. But the crew was something else: almost none of them had sailing experience and half of them were sick when they came aboard—the dregs of the dregs of the New York waterfront.

The ship entered the Golden Gate flying its distress flag on October 29, 1851. As it lay at anchor in the bay for two days, waiting for a berth at the crowded Pacific Street Wharf, word spread that nine of the fifty-six-man crew had died during the trip, eight men were in irons for attempted

FIG. 1-6
The New York–built clipper ship *Challenge*, 1851–1877. The maiden voyage from New York to San Francisco resulted in the mistreatment and death of seamen to such a degree the ship was branded a "hellship." Courtesy of the Library of Congress.

mutiny, and a dozen more were in the ship's infirmary unable to walk. The sailors came ashore with tales of terror: the *Challenge* was a hellship—the term sailors applied to ships where they had experienced extraordinary cruelty or harsh conditions. Waterman had shot men out of the rigging; Douglass had nearly beaten a man to death and had then thrown him overboard while still alive; every man had been savagely beaten.

On November 1, the day the *Challenge* was towed to the wharf, an editorial appeared in the *California Courier* branding Captain Waterman a monster:

> The ship *Challenge* has arrived, and Capt. Waterman, her commander, has also, but where are nine of his crew? And where is he and his guilty mate? The accounts given of Capt. Waterman towards his men, if true, make him one of the most inhumane monsters of this age. If they are true, he should be burned alive—he should never leave this city a live man. Nine of his men are missing, and the sailors who are here declare that four were shaken from the mizzen-topsail yard into the sea, where they drowned, and five of them died from the effects of wounds and ill treatment. The scene at this time on board of the ship beggars all

description. Five of them are mangled and bruised in the most shocking manner. One poor fellow died today, and five others, it is expected, will soon be in the brace of death. One of the men now lying on his death-bed has been severely injured in his genitals, by a kick from this brute in human form. Had these poor men been put in a den with bears and panthers, they could not have been much more inhumanely and shockingly maimed. They are all now lying in the forecastle of the ship. The captain, vile monster, has made his escape, and so has his brutal mate. It is an infamous outrage to have such a bloody murderer to command a ship. He is noted for his cruelty everywhere, and in the streets of New York he dare not show himself, nor dare he hereafter show himself in this city. We hope that the respectable house to which he is consigned here will not only disavow his conduct, but if they have the power, remove him from command. If he is not removed, we hope this community will not permit such a monster to sail out of this port as captain of any vessel. In all sincerity, we hope the monster may be caught, and dealt with in the severest manner. We did hear last night, that the mate had been taken, and now we trust that all humane men will turn out and pursue the captain until he is captured and punished.

As the *Challenge* tied up, a drunk and unruly crowd of more than one thousand men gathered at the ship's gangway, calling for Waterman's head. The captain puffed himself up to his full potential for authority and calmly strode down the gangway toward the crowd, his head held high. The mob taunted him, but parted to let him pass as he made his way to the Alsop Building on California Street, which housed the San Francisco agents for N. L. & G. Griswold, owners of the *Challenge*. There he met with Charles Griswold, to whom he gave the ship's manifest. The voyage had taken 108 days, much more than the ninety days Waterman needed to receive a $10,000 bonus, but still not bad for a winter passage around Cape Horn, and the *Challenge* had beaten the clipper *Telegraph*, which had left New York the same day. This might have been satisfactory for an ordinary captain, but Waterman was the clipper captain—he held the record for the fastest passage from Canton, China, to New York, and he had never lost a mast, much less a ship. He had an uncanny knack for finding good wind and novel routes, and knew how to get the most out of a ship—and a crew—from anchor to anchor.

While Waterman met with Griswold, the mob had watched as sailors were taken in stretchers from the *Challenge* to the Marine Hospital.

Waterman escaped up to the roof just as a delegation from the mob entered the Alsop Building. Captain John Land, who was to take the *Challenge* on the next leg of its voyage to China, was grabbed and dragged out to the street by men who threatened to hang him if Waterman was not produced. Mayor Charles Brenham, a former ship captain, arrived with a private militia and gave the crowd ten minutes to go home. "If you fail to comply, I shall order every last one of you to be incarcerated in the city Bastille," Brenham shouted. "In other words, I will put every damned one of you in jail!"

The tolling of the bells of the Monumental Engine Company signaled the arrival of the vigilance committee, an army of private citizens organized in 1851 to maintain law and order in San Francisco. With that, members of the mob, some of them swinging hangman's nooses, dispersed. Waterman waited until darkness and then slipped out of the city and across the bay to his ranch in Fairfield. Douglass had a tougher time. Still on board the *Challenge* while her cargo was removed, Douglass waited for a quiet moment and then jumped into a rowboat. A half dozen other rowboats filled with shouting men spotted him and gave chase, but they lost Douglass in the ship graveyard of Yerba Buena Cove.

Less than a week after the *Challenge*'s arrival, US Attorney Calhoun Benham issued the first indictments against Waterman and Douglass for cruelty to seamen. Posters around the city announced that arrest warrants had been issued for both men with a reward of $500 each. Douglass was found soon enough: the day after his escape from the *Challenge*, he was discovered drunk and asleep in a cart about ten miles south of San Francisco, on the road to Monterey. "Sheriff Jack Hayes and a couple of aides bound Douglass's hands behind his back, slipped a lariat round his shoulders, and led him back to the city. Still unrepentant, Douglass muttered 'I whipped 'em and I'll whip 'em again,'" A. B. C. Whipple recounted in his 1987 book *The Challenge*.

Henceforth the lawsuits began to fly: a grand jury indicted Waterman and Douglass for the murder of sailor George Lessing; Waterman for assault of four different crewmen; and Douglass for the murder of an Italian sailor known as PawPaw and for "malicious cruelty" to six others. Hugh Patterson, the second mate, was charged with two counts of assault for kicking one man off a yardarm and another on deck. And eight crew members were arrested and charged with attempted mutiny, including the third mate, Alex Coghill.

The district court's courtroom on Merchant Street was packed as eight jury trials were held from November 1851 through February 1852. It was probably the first look most locals had at young Judge Hoffman and their first taste of what kind of justice a federal court might offer a do-it-yourself town like San Francisco. Hoffman had the arduous task of scraping together not one but eight impartial juries. Everyone had heard of "Bully" Waterman, "Black" Douglass, and the "hellship" *Challenge*. And once found, jurors were far from reliable: the day after Christmas, the court had to be adjourned because two of the jurors were still drunk from the previous night's celebrations.

A sailor suing a ship's officers for abuse was not novel in the 1850s. The wharves of New York and San Francisco were full with "sea lawyers" ready to take on sailors' claims of mistreatment. Conditions on board the merchant ships of the day were notoriously perilous, and sailors served at the whim of masters and mates. Excessive force, cruelty, and sadism from officers were risks a sailor encountered along with the everyday dangers of life at sea. Discipline and routine were what made a ragtag group of men, usually from different countries, able to work together to coordinate the complicated job of tending to the many sails of the tall clipper ships of the day. In order to keep a ship and its crew safe, a captain had to preserve a system of obedience in which orders were carried out on command. A captain's authority was absolute—he was dictator, father, taskmaster, judge, and jury. "He stands no watch, comes and goes when he pleases, and is accountable to no one, and must be obeyed in everything, without a question, even from his chief officer," wrote Richard Henry Dana Jr. in his 1840 classic *Two Years Before the Mast*. "The prime minister, the official organ, and the active and superintending officer, is the chief mate. He is first lieutenant, boatswain, sailing-master, and quarter-master. The captain tells him what he wishes to have done, and leaves to him the care of overseeing, of allotting the work, and also the responsibility of its being well done." Dana had dropped out of Harvard to sail around Cape Horn to California in 1834, a two-year voyage aboard the ship *Pilgrim* that enabled him to articulate the perils and possibilities of the ordinary sailor. Later, he went to law school and became an advocate for sailors' rights.

The charges against Waterman and Douglass centered on whether the officers had gone to extremes in disciplining the crew, and whether Douglass had acted alone or on the captain's orders. The mutiny charges against the crew members were serious. Until 1835, mutiny was considered an act of piracy and punishable by death. But contemporary laws allowed variant sentencing depending on the circumstances of the mutiny, and provided protection for the crew against cruel punishment by the captain and officers. Imprisonment, beatings, and the withholding of adequate nourishment, if done "from malice, hatred or revenge, and without justifiable cause" by an officer, could be punished by a fine of up to $1,000 or five years in prison. "The silent operation of this statute has sheathed many a knife and quelled many a mutiny," wrote Dana in "Cruelty to Seamen," an article in *American Jurist and Law Magazine* in 1839. The problem, Dana wrote, was that officers rarely received serious sentences, even in outrageous cases of abuse.

It was widely assumed that captains had to be tough and that sailors were born liars. Even so, the *Challenge* cases began to tip the balance of the courts—and public opinion—in favor of sailors being treated more humanely. The cases were built around charges of outrageous and gratuitous cruelty by Waterman and Douglass. Waterman's defense was that the crew was inept and lazy, and that he and his officers did only what was necessary to keep the ship from sinking in heavy seas around Cape Horn.

During the mutiny trial, Waterman told the court:

> When my ship *Challenge* was in the neighborhood of Rio de Janeiro about thirty of the crew fell on the first mate, Jim Douglass, with the declared intention of killing him, and, afterward me. This is an act they later confessed to, which signed confessions I have in my possession at this time.
>
> On the occasion in question, I was on the bridge taking observations while the mate Douglass stood forward at the galley. Mutinous leaders of the incident stabbed Mr. Douglass and had beaten him shockingly before I could get to him. I struck down three of the mutineers with my sextant, rescued the mate and quelled the mutiny. I flogged eight of the confessed mutineers. Off Cape Horn, three men fell from the mizzen tops'l yardarm and were killed, and after a few weeks four more men died of dysentery and syphilis; none of them, however, were among the mutineers. For most of the voyage, thereafter, I was sole in command since the mates, Jim Douglass and Hugh Patterson, were still unable to attend their regular duties, having not yet recovered from the beatings of the mutinous crewmen. So for eighteen days I was continuously on duty, not once going below to my cabin for rest since no available helmsman could be trusted alone at the wheel.

Upon reaching San Francisco, some of the blacklegs, or mutineers in the crew, the better to conceal their own guilt, spread slanderous falsehoods and outlandish stories to the newspapers, as has been proven, so that a mob of idlers, many bolstered with free rum, were out to with the aim of stringing me up....

Now it can and will be shown that the toughs of the crew of the *Challenge* received only such ill treatment—severe as it seemed to be—as was necessary for the successful operation of the ship and the safety of the forty-two passengers aboard.

First Mate Douglass testified that off Rio de Janeiro, "I was ordered to make a search of the trunks in consequence of reports that property had been stolen from some of the crew. I was standing on deck seeing the chests overhauled when I was seized from behind and thrown down. About all of the crew were present. While I was falling, I received a wound. I felt a knife as I fell, but did not see who struck me with it. There was several men kicking me." Passenger William Marsten swore he saw sailor Fred Birkenshaw grab Douglass from behind as sailor George Smith stabbed him. Waterman then jumped into the melee, hit Smith on the head with his sextant, and tied him up. Birkenshaw slipped away as Douglass, thigh bleeding from his wound, picked up his fallen heaver (a heavy club hammer) and attacked the still gathered crew.

Despite the severity of the attack against Douglass, the defense attorneys compellingly argued that this was not a premeditated mutiny, but rather an unplanned response to Douglass's reign of terror. One by one, sailors took the stand and told of unprompted beatings. "I was beat with a club myself," said Charles Flanders. "I did not disobey orders. The first intimation I had was a crack on the head." John Leggett claimed that Birkenshaw only reacted after Douglass hit him suddenly with the heaver while the sea chests were being inspected. Alex Coghill sided with the sailors and denied the charges of mutiny. "I know nothing of any revolt, mutiny, disobedience of orders, or attempts to do so," he testified, praising Birkenshaw—who had originally fingered Coghill as an accomplice—as an obedient and fine sailor. The jury found Birkenshaw not guilty of mutiny and dismissed the conspiracy charges against Coghill.

Douglass and Waterman stood trial for murder and assault against various sailors, among them George Lessing, a twenty-year-old Irish sailor. During a storm off Cape Horn, Douglass ordered Lessing into the rigging. Terrified, Lessing refused to climb, claiming to have dysentery.

Sailors testified that Douglass then brought him aft to see the captain, who would "cure" him. Waterman grabbed Lessing and threw him into the lee scuppers, where the water drains from the ship's deck. Douglass held him under freezing water and then tied him to the ship's weather rail on the side being pounded by wind and waves. Lessing, barefoot and wearing only a flannel jacket and pants, was left there anywhere from ten minutes to an hour, depending on the testimony, until Douglass cut him down and let him go below. Within days, he did have dysentery and grew increasingly weak. He died twelve days later. The charges were dismissed after the trial ended with a hung jury.

Waterman's charges included allegations of mistreatment of foreign sailors, particularly two called PawPaw and Smiti. PawPaw was an old Italian sailor who spoke no English. He arrived on board with no shoes and would shake his head *no* when given orders. Waterman allegedly beat him with a belaying pin when the man didn't respond to an order to let go of a rope, nearly fouling one of the ship's tacks near Cape Horn. After PawPaw refused to come up on deck, complaining of frostbitten feet, Douglass beat him in his bunk, where he later died.

Waterman was accused of beating Smiti, a Finnish sailor, when he refused to scrub the deck. "Yes, I ordered the mate to give him a rope's end and I think he deserved it," said Waterman. Smiti was "lazy, dirty, indolent, and always skulking," Waterman testified. When reminded by witnesses that Smiti's legs and feet were so swollen with scurvy that he couldn't move, Waterman said, "He appeared to walk well enough when going to the galley for his tea."

Not all of the sailors who appeared as witnesses actually aided their own causes. "US Attorney called to the stand Plaintiff Nicoll," reads the January 30, 1852, record for *United States v. Jim Douglass and Robert Waterman*. The charge was the beating of sailor Nicoll. "As the witness commenced his testimony he betrayed manifest symptoms of intoxication and declared in a loud voice that Birkenshaw, also a witness, was drunker than he was. On motion of the US Attorney for 'nole contendre' [*sic*] the case against the defendants was dismissed."

A handwritten note entitled "Points for Mate" in the case file appears to be written in Judge Hoffman's handwriting and was probably used to instruct the juries. "Very much stronger evidence is necessary to convict the mate under this statute when he obeys the orders of the Captain.... The jury must consider an act of the mate in obedience to the commands of the captain as prima facie, and not done 'with hatred, revenge, or malice' and 'without justifiable cause.'"

Ultimately, most of the charges against Waterman and Douglass were dismissed, either because the juries couldn't reach a verdict or because the witnesses were too drunk. Waterman was cleared for the beating of PawPaw, convicted of one count of beating Smiti, the Finnish sailor, and fined $400. Douglass was fined $50 after being found guilty of two counts of beating sailors and fined $200 for the death of PawPaw. Patterson, the second mate, was found guilty of one count of assault for a kick to the groin that left sailor John Brown "emasculated." In lieu of a fine, he was sentenced to thirty days in prison.

Waterman retired to his ranch and never showed any signs of remorse for his treatment of the *Challenge*'s crew. He later served as the Inspector of Hulls for the Port of San Francisco and prospered as a rancher and farmer. He is credited with introducing eucalyptus trees into California from their native Australia and pioneering soybean production. Douglass slipped into ignominy. Patterson was shot under mysterious circumstances at an 1858 New Year's Eve party at Waterman's ranch, an event attended by a number of San Francisco's notable residents, including Judge Hoffman. Waterman suspected that the gunman was a sailor from the *Challenge*, an Englishman named McCorkle, later tracked down in a Liverpool bar. After bragging of the killing, the man was arrested by British police.

The *Challenge*, beautiful and fast though she was, received the ultimate sentence: she was branded a hellship, which meant should would forever have trouble getting a decent crew. Captain Land finally had to pay $200 a head to get a crew together for the ship's voyage from San Francisco to China. She made the return trip to San Francisco in a record thirty-four days, after a near mutiny was quelled by US marines near Hong Kong. She hauled Chinese laborers, slaves, and even guano before she grounded and broke up off the coast of France in 1877.

White Swallow: The Gentle Mutiny

Hoffman's rulings on sailor abuse cases in the 1850s and 1860s were the first American challenges to the abominable working conditions aboard nineteenth-century sailing ships. "I feel it is among the most important sacred duties of the court to protect, so far as it may, seamen from injustice, tyranny and oppression, and to restrain within the limits of humanity and justice the…irresponsible authority of the master," he wrote. However, Hoffman could only impose a sentence after a jury returned a guilty verdict, and San Francisco juries tended to find captains and officers not guilty. An 1864 law changed this by allowing federal district judges to hear minor charges of physical violence by officers or crew members without a jury. From this point onwards, Hoffman

FIG. 1-7
In 1865, a bloodless and orderly mutiny occurred aboard the *White Swallow* clipper ship en route from New York to San Francisco. The *White Swallow* case was decided in favor of the crew, the first mutiny case that found a crew justified in taking command from a ship's captain and its officers. This advertisement for the ship was printed by G. F. Nesbitt and Company. Courtesy of The Bancroft Library, University of California, Berkeley.

tended to punish officers relatively severely, with sentences ranging from six months in prison to six years hard labor. His decisions helped reform the industry.

In 1866, Hoffman heard the case of the "gentle mutiny" aboard the ship *White Swallow*. The *White Swallow* left New York in September 1865 with a crew of sixteen, eleven of them able-bodied seamen, the term for professional sailors, bound for San Francisco. During the voyage, six of the crew overpowered the captain as well as the first and second mates, imprisoning them for several days until the captain promised the men would be treated better. The sailors also wrote and signed a document admitting to the mutiny and outlining the reasons for it. Arriving in San Francisco in late January, the leaders of the revolt were arrested and a federal grand jury issued an indictment for charges of mutiny. The six men pleaded not guilty.

The *Daily Evening Bulletin* covered the indictment in its January 31, 1866, issue:

> It is charged that when the ship was off the coast of South America, below the equator, the crew made a simultaneous uprising, as if by a preconcerted arrangement, and secured the captain and mates, whom they put in irons and kept in confinement as prisoners for four days. They obtained possession of the ship's arms and ammunition, which they brought out of the cabin.... [C]onvinced of their inability to manage the elephant which they had taken upon their hands [they] accordingly gave up the command to the officers, after having extorted from them a written guarantee that they should suffer no punishment for the offence upon arrival in port. Upon the facts becoming known to the consignees of the ship, a prosecution was insisted upon for the safety of the mercantile marine service.

On the next day, however, the *Bulletin* published an extensive "Sailors Side of the Story":

> We yesterday published a statement concerning the alleged mutiny aboard the clipper ship White Swallow as given by the prosecution. Since then we have heard the defense of the seamen charged, and if their statements be true, the offense, if any has been committed, is but a technical one at the most, and their action would be sanctioned as justified by many people. The men say that immediately after the ship left New York they were subjected to the most cruel treatment imaginable,

the ship being transformed into a perfect hell, from the cruelty of the officers. Men were knocked down with belaying pins, deck scrapers and anything which happened to be handy to the officers, without any cause whatever, and out of pure malice and devilishness....Then when they had returned to their forecastle they held a meeting and discussed their situation and it was determined by united action to save their lives and to secure to themselves decent treatment during the voyage. With this object and none other they put the captain and first and second mates in irons until they had obtained control of the ship's armament and thrown overboard the brass knuckles and other implements which had been used as instruments for their torture. None of the officers were ill-treated. The captain directed the course of the ship every day, took the sun and gave directions for the ship's management which were fully obeyed, but he was only confined sufficiently to enable them to obtain a guarantee for their future good treatment, in which they succeeded in three days time, when the officers having given the requisite promise, were released, and during the balance of the voyage everything worked harmoniously. The men under arrest are a fine looking crew, and appear to be intelligent for men of their class.

Testimony revealed that the crew had been regularly beaten for no apparent reason by the first and second mates. "This was my first voyage to sea and I hope it will be my last," said James Welsh, who worked as a crew member to pay his passage to California, according to the *Bulletin*. "I was often badly treated by the first mate, he often called me a 'd----d Irish son of a b---h.' Both the first and second mates were in the habit of calling the men vile names....I do not think [the mutineers] went into counsel to do any bodily injury to the any of the officers, or any injury to the cargo, but merely to protect themselves." Other sailors testified that officers made little effort to save two men who fell overboard, and told the court they feared that more of them might die. They said the first mate told the crew, "It's just fun for me to lick you fellows, and if I can't lick you I'll shoot you." The captain, they said, appeared not to take seriously any of their charges of mistreatment.

Captain Elijah E. Knowles contended that the crew had never made any formal complaints to him. When seized by the men, he was told that they had nothing against him but were angry at the first and second mates. Knowles told the court he was released the second or third day. The mates were released the following day. He claimed the crew was well-treated and had the same quantity of water and the same kind of food as the officers. During his confinement, the captain was allowed to navigate and his orders were followed. The mutineers did not even increase their water rations.

Defense attorney J. B. Manchester told the court that the alleged mutiny was done in self-defense, to save the crew's lives. "Time was when Jack had no rights and could be maltreated by the officers with impunity, but that time had passed, and the time was now approaching when the sailor was to have his rights as well as any other men," he proclaimed. When applause broke out, Judge Hoffman warned spectators he would clear the court if they could not sit still. In his instructions to the jury, Hoffman reminded them of the extraordinary features of the *White Swallow* case: six sailors had confessed to one of the gravest crimes in maritime law, and none of the facts in the case were in dispute.

"Certainly it presents a novel instance in the history of seamen, that when they got possession of the ship they should be guilty of no outrage or excess—that they should perform their duties in a regular and orderly manner, and should take the precaution to lock up the room where the liquors were kept and even throw overboard a cup of whiskey that one of them had obtained, in order to remove all cause of disturbance," Hoffman told the jury. "The question, then, that you are to determine upon the evidence, and upon a careful, calm, thorough review of the relation of master and seaman, is, were the men justified, under the circumstances of this case, in doing what they did?"

The six men were acquitted of all charges and made maritime history: the *White Swallow* case was the first mutiny case where a crew was found justified in taking command from the ship's captain and its officers. The verdict shocked the maritime community. There will be "serious apprehensions" wrote the *Bulletin,* as to the effect the verdict might have upon future crews "inclined to be mutinous....There is no class of people who will read this trial with more attention...than sailors, and they cannot fail to see that the only ground on which the jury and the public justify the crew of the White Swallow lies in the fact that their moderate, judicious, and sober conduct after the mutiny proved that there was no felonious intent in the revolt, and that, when they had attained the sole object for which the mutiny is justifiable in law—self-protection—they were willing to restore the ship to the command of the officers. Had there been any excesses committed the result of the trial would have been far different."

The San Francisco Committees of Vigilance

Outraged by crime and corruption, local citizens formed a vigilance committee—an armed militia and pseudo judicial system—to bring order to the city in 1851 and again in 1856. The San Francisco Committee of Vigilance took as its motto *Fiat justitia ruat coelum*: "Let justice be done though the heavens fall."

Taking the law into one's own hands was a California pastime—and occasional necessity—that predated the federal district court. Frontier justice was the only practical option in the Wild West, which was settled before the establishment of local, state, and federal judicial systems. There were no courts, there were rarely jails, and the population was essentially transient until the early 1850s. Travel to a town large enough for legal niceties was also often impractical. So when a horse thief or murderer was caught, justice was often immediate.

What made the San Francisco vigilance movement of the 1850s different from frontier justice was that local judicial institutions were already established when popular militias were formed to clean up the city. Organizers were not miners and frontiersmen but the city's most prominent citizens: merchants, shippers, lawyers, bankers, doctors, publishers, and politicians. These men were so outraged by the city's rampant crime and so disgusted with corruption among its officials that they usurped elected politicians and the police force as the city's central authority. The committees were highly organized and gave themselves the hallmarks of legitimacy by passing bylaws, arresting criminals, holding trials, carrying out sentences, and leading the city during a vacuum of leadership. The vast majority of the city's residents supported them.

"San Francisco has been through its season of Heaven-defying crime, violence and blood," wrote Dana, "from which it was rescued and handed back to soberness, morality and good government, by that peculiar invention of Anglo-Saxon Republican America, the solemn, awe-inspiring Vigilance Committee of the most grave and responsible citizens, the last resort of the thinking and the good, taken to only when vice, fraud and ruffianism have intrenched [*sic*] themselves behind the forms of law, suffrage, and ballot, and there is no hope but in an organized force, whose action must be instant and thorough, or its state will be worse than before."

These two short-lived but effective committees of vigilance captured, tried, convicted, and executed criminals, acting as defense, prosecution,

FIG. 1-8
The 1856 San Francisco Committee of Vigilance converted a sandbagged warehouse on Sacramento Street between Front and Davis Streets into their headquarters. Nicknamed Fort Gunnybags, the location also served as the committee's arsenal. Courtesy of the California Historical Society, FN-21027/CHS2013.1139.

judge, and jury. In all, eight men were convicted and hanged for murder, at least one committed suicide while awaiting trial, and dozens were banished from California under threat of execution. The members justified their extra-legal conduct by pointing to the impotence of the police and courts and the brazenness of the criminals.

While the 1851 committee (sparked by the rampages of Australian felons called the Sydney Ducks) played its role in the *Challenge* trials by heading off the lynch mob looking for Captain Waterman, the 1856 Committee of Vigilance was the largest and more powerful of the two. It seized complete control of the city, executed four men, banished dozens more (two of whom would later file suit in the district court), and imprisoned and tried in their court the chief justice of the state supreme court, David Terry. The federal district court and the circuit court would be the only institutions—judicial or otherwise—that would stand up to the committee's extra-legal activities.

Judge Hoffman was in the minority in publicly opposing the committees. But it wasn't until 1856 that he would be called to address the authority of this popular movement, together with Judge McAllister of the circuit court. When Hoffman arrived in San Francisco in the spring of 1850, the city was experiencing its first economic depression and crime had exploded. The number of reported burglaries jumped from three in the first half of 1850 to forty-nine in the second half to fifty-three in early 1851. Murders likewise increased. "Who is safe when the store of a peaceable citizen can be entered and the proprietor almost murdered?" asked the *Alta California* in 1851 after an audacious downtown robbery. "Is it worthwhile if caught to offer [the criminals] a trial in our courts?" questioned the *California Courier*, which wrote that thieves use their loot to pay "pettifogging" attorneys to get them released. "Is it not better to make examples of them, if found, by hanging them at once?"

A real city jail was still being built in the early 1850s, and temporary jails were inadequate, with escapes being commonplace. Even so, there were a number of prominent residents who could not justify what was essentially a military coup d'état. Chief among them was Judge Hoffman, an ardent federalist who abhorred violence and believed above all in the rule of law and its institutions to maintain order. He actively opposed both vigilance committees by supporting the anti-vigilance Law and Order Party. San Franciscans learned of his appointment to their federal district court the same month he publicly defended a state judge critical of the 1851 committee.

By 1853, San Francisco's government had been infiltrated by malleable politicians and "hounds," the contemporary term for ex-convicts. Imports from New York's corrupt Tammany Hall and Bowery gangs had inserted themselves in the city's nascent public infrastructure and were milking the city of cash. City expenditures that year were $2,646,000. Under a reform following the 1856 committee, "the city got along in good shape with the expenditure of $353,000," according to a 1925 edition of the *San Francisco Newsletter*, in the collection of the Virtual Museum of the City of San Francisco.

The formation of the 1856 committee was sparked by two events: the killing of a US marshal and the murder of a crusading newspaper editor. On November 18, 1855, the marshal for the Northern District, William H. Richardson, was shot by Charles Cora, a notorious gambler. Richardson was not on duty at the time. He had been drinking heavily and taken offense to something that Cora had said as he passed him entering the Blue Wing, a Montgomery Street saloon popular with politicians. "Cora was a gambler, yet he did not look the character. He was a low-sized, well-formed man; dressed in genteel manner, without display of jewelry or loudness; was reserved and quiet in his demeanor; and his manners and conversation were those of a refined gentleman," wrote pioneer journalist James O'Meara in his account of that turbulent year. "General Richardson was a morose and at times a very disagreeable man. He was of low stature, thick set, dark complexion, black hair, and usually wore a bull-dog look. He was known by his intimate friends to be a dangerous man as a foe, and he always went armed with a pair of derringers."

On the night of the shooting, O'Meara was drinking with John Monroe, Hoffman's clerk of court, and some other men in the Court Exchange when Richardson came in. Still obsessing about the presumed insult, Richardson "became sullen and, as we all knew his nature, it was quietly agreed among ourselves that we would leave and try to get him away." They walked him toward his home south of Market, where he insisted on one last drink. There they left him. Richardson soon headed back toward the Blue Wing to find Cora. He asked Cora outside and "walked with him around the corner into Clay street…and so managed as to put Cora on the iron grating, of the sidewalk inside, with his back to the brick wall of the store. Cora had not the slightest idea that Richardson had taken offence at his remark on Thursday night," wrote O'Meara.

Thus cornered, Cora shot him dead. He claimed self-defense and, despite public prejudice against him, a local jury was unable to arrive at a verdict. Cora was back in jail awaiting a retrial the following May when a man named James King of William was shot on Montgomery Street by James Casey, a former city supervisor and rival publisher. King, the crusading editor of the anti-corruption *Daily Evening Bulletin*, had written that Casey had served time in Sing Sing Prison in New York. The wounded King lingered for several days while Casey was put in jail by the corrupt sheriff David Scannell, a friend, for his own safety. An angry crowd gathered at the jail calling for Casey's head.

The next day, May 14, various citizens had reorganized the Committee of Vigilance, adopted a new constitution, and purchased a building at 41 Sacramento Street between Front and Davis Streets. It would become known as Fort Gunnybags for the eight-foot-high sandbag fortifications erected around it. William Tell Coleman, an influential member of the

1851 committee, was appointed the leader of some five thousand members, about 10 percent of the city's population. The city effectively fell under the military control of the committee. Coleman sent a large contingent of armed men and a cannon to the jail to remove Casey and Cora. Within two days, King died and both Cora and Casey were tried by the Committee of Vigilance court. They were convicted and sentenced to hang. On May 22, 1856, as King's funeral procession wound through town, two beams were rigged to the roof of Fort Gunnybags, where Casey and Cora were hanged with armed detachments in military regalia and a large crowd assembled below.

"We all thought the matter had ended there, and accordingly the Governor returned to Sacramento in disgust, and I went about my business," wrote William Tecumseh Sherman in his memoirs. Sherman, a San Francisco banker and retired army captain who would lead the Union forces during the Civil War, had recently been appointed by California governor J. Neely Johnson to lead the San Francisco division of the California militia. "But it soon became manifest that the Vigilance Committee had no intention to surrender the power thus usurped....[They] employed guards and armed sentinels, sat in midnight council, issued writs of arrest and banishment, and utterly ignored all authority but their own."

On June 2, Governor Johnson declared San Francisco to be in a state of insurrection and asked Sherman to activate the San Francisco militia. But not enough men answered the call to challenge the well-armed vigilance forces. Johnson attempted to bring the army to San Francisco, but President Franklin Pierce had no interest in sparking a civil war in San Francisco. Although it wouldn't send soldiers, the federal government did agree to provide the state with its annual quota of arms from the federal arsenal. Three members of the state militia, John G. Phillips, James Reuben Maloney, and James McNabb, were sent to collect the arms—113 muskets, one saber, and two bullet molds—and bring them back to San Francisco on the schooner *Julia*.

The committee got wind of the plan and sent a group, led by former policeman John L. Durkee, to intercept them. Durkee and his men seized the arms along with the three militia men on June 21. After Durkee delivered the muskets to the committee, he released the men as ordered. Phillips promptly swore out a complaint against Durkee for piracy in the circuit court, and a warrant was issued for his arrest. Upping the ante, the vigilance committee soon issued its own arrest warrant for

James Maloney. During a fight to capture Maloney, California Supreme Court justice David S. Terry severely wounded vigilance committee member Sterling Hopkins with a bowie knife. (Terry was a violent hot-head, known for his trademark bowie knife, which he wore even under his robes. In 1859 he would kill state senator David Broderick in a duel, and he would be killed himself by a deputy US marshal in 1888 when he attacked Supreme Court justice Stephen Field.) Maloney, Terry, and their supporters retreated to the armory, which was soon surrounded by the vigilance committee. Vigilantes soon overran the armory and took Maloney, Terry, and hundreds of weapons into custody.

The prisoners were held in Fort Gunnybags while armed details were sent out to overpower the city's other Law and Order Party militias. The Committee of Vigilance now had complete control of the city of San Francisco and held a California Supreme Court justice in its jail. Word on the street was that Terry would be hanged if Hopkins died, banished if he pulled through. Meanwhile, US Navy Commander E. B. Boutwell had tied up his ship, the USS *John Adams*, at the Sacramento Street wharf to lend "moral" support to the state's forces. Terry wrote to Boutwell on June 27, begging him to intervene. Boutwell requested that Justice Terry be treated as a prisoner of war and placed aboard his ship to await trial. The committee refused. "I could destroy the city of San Francisco with the guns of the John Adams, but in the ruin, friends as well as others would suffer....If I demand [Terry's] release, and they fail to give him up, I must either batter the town down or render myself ridiculous," Bout-well wrote to Governor Johnson.

Between the impending federal trial of Durkee for piracy and the vigilance trial of Justice Terry, many senior committee members began to feel as if the whole situation had gotten out of hand. As vigilance committee executive member James Dows described the Terry situation, "We started in to hunt coyotes, but we've got a grizzly bear on our hands, and we don't know what to do with him." The idea of hanging a state supreme court justice was serious enough to give even the most virulent vigilantes pause. Luckily, Sterling Hopkins recovered. He testified against Terry at the committee trial where Terry was convicted of resisting arrest and two counts of assault. He was released August 7 with the recommendation that he resign his office. He was whisked aboard the USS *John Adams*, and within a few days he had returned to his seat on the California Supreme Court in Sacramento.

On August 18, the Committee of Vigilance held a parade through the streets of San Francisco. As it was cheered by thousands, the group officially disbanded. In a farewell message printed on hundreds of posters, they reserved the right to reassemble to fight abuses, mete out justice, and protect "any member of the Committee from violence or malicious prosecution, arising out of any act performed by authority of the Committee."

This not-so-subtle warning had little effect on Judge Hoffman and Judge McAllister as they convened a circuit court grand jury later that year. Durkee and his accomplice, a man called Rand, were each charged with piracy for boarding the *Julia*, assaulting its crew, and stealing muskets belonging to the state of California. The men faced a mandatory death sentence if convicted.

Former members of the vigilance committee watched the proceedings carefully. When bail was denied, the vigilance guard was put on notice. While many admired the judges' courage, just as many felt it was foolhardy to twitch the tiger's tail. "I would not have the judge to swerve one iota from the course he would pursue in times of quiet, but it would be well not to arouse these men who think they have saved the country from the control of rowdies," wrote William T. Sherman in a letter to his bank partners in St. Louis. "At the same time I don't see how we are to escape the necessity of putting down this spirit of resistance to the Law, for it will be repeated again and again until subdued by force or until some outrage causes the more peaceable inhabitants to rebel against the assumed authority of their Executive Committee."

Within days, James Dows, a member of the vigilance committee's executive committee, publicly threatened the judge and jury, saying, "If [Durkee and Rand] were convicted, that Judge McAllister and the Jury, and the United States Marshal would be hung out the windows of the court house."

The threat of violence was real enough for the US marshal to write to General John Ellis Wool, military commander of US forces on the Pacific coast, and request protection, if needed, for the prisoners and the court. Wool replied that he would need a request from the court itself. The judges promptly sent an official request:

Chamber Circuit Court United States
District of California, San Francisco
September 9, 1856

Sir: There are two prisoners in custody of the marshal of the United States against whom true bills for piracy have been returned by the grand jury. These men will be placed on trial to-morrow, and the investigation will occupy two or three days. The marshal reports that, with the force ordinarily at his command, he is unable to ensure the safe-keeping of the prisoners, or command respect for the process of the court. It is unpracticable [sic] for us to deem it proper to learn from you whether you have any orders which, in your opinion, will authorize you to extend any aid to the marshal for the purpose of maintaining the laws, in case an attempt shall be made to nullify the process of the court.

We have the honor to be, very respectably, your obedient servants,

M. Hall McAllister
Circuit Judge United States

Ogden Hoffman
District Judge

General Wool refused. "I have no orders whatever applicable to the subject in question. I must refer you to the laws of the United States, by which I am totally governed."

Court opened the following day with Judge McAllister announcing that no member of either the vigilance committee or the Law and Order Party would be allowed to sit on the jury. The facts in the case were not in dispute. Durkee and Rand admitted that they boarded the *Julia* and took the arms. The question was whether they did so with felonious intent—that is, to profit from their act of piracy. Without this intent, their attorneys argued, they should be found not guilty. Vigilance committee member George Ward testified that the seized muskets had never been used and would be returned in their original packages at the "appropriate time." This provoked McAllister to utter, "You mean that you will give them up, when you please to do so." US Attorney William Blanding argued that a conviction for piracy didn't require "pecuniary gain to the person who took the property," while the defense maintained that Durkee had acted to prevent civil war in San Francisco. Defense attorney William Duer reminded the jury "the objects of the committee were noble ones." In closing, he added that he hoped the jury would "restore peace to the city by a conscientious verdict."

In instructing jurors, McAllister said that they should disregard the notion that Durkee was simply following orders because the committee was "unauthorized by and banded together in violation and defense of the laws." Durkee was on trial solely for piracy—robbery of a vessel within the ebb and flow of the sea. But McAllister said that intent was lacking if the robbery was not for personal profit or if permanent deprivation was not intended. After an exhausting review of American and English case law, he summarized: "If you shall believe that he did not take the arms for the purpose of appropriating them, or any part thereof, to his own use, and only for the purpose of preventing their being used on himself or his associates, then the prisoner is not guilty." The courtroom crowd broke out in applause. Within three minutes, the jury returned a verdict of not guilty. The court discharged the prisoners.

McAllister was the first American judge to be faced with the application of federal piracy statutes to domestic insurrections. Not until the Civil War would circuit court judges in New York and Philadelphia face similar questions in regard to Confederate privateers. McAllister apparently changed his view of the case as the trial progressed. No one intending to deliver a charge of acquittal would need to request federal troops, yet Judge McAllister did. In "Authorized By No Law," Gordan suggests that this apparent flip-flop, from denial of bail to essentially an order to acquit, was the result of General Wool's refusal to provide military aid in the event of a conviction. "Given the consistency of his opposition to the committee up to that time, the inference is fairly compelling that when he wrote to General Wool on September 9 Judge McAllister contemplated jury instructions of a radically different tenor than the direction to acquit he actually delivered on the 11th. Evidently, something happened between the 9th and the end of the trial to change his mind," Gordan wrote. When faced with the reality of the general's refusal to come to his court's aid in the event of a third vigilance committee—a likely possibility if there had been a conviction—perhaps he questioned whether a conviction would do more harm than good.

Did this apparent change of heart make Judge McAllister a coward? Or did he feel that Durkee's trial had made the point that the federal courts would stand outside of local politics to uphold the law? If the federal courts—or its judges—had been physically attacked, General Wool would have had no choice but to come to their defense and there might indeed have been civil war in San Francisco. Instead, there never was a third vigilance committee.

The Banished

One of the 1856 vigilance committee's early actions was to single out a group of about thirty undesirable men, "notorious ballot-box stuffers and other desperate characters," who were kidnapped, tried, and sentenced to exile from California, under penalty of death if they returned. Charles P. Duane and Martin Gallagher were two of the banished men. "Dutch Charly" Duane was placed on a ship bound for Panama, and Gallagher on one bound for Hawaii. It took them two years or longer to make it back to San Francisco, but when they did they brought suit in federal court against the committee and the captains of the ships they were placed on. These cases would be the first legal challenges to the committee by its victims. The district court would be the lone court in the state where committee members were prosecuted.

Duane was a well-known political muscleman who had been the chief engineer of the San Francisco Fire Department. He was in league with California Democrats and had been charged, though rarely convicted in local courts, of numerous assaults and shootings—including one of a committee member—before his 1856 banishment. Gallagher was a night watchman employed by the US Customs House. The committee accused him of also being part of the city's corrupt political patronage machine.

When Gallagher finally arrived back in San Francisco, he filed federal suit against James Smith, master of the barque *Yankee*, and the executive members of the vigilance committee for kidnapping on the high seas. He asked for $25,000 in damages. In court, Gallagher testified that on the night of May 25, 1856, he was on duty patrolling the waterfront when he was surrounded by a group of armed men who seized him and brought him to the vigilance committee building. He was kept incommunicado in a cell in the basement for several days. Finally, he was brought upstairs for his "sentencing," where he was told he was a disturber of the peace and a "promoter of quarrels at the polls" on election days. "You are a bad man and you are banished from the State of California, never to return under the severest penalties," he said committee member George R. Ward told him. At two o'clock in the morning on June 5, Gallagher said he and a number of other prisoners, including Duane, were put in irons and taken out the rear of the building into an alley. There, with a line of armed men on each side, the prisoners were marched down California Street to the wharf where they boarded the steam tug *Hercules*. Outside the Golden Gate, she waited while the *Yankee* sailed toward them. Gallagher and two other men were placed in a boat alongside the *Hercules*. As they approached the *Yankee*, Captain Smith called out "Are you bound for Honolulu?"

"No," Gallagher said he replied in a clear voice before being forced to board the *Yankee*. Captain Smith again asked the men if they were bound for Honolulu. Gallagher requested that he be returned to San Francisco. By then, the tender was gone and the *Yankee* got under way. During the voyage, Smith told his prisoner that he was a member of the vigilance committee that had arranged for Gallagher's passage. Eleven days later, they arrived in Honolulu. Gallagher testified that he was subject to ridicule in the streets until a Good Samaritan took him in for several months. Using an assumed name, he was finally able to board a ship bound for Puget Sound, Washington, and from there return to San Francisco, where he arrived in November 1856. He was unable to get work since he was on the committee blacklist, so he went to Callao, Peru, where he found employment until his identity was discovered.

In 1858, Gallagher returned to San Francisco, determined to right the wrong done to him. He filed his suit in district court in March. "One by one these miscreants are returning to the city," noted the *Alta California* when the lawsuit was filed. It admonished Gallagher and others to "let lawing [*sic*] alone, eschew political matters and attend to some regular work to earn an honest living." Few, if any, state judges were brave enough to take on a case against the committee, even after it disbanded.

Hoffman rejected the defense's claim that under California law Gallagher only had one year to file his cause, noting the circumstances of the banishment and the reluctance of state courts to take on the matter. He said that while he had no jurisdiction over Gallagher's confinement on land, he certainly did in regards to his deportation by an American vessel. "So long as our country remains under the dominion of law, and so long as the great constitutional provisions which secure the citizen his life, liberty and his property until deprived of them by due process of law, are prized by the American people, and are enforced by the courts, the deportation of a citizen to a foreign country in an American ship, commanded by an American master, in pursuance or execution of a sentence of an illegal and self-constituted body of men, must remain a marine tort of the most flagrant character," Hoffman wrote.

The judge awarded Gallagher $3,000 plus expenses. He admonished the shipping industry not to take part in extra-judiciary efforts. "Masters and agents of ships should learn, that whatever be the power that in

SHIPMENT OF THE PRISONERS.

FIG. 1-9
An 1856 illustration by T. C. Boyd showing the Committee of Vigilance exiling "undesirables," including Charles P. Duane. Courtesy of the California Historical Society, FN-13071/CHS2013.1138.

moments of popular excitement, illegal bodies of men may usurp…yet on American vessels on the high seas the laws of the United States are still supreme." Hoffman was roasted in the press for his decision. Both the *Alta* and the *Bulletin* accused him of going out of his way "to strain law and facts in favor of the worthless individual" and predicted that the Supreme Court would teach Hoffman a "judicial lesson" by reversing him. The judge, they charged, was guilty of poking a sleeping dog. "Just as the bitterness of the past was fading out, this Federal Judge transcends his duty to stir up the embers, and again fan the fire into a consuming blaze," said the *Bulletin* on January 19, 1859.

The blaze came in the form of a half-dozen more lawsuits directed against the actions of the 1856 vigilance committee. In 1860, Duane filed a series of lawsuits against the masters of the ships *Hercules, Golden Gate,* and *John L. Stephens.* "There have been two Vigilance Committees, there may be a third," said Duane's lawyer. "Masters and companies need to know what liabilities they meet by kidnapping citizens."

Coincidentally, Judge McAllister encountered Duane while returning to San Francisco from Mexico in June 1856. He was traveling with his son Cutler, the circuit court clerk, on the steamship *John L. Stephens* when the ship's captain, committee member Robert H. Pearson, transferred Duane to the southbound *Sonora*, to stop his return. When Pearson sent orders that Duane be brought aboard the *Sonora*, Duane hid but was eventually cornered. "I had a knife which a passenger lent me. I drew it and said I was ready to defend myself," Duane testified in court. "On the promenade I met Cutler McAllister, who advised me not to resist, they were determined to take me....The first mate was in charge. I drew my knife again....I said the captain had no authority to seize me and put me off the steamer....I backed up so that they couldn't get behind me. The passengers appeared to arm themselves, and said they must not interfere with me; told me not to be afraid; they would defend me. I had to plead very hard to stop them; told them I didn't wish a mutiny on board on my account; saw the mate cocking his pistol; said shoot away, you can't intimidate me....I remained in this position for some fifteen or twenty minutes."

Then Judge McAllister came through the crowd and said, "Duane, put your knife away; don't cut anybody, or the captain will hang you at the yard-arm, as he has done so before." Duane testified, "I knew he was a friend. I took his advise [*sic*]; put my knife away, and cried like a child. I couldn't help it. They came and dragged me away to the side of the ship. There was a great confusion on board; passengers cried 'Shame! Shame!' Judge McAllister said to the mate, 'You shall be held responsible for this high-handed measure on the high seas.'"

Duane was taken aboard the *Sonora* and ended up back in Acapulco. Hoffman awarded Duane $4,000 damages in his case against Captain Pearson, who was defended by another of Judge McAllister's sons, Hall. Judge McAllister never sat on any of Duane's cases, but he did find for Martin Gallagher when Gallagher sued the master of the *Hercules* in the circuit court. Gallagher's sentence of banishment was "issued by a body of men authorized by no law, and who substituted their private judgements for the action of those judicial tribunals to which constitution and laws of their country had confided solely the distribution of justice," wrote Judge McAllister.

These decisions, by the district court and circuit court, finally put an end to vigilantism in San Francisco.

CHAPTER 2

THE GOLD RUSH AND THE LAND GRAB

FOUR DAYS AFTER the first flakes were found in the mud beneath John Augustus Sutter's new sawmill near Sacramento, Sutter's employee James Marshall nervously unwrapped the mysterious material he had collected. On January 28, 1848, Sutter weighed and tested the substance, looked up at Marshall, and said, "It's gold."

Sutter tried to keep the find a secret, because he knew once word leaked out, he would lose the workers he needed to build his planned agricultural empire. But within days, rumors began to spread. Within weeks, Mormon entrepreneur Samuel Brannan ran down the streets of San Francisco shaking a glass vial and yelling, "Gold! Gold! Gold from the American River!" By the end of 1848, President James K. Polk confirmed the "abundance of gold" found in the hills more than one hundred miles northeast of San Francisco, near present-day Coloma. California—and the world—would never be the same.

"Over all California the excitement was prodigious," recalled *The Annals of San Francisco*. "Spaniard, American, and foreigner were all alike affected. The husband left his wife; the father, his family; men deserted their masters, and these followed their servants—all hurried to Sutter's Mill."

The effect on John Sutter's enterprises was immediate and calamitous. He possessed no mineral rights to the gold, and prospectors and squatters soon overran his land. "By this sudden discovery of the gold, all my great plans were destroyed," he wrote in 1857. "From my mill buildings I reaped no benefit whatever, the mill stones even have been stolen and sold. Had I succeeded for a few years before the gold was discovered, I would have been the richest citizen on the Pacific shore; but it had to be different. Instead of being rich, I am ruined."

PREVIOUS PAGE
See Fig. 2-4 for caption.

An early pioneer and a delegate to California's constitutional convention in 1849, Sutter continued to reap nothing but ruin from the rush that created modern California. When California was part of Mexico, all that was needed for legal title to land was a crude *diseño*, or sketch, of a property's vague boundaries, a letter from the governor, and the honor of a gentleman. After statehood, granted in 1850, Sutter and other landowners, including cities, would have to prove to the US courts that their lands had been officially granted to them by the Spanish or Mexican governments, otherwise they would become public domain. A three-tiered approval system was set up by Congress in 1851 to separate private from public land. Claims were made to the US Board of Land Commissioners, automatically appealed to the district court, and could then be appealed to the Supreme Court. The costly legal process took years, and landowners were often left with just a portion of their original holdings. Judge Hoffman and the district court would decide most of the state's more than eight hundred claims for private land grants, including four made by Sutter and many made by the state's cities.

Sutter was born in Kandern, Baden, Germany, near the Swiss border, in 1803. He abandoned his wife and four small children to escape debtors' prison in Switzerland and arrived in California in 1839. Two years later, after becoming a Mexican citizen, Sutter was granted nearly 49,000 acres of land by Mexican governor Juan B. Alvarado. In exchange, Sutter was to cultivate the land and secure it from hostile Native Americans.

Sutter's was just one of nearly five hundred ranchos, or large land grants, that Mexican governors handed out between 1823 and 1846 to encourage settlement of Alta California and in return for political and material favors. Altogether, Spanish and Mexican land grants comprised

Early California Land Measurement

The Spanish and Mexican system of land measurement was based on the *vara*, or Spanish yard, approximately thirty-three inches long depending on the locale. This fluid measurement system led to the notation of *poco mas o meno*, "more or less," being included in most land grants. The *legua*, or square league, was the equivalent of about 4,439 acres in California (slightly less in Texas). In the 1850s, the US Surveyor fixed the *vara* at 33.3 inches for the purposes of land patents.

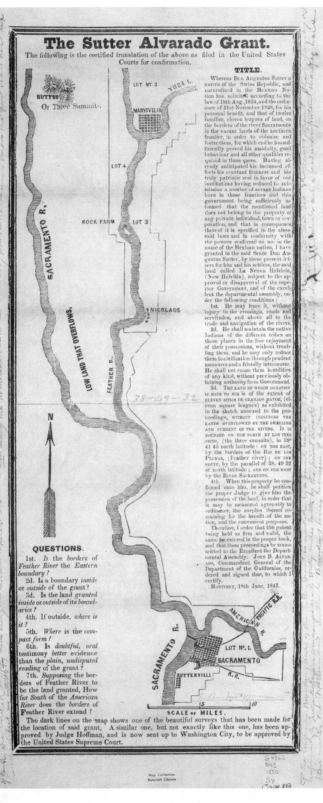

The Sutter Alvarado Grant.

The following is the certified translation of the above as filed in the United States Courts for confirmation.

BUTTES
Or Three Summit.

LOT Nº 3
YUBA R.
MARYSVILLE
LOT 4
SACRAMENTO R.
HOCK FARM   LOT 2
LOW LAND THAT OVERFLOWS.
FEATHER R.
NICOLAUS

38—49—32

N

QUESTIONS.

1st. *Is the borders of Feather River the Eastern boundary?*

2d. *Is a boundary inside or outside of the grant?*

3d. *Is the land granted inside or outside of its boundaries?*

4th. *If outside, where is it?*

5th. *Where is the compact form?*

6th. *Is doubtful, oral testimony better evidence than the plain, undisputed reading of the grant?*

7th. *Supposing the borders of Feather River to be the land granted, How far South of the American River does the borders of Feather River extend?*

TITLE.

Whereas Don Augustus Sutter a native of the Swiss Republic, and naturalized in the Mexican Nation has solicited according to the law of 18th Aug., 1824, and the ordinance of 21st November 1828, for his personal benefit, and that of twelve families, eleven leagues of land, on the borders of the river Sacramento in the vacant lands of the northern frontier, in order to colonize and foster them, for which end he hassufficiently proved his assiduity, good behaviour and all other qualities required in those cases. Having already anticipated his increased efforts his constant firmness and his truly patriotic zeal in favor of our institutions having reduced to submission a number of savage Indians born in those frontiers and this government being sufficiently informed that the mentioned land does not belong to the property of any private individual, town or corporation, and that in consequence thereof it is specified in the aforesaid laws and in conformity with the powers conferred on me in the name of the Mexican nation, I have granted to the said Señor Don Augustus Sutter, by these present letters for him and his settlers, the said land called La Nueva Helvitia, (New Helvitia,) subject to the approval or disapproval of the superior Government, and of the excellent the departmental assembly, under the following conditions :

1st. He may fence it, without injury to the crossings, roads and servitudes, and above all to the trade and navigation of the rivers.

2d. He shall maintain the native Indians of the different tribes on those places in the free enjoyment of their possessions, without troubling them, and he may only reduce them to civilization through prudent measures and a friendly intercourse. He shall not cause them hostilities of any kind, without previously obtaining authority from Government.

3d. THE LAND OF WHICH DONATION IS MADE TO HIM is of the extent of ELEVEN SITIOS DE GRANADO MAYOR, (eleven square leagues) as exhibited in the sketch annexed to the proceedings, WITHOUT INCLUDING THE LANDS OVERFLOWED BY THE SWELLING AND CURRENT OF THE RIVERS. IT IS BOUNDED ON THE NORTH BY LOS TRES PICOS, (the three summits), in 39º 41 45 north latitude : ON THE EAST, by the borders of the RIO DE LOS PLUMAS, (Feather river) ; ON THE SOUTH, by the parallel of 38, 49 32 of north latitude ; AND ON THE WEST by the RIVER SACRAMENTO.

4th. When this property be confirmed unto him, he shall petition the proper Judge to give him the possession of the land, in order that it may be measured agreeably to ordinance, the surplus thereof remaining for the benefit of the nation, and the convenient purposes.

Therefore, I order that this patent being held as firm and valid, the same be entered in the proper book, and that these proceedings be transmitted to the Excellent the Departmental Assembly. JOHN B. ALVARADO, Commandant General of the Department of the Californias, ordered and signed thus, to which I certify.

MONTEREY, 18th June, 1841.

AMERICAN R.
PACIFIC R.R.
SACRAMENTO R.
LOT Nº 1.
SACRAMENTO
SUTTERVILLE
R. R.

SCALE OF MILES.
5   10

The dark lines on the map shows one of the beautiful surveys that has been made for the location of said grant, A similar one, but not exactly like this one, has been approved by Judge Hoffman, and is now sent up to Washington City, to be approved by the United States Supreme Court.

19,000 square miles (13 percent of the state's total area) of California's best land along the coast from San Diego to Mendocino, around San Francisco Bay, and along the major rivers.

Sutter's property sat at the fork of the Sacramento and American Rivers, close to the major overland trails into California from the Midwest. There Sutter built the first European settlement in the Sacramento Valley, which he called Nueva Helvetia, or New Switzerland. Sutter's Fort—a five-acre walled compound—prospered as Sutter acquired supplies and animals, planted crops, fought off Indians, and acted as a government representative in the area. He also became known as a generous benefactor and played a key role in rescuing the survivors of the ill-fated Donner Party in 1846.

But by 1848, Sutter was deep in debt, overleveraged in his agricultural expansion. The discovery of gold would undo his plans as it accelerated California's integration into the United States. California would skip territorial status and go directly from American occupation in 1846 to statehood in 1850. Gold made California the United States' premier property. The fact that the Americans—not the English, French, or Russians, who had also been eyeing California—were the ones who took California from Mexico would complete the nascent country's westward expansion and change the world's immigrant and economic patterns for decades to come.

Sutter's oldest son, John Augustus Sutter Jr., arrived in California coincidentally just after gold was discovered in 1848. He worked ardently to put his father's financial house in order, but neither man was suited to the cutthroat speculation that came with the gold rush. To raise money, Sutter Jr. laid out a town at a key landing on the Sacramento River, and sold lots from his father's holdings. He founded Sacramento, paid off most of his father's debts, and brought the rest of the Sutter family to California from Switzerland. But John Sutter was furious because his son's success put an end to his own plans for a town down the river, to be called Sutterville. Their relationship disintegrated, fueled by investors who stood to gain by estranging the father and son. Both Sutters were

FIG. 2-1 (OPPOSITE)
Certified translation of the Sutter-Alvarado grant, as filed in the United States court in Monterey for confirmation on June 18, 1841. "The dark lines on the map," the document explains, "show one of the beautiful surveys that has been made for the location of said grant. A similar one...has been approved by Judge Hoffman, and is now sent up to Washington City, to be approved by the United States Supreme Court." Courtesy of The Bancroft Library, University of California, Berkeley.

gullible and trusting of shark-like advisers, who made off with most of their land and money.

"I respected him for his intrepid courage, his gentle manners, his large heart, and his unbounded benevolence," wrote Justice Stephen J. Field of John Sutter in his 1877 memoir *Personal Reminiscences of Early Days in California*. A forty-niner, Field was a frontier lawyer and politician who helped write California's civil and criminal codes. He was elected to the state supreme court and later served as the first Supreme Court justice from California. He wrote of Sutter, "I pitied him for his simplicity, which, while suspecting nothing wrong in others, led him to trust all who had a kind word on their lips, and made him the victim of every sharper in the country."

Sutter Jr., ill and disgusted with his gold rush experience, left Sacramento in 1850 for Acapulco, where he married and eventually became US consul, never to return to California. For all the grief and strife he encountered, he only received $35,000 on property that, even then, was worth hundreds of thousands of dollars.

In 1852, John Sutter filed claim No. 92 with the land board for the New Helvetia grant, more than 145,000 acres in Yuba and Sutter counties. In addition to the original grant in 1841, Sutter received 96,000 acres from Governor Manuel Micheltorena in 1845. The board confirmed Sutter's claim in 1855, and the district court confirmed it upon appeal from the federal government. But the US Attorney appealed the decision to the Supreme Court. Sutter bitterly resented the final appeal.

The Supreme Court ruled in 1857 that Sutter's 1841 grant was valid, but it rejected the 1845 grant. The court determined that Micheltorena had signed the grant under duress (during a civil war in which Sutter supplied him with a foreign militia) and that Sutter never registered the grant with the successive Mexican administration.

Despite having his legal title to a large portion of his land confirmed, Sutter lost most of it to swindlers, squatters, and legal costs incurred while defending his title. He had to sell off or trade land to pay lawyers and court costs. A fire in 1865, believed set by a squatter, destroyed his Victorian redwood home on Hock Farm, near Marysville, where he had retired. Afterward, he and his wife and several grandchildren left California. From there, he traveled frequently to Washington to petition Congress for restitution for his property, which he charged the government had failed to protect when it acquired California. Sutter died in 1880 as Congress was considering legislation that would have awarded him $50,000.

"Sharpers robbed him of what the squatters did not take, until at last he was stripped of everything; and, finally, he left the State, and for some years has been living with relatives in Pennsylvania," Field wrote of Sutter's last years. "Even the stipend of $2,500, which the State of California for some years allowed him, has been withdrawn, and now in his advanced years, he is almost destitute....Yet, in his days of prosperity, he was always ready to assist others. His fort was always open to the stranger, and food, to the value of many thousand dollars, was, every year, so long as he had the means, sent out by him for the relief of emigrants crossing the plains. It is a reproach to California that she leaves the pioneer and hero destitute in his old age."

District Court Marshal Francis Bret Harte, Gold Rush Writer

Writer and poet Francis Bret Harte was born in New York in 1836 and moved to California in 1854. He worked a number of odd jobs in San Francisco to support his writing, including a stint in 1862 as a US marshal for the Northern District Court. He was sworn in by Judge Hoffman on his twenty-eighth birthday and was issued a badge and a six-shooter. He later served as secretary to the US Mint in San Francisco before moving back to New York in 1870.

In his 1868 story "The Luck of Roaring Camp," which propelled him to national fame, he writes about frontier life:

> The assemblage numbered about a hundred men. One or two of these were actual fugitives from justice, some were criminal, and all were reckless. Physically they exhibited no indication of their past lives and character. The greatest scamp had a Raphael face, with a profusion of blond hair; Oakhurst, a gambler, had the melancholy air and intellectual abstraction of a Hamlet; the coolest and most courageous man was scarcely over five feet in height, with a soft voice and an embarrassed, timid manner. The term "roughs" applied to them was a distinction rather than a definition. Perhaps in the minor details of fingers, toes, ears, etc., the camp may have been deficient, but these slight omissions did not detract from their aggregate force. The strongest man had but three fingers on his right hand; the best shot had but one eye.

Who Owns California?

"In the early days of California there were two important issues, one legal and one economic, both of which were encompassed in the question: Who owns the land in California?" wrote Kenneth Johnson in the 1975 introduction to Judge Hoffman's 1862 book, *Hoffman's Reports: Land Cases,* which collected his decisions on appeals from the land board. Indeed, who? The rights to this land spanned five hundred years of exploration, conquest, and war. The native California Indians were already established in the region when Spanish explorers first visited what they would call Alta California in the 1500s. Not until the late 1700s would Spain colonize the isolated area, establish a Roman Catholic mission system, and issue about one hundred private land grants. California would be Spain's last colony.

After Mexico gained independence from Spain in 1821, Alta California, along with most of the present American Southwest, became a Mexican province. Mexico liberalized trade and immigration rules in Alta California, allowed foreigners to receive land grants, and shut down the mission system.

As in the former Mexican territory of Texas, this new liberal immigration policy led to a growing number of American settlers in California. By the 1840s, many settlers and leading Californios—California-born descendants of Spanish and Mexican settlers—were tired of the Mexican government's neglect and longed for independence or an alliance with the United States or England. In 1845, President Polk's administration offered Mexico $25 million to purchase California and other parts of the Southwest. But after his personal envoy was snubbed, Polk sent four thousand soldiers to the disputed borderline along the Rio Grande River in southern Texas, sparking a fight with Mexican troops. Congress formally declared war against Mexico in May. It took several months for this news to reach California, which was in the middle of the Bear Flag Revolt, a short-lived bid for independence based in Sonoma, north of San Francisco, and led by surveyor John C. Frémont and a group of American settlers. Frémont would be California's first, albeit brief, military governor and one of its first US senators. His claim for the Las Mariposas rancho would be the first case filed with the land board and the district court.

On July 7, 1846, US forces seized Alta California's capital, Monterey, without firing a shot. Two days later, the American flag was raised in

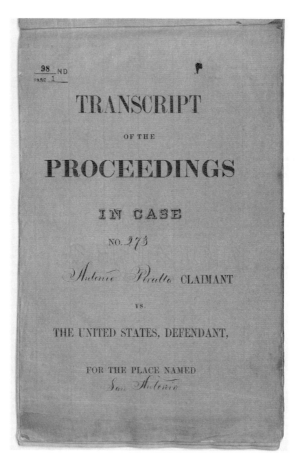

FIG. 2-2
Title page of the transcript of the proceedings of *United States v. Antonio Peralta,* from the San Antonio land grant case files (Case No. 98, US District Court, Northern District, 1852–1871), pertaining to the adjudication of private land claims in California. Courtesy of The Bancroft Library, University of California, Berkeley.

the plaza of the pueblo of Yerba Buena (now Portsmouth Square in San Francisco) and the Bear Flag was replaced with the Stars and Stripes in Sonoma. The Mexican-American War ended in September 1847 after American forces took control of Mexico City. The two sides signed the Treaty of Guadalupe Hidalgo in 1848, coincidentally just days after gold was discovered at Sutter's Mill. In the document, Mexico gave up nearly half of its territory, including all or part of present-day California, Arizona, New Mexico, Nevada, Utah, Wyoming, and Colorado, in return for peace as well as $15 million and a new border. The treaty also promised that Mexican and Spanish settlers in the new American territories—about ten thousand people in California—would be able to keep their land.

But in order to keep it, the Californios would need to survive the US land grant approval process. Spanish and Mexican law was in effect until April 1850, when the first California legislature adopted English common law and the state courts were established. Statehood brought with it the creation of the California federal courts. Although much of the district court's extraordinary jurisdiction was revoked in 1855, when Congress created a special California circuit court, land claim appeals stayed with the district court.

Judge Hoffman heard almost all of the California land claims in San Francisco, where the Board of Land Commissioners met and all court records for the state were kept. The California Land Act, passed by Congress in 1851, required a claimant to provide documentation, witnesses, and maps of their land as evidence. The land board and courts looked to the treaty with Mexico, Spanish and Mexican law, and the customs of the era for guidance in making decisions, but the process was painfully slow, taking an average of seventeen years. Once approved by the courts, land had to be formally surveyed and registered in Washington, DC, before a patent, which served as a deed, could be issued. Of 809 claims filed with the land board, all but 19 were appealed to the district court, according to W. W. Robinson's 1948 book, *Land in California*. Once a patent was issued, this only settled the fact that the land was privately owned and not part of public domain. Lawsuits by private parties could—and did—continue in state court and squatters were emboldened by unsettled titles.

The land-rich but cash-poor Californios had a difficult transition from the Spanish-speaking, informal bureaucratic culture of a colonial outpost to the English-speaking, impersonal legal structure of a new American state. They were reviled in their own home for their race and their vast land holdings. "Up and down California, during the five years of the board's activities, Californians gathered up all the papers they could to prove to the gentlemen of the board that they owned the land that they had been living on for so many years," wrote Robinson, who continued:

> They looked into their leather trunks for original grants from Mexican governors. They called upon their friends and relatives to testify to long residence and to the number of their cattle. They went to Yankee lawyers for help. They sent to the Surveyor General's Office in San Francisco for

copies of the archive files relating to particular ranchos. They made journeys and drew upon their slender fund of cash. They sometimes mortgaged their lands and their futures or conveyed "undivided" interests to their attorneys. Town officials bestirred themselves to prove pueblo titles. Mission claimants did likewise. Indians, quite unaware of what was happening, did nothing about the lands they were occupying.

The Mexican laws the commission looked to were clear about the requirements needed to receive a grant of land. First, a person, be they Mexican or foreign, had to petition the Alta California governor for specific lands, describe the land, and provide a *diseño*. Second, the governor had to sign a grant, a document that served as title, to the person and then record the petition, grant, and *diseño* in the state archives in Monterey. Third, these grants had to be approved by the Territorial Deputation, or the supreme government, in Mexico City. Grants to *empresarios* (entrepreneurs such as Sutter) for colonization also required approval from the supreme government. Failure to occupy or cultivate the land within a prescribed time voided the grant. Proof of occupancy or cultivation had to be presented to nearby municipal authorities, the *alcaldes*, in order to secure ownership and to authorize any sale. Unfortunately for the claimants—and the courts—few of the Mexican grants fully conformed to Mexican law. Alta California's rotating Mexican governors (twelve in twenty-three years) were lax in their filings and slow in documenting titles. Documents were misplaced, lost in the mail, and destroyed in fires or shipwrecks, leaving claimants to rely heavily on verbal testimony rather than documentation.

The land board and the courts had great discretion in how closely they followed Mexican legal requirements or the laxity of the era's customs. However, decisions based on informal customs fueled suspicions of fraud in a political environment that already strongly resented the Californios' vast amounts of land. But the Treaty of Guadalupe Hidalgo, which stated that "property of every kind, now belonging to Mexicans…shall be inviolably respected," was very clear that Mexican citizens who owned property needed to be respected as if they were Americans.

Although the Californios and their ranchos drew the most attention, they were not the only ones to receive land grants. The bulk of the more than eight hundred claims filed with the land board were from settlers of more humble origins, many of them retired soldiers. Not all of these landowners filed claims under the new American government; some people were unaware of the process or of the two-year deadline or didn't have the resources to finance a claim.

The California Land Act also confirmed corporate authorities to any city, town, or village that existed on July 7, 1846, the day the American flag was raised in Monterey. This meant that municipal authorities of existing pueblos could petition the land board for the four square leagues (nearly 18,000 acres) of land due to them under Mexican law. The civic pueblos of San Jose, Los Angeles, and Sonoma and the military pueblos of San Francisco, Santa Barbara, San Diego, and Monterey all petitioned the board for various amounts of land. All eventually received patents for some pueblo lands. Los Angeles asked for sixteen square leagues and got four; meanwhile, the gold rush land grab caused a dramatic and lengthy legal battle for San Francisco's pueblo land.

California's Native Americans did not fare so well. The US government negotiated eighteen treaties with the chiefs of a number of California Indian tribes after California's admission to the Union. The tribes agreed to cede their rights to lands in exchange for use and occupation of a number of specific areas, plus support for their communities in the form of buildings, tools, clothing, livestock, seeds and rootstocks, and teachers. But the Senate, after the urging of the California legislature, later refused to ratify a single one of the treaties. California Indians were left with nothing. Many became homeless wanderers, subject to persecution, starvation, exploitation, enslavement, and massacre. Only a handful of claims on behalf of individual Native Americans were presented to the land board.

Meanwhile, frontier lawyers grabbed land too. Henry Halleck, California's first secretary of state, wrote the first of two reports to Congress on California land that preceded the passage of the California Land Act. Halleck had been the first American official to review the Mexican archives in Monterey, where the land grant records were kept. He took a critical overview of California's land titles, concluding that most were "at least doubtful, if not entirely fraudulent" because they did not conform to the letter of Mexican law. Halleck wrote that the state's land-claim system was wide open to fraud. He noted that much of the claimed land had already been subdivided by the owners and sold to speculators who would jack up the price before selling it to new settlers.

While Halleck recommended critical scrutiny for rancho titles, he advised that *alcalde* grants be summarily confirmed. Between 1846 and

1850, when California was an American territory, land grants could be made under the *alcalde* system, where an official who was a sort of mayor and justice of the peace could grant land within his jurisdiction. Halleck owned the 30,000-acre Rancho Nicasio in Marin County and a number of valuable lots in San Francisco that had been granted by the *alcalde*. Halleck also acted as the purchasing agent for a number of ranchos for new settlers, and was director of the New Almaden Quicksilver Mine in San Jose, the subject of a bitter land grant dispute. Halleck's law firm, Halleck, Peachy, and Billings, represented many prominent Californios in their land claims, including Mariano Vallejo, José de la Guerra y Noriega, and Andrés Pico.

Another attorney, William Carey Jones, filed a similar report, but while he confirmed that many of the grants did not perfectly comply with Mexican law, he reasoned that few people followed such formalities during the heyday of California colonization. "The law of custom, with the acquiescence of the highest authorities, overcame, in these respects, the written law," wrote Jones in his *Report on the Subject of Land Titles in California*. He advocated a speedy approval process that reserved government opposition only on truly suspect claims. But Jones, too, had a land claim himself. He had purchased a 53,000-acre rancho in San Diego County while researching his report.

In the end, the California Land Act was written by Democrat William Gwin, California's other first senator (he served together with John Frémont), and a champion of the rights of settlers, not landed Californios. The law reflected Halleck's skepticism—the burden of proof was on those who claimed a right in the land and could establish it by acceptable documentation.

In the mid- to late 1850s, when most of the land cases came to the district court, Judge Hoffman was often the only sitting district judge for the entire state, so most appeals from Southern California ranchos were heard in his San Francisco court as well. Travel was by horse or stagecoach until the 1870s, when railroads finally connected key cities. Anyone filing a land claim, regardless of whether their property was in Mendocino, San Mateo, or San Diego Counties, would have to make the long and expensive journey to San Francisco.

Hoffman was overwhelmed by the deluge of land grant appeals atop an already crushing court caseload. He wrote to US Attorney General Caleb Cushing asking for help in 1853: "After two years and a half of almost uninterrupted toil at a compensation very less than the smallest professional income of respectable lawyers, I should at length have an opportunity for occasional leisure and relaxation, and should no longer be discouraged by the anticipation of unremitting and unrelenting labor." By 1854, Hoffman was sick and near collapse from the strain. In 1855, Hoffman finally got a raise—from $3,700 to $5,000 annually—as well as help in the form of the special California circuit court. Starting in 1856, circuit court judge Matthew Hall McAllister also sat with Hoffman to hear land claim appeals.

Though the land board was disbanded in 1856, many cases dragged on for decades and were ultimately resolved by the Supreme Court. Hoffman, though he diligently followed precedent, often found his decisions reversed by the Supreme Court, which vacillated in how strictly it interpreted Spanish and Mexican legal requirements.

Spanish Roots of California

Crucial to a judge's ability to rule on California's land titles was an understanding of the practices and customs in effect during Spanish colonization; of Spanish and Mexican laws, including the Laws of the Indies and the *Regalamento*; as well as of the Treaty of Guadalupe Hidalgo.

Spain had waited nearly two hundred years before finally colonizing California in the 1770s. While Spain desperately needed northern ports for her fleets of galleons making the spice run from the Philippines to Acapulco, it was the fear that England, Russia, or France might try to take California that finally made Spain act. (Ironically, this same fear—that a foreign entity might grab the isolated prize—was what pushed President Polk seventy years later to provoke the Mexican-American War.) California was an expensive proposition for any country in the eighteenth and nineteenth centuries: isolated, on the other side of the world from the European and American seats of government, with few settlers, many hostile natives, no economic activity to speak of, and an uncertain future despite its fabulous natural harbors, varied vegetation, and mild climate. But the Spanish Empire was over-extended in its colonial activities and stretched to its financial limits. California would be her last colony, held for a mere half century.

Spain's relationship with the Roman Catholic Church was the key to its colonization of California. Missionary priests were common on voyages

FIG. 2-3
Walter Colton, *alcalde* (chief magistrate) of Monterey, described a pastoral scene in *Three Years in California,* his account of California before the gold rush. This illustration from the book depicts couples on horseback riding through bucolic woods on their way to a picnic (*marrienda*). Courtesy of the California Historical Society Collections at the University of Southern California.

to the New World, providing the dual task of Christianizing natives and solidifying military and civic colonization efforts. The Spanish monarchy acquired the rights to most of the New World from Pope Alexander VI in 1493. This included Mexico, most of North America, much of Central and South America, and parts of the Caribbean. Starting in 1535, the Mexico City–based Viceroyalty of New Spain controlled nearly everything north of the Isthmus of Panama, including present-day Mexico, California, Nevada, Utah, Colorado, Wyoming, Arizona, Texas, and New Mexico.

In Alta California, missionaries from the Franciscan order, led by Fray Junípero Serra, and the natives—for all intents and purposes enslaved by the missionaries—built a string of twenty-one missions from San Diego to Sonoma that would be the backbone of California's development. Serra was a part of the 1769 overland expedition led by Spanish Captain

Gaspar de Portolà, who established presidios in San Diego and Monterey and brought Franciscan missionaries to build the missions. On October 31, 1769, Portolà, coming by land from the south, found San Francisco Bay, whose narrow, fog-shrouded entrance had eluded discovery by ship. The San Francisco presidio and the mission of San Francisco de Asís (Saint Francis of Assisi), also known as Mission Dolores, were both founded there in 1776.

The twenty-one missions formed a chain of outposts along the six-hundred-mile-long El Camino Real trail (the Royal Highway, now Highway 101), all within a day's ride from the coast and each other. Soldiers and their families settled military presidios in San Diego, Monterey, Santa Barbara, and San Francisco and civilian pueblos in San Jose, Branciforte (Santa Cruz), and Los Angeles. The presidios provided protection for the missions and the missions provided food for the presidios.

The mission system was meant to be temporary—Spanish law dictated that the missions and their lands were being held in trust for the Indians until they became *gente di razón* (people of reason—civilized citizens). Then the missionaries were to be replaced with parish priests and the community was to become a pueblo with each Indian having the right to his own land. But that never happened. Only a handful of California's Indians ever received title to any land. Despite the good intentions of the mission movement, the only thing it offered most California Indians was death, mostly from European diseases such as smallpox, measles, typhus, and influenza, to which they had no immunity.

As California's population slowly increased, the interests of the ranchos and pueblos increasingly clashed with those of the missions. The priests protested as ranchos were carved out of the edges of "their" land, which they claimed they needed for the Indians. For example, San Francisco's Mission Dolores had been using parts of the Rancho San Antonio (present-day Oakland, Berkeley, Alameda, Emeryville, Piedmont, Albany, and San Leandro) for sheep grazing. The priests protested when the land was ceded to Luis María Peralta by Spanish governor Pablo Vicente de Solá in 1820.

When Mexico gained independence from Spain in 1821, it took almost a year for the news to reach Alta California. The new government allowed free trade, granted land to foreign settlers (after they had converted to Catholicism), and dismantled the mission system, leading to a new land rush. The number of land grants issued by the Mexican government jumped after 1834, the year the missions began to close. By the end of 1836, there were more than one hundred in total; by the 1840s, one hundred or more were being granted each year. When Joseph Sodoc Alemany, San Francisco's first Roman Catholic archbishop, filed claims with the land board in 1853 for land at all twenty-one missions, the total was for just over forty thousand acres, a paltry shadow of the church's earlier land holdings. The US patents issued to the church were mostly for the immediate land that contained the churches, cemeteries and gardens, ranging from 6.48 acres in Marin County at Mission San Rafael Arcángel to 283 acres at Mission Santa Barbara.

Because missions were created to bring Christianity to the Native Americans, some of the mission land was distributed to Indian families. A few short-lived Indian pueblos and a number of baptized Indians received Mexican land grants. By and large, though, the Indians were left to fend for themselves in a new and confusing world: many had grown up in the missions and had little knowledge of traditional ways of living (plus their hunting and gathering grounds continued to shrink with the growth of settlement and immigration), and now not even the missions were there to shelter them.

The missions and their famed vineyards were abandoned or fell into disrepair. The mission era gave way to the rancho era, an economy based on cattle. By 1846, close to five hundred ranchos had been established. They ranged in size from less than 20 acres to the 115,000 acres of the former Mission of San Fernando. One man, José de la Guerra y Noriega, of Santa Barbara, had four ranchos—Simi, San Julian, Conejo, and Las Posas—totaling nearly 216,000 acres. The rancho era was a time of pastoral living when landed Californio families lived in sprawling haciendas with gardens and thousands of heads of cattle. The lives of rancho families were filled with picnics, horsemanship, bear hunts, target practice, long meals, family gatherings, and dances. They would take turns hosting days-long fiestas such as rodeos and fandangos to celebrate a roundup or a saint's feast day. But this life would last less than a generation. Most of the rancho families were wiped out financially during the 1850s land grant approval process or by the alternating droughts and severe flooding of the mid-1860s that littered Southern California with the bloated bodies of drowned cattle.

Under Mexican law, only a Catholic could petition the government for a land grant. But many non-Hispanic immigrants, including American,

English, Irish, Dutch, and Swiss, became Mexican citizens, converted (if necessary) to Catholicism, married into local families, and received land grants. Some of these foreigners, such as Yerba Buena pioneers William Richardson and Jacob P. Leese, received grants that were later approved by the district court. Richardson, who established the first trading post in Yerba Buena, made a claim to a grant of ten-by-two leagues in Mendocino County and for the Rancho Saucelito in Marin County, which were both confirmed by the land board. Leese, who built the second house in Yerba Buena, filed a land-grant claim for 200-by-100 *varas* in San Francisco, which was confirmed in 1856. His 3.38 acres near the corner of present-day Grant Avenue and Clay Street would prove to be worth a fortune as the village of Yerba Buena exploded into the city of San Francisco during the gold rush. In 1852, he bought the Rancho Sausal (near present day Salinas in Monterey County). His claim was upheld by the district court and patented in 1857.

Shotgun Titles

A clear title didn't necessarily give one peace of mind during California's heyday. Squatters and "shotgun titles" reduced the toughest man's legitimate claim from a blanket to a handkerchief. Archibald Ritchie was one of those men. A retired clipper ship captain who came to California in 1848 at the age of forty-two, he set up a shop outfitting miners in San Francisco. Delaware-born Ritchie had run away to sea at age thirteen and was a captain by nineteen. He made considerable money in the China tea trade, but "swallowed the anchor" (retired from the sea) in 1838 and worked as a shipping agent in Canton, China, before coming to California. Once here, he set about investing his large capital in land.

Henry Halleck handled Ritchie's 1850 purchase of a large parcel in Benicia (briefly the state capital in 1853). Ritchie then acquired the Guenoc and Loconma (Collayomi) ranchos in Lake County, 150 acres in Napa County, the Calistoga grant in Sonoma County, and the Rancho Suisun in Solano County, plus property in San Francisco. He built a handsome residence in the city's fashionable South Park neighborhood near Rincon Hill, where he lived with his wife and seven children. His claims were all confirmed by the district court.

The tangled title of the Rancho Suisin is a good example of what the land board and the district court faced in deciding some of its claims and the severity of the squatter problem. The rancho had been one of the few granted to a Christianized Indian. "Whereas the native Francisco Solano, Chief of the Suisunnes of the Yokut Indian nation, has claimed for his personal benefit and that of his family and tribesmen, that tract of land known by the name of Suisun, of which he is a native and Chief of the tribe on the frontier of Sonoma, in the name of the Mexican Nation has deeded him the said land," stated the grant signed by Mexican governor Juan Alvarado in 1842. Just four months later, the chief sold the nearly 18,000-acre rancho for $1,000 to his friend, General Mariano Vallejo, prompting more than a century of suspicion that Solano was really fronting for Vallejo all along. In 1850, Vallejo sold the Suisun Rancho to Ritchie for $50,000. Ritchie filed his claim for Rancho Suisun in 1852. It was the third claim filed with the board, which confirmed it a year later. The district court upheld it in 1853 and the Supreme Court confirmed it in 1855.

Despite his legal title to the Suisun Rancho, Ritchie had a problem common to land owners in gold rush California: squatters. Shotgun titles

FIG. 2-4
California artist Charles Nahl's sketch *Bogue Ejecting the Squatters* was published in *Old Block's Sketch-Book*, a collection of tales of gold rush California, in 1856. The shotgun and the fist were common resources used by both gold miners and squatters to secure their possessions. Courtesy of the California Historical Society, FN-30963/CHS2013.1142.

usually proved stronger than paper ones. Ritchie wrote a series of letters on the problem to both lawyers and politicians while his title wound its way through the labyrinth of the approval process. He wrote:

> You are aware that the whole of this property of mine has been taken possession of by 'Squatters,' to the number of more than 150 preemption claimants that they have expelled me from it, by threats and a demonstration of loaded rifles! & have formed themselves into an association, professing...a determination never to give up the lands in question, even if my Title is confirmed, & in regard to said Title, H.W. Halleck Esq. pronounces it perfect.
>
> I may add that many of the Squatters on Suisun, were men of considerable property, when they settled there, several of the claims being held by merchants, Doctors & I believe one or two calling themselves lawyers! Tho a majority are young men without families which reminds me that I have a wife and seven children, that the hard earnings of thirty years, mostly passed on the ocean ($50,000) are invested in Suisun lands... Captain Halleck says, 'It is impossible for our Gov't or our US Courts to violate or disregard the solemn provisions of a treaty, and that all will come out right in good time,' but I have so long 'been hoping against hope,' that I must confess, I have of late been inclined to despair.

Squatters had prevented any surveys being done of the property, delaying the issuance of a patent. Finally US marshals had to be sent to enforce the order. In 1856, with his title finally clear but with squatters still on his property, Ritchie suffered a fatal stroke in his carriage on the road from Sonoma to Napa and died. A patent for the Rancho Suisun was finally issued the following year.

Squatters plagued private and public owners. Possession was considered the best legal remedy. Riots over land became commonplace in the 1850s. Sacramento was the site of the deadliest one in the muggy August of 1850. Squatters had settled all over lots previously sold by the Sutter family. After several squatters' homes were demolished, a series of confrontations led to a waterfront riot that left the city assessor and a number of squatters dead and scores of others wounded, including the mayor and sheriff.

In San Francisco, soldiers had to be dispatched from the presidio to oust squatters on government land at Rincon Point and other areas. In 1853, a battle over a lot at Third and Mission Streets left two men dead and five wounded. Wealthy landowners hired private police or caretakers to keep their lots occupied and protected. Others were at the mercy of the mob. "A poor woman, who owned a solitary house on a small lot, had her house burned down, the land fenced in and herself turned out into the street to starve," reported *The Annals of San Francisco* on the aggression of the city's squatters. "The problem went unchecked by the authorities; riot followed riot; the squatters armed themselves and threatened to kill whoever should attempt to dispossess them."

Squatting was fueled by resentment. New immigrants expected that there would be ample free and good land for homesteading as there had been in the Oregon and Washington Territories and that the US government would allow it. The fact that vast amounts of prime land were already in private hands in a new state outraged many. The call of "Free land for Americans!" echoed throughout the state. By 1856, the squatter's lobby was so influential that the California state legislature passed a law stating that all lands were to be regarded as public land until legal title proved it was privately owned. (This was later struck down by the Supreme Court as unconstitutional.) The amount of time it took for land grants to clear the courts only strengthened squatters' resolve and influenced their settlement patterns. If the land board rejected a claim, squatters would swarm the area once word got out. If that claim was later upheld by the district court, some might move, but most refused.

Law or Customs?

It was precisely this choice between law and customs that was presented in the first claim filed with the land board and the first case reversed by the district court. John C. Frémont, the famous explorer, cartographer, writer, and soldier, filed the claim on Las Mariposas, a 44,387-acre rancho named after the butterflies that inhabit the area. Technically, the grant did not comply with Mexican law, as Frémont never lived on the rancho. In fact, he never even wanted to buy it.

In 1847, Frémont gave $3,000 to Thomas O. Larkin, the US consul to Alta California, to buy a rancho near San Jose. Instead, Larkin purchased the rancho for himself and bought for Frémont a massive tract of wild land in Indian country, one hundred miles from the nearest settlement. (The land encompasses present-day Mariposa County, in the Sierra foothills on the way to Yosemite National Park.) Frémont and his wife, Jessie Benton, were not pleased—until the discovery of gold in deposits near

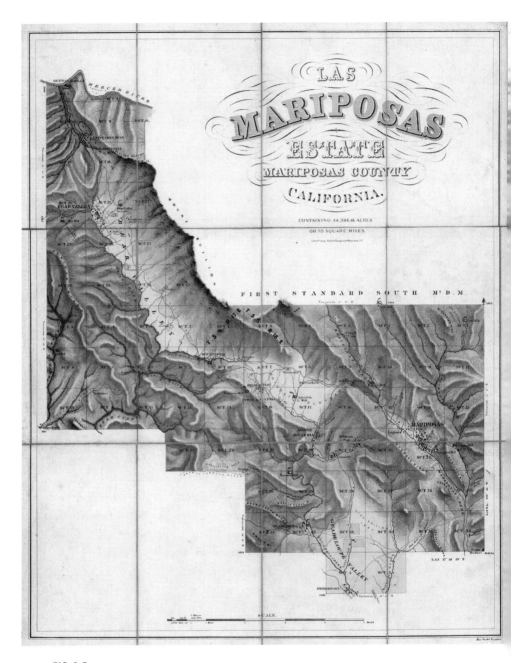

FIG. 2-5
This 1861 map of John Charles Frémont's Las Mariposas estate in Mariposa County shows a large portion of California's gold country. Frémont's efforts to secure Las Mariposas became the first California land claim to reach the United States Supreme Court, in 1854. Courtesy of Barry Lawrence Ruderman Antique Maps, RareMaps.com.

his property suddenly made it worth a fortune. Because Las Mariposas was a floating grant, where the grantee could choose his land from within a larger area, Frémont was able to fudge the borders a little so as to also include gold deposits discovered by others. It was known as the Frying Pan Grant for the shape of the grant's official survey, which included a slice of the Mother Lode gold belt.

Frémont's claim was based on the original 1844 floating grant from then governor Manuel Micheltorena to former governor Juan Alvarado. The conditions of the grant required that Alvarado build and inhabit a house and, within a year, survey the property and get a patent from the local *alcalde*. Alvarado had done none of these things at the time of the sale of the property to Frémont. Furthermore, the grant had never been approved by the supreme government and a *diseño* had never been filed in Monterey. In other words, this grant was not valid according to Mexican law.

At the time, Frémont was one of the most famous men in America. Nicknamed "The Pathfinder" for his extraordinary mapping expeditions of the Midwest and Far West, Frémont had led the Bear Flag Revolt and set the stage for the American takeover in 1846. He was an author and internationally respected scientist who had advanced the fields of cartography, geology, botany, and astronomy. And he was politically connected, married to the daughter of Senator Thomas Hart Benton of Missouri. But Frémont was reviled by Californios for his vicious execution of the de Haro brothers, twin sons of Francisco de Haro, San Francisco's first Mexican *alcalde*. The two unarmed men and their uncle stumbled into the Bear Flag Revolt in Sonoma and were ordered shot by Frémont.

In 1852, Frémont presented his case to the land board at its first hearing. The board, undoubtedly respectful of Frémont's fame and service to his country and California, confirmed the claim. But when the government appealed to the district court, Judge Hoffman concluded that the requirements of the grant had clearly not been fulfilled and reversed the board's decision. Frémont was furious. One of his legal advisers, Montgomery Blair, said Judge Hoffman's ruling was no surprise given he was "a violent partisan and unfriendly to Frémont, Benton and that whole political connation [sic]."

In 1854, Las Mariposas became the first California land claim to reach the Supreme Court, as *Frémont v. United States*. The justices ruled six to two in Frémont's favor, overturning Judge Hoffman's ruling, and even added mineral rights to the grant, which under Spanish and Mexican law would have been retained by the government. Chief Justice Roger Taney wrote the majority opinion. In previous test cases out of Florida and Louisiana, Taney had strictly interpreted Spanish law, but here he focused on "customs and usages" and California's uncertain sovereignty at the time of the Frémont purchase. President Franklin Pierce personally presented Frémont with the patent for Las Mariposas at the White House.

The decision, in effect, lowered the bar for claimants, giving much greater weight to usage and custom than the letter of the law. After *Frémont*, Judge Hoffman found himself bound by precedent to take a

John Charles Frémont

John Charles Frémont was born illegitimate in 1813 to a Virginia society woman and a penniless French refugee. After assisting on a series of explorations and surveys of the upper Missouri and Mississippi Rivers, Frémont was assigned the mapping of the Oregon Trail through the Rockies by the South Pass. Frémont's first expedition was a success—his account of the 1842 trip (widely believed to have been written mostly by his wife, Jessie Benton) was published by Congress and became a bestseller. His second report was on his 1843–1844 winter crossing of the ten-thousand-foot Sierra Nevada into California. His fame and popularity grew, and he was presented with honors by many European scientific societies. By all accounts Frémont was a great leader. "His men all loved him intensely. He gave his orders with great mildness and simplicity, but they had to be obeyed. There was no shrinking from duty. He was like a father to those under his command," wrote Peter H. Burnett, California's first governor. But Frémont routinely overstepped his authority, which kept him in near constant trouble with his superiors. In 1856, Frémont was the first presidential candidate for the new Republican Party. He campaigned under the slogan "Free Speech, Free Press, Free Soil, Free Men, Frémont and Victory." He carried the North, but lost to Democrat James Buchanan. Republican president Abraham Lincoln appointed Frémont a major general in Missouri, a slave state. Frémont declared martial law and issued an emancipation proclamation that freed all slaves in the state. The ensuing uproar forced Lincoln to rescind the order and remove Frémont from command the night before a major battle. He died in New York City in 1890. The town of Fremont, California, and streets in San Francisco and Las Vegas are named after him.

much more lenient view of fulfillment of Mexican legal requirements. The litigation surrounding Las Mariposas also helped clarify just what, if any, were the mineral rights inherent in California land. Under Mexican and Spanish law, mineral rights were retained by the state unless expressly designated to the owner. Under the Treaty of Guadalupe Hidalgo, therefore, those rights went to the US government until the issuance of a patent, which then conveyed full title and mineral rights to the owner. *Frémont* established much of the legal precedent for mineral rights in the West.

While John Frémont benefited from the lenient view the courts took of grant requirements, another famous Californio, General Mariano G. Vallejo, did not. Vallejo had occupied most of Alta California's important military positions during his life, culminating with commandant general in 1838. His life straddled California's transition from Spanish to Mexican to American rule. He was born in Monterey in 1808 and entered military service while a teenager. In 1834, he was sent to secularize California's northernmost mission, San Francisco Solano. He laid out a town around the church and gave it the name Sonoma, the Indian word for the area that means "valley of the moon." As director of colonization, he was given authority to issue land grants to settlers. He convinced a number of families to settle there and briefly moved the San Francisco company of soldiers from the presidio to Sonoma. When the Mexican government ran out of money to pay his soldiers, Vallejo paid them out of his own pocket. In 1835, Governor José Figueroa granted him a 150-by-300-*vara* lot in the town of Sonoma. By 1837, he was one of the richest men in the state, with ten thousand cattle, five thousand horses, and many thousand sheep. The hospitality of his large home on Sonoma's plaza was legendary.

In 1843, Governor Micheltorena granted Vallejo the 66,622-acre Rancho Petaluma in Sonoma County and the Suscol Rancho in Solano County. Vallejo built a large adobe hacienda on his Petaluma land, which is now a state museum. While Vallejo had objected to the expansionist activities of the Russians in Bodega Bay and of John Sutter in Sacramento, he supported the American takeover of California, and served as a delegate to the constitutional convention in Monterey. He was the lone Californio elected to the state's first senate.

Vallejo filed six claims with the land board, three for his direct grants and three for additional properties in Sonoma and Napa Counties that he had purchased before the American takeover. The board and the district court upheld his direct grants. Judge Hoffman was undoubtedly well familiar with Vallejo's reputation as a man of honor and of the services and loyalty he had shown the Americans. Vallejo's claim to the Rancho Yulupa, land that bordered his Petaluma land, was rejected by the board but upheld by Hoffman, even though the original grant from Micheltorena to Juan Alvarado had never been registered in the California archives. The judge knew the man and knew that forgery was beneath him. The government appealed, however, bringing *United States v. Vallejo* before the Supreme Court, which reversed Hoffman, evidently relying on the letter of the law—no registration, no valid claim. Unlike the *Frémont* decision, which seemed to bend the rules for services rendered by a California pioneer, the *Vallejo* decision was a slap in the face to the already dying breed of honorable Californios. Vallejo still had thousands of acres of land, but he passed his later years in relative poverty. The town of Vallejo is named after him, as is a street in San Francisco. The town of Benicia was named after his wife, Doña Francisca Benicia.

New Almaden Quicksilver Mine

Mining rights, the Civil War, and eminent domain would all combine in the bitter case of the New Almaden Quicksilver Mine, which spawned twenty years of litigation in the federal and state courts.

Quicksilver, another name for mercury, is a magnet for gold that significantly speeds up the process of gold refining. Early miners would line their sluices, or even creek beds, with the liquid metal to amalgamate their gold. Later, the amalgam was heated in a kiln until the mercury turned into gas and was carried off to a cooling tank to turn back into a liquid. Gold would be left behind. Luckily for the forty-niners, the largest quicksilver mine in the United States was in San Jose, near today's Silicon Valley, just a few hundred miles south of the major gold diggings. The mine was discovered by Andrés Castillero, a Mexican cavalry officer and chemist, during an 1845 expedition from Mexico. Castillero recognized the red rocks near Mission Santa Clara as cinnabar, a sulfide that contains mercury. Native Americans had used the red dust for ceremonial decorations and currency for centuries. He received title to the mine, including three thousand *varas* of land in all directions from the mouth, from the local *alcalde* in 1845. The president of Mexico approved it the following year.

FIG. 2-6
The New Almaden Quicksilver Mine opened in 1845 and was California's first mining operation. It achieved world-wide fame during the gold rush and was the subject of a bitter land grant dispute. During the 1860s, the prominent California photographer Carleton Watkins was invited to document the mine. Courtesy of the California History Room, California State Library, Sacramento, California.

Castillero created the Santa Clara Mine Company, but stalled on starting operations. He returned to Mexico City, and then war broke out with the United States. He was unable to return to California and sold part of his interest in the mine to two British men. Together they formed a new company and re-christened the mine New Almaden, after the famous quicksilver mine in Spain. Production began in 1847, and during the gold rush quicksilver was shipped north through San Francisco Bay and then upriver to the diggings. Henry Halleck, who was an engineer as well as a lawyer, became superintendent in 1850, modernized the mine, and greatly increased production.

Castillero and the New Almaden Quicksilver Mine filed a claim with the land board for the mine and surrounding land. The land board confirmed his title to the land in 1856, but rejected title to the mine. Meanwhile, the US government became concerned that the largest quicksilver mine in the country was in the hands of British subjects. An injunction to stop work in the mine until the title was settled was issued by the circuit court in 1858. On appeal in the district court, Judge Hoffman confirmed the title to the mine and lifted the injunction but rejected the claim for the land. Both sides appealed Hoffman's ruling. The Supreme Court sided with the government in 1863, denying the claim to both

Juana Briones

Doña Juana Briones de Miranda was one of the few California women who filed a land claim in her own name. Briones was a singularly independent woman for her era. Although unable to read or write, she became a successful businesswoman and obtained a legal separation from her husband at a time when divorce was illegal. She established her own farm near what is now Washington Square Park in San Francisco and was a respected healer and midwife who cured Indians, Californios, and foreigners alike. Her hospitality, generosity, and business sense won her the respect and friendship of many foreigners who later helped her navigate the land claim process. The land board and the district court upheld her title to her San Francisco and Santa Clara properties.

Briones, whose family had come from Mexico in the 1770s, was born in the short-lived pueblo of Branciforte (near Santa Cruz) in 1802. She grew up in the Presidio of San Francisco, where her father was stationed. In 1820, she married Apolonario Miranda, a cavalryman. Together they had eleven children and settled in the Ojo de Figueroa, an area bordering the present Presidio District, near Green and Lyon Streets. In 1835, Briones received permission from the bishop and the *alcalde* to separate from her husband because he was a heavy drinker. She settled with her children in Yerba Buena, the growing port on the east side of San Francisco, and built an adobe house on what is now the northwest corner of Washington Square. She put the title to the land in her own name, raised cattle, and sold milk, produce, and eggs to crews of visiting sailing ships. The nearby beach (now North Beach) was known as La Playa di Juana Briones. In 1844, she bought the 4,437-acre Rancho la Purísima Concepción in Santa Clara County. After statehood, she picked advisers and lawyers to represent her in the land claim process and received title to her rancho and the North Beach tract as well as the presidio property that she and her children inherited after her husband died. She retired to Palo Alto, where she lived until her death in 1889.

the mine and the land on the grounds that Castillero had not properly registered the grant and therefore the mine and lands were government property due to their strategic importance. President Lincoln ordered that the mine be taken over by the US government. It was seen as vital to national security in the midst of the Civil War; without readily available mercury, western mines wouldn't be able to pump out gold and silver fast enough to help finance the Union cause.

C. W. Rand, the US marshal for the Northern District in San Francisco, had orders to empty the mine of all workers and secure it. But Rand and his cavalry detachment were forced to retreat after they were met by an armed mob of mine workers. Lincoln was lambasted in the West as a tyrant and faced a revolt by California and Nevada amid rumors that the government would begin seizing mines all over the West. Under pressure from the war, Lincoln thought better of it and rescinded the order, returning the mine to private ownership. The mine continued operating under various owners until 1976. The area is now a Santa Clara County historical park.

The Land Grab: San Francisco's Early Years

The effect of the gold rush on California was perhaps nowhere as dramatic as in San Francisco. Almost overnight the city mushroomed from fifty dwellings on a sandy, windswept harbor to a metropolis of buildings, tents, transient men, rotting ships, saloons, gambling halls, merchants, and lawyers. At the time of the American occupation in 1847, the pueblo contained some four hundred souls; by the end of 1848, the city held nearly two thousand. During the first six months of 1849, fifteen thousand men and two hundred women arrived. The rest of that year saw some four thousand immigrants arrive in San Francisco each month. By the spring of 1850, when Ogden Hoffman Jr. first arrived, another thirty-six thousand had been added to the population.

Spanish colonialists had founded the Presidio of San Francisco near the entry to the bay and Mission San Francisco de Asís in the interior in 1776. Ships frequently anchored in Yerba Buena Cove on the protected eastern shore away from the windy presidio. Yerba Buena, "good herb" in Spanish, was named after the wild spearmint that grew on the hills. By 1834, the presidio had been officially recognized as a Mexican pueblo and Yerba Buena was within the four square leagues (more than seventeen

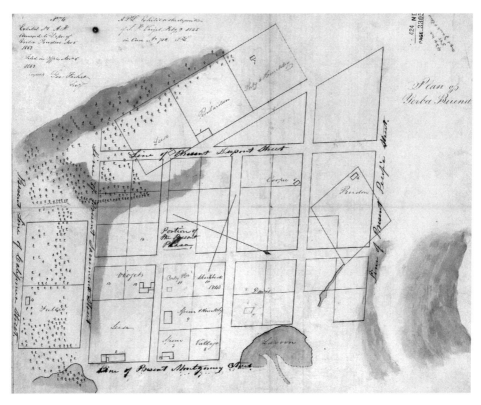

FIG. 2-7

In 1839, Jean Jacques Vioget, a sea captain with an engineering background, was asked to survey the settlement of Yerba Buena (San Francisco). Using a sextant and compass, he "made an observation so as to fix one point, and then drew off the future metropolis of the Pacific, with the greatest ease and the most remarkable celerity," M. G. Upton observed in the *Overland Monthly* in 1869. Courtesy of The Bancroft Library, University of California, Berkeley.

thousand acres) measured from the Presidio Plaza. Settlers began arriving after the first trading post opened in 1835.

By 1839, Yerba Buena was large enough that *alcalde* Francisco de Haro commissioned Jean Jacques Vioget, a French sea captain turned grocer, to map out city streets. Vioget's map included the central area founded on the cove, bounded by Pacific, California, Montgomery, and Dupont (now Grant Avenue). A freshwater pond, *la laguna dulce*, interrupted Montgomery Street at the foot of Sacramento Street. This map was kept pinned to the wall at Bob Ridley's billiard saloon. When lots changed hands, the map would come on top of the bar and the old owner's name was erased and replaced by a new name—with drinks all around. A number of ranchos occupied the city's future limits, including the Visitación rancho

(Visitacion Valley), the Rancho San Miguel (about four thousand acres covering present-day Twin Peaks, the Castro, and the city's geographic center), and the Rancho Viejo, Rincon de las Salinas y Potrero Viejo, which included Bernal Heights and Potrero Hill. In 1847, the first American *alcalde*, Washington Bartlett, renamed the town San Francisco, after the mission's patron saint, Saint Francis of Assisi. About twelve hundred lots, each costing about $17, were granted or sold by American *alcaldes*. By early 1849, the same lot would sell for $6,000, and by 1850, $45,000.

Speculation, greed, and duplicity were rampant during the gold rush years. Even army officers, such as Captain Joseph L. Folsom, were known to have employed friends and employees as straw men to purchase lots in violation of limits on lot sales to individuals. Because the most valuable property was that closest to the commercial district, early on the city council staked out water lots in the mudflats of the cove and sold them, and the process of expanding the city by filling in the shallows of the bay began in earnest. Construction on the city's present seawall began in the mid-1860s.

Lawyers were frequent investors and speculators in city land despite the fact that San Francisco was little more than one great squatters' town. San Francisco lawyer and future California governor Henry H. Haight said in 1850 that virtually all the land granted or sold after 1846 was "of dubious legality" if not tainted by "fraud and corruption." Even so, Haight and a partner invested $22,000 in six water lots, according to Christian Fritz in the winter 1986 *Santa Clara Law Review*. Other investors included Hall McAllister, son of Judge Matthew Hall McAllister and a leader of the California bar, and Serranus Clinton Hastings, the first chief justice of the California Supreme Court and founder of the Hastings College of Law, California's first law school.

Another gold rush attorney, John McCracke, noted that because most every lawyer in town had some property of his own, clients could be assured they would work long and hard to see the titles upheld in litigation. One exception to this rule appears to have been Ogden Hoffman, who apparently never invested in property of any kind in California, making him either the era's most honest judge or a poor fool.

By 1852, the same year the city filed its claim for its pueblo land, the city was so deeply in debt that it began selling off public property, especially water lots, to pay its creditors. One of those creditors was Peter Smith, a physician who was contracted by the city to care for indigent residents during the cholera outbreak in the winter of 1850. When Smith

Fugitive Slaves in California

By the late 1840s, America was deeply divided on the issue of slavery: thirteen states whose economies had been built upon slave labor permitted it, and thirteen did not. During the gold rush, many Southerners brought their slaves with them to California. Despite an 1823 law banning slavery, early California settlers continued these practices, notably with Native Americans. But by the gold rush, many Californians feared the Southern aristocracy would transplant itself to California and use slave labor to mine gold, so the State Constitution of 1849 outlawed slavery. Congress passed the Fugitive Slave Act of 1850 as an attempt to compromise the interests of the Southern slaveholding states and abolitionists in the North. The act required the arrest of anyone in a free state suspected of having crossed state lines to escape a Southern master. In 1858, California's most famous fugitive slave case came to Sacramento and San Francisco. Nineteen-year-old Archy Lee had been brought to California by Charles Stovall from Mississippi. Lee ran away when Stovall decided to send him back to the South. Lee was caught and arrested, but a Sacramento judge declared him a free man. Lee was promptly arrested again on order of California Supreme Court justice David Terry. A fellow Southerner, Terry ruled that Lee indeed belonged to Stovall, who claimed he was just visiting California and was therefore able to keep his slave. By now, California's free black community (about five hundred residents in Sacramento and nearly one thousand in San Francisco) was in an uproar. Meanwhile, Stovall had secretly brought Lee, under heavy guard, to San Francisco, where he planned to put him on a ship bound for Mississippi. As they tried to board the ship, a deputy sheriff served Stovall with a writ of habeas corpus for Lee and an arrest warrant for kidnapping. A San Francisco judge overturned Terry's decision and freed Lee, who was immediately re-arrested in the courtroom by a US marshal. A near-riot broke out as Lee was brought through the city streets from City Hall to the Merchants Exchange Building, where the federal courts were housed. Stovall claimed Lee under the Fugitive Slave Act, but US Commissioner William Penn Johnson ruled that Lee was not a fugitive slave. Johnson determined that Lee had crossed no state lines, and set him free. Lee was released from the San Francisco jail to the joy of his supporters. He later joined a migration of San Francisco blacks to start a colony in British Columbia, but returned after the Civil War. For a time he worked as a barber in Washoe, Nevada. He is believed to have died near Sacramento in 1873.

presented a bill for $64,000, the city didn't have enough cash, so he was paid in land scrip, at 3 percent interest per month, which he in turn sold. But sales revenue was surprisingly low—many Smith lots sold for as low as eleven cents—and there was widespread speculation that the bidders, including many prominent politicians, merchants, military men, and lawyers (or their straw men), colluded to keep the bidding down. "One thing only seems certain—the 'manifest destiny' of San Francisco is to be plundered at all hands, and to yield easy and quickly won fortunes to her 'most prominent citizens,'" wrote *The Annals of San Francisco*. Dr. Smith died before his bill was fully paid, and the legacy of the Peter Smith deeds, as these properties were called, would haunt San Francisco through nearly two decades of litigation and hold up the city's pueblo title. The stakes were high not just for owners of valuable property that dated back to *alcalde* grants but for thousands of settlers who had built on what they thought was public domain, not to mention the ability of the city to set aside land for public use or sell it off for revenue.

Not until 1865 did the circuit court—with Justice Field presiding—definitively uphold San Francisco's title to its pueblo land. In the meantime, the city laid the groundwork for its pueblo case by settling as many titles as it could. The board of supervisors passed the Van Ness Ordinance, which allowed anyone possessing land unclaimed as of 1855 to receive their titles without fear of a challenge from the city.

Although the ultimate fate of pueblo lands rested in the hands of the federal judiciary, the state courts' rulings affected the political climate, which in turn influenced the higher courts. One of these was the 1860 landmark case *Hart v. Burnett*. In *Hart*, Justice Field, sitting as chief justice of the state supreme court at the time, ruled that a pueblo held its land in trust for its residents and could not sell it to pay off debts. It could, however, make outright grants and sales of land that was not for common use. In other words, the Peter Smith deeds were not valid, but most grants and sales done under the American *alcalde* system were validated. This case marked the first time that the public trust was upheld in a California land dispute: tidelands, and certain other lands and waters, were held in trust for the public and could not be sold for private benefit, and, if granted to a private entity, the state retained the authority to regulate their use.

Hart left thousands of investors holding worthless titles. With the pueblo case still unresolved, the city was in an uproar—no title seemed safe. Squatting became a full-time business. "Men squatted for themselves and for hire, and did this over a twenty-year period," wrote the *Annals.* "Squatting implements were blankets and firearms. In the long run, the city of San Francisco was forced to recognize the claims of squatters in certain large areas...many a real estate fortune in San Francisco, and the rise of many a prominent San Francisco family, dates from this municipal recognition of possessory rights."

In 1854, the land board upheld San Francisco's pueblo claim, but for less than the full amount, based on pueblo boundaries described in a document that predated the city's 1851 charter. The city appealed to the district court. Meanwhile, two other claims, filed by James R. Bolton and Peter Sherrebeck, were pending before the board. If approved, either one would put serious holes in the fabric of San Francisco's claim.

Bolton's claim was for land near the commercial district that had been originally granted to a Mexican priest in 1846 but was now owned by the San Francisco Land Company. The land board ruled in favor of Bolton. In 1857, an appeal reached Judge Hoffman in the district court, but with no new evidence introduced, he entered a summary confirmation of the board's decision to hasten its review by the Supreme Court. Settlers living on Bolton's claim formed an association, raised money, and said they now had proof that the Bolton grant was a fake. They wrote Judge Hoffman and asked him to re-hear the case, then sent a petition with ten thousand signatures to the Supreme Court and each member of Congress urging its invalidation due to fraud. In 1860, the Supreme Court ruled on *United States v. Bolton* and rejected Bolton's claim on the grounds that its validity had not been fully established. The justices noted that their decision was the only fair one to settlers who had bought the land without notice of any private ownership.

Sherrebeck's claim for El Rincon included part of the downtown area along the bay just south of Market Street, which he said had been part of Yerba Buena's commons (*ejidos*) and therefore grantable under the *alcalde* system. The board found that Sherrebeck had an authentic Mexican grant, but still rejected the claim on the grounds that there wasn't enough evidence that the land had been part of the commons. Sherrebeck appealed to the district court, where Judge Hoffman felt compelled by the evidence to reverse the board, ruling in his favor in 1859. Within a year, the Supreme Court reversed his decision in *United States v. Sherrebeck.*

Judge Hoffman carefully followed Mexican and Spanish law as well as US legal precedents to reach his rulings. Even so, the Supreme Court reversed him on a number of important cases, such as *Frémont, Bolton,* and *Sherrebeck.* In nearly all these cases, the justices also took into account the weight and context of larger political and economic issues. Hoffman was a solid, fair, scrupulously honest, but fastidiously literal judge. And once the San Francisco land cases began entering his court, he was thrust into a world in which he was poorly equipped to operate: frontier land politics. The city's boosters, led by Justice Field, then chief justice of the California Supreme Court, had an aggressive and pragmatic approach to the economic and political realities of the situation and ultimately saw Hoffman as an obstacle to the resolution of land titles and the city's progress.

Limantour: US Victory against Fraud

The most serious threat to San Francisco's pueblo land came in 1853 from a French sea captain and trader, José Yves Limantour, who suddenly filed claims for most of San Francisco and its bay islands. "San Francisco, which had survived the…Colton grants, the Peter Smith sales, and other legalized robberies and 'squatters' without number…was now threatened by a claim, which if held valid, would turn over to a single individual one-half of its real estate, owned partly by the city itself, and partly by thousands of onerous and bona fide holders, who fancied their possessions were their own by the strongest legal titles." So recorded the *Annals* on the day in 1853 that Limantour presented his claim to the land board, just a few months shy of the filing deadline.

Limantour filed eight claims for a total of nearly six hundred thousand acres. The first was for about fifteen thousand acres, which included most of San Francisco; the second was for the bay islands of Yerba Buena and Alcatraz, Point Tiburon in Marin County, and the Farallon Islands outside the Golden Gate. The others included a huge rancho in Mendocino County, the city of Stockton, and the vineyard of Mission San Francisco Solano. Limantour said Governor Micheltorena had granted the lands to him during 1843 and 1844 in return for military supplies and cash he had supplied to the Mexican government, worth some $40,000. For his San Francisco claim, Limantour presented the board with all the required necessary documents, including a grant signed by the governor and a *diseño*.

In 1856, San Franciscans were shocked to find that the land board upheld Limantour's claims to the city and its islands. His other six claims were rejected. The government appealed to the district court. Peter Della Torre was the US Attorney, assisted by Edwin M. Stanton; General James Wilson represented Limantour. The new land baron did not appeal the six rejected claims but began collecting the "Limantour Tax," a 10 percent fee to relieve property owners on "his" San Francisco land from the threat of lawsuits. In all, Limantour was said to have collected about $300,000 from individuals.

Meanwhile, a pamphlet was published and distributed in San Francisco that accused Limantour of forgery and fraud. In it, Limantour's former employee Augustus Jouan charged that he took part in the fraud by changing the dates on the grants at Limantour's request. Francois Jacomet, Limantour's former clerk, said another man, named Letanneur had forged one of the grants in 1852. Limantour responded to the charges by publishing his own pamphlet, written by well-known *Alta California* scribe John S. Hittel, defending his claims and describing how he assisted California's government when it was in desperate need of cash and arms. The grant for San Francisco had been signed by Micheltorena in Los Angeles in 1843. Limantour's attorney insisted that "Fraud is to be proved, not inferred." As it would turn out, of all the land claims, the Limantour case would be the US government's greatest victory against fraud and mark a turning point in the land claims process. From Limantour forward, fraud was nearly always suspected.

When the appeal reached Judge Hoffman in 1858, the current value for Limantour's half of San Francisco—which included most of the northern portion of the city, including the town itself—was estimated at $15 million. Della Torre contended that all of Limantour's documents were forgeries, fabricated long after the American occupation in 1846. Jacomet came from Mexico and testified before the grand jury, corroborating Jouan's testimony. Letanneur testified and confirmed that he had written one of the grants himself. Della Torre then dramatically showed the court how the official Mexican government watermark and seal on Limantour's grant was from a different year than the one it was supposed to have been signed in. A US marshal tapped Limantour on the shoulder. He looked up. He was to be charged with forgery and perjury. Bail was set at $10,000, which he paid. After being freed, he disappeared from San Francisco. Judge Hoffman called the fraud "without parallel in the judicial history of the country." Limantour died in Mexico City in 1885, but he left his mark. Limantour Beach, in Point Reyes National Seashore, is named for the site where his ship wrecked in 1841.

The City of San Francisco v. United States entered Hoffman's docket in 1856 and sat there until 1864, when an act of Congress transferred all pending pueblo cases to the United States Circuit Court for California. Justice Field did not trust Judge Hoffman to rule the right way on such an important case, so he and Senator John Conness wrote legislation that would take the district court out of the pueblo loop and transfer San Francisco's cases to the federal circuit court where Justice Field presided. The only pueblo cases pending in the district court at the time were those

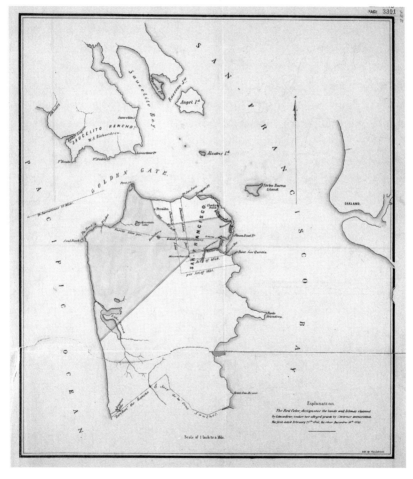

FIG. 2-8

José Y. Limantour fraudulently claimed title to lands and islands around San Francisco that constituted some of the city's most valuable areas. This map, in the district court's files for Land Case No. 424, shows claims for two grants made by Manuel Micheltorena, Mexican governor of Alta California (1842–1845), on February 27 and December 16, 1843. Courtesy of The Bancroft Library, University of California, Berkeley.

of San Francisco and Sonoma. The district court's authority to review and approve land surveys was also removed and given to the Surveyor General's office in Washington, DC.

In the circuit court in 1864, Justice Field ruled that San Francisco's pueblo status was well established under Spanish and Mexican law and therefore it was entitled to its four square leagues, with some limitations for the public trust. Judge Hoffman, who would normally have sat with the circuit court judge in such a matter, was conspicuously absent that day. "For some reason I do not now recall, the District Judge was unable to sit with me, and the case was, therefore, heard before me alone," Field wrote coyly of the San Francisco pueblo case in his *Personal Reminiscences*. This came as no surprise to insiders who knew that Field and Conness had also written legislation that would have removed Hoffman from his bench, legislation that was never passed by Congress, and which provoked an outpouring of support from San Francisco's business and legal communities for Hoffman's honesty, integrity, and independence. "Is it not better that the Judge be righteous than right? Should we feel ourselves, or our property or even our lives safe for a moment if we had known or even suspected that he decided against his conviction and in accordance with public clamor?" wrote the *Alta California* in 1864. "If Judge Hoffman has committed errors, let him be impeached. This thing of legislating him out of office...is a deadly blow aimed at the Federal Judiciary everywhere."

But San Francisco's pueblo title was still far from settled. The federal government, having already declared the presidio, Fort Point, Point San Jose (present day Fort Mason), and Alcatraz, Angel, and Yerba Buena Islands to be military reservations, withdrew an initial appeal to the Supreme Court within a month, but then asked for a rehearing in the circuit court on the grounds that the government's brief had been suppressed by the clerk of court. A technical tug-of-war continued between Field and US Attorney Delos Lake, with repeated motions for appeal denied by Field. In his May 1865 denial for appeal to the Supreme Court, Field pointed out that under the provisions of the 1864 law (which Field wrote), the Supreme Court had no jurisdiction in the case. "The decision not being subject to appeal, the controversy between the city and the Government is closed, and the claim of the city stands precisely as if the United States owned the land and by an Act of Congress had ceded it, subject to certain reservations, to the city in trust for the inhabitants. Motion to allow an appeal is denied." A year later, Congress

Justice Stephen Johnson Field

Born in Connecticut in 1816, Stephen J. Field was one of eight children of a Puritan minister. He attended Williams College in Williamstown, Massachusetts, and traveled extensively in Europe, living a year in Turkey with his missionary sister. He practiced law with his older brother, the well-known New York attorney David Dudley Field, before coming west.

Field arrived in San Francisco in 1849 with $10 in his pocket. He spent $7 just to get his trunks ashore and $3 for breakfast. Nevertheless cheery, he met numerous acquaintances from back East on the muddy streets of this "glorious country," as he wrote in his 1877 memoir. Field sold the eastern newspapers he carried and ended up with $32. After collecting a $400 debt owed to his brother by a merchant, Field headed for the mining country and began speculating in real estate and practicing law. He settled in the town of Marysville, where he was elected its first *alcalde* within three days of his arrival. He quickly amassed $14,000 from his land investments. He took to the *alcalde* role of judge, justice of the peace, and feudal lord with a relish, and acquired a reputation as a hothead. He went about armed with a bowie knife and pistol, and was said to have even brandished them in court in Marysville when a losing defense attorney pulled his guns.

From this tiny town about 125 miles northeast of San Francisco, Field was elected to the first California State Legislature in 1850, where he wrote much of the state's civil and criminal codes. He unsuccessfully ran for state senate and for governor, but was elected to the California US Supreme Court in 1859, later becoming its chief justice. President Lincoln appointed him to the Supreme Court in 1863.

Field was impulsive, aggressive, clever, arrogant, and vindictive. He had "a singular capacity for making enemies," according to Carl Brent Swisher's 1930 book *Stephen J. Field: Craftsman of the Law.* One of his first acts when he was elected to the state assembly in 1850 was to re-organize the state courts and send Judge William R. Turner from Marysville to the remote wilderness of Klamath County. Turner was a state district judge who had formed an immediate hatred of Field and had him fined, imprisoned, and briefly disbarred for contempt. The judge had also continued to threaten him physically. Wrote Field, in *Personal Reminiscences:*

> When I came to California, I came with all those notions, in respect to acts of violence, which are instilled into New England youth; if a man were rude, I would turn away from him. But I soon found that men in California were likely to take very great liberties with a person who acted in such a manner, and that the only way to get along was to hold every man responsible, and

resent every trespass upon one's rights. Though I was not prepared to follow Judge Bennett's suggestion [to shoot Judge Turner first], I did purchase a pair of revolvers and had a sack-coat made with pockets in which the barrels could lie, and be discharged; and I began to practice firing the pistols from the pockets. In time I acquired considerable skill, and was able to hit a small object across the street. An object so large as a man I could have hit without difficulty. I had come to the conclusion that if I had to give up my independence; if I had to avoid a man because I was afraid he would attack me; if I had to cross the street every time I saw him coming, life itself was not worth having.

Field ran for president twice on the Democratic ticket, in 1880 and 1884. Both times he failed to receive the California party nomination. He served on the Supreme Court until 1897 and died two years later.

passed a law relinquishing to the city the confirmed land and effectively closing the case.

In *Personal Reminiscences*, Field takes full credit for getting San Francisco its pueblo land in a timely manner.

> On the 18th of May, 1865, the decree was finally settled and entered. Appeals from it were prosecuted to the Supreme Court both by the United States and by the city; by the United States from the whole decree, and by the city from so much of it as included certain reservations in the estimate of the quantity of land confirmed. The case on appeal in the meantime was not reached in the Supreme Court, and was not likely to be for a long period. Ascertaining from General Halleck that the Secretary of War would not recommend any further reservations to be made from the municipal lands, and that probably none would be made, I drew a bill to quiet the title of the city to all the lands embraced within the decree of confirmation, and gave it to Senator Conness, who being ready, as usual, to act for the interests of the city, immediately took charge of it and secured its passage in the Senate. In the House Mr. McRuer, Member of Congress from California, took charge of it, and with the assistance of the rest of the delegation from the State, procured its passage there. It was signed by the President and became a law on the 8th of March, 1866....
>
> The title of the city rests, therefore, upon the decree of the Circuit Court entered on the 18th day of May, 1865, and this confirmatory

act of Congress. It has been so adjudged by the Supreme Court of the United States. The title of the city being settled, the municipal authorities took measures…to set apart lands for school-houses, hospitals, court-house buildings, and other public purposes, and…the Ocean Park, which looks out upon the Pacific Ocean and the Golden Gate, and is destined to be one of the finest parks in the world, was set apart and secured to the city for all time.

Justice Field and Judge Hoffman: A Love Story with Pirates

The dislike that Judge Hoffman and Justice Field nurtured for each other blossomed into true contempt during the resolution of San Francisco's land titles as the two men's personal styles and judicial objectives collided. "Hoffman's pride, stubbornness, faithfulness to strict textual analysis, and judicial restraint collided with Field's aggressive, free-wheeling, and openly political behavior," wrote Fritz. "This contrast prompted an attempt—supported by Field—to strip the district judge not only of his judicial power but of his office itself."

Hoffman was bitterly disappointed that Field, not himself, was the West's first appointment to the Supreme Court. He had long dreamed of higher judicial office and expected that his stature as the first federal judge in California would have made him the first pick. Field, enjoying his reign as chief justice of the state supreme court, had turned down an offer of circuit court judge but made it known that he was open to an appointment to the Supreme Court, which he was offered in 1863. Field had been mortified at Hoffman's slow deliberations and rulings in several important cases, chiefly the *Bolton* and *Sherrebeck* claims, but it was *United States v. Greathouse,* California's Civil War treason case, that would prompt him to seek Hoffman's dismissal.

Ridgely Greathouse, Asbury Harpending, and Alfred Rubery conspired to raid gold shipments leaving San Francisco Bay and use the money to aid the South. Harpending, a twenty-three-year-old Kentuckian, was authorized by the Confederate government in Virginia to operate as a privateer. They purchased the *J. M. Chapman,* a ninety-ton schooner, and outfitted her with a cannon, rifles, pistols, and a crew of twenty. They set off from San Francisco on March 14, 1863, to start pirating. But federal authorities had gotten word of their plans and trapped the boat at dawn the next morning.

Greathouse, Harpending, and Rubery were taken into custody and charged with treason. Just a year earlier, Congress had enacted a statutory form of treason where the punishment was limited to imprisonment and fines instead of death. Justice Field, in his first case sitting in the circuit court as a Supreme Court justice, together with Judge Hoffman, presided at the 1863 trial. After a two-week trial and four minutes of deliberation, a jury found all three men guilty. Field imposed the maximum sentence on each man: ten years in prison and a $10,000 fine. While this barely quenched the public's thirst for punishing the pirates, it was harsh in light of President Lincoln's policy of forgiveness and reconciliation for Confederates. After Lincoln's amnesty proclamation in December 1863, Greathouse's lawyers moved for his release. When word reached Lincoln, he telegraphed Judge Hoffman and explained that the amnesty was intended for people who voluntarily took an oath of loyalty to the United States and not for those "constrained to take it, in order to escape actual imprisonment or punishment."

Hoffman, literal as always, informed the president that nothing in the language of his proclamation excluded convicts and that he was bound to interpret the document as it was unless the president clarified in "an equally formal document." None came. Though reluctant, Hoffman released Greathouse on a writ of habeas corpus in 1864. Hoffman was roasted for his decision, which made national headlines. The *Missouri Democrat* called him a "copperhead judge," the nickname for Northern sympathizers of the Southern rebellion. Field and Senator Conness were incensed and took Hoffman's bad press as the opportunity to pounce, drafting punitive legislation that would reorganize California's federal district court, remove Hoffman, and replace him with a friend of Field's.

Hoffman fought back through his family's contacts in Congress, firing off letters of protest like the one he sent to Senator William P. Fessenden, Republican of Maine and chairman of the Senate Finance Committee, declaring he would not "submit to be the victim of a political intrigue." This lobbying, and the support of San Francisco's business community, succeeded in removing the portions of the law that would have replaced Hoffman. Field did get Congress to pass a law in 1864 that removed the district court—and Hoffman—from overseeing the pueblo land cases. So in the end, they each got what they wanted: Field got San Francisco its land and Hoffman kept his job and honor intact.

CHAPTER 3

THE CHINESE HABEAS CORPUS MILL

THE STEAMSHIP GROANED as it pulled alongside the Pacific Mail Steamship Company docks in the early morning fog. Inside the ship, dozens of Chinese men, and a couple of women, gathered their belongings and huddled together, anxious to breathe fresh air and feel solid ground under their feet again. Most of them had come from neighboring villages in the Guangdong (Canton) or Fujian Provinces on the South China Sea. As soon as they filed off the gangplank, they were herded into the *Tongsaan Matau*, or "China dock," a bleak, dilapidated wooden building known to whites as "The Shed."

The Shed was a "cheap, two-story wooden building…where the odors of sewage and bilge are most offensive; unclean, at times overrun with vermin, and often inadequate to the numbers to be detained," as Mary Roberts Coolidge described it in her 1909 book, *Chinese Immigration*. Immigrants were not separated by class, as was customary at the time, only by sex, and sometimes the wives and children of merchants were "imprisoned with women held as professional prostitutes," which was considered an outrage and an insult.

Between 1850 and 1882, 322,000 Chinese immigrants came to the United States, most of them through San Francisco. On a single day in 1852, some 2,000 arrived. People were detained in the Shed for days, weeks, and sometimes months before their immigration status was determined and they were either deported or allowed to finally walk anxiously toward Chinatown. Inside, they were denied contact with any local relatives or friends and subjected to a series of physical examinations and

FIG. 3-1 (PREVIOUS PAGE)
In this lithograph illustrating the relentless tide of Chinese arrivals to San Francisco, streams of Chinese immigrants make their way from the Pacific Mail Steamship Company (left) and the Canadian Pacific Steamship Company (right). Courtesy of The Bancroft Library, University of California, Berkeley.

Songs of Gold Mountain

American law, more ferocious than tigers
Many are the people jailed inside wooden walls
Detained, interrogated, tortured
Like birds plunged into an open trap
Had I only known such difficulty in passing the Golden Gate...
I regret my journey here

—poem by an unknown Chinese immigrant to San Francisco in the early twentieth century, from *Songs of Gold Mountain,* edited by Marlon Kom

interrogations, often with an interpreter who understood little of their native dialect. The Shed processed Chinese immigrants arriving in San Francisco from the 1850s until 1910, when a new, larger—but still bleak—facility was built on Angel Island.

The district court in San Francisco was ground zero for the battle over Chinese immigration that would engulf the city, the state, and eventually the entire nation in the last half of the nineteenth century. Chinese immigrants made effective use of the court by appealing numerous discriminatory local and state laws. The desire of California's white immigrants to remove competition from Chinese labor would be the impetus for the most restrictive immigration laws ever passed in this country: the Chinese exclusion laws of the 1880s. For the first time in America's history, an immigrant group was denied entry to the country or deported solely on the basis of race. Ironically, because the Chinese were treated separately from all other immigrants under the exclusion laws, they were able to continue petitions and appeals to the federal courts when others were not.

Coming to America

While America is a nation of immigrants, restrictions on who could come here and who could become a citizen began as early as 1790 with the passage of the Naturalization Act, which set the stage for whites

Habeas Corpus: The Sacred Document of Personal Freedom

A writ of habeas corpus, literally "that you have the body" in Latin, is a court order from a judge to bring a prisoner before the court to determine the reason for his imprisonment. Habeas corpus was part of English common law and recognized in the US Constitution as a fundamental right to challenge arbitrary imprisonment. "That any human being claiming to be unlawfully restrained of his liberty has a right to demand a judicial investigation into the lawfulness of his imprisonment is not questioned by any one who knows by what constitutional and legal methods the right of liberty is secured and enforced by at least all English-speaking peoples," district court judge Ogden Hoffman wrote in 1884. It is, he said, the "most sacred" document of personal freedom and is available to everyone "no matter what his race or color."

---

to be considered legally and politically superior to other races. The act excluded African Americans and Native Americans from becoming naturalized citizens. While it did not specifically exclude Asians, they were later added to the list of non-white groups considered ineligible for naturalization.

With the Page Act of 1875, Congress outlawed the immigration of convicts, prostitutes, "idiots," and those who might become a ward of the state, but local customs authorities had broad discretion in picking these people out from arriving vessels. But the Chinese were the only racial group specifically excluded from immigration by a number of states and by the federal government, starting with the Chinese Exclusion Act of 1882. When Chinese immigrants did arrive in San Francisco, they were detained and frequently deported. The Northern District Court and the old circuit court were nearly always the first choice of legal recourse for the thousands of Chinese who challenged their detainment, mainly through writs of habeas corpus. Petitioners could file writs of habeas corpus in either court, but the majority were filed in the district court. More than seven thousand habeas writs were filed by Chinese plaintiffs in the court between 1882 and 1891.

California: Gold Mountain

The gold rush coincided with a period of decline in China. Southern China in particular suffered from widespread poverty and political instability caused by the fallout from the Opium Wars in the 1840s and 1850s and the Taiping Rebellion between 1850 and 1864. Droughts, famines, and floods added to the push for emigration, which had previously been a crime punishable by death. Thousands of men, mostly from Guangdong, made the trip east across the Pacific Ocean to come to *Gum Saan*, "Gold Mountain," the popular Chinese term for California. The Chinese were briefly welcomed, then reviled.

FIG. 3-2
More than ten thousand Chinese railroad workers laid tracks, bored tunnels, leveled roadbeds, and blasted the mountainsides of the Sierra Nevada for the Central Pacific Railroad's transcontinental line. Courtesy of the Library of Congress.

Timeline of the Chinese in California

1839   The First Opium War begins between China and Great Britain. China had outlawed opium, but Britain continued to smuggle the drug into China. American interests and shipping companies also benefited from this trade. China confiscated and destroyed three million pounds of the drug from British traders. The British responded by sending warships and attacking coastal towns. The war ended with the Treaty of Nanking in 1842.

1850   Five hundred Chinese arrive in California in a first wave of gold rush immigrants.

1850   California imposes a twenty-dollar monthly tax on each foreign miner.

1852   Up to twenty thousand Chinese are living in California.

1854   The California Supreme Court rules that a white man charged with murder cannot be convicted on the testimony of a Chinese witness (*People v. Hall*).

1856   The Second Opium War begins between China and Great Britain and France. At issue is the opening of further ports to western trade, respecting the rights of Christians, legalizing the "Coolie Trade," and establishing embassies for Britain, France, the United States, and Russia. The war concluded in 1860.

1860s   Formation of the Chinese Six Companies in San Francisco. They represent Chinese interests and later provide legal assistance to Chinese immigrants and residents.

1863   Construction begins on the Central Pacific Railroad.

1865   Passage of the Fourteenth Amendment allows for citizenship for all US-born children.

1865   Railroad baron Charles Crocker hires fifty Chinese men in response to threats of a strike by white workers; within two years, 90 percent of railroad workers are Chinese.

1867   Chinese laborers win wage concessions from the railroad companies.

1867   Dennis Kearney forms the Workingmen's Party in San Francisco with an anti-Chinese platform. Mobs attack Chinese people.

1868   China signs the Burlingame Treaty, an American effort to ensure trade access on par with Great Britain's. The treaty gave most-favored nation status to Chinese subjects and allowed for their free migration to the United States for the purposes of tourism, trade, or residency.

1870   The Foreign Miners Tax makes up 25 to 50 percent of state revenue. The Chinese are the state's largest ethnic group, making up 9 percent of the total population and 25 percent of the labor force. Thirty-five hundred Chinese women now live in the state; 61 percent are listed as prostitutes.

1870s The transcontinental railroad's completion leads to record unemployment in California. Chinese labor moves to agriculture, fishing, and trades in towns and cities.

1871 Fifteen Chinese people are lynched and four are shot in Los Angeles during anti-Chinese riots.

1880 The Burlingame Treaty is amended to limit the arrival of Chinese laborers who might be injurious to public interest or endanger public order in communities.

1882 The Immigration Act centralizes immigration policy as a federal responsibility, but the states maintain day-to-day control over entry. The act also forbids the entry of convicts, lunatics, idiots, and paupers.

1882 On May 6, the Chinese Exclusion Act freezes the immigration of any Chinese laborers into the United States for ten years.

1884 On July 5, the Exclusion Act is modified to require that Chinese laborers may offer a return certificate issued by the federal government as "the only evidence permissible to establish his right of re-entry" for those residing in the United States on November 17, 1880, who had departed by sea prior to May 6, 1882, and remained out of the United States until after July 5, 1884.

1888 On October 1, Congress amends the Exclusion Act to forbid any Chinese laborers from entering the United States, regardless of whether they had previous return certificates issued under the earlier legislation.

1891 Congress passes the Immigration Act, which moves immigration jurisdiction from the federal courts to the new Office of the Superintendent of Immigration, under the Treasury Department. All decisions made by the department are to be final.

1892 The Geary Act extends the Chinese Exclusion laws for another ten years.

1902 The Chinese Exclusion Act is made permanent.

1905 The Federal Bureau of Immigration is created.

1906 The Great Earthquake and Fire in San Francisco destroys all birth records for city residents. Many immigrants claim naturalization by birth; many claims are doubted. Chinese relatives continue to try to join their families.

1906 The San Francisco School Board orders the segregation of Asian children. Japan protests that this violates its treaty with the United States.

1907 President Theodore Roosevelt convinces the San Francisco School Board to rescind Asian segregation; Japan agrees to a revised treaty that bars Japanese and Korean laborers from coming to the United States, effectively extending the exclusion laws to all Asians.

1910 The Angel Island detention center is set up to process and detain Asian immigrants.

1943 China becomes an ally against Japan in World War II. In December, the Chinese Exclusion Repeal Act ends the Chinese exclusion laws.

The first Chinese to arrive during the gold rush were seen by the white miners as just another of a multitude of exotic races. Many had experience mining in their homeland and could offer advice to the often-ignorant Americans. Even for those working outside the goldfields, the Chinese were not only welcomed but also considered indispensable. "Here were men who would do the drudgery of life at a reasonable wage when every other man had but one idea—to work at the mines for gold. Here were cooks, laundrymen, and servants ready and willing. Just what early California civilization most wanted these men could and would supply," wrote Henry K. Norton in his 1924 memoir, *The Story of California from the Earliest Days to the Present*. The Chinese were praised for their hard work and good habits. *The Annals of San Francisco* noted the opening of the city's first Chinese restaurant in 1850 on Jackson Street by "the Celestial Jon-Ling." The Chinese even took part in the parades that celebrated California's admission to the Union in the fall of 1850. But this fascination and tolerance was short-lived. Norton described this change of heart, writing:

> The Chinaman was welcomed as long as the surface gold was plentiful enough to make rich all who came. But that happy situation was not long to continue. Thousands of Americans came flocking in to the mines. Rich surface claims soon became exhausted. These newcomers did not find it so easy as their predecessors had done to amass large fortunes in a few days. California did not fulfill the promise of the golden tales that had been told of her. These gold-seekers were disappointed. In the bitterness of their disappointment they turned upon the men of other races who were working side by side with them and accused them of stealing their wealth. They boldly asserted that California's gold belonged to them. The cry of "California for the Americans" was raised and taken up on all sides. Within a short time the Frenchman, the Mexican and the Chileño had been driven out and the full force of this anti-foreign persecution fell upon the unfortunate Chinaman.

A few hundred Chinese immigrants lived in California in 1849. By 1850, 789 lived in the state; by 1851, it was 4,000, and by 1852, 25,000. "In China, the California fever seems to have reached an unprecedented height, and the long tailed and curious denizens of that strange world evinced as great eagerness to reach our magic land as ever exhibited by *our own countrymen* from the Eastern United States. They are flocking in upon us by the hundreds, every ship arriving from thence, bringing from one hundred and fifty upwards," noted San Francisco's *Evening Picayune* in April 1852.

There were 151,000 Chinese in the United States by 1876; 116,000 of those lived in California, constituting about 9 percent of the state's population. The vast majority of these were men; financial and immigration restraints meant few wives could join their husbands. Miscegenation laws meant Chinese men were forbidden from marrying white women, and the few Chinese women who made it to California were mostly sex slaves—usually peasant girls sold by their parents—who would become prostitutes in San Francisco's Chinatown or the mining camps. In 1870, there were only 3,500 Chinese women in California and almost two-thirds of them worked as prostitutes.

The Rise of Anti-Chinese Sentiment

Discrimination against the Chinese in California paralleled the state's economic development. When work was plentiful, there were lulls in discrimination; in economic downturns, the racism was virulent and unforgiving. Because the Chinese were generally so successful at whatever enterprise they undertook, lived frugally in bachelor communities, and took jobs for lower pay than whites did, they offered an easy target for the frustrations of white laborers who felt squeezed by capitalist railroad barons on the one hand and lower-cost Chinese labor on the other. In particular, Irish laborers, who had come to California in great numbers in the late 1840s to escape the potato famines in Ireland, hated the Chinese. Anti-Catholic bigotry had driven many Irish from Eastern cities like Boston and Philadelphia, and now they returned the favor to Chinese immigrants in California. Anti-Chinese bigotry served as the glue that brought together disparate California labor unions, making them a powerful force in state and national politics for decades to come. The Chinese population achieved great numbers at an inopportune time and were conspicuously un-American in appearance, customs, and manners. Starting with early expulsions from California mining camps, this resentment would grow for three decades, culminating in a nationwide ban on Chinese immigration in 1882.

In April 1850, the state legislature passed its first anti-Chinese legislation: the Foreign Miners Tax, which imposed the princely sum of twenty dollars per month on any miner who was not a naturalized citizen. This was routinely enforced only against Chinese, Mexican, and Chilean miners. But the law hurt gold production, so it was repealed and later replaced with a four-dollar-per-month version. California governor John Bigler gained political capital by seizing on early anti-Chinese sentiment in the mines. In the spring of 1852, he asked the legislature to outlaw Chinese laborers, characterizing them as "coolies" who weren't interested in integrating or making lives in America but only in taking American gold back to China.

But the Chinese immigrant community also included merchants, scholars, and diplomats, some of whom had been educated by American missionaries in Asia. Two men, Hab Wa and Long Achic, replied to Governor Bigler's call in a letter reprinted in the July 1852 issue of *Living Age* magazine. In it, they informed the governor that most Chinese laborers in California were not coolies but common laborers. "The Irishmen who are engaged in digging down your hills, the men who unload ships, who clean streets, or even drive your drays, would, if they were in China be considered 'Coolies,'" they wrote.

The governor did not respond.

State courts soon joined the campaign against the new immigrants. The California Supreme Court, in *People v. Hall* (1854), ruled that Chinese, like blacks and Indians, were not allowed to testify against a white person in criminal court. The rationale was that "the name of Indian, from the time of Columbus to the present day, has been used to designate, not alone the North American Indian, but the whole of the Mongolian race."

In the district court, the earliest cases involving Chinese plaintiffs were for non-payment of sailors' wages or breach of contract. In 1852, the Chinese agent for the San Francisco firm of Heung Mow Company sued the ship *Robert Small* for breach of contract in admiralty court. The ship had been chartered to bring Chinese immigrants to California, but after landing them, the captain refused to release their belongings and other cargo worth $750. The case was settled before a trial, and no one questioned the ability of the Chinese merchants to sue the white ship owners.

The discovery of the Comstock Lode near Virginia City, Nevada, in 1859 set off a Silver Rush that lifted the California economy and briefly eased anti-Chinese sentiments. But by 1862, the California legislature passed the Anti-Coolie Act to "Protect Free White Labor against Competition with Chinese Coolie Labor, and to Discourage the Immigration of the Chinese into the State of California." The act created what was

No Term of Endearment

Coolie was a derogatory term for unskilled Chinese laborers and used on a par with the term "nigger." The word comes from the Hindi *qūlī*, which means "hired labor." Coolie workers were often indentured servants brought to the United States to work under contracts of various lengths. Most California Chinese, however, were just day laborers escaping poverty and war in China.

---

known as the Chinese Police Tax. Every person of Mongolian descent aged eighteen and older needed a license to work that cost a monthly tax of $2.50. Chinese workers involved in the production of essentials such as rice, sugar, and tea were exempt from the tax.

Construction of the Central Pacific Railroad began just east of Sacramento in 1863. Two years later, a strike threatened by the workers—most of whom were Irish—led railroad financier Charles Crocker to hire fifty Chinese men to do the backbreaking and dangerous work of punching through the Sierra Nevada. Eventually, the railroad employed some twelve thousand Chinese, about 90 percent of the workforce. They were nicknamed "Crocker's pets." California governor Leland Stanford, who was on the board of directors of the Central Pacific, reported to President Lincoln in 1865 on Chinese laborers: "As a class they are quiet, peaceable, patient, industrious, and economical. Ready and apt to learn all the different kinds of work required in railroad building, they soon became as efficient as white laborers."

On May 10, 1869, the Central Pacific Railroad met the Union Pacific Railroad at Promontory Point, Utah, and the nation opened its first transcontinental railroad. The completion of the railroad meant the migration of thousands of Chinese from the mountains to the valleys, towns, and cities to look for work. Some went on to build more railroads. The Union Pacific in Wyoming hired Chinese workers in 1870 for $32.50 per month instead of paying the $52 per month demanded by white workers. Wherever the Chinese settled, they were successful, be it in agriculture, fishing, commerce, manufacturing, or other trades.

The year 1869 also marked the creation of the United States Circuit Court for the Ninth Circuit, which had trial and appellate jurisdiction in California, Oregon, and Nevada, and later Montana, Washington, and

Idaho. California had been without a full-time circuit court judge since Matthew Hall McAllister had retired from the special California circuit court in 1862. In 1870, Judge Lorenzo Sawyer, then chief justice of the California Supreme Court, was appointed by President Ulysses S. Grant to serve as the first Ninth Circuit Court judge. He served as the circuit's only appointed judge from 1870 until his death in 1891, and sat with Supreme Court justice Stephen J. Field and the circuit's district judges Ogden Hoffman, Matthew P. Deady of Oregon, and George Sabin and Edgar Hillyer of Nevada. In 1891, Congress replaced the circuit court with the United States Court of Appeals for the Ninth Circuit and appointed Joseph McKenna to replace Sawyer.

The Octopus

Many on the frontier resented railroad companies for bringing the "scourge" of Chinese labor to California and for taking large tracts of public land. In much the way the Spanish and Mexican governments had gifted vast amounts of land to private individuals in return for investments, so too did the US government give land to the railroads at the end of the nineteenth century. Construction of four of the five major American railroads were mostly financed by land grants. Congress gave companies millions of acres to build the railroad tracks and sold lands adjoining the right-of-ways to finance the construction. Completion of the transcontinental railroads permanently linked California to the East. What had been a dangerous journey taking several months was now a comfortable six-day trip. For the first time, an established distribution network made a national economy possible. But it was not an easy road. Besides the "Chinese Question," railroad barons in California were villainized for their vise-like monopoly of virtually all the state's transportation, from rail to ferry to stagecoach, for fixing freight prices, and for evicting settlers from their land. Farmers and settlers established leagues to legally challenge the seemingly limitless power of the railroad companies to dictate the price and availability of land within their right-of-ways. In California, the Southern Pacific Railroad was demonized in the popular press as an octopus with tentacles strangling every part of the economy. In 1901, Frank Norris published *The Octopus: A Story of California*, a novel based on the battle between the interests of the Southern Pacific railroad and wheat farmers in California's Central Valley:

The great struggle had begun to invest the combatants with interest. Daily, almost hourly, Dyke was in touch with the ranchers, the wheat-growers. He heard their denunciations, their growls of exasperation and defiance. Here was the other side—this placid, fat man, with a stiff straw hat and linen vest, who never lost his temper, who smiled affably upon his enemies, giving them good advice, commiserating with them in one defeat after another, never ruffled, never excited, sure of his power, conscious that back of him was the Machine, the colossal force, the inexhaustible coffers of a mighty organization, vomiting millions to the League's thousands.

Bankruptcy: Ghirardelli, The Chocolate King

Around this time, one of the district court's early bankruptcy proceedings was filed by Domenico Ghirardelli in San Francisco. Ghirardelli was the founder of the Ghirardelli Chocolate Factory, whose building still stands on the San Francisco waterfront. Ghirardelli was born in Rapallo, Italy, in 1817 and came to San Francisco during the gold rush via Lima, Peru, where he had set up his first confectionary shop. He built one of San Francisco's first hotels, the Europa, which was destroyed in the Great Fire of 1851. He opened a new confectionary store the following year on Kearny and Washington Streets called Mrs. Ghirardelli & Co. In 1856, he built his first chocolate factory at 415 Jackson Street, which operated until he and his sons began construction on the Victorian factory at North Point and Polk Streets (Ghirardelli Square) that remains today. During the 1860s, he discovered and patented the Broma process for making dry, powdered chocolate. After the federal government passed the Bankruptcy Act of 1867, Ghiardelli filed for bankruptcy in the district court. According to former court clerk Carl Calbreath, Ghiardelli and his estate opened and closed bankruptcy proceedings a number of times from the early 1870s until 1912. "The bankrupt seemed to have bought a lot of water lots on and around the bay and it is believed that he did not know just how many he owned or their location. As these water lots were discovered, it was necessary to reopen the proceedings, sell the lots and thereby the purchaser obtained a clear title," the clerk wrote. Ghirardelli died in 1894 during a visit to his hometown in Italy. His chocolate is still made in the US.

FIG. 3-3

In 1882, the satirical weekly *The Illustrated Wasp* published G. Frederick Keller's depiction of the Southern Pacific railroad monopoly as an octopus whose tentacles clutched the state's key economic drivers. Courtesy of The Bancroft Library, University of California, Berkeley.

A trio of cases in the circuit court laid the groundwork for the railroad companies' influence. In *Southern Pacific Railroad Co. v. Orton* (1879), settlers from the San Joaquin Valley challenged the validity of the Southern Pacific's land grant. When Judge Sawyer ruled in favor of

Patents: Andrew Hallidie's Cable Car

Legend has it that the sight of horses being whipped while trying to pull a load up one of San Francisco's famous hills was the inspiration for Andrew Smith Hallidie's idea of replacing animals with a wire cable railway. Hallidie was born in London but came to California for his health in 1852 and stayed. His father held several patents for the manufacture of wire ropes, so young Hallidie followed suit, becoming the first person in California to manufacture wire rope and the first to supply mines with hauling systems. He also built a number of suspension bridges. Hallidie did not invent the cable car, however. A man named Benjamin H. Brooks had received the franchise from the city of San Francisco in 1870 for an "endless rope" street railroad. (Brooks was also one of the few white attorneys to regularly represent Chinese clients.) When Brooks was unable to get financing for construction, he sold the franchise to Hallidie, who added the crucial element to the system: a special grip wheel that allowed a trolley car to hold onto the cable without it slipping. Hallidie received US Patent 110,971 in 1871 for his endless wire ropeway, and Patent 129,130 the next year for his cable grip.

"The rope is grasped and released at pleasure by a peculiar gripping device attached to the passenger car, and controlled by a man in charge," wrote Hallidie in an 1881 issue of *Scientific American*. "The car is more smoothly started than by horses, and instantly stopped on any part of the road; its mechanical construction is simple and easily controlled, and on the streets it does not frighten horses or endanger lives."

Hallidie and his partners built a test railroad along Clay Street, from Kearny Street to the summit of the 307-foot-tall hill at Leavenworth Street. The Clay Street Hill Railroad, the world's first grip-operated cable car system, was a huge success. The system was quickly expanded in San Francisco and led to greater areas of the city being developed. Hallidie died in 1900, late enough to see international success. Today San Francisco is the only city in the world that still has traditional manual-operated cable cars. Hallidie Plaza in downtown San Francisco is named after him.

the Southern Pacific, railroad employees offered to buy settlers out or quoted them a high, railroad-set appraisal price for title to their land. In 1880, when farmers refused to vacate their lands and instead confronted the railroad officials, a shootout escalated to what became known as the Battle of Mussel Slough. Two deputy US marshals and five ranchers were killed.

In the Railroad Tax cases—*San Mateo County v. Southern Pacific* and *Santa Clara County v. Southern Pacific*—Justice Field and Judge Sawyer ruled that corporations have the same constitutional rights to due process as individuals. In *Santa Clara* (1883), the county sued the railroad to recover its share of unpaid property taxes. Justice Field declared that corporations were essentially people and thus protected by the Fourteenth Amendment: the state could not assess land owned by a corporation differently than that of private individuals. Sawyer, a shareholder in the Southern Pacific, concurred. Both he and Field were close with numerous Southern Pacific directors, and were criticized for those connections. The Railroad Tax cases are often cited as the underpinning of the Supreme Court's 2010 decision upholding the First Amendment rights of corporations in *Citizens United v. Federal Election Commission*.

The Perfect Storm

Conditions in the 1870s created a perfect storm for the Chinese discrimination that had been building since the gold rush: the completion of the railroads, the end of the mining booms, drought in California, and a national depression that brought more Easterners to the West in search of work that wasn't there. The Chinese competed with white immigrants for day labor, domestic work such as cooking and laundry, and light manufacturing such as cigars and shirts. The cities were full of out-of-work white men begging or seeking public assistance, while it seemed that the Chinese were always the last to be unemployed. Meanwhile, Chinese immigration continued: by 1870, Chinese immigrants made up 25 percent of California's labor force. In San Francisco, the manufacturing capital of the state, they constituted nearly 50 percent of workers in the four main industries.

The court records tell the tale of an evolving pattern of discrimination in whatever industry Chinese immigrants succeeded, including mining, cigar making, and laundries. As the number of Chinese-owned enterprises rose in an industry, local or state governments enacted laws to restrict their activities or put them out of business. The Chinese were also frequent targets of the US Attorney for violations of revenue laws in the 1860s and 1870s. The cigar industry was a case in point.

By 1866, more than half of San Francisco's cigar factories were Chinese-owned, and up to 90 percent of the workforce was Chinese. They had lower labor costs and came to dominate the industry. Labor leaders charged that the Chinese workers had replaced white women workers, who had no work to turn to but prostitution. Wrote *The Truth*, a local pro-labor newspaper, in 1882:

> Six years ago, six thousand white Americans with wives, with sisters, with little babes—four thousand men and two thousand women were working in this city manufacturing cigars. To-day there are but one hundred and seventy-nine! Where have they gone? What had become of the free Americans? WHERE HAVE THEY GONE? Replaced by Chinese, those men who lived became thieves, tramps, vagrants, paupers, or at best, common laborers. The women,—oh, SHAME on the people, the press and the laws that permit it—to day sell their bodies as COMMON PROSTITUTES.

By the late 1870s, the Chinese had become the principal targets in revenue violation cases brought by the US Attorney, usually for technicalities that ensured tax collection. By 1879, mandatory minimum sentences and fees associated with these violations had raised the stakes considerably for Chinese cigar makers: a conviction could mean the confiscation of the entire factory by the government. From 1879 to 1881, more than six hundred cases of revenue violations related to cigar and match production were filed in the district court. More than 70 percent of the cases involved Chinese defendants, who were convicted twice as often as white defendants, according to Christian Fritz in *Federal Justice in California* (1991). They were also far less likely to have their cases dismissed. The Chinese were effectively forced out of the cigar industry by the mid-1880s.

The debate over the Chinese Question raged in California cities throughout the decade, amidst the most virulent racism the Chinese had yet experienced, be it by mob or local and state laws. Los Angeles was the site of California's most violent anti-Chinese incident: an argument between two Chinese men over a woman in 1871 escalated into a city-wide anti-Chinese riot in which nineteen Chinese were lynched and four others shot. The city's Chinese population at the time was only two hundred.

While fellow workers increasingly detested the Chinese, they were cherished by employers for their hard work, low pay, and reliability. Trade with Asia and cheap Chinese labor built many an American fortune, so despite anti-Chinese sentiment in California, there was widespread support for Ambassador Anson Burlingame's diplomatic mission to China, which led to the Burlingame Treaty of 1868. The treaty secured most-favored nation status for China, encouraged commerce and trade, promised reciprocal exemption from persecution of religion, and provided for the mutual free immigration of both American citizens and Chinese subjects for the purpose of "curiosity or trade or as permanent residents." The Burlingame Treaty also promised that Chinese subjects in the United States would be accorded all the "privileges, immunities and exemptions in respect to travel and residence…to citizens…of the most favored nation." But almost as soon as the treaty was signed, fierce lobbying began to amend it to restrict Chinese immigration.

A serious depression in the mid-1870s led to widespread unemployment and reduced wages. Nascent labor movements resented capitalists' growing use of Chinese labor, especially when they began importing Chinese workers to manufacturing centers on the East Coast in the 1870s. The Chinese were particularly hated for their ability to live so frugally as to permit them to send nearly all their earnings back to China. This, it was said, took money out of the local and state economy.

Many politicians felt that local action was the only way to discourage Chinese immigration. "The general government has so tied our hands by the treaty with China, that we must depend entirely on local legislation to discourage immigration of Chinese, who are coming here at the rate of two thousand a month," stated San Francisco supervisor Robert Goodwin during an 1873 board session. He proposed three anti-Chinese ordinances: the Queue Ordinance, the Cemetery Ordinance, and the Chinese Laundry Tax. The Queue Ordinance would cut the queues (ponytails) of any Chinese convicted of a crime; the Cemetery Ordinance would require permission from the city coroner before any body could be removed from county cemeteries; and the laundry tax would charge fifteen dollars per quarter for each male employee and an additional tax for laundries that deliver without a horse and wagon (i.e., all Chinese laundries). The *San Francisco Bulletin* outlined the intent of the ordinances:

> It is generally known that to deprive a Chinaman of his queue is to humiliate him as deeply as is possible. It is also very generally known, that the bones of no Chinaman are permitted to remain in a foreign land, and that all Chinese, before leaving their country, feel assured that, after death, no matter where they die, their bones will be taken back to mingle with their native sod. So strict are all Chinese on these two points, that it is believed, if they were prevented from wearing their tails here, and if after death their bones were denied transportation to their native land, the immigration of this superstitious people would be effectually stopped.

At least one member of the Board of Supervisors opposed the ordinances. "The whole letter and spirit of these resolutions are illegal, narrow-minded, contemptible, and utterly unworthy of the sanction of this body," Supervisor Andrew B. Forbes said at the 1873 meeting where the ordinances were passed. "We ought not to do an illegal act by imposing unequal taxation, which the celebrated 'one-horse' ordinance contemplates, nor should we permit ourselves to favor the passage of the barbarous orders, as to queue cutting and disinterments, which breathe a spirit only worthy of savages." But even the enlightened Forbes had to throw his bone to the anti-Chinese lobby. "Nor do I propose to make a plea in favor of Chinese emigration, per se; I do not favor their coming, but they are here—here under the provisions of a treaty, and in common with others, have rights."

San Francisco mayor William Alvord refused to sign the Queue Ordinance into law and sent it back to the board, writing:

> With respect to the wisdom and policy of encouraging Chinese immigration, reasonable and honest differences of opinion exist; but this fact should not induce any of us to attempt to defeat the operations of the Federal Government in reference to this or any other class of foreign immigration. As Justice Field has observed, in a charge given by him to a Grand Jury in this district: "If public policy requires that the Chinese should be excluded from our shores, let the general government so provide and declare, but until it does so provide and declare, and whilst here, they are entitled, equally with all others, to the full protection of

the laws." I trust, that after having considered the above quoted laws and legal authorities, your honorable body will concur with me in the objections now submitted.

Justice Field, frequently attacked for his rulings in favor of Chinese plaintiffs in the circuit court, openly advocated for Congress to change the laws to legally restrict Chinese immigration.

It would take three years before the "pigtail order," as the Queue Ordinance was known, came up for a vote again. This time, Supervisor Frederick A. Gibbs wrote it up as a "health precaution" and made it applicable to all prisoners. By this time it elicited little debate—nearly every politician was against the Chinese. It was passed in 1876 on a ten-to-two vote and signed into law by Mayor Andrew J. Bryant. The new ordinance required that every man imprisoned in county jail have his hair cut to within one inch of his scalp. The impetus for this law was the fact that many Chinese, faced with fines for infractions of any number of discriminatory laws, often preferred to serve jail time instead of paying a fine. One prisoner, Ho Ah Kow, whose queue was cut, sued San Francisco sheriff Matthew Nunan for $10,000 in damages in the old circuit court.

FIG. 3-4
This cartoon, titled "Judge Righteous Judgment," and published in the satirical magazine *The Wasp*, depicts Justice Stephen Johnson Field cutting off the queue of a Chinese man holding an opium pipe. Courtesy of The Bancroft Library, University of California, Berkeley.

Ho had been convicted of violating the state Cubic Air Law, also passed in 1876, which made it a misdemeanor for any person to sleep in a room with less than five hundred cubic feet of space per person. The fine was either cash, ranging from ten to fifty dollars, imprisonment, or both. This law was aimed at Chinese lodgings and flophouses, which packed in sleepers like sardines. In 1878, Ho was given the choice between a ten-dollar fine and five days in county jail. Failing to pay the fine, he was brought to San Francisco's county jail, where Sheriff Nunan processed him and cut off his queue.

During the trial, Ho told the court that the lack of a queue is regarded as a mark of disgrace in Chinese culture and that his religion promises misfortune and suffering in the afterlife because of it. He said that the sheriff was aware of the sacred significance of the queue and that Ho professed his religion. Since his release, Ho alleged he had suffered mental anguish and had been ostracized by his community. Nunan defended his action on the grounds of the city's Queue Ordinance. Sitting on the circuit court, Justice Field and Judge Sawyer found that the Board of Supervisors had overstepped its authority by adding additional punishment to a state crime. Furthermore, they determined that the measure was discriminately pointed at the Chinese and violated the Constitution's Fourteenth Amendment. For Chinese prisoners, Field concluded in his 1879 opinion that the enforcement of the Queue Ordinance was cruel and unusual punishment:

> The cutting of the hair of every male person within an inch of the scalp, on his arrival at the jail, was not intended and cannot be maintained as a measure of discipline or as a sanitary condition....It was done to add to the severity of the punishment....It is special legislation, on the part of the supervisors, against a class of persons, who, under the constitution and laws of the United States, are entitled to the equal protection of the laws. The ordinance was intended for the Chinese in San Francisco. This was avowed by the supervisors on its passage, and was so understood by everyone. The ordinance is known in the community as the 'Queue Ordinance,' being so designated from its purpose to reach the queues of the Chinese, and it is not enforced against any of other persons. The reason for its adoption...is that only the dread of the loss of his queue will induce a Chinaman to pay his fine....Probably the bastinado, or the knout, or the thumbscrew, or the rack, would accomplish the same end; and no doubt the Chinaman would prefer either of these modes of

torture to that which entails upon him disgrace among his countrymen and carries with it the constant dread of misfortune and suffering after death. It is not creditable to the humanity and civilization of our people, much less to their Christianity, that an ordinance of this character was possible.

Justice Field urged local lawmakers to turn to the federal government for an actionable remedy for the "apprehended evil" of Chinese immigration:

We are aware of the general feeling—amounting to positive hostility—prevailing in California against the Chinese....Their dissimilarity in physical characteristics, in language, manners, and religion would seem, from past experience, to prevent the possibility of assimilation with our people. And thoughtful persons, looking at the millions which crowd the opposite shores of the Pacific, and the possibility at no distant day of their pouring over in vast hordes among us, giving rise to fierce antagonisms of race, hope that some way may be devised to prevent their future immigration…the appeal must be made to the general government; and it is not believed that the appeal will ultimately be disregarded. Be that as it may, nothing can be accomplished in that direction by hostile and spiteful legislation on the part of the State, or any of its municipal bodies, like the ordinance in question—legislation which is unworthy of a brave and manly people. Against such legislation it will always be the duty of the judiciary to declare and enforce the paramount law of the nation.

Justice Field was lambasted and ridiculed in the press for his ruling. A cartoon in the *Illustrated Wasp* depicted him carefully braiding the queue of a Chinese man smoking an opium pipe with the caption "Judge Righteous Judgment." This did not sit well with Field, who was readying himself for his first run for president in the 1880 election. He failed to win the endorsement of the California Democratic delegation, a matter he later blamed on his Chinese rulings.

The hot-button issue of Chinese immigration became the measuring stick by which all local and state politicians were judged, and few could turn away from the groundswell of anti-Chinese sentiment. State Senate hearings in 1876 regarding the Chinese Question proclaimed that:

The male element of this population, where not criminal, comes into a painful competition with the most needy and most deserving of our people—those who are engaged, or entitled to be engaged, in industrial pursuits in our midst. The common laborer, the farm hand, the shoe-maker, the cigar maker, the domestic male and female, and workmen of all descriptions, find their various occupations monopolized by Chinese labor, employed at a compensation upon which white labor cannot possibly exist.

Many people also felt that the Chinese labored under a system similar to slavery, which had only recently been abolished. "When the Coolie arrives here he is as rigidly under the control of the contractor who brought him as ever an African slave was under his master in South Carolina or Louisiana," wrote the *San Francisco Chronicle* in 1879. While many Chinese immigrants were slaves—taken to Cuba and Peru to work in the mines and guano trade—most American-bound Chinese were free immigrants, or semi-free, in the sense that many labored under the so-called credit-ticket system by which individuals were in debt bondage to pay back their tickets. Various individuals—such as returned emigrants, Chinese merchants, Western labor recruiters, and ship captains—as well as Chinese fraternal associations provided emigrants with tickets on credit for the voyage abroad. The emigrants were then obligated to repay the fares from their future earnings upon arrival at their destination, often at a high interest rate. This system, coupled with the sex slave trade of Chinese prostitutes, was another black mark against the Chinese as far as public opinion was concerned.

The state commissioner of immigration could require a five-hundred-dollar bond from the master of a ship for any alien deemed "lewd and debauched" (i.e., a prostitute) or thought likely to become a public charge. The commissioner received 20 percent of the fees and the remainder went to the state fund for indigent citizens (not aliens). This was challenged by a Chinese woman, Chy Lung, who had been detained in San Francisco. The Supreme Court found the law to be unconstitutional in 1875: "Its manifest purpose, as we have already said, is not to obtain indemnity, but money…whether a young woman's manners are such to justify the commissioner in calling her lewd may be made to depend on the sum she will pay for the privilege of landing in San Francisco….In any view we can take of this statute, it is in conflict with the Constitution of the United States, and therefore void."

That same year, Congress passed the Page Act. It was the beginning of the federal push to remove immigration control from the states. The Page Act gave a nod to California's concerns about Chinese immigration, making it a felony to import women for the purpose of prostitution and to bring contract laborers to the United States. It also forbade the importation of any Asian workers against their will and forbade the entry of convicts (except those convicted of political crimes). It empowered the collector of customs for each port to inspect arriving vessels and order the detention of any suspected "obnoxious persons." Masters of vessels were required to post a five-hundred-dollar bond to secure the deportation of any suspects within six months.

The year 1877 was the watershed moment for anti-Chinese sentiment in California. The economic depression had been exacerbated by a vicious drought. In this fertile soil of animosity, prejudice, and desperation bloomed the Workingmen's Party of Dennis Kearney, an Irishman who had come to California from New York with the battle cry of "The Chinese Must Go!" Kearney also denounced the millionaire monopolists who had built the railroads with Chinese labor and controlled much of California's economy to the detriment of farmers and laborers.

Around a strident anti-Chinese platform, the Workingmen's Party galvanized California labor into a coherent political force. In 1878, party candidates won a third of the 152 seats to the state constitutional convention in Sacramento. The new California constitution, adopted in 1879, reflected the party's influence in its strong anti-Chinese language: Chinese people could not own property or be elected to public office. They could not be employed by the state or any municipality, or any California-based corporation. Many who had feared that the anti-Chinese lobby would resort to mob law to achieve its objectives were both surprised and horrified by the Workingmen's Party's success. "Curiously, however, it was to regular legal procedures rather than to lynch law that the Sand-Lotters appealed....[The] new constitution for the state... embodied most of their radical ideas," noted John D. Hicks in his 1937 book, *The American Nation: A History of the United States from 1865 to the Present.*

The conflict between California's new constitution and the 1868 Burlingame Treaty, which promised that Chinese subjects would be respected, collided in the 1880 case of Tiburcio Parrott. Born in Mazatlan, Mexico, in 1840, Parrott was the illegitimate son of US consul John Parrott. Educated in the United States and England, he came to California in 1862 to work for his father and became a successful banker and financier. Parrott owned the Sulphur Bank Mine in Lake County, north of San Francisco, which started producing quicksilver in 1874. The majority of the Sulphur

Address by Dennis Kearney, 1878

In our golden state all these evils have been intensified. Land monopoly has seized upon all the best soil in this fair land. A few men own from ten thousand to two hundred thousand acres each. The poor Laborer can find no resting place, save on the barren mountain, or in the trackless desert. Money monopoly has reached its grandest proportions. Here, in San Francisco, the palace of the millionaire looms up above the hovel of the starving poor with as wide a contrast as anywhere on earth.

To add to our misery and despair, a bloated aristocracy has sent to China—the greatest and oldest despotism in the world—for a cheap working slave....Their dress is scant and cheap. Their food is rice from China. They hedge twenty in a room, ten by ten. They are whipped curs, abject in docility, mean, contemptible and obedient in all things. They have no wives, children or dependents.

They are imported by companies, controlled as serfs, worked like slaves, and at last go back to China with all their earnings. They are in every place, they seem to have no sex. Boys work, girls work; it is all alike to them. The father of a family is met by them at every turn. Would he get work for himself? Ah! A stout Chinaman does it cheaper. Will he get a place for his oldest boy? He can not. His girl? Why, the Chinaman is in her place too! Every door is closed. He can only go to crime or suicide, his wife and daughter to prostitution, and his boys to hoodlumism and the penitentiary.

Do not believe those who call us savages, rioters, incendiaries, and outlaws. We seek our ends calmly, rationally, at the ballot box....

We are men, and propose to live like men in this free land, without the contamination of slave labor, or die like men, if need be, in asserting the rights of our race, our country, and our families.

California must be all American or all Chinese. We are resolved that it shall be American, and are prepared to make it so. May we not rely upon your sympathy and assistance?

With great respect,
for the Workingman's Party of California.
Dennis Kearney, President
H. L. Knight, Secretary

(From the *Indianapolis Times*, February 28, 1878)

Bank miners were Chinese, who worked under dangerous conditions in unbearable heat and amid poisonous fumes. During one incident in the early 1880s, a number of Chinese miners were scalded to death when they struck an underground geyser. Many white miners refused to work in the more dangerous underground shafts. The new state constitution thus had a paralyzing effect on the state's quicksilver mines, whose owners had great difficulty finding any non-Chinese miners. Parrott deliberately defied the law, refusing to fire his Chinese miners, and was arrested,

---

California Constitution of 1879

ARTICLE XIX

Chinese.

SECTION 1. The Legislature shall prescribe all necessary regulations for the protection of the state...from the burdens and evils arising from the presence of aliens who are or may become vagrants, paupers, mendicants, criminals, or invalids, afflicted with contagious or infectious diseases, and from aliens otherwise dangerous and detrimental to the well-being or peace of the State, and to impose conditions upon which such persons may reside in the state, and to provide the means and mode of their removal from the state upon failure of refusal to comply with such conditions; *provided,* that nothing contained in this section shall be construed to impair or limit the power of the Legislature to pass such police laws or other regulations as it may deem necessary.

SECTION 2. No corporation now existing, or hereafter formed under the laws of this State, shall, after the adoption of this Constitution, employ, directly or indirectly, in any capacity, any Chinese or Mongolians. The Legislature shall pass such laws as may be necessary to enforce this provision.

SECTION 3. No Chinese shall be employed on any State, county, municipal, or other public work, except in punishment for crime.

SECTION 4. The presence of foreigners ineligible to become citizens is declared to be dangerous to the well-being of this State, and the Legislature shall discourage their immigration by all the means within its power.

tried, and found guilty by state courts. He appealed to the circuit court on a writ of habeas corpus.

Judge Sawyer and Judge Hoffman heard the case, which centered on how far the state could go in regulating the actions of corporations. They took a strong stand against the new state constitution. Hoffman, in his opinion, wondered, "Would it be believed possible...that such legislation as this could be directed against a race whose right to freely emigrate to this country, and reside here with all the 'privileges, immunities, and exemptions of the most favored nation,' has been recognized and guaranteed by a solemn treaty of the United States, which not only engages the honor of the National Government but is by the very terms of the Constitution the supreme law of the land?" He wrote that if a state has the power to pass such a law, "it might equally well have forbidden the employment of Irish, German, or Americans, or people of color, or it might have required the employment of any of these classes of persons to the exclusion of the rest....Such an exercise of legislative power can only be maintained on the ground that stockholders of corporations have no rights which the Legislature is bound to respect."

Banks, churches, and hospitals would be unable to employ Chinese interpreters or nurses; only private citizens might employ them, Hoffman noted, pointing out that this was one of many recent attempts to undermine the treaty with China. "The attempt to impose a special license tax upon Chinese for the privilege of mining, the attempt to subject them to peculiar and exceptional punishments commonly known as the Queue Ordinance, have been frustrated by the judgments of this Court. The attempt to extort a bond from ship-owners as a condition of being permitted to land those whom a Commissioner of Immigration might choose to consider as coming within certain enumerated classes, has received the empathetic and indignant condemnation of the Supreme Court." Hoffman added that the "growing evil" of Chinese immigration was an opinion held "by most thoughtful persons." But, he wrote, while the Burlingame Treaty existed, "the Chinese have the same rights of immigration and residence as are possessed by any other foreigners. Those rights it is the duty of the courts to maintain, and the Government to enforce."

Judge Sawyer reminded the state legislature that the Constitution, laws, and treaties of the United States "are as much a part of the law of every State as its own local laws and constitution." He further pointed out that a state cannot deny a person the right to labor for subsistence: "As to by far the greater portion of the Chinese, as well as other foreigners who land upon our shores, their labor is the only exchangeable commodity they possess. To deprive them of the right to labor is to consign them to starvation." The real aim of this legislation, Sawyer said, was not to regulate corporations but rather to evict the Chinese from California. He concluded with a warning: "In view of recent events transpiring in San Francisco...I deem it not inappropriate in this connection to call attention to the fact, of which many are probably unaware, that the Statutes of the United States are not without provisions, both of a civil and criminal nature...to enforce the Fourteenth Amendment...which guarantees to every 'person'—which term, as we have seen, includes Chinese—'within the jurisdiction' of California, the 'equal protection of the laws.'"

The circuit court declared Article XIX of the California Constitution unconstitutional and void. Parrott was released from custody in 1880. (He went on to build a palatial Victorian estate, Miravalle, near the Napa Valley town of St. Helena in the early 1890s, which was the setting of the TV soap opera *Falcon Crest* nearly a century later.)

Chinese dignitaries respectfully tried to dissuade the Americans from violating the Burlingame Treaty. Chinese Foreign Minister Wu Tingfang wrote Congress that if the American people wanted to restrict the Chinese, they should do so, but only if they restricted all foreigners as well. "Justice would seem to demand equal consideration for the Chinese on the part of the United States," he wrote. "China does not ask for special favors. All she wants is enjoyment of the same privileges accorded other nationalities. Instead, she is singled out for discrimination and made the subject of hostile legislation. Her door is wide open to the people of the United States, but their door is slammed in the face of her people."

In 1879, Democrats controlled both houses of Congress. The California delegation drafted a Fifteen Passenger Law that would have limited steamships to carrying no more than fifteen Chinese passengers per vessel. The resolution passed, but was vetoed by Republican president Rutherford B. Hayes on the grounds that it violated the Burlingame Treaty. Hayes amended the treaty in 1880 with new provisions that allowed China or the United States to restrict immigration whenever it "affects or threatens to affect the interest of that country or endangers the good order...or of any locality within the territory thereof." Chinese subjects already in the US were "allowed to come and go of their own free will and allowed...all the rights, privileges and amenities...accorded to the citizens and subjects of the most favored nation."

After the 1880 election, the California delegation drafted a bill that would ban Chinese immigration for twenty years. It passed, but was vetoed by President Chester A. Arthur. The next version was a ban for ten years. The act decreed that only laborers who were residents on November 17, 1880, would be allowed to stay in the United States. Any Chinese person departing the United States was required to get a return certificate from the port customs collector stating the person's name, age, residence, and physical description. Any non-laborers wishing to immigrate needed a certificate from the Chinese government—a so-called Canton certificate—vouching for their status as a merchant, student, or scholar. Upon landing in any US port, shipmasters were required to submit a list of all Chinese passengers along with a statement that their certificates were in order. The law, enacted as the Chinese Exclusion Act of 1882, was renewed for another ten years in 1892 and renewed indefinitely in 1902.

The Shed

As steamships tied up in San Francisco and Chinese immigrants waited for clearance to land, many were held in the Shed while their status was being determined. Most of these fell into three categories: laborers claiming former residence, applicants with Canton certificates, and children trying to join their parents. San Francisco's Chinese population, though thoroughly isolated culturally, did not passively submit to legal discrimination but used the courts to press for their rights under the US-China treaties and the Constitution. The formation of the Chinese Benevolent Society, better known as the Chinese Six Companies, in the 1850s provided a source of legal aid and attorneys for this community. The Six Companies also acted as an informal form of government, police, and legal system, resolving disputes and punishing transgressors. New immigrants, usually brought to America through a family association in China, registered with the Six Companies upon arrival and were required to pay fees and any debts before departing for China. The organization provided temporary housing, helped arrange for the shipping of bodies back to China, and mediated disputes.

When the customs collector forbade a Chinese immigrant to land, a representative from the Chinese Six Companies would hire an attorney to challenge the exclusion laws by petitioning the federal courts for a writ of habeas corpus. Between 1882 and 1891, more than seven thousand writs of habeas corpus were filed in the district court by Chinese detained under the exclusion laws, according to Fritz. Despite hatred of the Chinese and support of anti-Chinese legislation by the leading politicians, lawyers, and judges of the day, the district court ruled in favor of the Chinese in the vast majority of habeas cases. "With the aid of attorneys who transformed Chinese complaints into recognizable legal claims, Chinese immigrants repeatedly turned to the federal courts at San Francisco to contest the enforcement of the Chinese exclusion and general immigration laws and enjoyed remarkable success," wrote Lucy E. Salyer in her 1995 book, *Laws Harsh as Tigers: Chinese Immigrants and the Shaping of Modern Immigration Law.*

Many of the habeas cases of the 1880s addressed the validity of return certificates and whether the 1884 and 1888 modifications to the Chinese Exclusion Act affected Chinese residents who had left the United States before the legislation was enacted. Judge Hoffman and Judge Sawyer wrote that Chinese residents seeking to return should not be required to possess a return certificate if it wasn't required when they left. Justice Field was another story.

The case of Chew Heong was a test case that sharply illustrated the divisions between Field and his colleagues on the bench. Chew was a San Francisco resident in 1880. He left for Hawaii in 1881 and stayed there for three years. When he returned to San Francisco in 1884, he was denied entry for lack of a return certificate. Chew petitioned for a writ of habeas corpus and sought re-entry based on prior residence. Judges Hoffman and Sawyer had consistently ruled that the 1882 act was not intended to be retroactive, and therefore return certificates were not required. In fact, it was the Northern District Court's frequent findings for the Chinese that led Congress to amend the act in 1884 so that oral testimony from other Chinese was disallowed and return certificates were the only permissible evidence in court to establish prior residence.

Whatever their personal views on race, Hoffman and Sawyer believed in the rights of the accused regardless of the color of their skin. In 1884, defending his continued collection of testimony from Chinese plaintiffs, Hoffman wrote:

> By the constitution and laws of the United States, Chinese persons in common with all others, have the right 'to the equal protection of the law' and this includes the right 'to give evidence' in courts. A Chinese person is therefore a competent witness. To reject his testimony when

consistent with itself, and wholly uncontradicted by other proofs, on the sole ground that he is a Chinese person, would be an evasion, or rather violation, of the constitution and law, which every one who sets a just value upon the uprightness and independence of the judiciary, would deeply deplore.

Justice Field returned to California in the fall of 1884, just months after once again failing to receive the state nomination for president, determined to bring his colleagues into line with Congress's intent. Sitting on a judicial panel composed of Judges Sawyer, Hoffman, and George Sabin, Field was in a position as the circuit justice to control the rulings even in the face of their dissent. He made sure that the Chinese Exclusion Act was strictly and more broadly interpreted to disallow the return of any Chinese resident. In the case of Chew Heong, Field was creative in his interpretation not only of the letter of the law but as to the intent of Congress in writing it. In a back-and-forth exchange with Thomas D. Riordan, Chew's attorney, Field insisted that the 1884 act allowed only a certificate. "Congress never supposed that Chinamen intended to go back to China and stay several years. If they do not come back at once they should not be allowed to come at all. We can't have them going away and staying as long as they want to," Field said, according to the *Alta California* newspaper. To this, Riordan replied, "Then I suppose, your Honor, there is no use in arguing the case further."

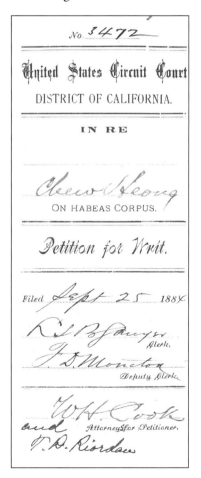

FIG. 3-5
Petition for writ of habeas corpus, September 25, 1884, US Circuit Court for the Northern District of California, Ninth Circuit, Case File No. 3472, *In Re: Chew Heong on Habeas Corpus*. Courtesy of the National Archives and Records Administration, San Bruno, California.

"Not in the least," retorted Field. "My mind is made up on the matter." He advised Riordan to take his case to the Supreme Court or to the Chinese ambassador for further review.

In rejecting his colleagues' earlier opinions, Field asserted that the 1884 act was meant to cover only those Chinese laborers who were in the United States at the time of its passage. Those who had already departed were to be excluded from re-entry. In other words, Field said that Hoffman and Sawyer had been subverting the purpose of the Exclusion Act. In a lengthy dissent on behalf of himself, Hoffman, and Sabin, Judge Sawyer wrote that he saw no merit in the argument that prior Chinese residents be required to produce certificates they could not have obtained. Sawyer contended that Field's decision was at odds with the treaty with China, while the court's previous decisions had both respected the letter of the law and treaty obligations while also leading to an overall decline in the number of Chinese in California.

Chew's case was appealed to the Supreme Court, which reversed Field in a seven-to-two decision based on points similar to Sawyer's. "It is some consolation, after all the lying, abuse, threatening of impeachment etc. as to our construction of the Chinese [Exclusion] act, and the grand glorification of our brother Field for coming out here and so easily, promptly and thoroughly sitting down on us and setting us right on that subject to find that we are not so widely out of our sense after all," Sawyer wrote to Oregon District Court judge Matthew Deady in 1884. The letter was titled "Confidential—Destroy."

Hoffman's Star Chamber

In 1888, Judge Hoffman went head-to-head with John S. Hager, San Francisco's collector of port. Hager was a former senator and zealous anti-Chinese advocate who on his appointment swore not to tolerate "interference" from meddlesome, Chinese-loving federal judges. He insisted that the Chinese had no right to a review in the federal courts and that he, as collector, passed judgment on matters of law and fact. This question was put to the test in the case of *United States v. Jung Ah Lung*. Jung, who claimed to be a California resident re-entering from China without a return certificate, had been detained by Hager. Jung sought a writ of habeas corpus in the district court. US Attorney Samuel Hilborn, under pressure from Hager, challenged the writ, arguing that the court had no jurisdiction. Hoffman was outraged at the government's presumptuousness. "The petitioner is a free man, under our flag, and within the protections of our laws," wrote Hoffman in *In Re Jung Ah Lung*. Requiring the court "in its investigation to be governed by the decision of an executive officer, acting under instructions from Washington" would be "an anomaly wholly without precedent, if not a flagrant absurdity." The Supreme Court upheld Hoffman's ruling. Yet Congress would approve precisely this removal from judicial review just a few years later.

Despite his adamant defense of the Chinese and their right to habeas corpus, Hoffman also believed them to be able liars. He initiated some unusual extrajudicial procedures in reviewing their cases. Starting in 1888, Hoffman allowed Chinese habeas petitioners to be interviewed by the US Attorney without a lawyer present and admitted these interviews as evidence in court. These so-called Star Chamber proceedings were reportedly necessary to speed the processing of immigration court. "We are buried out of sight in Chinese habeas corpus cases," wrote Judge Sawyer in 1888. Hoffman was gravely ill during this time, in part because of the "physical distress and the mental strain caused by a day's conscientious attention to these Chinese cases." This was the peak year for what was known as the habeas corpus mill: more than three thousand habeas cases were filed in that single year. Judges Sabin and Deady helped out until Congress authorized special commissioners to also hear habeas cases. Even so, Hoffman would review each case's testimony and the commissioner's recommendation before arriving at his own, sometimes divergent, opinion.

The combination of election year politics and China's refusal to ratify a new treaty led to the 1888 Chinese Exclusion Act, which forbade re-entry of any resident Chinese laborer and voided all previously issued return certificates. Immigration of any new Chinese laborers was outlawed. President Grover Cleveland signed the act into law and within twenty-four hours San Francisco's federal judges and customs house officials received a telegram from Washington that it was to be enforced at once.

The 1888 act potentially affected some thirty thousand Chinese who had left the country with return certificates. Within two weeks, a test case arrived. Chae Chan Ping was a laborer who lived in California from 1875 to 1887, when he left for China with a return certificate. During his passage back to San Francisco, the 1888 act became law. He arrived

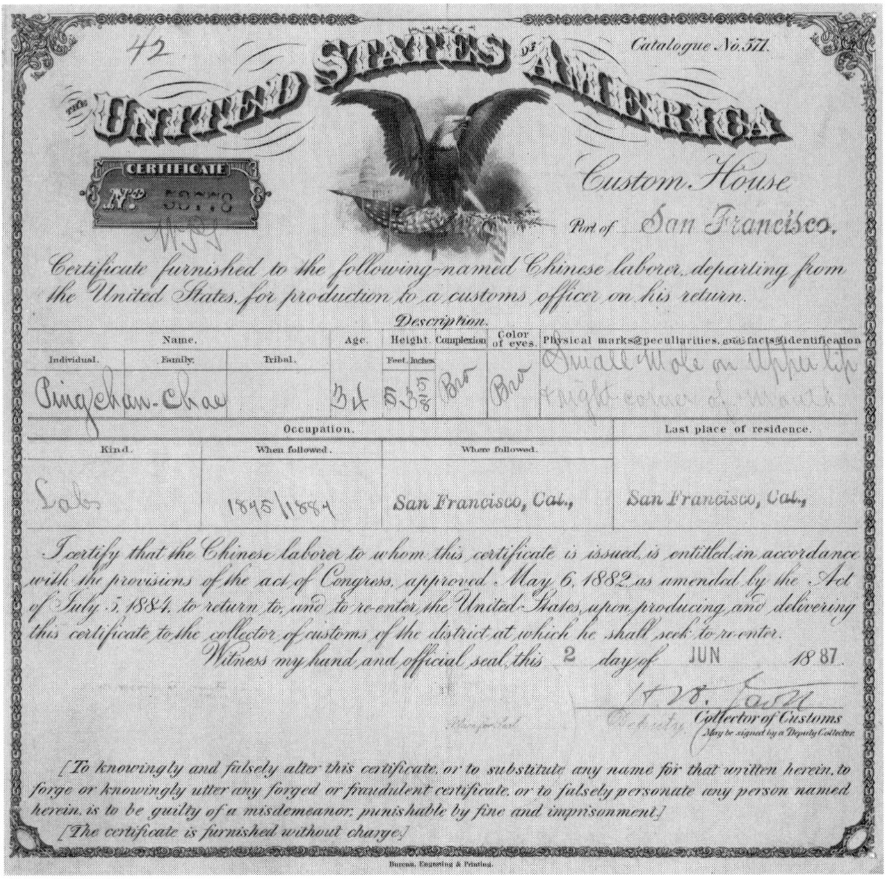

FIG. 3-6
Chae Chan Ping's "Red Eagle" Laborer's Return Certificate, issued June 2, 1887; US Circuit Court for the Northern District of California, Ninth Circuit, Case No. 10100, *In Re: Chae Chan Ping on Habeas Corpus*. Courtesy of the National Archives and Records Administration, San Bruno, California.

in San Francisco and was denied entry. Aboard the steamship *Belgic* in San Francisco Bay, Chae applied to the circuit court for a writ of habeas corpus. Judges Sawyer and Hoffman ruled that under the 1888 act, Chae was denied re-entry to the United States. "We have, heretofore, found it our duty, however unpleasant, at times, to maintain, fearlessly, and steadily, the rights of Chinese laborers under our treaties with China, and the acts of Congress passed to carry them out," wrote Sawyer in *In Re Chae Chan Ping*. Ping appealed to the Supreme Court, contending that the act violated the existing treaties with China. Justice Field delivered the opinion of the court, which vigorously upheld Sawyer's decision.

Judge Lorenzo Sawyer

Lorenzo Sawyer was the first judge appointed in 1870 to the newly organized United States Circuit Court for the Ninth Circuit. He was born in 1820 on a farm in upstate New York and was educated at Western Reserve College near Cleveland. He practiced law in Chicago and Wisconsin in the late 1840s and crossed the plains to California in 1850, where he set up shop in Sacramento and San Francisco. He was San Francisco's city attorney in 1854 and practiced law in San Francisco and Virginia City, Nevada, during the heyday of the Comstock silver lode in the early 1860s. He became a state court judge in 1862 and was elected to the California Supreme Court in 1863. Sawyer was chief justice from 1868 to 1869. He was president of the board of trustees of Stanford University when the cornerstone was laid in 1887. Sawyer was reassigned to the United States Court of Appeals for the Ninth Circuit upon its creation from the circuit court in 1891. He died less than three months later.

Though Judges Hoffman and Sawyer agreed in principle with Justice Field on the Chinese Question, their interactions with the Chinese in court and, perhaps, their personalities led them to different conclusions and to render decisions that put them at odds with Field and the politics of the time. "The Chinese are vastly superior to the Negro, but they are a race entirely different from ours and never can be assimilated, and I don't think it's desirable that they should and for that reason I don't think it desirable that they come here. I think we made a mistake when we opened our door of immigration to them," Judge Sawyer said in his 1888 oral history, recorded by the Bancroft Library at the University of California. But the thousands of separate habeas hearings forced Sawyer and Hoffman to see the Chinese as "human beings with distinct explanations and histories that had to be appraised," wrote Fritz. Field, on the other hand, "heard only test cases in which the Chinese petitioner at hand was largely incidental and symbolic of many others....Hoffman and Sawyer could not maintain Field's detachment."

Supporters of the exclusion laws saw habeas corpus as a dangerous loophole that allowed the release of thousands of illegal, and certainly unwanted, immigrants. "The future historian will find one of the most interesting chapters on the jurisprudence of the American Republic to consist in a description and analysis of the writ of habeas corpus as applied to landing Chinamen in violation…of Restriction Acts in the United States courts of California," predicted the *San Francisco Evening Bulletin* in1888. It was widely assumed that Chinese plaintiffs and their witnesses lied in court and that untold thousands of "paper sons," those with forged nativity papers, were allowed to remain in California.

The success of the Chinese in San Francisco's habeas corpus mill was so legendary that in 1905 Congress took immigration almost entirely out of the courts by vesting it in the newly fortified Bureau of Immigration. If immigrants were refused entry, they were no longer given their day in federal court but only an administrative hearing. But did aliens give up all rights to any judicial proceedings once they entered the realm of the Bureau of Immigration? This question has been the main source of immigration litigation of the last century.

"The successful litigation by Chinese provided the main impulse for taking away the jurisdiction of the federal courts in immigration matters and for placing immigration regulation, instead, under the firm control of the administrative agency," wrote Lucy Salyer. "The Bureau of Immigration had the distinct advantage of being free of traditional legal constraints and being more accountable to public opinion." This decision— forced by the Chinese Question in California—changed the course of American immigration policy. To this day, the Bureau of Immigration or its successors have had powers that often put it above and beyond the reach of the courts in many matters.

Yick Wo v. Hopkins: Equal Protection Under the Law

San Francisco's local laws were always at the forefront of Chinese discrimination. A plethora of laws were passed to restrict the movement, activities, commerce, and culture of Chinese immigrants. In 1870, the city announced that no Chinese would be hired for the improvements to Yerba Buena Park; the use of "yeo-ho" shoulder poles for transporting goods was outlawed; and gongs could not be rung in theaters. An 1873 law enacted a special tax on laundries: those with animal-drawn carts had to pay a two-dollar license fee, and those without (the Chinese) had to pay fifteen dollars. In 1880, there were about 320 laundries in San Francisco, of which 310 were in wooden buildings and 240 were owned and operated by Chinese. Under the guise of protecting the city from fire, the city Board of Supervisors passed the Chinese Laundry Laws in

1880, which stated that laundries could only be operated in brick or stone buildings.

Yick Wo had come to California in 1861 and had operated a laundry in the same wooden building for twenty-two years. His building had always passed the fire warden's inspection laws. In 1885, he was refused permission from the Board of Supervisors to continue his business on the basis of the new law. Yick Wo was one of more than two hundred Chinese laundry owners who were refused licenses. All but one of the ninety non-Chinese laundry owners who operated in wooden buildings

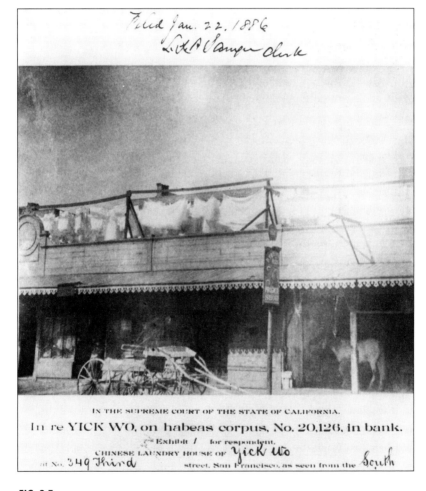

FIG. 3-7
The Yick Wo laundry in San Francisco was the focus of a landmark 1886 Supreme Court ruling applying the Fourteenth Amendment's equal protection and due process clauses to non-citizens. Courtesy of the ACLU of Northern California.

were given permission to continue their businesses. Yick Wo and more than 150 other Chinese owners ignored the law and continued operating. They were arrested, tried, found guilty, and fined ten dollars. Yick Wo refused to pay and was confined to the city jail. He petitioned the California Supreme Court to order San Francisco sheriff Peter Hopkins to release him. The court affirmed the Board of Supervisors' authority to regulate businesses within its jurisdiction. Wo Lee, a fellow Chinese laundry owner imprisoned with Yick Wo, appealed to the circuit court for a writ of habeas corpus. Both Yick and Wo declared in the lawsuit that "those who are not subjects of China, and who are conducting eighty odd laundries under similar conditions, are left unmolested and free to enjoy the enhanced trade and profits arising from this hurtful and unfair discrimination. The business of your petitioner and of those of his countrymen similarly situated, is greatly impaired, and in many cases practically ruined by this system of oppression to one kind of men and favoritism to all others."

The second clause of the Fourteenth Amendment states that "no state shall…deprive any person of life, liberty, or property, without due process of law; nor deny to any person within its jurisdiction the equal protection of the law." After pointing out the power that the laundry laws gave the Board of Supervisors to arbitrarily regulate any business or activity in the city, Judge Sawyer, in his circuit court opinion, pointed out the unconstitutionality of the law:

> The necessary tendency, if not the specific purpose, of this ordinance, and of enforcing it in the manner indicated in the record, is to drive out of business all the numerous small laundries, especially those owned by Chinese, and give a monopoly of the business to the large institutions established and carried on by means of large associated Caucasian capital.…If the facts…indicate a purpose to drive out the Chinese laundrymen, and not merely to regulate the business for the public safety, does it not disclose a case of violation of the provisions of the Fourteenth Amendment to the National Constitution, and of the treaty between the United States and China?…That [the law] does mean prohibition, as to the Chinese, it seems to us must be apparent to every citizen of San Francisco who has been here long enough to be familiar with the cause of an active and aggressive branch of public opinion and of public notorious events. Can a court be blind to what must be necessarily known to every intelligent person in the State?

The Fourteenth Amendment

Passed by Congress in 1868, just a couple of years after the conclusion of the Civil War, the longest amendment to the Constitution was directed at the protection of the rights of newly freed African American slaves. It stated that "all persons born or naturalized in the United States, and subject to the jurisdiction thereof, are citizens of the United States and of the state wherein they reside." Under it, no state may restrict the rights of people within its boundaries or deprive them of "life, liberty, or property without due process of law, nor deny...equal protection of the laws." Its Republican authors considered the recognition of the absolute equality of all persons before the law the "divinest" feature of the Constitution. While aimed at African Americans, this amendment paved the way for the recognition of civil rights for many other minorities in the United States, particularly Chinese immigrants and Chinese Americans when they were under attack during the heyday of the anti-Chinese laws of the 1880s and 1890s.

Even so, Sawyer deferred to the ruling of the California Supreme Court in *Yick Wo*, discharged the writ, and remanded Wo Lee to jail. Both men appealed to the US Supreme Court in 1886. The court combined both cases on appeal and "severely reversed" the rulings of the circuit court and state supreme court, declaring the ordinance in violation of the Fourteenth Amendment. "Though a law be fair on its face and impartial in appearance, yet, if it is administered by public authority with an evil eye and an unequal hand, so as practically to make illegal discriminations between persons in similar circumstances, material to their rights, the denial of equal justice is still within the prohibition of the Constitution," wrote Justice Stanley Matthews for the majority.

The court also reminded California that, "the guarantees of protection contained in the Fourteenth Amendment to the Constitution extend to all persons within the territorial jurisdiction of the United States, without regard to differences of race, of color, or of nationality.... Those subjects of the Emperor of China who have the right to temporarily or permanently reside within the United States, are entitled to enjoy the protection guaranteed by the Constitution and afforded by the laws."

Hall McAllister, son of Judge Matthew Hall McAllister, was one of the lawyers representing Yick Wo and Wo Lee in their appeal to the

Supreme Court. Yick Wo Elementary School in San Francisco's North Beach neighborhood is named after the man and the landmark civil rights case.

Born in the USA

Congress had excluded the Chinese from immigrating or becoming naturalized citizens, but the Fourteenth Amendment broadened citizenship to include all people born in the US. In 1895, the Northern District Court was called upon to decide whether an American-born Chinese person could be excluded from the country based on race. Wong Kim Ark had been born in San Francisco but was refused re-entry to the United States after a visit to China. At issue was whether a child born in the United States to parents who were not citizens was still entitled to citizenship under the Fourteenth Amendment. And if that child was Chinese, of Chinese parents, would the Chinese exclusion laws apply to him?

Under the Civil Rights Act passed by Congress in 1866, all persons born in the United States, plus former slaves brought here, were entitled to the same rights as white men:

> That all persons born in the United States and not subject to any foreign power, excluding Indians not taxed, are hereby declared to be citizens of the United States; and such citizens, of every race and color, without regard to any previous condition of slavery or involuntary servitude, except as a punishment for crime whereof the party shall have been duly convicted, shall have the same right, in every State and Territory in the United States, to make and enforce contracts, to sue, be parties, and give evidence, to inherit, purchase, lease, sell, hold, and convey real and personal property, and to full and equal benefit of all laws and proceedings for the security of person and property, as is enjoyed by white citizens, and shall be subject to like punishment, pains, and penalties, and to none other, any law, statute, ordinance, regulation, or custom, to the contrary notwithstanding.

As Chinese could not become naturalized citizens, nativity was the only way. Wong Kim Ark was born in 1873 at 751 Sacramento Street in San Francisco's Chinatown. In 1890, he and his parents traveled to China. The parents remained there, but Wong returned to San Francisco later that year. The customs collector permitted him to land on the grounds that he was a native-born citizen. In 1894, Wong once again traveled to

China to visit his parents. He returned the following year but was denied re-entry under the exclusions laws by the customs collector and detained aboard ship. Thomas Riordan, attorney for the Chinese consulate in San Francisco and the Chinese Six companies, filed a writ of habeas corpus on behalf of Wong in district court. At the hearing, the US Attorney argued that because Wong "has been at all times, by reason of his race, language, color, and dress, a Chinese person," he should be denied entry under the Chinese exclusion laws and deported. Riordan argued that because Wong was born in the United States of parents who were residents and that he "has not, either by himself or his parents acting for him, ever renounced his allegiance to the United States, and that he has never done or committed any act or thing to exclude him therefrom," he was a US citizen and therefore not subject to the Chinese exclusion laws.

Judge William Morrow, who had become district judge after Judge Hoffman's death in 1891, ordered Wong's release on the grounds that he was a US citizen. The US Attorney appealed the case to the Supreme Court. *The San Francisco Call* described the importance of the case in an 1896 article:

> The question at issue is not one that affects American-born Chinese only, but every American-born son of a foreign-born father who did not become a naturalized citizen of this country. In this view of the case one sees at a glance that many thousands of voters all over the United States are deeply interested in the knotty legal problem, though of course if the United States Supreme Court reverses the ruling of Judge Morrow, as it is confidently expected that it will, the American-born Chinese will be the only ones ultimately deprived of citizenship. Sons of non-naturalized Caucasians will merely have to secure naturalization in the ordinary way. But the Mongolians, while the existing Chinese restriction laws are in force, will be forever barred from citizenship.

In *United States v. Wong Kim Ark*, the Supreme Court supported Judge Morrow. "The Fourteenth Amendment affirms the ancient and fundamental rule of citizenship by birth within the territory," wrote Justice Gray for the majority, who ruled that the Fourteenth Amendment applied to all people born in the United States "regardless of race or color" and even if their parents were foreign-born and not citizens. *Wong Kim Ark* became one of the most far-reaching cases in immigration law and would pave the way for generations of children of immigrants of all races to become American citizens.

End of the Century

The close of the nineteenth century brought about a major shift in the national vision of who should be allowed to come to America and what rights aliens should possess. Led by California's move to restrict the Chinese, Congress—and the federal courts—moved from supporting free immigration, in the form of the Burlingame Treaty with China and other treaties, to sharply curtailing it. By 1891, the majority of immigration cases were decided not by federal judges but by administrators in the newly created Bureau of Immigration, then part of the Treasury Department. "Courts and judicial methods were rejected in favor of an agency with broad discretion, operating according to summary administrative proceedings," wrote Salyer. The Supreme Court "began with the premise that Congress had the inherent sovereign power to exclude and deport aliens for any policy reasons it chose....Congress also had the power to devise whatever procedures it desired to implement its policies. Aliens, who entered and remained in the United States at the sufferance of Congress, were not protected by explicit constitutional procedural guarantees. They enjoyed only those privileges the government expressly allowed them. The only procedural restraint the Court imposed was that aliens should have a fair opportunity to be heard in immigration proceedings."

FIG. 3-8
In 1900, a barbed-wire barricade was erected around San Francisco's Chinatown—believed to be the source of a bubonic plague outbreak—effectively creating a fourteen-block ghetto. Courtesy of The Bancroft Library, University of California, Berkeley.

San Francisco tried to ghettoize its Chinese residents in 1890 by passing the Bingham Ordinance, which required all Chinese inhabitants, including citizens, to "remove from the portion of the city heretofore occupied by them, outside the city and county, or to another designated part of the city and county." It also made it unlawful for Chinese to work in the city, except in specified zones. Chinese residents were to move within sixty days of the passage of the law. Judge Sawyer in the circuit court declared this unconstitutional and voided the law in the 1890 case of *In Re Lee Sing*:

> The obvious purpose of this order, is, to forcibly drive out a whole community of twenty-odd thousand people, old and young, male and female, citizens of the United States, born on the soil, and foreigners of the Chinese race, moral and immoral, good, bad, and indifferent, and without respect to circumstances or conditions, from a whole section of the city which they have inhabited, and in which they have carried on all kinds of business appropriate to a city, mercantile, manufacturing, and otherwise, for more than forty years. The discrimination against Chinese, and the gross inequality of the operation of this ordinance upon Chinese…are so manifest upon its face, that I am unable to comprehend how this discrimination and inequality of operation, and the consequent violation of the express provisions of the constitution, treaties and statutes of the United States, can fail to be apparent to the mind of every intelligent person, be he lawyer or layman.

In 1900, the bubonic plague enveloped San Francisco, and the Chinese were widely believed to be the source and carriers of the disease. In May, after nine deaths in Chinatown that were attributed to the plague, the city health department and Board of Supervisors adopted a resolution to quarantine the fourteen-block area bounded by Broadway, Kearny, California, and Stockton Streets. The city erected barriers around Chinatown; no one was allowed in or out.

One man who lived within the quarantined area, Jew Ho, challenged the enforcement of the quarantine. Jew, who lived above his grocery store at 926 Stockton Street, claimed in circuit court that his business had been essentially shut down because of the quarantine at a great financial loss. He also alleged that while the quarantine was supposed to apply to all residents within the area, it was only being enforced against the Chinese. Police let non-Chinese residents and business people come and go, while physicians attending Chinese residents were not even allowed to enter. Jew charged that none of the Chinatown deaths were from bubonic plague. He presented a letter from a local physician that stated that the contagious nature of the plague would have caused thousands of deaths in crowded Chinatown had it really been present. Jew sought an injunction to end the quarantine. Circuit court judge William Morrow and district court judge John J. DeHaven agreed in *Jew Ho v. Williamson* that the quarantine was of dubious health safety value and discriminatory.

"If we are to suppose that this bubonic plague has existed in San Francisco since the 6th day of March, and that there has been danger of its spreading over the city, the most dangerous thing that could have been done was to quarantine the whole city, as to the Chinese, as was substantially done in the first instance," wrote Morrow. "The next most dangerous thing to do was to quarantine any considerable portion of the city, and not restrict intercommunication within the quarantined district. The court cannot but see the practical question that is presented to it as to the ineffectiveness of this method of quarantine against such a disease as this."

Morrow determined that the Chinese were once again on the short end of San Francisco regulations. "The evidence here is clear that this is made to operate against the Chinese population only, and the reason given for it is that the Chinese may communicate the disease from one to the other," he wrote. "That explanation, in the judgment of the court, is not sufficient. It is, in effect, a discrimination, and it is the discrimination that has been frequently called to the attention of the federal courts where matters of this character have arisen with respect to Chinese."

The judge declared the quarantine in violation of the Fourteenth Amendment and granted the injunction. Morrow then dipped his toes into the waters of the larger political debate as to whether or not bubonic plague actually occurred in San Francisco at all. The business community and most city and state politicians denied a plague existed. They worried it was bad for business. Morrow noted that the physicians who examined the dead found no signs of plague, but that Board of Heath physicians determined it did exist: "So that in this case the court does not feel at liberty to decide this question, although, as I have said, personally the evidence in this case seems to be sufficient to establish the fact that the bubonic plague has not existed, and does not now exist, in San Francisco." A related case, *Wong Wai v. Williamson*, in which the city sought to force experimental plague inoculations on Chinese residents, was likewise found unconstitutional and based on dubious science.

Judge William Morrow

William W. Morrow was a schoolteacher, miner, and lawyer before becoming the district court's second judge. He took the bench on August 11, 1891, just days after Ogden Hoffman's death and in the waning years of the habeas corpus mill. Republican president Benjamin Harrison gave Morrow a recess appointment, and the Senate confirmed him in 1892. Morrow ushered in a second era for California's federal courts: he replaced Hoffman, who had sat for forty years on the bench, in the same year that Joseph McKenna replaced Lorenzo Sawyer on the circuit court. To get the nomination, Morrow gathered letters of support from six senators and more than one hundred lawyers, politicians, and friends. "I know of no person who would be more likely to forget personalities and decide all cases upon their merits, than Mr. Morrow," wrote attorney James A. Waymire from the New Chronicle Building to President Harrison in early 1891. "He has the courage too, I think, to decide according to what he believes to be right, without fear of personal consequences." Another lawyer, Morris Estee, wrote, "He returned home a few days ago, with his family, after six years faithful service in Congress, and although he once had a splendid practice, his clientage is now scattered, and it will require active and earnest efforts on his part to build up within a reasonable time, a new business."

Only one letter, from attorney Hugh K. McJunkin, opposed the appointment. He wrote: "Mr. Morrow is a very apt politician, but does not possess the slightest qualification for a judge—either natural or acquired. If you wish to 'take care of him' give him any political office you wish, but do not appoint him as a judge."

Morrow was born near Milton, Indiana, in 1843, and moved to California in 1859. He volunteered for the Union Army, fought in the Civil War, and was appointed a special agent of the treasury in 1865 and assigned to California. He passed the bar in 1869 and began private practice in San Francisco. Morrow was a mover and shaker: he helped organize the San Francisco Bar Association in 1872, was active in the state Republican party, and was elected to Congress in 1885, where he served until his judicial appointment.

After five years on the district court, he was appointed in 1897 to the reorganized Court of Appeals for the Ninth Circuit, where he served until his death, in 1929. Morrow was one of the incorporators of the American Red Cross, in 1905, and was president of the California chapter of the Red Cross during San Francisco's 1906 earthquake.

Judge John J. DeHaven

John Jefferson DeHaven replaced William Morrow in 1897 and became the Northern District Court's third judge. He was nominated by President William McKinley in 1897 and served until his death in 1913. DeHaven was born in St. Joseph, Missouri, in 1849, and moved to California at age four. He read law in 1866 and practiced in Eureka on and off until his appointment to the federal bench. He also served as the Humboldt County district attorney and the Eureka city attorney. DeHaven was elected to the California Assembly and the Senate, and became a state superior court judge. He served in Congress in 1889 and 1890 and was then elected to the state supreme court.

From Celebrity Divorce to *In Re Neagle*

Headlines in the 1880s weren't all about the Chinese Question. California's first celebrity divorce trial took place in the old circuit court. The case had everything the tabloid press still reveres today: money, fame, salacious sex, voodoo, an older respectable ex-senator and a younger woman, courtroom drama, and a grand finale.

William Sharon was one of the richest men in San Francisco—and that was saying something in the gilded age of the 1880s. A Comstock Lode millionaire, owner of the Palace and Grand Hotels in San Francisco (some would say he stole the Palace from the estate of his former partner William Ralston, who built it), and former United States senator from Nevada, Sharon was a widower who was known to have had a series of attractive young companions. But there was shock and surprise all around in 1883, when the charming thirty-year-old Sarah Althea Hill claimed to have been secretly married to the sixty-three-year-old Sharon three years earlier. She had him arrested for adultery and was suing for divorce and alimony in state court. The marriage contract included a clause in which Hill promised not to reveal the union for at least two years unless Sharon approved.

Sharon kept a vast suite in the Palace and had set Hill up with rooms at the Grand, stock tips, and spending money. The Grand and Palace Hotels were joined across New Montgomery Street by an elevated covered walkway, which the couple used to visit each other's rooms. The press nicknamed it the Bridge of Sighs, alluding to the romantic trysts it enabled. But their union cooled after a year. Sharon suspected Hill of rifling through his papers. Hill claimed he offered her $500 per month to sign a document saying they were never married, and threw her out of the hotel when she refused. Their messy relationship ended up in the circuit court when Sharon, a Nevada resident, filed a suit enjoining Hill, a California resident, from using the marriage contract, which he claimed was a fraud, as a basis for action against him. Justice Field and Judge Sawyer tried to contain the circus.

Hill was either a scheming woman from the wrong side of the tracks or a compromised girl from a good family, depending on who described her. She had moved to San Francisco from Missouri in 1871 and met Sharon at the Bank of California, which he owned and where she held an account. During the trial, the attractive Hill carefully cultivated her public image as a wronged, albeit unconventional, woman, one willing to fight for her rights (and her money). The salacious details of the case scandalized San Francisco's Victorian community, but few residents could get enough of the story. The press dubbed her the Rose of Sharon.

One of Hill's attorneys was David Terry, the infamous lawyer and former California Supreme Court justice who resigned from the bench in 1859 in order to fight a duel with Senator David Broderick, whom he killed. Terry took the Hill divorce case to superior court in 1884. In closing arguments before Judge Jeremiah F. Sullivan, Terry spoke for four and a half days on behalf of Hill, concluding, "She goes from this courtroom either vindicated as an honest and virtuous wife or branded as an adventuress, a blackmailer, a perjurer, and a harlot." This was six months and one week after the trial began. Testimony filled more than one thousand pages. Judge Sullivan ruled in Hill's favor on Christmas Eve before a packed courtroom: the marriage contract was valid.

Sullivan said that Sharon was "a man of unbounded wealth, possessed of strong animal passions that from excessive indulgence had become unaccustomed to restraint." Wrote Sullivan of the millionaire: "Whatever he had undertaken in his career he had in great measure accomplished. His passion may have been stronger than his judgment. He may have considered as a trifle, as weak as air, the miserable bit of paper with which a weak woman could shelter her virginity and her claim to standing in the community." Sullivan dissolved the marriage and ordered a referee to handle division of community property. The new divorcée celebrated with a shopping spree. Hill bought gifts for herself and her many friends and admirers, telling shop clerks to "Charge it to Mrs. William Sharon." But the California Supreme Court later denied her any alimony until the federal circuit court case was finished.

Hill had little luck in the federal case. In the circuit courtroom of the old Appraiser's Building on Sansome Street, Judge Sawyer denied a motion for dismissal by Hill's lawyer on the grounds that a similar suit was pending appeal in the state courts. Sawyer contended that because each case had a different plaintiff and each was seeking different relief, the lawsuits were not identical. The trial was filled with histrionics and drama: Hill refused to submit the marriage contract and "Dear Wife" letters as evidence for the federal trial, fearing they would be destroyed. She was held for twenty-four hours in the Broadway jail for contempt. While there, she composed a poem to Judge Sawyer, which she happily gave to the newspapers upon her release to a jubilant crowd of five hundred people. Mammy Pleasant, a successful African American madam and businesswoman with numerous political connections in white San Francisco, took Hill under her wing and accompanied her to court daily. Their friendship led to stories that Hill, under Pleasant's tutelage, had used voodoo and racy sex, including a ménage à trois with a younger friend, to try to entice Sharon back to her.

Hill accused the federal judges of bias against her because of their well-known differences with Terry and connections with Sharon. Terry was known to be a hothead who always sported a bowie knife, even in court. At the age of thirty-four, he became chief justice of the state supreme court, which he swore Field onto in 1857. While Terry, Field, and Broderick were all Democrats, the politics of slavery that led to the Civil War created deep divisions within the party in California. Terry and Broderick ended up on opposite sides of the debate, which soon assumed a very personal aspect, and led to Terry's resignation and his calling out Broderick. On September 13, 1859, the two men met amid the sand dunes and cypress trees of Lake Merced on the outskirts of San Francisco. They paced off with pistols drawn and turned to face each other. In a moment, Broderick lay on the ground, mortally wounded. (Visitors to the park today can face off from two stone obelisks.) Broderick was a close friend of Field, who was elevated to chief justice of the California Supreme Court in 1859 and to associate justice of the US Supreme Court in 1863.

Several of Sharon's attorneys had supported Field in his unsuccessful bids for the Democratic presidential nomination in 1880 and 1884. Terry had been one of the most vocal opponents of Field's nomination in

1884. After the vote, Field was said to carry a personal blacklist around in his hat of several hundred California "communists," as he called them. Terry was atop the list.

Just as the slavery issue had divided California's legal community in the 1860s, the expansion and power of the railroads divided it again in the 1880s. Those who supported the railroads included Field, Sawyer, and Sharon. Those who thought that manufacturing and agriculture could only grow if the railroads were subject to tighter controls included Terry.

Now Terry was to face Field in federal court to defend the honor of Sarah Hill, who was now also his wife: they married after Sharon's sudden death in November 1885 of an apparent heart attack. Just days earlier, Sharon had sworn in a newspaper interview that he would never give up the case and would fight Hill to the bitter end. His estate was estimated at $10 million, of which he left $50,000 to the city for the building of

FIG. 3-9
Sarah Althea Hill Sharon was the source of a celebrated divorce case in the 1870s. Hothead state judge David S. Terry became her lawyer and later married her. Sharon appeared before Justice Stephen J. Field in a legal dispute arising from her first marriage. Terry later attacked Justice Field and was killed by a US marshal. Courtesy of The Bancroft Library, University of California, Berkeley.

Golden Gate Park. Sharon's son, Frederick, executor of his father's estate, continued the lawsuit.

Mr. and Mrs. Terry were a tabloid match made in heaven. One day in court, Mrs. Terry threatened to shoot one of Sharon's lawyers, William Stewart, for insinuating that she was a tart. "With a glance at Stewart [she] said, 'I can hit a four-bit piece nine times out of ten.' She then was quiet for a while until she suddenly pulled a small gun out of her reticule, aimed nonchalantly at Oliver P. Evans, another of Sharon's attorneys, and then dropped it to her lap. Sarah handed over the pistol to the examiner Houghton, who reported it to the court," according to Robert Kroninger in his 1964 book, *Sarah and the Senator.*

In 1888, Field ruled for Sharon and declared the marriage contract a forgery. It was to be given to the court and destroyed. Hill was nothing more than a mistress to Sharon. As Kroniger recounted, not halfway through reading his opinion, Mrs. Terry stood up and interrupted Justice Field to challenge him:

"Are you going to take it upon yourself to order me to give up that contract?" she yelled.

After an indignant pause, Field replied, "Sit down, Madam."

Hill started to sit, but continued talking back to the bench.

"Marshal, put that woman out!" the justice ordered.

Hill yelled back: "Judge Field, how much have you been paid for that decision? I know it was bought!"

"Marshal, put that woman out," Field repeated.

Court spectators stood up to get a better look.

"Don't put a finger on my wife," said Terry, still seated at counsel's bench. He said he would walk her out himself.

The marshal hesitated, then tried to push past Terry, who punched him in the face, knocking out several teeth. Bystanders jumped on Terry, who was reaching inside his coat, presumably for his knife, and pinned him down. Mrs. Terry was relieved of her purse, which held a small six-shot revolver loaded with five bullets, and led her away to the marshal's anteroom.

Terry, now restrained, said quietly, "I only want to accompany my wife."

Justice Field had remained stone-faced throughout the melee. After a brief sip of water, he finished reading his opinion.

When Terry tried to enter the marshal's room and found it barred by a deputy, he drew his knife and fighting resumed. A bystander named

David Neagle wrestled the knife from Terry's hand. Both Terrys were placed under arrest for contempt of court. That afternoon, Field reconvened court—without Mr. and Mrs. Terry—to decide on their punishment. They later found out their sentences from reporters: Mrs. Terry would spend thirty days in the Alameda County Jail; Terry would get six months. "I'll go with you," he said to Sarah, softly stroking her cheek.

The next day, the two held hands on the ferry going across the bay, where they would serve their sentences. They were allowed to share a cell and received gifts and numerous visits from supporters. After Sarah completed her thirty days, she stayed at a nearby hotel and visited Terry each day. Terry's friends suggested that he petition Field to remand part of his sentence. Terry wrote a letter of apology, but Field refused to shave even an hour off of the sentence. Because Terry was a federal prisoner, he was eligible to receive time off for good behavior, up to five days per month, but Judge Sawyer ruled Terry was ineligible because he was serving time in a state prison for a federal offense. Terry spent his time in jail reading, writing, and brooding over the injustices he felt Field had delivered him. Both Terrys made frequent threats against Sawyer and Field, which made it into the newspapers and back to Washington. Field remarked that Terry was "under great excitement and unless he cools down before his term of imprisonment is finished, he may attempt to wreak bodily vengeance upon the judges and officers of the court."

After Terry's release from prison, the couple retired to their country home near Fresno, but made regular trips north to San Francisco. On one trip, Sarah encountered Judge Sawyer on the train. She pulled his hair and threatened to shoot him. When Field returned to California for his circuit court duties in 1889, it was with a bodyguard—the US attorney general had authorized protection for Field, an unprecedented action. David Neagle, the bystander who had grabbed Terry's knife, accompanied Field as a deputy marshal. On August 13, after sitting in court in Los Angeles, Field and Neagle boarded the overnight train for San Francisco. Early the next morning, Neagle saw the Terrys get on the train at the Fresno stop. They were scheduled to appear in court in San Francisco the next day on pending criminal charges related to the courtroom melee.

Neagle alerted the conductor and asked that they wire the next station, where the train would stop for breakfast, to have a constable ready in case of trouble. The train stopped at Lathrop, in San Joaquin County, where passengers disembarked to the station dining room. Field and Neagle sat at a table in the middle of the room, facing the door. A few minutes later

Mr. and Mrs. Terry entered the room. As soon as she saw Field, Sarah wheeled around suddenly and left the room. Terry walked past and took a seat at a nearby table. Field began eating his breakfast.

"In a moment or two afterwards I looked round, and saw Judge Terry rise from this seat," Field later testified. "I supposed at the time he was going out to meet his wife, as she had not returned; so I went on with my breakfast. It seems, however, that he came round back of me—I did not see him—and he struck me a violent blow in the face, followed instantaneously by another blow....I heard 'Stop! Stop!' cried by Neagle. Of course, I was for the moment dazed by the blows. I turned my head round, and I saw that great form of Terry's, with his arm raised, and his fists clinched to strike me. I felt that a terrific blow was coming, and his arm was descending in a curved way as though to strike the side of my temple, when I heard Neagle cry out, 'Stop! Stop! I am an officer!' Instantly two shots followed."

Neagle claimed that Terry was reaching for his knife when he fired, killing him.

Meanwhile, Sarah had found her purse with her pistol and was returning to the dining room when news of her husband's death reached her. Distraught, she called Field and Neagle murderers and threatened to kill them herself. She was disarmed but quickly swore out complaints against both Neagle and Field for murder. Both were arrested in the station by the local constable. Field was released on his own recognizance and continued to San Francisco alone, without a bodyguard. Neagle was held in the Stockton county jail. The murder charges against Field were quickly dropped by the San Joaquin district attorney after prompting from the governor and state attorney general.

Neagle petitioned the circuit court for a writ of habeas corpus on the grounds that he was a federal officer arrested in the performance of his duty. At issue was whether a deputy marshal could exercise powers that normally were reserved to state law officers and whether he was guilty of murder or justifiable homicide. Judge Sawyer granted the writ. The Supreme Court affirmed the decision. *In Re Neagle* set the precedent that even though there was no explicit law giving the attorney general the power to assign bodyguards to judges, the action assured that the nation's laws would be carried out. Under these circumstances, the US marshal had the same authority as state sheriffs and deputies to protect a judge's life. Neagle was cleared of charges. Sarah was prostrate with grief and never remarried. She reportedly went insane by age forty and was committed to the Stockton State Hospital, where she lived until her death in the 1930s.

The Mint Robber

Walter Dimmick was a trusted employee of the US Mint in San Francisco. In 1901, his supervisor, Frank A. Leach, questioned him about the balance of one of their accounts. Dimmick told his boss that the next day he would reconcile the account right to the dollar. But the next morning Dimmick pleaded, "Mr. Leach, for the first time in my life I have told a lie. I could not sleep all night. Don't ask me for that money, for if you do, it will make me an embezzler." Dimmick explained that during recent hard times he had borrowed some of the mint's money, but he had always replaced it by the end of the quarter, when the accounts were to be balanced. "I told him that whatever his purpose in using that money, he had committed a criminal act and nothing of the kind justified him...when he commenced crying and said he supposed he would have to go to San Quentin for this," Leach testified at Dimmick's trial. Leach said he gave Dimmick a number of days to bring back the missing $1,338, but told him he could no longer work there. Dimmick did return the money but was convicted by Judge DeHaven for "knowingly, willingly, and feloniously failing to deposit certain money belonging to the United States." Dimmick had also been charged with stealing gold from the mint, but the gold was never found and he was not convicted of those charges. Dimmick was sentenced to two years in San Quentin Prison. The decision was upheld by the court of appeals.

"Many years ago I waited on a man who came to the counter in the clerk's office," wrote Carl Calbreath, the former clerk of court. "He asked to see the case of *United States v. Dimmick* and I casually said, 'Oh, yes, that is the man who robbed the mint.' With a rather stern face, the man corrected me: 'He was *charged* with robbing the mint.' I immediately knew that I was talking to Mr. Dimmick. It seemed he was applying for a restoration of civil rights, commonly called a Pardon. I thereupon secured the file and gave him the necessary information he needed in filling out his application. Some six months later he again came to the counter and showed me the 'restoration to civil rights' and asked if I would make a note on the docket page of his case that a 'Pardon' had been granted to him. This I readily did."

An Early Victory for the Environment

Amidst the habeas corpus mill of the early 1880s came a court case that brought to a head the state's twenty-year struggle between gold and grain, the interests of the mining industry versus the potential of agriculture. California was becoming the breadbasket for the world, and its fertile Central Valley, aided by new water delivery systems, was the epicenter of unsurpassed agricultural productivity. Water revealed gold to the early miners, and after easy placer mines grew thin during the mid-1850s, water was used to find more gold. Hydraulic miners employed water from high-pressure hoses to blast away hills and mountains in their quest for fortune. The process sent dirt and gravel down sluices, where the heavier gold would drop out. But tailings—mining debris such as mud, sand, and gravel—would continue down rivers or streams, ultimately fouling them and nearby fields.

Hydraulic mining continued twenty-four hours a day, seven days a week, because the high-pressure hoses could not be easily turned off. By 1870, more than forty thousand men had joined the hydraulic mining industry in the Sierra Nevada, which sped the sedimentation of area waterways. A single hose—more like a cannon—shot more than one million gallons of water each hour. Whole mountains were washed away, the sand and gravel pushed downstream, where it would settle and ultimately fill riverbeds. Within a couple of years, few boats could navigate nearby rivers. Floods in the rainy season meant that water and mining debris overflowed onto nearby farmland, ruining fields and choking fruit trees. Massive flooding in the Central Valley caused farmers and townspeople to build huge levees to protect themselves. Marysville, a gold rush freshwater port on the Yuba River that received steamboats bringing supplies from the East Coast and shipped out grain grown in the valley, built its first levee in 1868, and made it higher each year. In 1875, its levees broke and Marysville was flooded by four feet of water and thick mud.

The effects of hydraulic mining followed the water downstream, from the mighty Sacramento River to San Francisco Bay. By the early 1880s, agriculture was becoming more important to the state economy than mining, but farmers did not have as much political clout as miners. Edward Woodruff filed suit in the circuit court in 1882 against the North Bloomfield Gravel Mining Company to stop the company's hydraulic mining and release of debris down the Yuba River. Woodruff claimed that the sedimentation caused by hydraulic mining had damaged his livelihood by preventing navigation on the Yuba River and causing flooding on his adjacent farmland. The complaint alleged that debris from hydraulic mines "largely and materially fouls and adulterates the waters of the Yuba and Feather Rivers." Woodruff asked for an injunction to stop North Bloomfield and other mines from discharging debris into the rivers. Lawyers for North Bloomfield maintained that it was impossible to tell if the sedimentation had come from their operations. The company argued that it had made an effort to curtail its discharges into the South Yuba River by building a levee to hold them back.

Sawyer, a former miner and frontiersman, heard the complaint. During two years of litigation, more than two hundred people testified. When he finally issued his opinion in 1884, the whole state was watching. Sawyer recognized that "hydraulickin'" still supported the economy of many a Sierra town and declined to outlaw it. But he described the technique as a "public and private nuisance, destructive, continuous, increasing, and threatening to continue, increase, and be still more destructive." Sawyer issued an injunction to stop discharging debris into the rivers, but left an escape clause in case the state's economy once again needed mining income. The ruling effectively killed the practice of hydraulic mining in California, although some hydraulic mines were allowed to operate for decades longer provided they had safety nets to catch debris.

The Disaster of the SS *Rio de Janeiro*

On the morning of Friday, February 22, 1901, the SS *Rio de Janeiro* was heading into San Francisco Bay in a heavy fog when it struck the rocks off Fort Point. It sank with 220 people aboard, 138 of whom died. It was San Francisco's worst maritime disaster. District court judge John J. DeHaven would decide whether the steamship's owner, the Pacific Mail Steamship Company, could seek protection in admiralty court from lawsuits arising from the tragedy.

The steamship left Hong Kong and stopped in Shanghai, China, and the Japanese cities of Nagasaki, Kobe, and Yokohama before reaching Honolulu. As the *Rio* approached the Northern California coast, it encountered heavy fog and rain. Though the ship's captain couldn't see a thing, depth soundings and positioning indicated that they were just outside the Golden Gate. Captain William Ward gave the order to drop anchor until a harbor pilot showed up to lead the ship through the narrow straits. At thirty-eight, Ward had been master of the *Rio* since 1896 and knew the iron-hulled, 368-foot ship inside and out, her strengths and her weaknesses. But just as the passengers were impatient to reach home port, so was Ward. His fiancée, Lena Jackson, awaited him in San Francisco.

At this time, ships still navigated by sight, sound, and soundings. If visibility was poor, foghorns, bells, whistles and lights (each with a signature sound or flash), and buoys were used to gauge approximate location. Soundings to check depth were made by throwing a weighted line overboard until it hit bottom. The Golden Gate, the narrow, mile-wide entrance to San Francisco Bay, has swift currents. Combined with thick fog, it made for a risky passage.

The bar pilot, Captain Frederick W. Jordan, had been guiding ships in and out of the bay for twelve years and sailing ships there for twenty-five years. He had never had an accident. Jordan testified that he boarded the *Rio* about four o'clock on the afternoon of February 21. Jordan and Ward were friends and had worked together before, navigating the Golden Gate. The weather was still uncooperative: the fog had not lifted and a heavy swell and high wind remained. Jordan had brought many ships through the Gate in this kind of weather; in fact, some of them had been Ward's. He suggested they lift anchor and move ahead. But Ward didn't like the thick fog and said they should wait. Jordan was surprised at Ward's caution, but acquiesced.

They repositioned the *Rio* slightly closer to land and anchored again about four miles offshore from the Cliff House at Point Lobos at about six o'clock that evening. Some of the passengers held a second-to-last-night-at-sea party; others finished packing; the ship's officers organized their paperwork. Jordan continued to needle Ward that they could slip under the fog and into the Gate without a problem. Ward finally relented and told Jordan that he would give it a try in the morning if visibility improved. Jordan gave him a pat on the back and notified the main deck watchman, James Russell, to wake him when the fog lifted enough so that the lighthouse at Point Bonita was visible. While socializing with the passengers after dinner that night, several of them asked the captain why they couldn't head into San Francisco that night. Ward politely told them all that the fog was too thick and not worth risking the ship.

At four o'clock on the morning of February 22, the fog had lifted enough to see the Point Bonita light, so Russell woke the captain and Jordan. Drinking their coffee on the bridge, they could also clearly see the light at Fort Point and the twinkling city lights of the Richmond

District of San Francisco. "Let her go," Ward declared. As pilot, Jordan took command of the *Rio*, and at 4:30 a.m. they started ahead against an unusually strong current of about six knots. The ebb tide was shooting out of San Francisco Bay, swollen by recent winter rains. Shortly afterward, they slowed and stopped. "Daybreak came and I could see the fog up the bay and I stopped for a few minutes and then hove up again and started," Jordan later testified. Within fifteen minutes, the fog from the bay spilled out of the Gate and enveloped the ship. The water there was deep and difficult to anchor in, and the pilot felt it would have been more dangerous to anchor than move ahead. They were on a northeast course. "Easy as she goes," Jordan told the helm.

"I saw the light just as she struck, the Fort Point light," Jordan said. It was 5:19 a.m. He said he had been able to hear the Lime Point (the Marin County anchorage of the future Golden Gate Bridge) whistle the whole time, but never heard the Fort Point bell until just before they struck. The *Rio* came to a bone-crunching stop. The sound of grinding metal and breaking wood convulsed the ship. The ship had hit rocks off Fort Point, just to the right of the entrance to the Golden Gate.

Captain Ward immediately issued orders for damage reports and readied lifeboats. Already there was twelve feet of water in the forward part of the ship and more than twenty feet amidships. The bottom of the ship had been ripped open on the rocks. "Everyone to his station," Ward ordered calmly. "Lower the boats and save the passengers." Two sharp blasts were blown on the ship's whistle, and then it was tied down to blow continuously.

Except the officers, who were white, the majority of the *Rio*'s crew was Chinese, few of whom spoke English. Only one of the white officers could speak any Chinese. There were also fifty-three Asian passengers in steerage, where the water first flooded the passenger cabins. Panic ensued when the lights went out as passengers scrambled to reach the main deck and the lifeboats. Ward admonished the passengers and crew to stay calm and to make way for women and children in the lifeboats. One passenger, Kate West, testified that Ward helped her find her way to a lifeboat. Then she watched him enter his stateroom and close the door. The captain went down with his ship.

In the confusion, only three of the eleven lifeboats were launched. Passengers, some with life vests and many without, jumped into the fifty-degree water to save themselves. At least one lifeboat filled with water and sank; another was destroyed when struck by the mast of the ship as it went down. The remaining boat and life rafts circled around in the early dawn darkness to pick people out of the water. Others floated with life preservers or clung to debris and waited. Cries and moans filled the air. A passing Italian fishing boat spotted the wreckage, rescued four people, and was the first to report the ship's sinking about an hour later. Bodies and survivors began washing up on Baker Beach in San Francisco. Some survivors suffered broken arms and legs; others suffered from hypothermia and shock. Many had been in the water for more than an hour.

When the ship went down, Jordan was thrown into the water. "I was floating on a mail sack at first and a small piece of board…until I was assisted up on a larger piece of wreckage by a Chinese." An Italian fisherman later picked him up. As word of the disaster spread, dozens of ships went out to search for survivors.

Most of the white passengers landed at Meiggs' Wharf at the foot of Powell Street. They were interviewed and put up in hotels by the Pacific Mail Steamship Company if they weren't city residents. The Asian passengers and crew were held in the immigration building.

By eight o'clock, the fog had lifted, the sun was shining, and nothing but floating debris and the occasional oil slick gave any indication of the horror that had taken place just a few hours earlier. By midday, the bodies of three white men, three white women, one Japanese man, and six Chinese men were recovered and brought to the morgue for identification. The whole south shore of San Francisco was put under guard, and customs officers watched for cargo that might float ashore. But besides the carcasses of a crewman's dog and a number of pigs from the ship's stores that washed up near Fort Point, no more bodies were found until early March, when the body of a Chinese sailor washed up on a beach near San Rafael. In the end, only 82 of a total of 220 passengers and crew would live to tell the tale of the *Rio*.

Then came the issue of salvage. The Pacific Mail Steamship Company retained its rights to the vessel, but was unable to locate it. Rumors that the ship had also carried gold and silver prompted several private salvage divers to try to locate the wreck. All were unsuccessful. Meanwhile, surviving passengers began to file lawsuits against the company. Mrs. Sarah Guyon, the widow of passenger Henry Guyon, sued for $25,000 in damages for the death of her husband. Others filed for the value of lost luggage and for the deaths of relatives. There were a total of eighteen claims against the company, totaling $224,352.

The Pacific Mail Steamship Company filed for limitation of liability protection in the district court's admiralty court. Limitation of liability is a doctrine of admiralty law whereby a ship owner can restrict liability from a shipwreck to the value of the vessel plus any freight and passage due as long as the owner is not found to be personally negligent. It is a kind of reverse lawsuit, where if a company knows it will be sued for loss of life and damages, it can ask the protection of the admiralty court to limit its financial liability.

The families affected by the *Rio* tragedy vigorously protested this. Admiralty attorney William Denman—who would be appointed to the Ninth Circuit Court of Appeals in 1935 by Franklin Roosevelt and serve as chief judge from 1948 to 1957—represented many of the plaintiffs and told Judge DeHaven that the crew, most of whom were Chinese and spoke no English, had not been properly trained in lowering lifeboats and could not understand the commands of their English-speaking officers in an emergency situation. He argued that the Pacific Mail Company was negligent in not providing enough translators among the crew to make sure that the Chinese sailors could follow orders. "This deficiency…was the cause of the loss of life in the families of the relatives we represent and that the company should not limit its liability," Denman told the court. Denman offered the depositions of surviving Chinese crew members, most of whom had gone back to China, including Pung Wah, a second boatswain. Through an interpreter, Pung had said that none of the deck department spoke English and that they had never done a boat drill, only fire drills.

In 1903, Judge DeHaven granted the petition of limited liability to the Pacific Mail. His decision was reversed a year later in the Court of Appeals on the grounds that the company had not provided an adequate number of translators for the Chinese crew. In 1904, Judge DeHaven ordered the Pacific Mail Company to pay damages: Sarah Guyon received $7,000; the heirs of William Henshall, $6,000; Maria Gussoni, $5,000; the brother of Mrs. Leticia Wildman received $1,200 for her death and $1,000 for her lost luggage; and surviving passenger Kate West received $750 for lost baggage and "loss of time due to injury."

Rumors persisted through the decades that the *Rio* was carrying $2 million worth of silver and gold. Fueled by the mystery of the *Rio's* final resting place, treasure-hunting schemes came and went, but definite remains of the wreck have never been found. In 1947, an oceanographer named William Gibson, taking soundings near the Marin headlands, noted an unusual pattern in the readings indicating that a large object was resting on the bottom. Gibson suspected it to be the wreck of the *Rio* but was unable to finance a dive. In 1985, Gibson's son took up the task. Using more sophisticated technology, he was able to locate a wreck similar in size to the *Rio*. It is resting upright in three hundred feet of water near the Marin side of the Golden Gate Bridge. This would indicate that the *Rio* likely struck the reef off Fort Point and was then carried by the current across the channel until she hit bottom. Her cargo manifest showed she carried rice, sugar, raw silk, hemp, opium, and tin ingots. It is true that in Honolulu, $75,000 in gold had been placed on the ship for transport to San Francisco, but no silver.

CHAPTER 4

THE NEW COURTHOUSE

WILLIAM MORROW'S DREAM of a grand palace of justice was realized in 1905 with the dedication of the new United States Post Office and Courthouse. Morrow, who had first promised to secure money for a new federal building when he ran for Congress in 1884, was the ideal speaker on the day the Beaux Arts beauty officially opened at the northeast corner of Seventh and Mission Streets on August 29. For it was Morrow who obtained more than $1 million to purchase the site and $2.5 million for construction. And it was Morrow who would occupy the building along with the other appeals court judges and district court judge John DeHaven.

San Francisco had actually needed a new federal building since the 1868 earthquake substantially damaged the Post Office and Custom House and the Merchants Exchange. The early buildings on Battery Street needed to be torn down and replaced, but not enough money was available, so cracked walls were bolted with iron reinforcing rods and braced. In 1887, the government finally found enough money to purchase a site for a new federal building. It was a curious location, a full mile from San Francisco's prospering downtown district on a sandy parcel of land in a downtrodden immigrant district south of Market Street.

Construction of the three-story building began in 1897. The $2.5 million appropriation was enough to bathe the courtrooms in Italian marble, mahogany, redwood, and oak, and fill the corridors with bronze doors, Venetian glass, porcelain, and ceramic tile. The building, one of the most ornate west of the Mississippi River, was constructed in the manner of the Italian Renaissance, but also showed hints of the US Capitol

FIG. 4-1 (PREVIOUS PAGE)
The new Post Office and Courthouse, designed by James Knox Taylor and built on the corner of Seventh and Mission Streets, was dedicated in 1905 and survived the 1906 earthquake and fire. Courtesy of the San Francisco History Center, San Francisco Public Library.

FIG. 4-2
Fire engulfs the Call Building on Third and Market Streets after the 1906 earthquake. The court heard numerous cases involving compensation for property damaged by the fire. Courtesy of the California Historical Society Collections at the University of Southern California.

in Washington, DC. It was designed by James Knox Taylor, supervising architect of the Treasury Department, who said, "The experience of centuries has demonstrated that no form of architecture is so pleasing to the great mass of mankind as the classic." This was Taylor's masterpiece, a huge structure that harkened back to Europe but proclaimed the federal government's power. With thick granite walls and Ionic columns topped by American eagles, this was the people's palace: a grand post office on the first floor, fancy chambers for judges on the second floor, and sumptuous courtrooms on the third. The building certainly demonstrated that Washington, DC, was committed to the land by the Golden Gate and could perform cross-country miracles.

Speaking at the dedication, Morrow talked about the building's setting and the history that had led to this moment:

> I am informed that it is the most perfect building for post office purposes ever constructed. The part assigned to the United States Courts has been finished in a manner so artistic and substantial as to be beyond my powers of description. It is sufficient to say that it is as substantial as the Congressional Library at Washington, and second only to that marvelous building in elegance and artistic finish.
>
> The growth of a great city, like the growth of a great individual, is usually in the beginning a struggle with adverse conditions. Indeed, it seems to be a law of nature that real substantial strength and power comes from efforts employed in overcoming great difficulty....In early days, [San Francisco] had to contend with many difficulties. It had some advantages, it is true, but it had also many disadvantages. It was a long distance from anywhere. It took a long time to get here. It was on the edge of the continent, with its principal trade and commerce projected inland and eastward, and not to all points of the compass, as is usually the case with great trade centers.
>
> In the early days, we were not in very close touch with the general government, and we grew up with our manners, customs, currency, and business system. We were a law unto ourselves. But we grew, and poured the wealth of our resources into all the channels of trade and commerce, bettering the conditions, and adding to the comforts of mankind in all parts of the globe.
>
> And now San Francisco has grown to such dimensions that she cannot be ignored. As a community we are beginning to attract attention, and our Uncle Samuel is taking notice of us. In this magnificent building he has made a splendid investment in our midst for himself and in his own name, but for our benefit, and for the benefit of those who shall come after us, and we have assembled here today to look it over and see how we like it, and make suitable acknowledgment for his generosity and good taste.

Less than eight months later, the city that surrounded the people's palace lay in ruins. The Great Earthquake struck on April 18, 1906, and between the quake and the fires that consumed much of the city for three days, thousands of Northern Californians died, most of them in San Francisco, and an estimated twenty-eight thousand buildings were destroyed. Only a few dozen major buildings were salvageable, but the new Post Office and Courthouse was one of them. In the upstairs chambers and courtrooms, "the only thing which the earthquake had disturbed was an office safe, which was on four wheels and had rolled across the office, but no real damage was done to the office," wrote Carl William Calbreath, who served as district court clerk from 1943 to 1960. At the time of the earthquake, Calbreath was a sixteen-year-old petit clerk who had managed to make his way around the military guard that was thrown up to protect the building.

Fires, however, did scar the building. One blaze from a nearby building caught the drapes in Judge DeHaven's beautiful second-floor redwood-paneled library, but workers stamped out the fire before it took hold. "The Post Office may collapse at any time," custodians wired Washington the next day. The building took on the appearance of a schooner adrift on a wind-tossed sea as the streets around it buckled and broke. Mission Street dropped more than three feet, and Seventh Street sank too. The first-floor post office suffered the most damage. Eyewitnesses reported that first-floor ceilings and arches dropped, marble split, and walls crumbled. Mosaics fell to the floor and furniture was destroyed. The structure survived, but barely, and it almost crumbled five days later during the demolition of the nearby Odd Fellows Building. Explosives used to blast away the foundation of the Odd Fellows knocked out every pane of glass of the courthouse, blasted off part of the marble cornice, and dropped more mosaics. It took almost four years to repair the building.

But decisions made there—by the district and circuit courts—helped San Francisco rebuild. William Cary Van Fleet, who in 1907 became the district court's fourth judge, consistently ruled for San Francisco property owners whose insurance claims were initially denied. Proprietors of most of the insurance companies argued that clauses in their policies exempted them from earthquake damage. But property owners countered, arguing that most of the damage was caused by the sixty or so fires that started after the quake. These complicated cases came before Van Fleet, who, along with juries, decided exactly how the fires around the city started following the sixty-second quake. Was the property damaged by fires that were a direct result of the earthquake? Or was the property damaged by fires that started independently? Because of the extensive destruction, little evidence was left and answers were hard to find. But Van Fleet usually sided with the property owners, starting with a key case filed by Leon Willard and Company against the Williamsburgh City Fire Insurance Company. He made it clear to the jury that the insurance company must prove that the destruction of the building was directly caused by the earthquake: "In reaching your conclusion in this case as to the cause of the fire which destroyed plaintiff's property, you will bear in mind that the law does not require demonstration—that is, such a degree of proof as, excluding possibility of error, produces absolute certainty—because such proof is rarely possible. Moral certainty only is required, or that degree of proof which produces conviction in an unprejudiced mind." In other words, the burden of proof was on the insurance company.

One of the first insurance trials started just five months after the earthquake. Levi Strauss Realty Company filed a lawsuit in circuit court against the Transatlantic Fire Insurance Company of Hamburg, Germany, demanding that the insurer pay $10,000 for the company's fire-ravaged brick building on Battery Street between Bush and Pine Streets. To pinpoint the cause of the fire, Levi Strauss attorneys went to great lengths to set the scene of San Francisco's most fateful day.

The plaintiffs called San Francisco Mayor Eugene Schmitz, who said he was awake when the earthquake struck at 5:14 a.m. "Naturally, there was a commotion that would exist under these conditions," Schmitz told the court. "There is commotion always when we have a fire of any kind. This was a very extraordinary fire compared with anything I have ever known before. It was a remarkable earthquake." Schmitz, who issued an order that day declaring that looters be shot on sight, was defensive on the stand, trying to appear that he was in charge during the unfolding disaster. "The only looting that came to my knowledge was three boys had looted a store, had stolen something," he testified. "I issued a proclamation with reference to the matter of looting; the proclamation was issued with a view of anticipating the possibility of looting under the condition that existed at that time, and also issued to prevent a possibility of any breaches of the law."

M. H. de Young, proprietor and editor of the *San Francisco Chronicle*, testified that San Francisco was eerily quiet on the day of the earthquake:

"Coming down in my automobile and going backwards and forwards during the day all over town, I had an opportunity to see the center of the town pretty thoroughly," he told the court. "There was very little damage except to certain buildings where the firewalls went down. In some few instances chimneys were down. The larger commercial houses were not injured at all. My own building was not injured."

De Young painted a surprising picture of a passive San Francisco just after the quake. He said he saw firemen putting out blazes on the waterfront, and soldiers arriving to help keep order. "Otherwise there was nothing going on," he said. "Everything was perfectly quiet, even more quiet than on an ordinary day. No excitement among the people during those two days. I never saw anything so quiet." De Young said people were calm. "I had occasion to go through Market Street from Kearney to Sixth or Seventh, on April 18 or 19. No excitement. People were standing looking at the fire. No crowds. Was surprised at that. Everyone was around their own home I suppose. No crowds around DuPont or Stockton streets, very few gathered there. They seemed to be distributed."

Edward Whitson, a district court judge from the Eastern District of Washington who presided over the Levi Strauss case, thought the evidence was clear. Testimony indicated that the fires were not the direct result of the quake. At the end of the testimony, Whitson said, "Gentlemen of the jury, there can be but one verdict in this case. If you should return a verdict for the defendant, the court would be compelled to immediately set it aside. On the undisputed facts and omissions here the plaintiff is entitled to a verdict for the full amount of its claim."

By early 1909, federal judges had assessed judgments of more than $500,000 against insurance executives who balked at the claims. By then, 104 earthquake damage cases had been filed in circuit court against insurance companies. Eighty-eight of them were quickly decided in favor of property owners; the others went to trial.

About 90 percent of the properties in San Francisco were covered by fire insurance, including most of the demolished buildings. Some 130 fire insurance companies, including fifty foreign companies, wrote policies in the city at the time, according to a study issued a century later by the Swiss Re reinsurance company. Almost all of the policies excluded earthquake damage, but only a few specifically excluded damage by fire resulting from earthquakes. In the end, forty-three companies paid a total of about $235 million in claims, according to the study.

Two years after the quake, casualty actuary Albert W. Whitney reported that 80 percent of the fire liability limits had been paid by insurance companies. "Taken all in all, the insurers have done remarkably well," he wrote. "An immense sum of money has been paid into this city, a far larger sum than insurance companies have had to pay at any one time before." Unsurprisingly, first-class companies paid the fastest. "The second class, on the other hand, was less homogeneous," he wrote. "It included some companies that were so 'hard hit' as to be unable, at that time at least, to contemplate payment in full."

Interestingly, Judge Van Fleet, part of Northern California's moneyed elite, sided with property owners in their legal fight against insurance companies. In 1887, he married Lizzie Crocker, a member of the prominent Crocker family that had helped build the Central Pacific Railroad. His connection to California's aristocracy ran counter to the emerging populist movement then developing throughout the state. But Van Fleet came from humble origins. Born in Maumee City, Ohio, in 1852, he moved to Sacramento at age seventeen. He read law and was admitted to the bar four years later. He first practiced in Elko, Nevada, but soon returned to Sacramento and then took a series of two-year jobs: serving as Sacramento County assistant district attorney from 1878 to 1879, Republican member of the California House of Representatives from 1881 to 1882, and director of the California State Prisons from 1883 to 1884, when he won election as a California Superior Court judge.

"Judge Van Fleet has the reputation of being a good lawyer, sound in practice, active and diligent in his attention to the interests of clients, and deeply read in all branches of the law," William J. Davis wrote in the 1890 *An Illustrated History of Sacramento County, California*. "As a judge he is fair and impartial, firm and fearless in his determinations, bringing to bear upon all points an accurate knowledge of the minute technicalities, as well as the broader principles of the science of law."

Van Fleet was popular, regarded even then as a judge destined for higher office. He was "fitted by birth and personal characteristics to fill any position to which he may be called," wrote Davis. In 1891, Van Fleet was encouraged by friends to seek the position of district court judge to replace Ogden Hoffman, but he lost to William Morrow. Van Fleet was restless; he served on the superior court until 1892 and then resigned to practice law in San Francisco. Two years later, he was appointed to the California Supreme Court by Governor Henry H. Markham. Van Fleet's appointment was lauded by the *San Francisco Chronicle,* which wrote that the young lawyer had become renowned for his excellent judgment. But Van Fleet's first years on the court were marked with controversy concerning his judgment. The *San Francisco Examiner* excoriated the judge when he set aside a jury decision to award $6,000 to a family whose son was struck and killed by a train in Oakland. "The decision was an impudent encroachment on the rights of a jury to assess damages, and all the special pleading of lawyers from now until the crack of doom will not make it otherwise," the paper editorialized. "Justice Van Fleet is a member of the Southern Pacific family. It is not surprising, therefore, that his sympathies should lie with the corporation." (The Central Pacific had been leased by the Southern Pacific since 1885.)

Van Fleet sought election to the California Supreme Court in 1895 on the Republican ticket but was defeated. Instead of running for political office, he became an insider, taking the helm of the state Republican Party, which endorsed Theodore Roosevelt in his 1904 campaign for president. Three years later, Roosevelt returned the favor by nominating Van Fleet to fill the recently created second seat on the district court. The *San Francisco Call* described how Van Fleet won the nomination with the help of railroad magnate E. H. Harridan and William Herrin, head of the Southern Pacific's powerful political bureau. Van Fleet received a recess appointment from Roosevelt. The addition of a second judge changed the nature of the Northern District. No longer was it a single-judge court. No longer was one man the law in Northern California. Van Fleet's induction was marked by "extreme simplicity," according to the *Bulletin.* Judge DeHaven led Van Fleet into chambers "comfortably filled" with lawyers and government officials. DeHaven unrolled an engraved parchment and administered the oath. "The whole ceremony hardly consumed five minutes, but at its conclusion the United States had a new judge and Van Fleet, who had entered the court an ordinary citizen, had been endowed with tremendous powers," wrote the *Bulletin.*

Perhaps because he was part of the Crocker family, Van Fleet garnered criticism quickly when his opinions ran counter to the populist sentiment of the age. A few months after his induction, he was berated for siding with the San Francisco Gas and Electric Company when it sought concessions to keep from falling into bankruptcy. "The decision of Judge Van Fleet in the gas rate case does not impress the impartial mind as an example of judicial wisdom," wrote the *Call.* "In order to reach his conclusion it was necessary for the court to ignore and discredit the whole body of testimony offered on behalf of the rate payers and the city."

And in 1916, Van Fleet was accused of bias in the reorganization of the Western Pacific Railroad. When the Equitable Trust Company sought to foreclose on the railroad's mortgage, the judge was placed in charge of determining the minimum price a seller would entertain as a bid for the railroad. Equitable Trust attorneys questioned whether Van Fleet could determine a fair figure because of his family connection to the Southern Pacific. But Van Fleet doggedly refused the suggestion that he recuse himself.

"This court will not permit itself in this case of the Western Pacific to be driven from what it conceives to be its duty by such an attack," Van Fleet declared from the bench. "Were it to do so without any response it would certainly be subject to the characterization of being cowardly. I don't think anybody ever has accused me of being a coward in the performance of my duty."

Later that year, Van Fleet began a bizarre trial: he put *himself* on trial to prove that he could hear the case in a fair manner. "Van Fleet Begins Quiz of Own Mind," the *Examiner* headlined its front-page story. The paper wrote:

> One of the most singular proceedings ever heard in a federal court began before Judge William C. Van Fleet in the United States Court yesterday.
>
> Judge Van Fleet began the trial of his own "state of mind" in the Western Pacific Railroad reorganization tangle.
>
> He filed an affidavit with himself in which he denied all the allegations as to his unfitness to sit in the reorganization cases, which were made last week by Lyman Rhoades, vice president of the Equitable Trust Company of New York.
>
> Then he heard testimony regarding the legal sufficiency of the Rhodes affidavit and listened while his personal attorney, Garret W. McEnerney, argued to convince him that his judicial discrimination was intact.

A day later, Van Fleet unsurprisingly ruled that he was unbiased. But the Circuit Court of Appeals soon demanded that Van Fleet show why he should not be disqualified from the trial. Van Fleet's attorneys went to work again, convincing three circuit court judges to leave Van Fleet on the case. Once vindicated, Van Fleet withdrew from the case, transferring it to another judge.

The Case That Rocked the Region

In 1913, Judge Van Fleet presided over the first sensational district court trial of the twentieth century, when Sacramento residents Maury Diggs and F. Drew Caminetti were indicted on federal charges for violating the Mann Act. Passed by Congress in 1910 to lessen the thriving business of prostitution, the act was designed to stop the transportation of women across state lines for "immoral purposes." Diggs and Caminetti were charged with taking two nineteen-year-old women on a train from Sacramento to Reno, Nevada, for a sexual fling. Both men were married, and Caminetti had young children.

Diggs, the California state architect, and Caminetti, who worked as a clerk for the State Board of Control, both came from prominent political families—Caminetti was the son of Anthony Caminetti, a former state senator, who had just been named by President Woodrow Wilson to serve

FIG. 4-3
The repaired courthouse at Seventh and Mission Streets was the site of "the case that rocked the region." This photograph was made not long after the 1906 earthquake. Reproduced courtesy of the US District Court for the Northern District of California.

in Washington as the federal commissioner general of immigration—so the case became major news the moment the four were reported missing in Sacramento. The *Examiner,* in an article entitled "Prominent Men and Society Girls Gone," reported that "Sacramento society was shocked to its foundations to-day when it became known that two prominent young men, both married, had disappeared, and that two of the best known society girls had also left their homes. The whereabouts of the four are unknown."

A few days later, police found Diggs and girlfriend Marsha Warrington and Caminetti and girlfriend Lola Norris living together in a Reno cottage. They were transported back to Sacramento, where authorities filed federal charges against Diggs and Caminetti. Speculation was rife that they might get off easy because of their influential families. John L. McNab, the US Attorney for the Northern District of California, countered by declaring to the *Sacramento Bee*: "The US district attorney's office has taken charge of this prosecution and will conduct it to the finish. Those who ridicule the prosecution of these men know little or nothing of the precision and effectiveness of the federal court. Enough facts are already in my possession to send both of these men to the penitentiary. Under the evidence in my possession, that is where I expect to see them land."

Other Well-Known People Prosecuted Under The Mann Act

- Architect Frank Lloyd Wright. In 1925, he and his live-in lover, Ogivanna Hinzenberg, were charged with violating the Mann Act in Minnesota. The charges were dropped the following year. The couple married in 1928.
- Boxer Jack Johnson. The African American heavyweight champ was convicted in Chicago of violating the Mann Act because he sent interstate railroad tickets to his white girlfriend, Belle Schreiber. He was sentenced to a year in prison.
- Actor Charlie Chaplin. Charged with violating the Mann Act during a 1944 paternity suit, he was later aquitted.
- Musician Chuck Berry. Convicted for transporting a fourteen-year-old girl from Texas to Missouri in 1959, Berry served a two-year prison term.

Indictments followed swiftly. But US Attorney General James C. McReynolds slowed down the process, wiring McNab from Washington for a full report. "Take no further affirmative action in respect of same until you receive advice from me," the attorney general wrote. Was the fix in?

McNab responded with a twelve-page report, which included a request to proceed immediately. "I trust that you will not misunderstand the unfortunate situation which will arise here if the case is permitted to go over from week to week," he wrote. "The well-known political prominence of the defendants' relatives will subject this office to the public criticism that this office is unduly favoring these defendants."

McReynolds wired back agreeing that McNab should proceed. But a few weeks later, the attorney general wrote that McNab should postpone the trial until autumn because Commissioner Caminetti was needed in Washington. Later that day, the attorney general sent another wire ordering McNab to postpone the trial of two directors of the Western Fuel Company. They had been indicted earlier in the year, along with three other directors, of conspiracy to defraud the government. McReynolds wrote that the attorney general's department had "grave doubt" as to the guilt of the two men, who were only directors of the company.

Angry at this turn of events, McNab resigned. He sent two telegrams, one to McReynolds and one to President Woodrow Wilson. "In bitter humiliation of spirit I am compelled to acknowledge what I have heretofore indignantly refused to believe, namely, that the Department of Justice is yielding to influences which cripple and destroy the usefulness of this office," McNab wrote to the president.

His letter was severely critical. "I cannot consent to occupy this position as a mere automaton and have the guilt or innocence of rich and powerful defendants, who have been indicted by unbiased grand juries on overwhelming evidence, determined in Washington on representation on behalf of the defendants without notice to me," McNab wrote. "I seem unable to convey to the department an understanding of the serious situation in which its action will leave this office. If the department in the future is to review the findings of grand juries and nullify their indictments, then this office might as well be abolished, for its functions will have ceased to exist. Neither my private honor nor sense of public duty can permit me thus to destroy the prestige of this office."

McReynolds, a Democrat, responded with "A Republican District Attorney has resigned and I am shedding no tears." President Wilson, also a Democrat, accepted McNab's resignation. He exonerated McReynolds and ordered the trials of Diggs and Caminetti to start soon.

The battle was far from over. The federal grand jury that had returned the indictments in the Western Fuel case took up McNab's cause. All twenty-four members of the jury sent a letter to Wilson protesting the decision to postpone the Mann Act trial. Jurors wrote that "We cannot refrain from expressing our protest that after ten days of earnest labor devoted to the consideration of evidence against these defendants our work is swept away by the authoritative act of an administrative official."

The grand jury was particularly critical of McReynolds and Wilson. "The defense of the attorney general, in view of the correspondence, is unfortunately weak," the grand jury concluded. "The action of the president in sustaining in one breath the position of the attorney general and in the next breath taking steps in exact consonance with those demanded by District Attorney McNab is, in the opinion of the grand jury, to say the least, a most astonishing method of disposing of a serious case, and we are forced to view in sadness and regret the remarkable closing of this chapter."

Judge Van Fleet refused to formally accept the grand jury's written report. He told the jurors to delete the criticism of the attorney general and resubmit the report. "It would not comport with the dignity of the court, nor with the proprieties to permit any report to be filed here which contained anything which would reflect upon the department of the government of which this court constitutes a part," the judge wrote.

Van Fleet was rebuked for his response. In an editorial entitled "The Grand Jury Was Right," the *San Francisco Call* wrote, "On what basis of common sense is it possible that it is right and proper for a federal judge to attempt to place a president, an attorney general, or even himself, above the criticism of a federal grand jury?" The editorial concluded that the grand jury was actually mild in its criticism, noting that "For a grand jury to 'view in sadness and regret' can hardly be taken to be a savage or ferocious attack on the dignity and sanctity of the courts or upon the president of the United States."

The Diggs-Caminetti case had all the elements of a juicy trial: sex, lust, lost innocence, clandestine romance, and influence peddling. Even the details—from Maury Diggs's Cadillac torpedo, which he called the Joy Machine, to the bloody sheets found in Lola Norris's bed in Reno—were racy. "For a brief while, however, in the spring and summer of 1913, the names of Maury Diggs and Drew Caminetti practically became household words," wrote Robert L. Anderson in his 1990 two-volume book,

The Diggs-Caminetti Case, 1913–1917: For Any Other Immoral Purpose. "Newspapers reported in detail their prosecutions under the White Slave Traffic Act. Their lives and those of their families were closely scrutinized. Their names were raised in the halls of Congress. They and some of the other principal actors in the drama were pursued in and about the streets of San Francisco by 1913's version of paparazzi. There were even offers of lucrative vaudeville contracts in what was apparently some show business entrepreneur's scheme to capitalize on the prurient appeal of the 'white slave' cases."

But the heart of the trial was the legality of the Mann Act, also known as the White Slave Act. Named after Representative James Robert Mann of Illinois, the act read:

> Any person who shall knowingly transport or cause to be transported, or aid or assist in obtaining transportation for, or in transporting, in interstate or foreign commerce, or in any Territory or in the District of Columbia, any woman or girl for the purpose of prostitution or debauchery, or for any other immoral purpose, or with the intent to induce, entice, or compel such woman or girl to become a prostitute or to give herself up to debauchery, or to engage in any other immoral practice…shall be deemed guilty of a felony, and upon conviction shall be punished by a fine not exceeding five thousand dollars, or by imprisonment in the discretion of the court.

Judge Van Fleet emphasized that the act went beyond prostitution to include debauchery—meaning to lead a person away from purity, to corrupt in character. "A man debauches a woman when…he gains her confidence and love, and then, by taking her to questionable resorts, plying her with intoxicating drinks or other similar methods, he breaks down her sense of delicacy, perverts her moral nature and arouses her animal passions, and thus seduces her to lewd actions such as illicit sexual relations or commerce," the judge said.

There was little dispute of the facts during the two trials. The trial of Maury Diggs began in August 1913 in Van Fleet's courtroom in the rebuilt courthouse at Seventh and Mission Streets. Two former US district attorneys, Marshall Woodworth and Robert Devlin, and three other attorneys represented Diggs. Special prosecutors Matthew I. Sullivan and Theodore Roche and three other attorneys represented the government.

The key witnesses, of course, were Marsha Warrington and Lola Norris. Under questioning by the special prosecutor, Warrington unfolded the entire love story, from the day she met Diggs as they waited for a streetcar in Sacramento in September 1912 to their arrest in Reno six months later. Warrington, who lived with her parents and worked as a stenographer, said she and Lola knew that the two men were married when they started going for long rides in Diggs's car. The trips got longer and longer, eventually lasting several days—and nights. She told the packed court that she was first seduced by Diggs and champagne in his office in November.

"You remember the occurrence, do you?" prosecutor Roche asked her.

"Yes," Warrington replied. "The occurrence is vividly impressed upon my mind because it was the first time I had sexual intercourse with anyone."

She was then asked by Roche: "At the time you had sexual intercourse, and which you say was the first time you had intercourse in your life, in what condition were you as a result of the champagne?"

"I was rather intoxicated," she replied.

It was the first of many office trysts. "Sexual intercourse took place between Mr. Diggs and I more than once at his office," she said.

Lola Norris, who worked in the California State Library, told a similar story of the car rides and overnight trips. However, she did not submit to Drew Caminetti until the Reno trip. She testified that she had never been intimate with a man until then.

"When you entered into these relations with Mr. Caminetti, you believed that he would marry you?" Roche asked her.

"Yes, Sir," she answered.

The jury took five hours to return guilty verdicts on four of the six counts of the indictment.

Almost a week later, Caminetti's trial began in Van Fleet's courtroom. The same cast of characters played out this second drama. Norris testified that Caminetti did not suggest the Reno trip to her for the purpose of having sexual relations or to be his mistress. She refused his advances several times before the Nevada trip and again on the first night in Reno. But then, "Upon the three nights that I occupied this rear room with Mr. Caminetti, upon retiring, we both disrobed," she said. "I don't know whether that is true also of Miss Warrington and Mr. Diggs. During the three nights that I was there in that bungalow I had sexual intercourse with Mr. Caminetti." Drew Caminetti took the stand but lasted only twenty minutes because he was uncomfortable with the questioning. His brother, Anthony Caminetti Jr., was far more eloquent, telling the jury that it was Maury Diggs who had planned the Reno trip. His brother left for Reno to avoid publicity, not to debauch any woman, he argued. Anthony concluded his twenty-five-minute plea to the jury by saying, "Whatever my brother has been, whatever he has done, gentlemen of the jury, he is not a white slaver."

The trial turned out to be more about morals than the violation of a federal statute. "If you believe in the sanctity of the home, if you believe in upholding the moral law, if you believe all laws should be enforced independent of position, influence, or wealth your verdict must be guilty," Special Prosecutor Sullivan told the jury, referring to the fact that Caminetti was married. The jury took five hours to find him guilty of one of the four counts of the indictment.

Van Fleet, who said he was satisfied with the verdicts, told the men that by law he was not able to keep them from the penitentiary. "I would do it, not only because of the fact that this is your first offense, but I would do it on account of your family. But, in my judgment, I am not left any discretion in that regard." Diggs was sentenced to two years in prison and fined $2,000. Caminetti was sentenced to eighteen months and fined $1,500. Both men lost appeals in the Ninth Circuit Court and the Supreme Court. Diggs and Caminetti hoped President Wilson would pardon them before they served time, but he fell silent on the case despite a petition for a pardon signed by two thousand people, including ten members of the jury. Wilson wrote Mrs. Anthony Caminetti that "It tears my heart to have to say to you that I cannot see my way clear to pardon your son. If I followed the dictates of my heart or allowed myself to be influenced by my genuine friendship for yourself and your husband, I would of course do it; but in matters of this sort it seems to me my imperative duty to leave personal feelings and connections out of the question entirely."

Caminetti served six months and Diggs served eight months in prison on McNeil Island, Washington. Caminetti temporarily reconciled with his wife, Elizabeth, and later became an Oakland businessman and a rancher. Elizabeth filed for divorce in 1927, charging him with philandering. "I tried everything humanly possible to make him mend his ways," she said, "but he would not listen." He remarried the following year. He married two more times and died in 1945.

Diggs returned to architecture during the appeal period. He divorced his wife, Lina, in 1914, and married Warrington in 1916, announcing, "I think that Marsha Warrington is one of the sweetest girls that ever lived. I'm sure we're going to be very happy." They apparently were, and lived to old age together. He is credited with taking part in the design of San Quentin State Prison, the Fox Theater in Oakland, and several horse racing tracks, including Bay Meadows Race Course in San Mateo and Golden Gate Fields in Berkeley. He died at age sixty-six in 1953, survived by Marsha, a daughter, and three grandchildren.

John McNab practiced law in San Francisco for most of his career. He made the nominating speech for Herbert Hoover at the 1928 Republican Convention and was given a job as Hoover's personal adviser on Prohibition prosecutions. James McReynolds was elevated to the Supreme Court in order to remove him from Wilson's cabinet, according to Albert Lawrence in the *Journal of Supreme Court History.* McReynolds served from 1914 to 1941, developing a reputation as the most conservative justice ever to sit on the court. "He was also labeled a racist, an anti-Semite, a misogynist, lazy, irascible, an obstructionist, and unpleasant," wrote Lawrence in 2005. McReynolds recused himself when the Diggs-Caminetti cases made it to the Supreme Court.

Beyond San Francisco

In early 1913, Judge DeHaven suffered a cerebral hemorrhage and died in Yountville, just north of Napa. DeHaven had had a nervous breakdown around 1911 and been in poor health since. In late 1912, he retired to his country home to rest and recharge, but he died not long after. Judge Van Fleet eulogized DeHaven at his funeral: "While regarded by some, from a mere outward semblance, as a man of somewhat cold nature or demeanor, when you got beneath the outer crust of Judge DeHaven's manner he was found to be as gentle and kindly as a woman; and especially was he a helpful man to be associated with."

Maurice Timothy Dooling, whose outward semblance was friendly and whose demeanor was warm, was appointed to fill DeHaven's seat. Dooling, the court's fifth judge, was the first from California. He was born in 1860 in Moore's Flat, a tiny gold mining community northeast of Sacramento. Both of his parents were Irish immigrants. His father had worked in the California gold mines for three years, where he made a substantial amount of money, according to a family history. In 1867, Dooling's family moved to San Francisco. The following year, they purchased a small ranch near Hollister, about ninety-five miles southeast of San Francisco in San Benito County.

Maurice, known as Bob most of his life, impressed neighbors with his intellectual ability at an early age. He attended and taught at St. Mary's College in San Francisco, where he received a bachelor's degree in 1880 and a master's degree in 1881. He read and spoke at least six languages. For fun, Dooling translated much of Dante's *Inferno* into English and then back into Italian. Years later, he received a PhD from Santa Clara College.

In 1883, Dooling returned to Hollister to read law. He was admitted to the bar two years later and distinguished himself as a lawyer who stood up for the common man. A would-be client came to Hollister looking for the young barrister with a reputation. "I heard if you have no money but Dooling feels your case is a worthy one, he'll take your case and will even pay the court costs," the man said. The client was correct.

"In the early 1900s, the first Chinese immigrant child to enroll in the Hollister school was not admitted until Judge Dooling took the boy, Wong U. Fong, with his queue hanging down his back, to the office of the superintendent of schools and told them they must either admit the child or start a school for him," the *Hollister Bee* reported. "Fong became a close friend of the Dooling family, graduated from Hollister High School with honors and went on to the University of California where he secured a PhD in science."

But Dooling developed a drinking habit that threatened his success. "By the time he was at St. Mary's College, Maurice Dooling knew that alcohol affected him differently than it did most of his friends," Alma Dettweiler wrote about her paternal grandfather. "He would not take a drink for several weeks, but then he'd have a drink with the boys and would keep drinking until he was so drunk they'd have to take him home and put him to bed." Fortunately, she wrote, Dooling would go months without taking a drink, so his occasional binges did not seriously threaten his career. In 1887, Dooling married Ida Mae Wagner, but his alcohol addiction raged on. "The early years of their marriage were marred by Bob going on periodic drinking bouts," Dettweiler wrote. "But when their sons were about ages five and three, Bob Dooling gave up drinking and never took a drink in the remaining thirty years of his life."

Active in Democratic politics for decades, Dooling served as a member of the California House of Representatives from 1885 to 1887. He was elected district attorney of San Benito County in 1892, and served as a judge in the Superior Court of San Benito County from 1897 to 1913.

During those sixteen years, Dooling displayed such a statewide reputation for fairness that few criminal defendants or civil attorneys sought juries in his court. In 1908, Dooling presided over the first graft trial of San Francisco political kingpin Abraham Ruef. The jury failed to agree whether Boss Ruef was guilty of offering a bribe to a San Francisco board supervisor. Later that year, Ruef was convicted of bribery and sentenced to fourteen years in prison.

Dooling was nominated to the district court by President Wilson to take the seat vacated by Judge DeHaven. Dooling, who had supported Wilson in the 1912 primary, was confirmed by the Senate in July 1913.

"Miss him? Everyone will miss him," wrote the *Hollister Bee* following Dooling's appointment. "There is not a mother or a father in the county who at some time or other has not sought his advice and always acted on it. When in any kind of domestic trouble or public dilemma you asked your neighbor what was best to be done, the answer has always been, 'You'd better ask the Judge. He knows best.' And he never refused his opinion, counseling patience in adversity, honesty in action, hope in the future, and trust in The Great Judge of all. Yes, we shall miss him, for the lawyers who have pleaded before him to the humblest citizen in the county unable to speak English."

Dooling was an approachable, casual pillar of the community. He often wore a soft-collared colored shirt under a brown or gray suit, the paper noted, instead of the stiff-collar shirts that were in vogue. "His old friends were taking bets on whether or not Judge Dooling would dress in the fashion of that day when he was sworn in on the US District Court," the *Bee* reported. "He arrived in his usual outfit and when he started to enter the courtroom, the bailiff thought he was a lowly citizen and refused to let him enter until someone who knew Judge Dooling told him that this was the new judge."

As a federal judge, Dooling was known for giving first offenders a second chance. "I try to put myself in the other fellow's place," he told a reporter in 1921. "I've been here eight years. I don't believe I have seen the same fellow up here before me twice." And he was known for creating a calm, informal atmosphere in court. "One of the foundations upon which Judge Dooling's prestige rests is his remarkable expertness in criminal psychology, and the peculiar quieting effect he had on defendants who come before him," wrote Dick Martinsen in the *San Francisco Daily News* in 1921. "A US attorney recently declared that his honor was possessed with a 'magic eye.' 'Two minutes after a defendant is seated near the judge he relaxes, and his whole attitude changes,' is the way lawyers who have worked under Dooling put it. 'It's really a very simple thing,' says the judge, quietly. 'I simply try to make them understand that I am quite the opposite of hostile in my attitude towards them.'"

Dooling's last years on the court were difficult. He broke his pelvis when his car overturned on top of him in 1917, and he never recovered. He caught influenza in 1923, which weakened him, but he managed to return to San Francisco in late December to set bail for prisoners before the holidays. "His mind never lost its vitality," noted his obituary. "In his last days he amused himself reading the gospels in Greek, comparing them with the Latin and King James versions." Dooling died in late 1924. His burial, in Hollister, was scheduled after the eleven o'clock train arrived from San Francisco packed with his city friends, including Judge John Partridge and US Attorney Sterling Carr.

"The whole countryside attended the funeral service in the old white Catholic church and followed the body to the grave," one paper reported. The article continued:

> Mingling with the men from the city were those who had known Judge Dooling long before the city ever heard of him. They included descendants of the old Spanish settler from whom the jurist had learned his fluent Spanish, cowboys who had ridden through the passes, ranchers who have grown prosperous in San Benito County, and business men of the now flourishing town.
>
> To them, it was a tribute to an old friend—to the quiet country judge whose repute was such that no juries were needed when he held court. To them, it was a home-coming of an old friend. The fact that he had won honor in San Francisco and marked recognition upon the high federal bench was merely incidental.

New Directions

The district court transformed in subtle and not-so-subtle ways during the first two decades of the twentieth century. In 1905, the court moved into its magnificent new San Francisco quarters, and in 1907, the number of judges doubled. In 1910, the district and circuit courts were required by law to hold at least one term each year in Sacramento. And six years later, Congress divided the Northern District into two divisions—the Southern Division in San Francisco and the new Northern Division in Sacramento, where district court was held first at the Sacramento County Courthouse and later in the State Capitol Senate Chambers. For the first time, two dockets were kept, one for each division. And for the first time, a term was mandated to be held annually in Eureka, about 450 miles north of San Francisco not far from the Oregon border.

Bigger changes occurred in 1914, when Annette Abbott Adams became the first woman appointed as an assistant United States district attorney in the Northern District of California and the first woman hired as a lawyer in any district attorney's office in the nation. It wasn't an easy appointment. Northern California's US Attorney John W. Preston submitted Adams's name along with those of three men to US Attorney General James McReynolds, who had clashed with the district court in

FIG. 4-4
California native Annette Grace Abbott Adams (1877–1956) was the first female assistant attorney general in the United States. In 1950, by special assignment, she became the first woman to sit on a case in the California Supreme Court. Courtesy of the Library of Congress.

the Diggs-Caminetti cases. McReynolds approved the appointment of the men but refused to sign off on Adams because he was opposed to the idea of any woman serving in the office. Preston stood firm, waging a campaign for Adams's appointment, and won the job for her soon after McReynolds was appointed to the Supreme Court. "Though the three other assistants were getting $2,150 a year, the salary of Mrs. Adams was fixed in Washington at $1,800, a circumstance that ought to be pondered by the few feminine anti-suffragists left in the world," wrote newspaper columnist John D. Barry.

Adams was a path breaker. Born in 1877 in Prattsville, about two hundred miles northeast of San Francisco, she graduated from Chico Normal School and taught school from 1897 to 1900. She entered the University of California at Berkeley in 1900 and studied law at the school's Boalt Hall, receiving a bachelor of laws degree in 1904. At the time, most women with law degrees were discouraged from practice. Only a few worked as attorneys; most opted for a career in social services. Unable to get a job as a lawyer, Adams returned to education, teaching grammar school in Modoc County and serving as one of the state's first female school principals, at Modoc County High School. She returned to Boalt Hall in 1910 to continue her law study and received a juris doctor degree in 1912. She established a law partnership in San Francisco the following year.

Adams's first visit to the Northern District Court was in 1914, when she appeared as a defense attorney for a client charged with violating the Mann Act. Arthur Dunn described her performance in a *Sunset* magazine article entitled "A Portia in the Federal Court":

> Mrs. Adams addressed the court in the frankest fashion on behalf of her client. She did not attempt to give him a lily-white reputation or to exhibit his angel wings just sprouting where such wings are expected to grow. She didn't quibble or quiver over the question; there was no evasion or evanescing—just facts. The prosecutor listened attentively. The judge manifestly was interested. Mrs. Adams's client was sentenced to a term of six months imprisonment, the judge declaring from the bench that the statement of his counsel had won for the client the court's clemency. It had been in the mind of the court to make the sentence a term of years.

Adams's defense so impressed Preston that he asked her to join his staff. During her first years in the office, defense attorneys often called attention to Adams's gender. They would ask potential jurors if they would be prejudiced if a woman asked witnesses "some nasty questions." One time, Adams countered, asking jurors if they would be bothered if her opponent, a young attorney, asked nasty questions. Adams soon became known as a loud feminist voice in San Francisco. She campaigned vigorously for the right of women to vote. She was unwavering in her belief that women were as qualified as men to hold professional positions. "Many of the currently accepted opinions about the two sexes have been overturned in my own mind in recent years," she told a lunch group at the Fairmont Hotel in 1922. "I do not think that women's minds are as coldly logical or unemotional [as] men's. I know. As a prosecuting attorney I have seen attorneys and other influences play upon the emotions of the male juror many times. But let a reasoning woman take a firm stand upon a case and the men of the world will characterize her as stubborn." Actually, women are *more* logical and orderly than men, Adams asserted. "If anyone does not think so, just visit the august United States Senate in session," she said. "Their ideas of the businesslike precision with which men conduct the affairs of the nation will be badly shattered."

In 1918, Adams was appointed as temporary US Attorney and began running an office with seven assistants. "It is said, by the way, that her appointment was regarded as a joke in Washington," wrote columnist Barry. "It is no joke in San Francisco. Humor depends very largely on the point of view. There are lawyers in San Francisco who think a woman has no right to hold that job. They are indignant." In 1919, she was nominated by President Wilson to serve as US Attorney for the Northern District. She was the first woman to be given a presidential appointment as a US Attorney, according to the *San Francisco Examiner*.

Adams left the Northern District the following year when she was appointed deputy United States attorney general. She served in Washington for one year before returning to San Francisco to practice law on her own. She was surprised when she was met at the ferry by supporters and then spirited off to a reception for tea at the Fairmont Hotel that included hundreds of women. In 1935, Adams was considered to fill a federal court vacancy in California left by Judge Frank Kerrigan, but she was never nominated. She joined Preston in a law partnership and continued working with him until 1941. The next year, she was named presiding justice of the Third District Court of Appeals of California, a position she held for ten years until her retirement. Adams died in 1956. Her *New York Times* obituary noted her "long and brilliant career."

The Hindoo Conspiracy

Annette Abbott Adams played a leading role in two major World War I cases. Both revolved around Franz Bopp, the German consul general in San Francisco. In 1914, after the Great War began, President Wilson declared that the United States would maintain a neutral stance. Two years later, a federal grand jury indicted Bopp and thirty others, accusing them of conspiring to slow down the manufacture and transportation of weapons made in the United States and Canada and shipped to the allied war effort. They were charged with taking part in a grandiose plan to blow up munitions-carrying ships in Washington State and freight railroad facilities in Canada, including the tunnel under the St. Clair River that connects Port Huron, Michigan, to Sarnia, Ontario. They were also charged with shipping war material—from coal to sauerkraut and beer—to German ships in the Pacific Ocean. In short, they were charged with plotting to undermine American neutrality. Bopp and three others were found guilty in 1917 and sentenced to two years in prison. The following year, Bopp and twenty-eight others were found guilty of conspiring to foment revolution against British rule in India in one of the district court's most sensational cases, known as the Hindoo Conspiracy Trial.

Mrs. A. A. Adams, as she was known on legal papers, was John Preston's leading assistant in the prosecution of Bopp and 104 other defendants charged with conspiring to help India revolt against British rule. Bopp and the Germans knew that revolution in India would siphon British military manpower and money from the European fronts. He was joined by a contingent of pro-nationalist Indians who lived in the United States and Canada. The group's leader, Ram Chandra, was the editor of the western-based *Hindustan Ghadar* newspaper, which called for an uprising and revolt against British rule starting in 1913. "The time will soon come when rifles and blood will take the place of paper and ink," the paper declared in its first issue. In 1914, Chandra organized a group of sixty Punjabi expatriates to smuggle arms back to India for the planned revolution, but the group was arrested as soon as it landed in Calcutta, and the arms were confiscated.

On April 6, 1917, the day the United States formally declared war on Germany, the US government started rounding up Indian expatriates who were believed to be working to overthrow British rule in India. Chandra and sixteen other Indians were arrested in San Francisco. Others connected to the cause were arrested for conspiracy in Chicago and

New York. Three months later, a San Francisco grand jury returned secret indictments against 105 men, charging them with conspiracy to violate United States neutrality.

"The advantages the government has in a conspiracy trial were exploited fully in San Francisco," Joan M. Jensen wrote in a 1979 reassessment of the case in the *Pacific Historical Review*. "The charge of conspiracy branded the East Indians with the image of secrecy and evil plotting, which heightened apprehensions already present in San Francisco during the first winter of the war. Hearsay evidence rules were relaxed to allow the words of alleged conspirators to be used against each other. The defendants were confronted with the recitation of a hodgepodge of alleged acts and the statements of others, which the government hoped might persuade the jury of the existence of the conspiracy. All the government had to prove was that two defendants conspired to bring about some illegal act and that one person then made an overt act to further that conspiracy. The government did not have to prove actual criminal acts."

The trial, before Judge Van Fleet, started in November 1917 and ended on the most dramatic day in the history of the Northern District court. On April 23, 1918, Ram Chandra was shot and killed by fellow defendant Ram Singh in Courtroom 1 at the district courthouse. After Chandra dropped to the foot of the witness stand, Marshal James B. Holohan rose and fatally shot Singh. The *San Francisco Chronicle* reported that Singh, a wealthy Canadian landowner who had given thousands of dollars to Chandra as editor and leader of the Ghadar Party, became convinced that Chandra had abandoned the cause.

Carl Calbreath, who then was a young assistant clerk, described what happened:

> It late developed that among the forty Hindus on trial there were two factions: one headed by Ram Chandra and the other by Ram Singh. It is believed that the attorneys for the Hindu defendants knew of the existence of this feud, but did not believe that there would be any shooting, especially in the courtroom.
>
> To set the scene in the courtroom prior to the shooting—the noon recess had been declared by Judge Van Fleet; the jury had filed out of the courtroom before any one else left the room, then Judge Van Fleet left the bench. The room was still packed with defendants and attorneys and spectators and newspaper men. Ram Chandra was a small man, about five feet five inches tall and very thin. He was standing with his

back to the rear of the room and talking with his attorney, Stanley A. Moore. Mr. Moore was a rather large man and towered over little Ram Chandra. Ram Singh came across the room and up in back of Ram Chandra and holding the revolver not more than two or three feet from Ram Chandra's back fired one bullet. Ram Chandra dropped to the floor immediately. Many have wondered why the bullet did not go through Ram Chandra and enter the body of Mr. Moore, but it did not. It was felt that the bullet had not had time to gain maximum velocity. Marshal Holohan was about ten or twelve feet away when he shot over the heads of the attorneys standing in front of him. His bullet entered the heart muscle of Ram Singh.

Pandemonium broke out in the room with spectators and defendants trying to leave the room by the double rear doors. I had taken the court session from 10 a.m. to about 11 a.m. when I was relieved by deputy clerk Lyle S. Morris (now deceased). When I heard the shots in the clerk's office which was adjacent to the courtroom I hurried to the rear door of the office, which door is almost opposite the rear doors of the courtroom and was standing in this door when I saw the military guard running down the small corridor with drawn guns. Certain of the German and Hindu defendants were under military guard and were held at the military prison on Alcatraz Island. Everybody who could or tried to leave the courtroom were stopped by the guards. When the courtroom had been cleared of all persons except the defendants, the US marshals, military guards, and two British secret service men and the two dead defendants, I entered the courtroom. In a moment or two Charles Goff, captain of the San Francisco police department, who was in the building and hearing the shots hurried to the courtroom. He started to clear the room of persons whom he did not know and when he started to remove the two British secret service men I advised him who they were, and since he and I had been friends for many years he refrained from further action with them.

The question has often been asked; since all of the defendants, particularly the Hindus and Germans, whether in custody or not, had been searched as they entered the courtroom in the morning and again at 2 p.m., how was it that Ram Singh got possession of a revolver. The most plausible explanation seems to be that during the eleven o'clock a.m. recess the defendants were free to leave the courtroom and walk up and down a small corridor, at the other end of which stood the military guard and US marshals. However, off this corridor was a men's toilet. It is felt that on this particular day Ram Singh entered the toilet and in there was an accomplice, who had entered the toilet as a spectator and he passed the gun to Ram Singh while he was in the toilet. After the shooting, one of the attorneys for the Hindus was found under the clerk's courtroom desk; Mrs. Adams, the assistant US attorney, lost her slipper while she was running in back of the judge's bench to go out the rear door.

Moments later, Adams came out from behind Van Fleet's desk and announced, "He's still alive," as she pointed toward Chandra. But another woman felt his pulse and told the crowded court that a physician was not necessary. Chandra died a few moments later.

A *San Francisco Chronicle* reporter wrote that Chandra was survived by a wife and two children. "I have no desire to tell of her appearance in the courtroom after her husband lay dead," the reporter wrote. "A heart in the breaking is a grievous thing."

The jury came back to the courtroom at two o'clock to receive instructions and retired at dinnertime. It returned a verdict moments before midnight. Of the original 105 defendants, 29 were convicted, but they received short prison terms. One was found insane, and one—shipbuilder John T. Craig of Long Beach, California—was found not guilty of the conspiracy. Three other defendants had entered guilty pleas. The other 71 defendants either fled the country or won freedom by cooperating as government witnesses.

Morals and a World War

Van Fleet did his part to help the United States win World War I. In the months that followed President Wilson's declaration of war against Germany, the judge stepped up to protect young GIs based at the presidio army stations and the Yerba Buena Island naval training stations. During those years, bar owners in the Embarcadero and Barbary Coast neighborhoods had developed a reputation for serving liquor to minors, and local judges had developed a reputation for turning a blind eye. This had to stop, according to Van Fleet. The judge felt strongly that serving liquor to young soldiers and sailors was a threat to the war effort. "The lives and characters of the men in the Army and Navy are at stake," he wrote. "Traffickers in liquor must understand that they have to obey the law, and this law of all others. The very life of the nation depends upon it."

The *Examiner* praised Van Fleet's tough stand. "The Police Commission is not the only arm of the municipal government which has been helping to bring the city into disrepute with the federal government," the newspaper wrote in a 1917 editorial. "The gross indifference of the police court judges toward the efforts of the morals squad to enforce the city's own ordinances regarding the immoral resorts has also become a subject for general notice."

One of the most sensational World War I cases did not come to trial until almost two years after the armistice that ended the conflict. In 1920, William H. Dempsey, better known as Jack Dempsey or the Manassa Mauler, was found not guilty of evading the draft during World War I by a jury in the courtroom of Maurice Dooling. Dempsey, who won the heavyweight championship by defeating Jess Willard in 1919, was indicted by a grand jury after his former wife, Maxine, called him a draft dodger. In a letter published in the *San Francisco Chronicle,* she accused him of lying to get 3-A status. Dempsey received deferred classification for military service from his draft board on the grounds that he was married and had six dependents—his wife and two children, and his father, mother, and widowed sister. Maxine wrote that he did not support her during the war but rather that she had supported him by working in a dance hall.

Dempsey's status during the war became national conversation. For years, the boxer was plagued by reports that he had wiggled his way out of the war. The day after he was crowned heavyweight champ, Grantland Rice wrote in the *New York Tribune,* "It would be an insult to every young American who sleeps today from Flanders to Lorraine, from the Somme to the Argonne, to crown Dempsey with any laurels of fighting courage." Some American Legions formally condemned Dempsey. Even the *New York Times* weighed in, editorializing, "Dempsey, whose profession is fighting, whose living is combat, whose fame is battle; Dempsey, six feet one of strength, in the glowing splendor of youth, a man fashioned by nature as an athlete and a warrior—Dempsey did not go to war, while weak-armed, strong-hearted clerks reeled under pack and rifle; while middle-aged men with families volunteered; while America asked for its manhood."

Back in San Francisco, Dempsey was ready for this fight. He reportedly paid $50,000 to San Francisco attorney Gordon McNab, brother of former US Attorney John McNab, to defend him against the criminal charges. Before the trial, McNab convinced Maxine to change her story.

She met with assistant US Attorney Charles W. Thomas and denied her earlier charges, declaring Dempsey a "wonderful man and husband."

Despite their shaky star witness, prosecutors pushed the case to trial. They produced records showing that the members of Dempsey's family maintained jobs—even if temporary—during the war years, and called Maxine to the stand, where she said that Dempsey never sent her money. McNab countered, presenting evidence that Dempsey had sent Maxine $200 after one of his fights. He called Jack's sister, Celia Dempsey, who testified that the boxer's money kept her family intact. Dempsey finally took the stand, testifying he had attempted to join the service but had been turned down. He told the jury that he had no choice but to support his family during the war. The jury was out for only ten to fifteen minutes before returning with the not guilty verdict.

Dempsey became one of the greatest attractions during the sport's golden age in the 1920s, but the charges of being a slacker haunted him. He volunteered during World War II and served as a commander in the Coast Guard. In 1945, at the age of forty-nine, he saw action in Okinawa and finally put the draft dodger charges behind him.

A New Judgeship

The passage of the Eighteenth Amendment—which prohibited the manufacture, sale, or transportation of intoxicating liquors—and of the National Prohibition Act of 1919—which enforced the new laws—further expanded the work of the district court.

In 1923, President Warren G. Harding nominated John Slater Partridge to a new seat, the third, which was created to help the district court keep up with the ever-expanding volume of criminal cases surrounding Prohibition. Partridge was the first district court judge who grew up in San Francisco. His family moved to California during the gold rush, settling in Susanville, about two hundred miles northeast of San Francisco in Lassen County. Born in 1870, he moved to San Francisco with his family as a boy following the death of his father, who had worked as a civil engineer. The young Partridge attended Lowell High School and the University of California, receiving a bachelor's degree in 1892 and a master's degree in 1894. He taught school for five years, read law, and entered the bar in 1897. He spent the next twenty-six years in private practice in San Francisco, interrupted once for a two-year stint as an assistant city attorney and an unexpected run for mayor.

Challenging Prohibition

In 1920, a San Francisco bootlegger named Dillon challenged the constitutionality of the Eighteenth Amendment in a case that was decided in the Supreme Court. Dillon argued that Prohibition was illegal because Article Five of the Constitution, known as the amendment clause, contained no provisions for including a deadline for passage of a proposed amendment. The Eighteenth Amendment was the first to carry such a limit; it required that two-thirds of the states approve the amendment within seven years. The Supreme Court, in the case *Dillon v. Gloss,* upheld Congress's power to prescribe time limitations, and so held the Eighteenth Amendment to be legal.

Partridge's rise to the district court is steeped in early twentieth-century San Francisco history. It began in 1901, when Mayor James D. Phelan, a Democrat, broke a bitter Teamsters strike on San Francisco's waterfront by ordering police to protect strikebreakers. Phelan's action ended the strike and his five-year term as mayor. To fight Phelan, labor leaders created the Union Labor party and helped elect Eugene E. Schmitz, head of the Musician's Union, as San Francisco's new mayor. But Schmitz quickly mired himself in graft and corruption.

Four years later, the city's Republicans and Democrats united in an effort to stop Schmitz's reelection by creating the Fusion Ticket. Partridge, a promising lawyer and well known in Republican circles, wrote to Fremont Older, managing editor of the *San Francisco Bulletin,* who was in charge of choosing the coalition candidate. "He was an upright, upstanding young fellow, known to have lived a clean life and to be thoroughly reliable," Older wrote in his autobiography, *My Own Story.* "I invited him into my office and said to him, 'John, it's you for mayor. Don't say a word about it to any one.'"

The choice was a surprise, even to Partridge, who was more of a back-scenes player. "He was stunned," recalled Older, and asked how it could be done. "Never mind how it can be done," Older told Partridge. "You go up to the meeting and sit in there. Don't say a word, just watch it work out."

The moment Partridge left, Older sat down and wrote an editorial that detailed an earlier meeting he had had with Fairfax Wheelan and Gavin

FIG. 4-5
Two men appear to be guarding confiscated stills in front of the John C. Gordon San Jose Court House in 1925 during Prohibition. The unpopularity of the Eighteenth Amendment, repealed in 1933, led to a backlog of cases at the district court. Courtesy of the John C. Gordon Collection, MSS-1996-03-29, San Jose State University Special Collections and Archives.

McNab, leaders of the Republican and Democratic parties, respectively, who had conspired to find a candidate they could totally control. Older had rejected their plan. "I revealed every detail of the attempted felony of Wheelan and McNab, denounced them for it, washed my hands of the entire crowd, and cast them to the wolves." With this editorial in proof form, Older sent it to the Republican League. "I want Partridge nominated by two o'clock today," he told party leaders. "If he is not endorsed at two o'clock, this editorial will be published. Read it."

Partridge was nominated by both parties as the reform candidate, but Wheelan and McNab did little to help him in the election. Partridge spoke in all the districts of the city, railing against the graft of the Schmitz administration, but he suffered an overwhelming defeat. Partridge then withdrew from local politics and concentrated on his commercial law practice. When charges of graft and extortion started surfacing against Schmitz and Union Labor Party boss Abraham Ruef following the 1906 earthquake, Partridge became a symbol of opposition, but he never formally reentered politics.

Partridge "made his way to the federal bench by embracing the unsavory aspects of politics and yet by separating himself from what this politics implied," Joseph Franaszek wrote in "The Politics of Judicial Appointments," an unpublished manuscript. "While Partridge assumed active roles in a machine dominated Republican party, he distanced himself from the graft, power and ruthlessness such a role implied by becoming prominent in other activities: he began to speak for the party on national issues, avoiding local concerns and disputes; he attained distinction as an academic; he became prominent as a reformer in non-political endeavors, he displayed an empathy with the disadvantaged and used this empathy as an approach to public problems and as a guide to his own life."

Nine people were in the running for the district court judgeship in 1923, according to Franaszek. Republican senators Hiram Johnson and Samuel Shortridge each supported a different front-runner, and President Harding reportedly refused to choose until the senators agreed on one candidate. Unable to decide, both senators submitted their top four

A Man of Power

Gavin McNab, who defended actor Fatty Arbuckle in San Francisco Municipal Court, was one of the most prominent attorneys of his age. District court judge George Harris described McNab in his 1980 oral history:

> He was a large man, large proportions, and not too prepossessing in appearance and dress. He was cordial to a fault—a man of great cordiality and political attainment. Out of hand he practically ran the mayor's office, dictating policy from time to time. He was a man of intense power and held the power lightly.
>
> By that I mean he wasn't an oppressive boss type that you see in the literature of the courts. He was a benign—cut benign. He was a very lovely man with an intense charity, helped many people on their way, helped many a young lawyer, and was one of the real principle forces in the evolution of our legal process in the West, I think. Not that he was a great student, but he was a great humanitarian.

candidates. Partridge's name was listed third by each. After admiralty and patent lawyers campaigned for Partridge, the senators agreed on him.

The *Examiner* described the hubbub following the announcement of Partridge's nomination: "The telephone bell in the office, ringing constantly yesterday afternoon as scores of friends, learning of his nomination, called to offer their congratulations, and the busy door of his offices in the Foxcroft Building in Post Street, opening to attorneys, judges, and citizens bent on the same errand, further gave evidence of the popularity of President Harding's recommendation."

On the day of his appointment, Partridge was described by the *Examiner* as almost Lincolnesque in his build and attitude: tall and thin, almost gaunt, keen eyes, and a high forehead. The San Francisco Bar Association hosted a tribute to Partridge at the St. Francis Hotel on the night he was sworn in. Joining the celebration were former president William Howard Taft, who was chief justice of the Supreme Court at the time, and former New York senator Elihu Root, who won the Nobel Peace Prize in 1912. Both were in town visiting relatives and were admitted as honorary members of the Bar Association.

Partridge's first job was to help the court catch up on Prohibition cases. He promised "prompt and speedy justice," but refused to become a machinelike judge issuing verdicts without much consideration. He was, in fact, critical of both defendants and prosecutors who appeared in his court on liquor charges. He opposed the "booze lawyers" for using legal loopholes and delays to help their clients. "The situation here is unprecedented and one of the worst in the country," he told the *Examiner* in 1924. "All technicalities which are cited by attorneys are merely to shield the guilty. The practice is to be condemned." And he was critical of the government for using undercover Prohibition agents with fictitious names to obtain search warrants and appear as witnesses at trials. In 1925, Partridge threatened to dismiss hundreds of Prohibition cases if the practice continued. The government argued that the fake names were used to protect agents. Partridge did not buy the argument. "How can a man make a defense if he is accused by a person giving a fictitious name?" he asked.

The sheer volume of liquor cases caused a crisis at the district court. San Francisco patent attorney John H. Miller wrote the attorney general in 1922 that the illnesses of Judges Dooling and Van Fleet had made it impossible for him to try cases. Two years later, attorney Clinton L. White wrote Washington, DC, that "this division is so swamped with criminal cases that it is two years or more since any civil or equity case has been tried here." Attorney Harold C. Faulkner, who began his long legal career in the district court by defending bootleggers during the 1920s, recalled that Judge George M. Bourquin from the Montana district court was called in to help. "He would clean the calendar as though it was a child cleaning his teeth with a toothbrush, because the calendar would be nice and shiny because there would be no one left on it because he let everybody off easy," Faulkner recounted in a 1981 oral history. The secret: Bourquin gave Volstead Act violators small fines instead of prison sentences.

After the backlog of Prohibition cases was cleared, the three judges divided the work. One judge would hear criminal cases for one term, one would hear civil cases, and one would hear equity cases. Two months after Partridge took the bench, the *Examiner* reported that he would eventually assume the court's admiralty and equity cases and then rotate into other cases. The *Examiner* was complimentary of the new judge. "Among men, Judge Partridge might be a Keats or a Shelley—his face is finely chiseled, his figure is slim, his hands are small and his fingers taper—but among lawyers he has the mind of a Webster and the force of the elder Pitt," wrote Gilbert G. Weigle. "In matters of justice, the new federal judge has already from the bench sent a millionaire to jail, remitted the sentence of a poor man whom he believed he had unduly punished, and deplored that the statutes did not authorize him to give 'life' to a peddler of narcotics to young girls."

In that case, Partridge sentenced the drug dealer to five years in prison and fined him $2,000, the maximum for such a case. "There should be a law adequate to punish such monsters," Partridge said. "That man was worse than a murderer; he killed those young girls, body and soul." Partridge had little sympathy for dealers. "Anyone convicted of violating the federal laws relative to…narcotics will get the limit the law allows," he promised soon after his appointment. "There should be no halfway punishment…whether he be a gangster or a social leader." But he did have sympathy for addicts. "They are the ones who suffer," he wrote. "They should not go to prison. I believe laws should be passed giving the courts authority to commit such persons to some public institution for treatment." Watching narcotics cases unfold in his courtroom plagued Partridge. "I don't believe the half of this dope evil—this selling of narcotic drugs—has been told," he said. "I don't believe that the person in ordinary life has any conception of the dreadful consequences. God! I don't believe it is possible to exaggerate the dreadfulness of it."

Partridge's contemporary on the court was Frank Henry Kerrigan, a fellow Republican who rose through the ranks in a far different manner. Partridge was the reformer, who had soiled his hands but once in a political campaign. Kerrigan was a political pro who climbed the judicial ladder rung by rung. Kerrigan, appointed to the district court in 1924 to fill the seat vacated when William Van Fleet died, was raised in the Green Valley area of Contra Costa County. He first distinguished himself as an amateur bicycle rider in 1890s. "The noted jurist was a familiar figure in many of the great road races which were wont to be staged in this city and across the bay in the early days," noted the *Examiner*. "He was regarded as one of the brainiest riders of his time and disappointed many of his friends and admirers when he turned a deaf ear to the alluring professional offers that came his way during his career as a rider."

Kerrigan studied law in San Francisco and was admitted to the bar in 1889. Four years later, he won election as San Francisco's Justice of the Peace. Thus began a shrewd political career in which he won eight straight elections. Kerrigan was an adept politician who only ran for office at opportune times. He never ran against incumbents and only ran to fill vacancies. After winning three terms as justice of the peace, Kerrigan won a seat on the superior court bench, filling an unexpired term in 1899, and won reelection in 1903. Three years later, he won a seat on the First District Court of Appeals, filling an unexpired term, and won reelection in 1914. In 1922, he was elected to the California Supreme Court.

Kerrigan, who rose to power by aligning himself with the powerful Southern Pacific Railroad, somehow survived the rise of the progressives by attaching himself to the movement. In 1910, Kerrigan and two other justices reversed the extortion conviction of former mayor Eugene Schmitz. Kerrigan became a target of daily editorials from the *Bulletin*. He and his two colleagues became known as "the men who legalized blackmail," but the California Supreme Court later affirmed their decision.

According to Franaszek,

> Frank Kerrigan's charisma enabled him to become closely associated with the politics of the period. He did not attempt to separate himself from the unsavory aspects of partisan politics. Indeed, the charges of malfeasance and prejudice in office leveled against him, regardless of the validity of those charges, indicate how involved he was in that politics. Yet Kerrigan was able to transcend the corrupt politics of the period by indicating that the attempt to connect him with that politics was itself a

political act. By emphasizing his role in the established political order, by making a "hobby" of the politics of the period and by involving others in it and by exciting them with his ambitions—he secured the confidence of others in his ability to resolve public problems and concerns.

Kerrigan, nominated to the district court by President Calvin Coolidge, was supported by Republican senator Samuel M. Shortridge, of the old school, and Republican governor Friend William Richardson, who promised "sweeping retrenchment" to voters. But not everybody jumped on the Kerrigan bandwagon. The *San Francisco Daily News* protested his appointment, recalling Kerrigan's old association with corrupt boss Abe Ruef. "Judge Kerrigan may have lived down his pro-corporation record. But surely there is a capable judge with a better record whom the nation should reward with a place of honor," the paper opined.

"Both Partridge and Kerrigan considered elevation to the federal district court bench a fitting conclusion to their long careers of labor in the law," wrote Franaszek. "That each secured a place on the federal judiciary was unexpected by knowledgeable court watchers. Both were considered 'compromise' candidates for their appointment to the court."

Kerrigan worked tirelessly to win the nomination in a campaign that even included a letter to Supreme Court justice William H. Taft. "If I am so fortunate as to approach within hailing distance of your ideal as a federal district judge, I would regard it as a favor if you would, if and when consulted, express yourself as favorable to my candidacy," Kerrigan wrote Taft.

Like Partridge, Kerrigan's first charge was to help the district court clear thousands of Prohibition cases. He vowed that bootleggers were no longer going to be able to clog the court calendar. "Count that day lost whose low descending sun sees in my court no bootlegger on the run," he told a newspaper reporter. The judge promised to bring bootleggers who filed guilty pleas to trial within twenty-four hours, a plan the *Chronicle* applauded. Arraignment, plea, trial, triumph, and despair all in one day, the *Chronicle* wrote; "Excellent! Nothing else could do so much to discourage bootleggers. It follows reasonably that nothing else could do so much to discourage burglars, murderers—including the hit-and-run sort—and all other lawbreakers. Extend this rule to other cases and other courts—all cases and all courts. Nothing makes the criminal so sick and dizzy as the whirl of twenty-four-hour justice. And the innocent suffer less."

Kerrigan served on the district court until his death in 1935. Partridge, who was described as having boundless energy, served only three years. In May 1926, he took a vacation but returned early to check into St. Luke's Hospital because of a stomach ailment. An operation revealed that Partridge had an intestinal tumor. He died eight days later at the age of fifty-six.

Reporter Annie Laurie eulogized Partridge as beloved, respected, feared, and trusted. She recalled the day that Partridge himself paid the fine of three Berkeley boys he had found guilty of stealing a car, and the day a juror suddenly went insane in his courtroom. "It hurts a man in a good many ways to have it said that he's insane," the judge lectured reporters. "He may get perfectly well again—let's keep it a secret." Partridge was a man of grace, she wrote. "He'd smile that little, quiet, crooked smile of his to himself, maybe—when young Mr. Just-Called-To-The-Bar made the wrong motion at the wrong time—but he never corrected him publicly or said one word or gave one look to humiliate him."

Most important, Laurie wrote, was the way Partridge treated those in need. "Nobody ever saw a crippled, or an invalid, or a very old man go to jail from Judge Partridge's court—he always found a way out for the underdog," she wrote. Outside his courtroom, she wrote, he would donate to any cause. "What a line of charity seekers there always was at the door of his chambers, and there he'd sit smoking his little old dudheen and signing checks—always signing checks or putting his hand in his pocket and bringing it out with a fist full of silver—he didn't know how to say no when people told him about a lonely child or a sick man, or a forgotten old woman."

Partridge's friend, attorney Warren Gregory, announced the judge's death in the courthouse on May 20, 1926. A short time later, hundreds of attorneys, judges, and friends filled Partidge's courtroom for a memorial. Partridge's sudden death saddened the city. In his years as an attorney, politician, and judge, he had made a remarkable impression. His death was played on the front page of the *Examiner.* Above his photo ran the headline "To Highest Court."

CHAPTER 5

DEPRESSION
AND WAR

WITH HIS STERN DEMEANOR and sage appearance, Adolphus Frederick St. Sure was the face of the district court from Prohibition through the end of World War II. The conservative, white-haired St. Sure was respected, feared, and seldom challenged during his nearly quarter-century tenure.

Born in Sheboygan, Wisconsin, in 1869, a descendant of French voyageurs, St. Sure came to California with his family as an infant. His life was "almost a rags to riches story," wrote one newspaper. St. Sure's father died shortly after the family's arrival in Oroville, north of Sacramento in Butte County, and the young boy quit school at age thirteen to help his mother, who worked in the *Oroville Mercury* office. He swept floors, delivered newspapers, and served as an errand boy at first. Eventually, he worked his way up to print shop foreman and reporter. Tired of small-town life, St. Sure moved to Alameda at age twenty-one and took a job as the Alameda city correspondent for the *San Francisco Call* and later the *San Francisco Examiner.* In 1892, St. Sure ran for Justice of the Peace as a Democrat. He lost but was appointed the next year as the Alameda city recorder. To better understand his job, St. Sure started studying law and was admitted to the bar in 1895. For the next twenty-eight years, he practiced law in San Francisco and Oakland and continued his political career, serving as the Alameda city attorney from 1910 to 1917, as a judge in the Alameda County Superior Court from 1917 to 1922, and as an associate justice in the First District of the California Court of Appeals in 1923. During those years, he switched his political allegiance from the Democrats to the Republicans but remained a rock-ribbed conservative.

St. Sure was supported in his bid for the district court bench by California senator Samuel Shortridge, payback for the backing St. Sure gave

FIG. 5-1 (PREVIOUS PAGE)
John Paul Chase (right), an accomplice of Baby Face Nelson, is escorted by federal agents to a cell in Chicago. Chase was tried and convicted for the murder of a Justice Department agent and sentenced to life in prison on Alcratraz Island in 1935. © Bettmann/Corbis.

Shortridge during his 1920 election campaign. St. Sure convinced his close friend, and *Oakland Tribune* publisher, Joseph R. Knowland to help Shortridge's candidacy despite a long-simmering dispute between the two men. But St. Sure's nomination was delayed by efforts to push Mabel Walker Willebrandt, assistant US attorney general, to be the first woman on the federal bench. Willebrandt, a high-profile Justice Department attorney who specialized in the enforcement of Prohibition, met with President Coolidge in early January 1925 to discuss the judgeship. She was followed by Shortridge, who lobbied for St. Sure. On January 19, the *New York Times* reported that opponents of Mrs. Willebrandt had rallied. "Decision almost had been reached a week ago by President Coolidge and Attorney General [Harlan Fiske] Stone to nominate Mrs. Willebrandt to the vacant judgeship in the Northern District of California, but vigorous protest against such action by Senator Shortridge and several other members of Congress from California has caused a revision of plans."

Lady in Waiting

Mabel Walker Willebrandt, who was considered for a district court judgeship in 1925, wrote a highly critical letter about potential candidates to her boss, Attorney General Harlan Fiske Stone. Willebrandt, who was an assistant attorney general, wrote that she heard that the nomination of candidate Walter Perry Johnson was forwarded by Ku Klux Klan agents, and that Judge Frank Kerrigan, appointed the previous year, "has neither the ability nor the inclination to discharge the heavy and responsible duties of the office."

Willebrandt's letter is in the National Archives and Records Administration in College Park, Maryland, along with dozens of letters in support of and opposition to her failed candidacies in 1925 and 1927. San Francisco attorney John P. Beale wrote, "The writer wishes to recommend to you for this appointment, Mabel Walker Willebrandt, a woman who stands supreme throughout the West as a leading member of the bar of her sex."

Florence Ellinwood Allen was the first female federal judge, nominated by Franklin Roosevelt to the Circuit Court of Appeals for the Sixth Circuit in 1934. Burnita Shelton Matthews was the first female district court judge, appointed by Harry S. Truman to serve on the District of Columbia Court in 1949.

Shortridge and others publicly protested that Willebrandt was a Los Angeles resident. Privately, the issue concerned her gender. Coolidge nominated St. Sure on February 16, 1925, but his appointment was held up due to opposition from the powerful Anti-Saloon League, which considered St. Sure too liberal on Prohibition. When league officials confronted St. Sure with reports of his drinking at public functions, St. Sure demanded to face his accusers. "Thus was produced the extraordinary spectacle of an eminent jurist considering it necessary to appear before the Anti-Saloon League to defend himself and clear the way for his appointment to the federal bench," wrote the *Examiner.* When his accusers refused to confront St. Sure, the league withdrew its opposition. It was reported that St. Sure signed a pledge promising to abstain from drinking and to uphold the National Prohibition Act, but St. Sure denied he had signed any document. He did say that he had made a mental pledge to stay off liquor. He denied that he had promised to show no mercy for liquor violators, but said, "I don't see, however, if they are proven guilty why they shouldn't be given the limit."

St. Sure, who filled the seat vacated by Maurice Dooling's death, was confirmed by the Senate seven days after Coolidge nominated him in 1925 and received his commission the same day. After a subdued ceremony, he spent most of his first day with fellow judges Frank Kerrigan and John Partridge. At first, St. Sure heard only Prohibition cases, but he soon took on the full spectrum of district court work. During his twenty-four years on the bench, St. Sure was known for seldom showing mercy. "He was a crusty old so-and-so," recalled district court judge William Orrick, who appeared before St. Sure as an attorney. "He was the one who, for no matter what you did—steal a postage stamp, anything—he would put up his hand and say, 'Five years.'" After St. Sure's death, a reporter wrote, "The white-haired jurist was a stern disciplinarian in his courtroom, scolding and admonishing attorneys for dawdling and quibbling when necessary, smiling at them when a jest was courteously but cautiously offered."

Because of his severe nature, St. Sure's acts of kindness were striking. The judge cried and released a defendant when the man confessed he smuggled thirty dollars' worth of opium to support his wife and four children. St. Sure gave probation to a nineteen-year-old boy facing check kiting charges, saying, "I feel that this boy has never had a chance, and that this court would not be dealing justice should it sentence him on this charge and make him a 'two-time loser' before he reaches his majority." And in 1933, he gave twenty-two-year-old James J. Walsh a second chance after he was accused of trying to rob a post office. Walsh, who had spent his life bouncing among reform schools, jails, and prisons, expected at least a two-year prison term.

"From now on, James J. Walsh is officially dead," St. Sure told the man. "His past is dead. He is legally entitled to assume a new name and start anew."

Walsh didn't understand.

"You have said that it is hard to lead a crooked life," St. Sure told Walsh. "You'll find it easier to live straight."

When Walsh reported to his probation officer, he was given a new suit, shirt, socks, and a job.

"Tell the judge that I'll make good for him," Walsh told the probation officer. He never appeared in court again.

St. Sure had admirers and detractors. "He was a man of great stature in my opinion and carried the court almost single-handed for years," said George Harris, who served with St. Sure on the federal bench during St. Sure's final years. "Even when he was critically ill, he was hearing cases. He was quite an inspiration for many of the young lawyers." Attorney John Hays, who argued cases before St. Sure for decades, was not so kind. "He was a crusty individual and one had to be careful appearing before him not to suffer his impatience," Hays wrote.

The Federal Bureau of Investigation noted in 1939 that St. Sure was still industrious and still handled a large amount of litigation at age seventy. "He is, however, somewhat testy and gets out of patience with the attorneys appearing before him, which may be accounted for by his age," wrote Special Agent in Charge N. J. L. Pieper. "He may not be as alert physically and mentally as the two other judges in this district but he is not slow in making decisions or grasping situations." Despite St. Sure's cantankerous reputation, Pieper rated him as a model of fairness and consistency: "It is the general opinion that Judge St. Sure could not be influenced in administering his sworn duties by reason of his friendship or acquaintance with attorneys or others, or by reason of his political affiliation."

St. Sure made national news in the 1930s when he accepted guilty pleas from Jack Perkins and Joseph "Fatso" Negri, two members of Baby Face Nelson's gang. Nelson, born Lester M. Gillis, was a prime suspect in three bank robberies and the shooting deaths of at least five law enforcement officials. In 1932, Nelson escaped from an Illinois prison and fled to Sausalito, where he met John Paul Chase, who would become his accomplice. Nelson and Chase returned to the Midwest in 1933 to join John Dillinger's gang, but escaped to California again after Dillinger was shot to death while leaving Chicago's Biograph Theatre in the summer of 1934. Nelson was shot and killed in a gun battle near Chicago in November of the same year. Chase was eventually convicted in federal court in Illinois of the murder of a Justice Department inspector and sentenced to life in prison on Alcatraz Island.

Back in California, seventeen people were indicted for harboring Nelson on his West Coast trips. Four were found guilty in a jury trial conducted by a temporary district court judge. St. Sure later released Nelson's twenty-two-year-old widow, Helen Gillis, on a year's probation after she helped the government gather information against the former gang. "All I want is to have a chance," she told St. Sure. "I know I can make good and I want to go to work right away."

St. Sure made national news again in the 1940s when he consistently checked the federal Office of Price Administration. The OPA was established in 1942 to stabilize prices and stop inflation during the war, but its policies rankled the conservative judge. In 1943, St. Sure criticized the OPA for charging San Francisco's Union Pacific Restaurant with violating price ceilings. He read the indictment aloud in court and stopped when he read the charges that the restaurant raised the price of eggs from thirty-five to forty cents.

The Impeachment Trial

The district court judge who made the boldest headlines during the era between the two world wars was Harold Louderback, who became only the eleventh person in US history to be served with articles of impeachment. Like St. Sure, Louderback was backed by Senator Shortridge in his bid for the district court judgeship. Born and raised in San Francisco, Louderback came from a family of privilege. His mother, Frances Caroline Smith Louderback, was a California pioneer. His father, Davis Louderback, a forty-niner, was an attorney who served eight years as a San Francisco Police Court judge. An 1892 biography of Davis noted that "Judge Louderback made an honorable record on the bench, and won

FIG. 5-2
Harold Louderback (1881–1941) was the eighth Northern District judge and the only one to be impeached by Congress. Reproduced courtesy of US District Court for the Northern District of California.

the applause of all good citizens by his fearless manner in the punishment of hoodlumism."

Louderback received a bachelor's degree from the University of Nevada in 1905 and a law degree from Harvard Law School in 1908. He worked as an attorney in private practice in San Francisco from 1908 to 1917, then served as a captain in the army during World War I. He returned to private practice in 1919 and served as a judge in superior court from 1921 to 1928. While there he presided over the trials of movie star Roscoe "Fatty" Arbuckle, who stood accused of manslaughter in the 1921 death of starlet Virginia Rappe. Arbuckle's first two trials ended with deadlocked juries. After the third trial, a jury took only six minutes to acquit the star.

President Coolidge nominated Louderback—with the endorsement of Supreme Court justice William Howard Taft and California governor James Rolph Jr.—to the seat vacated by John Partridge in 1928. The new judge took the oath of office in a twenty-minute ceremony. "Let me bring an unbiased mind to the consideration of all problems," Louderback said, "and then have the courage to take the old, well-beaten path or break the untrodden trail. Give me the manliness that apologizes, the humanity that learns, and the honor that begets confidence."

What Louderback needed most during his first seven years on the court was not humility but a courtroom of his own. The district and appeals courts were expanding, and the building lacked space for additional full-fledged courtrooms until a new Mission Street wing was constructed, so Louderback was given a small, temporary courtroom. That space affected the judge, as attorney Harold Faulkner would recall decades later:

> Now, unlike Judge Kerrigan, who commanded respect the minute he sat on the bench, Judge Louderback had a different view. He felt that decorum, respect and all that should be pounded into the heads of the lawyers before him by the United States marshal. And he made it very difficult.
>
> Now his difficulties were often due to the fact that instead of having a spacious courtroom, he had a little cubby hole, you might say, and he was holding a dignified court in a very bad atmosphere with the noise of the street, the compactness of the room and all of those physical inconveniences.

When the new courtroom finally opened in 1934—with no furniture—one newspaper headlined its article with "Louderback Court In Good Standing."

But by then, he had made many enemies. Louderback's troubles started in April 1932, when the *San Francisco News* ran a series of exposés about the judge's curious appointments of friends and associates as attorneys and receivers in bankruptcy cases. (A receiver takes custody of a bankrupt business while it reorganizes its debts or liquidates its assets.) Soon after, a special subcommittee of the House Judiciary Committee was appointed to examine whether Louderback showed favoritism in appointing Samuel Shortridge Jr., son of the senator, and others to paid positions on bankruptcy cases before his court. The federal inquiry was initiated by Representative Fiorello H. LaGuardia, a reform-minded Republican from New York who had led House fights against four other federal judges. LaGuardia and two other congressmen met in September 1932 in San Francisco and recommended that the Judiciary Committee hold hearings on Louderback's conduct. In early 1933, Louderback was called to a closed-door session in Washington, DC, where he declared that he had not made any financial profit from the nineteen receiverships that had come before him.

After long argument, the Judiciary Committee voted to stop short of calling for Louderback's impeachment. In early 1933, in a report to the

House, the majority wrote, "The committee censures the judge for conduct prejudicial to the dignity of the judiciary in appointing incompetent receivers, for the method of selecting receivers, for allowing fees that seem excessive, and for a high degree of indifference to the interests of litigants in receiverships."

But LaGuardia, in a minority opinion, pressed for impeachment. Ten days later, he and Representative Hatton Sumners, the committee chairman, convinced the House to impeach Louderback of high crimes and misdemeanors. "Disregard of the interests of litigants, the granting of excessive fees, and practices involving favoritism by a federal judge constitute a high crime," argued Sumners. "Whenever a federal judge, holding his position for life, violates the ideals of judicial integrity it is time the House granted the people relief."

After a stormy debate in the House, the vote—183 to 142 to impeach—came as a surprise. Congress sent five articles of impeachment to the Senate accusing Louderback of "tyranny and oppression, favoritism and conspiracy." The articles claimed that Louderback "has brought the administration of justice in said district in the court of which he is a judge into disrepute, and by his conduct is guilty of misbehavior, falling under the constitutional provision as grounds for impeachment and removal from office."

The five articles—detailed allegations charging Louderback with hiring receivers and attorneys for "large and exorbitant fees," or hiring "incompetent, unqualified, and inexperienced" receivers—were based on bankruptcy cases in the early 1930s. They paint a strange picture of a man who left his wife to live in the Fairmont Hotel, and who depended on the advice of a mysterious friend, W. S. "Sam" Leake, a faith healer. Leake apparently suggested many of the receivers and attorneys who were hired in Louderback's bankruptcy court. In return, Leake may have received kickbacks. Louderback denied every substantial allegation in the impeachment articles and responded that they did not constitute an impeachable high crime and misdemeanor.

The Senate impeachment trial began on May 15, 1933. "Judge Louderback wore a blue suit, and sat almost rigid during the whole afternoon," the *New York Times* reported. "His eyes were hollow and underlined, his face pale, and the muscles of his jaw twitched nervously." House prosecutors outlined the case against Louderback for three hours, detailing the charges against the man they called an "unfit public servant." The prosecution called nineteen witnesses to the Senate chamber over the next three days. Louderback's attorneys countered with twenty-one witnesses over five days, including Leake, who had resisted appearing before the Senate. Leake, who claimed to be ill, was clad in pajamas as he was carried into the Senate chamber on a stretcher. From a reclining chair, Leake told the senators that he had taken "not one cent" in fees paid to receivers and attorneys in Louderback's court. He said he advised Louderback on appointments because the judge trusted him. But Leake admitted that he received more than $1,000 from the Shortridge family for favors he had performed for Senator Shortridge's wife.

Louderback then took the stand and once and for all told the Senate that he did not profit from fees handed out to receivers and their attorneys in his five years on the court. He said he appointed competent receivers and appointed the younger Shortridge only after litigants in two cases requested the appointment of the senator's son in writing.

The juiciest part of Louderback's testimony concerned his strange living arrangement, which remains mysterious to this day. Louderback testified that "due to certain domestic difficulties" he took a cheap room in the bachelors' section of the Fairmont. When it appeared that Louderback's separation with his wife would become permanent, the judge said he asked his brother, who lived in Contra Costa County, if he could live with him and the brother's wife. The couple welcomed Louderback. He moved his belongings to the new house and immediately registered to vote in Contra Costa County. But on his first night sleeping there, Louderback said he suffered a severe attack of asthma and returned to the Fairmont.

The representatives, who serve as prosecutors in Senate impeachment trials, thought the story strange. They badgered Louderback about his personal habits, which may have been based on reports that he had been seen around San Francisco with another married woman. The Senate trial turned into a morals court when Louderback took the stand.

"Where do you live?" Hatton Sumners asked the judge.

"I live at 107—if you mean by living that that is my residence—107 Ardmore Road, Kensington district, Contra Costa County, California."

"Where do you reside, to draw a distinction between where you live and where you reside?"

"If you mean where I sleep, I sleep frequently at the Fairmont Hotel."

"When you are not sleeping at your brother's home and not sleeping at the Fairmont Hotel, except in those instances where you go away on vacation or hold court out of San Francisco, where do you sleep?"

"I have no regular place of sleeping except the Fairmont Hotel in San Francisco."

"I am not talking about a regular place of sleeping. I want to know where do you sleep?"

"I do not know what you mean."

"I mean, when you go to sleep, when you shut your eyes or snore or something?"

"I have slept at the Hotel Fairmont and I do not know anything else you refer to."

After Louderback testified that he only paid rent at the Fairmont Hotel, Representative Randolph Perkins asked Louderback, "You do not pay rent at your brother's home because as a matter of honest-to-goodness fact you do not live over there, do you?"

"That is not true," replied Louderback. "If you mean by living over there that that is my domicile or my home."

"You have stayed there four nights in about three or four years, have you not?"

"Everything I have stated here regarding my presence there is true."

"Do you go there any more frequently now than you used to?"

"I go there once or twice a week on an average right straight along. It is necessary for me to do because I have to go there, for instance, if I'm going to use a tuxedo. My tuxedo is over there. If I wish to go away on a trip or in the summer, all my clothes are over there."

"Why don't you keep your tuxedo where you live? It would be handier, would it not?"

"The reason why I keep my property there is because I look upon it as my home and I have always hoped that I would be able to go over there and not have asthma."

Later, Perkins asked, "As a judge passing on the question, would you hold it to be the home of a person who could not live at that place?"

Louderback replied, "I understand residence once acquired remains with the person who acquires it until he acquires a new residence."

At the end of this cat-and-mouse game, the House managers conducting the prosecution called for impeachment. "The irrefutable facts of the record brand the respondent as a man totally destitute of the essential elements of judicial character and as a man that those people of a sovereign State and a sovereign district should be relieved of," Representative Gordon Browning told the senators. "It is only a political right we are asking you to take away from him. I insist that under the circumstances of this record it would be unfair to let him sit in judgment over a people that have brought these circumstances and these facts to you and laid them on your conscience to determine whether they shall be afflicted by an individual or whether they have a right to have someone administer justice in their courts of equity, their courts of bankruptcy, their courts of justice, about whom there is no suspicion and in whom they have confidence."

After the final speech, the senators met in an executive session and returned to vote on each of the five articles of impeachment. Louderback was found not guilty of the first four articles by a majority of the senators. Forty-five senators found Louderback guilty of the fifth article, a summary of all the charges, and thirty-four found him not guilty, but the roll call fell eight votes short of the two-thirds plurality needed to convict the judge. "I feel that it is a vindication," he told newspaper reporters.

Remarkably, Louderback recovered much of his prestige following the vote. He stopped at Chicago's Century of Progress exposition on his trip back to San Francisco, and when he returned to the courthouse on June 5, he was bathed in applause as he took the bench. About one hundred attorneys were there to greet him. Attorney M. M. Bourquin extended congratulations, and then attorney Ernest J. Torregano declared him "a martyr to the cause of independence and integrity in the judiciary." Louderback thanked everybody, adjourned court, and stepped from the bench. "This has changed from a session of the court to a reception," he said. "I am not going to say any more about the trial. You as lawyers have followed it or can read it in the *Congressional Record*. This has been a severe experience to me, regardless of the result. No matter what we feel or do, or how we justify ourselves, we want others to believe in us and have a kindly feeling."

Louderback continued on the court without further incident until his death in 1941. Because of his asthma, he preferred sitting in Sacramento, where the climate was generally drier than in San Francisco. In 1935, Louderback ruled that the owners of the British steamship freighter *Silver Palm* were as much responsible as the ship's skipper for the ship's 1933 collision with the cruiser USS *Chicago* in heavy fog off Point Sur. (The Court of Appeals reversed Louderback, and placed much of the blame on the navy.) In 1936, Louderback ruled that the Market Street Railway Company could operate one-man streetcars, contrary to a 1918 city law forbidding it. The decision came after the company president said the railroad would go bankrupt unless it could reduce labor costs because it was not allowed to increase the five-cent fare. (This case was also reversed by the court of appeals.) Federal officials continued to keep a close watch on Louderback. In 1939, Special Agent Pieper wrote to FBI director J. Edgar Hoover, "There appears to be an occasional rumble that comes to me which indicates that possibly Judge Louderback associates with the wrong kind of people, but nothing has ever come to my attention that would indicate he is dishonest or that any of the cases in his court have resulted in injustice because of any connections."

Thomas Mooney's Day in Court

On May 18, 1933, the fourth day of Judge Louderback's impeachment trial, San Francisco's most celebrated criminal, Thomas F. Mooney, was moved from San Quentin State Prison to San Francisco County Jail. Mooney was transferred so that he could go to trial, at his own request, on a World War I–era murder conviction. Louderback, when he sat on the superior court, was the last judge that Mooney had appeared before. Louderback had denied Mooney's request for a new hearing.

"Well, I see Judge Louderback and I are going to trial at the same time," Mooney told newspaper reporters. "Send him my regards."

Tom Mooney is largely forgotten now, but at one time he was a powerful labor boss and worldwide cause célèbre. He was convicted of the July 22, 1916, bombing of the Preparedness Day Parade, which killed ten onlookers and injured forty more on Steuart Street near Market Street. Prosecutors charged Mooney and his associates with carrying a suitcase bomb to the occasion. "The sixteen years Thomas J. Mooney has spent behind the walls of San Quentin Prison, overlooking the gray water of San Francisco Bay, have witnessed the writing of probably the longest and most bitter fight of any man in the United States to prove his innocence," wrote the Associated Press in 1933.

Mooney, a committed socialist, was the perfect suspect. He had previously been tried (and acquitted) of using explosives, and he was a vocal opponent to the United States' participation in the Great War. Five days after the explosion, Mooney, his wife Rena, assistant Warren K. Billings, and two other labor activists were charged with the murders. Billings was the first to be tried. He was convicted of second-degree murder in state court and given a life sentence.

At Mooney's trial, which began in California Superior Court in early 1917, several witnesses responding to a $5,000 reward came forth and claimed they saw Mooney and his associates drive down Market Street in a jitney. Witnesses said they saw Billings plant the bomb at 1:50 p.m. near the Ferry Building, just south of Market Street. Their testimony was contradicted by a photograph showing Mooney and associates watching the parade from the rooftop of a building far from the bombsite at about two o'clock. Three store clocks visible in the photo showed 1:58 p.m., 2:02 p.m., and 2:04 p.m. But the photograph did not help Mooney's case. The jury convicted him of murder and sentenced him to be hanged.

After the trial, key witnesses against Mooney denied their stories, and other witnesses were found to be lying. Letters published in the *Bulletin* indicated that the key prosecution witness was not even in San Francisco on the day of the parade. Three weeks before Mooney was scheduled to be executed, President Wilson asked California governor W. D. Stephens to reexamine the case. The governor commuted Mooney's sentence to life in prison. Mooney continued to fight for release in state and federal courts, but to no avail. He gathered a long list of supporters, which included George Bernard Shaw, John Dewey, Upton Sinclair, Theodore Dreiser, Sinclair Lewis, Sherwood Anderson, Carl Sandburg, six of his jurors, and even his trial judge, Franklin Griffin, who suggested that Mooney be pardoned. By the mid-1930s, Thomas Mooney was one of the best-known Americans in the world, ranking with Franklin Roosevelt, Charles Lindbergh, and Henry Ford.

Mooney presented a writ of habeas corpus petition to the district court in 1934, arguing that he was unlawfully imprisoned because his conviction in state court was obtained solely by perjured testimony. Mooney and his lawyers submitted a ninety-five-page brief and six hundred pages of exhibits. Judge St. Sure could have released Mooney, but he dismissed the writ, stating that Mooney had not exhausted his legal remedies in the state court, and that Mooney should instead apply to the California Supreme Court. If he failed there, he should take the case to the US Supreme Court. Later that year, St. Sure denied Mooney's second writ. "Clearly the petitioner has not exhausted all remedies available in the state courts," the judge wrote. State courts, he stated, are "as much bound as federal courts to see no man is punished in violation of the Constitution or laws of the United States."

Mooney was released from prison in 1939 after being pardoned by Governor Culbert Olson, who promised the pardon during his election

FIG. 5-3
In 1939, after serving twenty-two years in San Quentin Prison, Thomas F. Mooney was pardoned by Governor Culbert Olson for his role in the 1916 Preparedness Day bomb murders. Following his release, Mooney greeted supporters as he walked in a parade up San Francisco's Market Street from the Embarcadero to the Civic Center. Courtesy of the California Historical Society, FN-22611/CHS2013.1140.

campaign. Billings was released that year, too, but was not pardoned until 1961. Mooney came home a haggard old man. "These twenty-two long years have been moth-eaten," Rena said when her husband returned. "Life to me has been something like a cloak. There is little left but the tatters."

Mooney had hoped to resume his career as a labor leader, but he spent most of the next few years in the hospital. He died at age fifty-eight in 1942.

FDR's Men

Michael Joseph Roche was the first of three district court judges nominated by President Franklin Roosevelt. He was also the first district court judge to be a card-carrying union member, and he maintained a loyalty to labor during his two decades on the court. "Michael J. Roche came out of the loins of the labor unions," said district court judge George Harris. Actually, Roche came out of Ireland. Born in County Waterford in 1878,

Roche immigrated with his family to the United States in 1884. He grew up in the Midwest, primarily in Rock Island, Illinois, where he worked in foundries as an apprentice iron molder. He moved to San Francisco at the turn of the twentieth century and took a job in the Iron Molders' Union. He returned to the Midwest to earn his law degree from Valparaiso University School of Law in Indiana, and continued to support himself by working as a molder.

After graduating in 1908, Roche returned to San Francisco and took a job as an assistant district attorney. He began his political career as a Republican but soon switched to the Democratic Party. He served as a judge on the Municipal Court of San Francisco (then called the Justice Court) from 1910 to 1914, and as a judge in the superior court from 1918 to 1935, where he developed a reputation for old-school directness. In 1933, as a judge in divorce court, Roche declared, "A man who would stay home and cook for his wife is whipped." Roche told the *San Francisco News,* "Our real need is to get back to simple things. A wife should cook for her husband. If she refuses, in spite of the fact that he is doing the providing, then I think he is entitled to a divorce."

Directness aside, during those years, Roche was also called the jovial judge. A 1934 profile in the *San Francisco News* portrayed him as a man of the soil. "Clad in faded blue jumpers and a broad sombrero, superior court judge Michael J. Roche likes to tread through the acres of his peach ranch at Gridley, California, engaging in simple agrarian tasks. That is his hobby. Seeing growing trees thrills him, and as for driving a team of horses—it's more fascinating than flying an airplane. Milking cows, feeding chickens, and churning butter bring him contentment."

When Roche was nominated to the district court in 1935, the appointment received rave reviews. "The selection of Judge Roche was in the nature of a surprise to many outsiders," one newspaper wrote, "but is a tribute to a member of the San Francisco bench who has long served the people of San Francisco." The nomination, according to the paper, was primarily due to the support of Roche's close friend, Republican senator Hiram W. Johnson.

In 1938, Roche ruled that San Francisco could no longer sell the power it produced from the Hetch Hetchy Valley to the Pacific Gas and Electric Company. He determined that the city's contract with PG&E violated the Raker Act, which had permitted the building of the O'Shaughnessy Dam and the flooding of the Hetch Hetchy Valley in Yosemite National Park. The act banned the sale of any water or electric energy to a corporation for resale. San Francisco had been selling its electricity from Hetch Hetchy wholesale to PG&E, which then resold it at a profit.

Construction of the Hetch Hetchy water and power system was approved by Congress and President Woodrow Wilson in 1913 after years of debate and opposition by such environmentalists as John Muir. His declaration—"Dam Hetch Hetchy! As well dam for water tanks the people's cathedrals and churches, for no holier temple has ever been consecrated by the heart of man!"—became a rallying cry for the Sierra Club, which he founded. But Muir lost his battle. The Raker Act granted the city the right to build reservoirs to trap fresh mountain water from the Tuolumne River in the Hetch Hetchy Valley, about twenty miles northwest of the Yosemite Valley. Dams, reservoirs, hydroelectric stations, and aqueducts were built to supply drinking water and power to San Francisco and surrounding communities. The water was piped more than 150 miles from the Sierra to San Francisco, and the power was transmitted along power lines. In 1923, the city signed a contract to sell electricity generated from its hydroelectric powerhouse to PG&E. Although the deal violated the Raker Act, the city argued it was only temporary, until San Francisco finished building transmission lines and a distribution system. When San Francisco failed to pass bond issues to complete its distribution system, the city continued to sell its electricity to PG&E. In 1935, Secretary of the Interior Harold Ickes demanded the city establish its own municipal power system and stop selling electricity to PG&E. Roche agreed and gave San Francisco officials six months to figure out how the city could distribute its own power.

PG&E officials appealed Roche's decision. The Court of Appeals reversed his decision in 1939, saying that city leaders had no choice but to sell power because voters kept rejecting bond issues to build distribution facilities. The following year, the Supreme Court sided with Roche. Justice Hugo Black, in the official opinion of the court, wrote, "Congress clearly intended to require—as a condition of its grant—sale and distribution of Hetch Hetchy power exclusively by San Francisco and municipal agencies directly to consumers in the belief that consumers would thus be afforded power at cheap rates in competition with private power companies, particularly Pacific Gas and Electric." After several months of delay, the start of World War II put the contract dispute on hold. The debate continues today.

In 1941, Roche sent Alcatraz inmate Henri Young back to prison after he appeared in court, accused of murdering fellow convict Rufus

McCain, who had joined Young in a failed prison break two years earlier. The case against Young shed the first light on brutal conditions at "The Rock," and was one of the cases that led to the eventual closing of Alcatraz two decades later.

At the first hearing, Roche asked Young if he could afford an attorney. The defendant said no and then made an unusual request. "I should like to have the court appoint two youthful attorneys of no established

---

John Muir on Hetch Hetchy

John Muir, president of the Sierra Club, delivered this statement to the American Civic Association in 1908.

> At present the San Francisco board of supervisors and certain monopolizing capitalists are trying to get the Government's permission to dam and destroy Hetch Hetchy, the Tuolumne, Yosemite Valley, for a reservoir, simply that comparatively private gain may be made out of universal public loss.
>
> Should this wonderful valley be submerged as proposed, not only would it be made utterly inaccessible, but the sublime Tuolumne Canyon way to the heart of the high Sierra would be hopelessly closed. None, as far as I have learned, of the thousands who have visited the park, is in favor of this destructive and wholly unnecessary water scheme. Very few of the statements made by the applicants are even partly true.
>
> Thus, Hetch Hetchy, they say, is "a low-lying meadow." On the contrary, it is a high-lying natural landscape garden. "It is a common minor feature, like thousands of others." On the contrary, it is a very uncommon feature, and after Yosemite, the rarest, most beautiful, and in many ways the most important feature of the park. "Damming it would enhance its beauty." As well say damming New York's Central Park would enhance its beauty. "Hetch Hetchy water is the purest and the only available source of supply for San Francisco." It is not the purest, because it drains a pleasure ground visited by hundreds of campers with their animals every season, and soon these hundreds will be thousands. And there are many other adequate and available sources of supply, though probably they would be somewhat more costly; and so with all their bad, cunning arguments, boldly advanced under the general ignorance of the subject.

---

reputation for verdicts or hung juries," Young told the judge. "I want no attorney who has a reputation in San Francisco for receiving verdicts." Roche agreed to Young's request and appointed Sol Abrams and James M. MacInnis. They took up Young's cause in earnest, visiting him at Alcatraz and framing his defense around an argument that Young's act was not premeditated but was an impulsive reaction against a homosexual advance that McCain had made on Young, and that it was a response to inhumane conditions at Alcatraz. The defense lawyers subpoenaed warden James A. Johnston and called a number of inmates who spoke of beatings, straitjackets, and dungeons.

Young took the stand himself, telling the jury that because he refused to work in the prison laundry, he was stripped of his clothes by guards and placed in a six-by-nine solitary confinement cell with no bed and no other furniture. "It was like stepping into a sewer because of the bad plumbing," he said. After getting back his clothes, but not shoes, Young said he spent thirteen days in "the icebox," where he wavered on unconsciousness. "There is an old-type ventilator in the wall, open to the winds of the Golden Gate. I shivered all the time," he said. "I was in my stocking feet on concrete. At times I would get in a corner and put my coveralls around my head to keep warm. Then I would move them down around me." While there, Young said he had nightmares about McCain making sexual advances on him. When McCain did later insult him, Young said he snapped—knifing McCain to death during a state of unconsciousness. Young's attorneys argued that prison conditions drove their client insane.

The jury declared Young guilty of only manslaughter, not murder, and produced a document denouncing the prison. Foreman Paul Verdier read a statement that declared, "It is my duty to inform you on behalf of the jurors…that it is our added finding that conditions as concern treatment of prisoners at Alcatraz are unbelievably brutal and inhuman, and it is our respectful hope and our earnest petition that a proper and speedy investigation of Alcatraz be made so that justice and humanity may be served."

Roche was not so moved. He sentenced Young to the maximum for manslaughter: three years, to be tacked on to the end of his existing sentence. Roche also praised Warden Johnston's work. "So far as I know, the only mistake he ever made was in removing you from isolation, letting you go to the prison workshop, where you had the chance to…plan a cold-blooded, deliberate murder," the judge told Young. "You took a man's life without provocation. I've sentenced men to the gallows for far less."

One reporter wrote that "Young entered the courtroom with his lips wreathed in the same confident smirk that has characterized him throughout the murder trial. But the smirk had vanished utterly when he was finally hustled out of the courtroom, bound back to Alcatraz, branded in Judge Roche's scathing words as a 'cold blooded murderer.'" The incident and trial loosely served as the basis of the 1995 film *Murder in the First*, starring Kevin Bacon as Henri Young.

In 1938, the district court expanded to four judges after Congress passed a bill to provide for the appointment of a judge "whose official residence shall be Sacramento." Since 1933, the district court had been holding its annual Sacramento sessions in a large courtroom built on the fourth floor of the new classical-style United States Post Office, Courthouse, and Federal Building, which opened at 801 I Street. A year after signing the bill, President Roosevelt nominated Sacramento resident Martin Ignatius Welsh to the bench. Welsh, a life-long Democrat, was a logical choice because he had worked to lobby for the new judgeship, had worked in Sacramento as the US Commissioner for the district court, and had served as the mayor of Sacramento. Welsh became the last district court judge to be admitted to the bar by reading the law. Born in San Jose in 1882, he attended public schools and St. Vincent's

Mystery Court

In a 1989 oral history, admiralty lawyer John Hays looked back at the court during the early 1930s. The court was steeped in tradition during those years, and was a mysterious place, Hays recalled: "After a vessel had been seized in rem, at the appropriate time, usually on Mondays, which was sort of the 'law and motion' day in those days, you would show up and ask the clerk to read the proclamation. And he would get up and read in open court a formal archaic document which said that the vessel had been seized and that anybody who had an interest in her was given a certain date to file an answer or appear or be defaulted. I can remember that the reading of the proclamation regularly dumbfounded the civil lawyers that were in the courtroom at the time—they couldn't figure out what in the world was going on."

College in Cape Girardeau, Missouri, and started law school at Stanford University, but his legal education ended abruptly when his father, Garrett Welsh, died. Young Martin returned to San Jose, married Marie Eubanks, and started to make a living as a plumber. He resumed learning the law by reading law books borrowed from the California State Library. Years later, Welsh proudly recounted his days toting around law books and plumbing tools.

After joining the bar in 1912, Welsh started in private practice and climbed the legal ladder with breathtaking speed. In 1914, he took three successive jobs: Sacramento deputy district attorney, Sacramento County Superior Court judge, and commissioner. He stayed in the last post through 1919, when he returned to private practice. Welsh served as city councilman in Sacramento in 1928 and as the mayor in 1928 and 1929. He ran for lieutenant governor of California in 1930 on a Democratic anti-Prohibition platform, but was defeated. He was rewarded by being appointed once again to the superior court, where he served until his nomination to the district court bench eight years later.

Because the caseload in Sacramento was not busy enough to keep him occupied full time, Welsh often traveled to San Francisco to hear cases. In 1943, Welsh ruled against Harry Renton Bridges when Bridges filed a habeas corpus petition seeking release from the custody of the Immigration and Naturalization Service. It was the start of more than a decade of litigation against Bridges, the subject of the most intense witch hunt in district court history.

It is difficult to understand the enmity and support that Harry Bridges engendered in the 1930s as the leader of the International Longshoremen's Association. In 1934, he organized the West Coast Longshoremen's Strike, which nearly shut down shipping from the Pacific for eighty-three days and effectively made Bridges an enemy of the state. The Australian-born Bridges, who entered the United States legally in 1920 as a sailor, worked as a longshoreman in the Port of San Francisco and helped establish the militant ILA. The 1934 strike extended from the docks of Seattle to San Diego and led to closed-shop unionization at docks up and down the West Coast. Bridges and the union violently fought every effort to bring in strikebreakers to open the ports, and Bridges led a successful call for a general strike, which lasted for four days in the Bay Area. By defying powerful corporations and the Roosevelt administration, Bridges made a host of enemies, who conspired to curtail his power.

FIG. 5-4
Harry Bridges signs the register at San Quentin, the site of his deportation hearing, on August 25, 1939. Courtesy of the San Francisco History Center, San Francisco Public Library.

Their inaugural attempt came in 1938, when Bridges faced deportation because he was charged with being a member of the Communist Party. Bridges's hearing before the INS was exhaustive. It lasted for eleven weeks and included more than 7,700 pages of testimony and 274 exhibits. The government's evidence against the labor leader was shaky, based almost entirely on Harry Lundeberg, president of the rival Maritime Federation of the Pacific, who testified that Bridges had told him in 1935 that he was a Communist Party member.

Bridges took the stand and denied the charge. He discussed the blacklisting and discrimination that he saw as a young longshoreman, as well as the unsafe conditions at many docks. Men had to congregate every morning at six or seven o'clock on the sidewalks of the waterfront or in front of the Ferry Building with the hope of being picked up for work by straw bosses or gang foremen, he said. "It placed such amount of power in the hands of a petty foreman that he could exploit the men in many ways and did: collect part of their pay on percentage for giving them a job, require that they purchase liquor at this, that, or the other place, and such things as that."

The immigration inspector concluded that Bridges had ended his ties to the Communist Party prior to the start of the deportation hearing, so he dismissed the deportation warrant. To counter the decision, in 1940 Congress passed legislation directed at Bridges that amended deportation laws to include a provision that stated that aliens could be deported if they had been connected to any subversive organization at any time since their arrival in the United States.

Bridges was arrested again and brought before another INS hearing in 1941. This forty-two-day hearing produced 7,500 pages of testimony and 359 exhibits. This time, Bridges was ordered deported after it was determined that he was a member of the Communist Party of the USA and affiliated with the Marine Workers' Industrial Union, both of which were listed as subversive. The Board of Immigration Appeals then reversed the decision and ruled that Bridges could stay in the United States. That decision was reversed again by US Attorney General Francis Biddle, who stepped in and ordered Bridges's deportation.

In September 1942, Judge Welsh presided over Bridges's habeas corpus hearing. Bridges's attorneys argued that Biddle did not have the authority to overrule the appeals board and argued that the second round of deportation hearings constituted double jeopardy. Welsh ruled in 1943 that Biddle's order was made "after a fair hearing on substantial evidence." The judge, who upheld Biddle's deportation order, further wrote that Congress had not acted capriciously in its 1940 amendment to the deportation law.

Welsh's decision was affirmed in the Court of Appeals by a three-to-two vote; the court ruled that double jeopardy only applies to criminal proceedings. In his dissent, Judge William Healy showed sympathy to Bridges: "It is notable that the alien, in one fashion or another, had been under almost continuous investigation for a period of more than five years. Prior to and during the course of the second trial the Service had enlisted the powerful cooperation of the Federal Bureau of Investigation. The country had been scoured for witnesses, every circumstance of Bridges's active life had been subjected to scrutiny, and presumably no stone left unturned which might conceal evidence of the truth of the charges which the alien so flatly denied. The most significant feature of the inquiry, as it seems to me, is the paucity of the evidentiary product as contrasted with the magnitude of the effort expended in producing it."

Healy noted that Bridges openly admitted that he did accept the help of the Communist Party during the strike and had Communists among his associates. "The alien, who was nothing if not a forthright witness, made no effort to minimize or excuse the facts," Healy wrote. "He pointed merely to the reasons impelling his conduct. He would, he said, 'probably do the same thing again.' His concern was not with the opinions of men, but to win the strike."

Bridges prevailed. He won his seven-year fight when the Supreme Court ruled five to three to invalidate Biddle's order. The high court ruled that Bridges's affiliation with the Communist Party was not enough to deport him. "Individuals, like nations, may cooperate in a common cause over a period of months or years though their ultimate aims do not coincide," wrote Associate Justice William O. Douglas. "Alliances for limited objectives are well known. Certainly those who joined forces with Russia to defeat the Nazis may not be said to have made an alliance to spread the cause of communism."

Bridges's victory in the Supreme Court proved only temporary. His legal battles were far from over; he would face two more significant trials in the 1940s and 1950s.

Jury of One's Peers

San Francisco's Gilbert "Pete" Thiel changed the face of juries across the country when he challenged the district court's selection process in 1940. The Supreme Court's 1946 decision on *Thiel v. Southern Pacific Co.*, cited hundreds of times by federal courts, has helped define the way federal juries are chosen. The details of the case are recounted in "A Jury of His Peers," a 1997 paper by John Kelley, a student at the University of California's Hastings College of the Law.

The case is one of the strangest to make its way through the district court to the Supreme Court. Thiel, a twenty-eight-year-old San Francisco salesman, traveled to Reno, Nevada, in early 1940 to marry Billie Belle Brown. Just after the wedding, Thiel suffered something akin to buyer's remorse. He told his bride that he married her only to get back at his

A Woman's Place

In 1939, Judge St. Sure promised to put women on the district court's jury list, something that the California Federation of Women's Clubs had advocated for years. Women served as jurors in most other district courts but were barred from the Northern District Court supposedly because the federal building did not have adequate accommodations. But an annex with women's restrooms, built in 1937, solved that problem. That same year, Adelia C. McCabe became the first female US commissioner—a predecessor position to US magistrate—in the district court.

long-lost love, and confessed that he had no intention of being her husband. Following a drinking binge that lasted several days, Thiel—along with his new wife and a friend—eventually made plans for the return trip to San Francisco. Thiel later argued in his lawsuit that he was in an obvious state of intoxication while he waited for tickets at the Reno station. He said that railroad agents should have noticed his extreme nervousness, paranoia, and depression, and should have either refused to let him board the train or guarded him on the train. A ticket agent did suggest that Thiel and his companions take a private compartment, but the trio did not have enough money, so they purchased coach tickets.

About twenty-five minutes out of the station, near Verdi, Nevada, Thiel suddenly pulled open his train window and somehow managed to jump into the night. Thiel's friend grabbed his coat and held onto him for a minute or so while the train sped through the Nevada countryside at thirty-five miles per hour. Soon, however, Thiel fell out of his grasp and dropped onto the tracks. The moving train crushed him. The train braked, backed up to pick up the severely injured man, and transported him to a hospital in Truckee, California. Once called a hopeless case, Thiel made a remarkable recovery. Doctors had to amputate portions of both of his legs several times to stop the spread of infection, but Thiel left the hospital after eight months, learned to walk on artificial legs, and in time went to work in a factory.

After Thiel returned to San Francisco, he sued the Southern Pacific Company for $250,000, charging them with negligence for accepting him as a passenger despite the railroad agent's knowledge that Thiel was "out of his normal mind." The case originally came before Judge St. Sure, but he reassigned it to visiting judge John Clyde Bowen of the Western District of Washington. At trial in 1942, Thiel's attorney, Allen Spivock, made a motion to disallow the jury panel because it was made up of "mostly business executives or those having the employer's viewpoint." In those days, juries were composed primarily of men on club lists (such as members of the Bohemian or Olympic Clubs), association lists, or public lists. Spivock argued that his client's jury was largely made up of white businessmen who had little sympathy for the common man and who tended to side with big business. He called two attorneys who testified that filing personal injury lawsuits against large corporations had no chance in the district because of the jury selection process. One attorney stated that the typical federal court jury was made up of "all big businessmen, contractors, insurance company executives, practically all of them from California Street or Sansome Street, hardly any of them from the humble walks of life, no laboring people at all." Judge Bowen considered the motion. "I wish both sides to have the opportunity of producing all evidence that they feel is material on the plaintiff's charge that there was discrimination here in the selection of the jurors who were qualified," he said. But the judge denied Spivock's motion, and jury selection began. Once again, Spivock challenged the chosen jurors, charging that six of the twelve jurors were affiliated or connected to Southern Pacific. The challenge was denied. At the end of the trial, it took the jury only ten minutes to side with the railroad.

Thiel lost his appeal before the Ninth Circuit Court of Appeals but won his appeal before the Supreme Court. The court agreed there was an exclusion of a large class of wage earners. "The undisputed evidence in this case demonstrates a failure to abide by the proper rules and principles of jury selection," the court ruled. Associate Justice Frank Murphy, in the majority opinion, wrote:

> Both the clerk of the court and the jury commissioner testified that they deliberately and intentionally excluded from the jury lists all persons who work for a daily wage. They generally used the city directory as the source of names of prospective jurors. In the words of the clerk, "If I see in the directory the name of John Jones and it says he is a longshoreman, I do not put his name in, because I have found by experience that that man will not serve as a juror, and I will not get people who will qualify. The minute that a juror is called into court on a venire and says

he is working for ten dollars a day and cannot afford to work for four, the judge has never made one of those men serve, and so in order to avoid putting names of people in who I know won't become jurors in the court, won't qualify as jurors in this court, I do leave them out.... Where I thought the designation indicated that they were day laborers, I mean they were people who were compensated solely when they were working by the day, I leave them out." The jury commissioner corroborated this testimony, adding that he purposely excluded "all the iron craft, bricklayers, carpenters, and machinists because in the past those men came into court and offered that (financial hardship) as an excuse, and the judge usually let them go." The evidence indicated, however, that laborers who were paid weekly or monthly wages were placed on the jury lists, as well as the wives of daily wage earners.

The Supreme Court sided with Thiel only on the issue of jury selection, and remanded the case to the district court. This time, the court conducted a public drawing of jurors taken from a list of registered voters and telephone directories. Spivock once again challenged the jury selection process, but new judge George Harris denied his motion. Once again, the jury sided with the railroad. Thiel went on to live a fairly normal life, according to Kelley. He divorced his first wife, remarried, and lived until age seventy-eight. "While a number of puzzling questions about the Thiel case remain," Kelley wrote, "at least one answer is clear: Pete Thiel's loss at trial in 1942, and on appeal in 1945, became a catalyst for the implementation of fairer jury selection procedures throughout the country."

World War II

On July 2, 1940, ten months after Nazi Germany invaded Poland, the district court held a large open-air ceremony to publicly celebrate one of its most joyous functions, the swearing in of new US citizens. But with clouds of world tension swirling around the event, Judge St. Sure delivered sobering remarks to the crowd gathered on Treasure Island before asking the 150 foreign-born citizens to give their solemn declaration of citizenship. "There must be no thought in your minds of any divided allegiance," he told the immigrants. "We want no halfhearted American citizens. We demand your whole heart or none."

St. Sure's words, broadcast over the radio, focused on recent events of the world conflict and on the future he foresaw. He said that forces of hate, murder, and greed had been turned loose on the world and declared that these forces must be stopped. "Brute force has extinguished some of the lamps of civilization in Western Europe," the judge said. "These terrible happenings warn us that democracy is in danger. They sharply remind us that this land of ours, this America, may be imperiled; and that we may be called upon to defend the blessings of liberty and equality which we enjoy."

He then laid out a blueprint that foreshadowed the district court's stance during and after the war. "There can be no compromise between the American ideal of human liberty and that brand of barbarism spawned by National Socialism, fascism, or communism, which is bent on debasing liberty and exalting sheer power," St. Sure said. "There is no room in this country for any of these foreign isms, and any person tainted with the doctrines taught by them cannot be loyal to the American ideas."

FIG. 5-5
About eight thousand Bay Area Japanese American citizens and residents lived in temporary housing at the Tanforan Racetrack in San Bruno, California. Here, a woman sweeps out her new lodgings in a remodeled horse stall. Courtesy of The Bancroft Library, University of California, Berkeley.

Even before Pearl Harbor, the US government was making war plans in earnest. The district court oversaw efforts by the government to acquire hundreds of acres of land between Monterey Bay and San Francisco for the war effort in the late 1930s. In 1940, St. Sure approved the condemnation of a small parcel of land near Mussel Rock in San Mateo County after Secretary of War Henry H. Woodring said his department needed it "at the earliest possible time" for harbor fortifications. In 1941, St. Sure okayed the condemnation of 412 acres of land at Point Molate on the tip of the San Pablo Peninsula in Richmond to be used as a naval fuel supply depot. And in 1942, St. Sure signed a declaration giving the navy title to Treasure Island itself. The navy had been leasing the island and portions of nearby Yerba Buena Island since the close of the 1939 Golden Gate International Exposition. Naval Station Treasure Island became a major processing center for military personnel heading to or returning from the Pacific theater.

The only conflict St. Sure oversaw involved his 1941 decision approving the army's appropriation of seventy-two acres of Oakland's waterfront for use as its main Pacific supply depot. St. Sure denied Oakland's attempt to vacate the judgment. Oakland attorneys argued that the government did not have the authority to seize the land, calling the declaration a ruthless, arbitrary, and unconstitutional edict. "This action is destroying the Port of Oakland without even giving the Port of Oakland a chance for its day in court," argued attorney Charles A. Beardsley. St. Sure disagreed and ordered nineteen tenants on the property to leave.

Once the United States entered World War II, the district court's main war function was to pass on the federal government's plan to place Japanese Americans in internment camps. The drumbeat to segregate Japanese aliens and Japanese Americans began within weeks of Pearl Harbor. Roosevelt's top advisers were split on what to do with the Japanese, who were generally viewed with grave suspicion by the white majority. Secretary of War Henry L. Stimson sought their immediate incarceration. Attorney General Biddle, who worried about constitutional issues, and FBI director J. Edgar Hoover thought such extreme measures unnecessary. The debate grew public in January 1942 when Representative Leland Ford of Los Angeles urged that "all Japanese, whether citizens or not, be placed in inland concentration camps" to prevent sabotage, spying, and what he called "fifth column activity." Influential columnists Walter Lippmann and Westbrook Pegler soon took up the call. Lippmann called the Pacific Coast a combat zone, and wrote, "Nobody's constitutional rights include the right to reside and do business on a battlefield." Pegler wrote, "The Japanese in California should be under armed guard to the last man and woman right now and to hell with habeas corpus until the danger is over."

On February 19, 1942, only ten weeks after the bombing of Pearl Harbor, President Roosevelt issued Executive Order Number 9066, which gave military commanders the right to prescribe areas from which "any or all" people could be excluded. Early Japanese victories in the Pacific made it seem like an attack on the West Coast was imminent. Two weeks later, Lieutenant General John L. DeWitt issued Public Proclamation Number 1, which created Military Area Number 1: the western part of California, Oregon, and Washington and the southern part of Arizona. Military Area Number 2, created with the same proclamation, included the remaining parts of these states. DeWitt's Civilian Exclusion Order Number 34, issued on May 3, 1941, stipulated that all people of Japanese

---

Excerpt from Executive Order Number 9066

Authorizing the Secretary of War to Prescribe Military Areas

Whereas the successful prosecution of the war requires every possible protection against espionage and against sabotage to national-defense material, national-defense premises, and national-defense utilities....
Now, therefore, by virtue of the authority vested in me as President of the United States, and Commander in Chief of the Army and Navy, I hereby authorize and direct the Secretary of War, and the Military Commanders whom he may from time to time designate, whenever he or any designated Commander deems such action necessary or desirable, to prescribe military areas in such places and of such extent as he or the appropriate Military Commander may determine, from which any or all persons may be excluded, and with respect to which, the right of any person to enter, remain in, or leave shall be subject to whatever restrictions the Secretary of War or the appropriate Military Commander may impose in his discretion.

Franklin D. Roosevelt
The White House
February 19, 1942

---

ancestry had to leave Military Area Number 1. The order was founded on the belief—based on no facts—that Japanese people in America were helping Japan's cause through sabotage and espionage and that incarcerating them was a military necessity.

Those orders represented the culmination of decades of hatred and discrimination against Japanese immigrants in California that rivaled the state's hatred of Chinese immigrants. The first major wave of Japanese immigration to Northern California dates back to the early 1900s, when Japanese workers flocked to the state to fill a labor shortage on farms. Resentment over the success of Japanese farmers and worry about the "yellow peril" fueled anti-Japanese sentiment, and the government restricted Japanese immigration to the United States in 1908. By that point, a Japanese Exclusion League had formed in San Francisco and labor unions were taking up the chant against cheap Japanese labor. A few years later, the California legislature started passing laws to discourage immigration and beat back the success of Japanese farmers in the state. Laws such as the California Alien Land Acts of 1913 and 1920 barred Japanese and other "immigrants ineligible for citizenship" from owning land. The federal Immigration Act of 1924 put a stop to the flow of immigrants from Japan, and discrimination continued for those already in the country. First-generation immigrants from Japan, known as Issei, were barred by law from citizenship and prohibited from owning land. Classified as aliens before the war, they were known as enemy aliens after Pearl Harbor. Their American-born children, known as Nisei, were citizens at birth under the Fourteenth Amendment.

The alien land acts were disputed several times in the district court. The most significant challenge was *Webb v. O'Brien*, a case that successfully questioned a California law that forbade aliens from holding any interest in property. The Northern District Court ruled that Japanese workers could enter into "cropping contracts" with landowners and receive a portion of the farming profits, but the Supreme Court disagreed, ruling that a cropping contract was an interest in land and was therefore null and void because of the 1920 act. The act was not overturned until 1952.

More than 110,000 men and women of Japanese ancestry were removed from their homes during World War II and sent to temporary assembly centers at fairgrounds and racetracks. About one-third of them were Issei; the other two-thirds were Nisei, US citizens incarcerated without a trial. After the bombing of Pearl Harbor, these two groups were lumped together.

Excerpt from Civilian Exclusion Order Number 34

The Following Instructions Must Be Observed:

1. A responsible member of each family, preferably the head of the family, or the person in whose name most of the property is held, and each individual living alone, will report to the Civil Control Station to receive further instructions. This must be done between 8:00 a.m. and 5:00 p.m. on Monday, May 4, 1942, or between 8:00 a.m. and 5:00 p.m. on Tuesday, May 5, 1942.

2. Evacuees must carry with them on departure for the Assembly Center the following property:
   (a) Bedding and linens (no mattress) for each member of the family;
   (b) Toilet articles for each member of the family;
   (c) Extra clothing for each member of the family;
   (d) Sufficient knives, forks, spoons, plates, bowls, and cups for each member of the family;
   (e) Essential personal effects for each member of the family.

All items carried will be securely packaged, tied, and plainly marked with the name of the owner and numbered in accordance with instructions obtained at the Civil Control Station. The size and number of packages is limited to that which can be carried by the individual or family group.

3. No pets of any kind will be permitted.

4. No personal items and no household goods will be shipped to the Assembly Center.

5. The United States Government through its agencies will provide for the storage at the sole risk of the owner of the more substantial household items, such as iceboxes, washing machines, pianos, and other heavy furniture. Cooking utensils and other small items will be accepted for storage if crated, packed, and plainly marked with the name and address of the owner. Only one name and address will be used by a given family.

In *The Spoilage*, an influential study on internment released in 1946, just after the war, Dorothy Swaine Thomas and Richard S. Nishimoto addressed the citizenship issue:

> As early as December 8, the status of Nisei as American citizens was disregarded in favor of their status as descendants of the Japanese enemy. Thus the restriction on travel referred to "Japanese individuals" and was interpreted as applying both to aliens and citizens. This confusion of citizens with aliens became especially marked on the West Coast where about 90 percent of all persons of Japanese ancestry resided. In this area strategic points on highways were watched, and Japanese Americans, aliens and citizens alike, were stopped and questioned; many were held for days by local law enforcement officers, no charges being filed against them. Many Japanese Americans were dismissed from private employment; others were evicted from their residences. Grocery stores and other business firms refused to sell them goods, and extensive economic and social boycotts developed against them.

The stereotype started from the top. "A Jap's a Jap," General DeWitt was quoted as saying. "It makes no difference whether he is an American citizen or not."

From assembly centers, the Japanese prisoners were taken to one of ten remote relocation centers scattered across the United States. They were housed in tarpaper barracks surrounded by barbed wire fences and armed soldiers. But they did not go without a legal fight. Leading the effort was an unlikely figure, twenty-three-year-old Fred Toyosaburo Korematsu, who attacked the constitutionality of the laws that set the internment program in motion. He never intended to lead a constitutional battle. He just didn't want to leave his girlfriend.

Korematsu was arrested on March 30, 1942, and charged with a misdemeanor for violating Executive Order 9066 and Exclusion Order 34. Korematsu, a US citizen born and raised in Oakland, graduated from the Oakland public grammar schools and Claremont High School and worked as a ship welder until being fired after Pearl Harbor. He attempted to enlist in the navy but was rejected by the Selective Service Board because of a gastric ulcer. His parents, who reported for relocation, told their son that he must make his own decision as an adult whether to report. Korematsu refused. He had fallen in love with a young Italian American woman and came up with a plan to run away with her to the

Midwest, outside the military zones. He changed his name, attempted to disguise himself through minor plastic surgery on his eyelids and nose, and claimed to be of Spanish and Hawaiian descent. But he was captured three weeks after DeWitt's order. He was placed with the Wartime Civil Control Administration at the Tanforan Assembly Center in San Bruno, just south of San Francisco. He never saw his girlfriend again.

The American Civil Liberties Union, seeing Korematsu's arrest as a way to challenge the internment laws, came to his aid by providing attorneys. The San Francisco chapter of the ACLU, led by Ernest Besig, challenged the constitutionality of the executive order and DeWitt's proclamation by asking Judge Welsh to toss out the charges. Korematsu's first attorney, Clarence E. Rust of Oakland, argued that the exclusion acts were not dissimilar to the laws of Germany's Adolf Hitler or Japan's Hideki Tojo. "If this act is not erased from the statute books, a dangerous precedent will be established that will forever mock our declarations of equality before the laws," Rust stated.

In legal language that perhaps seemed like hyperbole at the time, Rust wrote, "This act will one day be celebrated not only for its structural deficiencies, but for the veiled fist it conceals and the grave injustice it wreaks upon innocent American civilians. It is a statute used as a lash to complete an exodus of American citizens. By its threat, it dispossesses, scatters and disinherits American citizens and deprives them of the privileges of national and state citizenship simply because their crime is that they are not pureblood white or Aryan stock."

US Attorney Frank J. Hennessy and his assistant, Alfonso Zirpoli, who would later become a district court judge, took the offensive. They wrote that the United States was in a new type of war that demanded new types of laws:

> Thus we find ourselves engaged in a war so vast and extensive that the field of military operation is no longer confined to the scene of actual physical combat, but includes as well our coast line, our harbors, our industrial and transportation centers, yes even our agricultural centers, in short a war whose success is dependent upon our operations in every state and hamlet in the Union. This total war calls not only for the mobilization of our manpower for combat service, but the industrial, economic, and moral mobilization of the nation as well. To conclude otherwise is to render ourselves blind to the lessons of this war already taught us by the ruthless, barbaric, and treacherous acts of our mortal

enemies, who would not only destroy us in combat, but would destroy and stamp out as well our democratic and constitutional institutions and our very way of life.

The US Attorneys wrote that one hundred thousand Japanese Americans lived within one hundred miles of the Pacific coast, many near army camps, posts, forts, arsenals, and naval installations, and that "the presence of this large number of persons of Japanese ancestry within this critical area constituted a serious threat to its security." Echoing popular stereotypes of the age, they wrote that the Japanese were especially suspect because they had refused to assimilate into America: "Their manners of thought and action, their traditional life patterns and their adherence to the customs and tradition of their oriental origins combined to make of them a people apart despite the provisions of the Nationality Code recognizing those born in this country as citizens. The fact of citizenship, thus conferred, bore little relationship to their status as loyal members of our body politic." These Japanese Americans, the attorneys concluded, had ample opportunity for sabotage if they were allowed to live near the West Coast. Furthermore, the evacuation would also protect them; the attorneys argued that Japanese Americans needed to be kept safe from the possibility of violent acts against them.

The government's arguments struck a chord with the judge, who was a member of an anti-Japanese group, the Native Sons of the Golden West. According to Peter Irons in his 1983 book, *Justice at War,* "Welsh had a reputation as an impetuous and lazy judge whose political ambitions colored his judicial behavior." Welsh rejected the ACLU challenge, deciding that the army had the right to evacuate Japanese-born residents from the West Coast and hold them in custody. Before leaving on vacation, Welsh assigned the case to Judge St. Sure, who, according to Irons, was a more independent and impartial judge.

Korematsu entered a plea of not guilty and waived his right to a jury trial. After his opening statement, prosecutor Zirpoli called only one witness, an FBI agent who produced signed letters from Korematsu admitting that he knew about the exclusion order and knowingly violated it. Irons, in his 1999 book, *A People's History of the Supreme Court,* described the short trial:

> After an FBI agent testified about Fred's draft-card forgery and plastic surgery, the soft-spoken defendant took the stand to explain his actions. His description of Dr. Bennett Masten's bargain-rate surgery drew smiles

in the courtroom. "I don't think he made any change in my appearance," he said, "for when I went to the Tanforan Assembly Center everyone knew me and my folks didn't know the difference." Fred told the judge that he had applied for military service before Pearl Harbor, but had been rejected on medical grounds. "As a citizen of the United States I am ready, willing, and able to bear arms for this country," he affirmed.

Korematsu's case was submitted to the court without argument. As expected, St. Sure found him guilty and ordered him placed on probation for five years. The judge set Korematsu's bail at $2,500, which the ACLU agreed to pay. According to Irons,

> There followed, however, what may be one of the few incidents in the history of the United States of armed revolt by the military against duly constituted judicial authority. It must certainly have been a bizarre scene to witness. After posting bail, Korematsu was entitled to leave the courthouse on his own, but he was arrested by a military policeman before he left the courthouse. Brought back to the courtroom, St. Sure raised the bail to $5,000, but Besig said he would meet this amount. Despite this, Korematsu was taken into custody, placed in local jail until being shipped to the Tanforan Assembly Center in San Bruno. He appealed the decision, but was eventually shipped to the Central Utah Relocation Center, at Topaz, Utah, where he remained through much of the war.

In 1942, Mitsuye Endo, who was confined at the Tule Lake War Relocation Center in Northern California, filed a writ of habeas corpus before Judge Roche seeking release from the internment camp. Endo, born in Sacramento, charged that being imprisoned at Tule Lake was violating her rights as a loyal and law-abiding US citizen. She was an excellent candidate to test the legal waters because she had a government job (as a clerical worker in the California Department of Motor Vehicles) and a brother serving in the military.

By July 1942, the government's military necessity argument was losing some of its punch. Japan's early victories all over the Pacific were now being countered by the United States. The Battle of Midway in June 1942 marked a turning point in the war, and fear of a Japanese invasion of the West Coast had greatly lessened. Judge Roche heard arguments on Endo's petition only eight days after it was filed. "Legal minds were attuned sharply today to a case in federal court here questioning the right of the government to intern American citizens of Japanese ancestry," the Associated Press reported.

Endo's attorney, James Purcell of San Francisco, argued that President Roosevelt and the military had no right to evacuate and detain citizens

FIG. 5-6
Mitsuye Endo filed a petition of habeas corpus to protest her detainment at the Tule Lake internment camp in Utah in April 1942. In *Ex parte Endo* (1944), the Supreme Court ruled that "loyal" internees be released from the internment camps. The decision facilitated the eventual closing of the camps between 1944 and 1946. Courtesy of the California State University, Sacramento, Library.

unless Congress enacted legislation allowing such actions, and suggested that DeWitt did not have the authority to detain Endo because citizens should not be detained without a hearing when courts are open. "So far as I know there never has been a decision of the Supreme Court of the United States upholding the right of a military commander to hold a citizen of the United States without hearing," he told the judge. He pointed out that no charge had ever been leveled against his client.

Roche was impressed. "When this matter was first brought up, I was of the opinion that it was a frivolous action," he said following Purcell's presentation. "I am no longer of that opinion." With that, Assistant US Attorney Zirpoli once again cited the military necessity of incarcerating the Japanese and called on Roche to look at the "factual background" of the situation. "In these times a court should be reluctant to take any action that would undo what the executive and military deem necessary," Zirpoli declared.

The judge normally ruled on habeas corpus petitions within two weeks, but Roche delayed his decision to watch similar internment cases wend their way through other courts. To forestall a decision against the government, Endo was offered release if she agreed to leave the restricted Western military area. She refused, demanding the right to return to her home and job in Sacramento. Finally, almost a year after she filed her petition, Roche ruled against her. She, along with Fred Korematsu, appealed to the Supreme Court.

On October 11, 1944, the two cases (*Ex parte Mitsuye Endo* and *Korematsu v. United States*) were heard by the high court in Washington, DC. Once again, the argument over the military necessity of interning the Japanese was the key to both cases, but this time—with the United States in full command of the war—the argument took on new overtones. Irons explained how the legal tactics changed before the Supreme Court:

> Government lawyers now claimed that mass internment was necessary to
> protect Japanese Americans against racial hostility, rather than to protect
> military installations against their hostile reaction to discrimination.
> No longer were DeWitt's orders a "reasonable" response to the dangers
> posed by disloyal Japanese Americans. They had in fact been designed
> to "prevent incidents involving violence between Japanese migrants"
> and Caucasians who blamed them for Pearl Harbor. "The belief of the
> military authorities in the danger of violence has not been shown to be

unreasonable," the government's brief weakly claimed. Fred Korematsu had not met "the burden which rested upon him" to disprove the evidence "of hostility to the evacuees, which lay at the basis of the decision to impose detention" on them. This about-face in the government's position reflected the fact that Japanese forces posed no threat to the West Coast after 1943, eroding arguments based on the danger of espionage and sabotage by Japanese Americans.

The Supreme Court upheld Korematsu's conviction by a vote of six to three. "We are not unmindful of the hardships imposed by it upon a large group of American citizens. But hardships are part of war, and war is an aggregation of hardships," wrote Justice Hugo Black. The high court did question the constitutionality of the Exclusion Order, but determined that it was proper in light of the "emergency and peril" of the war. Korematsu was not forced to leave home because of his race, Black wrote, but because of military need:

> He was excluded because we are at war with the Japanese Empire, because the properly constituted military authorities feared an invasion of our West Coast and felt constrained to take proper security measures, because they decided that the military urgency of the situation demanded that all citizens of Japanese ancestry be segregated from the West Coast temporarily, and finally, because Congress, reposing its confidence in this time of war in our military leaders—as inevitably it must—determined that they should have the power to do just this. There was evidence of disloyalty on the part of some, the military authorities considered that the need for action was great, and time was short. We cannot—by availing ourselves of the calm perspective of hindsight—now say that at that time these actions were unjustified.

The six justices in the majority did not see the racial overtones of the Exclusion Order. Citizenship has responsibilities as well as privileges, Black wrote. "To cast this case into outlines of racial prejudice, without reference to the real military dangers which were presented, merely confuses the issue."

All three opposing justices filed a dissent. Justice Owen Roberts wrote that no citizen should be imprisoned without evidence that indicates disloyalty. "I think the indisputable facts exhibit a clear violation of Constitutional rights," he wrote. Justice Frank Murphy was even clearer when he declared, "I dissent, therefore, from this legalization of racism." He wrote that the internment was one of the "most sweeping and complete deprivations of constitutional rights in the history of this nation in the absence of martial law," and added that "this exclusion of 'all persons of Japanese ancestry, both alien and non-alien,' from the Pacific Coast area on a plea of military necessity in the absence of martial law ought not to be approved. Such exclusion goes over 'the very brink of constitutional power' and falls into the ugly abyss of racism." And Justice Robert H. Jackson wrote that General DeWitt's evacuation and detention program had no place in law under the Constitution. "Guilt is personal and not inheritable," he wrote. Later he concluded, "I would reverse the judgment and discharge the prisoner."

On that same day, Mitsuye Endo won her unconditional release from the internment camp in Topaz, Utah, where she had been transferred from Tule Lake. The Supreme Court unanimously ruled that the government could not hold loyal citizens longer than was necessary. "We are of the view that Mitsuye Endo should be given her liberty," Justice William O. Douglas wrote in the court's opinion. "In reaching that conclusion we do not come to the underlying constitutional issues which have been argued. For we conclude that, whatever power the War Relocation Authority may have to detain other classes of citizens, it has no authority to subject citizens who are concededly loyal to its leave procedure."

The key was Endo's loyalty, which was never questioned by the Department of Justice. "A citizen who is concededly loyal presents no problem of espionage or sabotage," Douglas wrote. "Loyalty is a matter of the heart and mind not of race, creed, or color. He who is loyal is by definition not a spy or a saboteur. When the power to detain is derived from the power to protect the war effort against espionage and sabotage, detention which has no relationship to that objective is unauthorized."

The decision came on December 18, 1944, one day after the War Department announced that all loyal Japanese citizens would be released.

Correcting the Supreme Court

Almost four decades later, in 1983, Fred Korematsu filed a petition for a writ of error coram nobis in the district court, seeking to overturn his 1942 conviction. A legal team that included Peter Irons, who also worked as an attorney, and Oakland attorney Dale Minami, whose parents were interned, filed the lawsuit. In his Supreme Court history, Irons explained:

Normally, criminal defendants cannot ask judges to reopen their cases after appeals have been exhausted and sentences completed. The only exception to the "finality" rule stems from one of the "ancient writs" of English law, called the writ of error coram nobis. This term is legal Latin for "error before us," referring to the trial judges....In coram nobis cases, the former defendant must show that "prosecutorial misconduct" during the original trial deprived him or her of a fair trial. There are two grounds for coram nobis relief: one requires proof that government lawyers withheld "exculpatory" evidence that would show the defendant's innocence; the other involves the government's introduction at trial of false evidence of the defendant's guilt. The burden of proof on defendants is high, and coram nobis relief is rarely sought and even more rarely granted.

Irons and Minami argued that Korematsu's conviction was based on official misconduct. Key to the petition were Justice Department documents that Irons found through the Freedom of Information Act that showed that General DeWitt disregarded written information that contradicted his claim that Japanese Americans needed to be quarantined. Irons found memos from Edward Ennis, head of the Justice Department's Alien Enemy Control Unit, that reminded Solicitor General Charles Fahy of his obligation to tell the Supreme Court this information; Irons argued that Fahy's failure to do so constituted official misconduct:

> Ennis sent another memorandum to Fahy in September 1944, during his preparation for the *Korematsu* argument. Suspicious of General DeWitt's claims to have evidence of "espionage and sabotage" by Japanese Americans, Ennis had found more intelligence reports that refuted the charges DeWitt made in his "Final Report" on the internment program. Excerpts of DeWitt's report were included in the *Korematsu* brief that Fahy was about to file with the Court. Ennis urged Fahy to disavow the report's claims that "overt acts of treason were being committed" by Japanese Americans. "Since this is not so," Ennis wrote, "it is highly unfair to this racial minority that these lies, put out in an official publication, go unnoticed." Again, Fahy ignored Ennis and assured the justices that he vouched for "every sentence, every line, and every word" in DeWitt's report. Again, the Court accepted Fahy's assurances in upholding Fred Korematsu's conviction; Justice Hugo Black cited DeWitt's report as providing sufficient "evidence of disloyalty" among Japanese Americans to justify their mass evacuation from the West Coast.

The packed courtroom of district court judge Marilyn Hall Patel was filled with emotion as she held the coram nobis hearing in November 1983. "I still remember forty years ago when I was handcuffed and arrested as a criminal," Korematsu told the court in a brief statement. He recounted being reunited with his family at the Tanforan Racetrack after his first trial: "The horse stalls that we stayed in were made for horses, not human beings." Korematsu, who said he was speaking for all Japanese Americans who were "escorted to concentration camps," asked that the government apologize for its exclusion orders, "so this will never happen again to any American citizen of any race, creed, or color."

Patel granted Korematsu's writ and vacated his conviction. She wrote that the Supreme Court was misled. "Omitted from the reports presented to the courts was information possessed by the Federal Communications Commission, the Department of the Navy, and the Justice Department which directly contradicted General DeWitt's statements," she wrote. "Thus, the court had before it a selective record. Whether a fuller, more accurate record would have prompted a different decision cannot be determined. Nor need it be determined. Where relevant evidence has been withheld, it is ample justification for the government's concurrence that the conviction should be set aside. It is sufficient to satisfy the court's independent inquiry and justify the relief sought by petitioner."

The district court had come full circle.

Patel noted that no evidence was introduced that questioned Korematsu's loyalty to the United States, so he—and tens of thousands of other Japanese Americans—should never have been incarcerated:

> *Korematsu* remains on the pages of our legal and political history. As a legal precedent, it is now recognized as having very limited application. As historical precedent, it stands as a constant caution that in times of war or declared military necessity our institutions must be vigilant in protecting constitutional guarantees. It stands as a caution that in times of distress the shield of military necessity and national security must not be used to protect government actions from close scrutiny and accountability. It stands as a caution that in times of international hostility and antagonisms our institutions, legislative, executive and judicial, must be prepared to exercise their authority to protect all citizens from the petty fears and prejudices that are so easily aroused.

FIG. 5-7
Fred Korematsu (seated center), who had ignored the orders for the evacuation of Japanese American citizens and residents and had remained in Oakland before being arrested and tried in a case that went all the way to the Supreme Court, is surrounded by his legal team at a press conference addressing the reopening of his case in 1983. Courtesy of the Asian Law Caucus.

Modest and Unassuming

In the mid-1940s, long before Patel's ruling, district court judge Louis Earl Goodman had started making amends for what had happened to US citizens of Japanese ancestry during World War II. Goodman was the only judge to join the Northern District Court during the war. President Roosevelt nominated him to the seat vacated by Harold Louderback. Goodman, born in the tiny hamlet of Lemoore in the San Joaquin Valley in 1892, received his bachelor's degree from the University of California, Berkeley, in 1913 and his law degree from Hastings College of Law two years later. He worked in San Francisco as a lawyer in private practice from 1915 until his appointment to the district court in 1942. After Goodman, called "an ordinary business lawyer," was recommended by Democratic senator Sheridan Downey, columnist Herb Caen wrote in his "It's News to Me" column that Goodman was a "cincheroo" to fill the court vacancy. The Senate confirmed the nomination, despite opposition from California's Republican senator, Hiram W. Johnson. The Senate also passed legislation making the court's third seat permanent. Judge St. Sure swore Goodman in on the final day of 1942. Said St. Sure: "He appeals to me in that he is modest and unassuming."

Goodman, a practical man with liberal leanings, joined his fellow judges in helping the federal government press the war effort. From the start, Goodman did not hesitate to take tough cases. In 1943, he revoked

FIG. 5-8
A view of the Selective Service headquarters at the Tule Lake internment camp in California, where 420 men between the ages of eighteen and twenty registered for the draft. Courtesy of The Bancroft Library, University of California, Berkeley.

the citizenship of a German-born contractor who had praised Hitler. In 1944, he upheld the navy's seizure of 104 San Francisco machine shops. But Goodman courageously bolted from the prevailing sentiment in the district court and the nation on the issue of Japanese American internment. He ruled unconstitutional a California statute prohibiting inheritance of real and personal property by aliens residing in assembly areas. The state's new probate code was invalid and unconstitutional, he wrote, "because the State of California attempted, by the probate statute in question, to enter the field of foreign relations, a domain reserved exclusively to the federal government free from local interference."

He went further in fighting rules against the Japanese when the Selective Service announced it would induct Japanese Americans into the armed forces. About 2,800 Nisei registered for the draft, but another 315 refused to take the physical exam or register for the draft until their rights were fully restored. Goodman recognized the complicated plight of Japanese Americans in two lawsuits filed during and after the war. "I have no doubt that there was a complete lack of constitutional authority for administrative, executive, or military officers to detain and imprison American citizens at Tule Lake who were not charged criminally or subject to martial law," Goodman wrote in *United States v. Masaaki Kuwabara*. The lawsuit was filed in 1944 after a grand jury indicted Kuwabara and twenty-five other Japanese Americans imprisoned at Tule Lake for not reporting for a physical exam ordered by the Selective Service board in Modoc County. Kuwabara, a US citizen born in California, obeyed the Exclusion Order and left his San Pedro home in 1942. He was relocated to an internment camp in Jerome, Arkansas. From there, he was taken to Tule Lake, which was established to concentrate internees that the government categorized as not fully loyal to the United States. Kuwabara was placed there because, like hundreds of other prisoners, he sought repatriation to Japan after years of confinement. In 1943, the local selective service board classified Kuwabara as 1-A, available for military service. The following year, he was ordered to report for a physical exam.

Judge Goodman heard Kuwabara's case during a term in Eureka. The judge appointed two leading local attorneys to represent the twenty-six defendants and later granted motions to quash the indictments. Goodman ruled that because Kuwabara was not a free agent and could not receive due process, he and the twenty-six prisoners were not obligated to report for the pre-induction physical. "It is shocking to the conscience

World War II Cases

The Union Oil Company filed a lawsuit against the United States after a Japanese submarine sank its tanker off the Central Coast. On December 23, 1941, sixteen days after Pearl Harbor, a torpedo from a Japanese submarine struck the tanker and sunk it as it was pulling out of port at Avila Beach, near San Luis Obispo. The blast forced the crew to abandon ship in lifeboats. Judge Roche decided against the company. Later, the Matson Navigation Company filed a similar lawsuit after a Japanese submarine sunk the steamer *Lahaina* about eight hundred miles northeast of Honolulu. Four men were killed in lifeboats. Matson also lost in court.

John George Majus was charged with sabotaging a United States vessel in 1942 for using a hacksaw to damage the steering rod of a steamship at the Encinal Terminal in Alameda. Majus pled guilty and was sentenced to three years in prison. Later that year, Heinrich Roedel was charged with obstructing the war by attempting to set fire to a warehouse at the Richmond Shipyards. Roedel was tried before a jury and convicted. Judge St. Sure sent him to a penitentiary for thirty years.

The Tabor-Olney Corporation sued Cutter Laboratories, Inc., to stop Cutter from making blood plasma after the war ended. Tabor-Olney had a patent to manufacture blood plasma, and licensed Cutter to make plasma for use by GIs during the war without a fee. Cutter did not stop making the plasma at the end of 1945, as it had agreed to. A jury awarded damages to Tabor-Olney.

---

that an American citizen be confined on the ground of disloyalty, and then, while so under duress and restraint, be compelled to serve in the armed forces, or be prosecuted for not yielding to such compulsion," Goodman wrote. He was the only district court judge in the nation to side with the draft resisters. Most of the other resisters in other district courts were convicted of refusing induction and were sentenced to between two and five years in prison.

In 1947, President Harry S. Truman pardoned the internment camp draft resisters. That same year, Goodman ordered the release of 330 Japanese Americans who had renounced their American citizenship and were waiting in internment camps for deportation to Japan. Attorney Wayne

Collins asked that all the renunciations be declared null and void, and that the prisoners be released. Goodman agreed. He ruled that the renunciations had been signed under duress and coercion, and that the renunciation hearings lacked due process. He also ruled that the deportation code that related to losing United States nationality was unconstitutional.

"I am of the opinion that the detained applicants are not alien enemies within the provisions of the Alien Enemy Act of 1798 and hence may not be detained for removal or deportation from the United States, pursuant to said act," Goodman wrote in the 1947 *Ex parte Tadayasu Abo* decision. The judge took even further steps during the next few years as he restored the citizenship of more than four thousand Japanese Americans who had renounced their citizenship during what Goodman called "the unfortunate saga of Tule Lake." The reasons for the renunciations were complex. Some of the prisoners were repulsed by their treatment during the war and no longer wanted to remain US citizens. Others were intimidated by nationalist Japanese prisoners, who spread false rumors that signing renunciation papers could help them avoid deportation to Japan, avoid the military draft, help them stay together as a family, or stay safe in the camp as the war wound down.

The testimony of Ray Ibusuki followed these common themes. He testified in an affidavit that he feared he would be forced out of Tule Lake with no money and no protection and would be branded a Tule Lake activist unless he signed the papers. "I believed that my safety depended on renouncing so I could stay in the center for the duration and then be sent home unless the government decided to deport us," he said. "In case the government deported me I wanted to be able to arrive in Japan and not cause punishment for myself and of my family." He also stated that he feared for his safety in the camp if he didn't sign the papers. "I felt I had to renounce and make it look like I was pro-Japanese."

Goodman wrote that the government was aware of the fear, anxiety, hopelessness, and despair of the prisoners, yet accepted the renunciations as valid. He stated that the United States, "under the stress and necessities of national defense, committed error in accepting the renunciations." He did not blame the public officials who passed and instituted the internment. "The court is not unmindful of the heavy responsibilities and burdens resting upon the executive and military officials due to the war with Japan and the dangers particularly affecting the west coast of the United States," he wrote. "But even expediency cannot remove the taint of unfairness with which the renunciations, subsequently executed, were clothed."

Goodman called on the United States to correct the evils resulting from ignoring Constitutional safeguards. "The Government must be neither reluctant nor evasive in correcting wrongs inflicted upon a citizen," he wrote. "By so doing it demonstrates to the people of the world the fairness and justice of our form of society and law. The government need not sheepishly confess error; it must be stalwart and forthright in its recognition of injustice. By so doing, faith and confidence in our system of law will be maintained."

CHAPTER 6

AFTER
THE WAR

FLOTSAM FROM WORLD WAR II surfaced in the Northern District Court for many years after Japan formally surrendered in Tokyo Bay. After the war, Judge Adolphus St. Sure refused to help Tanforan Racetrack officials circumvent a government order that prevented them from reconstructing the San Bruno facility in time for the 1946 racing season, but the track soon returned to horse racing. During the 1980s, the district court ruled that fourteen Filipino nationals who fought for the United States during the war were not entitled to citizenship because they failed to apply for naturalization before the cutoff date. And as late as 2001, the court ruled against the son of a World War II veteran who claimed that his father should have been awarded three additional medals.

Hundreds of people filed war-related cases in the district court. The most sensational was the trial of Iva Ikuko Toguri D'Aquino, charged with treason for broadcasting radio messages from the Japanese government to GIs in the Pacific. She was known—incorrectly—as Tokyo Rose.

D'Aquino was born and raised in Los Angeles. She attended public schools in Los Angeles and received a degree in zoology from UCLA. D'Aquino's journey to the district courthouse on Seventh Street was a circuitous one. In 1941, she traveled to Japan to visit an ailing aunt. Before Pearl Harbor, she sought permission to return to the United States but was turned down by the State Department because she had no passport, and the department could find no proof of her US citizenship. D'Aquino did manage to book passage on a ship bound for the United States on December 2, 1941, but the vessel was turned back after the war started—and D'Aquino's woes began. The following year, she applied for evacuation through the Swiss Legation, but once again was denied because she had difficulty getting certification of her US citizenship.

PREVIOUS PAGE
See Fig. 6-6 for caption.

Out of work and out of money, she applied for a job at Radio Tokyo in 1943, and started work as a typist for the Japan Broadcasting Corporation. She soon began working as a scriptwriter and announcer on *The Zero Hour,* a daily radio show broadcast via short-wave radio across the Pacific. Following the war, she boasted that she took part in hundreds of *The Zero Hour* broadcasts because she felt she was something of a war hero. The object of *The Zero Hour* was to make GIs homesick and tired. D'Aquino said she conspired to make the broadcasts as harmless as possible. She saw the shows as mere entertainment for GIs.

"I knew that *The Zero Hour* was Japanese propaganda for the purpose of lowering the morale of the Allied troops, being beamed to them, and showing sportsmanship on the part of the Japanese by sending out messages from prisoners of war," she told investigators in 1946. "My purpose was to give the program a double meaning and thus reduce its effectiveness as a propaganda medium." D'Aquino said she was given freedom to write her own scripts, which were not checked before the shows went on air live. "I did not feel that I was working against the interests of the United States. I did not pay much attention, during my employment at Radio Tokyo, to the Japanese aims of the program, except that I knew all of their programs were propaganda."

At the conclusion of the war, D'Aquino agreed to give two Hearst journalists the exclusive rights to her story for $2,000. She later said she embellished her story and misidentified herself as Tokyo Rose. That was the name used by GIs to describe the seductive women announcers on Radio Tokyo who attempted to undermine the Allied war effort. No Tokyo Rose existed. D'Aquino used the names Ann and Orphan Ann. But after the war, she signed at least one autograph as "Iva I. Toguri, Tokyo Rose." That helped seal her fate.

Following the interview, D'Aquino was arrested in Japan by US troops in late 1945 and was held with other suspected war criminals for more than a year. During her confinement, she was interrogated by the Justice Department for two days without an attorney. Military authorities decided in May 1946 that she had committed no crime under military law, but they continued holding her until October. When she tried to return to the United States, powerful columnist Walter Winchell mounted a campaign against D'Aquino, calling her an "enemy of Democracy." She was arrested again in Tokyo in 1948 and taken back to the United States with a military escort. Upon her arrival in San Francisco, she was taken into custody by civilian police and indicted by a grand jury. She was charged with eight overt acts of treason for allegedly damaging the morale of US troops and giving aid and comfort to Japan.

D'Aquino's trial began in July 1949 in the courtroom of Michael Roche, who had been named the district court's first chief judge the previous year. A jury of six men and six women was chosen in less than three hours. The government used most of its jury challenges to remove African Americans. *Examiner* reporter Frances B. O'Gara wrote that the courtroom was transformed to look like a replica of war crime tribunals in Germany and Japan. "The unfamiliar courtroom trappings, with a record-player, amplifier, control panel, and earphones for judges and jurors, brought the promise of an intense legal battle even before the first witness was called," O'Gara wrote.

Prosecutors played five recordings of *The Zero Hour*, made at a Federal Communications Commission monitoring station at Portland, and called forty-six witnesses, including sixteen from Japan, to paint a picture that D'Aquino was a willing participant in the broadcasts. Two of the key witnesses were her former bosses at Radio Tokyo, who decades later admitted that their testimony was manufactured at the prodding of the US government. "Even though I was a government witness against her, I can say today that Iva Toguri D'Aquino was innocent—she never did anything treasonable," one of the key witnesses, who refused to use his name, told the *Chicago Tribune* in 1976. He said occupation army police told him he had no choice but to testify against D'Aquino. Another witness said the FBI forced him to "do what we were told" by harassment and threats.

Wayne Collins, who had joined the ACLU effort to defend Fred Korematsu, headed D'Aquino's defense. He called twenty-six witnesses, including D'Aquino, who took the stand for eight days to proclaim that she never broadcast sensitive war information on the radio.

The thirteen-week trial was the longest and costliest in the district court's history at the time. The jury reported, after three days of deliberation, that it was not close to a verdict, but Judge Roche ordered them to return, saying that the trial had cost more than $500,000. Finally, after eighty hours of deliberation, jurors found D'Aquino guilty of one of the eight acts of treason: "that on a day during October, 1944, the exact date being to the Grand Jurors unknown, said defendant, at Tokyo, Japan, in a broadcasting studio of The Broadcasting Corporation of Japan, did speak into a microphone concerning the loss of ships." Roche sentenced her to ten years in prison and fined her $10,000. As they left, the judge told the jury, "I want to comfort you by saying that no jury in the years of my experience has exercised any more patience and given a case more attention than each and every one of you."

D'Aquino became the seventh person convicted of treason in the nation's history. She served six years at the Alderson Penitentiary in West Virginia. Upon her release, she faced a deportation attempt. Newspapers reported that she was offered a chance to leave voluntarily or be deported. Her attorney argued that she could not be deported since she was a US citizen and immediately challenged the government's moves against her. D'Aquino lived in Collins's Presidio Avenue home until the government dropped its deportation plan in 1958. Almost two decades later, Collins's son, Wayne Merrill Collins, filed a presidential pardon petition for D'Aquino. President Ford, in one of his last acts before leaving office in 1977, granted the pardon. The elder Collins did not live long enough to see that day—he had died in an airplane crash in 1974. D'Aquino became the first person ever convicted of treason to receive a pardon.

New Judgeships

The district court nearly doubled in size during the last half of the 1940s as three new judgeships—the court's fifth, sixth, and seventh seats—were added. Eleven new judges joined the court between 1946 and 1959, remarkable because only twelve judges had served on the court between Ogden Hoffman Jr.'s appointment in 1851 and Louis Goodman's appointment in 1942.

Goodman was a leading figure in the court during the forties and fifties. His decisions to restore the citizenship of thousands of Japanese Americans marked him as an independent voice. He defied a congressional order to testify about a grand jury investigation in the early 1950s, and played a key role in the building of the new San Francisco Federal Courthouse—first known as Goodman's Towers while under construction. In addition, Goodman oversaw a major civil liberties case around the publication of Henry Miller's books *Tropic of Capricorn* and *Tropic of Cancer*. The case began in 1949 when San Francisco customs officials seized books sent from Europe by a Stanford University professor. Customs officials declared the books pornographic, and US Attorney Frank J.

Hennessy filed a lawsuit to ban them (*United States v. Two Obscene Books*). Meanwhile, Ernest Besig, director of the local American Civil Liberties Union chapter filed a lawsuit to get the books released.

Goodman was critical of the ACLU for taking on the case. "I am at a loss to perceive what could prompt the representative of the American Civil Liberties Union to urge the court to permit the introduction into this country of books of this kind," he wrote. "'Civil liberties' and 'freedom of speech' are certainly not synonymous with license and obscenity." In court, the defense produced eighteen reviews of Henry Miller's work and fifteen letters and two affidavits from critics to vouch for Miller's literary worth. Among the defenders was the San Francisco poet Kenneth Rexroth, who testified he was living at 187 Eighth Avenue, just south of the Presidio. Rexroth identified himself as the author of five books and the winner of two Guggenheim Fellowships. He wrote that he had read all of Miller's works. "They are realistic portrayals of life amongst young and poor writers and artists in America and abroad," Rexroth stated. "The use of common words for the parts and functions of the human body is considerably less frequent than occurs in actual life amongst the people described. The situations are no more erotic than those presented in hundreds of best sellers, and, under a glaze of censorship designed to suppress the offensive words but heighten the erotic appeal of the situation—in hundreds of motion pictures."

Miller was more honest than most contemporary writers, Rexroth wrote: "Those words and situations in his work to which objection is taken, are not for obscene purposes. That is, Miller is not interested in providing his readers with cheap sexual thrills, but quite the opposite. His books are very trenchant satires on the social evils of our time, from the point of view, not of foreign inspired political doctrine, but from a deeply religious, even mystical reverence for life and an intense and exceedingly American individualism." Rexroth compared Miller to Walt Whitman, whose work was also considered obscene by contemporaries. "It is absurd that the writer who is considered abroad as the greatest we now have in the USA should be banned in his own country," he concluded.

Goodman agreed that Henry Miller possessed literary skill, but the judge thought that the writer used pornography to build sales. "The filthy scatological portions are written in a bluntly different and distinct style from the pretentious metaphysical reflective manner of writing otherwise," the judge wrote. "Thus the conclusion is justified that either the alleged literary ability of the author deserted him or that he had his eye on 'the box office.'"

Goodman decided in 1951 that the books should be banned. Miller's language so shocked Goodman that he could barely cite it in his written opinion. "It is sufficient to say, however, that the many obscene passages in the books have such an evil stench that to include them here in foot-notes would make this opinion pornographic," he wrote. "For example, there are several passages where the female sexual organ and its function are described and referred to in such detailed vulgar language as to create nausea in the reader. If this be important literature, then the dignity of the human person and the stability of the family unit, which are the cor-nerstones of our system of society, are lost to us."

Goodman's decision was affirmed by the Court of Appeals, but Miller eventually had his day in court. The Supreme Court ruled in 1964 that *Tropic of Cancer* was literature, thus permitting its publication in the United States.

The highest profile case that Goodman heard during the 1950s involved Caryl Chessman. Although largely forgotten, Chessman was a cause célèbre in the fight to end capital punishment. Chessman was con-victed of being the Red Light Bandit, a man who posed as a police officer with a red light atop his car. The bandit attacked eight times in January 1948, accosting several couples in Los Angeles's lovers' lane and, on two occasions, kidnapping and sexually assaulting women. Chessman main-tained his innocence. He wrote four books during his years at San Quen-tin, including three popular memoirs—*Cell 2455, Death Row*; *Trial by Ordeal*; and *The Face of Justice*. *Cell 2455, Death Row* reportedly sold five hundred thousand copies and won Chessman worldwide support in his fight to avoid execution.

Chessman first appeared in Goodman's court in late 1955, after fil-ing a habeas corpus petition. Goodman denied that petition as well as another habeas corpus petition filed in 1960. Chessman's lawyers took fifteen appeals to the Supreme Court, but they all failed. Chessman was scheduled for execution by cyanide poisoning at ten o'clock on the morn-ing of May 2, 1960. His lawyers filed one last habeas corpus plea in the California Supreme Court. The justices met on the morning of May 2 and voted four to three to deny the plea. Moments later, they denied a request for a stay of execution so that the case could be heard by the US Supreme Court. Chessman's attorney, George Davis, rushed over to

Goodman's chambers to seek a one-hour stay of execution to allow time for a request seeking a writ of review from the Supreme Court.

Davis recalled years later that he and his associates frantically drove the six blocks from the California Supreme Court to the district court. There he presented Goodman with a fifteen-page document. "The judge took the petition, and he started to read it, page by page," Davis stated. "As he started to read it and turn the pages, I kept watching the clock....I saw that clock going from five minutes to ten, to four minutes to ten, to three minutes, and finally, when it got to just almost exactly one minute to, the judge said, 'All right, I'll grant the stay of execution.'"

Davis wrote that he offered to dial the direct number to the execution chamber to save time, but Goodman refused. The judge instead instructed his clerk, Edward Evansen, to ask his secretary, Celeste Hickey, to put a call through to the San Quentin warden. "I gave the number to the secretary," Davis recalled. "She walked into an adjoining office just a

FIG. 6-1
Guards at San Quentin State Prison lead convicted robber and rapist Caryl Chessman into the courtroom during an attempt to win his freedom from death row in December 1955. He was sent to the gas chamber four months later. Courtesy of the San Francisco History Center, San Francisco Public Library.

few feet away, and I thought 'Boy, this is the cliffhanger of all cliffhang-ers,' because now it's thirty seconds before ten, and she's dialing, but all it needs is to get to the warden. At about five seconds before ten, the secretary walks out and says, 'Could you give me that number again, Mr. Davis? I must have misdialed it.' I gave her the number again, she dialed it again, she got the warden." But it was too late.

"The prison number was passed along to Miss Hickey orally through several persons and somehow, in the noise and tension, a digit was dropped," Lawrence E. Davies reported in the *New York Times*. "She had to dial again after having verified the number." By the time she got through to the prison, associate warden Louis Nelson told her that the cyanide pellets had just been dropped. The execution had begun. Chess-man was pronounced dead at 10:12 a.m.

Truman's Judges

The first judge appointed to the district court after World War II was George B. Harris, who was also the first of six district court judges nom-inated by Democratic president Harry S. Truman. Born in 1901 in San Francisco, Harris was raised by his Irish-born grandmother following the death of his mother when he was four years old. He received his law degree from St. Ignatius College, now the University of San Francisco School of Law, in 1926, after years of attending night school and working by day. He learned the art of lawyering from Gavin McNab, one of San Francisco's ablest lawyers and the leader of the California Democratic Party. In 1941, Harris was appointed to the San Francisco Municipal Court, which he called the "most important court in the land" because it was where the "little people" had their day in court. During the war, Harris doubled his workload by patrolling the San Francisco waterfront as a member of the Coast Guard Port Security Force. He was appointed to the district court in 1946 after the Senate approved the establishment of a fifth seat. Harris won the nomination to the new seat with the sup-port of Democratic senator Sheridan Downey.

During his thirty-seven years on the bench, Harris brought a sense of majesty to the district court. With silver hair, a rugged face, and a deep voice, he looked and sounded like a federal judge. His chambers were filled with photos of celebrities—presidents, Supreme Court justices, opera stars, and the like—whom he counted as friends. Although not a legal scholar, Harris was a natural born judge who generally came up with verdicts that stand the test of time. In 1948, he ruled that prisoner Robert Stroud, known as the Birdman of Alcatraz, could communicate with his literary agent about publication of *Stroud's Digest of Diseases of Birds*. Assistant US Attorney Joseph Karesh argued that Stroud was "civilly dead" as a prisoner and should not be entitled to carry on business from the prison. Harris disagreed, saying that, "As a man, he may be civilly dead. But certainly he is not yet buried."

In 1961, Harris awarded film producer Samuel Goldwyn $300,000 in damages after he sued Twentieth Century-Fox Film Corporation and other film distributors for creating monopolies and forcing him to take less than fair compensation for the rights to show such films as *The Best Years of Our Lives*, *The Secret Life of Walter Mitty*, and *The Bishop's Wife*. And in his last years on the bench, Harris was determined to improve the "degrading conditions" at Soledad prison. He toured the facilities and found that prison officials had "abandoned elemental concepts of decency."

Harris followed Goodman as chief judge of the court, serving from 1961 to 1970. During those years, the new federal courthouse opened, the federal public defender system was established, and the jury selection system was reorganized. Harris assumed senior status in 1970 and worked as a senior judge until his death in 1983.

The case Harris perhaps found the most challenging centered around longshoreman leader Harry Bridges, who had spent months in the district court before Judge Martin Welch trying to avoid deportation. Welch ruled against him, but the Supreme Court ruled in 1945 that Bridges's connections to the Communist Party were not concrete enough to

A Getty in the House

In 1956, Judge George Harris's daughter, Gail, married John Paul Getty II, the son of oil billionaire J. Paul Getty, then considered the richest man in the world. The marriage lasted eight years. Their teenage son, John Paul Getty III, was kidnapped in Italy in 1973 and ransomed for more than $2 million. The senior Getty refused the initial demand, saying he'd have to pay ransom for all fifteen of his grandchildren if he responded. When kidnappers sent a lock of the boy's hair and the remains of one of his ears, the family agreed to the negotiated ransom. Harris's grandchild was severely traumatized by the incident.

warrant deportation. Bridges filed an application for naturalization on August 8, a week after the decision, and was later asked by superior court judge Thomas M. Foley, "Do you now, or have you ever, belonged to the Communist Party in the United States?"

"I have not; I do not," Bridges responded.

With that answer, Bridges became a United States citizen.

In 1948, Bridges led an acrimonious strike of twelve thousand long-shoremen and maritime workers that shut down the Pacific seaports for more than eight weeks. Soon after, a grand jury indicted Bridges on charges of perjury and conspiracy to fraudulently secure his natural-ization. Once again, the issue centered on whether Bridges had been a member of the Communist Party. Harris ruled that the three-year statute of limitations did not bar prosecution of Bridges, setting up a six-month trial, one of the longest and most bitterly contested criminal trials in the history of the court. His decision to allow the case to go to trial was likely bathed in government sentiment against the powerful union boss. "It was as difficult a case as I tried up to that time," Harris later recounted in an oral history. "It required a great deal of independent study, and it was a demanding case."

Bridges hired Vincent Hallinan, one of San Francisco's most success-ful attorneys of the era, who admitted years later that he was overconfi-dent and naive when he took the case. This was the start of a precipitous decline for Hallinan, who was later convicted in district court of tax evasion, fined, and sentenced to eighteen months in federal prison. The Bridges case radicalized the lawyer, who wrote a scathing denouncement of the justice system in his 1963 autobiography, *A Lion in Court*: "In dealing with many agents of the US government, you must assume, until the contrary is completely established, that these representatives might commit felonies, suborn perjury, conceal evidence, bribe wit-nesses, intimidate jurors, convey information to judges, and otherwise engage in practices which would be the cause for disbarment or impris-onment for a private attorney."

Before the trial opened, Hallinan tried to get Harris to disqualify himself, but the judge refused. The trial transcript reveals that Harris showed a determined enmity toward Bridges and the International Longshore and Warehouse Union. "Harris suffered all the limitations of a man who fights his way up from poverty into a self-conscious position in the upper middle class," wrote Charles P. Larrowe in the 1972 book *Harry Bridges: The Rise and Fall of Radical Labor in the United States.*

"In the thirties, Harris had run for municipal court judge in San Francisco on several occasions and, seemingly undisturbed by the shrill cries of Communists being hurled at Bridges, had solicited ILWU support. But in middle age, Harris married a rich Catholic and was converted to Catholicism, which may have brought on an unreasoning fear and hatred of Communism."

Right from his opening statement, Hallinan ran into a stone wall as prosecutors objected to his account of Bridges's former trials. "The judge upheld the prosecutor," wrote Larrowe. "And so it went, Hallinan persisting in telling his story to the jury, the prosecutor objecting, the judge upholding the objection, Hallinan lunging ahead anyway."

Two days into the trial, Harris shocked the courtroom when he declared that Hallinan was guilty of contempt of court and sentenced the attorney to six months in jail. After Harris ordered him taken into custody, Hallinan was seized by two marshals and dragged to the door. His co-counsel, James MacInnis, pleaded with the judge to delay Hallinan's jail term until the end of the trial. After a fifteen-minute recess, Harris announced that he would stay the execution of the contempt sentence until the end of the trial.

Harris's outrage was a major story around the nation. "It was a court day like no other in the memory of San Francisco lawyers, so violent was the exchange of personalities between Hallinan and the judge," Seymour Korman reported in the *Chicago Tribune*. "There was a time when government marshals actually were reaching for Hallinan to take him to jail at once." Lawrence E. Davies, of the *New York Times,* wrote a similar dispatch:

> During a court day which some of the lawyers with many years of experience termed "incredible," Mr. Hallinan sought unsuccessfully to file a formal motion and affidavit to disqualify Judge Harris on grounds of "personal bias and prejudice" from sitting further in the Bridges case, and to have another judge substituted. As an alternative he sought a mistrial.
>
> "You'll not file any affidavit before me in this division, Hallinan," the judge declared.
>
> "I'll file it upstairs," Mr. Hallinan retorted.
>
> "It will be stricken from the files," Judge Harris warned.

The government called seventeen witnesses, including eleven former communists. Several of Bridges's associates, who had refused to cooperate with federal investigators in the past, now placed Bridges at Communist Party meetings in the 1930s. Star witness John Schomaker testified that he worked with Bridges on the Communist Party newspaper *Waterfront Worker* and saw a Communist application card with the signature of H. R. Bridges. In almost two weeks of defense testimony, Hallinan called thirty-seven witnesses. Bridges recounted the story of his life and concluded that he was not being tried because he was a communist but because he was a union leader. "We are an effective union that packs a certain amount of economic and political weight," he said. "We get in people's way. We stop people from putting over their phony and crooked deals. Maybe we get into a lot of trouble because we put our nose into other people's business. We regard the trade union movement as our property."

The jury was out for five days before returning a guilty verdict against Bridges and two of his colleagues. Harris was pleased, telling the jurors, "You have finally found the golden truth shimmering in the fiery crucibles of this trial. Your deliberations have been marked by painstaking effort and a consciousness of the defendants' rights, as well as the rights of the Government of these United States." After the verdict was announced, Harris turned to attorneys Hallinan and MacInnis:

> I say to you that from the beginning of this trial you have embarked upon a course of conduct designed and calculated to contemptuously provoke the court in the hope that such provocation would lead the court to commit error or plunge the case into a mistrial.
>
> That such was your purpose has been entirely manifest to me. Such conduct is not alone an affront to the dignity of the judiciary of the United States, it is an affront to the dignity, good name and honor of a great profession. I said to you, and I repeat, that members of the bar are officers of the court. My experience has demonstrated that a vast majority of lawyers, in and out of court, conduct themselves with propriety, integrity, dignity and honor.
>
> Your assault on this court cannot go unchallenged, and I am determined, as far as I am able, in my humble capacity, that such behavior as displayed by you shall not be repeated in other federal courtrooms. America is justifiably proud of its judicial system, and anyone who attempts to degrade it or weaken it is working an injustice.
>
> With regard to you, Mr. Hallinan, I retrace my steps momentarily to remind you that on the 22nd of November 1949 the court adjudged you

guilty of criminal contempt, and thereafter regularly filed a certificate under the provisions of Rule 42(a) of the rules of Criminal Procedure. Thereafter, upon the request of your client, Mr. Harry Bridges, I permitted you to remain as counsel in the case and granted a stay of execution until termination of the trial.

The consent of the court was obtained upon the belief, reliance, and understanding that there would not be a repetition of such conduct. Unfortunately, within a comparatively brief period you deliberately launched into a series of acts and conduct again resulting in criminal contempt, which I have more particularly found and specified in a certificate. During the course of the trial and since the first adjudication, you have as a pattern of deliberate misconduct and in flagrant contempt of this court, the dignity thereof and the respect to it, sought to and did malign and abuse government witnesses, attorneys and agents in a loud, contemptible manner. It is difficult to portray by written word your intonation, gestures, and deportment, as well as the belligerent tone, mode, and manner created. It is difficult to portray by the written word the loud language used by you and the contemptible language used by you, both in and out of the presence of the jury; all of which conduct was designed to bring into disrepute this federal court, as well as the judge thereof charged with the administration of justice.

Harris sentenced Hallinan to six months in jail for contempt of court; he appealed his conviction to the Supreme Court but eventually served his term in 1952. MacInnis was given a three-month sentence for contempt. Harris sentenced Bridges to five years in prison and his colleagues to two years. The judge initially freed Bridges on $25,000 bond, but five months later, as the Korean War heated up, the government asked that the bond be canceled and Bridges be sent to jail. Harris agreed, calling Bridges "one of the most potent figures in the Communist Party in America." Harris was upset about reports that Bridges was telling union members that the United States should work for peace in the United Nations instead of resorting to war.

Bridges was defiant as he took the stand at his bond hearing: "Of all the senseless wars, I couldn't think of a worse one than a war started in Asia." After Harris's decision to jail Bridges, two deputies came to lead him out of the courtroom. His wife, Nancy, held on to him, and he said, "No tears now." As he was led out of the Federal Building, hundreds of people jeered. One man said, "You deserve this. You're a traitor." Bridges

lunged at the man but was held back by guards. Bridges was jailed in early August 1950 as a menace to national security.

Later that month, the court of appeals ruled that he should be released. "There is no showing that Bridges has in the present juncture committed any recognizable crime, or that he has himself counseled or advocated sabotage or sought to foment strikes or the establishment of picket lines on the waterfront or impeded by other means the prompt loading and dispatch of ships from the Far East," wrote Judges William Healy and William Orr. The appeals judges wrote that the effort to jail him was "as startling as it is novel."

Bridges's 1950 conviction was set aside by the Supreme Court three years later after the court determined that the three-year statute of limitations on perjury had already expired when he was indicted in 1948. Bridges's citizenship was restored.

Amazingly, the government went after Bridges one more time, with a civil suit seeking his denaturalization in 1956. Once again, witnesses were trotted out to testify for and against Bridges. But unlike previous trials, Judge Goodman put an end to the folly. "The testimony of the 'former Communists' was tinged and colored with discrepancies, animosities, vituperations, hates, and above all, with lengthy speeches and declarations of viewpoints," he wrote. The testimony of the witnesses did not add up to any proof: "To sift the truth from this welter of words of these witnesses is a task for the omniscient." Goodman concluded that the government failed to prove that Bridges was a member of the Communist Party, and the saga was over.

The Sacramento Seat

President Harry Truman nominated Dal Millington Lemmon to the district court bench in 1947 to fill the seat vacated by Martin Welsh. Although by statute Welsh was supposed to have lived in Sacramento, he actually divided his time between Sacramento, San Francisco, and other parts of the state. He apparently moved to San Francisco in 1946 due to health concerns before assuming senior status at the end of that year. Lemmon, a Republican appointed to sit in Sacramento, was a curious choice for Truman, a Democrat. Born in Newton, Kansas, in 1887, as a boy Lemmon moved with his family to Santa Rosa, in Sonoma County. His father was the editor of the *Santa Rosa Republican*. Young Lemmon received a bachelor's degree and law degree from Stanford University and moved to Sacramento in 1909 to work as the law librarian at the California State Library. He worked in private law practice in Sacramento from 1910 to 1933 and served on the Sacramento County Superior Court

Kidnapped

In 1958, William Heikkila was kidnapped by US immigration agents in San Francisco and put on a plane bound for his native Finland. Heikkila had lived most of his life in America but had never been naturalized. He admitted being a member of the Communist Party during the late 1920s and 1930s, and was tried for deportation in 1947. As he waited for an appeal, he was forced into a car by immigration agents as he left work, driven to San Francisco International Airport, and flown on a government plane to Vancouver, British Columbia, where he was placed in jail. Judge George Harris issued an order restraining agents from keeping Heikkila in custody or deporting him. But the next day, Heikkila was flown to Helsinki, Finland. Harris said the kidnapping "smacks of the Gestapo...the thumb and screw...things I don't approve of. We are a government of laws, not of men, and we want to keep it that way." Heikkila was eventually returned to the United States. He died at age fifty-four in 1960 while still appealing federal deportation rulings.

from 1933 to 1947. Lemmon was recommended to the district court by Republican senator William F. Knowland and Democratic senator Sheridan Downey. He was eventually the first district court judge to be elevated to the Ninth Circuit Court of Appeals, appointed there by President Dwight D. Eisenhower in 1954.

Truman nominated four other district court judges: Herbert W. Erskine, Oliver J. Carter, Edward P. Murphy, and Monroe M. Friedman. California Democratic party leader Harold I. McGrath detailed the inside story of these picks in a blunt 1970 oral history, which is at the Truman Library in Independence, Missouri. McGrath, who served as executive director of the Democratic State Central Committee, explained how Truman rewarded those who had helped him in the 1948 presidential campaign.

Herbert Erskine, a longtime litigator in the district court, figured he might be tabbed for a federal judgeship if he contributed and campaigned for Truman in the 1948 election. Active in Democratic Party politics, Erskine served as a delegate to the 1944 national convention that nominated Truman for vice president and helped the Democrats with financial planning in the 1948 election. "Herb Erskine simply appeared and said, 'I'm spending the next year, or the next x number of months campaigning for President Truman. Period.' He did and was of a great help to us," recalled McGrath. With the help of Monroe Friedman and others, Erskine put on a massive campaign rally for Truman in Oakland that helped the candidate take the state's twenty-five electoral votes. After Truman's victory, Erskine said he was tired of practicing law and publicly announced that he wanted to be a federal judge. He was steered to the position by McGrath and Oliver Carter, chairman of the California Democratic Party, who had run Truman's California campaign in 1948. When other powerful California Democrats started lobbying for their own candidates, McGrath contacted Truman again and campaigned behind the scenes.

"I saw to it that proper statements, not credited to me or Carter, appeared in the San Francisco paper that Herbert Erskine would have first refusal of any federal appointment on the federal bench," McGrath said in his oral history. "And that just pulled the plug out from anybody else. There was no further opposition, and he was appointed to the Federal District Court here, which is what he wanted, and where he served for, what, maybe two years, and then one day up and died. A damned shame; a delightful man."

Erskine, who was born in San Francisco in 1888 and worked as a corporate attorney from 1909 until his appointment, was the last link to the old court. At his installation in 1949, he announced that he knew all of the district court judges who preceded him except for Judge Ogden Hoffman. Erskine was nominated to the seat vacated by Adolphus St. Sure. As a district court judge, Erskine ruled in 1950 that Major General Claire Chennault, leader of the Flying Tigers during World War II, had legally purchased the Chinese National Aviation Corporation and Central Air Transport from the Nationalist Government in 1949 before it was driven from the mainland.

Erskine, who died in 1951 after suffering a heart attack, only served on the district court for two years. "I think Herbert Erskine, by reason of his extensive trial practice, was probably one of the best trial judges that we had in the United States," Judge George Harris said in his oral history. "He could handle any type of litigation and it was a joy to watch in court. However, I think, in turn also, he hastened his demise by reason of his tremendous activities. He refused to restrain himself and passed away very suddenly."

After Erskine's appointment, McGrath found that inserting a candidate into a district court judgeship was no longer so easy. In 1950, McGrath and Carter suggested attorneys Matthew Tobriner and Ben Duniway for the district court's two new judgeships, but Representative Patrick A. McCarran, chairman of the Senate Judiciary Committee from Nevada, rejected the names. McGrath recalled:

> Well, we got the word back that that was all very nice and we'd go along with you boys, but Pat McCarran says his friend Judge [Edward] Murphy, who was a Superior Court judge, his family friend, must get the first appointment or there won't be any approval. As simple as that. So, we tried to figure out a way to get around that and we couldn't because McCarran had the authority as the judicial chairman simply to just sit on the thing. There we were.
>
> So, in politics you do the art of the possible. Duniway and Tobriner both have magnificent law practices and were well off financially and didn't have any burning desire at this point to be judges; whereas Judge Carter, the son of the man who never had any shoes until he was seventeen years old, needed a paycheck, literally.

Oliver Carter was being groomed by the party to be California governor, a United States senator, or even the president, McGrath said. But he knew that Carter would be satisfied with the lifetime federal judgeship. "So we compromised with Senator McCarran," McGrath said, "and we said we will accept Murphy. Murphy is perfectly all right (except that he's a damned drunk) and for the two vacancies we'll take Murphy and Oliver Carter would be the other one. So, we submitted the names and that's the way they went through."

In September 1950, at age thirty-nine, Oliver Carter received a recess appointment from Truman to a new seat on the district court, the court's sixth, and was confirmed by the Senate in December. Carter, born in San Francisco in 1911, graduated from Hastings College of Law in 1935 and began working in private practice in Redding the following year. His father, Jesse Carter, was a civil libertarian who as an associate justice of the California Supreme Court became known as the greatest dissenter in the court's history. Oliver Carter, also considered a maverick, followed in his father's footsteps at the Shasta County district attorney's office and as a state senator. He served as assistant district attorney from 1938 and 1939, then returned to private practice until 1950. He was a member of the California State Senate from 1941 to 1949, distinguishing himself by standing up against the California Alien Land Law, which was directed against Asian immigrants.

Carter, who served as chief judge from 1970 to 1976, will always be remembered nationally for overseeing the 1976 trial of Patty Hearst. Around the courthouse, however, Carter will likely be remembered for his remarkably slow pace as a judge. He spent eighteen months deciding on a motion to dismiss tax evasion charges against Joseph Koret, head of the fashion firm Koret of California. He took two years to handle a habeas corpus petition from two Los Angeles men on death row in San Quentin State Prison. And he deliberated for twenty-two months on a motion for a verdict of acquittal notwithstanding the jury verdict in the case of a man convicted of illegally acting as a government agent. Warren Olney III, head of the Justice Department's criminal division, complained in 1956 that, "Leaving this man on tenterhooks…is a refinement of torture that has no parallel in the courts of the state of California." At one point, the Ninth Circuit Court intervened, telling the district court not to give Carter any new cases until he made headway on his backlog.

Carter said he deliberated slowly because he didn't want to be reversed. "Maybe I work too long or write too much," he told a reporter in 1968. "Maybe it's a strength, maybe it's a weakness." Carter, who arrived at the courthouse at 7:30 every morning, was proud of being reversed only six times in his first seventeen years on the bench. But until he took command in the Patty Hearst trial, Carter also had his detractors. He developed a reputation for being soft on sentencing and long on words. Lawyers jokingly referred to his long-winded dissertations in court as "the punishment by elocution in front of Ollie Carter." But he also developed a reputation as a patient, honest judge who worked hard to respond to every case that came before him. No verdict was predetermined in Carter's court.

In 1957, a man who described himself as a physicist tried to use Carter to stop the Atomic Energy Commission's nuclear testing in Nevada. "It was H. Wallace Hendricks versus the atom bomb yesterday—and the bomb won," wrote one newspaper. Hendricks appeared in Carter's court and said the bomb tests would cause "huge fractures in the earth's surfaces, radioactive geysers…even a chain reaction which would destroy the earth." Carter listened, but refused his request to end the tests. He told Hendricks that he was in the wrong jurisdiction, that he should take the case to Nevada.

In 1968, David Harris was found guilty by a jury in Carter's court for refusing military induction. Harris, husband of singer Joan Baez and leader of the Students for a Democratic Society at Stanford University, spoke eloquently against the Vietnam War as he challenged the constitutionality of the Selective Service Act, and said he could not kill anybody. Carter told Harris, "You are one of the most willful and deliberate violators of the law I have seen, and I think you will say 'hooray' to that."

"Thank you," Harris replied.

But then, Carter surprised the packed courtroom when he sentenced Harris to three years in prison.

"Miss Baez, who had been sitting in the front row and had maintained her composure throughout, buried her head in her hands for a few moments and a deep sigh from the spectators broke the stillness," wrote newspaper reporter David Hall. Harris was in jail most of the years of their marriage. They divorced in 1973.

Edward Preston Murphy, McCarran's choice, was nominated by Truman in 1950 to another new seat on the district court, the seventh. He and Carter received their commissions on the same day. Murphy was born in Austin, Nevada, in 1904, and attended Santa Clara University, earning a bachelor's degree in 1927, a law degree in 1928, and a juris doctor degree from the Santa Clara University School of Law in 1932.

He worked as a professor of law and public speaking at the university from 1928 to 1932, and then worked in private practice in San Francisco from 1933 to 1942. California governor Culbert Olson appointed him to the California Toll Bridge Authority in 1939 and to the San Francisco Municipal Court in 1942. Three years later, Murphy started serving as a judge in the Appellate Division of the California Superior Court.

Murphy died of a heart attack at age fifty-four while on a hunting trip in December 1958, but his eight years on the court were filled with colorful cases. In the early 1950s, Murphy tossed out a lawsuit filed by gangster Mickey Cohen seeking $11,500 in damages from San Francisco police chief Tom Cahill. Police inspectors had hauled Cohen from the Fairmont Hotel to the Hall of Justice so they could find out what he was doing in San Francisco. Cohen, who was considered the West Coast's mafia muscle, said at the time, "They treated me like a gentleman. They were gentlemen." But he later filed suit charging that his rights had been violated. The government argued that Cohen had agreed to go with the inspectors. Murphy called the lawsuit frivolous.

In 1953, Vincent Hallinan—the thorn in the side of Judge Harris—returned to the district court, this time as a defendant. Hallinan was convicted in Murphy's court of income tax evasion and sentenced to eighteen months in prison. Although he called the sentence harsh, Hallinan said Murphy had conducted a fair trial. Hallinan had run for president as a Progressive Party candidate in 1952, but the trial marked the end of his political career.

One of the more dramatic days in Murphy's court occurred in September 1954, when Basil "The Owl" Banghart was brought in from Alcatraz Prison to plead for his release. Banghart, a notorious machine gunner in a Chicago gang rival to Al Capone's, had been convicted in Illinois state court in 1934 of participating in the kidnapping of John "Jake the Barber" Factor and in federal court for robbing a US mail truck. He escaped from Stateville Penitentiary in Joliet, Illinois, in 1942, but was captured and shipped to Alcatraz. "Banghart, the jail busting, bank-robber kidnapper who once boasted that no cage could hold him, pleaded for his freedom from Alcatraz yesterday with all the bravado of a thoroughly whipped school boy," Dick Pollard wrote in the *Examiner.* "He was a time-beaten and vastly subdued man from the prohibition days, when he did the trigger work for Roger 'The Terrible' Touhy." Murphy denied the Owl's request for early release from Alcatraz.

FIG. 6-3
Burglar and prison escape artist Basil "The Owl" Banghart (center) attends a 1950 hearing with attorney Scott Stewart (front) and a bailiff. At the time, he was serving a term at Alcatraz for mail robbery. Courtesy of the Associated Press.

In 1952, Harold McGrath and California party leaders pushed for attorney Monroe Friedman to fill a vacant judgeship. But McGrath said Senator McCarran resisted, saying, "There'll be no Jew get through my committee in the West." Monroe Mark Friedman received a recess appointment from Truman in 1952 to the seat vacated by Herbert Erskine. But Friedman's service was terminated six months later after the Senate failed to confirm him. He had the shortest term in the district court's history. Friedman lost out on a permanent seat due to bad timing and his religion: his nomination came before the Senate Judiciary Committee just before it adjourned for the 1952 political conventions, McCarran's promise that his committee would approve no Jew held true, and Friedman's nomination was withdrawn after Eisenhower, a Republican, took over the White House.

For the record, Friedman likely would have made a fine district court judge. He later served as presiding judge of the Alameda County Superior Court from 1959 to 1971 and as senior judge from 1971 to 1975. On the superior court, Friedman presided over the trial of Black Panther founder Huey P. Newton, who was convicted in 1968 of the voluntary manslaughter of an Oakland police officer.

Runaway Grand Jury

One of the strangest chapters in district court history began in 1950 when a runaway grand jury tarnished the reputation of the entire court. The chapter began with little fanfare, as accusations of misconduct were leveled by the California Special Crime Study Commission against the Internal Revenue Bureau, the office that collected income tax in San Francisco. Some of those accusations were repeated later when the Senate's Kefauver Committee on organized crime held closed hearings in San Francisco. The star witness at the hearings told senators that he resigned as a Treasury Department investigator because his bosses in Northern California refused to prosecute tax evaders. The implication was that the mafia had infiltrated the bureau.

Soon after the hearing, a district court grand jury began looking into irregularities in the collector's office. The jurors were fueled by information provided by assistant US Attorney Charles O'Gara. But they were discouraged by O'Gara's boss, US Attorney Frank Hennessy. Jurors asked O'Gara to forward the information that he had collected. He did so on May 16, 1951, a day that was called Wild Wednesday at the federal courthouse.

That morning, O'Gara was assigned to talk to the new grand jurors by his boss, Robert B. McMillan, chief of the assistant US Attorneys. O'Gara presented evidence that the first grand jury had gathered on the revenue bureau and presented the grand jury with a bill of particulars that outlined charges against James G. Smyth, San Francisco's collector of internal revenue, and members of his staff. "In the midst of this presentation McMillan entered the jury room and ordered him to stop," Congressional investigators later wrote. "O'Gara was making wild charges against Hennessy and Judge Roche," McMillan told investigators. But O'Gara refused to stop. "McMillan urged the jurors to go and talk to one of the judges before proceeding further, whereupon O'Gara requested a vote as to whether they desired to hear him out, and the jury elected to have him continue at once."

McMillan called US Attorney Chauncey Tramutolo, who had taken over the office from Hennessy two days before, and found that O'Gara had been given no authority to direct the new jury to look into the revenue bureau. McMillan called Judge Louis Goodman, who sent a marshal to summon the jurors to appear in his courtroom. "Judge Goodman impounded the transcript of O'Gara's remarks and told the jurors that matters relating to the collector's office would be presented to them through the proper channels at some later date," investigators wrote. The judge told the grand jurors it was inappropriate for them to listen to O'Gara because he was not authorized to speak for the US Attorney's office, and he told the jurors that it was unwarranted for them to decide what to investigate.

About three weeks later, Judge Murphy dismissed the grand jury. Richard Seward, chairman of the jury, later said that Murphy submitted them to "quite an ordeal," testifying that "he was very critical. He used such words as 'self-appointed Gestapo' and said, 'The sovereignty of the United States is involved, and I am here to see it upheld.'"

The jury was disbanded, but not the controversy. Local newspapers doggedly continued coverage of the accusations surrounding the Internal Revenue Bureau. When the *San Francisco Call-Bulletin* reported in early 1952 that Judge Harris was named as a prominent figure in a real estate development associated with the revenue bureau scandal, Judge Carter took the offensive. He ordered a new grand jury to investigate whether the *Call-Bulletin* and other newspapers were "impeding justice" by publishing such news. He held a copy of the paper with the headline "US Judge Harris Named in Land Deal," handed the paper to the grand jury foreman, and declared, "I have submitted this to you because articles of this kind, the kind which will be referred to you, create a very serious problem in these courts in the administration of justice and the duties of this court in connection therewith." The judge then called on the grand jury to determine whether the newspaper publisher, editor, or writers were guilty of obstruction of justice.

Randolph Hearst, publisher of the paper, returned fire quickly with a front-page headline: "We Welcome The Grand Jury Investigation." The

Courthouse Hustlers

Westbrook Pegler, a columnist with Hearst's King Features Syndicate, took a dim view of the district court, writing in the *San Francisco Call-Bulletin* in 1955, "We accumulated a raffish roster of lame-ducks, loafers, courthouse hustlers, and miscellaneous bums in this jurisprudence during the foul regime, and the scant aristocracy of mediocrities seem Solonian by comparison."

Shooting Stars

In 1949, lineman William Radovich challenged the National Football League's reserve clause by suing the NFL and charging that the professional football league had conspired to monopolize and control the sport. Radovich played with the Detroit Lions in the NFL during the late 1930s and 1940s. He requested to be traded to the Los Angeles Rams to be closer to his ailing father in Los Angeles, but his request was refused. So Radovich took a job with the Los Angeles Dons of the All-America Football Conference. When he tried to return to the San Francisco Clippers of the NFL-affiliated Pacific Coast League as a player-coach, he was told that he was blacklisted. Radovich sought $105,000 in district court, but the case was dismissed. The Court of Appeals agreed with the decision, but the Supreme Court sided with Radovich in 1957 and ruled that the NFL was bound by antitrust laws.

In 1953, Frank Ciraolo, owner of the San Francisco Clippers football team, charged the NFL with monopoly and restraint of trade under the Sherman antitrust law. He said that the NFL promised him a franchise but gave it to the San Francisco 49ers instead. Ciraolo lost his case.

In 1963, Judge Lloyd Burke dismissed San Francisco Giants star Orlando Cepeda's $1 million libel suit against Look magazine. The judge ruled that a profile in the magazine was not libelous.

---

editorial below the headline stated that "It is a fair inference that there is some connection in Judge Carter's mind between his charge to the jury and the news story about Judge George Harris. We don't get it, frankly, or we'd be glad to discuss it."

California senator Richard Nixon entered the fray, saying that Carter's call for a grand jury investigation would be seen by many as "retaliation for the newspaper's embarrassing disclosures about the administration." He said he hoped the House Judiciary Committee would investigate "the San Francisco mess" soon. Within weeks, a subcommittee of the judiciary committee met in San Francisco, charged with determining why the district had been lax in prosecuting tax cases. "When we get through, Congress and the public will know once and for all whether justice has been obstructed and corruption covered up or whether innocent people

Ex-U. S. Grand Jurors Rap Judges, Prosecutor

Letters to Congressmen Charge Attempts to Influence Probe

By ED MONTGOMERY

The handling of Federal grand juries here by three Federal judges and the United States attorney's office was brought under direct attack yesterday by the Federal Grand Jury Association of Northern California.

Writing to two Congressmen, the association charged that the conduct of bench and prosecutors has "tended to compromise the independence of the grand jury and to make it subservient to the expedient impulses of the prosecuting attorney."

Further, charged the association, this conduct, "if persisted in, would break down and destroy the working of the grand jury system."

Action by the association came as deposed Collector of Internal Revenue James G. Smyth and three co-defendants prepared to plead in Federal court today to charges of conspiring to defraud the Government through the backdating of tax returns.

Attorneys for Smyth, John J. Boland, Paul V. Doyle and Attorney Lloyd J. Cosgrove are expected to file motions for a dismissal of the indictment, for an inspection of the grand jury minutes, for a bill of particulars and for a bill of discovery. The latter two motions call for an elaboration of the charges and the evidence presented the grand jury.

JUDGE NAMED——

The association suggested to Rep. Cecil H. King, chairman of the subcommittee opening hearings here February 4, that it "invite" Federal Judges Louis E. Goodman, Edward P. Murphy and Oliver J. Carter to appear as witnesses to defend their actions. These are the three judges who were involved in conflicts with grand juries during the long tax scandal investigations of 1951.

The association is made up of former grand jurors. Richard H. Seward, its president, who signed the letters to the two Congressmen, was foreman of one of the 1951 grand juries.

The second letter went to Representative Patrick J. Hillings, California Congressman who last week demanded a Judiciary subcommittee investigation here of the whole conflict.

ORDERS DIFFER——

In identical language, the two letters charged:

1—That orders from the bench to grand juries during 1951 "appear to be widely divergent and in fact contrary to long established precedent and rules" governing powers and duties of grand juries.

2—That the office of the United States Attorney during 1950 and 1951 showed "either a complete misconception as to the part which the grand jury plays in the democratic process" or made "a deliberate attempt to interfere with the orderly and proper functioning of the grand jury."

By mentioning 1950 as well as 1951, the association extended its criticism to include former United States Attorney Frank Hennessy. He was succeeded May 14, 1951, by Chauncey Tramutolo.

The former grand jurors said this conduct of bench and prosecutor has confused grand juries and "has acted to impair public confidence in the judicial process".

CONFLICT——

In proposing to Congressman King that the three judges be asked to testify, the association said:

"It is also suggested that the aforementioned judges may wish, in the public interest, to avail themselves of the opportunity to reconcile what appear to be serious discrepancies as between their recent decisions and instructions on the one hand, and the formidable body of opinion which exists supporting the traditional powers and duties of Federal grand juries on the other."

In another development yesterday, Tramutolo said that when the King subcommittee arrives, he will invite it to hold a closed hearing in the Federal grand jury chambers.

Tramutolo said he would propose that the hearing be attended by Attorney General Edmund G. Brown, District Attorney Thomas C. Lynch and himself. He did not explain further.

Meanwhile it was announced in Washington that Irvin Goldstein, special assistant to Attorney General who assisted in the recent grand jury tax office inquiry here, would leave for San Francisco today to reopen the internal revenue investigation.

Goldstein will concentrate on the affairs of Russell W. Duke of Portland, Ore. Duke, who testified before the Kessler grand jury here December 12, attempted suicide in his Portland home on December 20.

FIG. 6-4

On January 22, 1952, the *San Francisco Examiner* reported on accusations by the Federal Grand Jury Association of Northern California of "compromising" conduct by three federal judges and the United States Attorney's office in the Runaway Grand Jury affair. Courtesy of the Historical Society and Archives, US District Court for the Northern District of California.

have been smeared," said Representative Patrick J. Hillings, a Democrat from California who said that grand jurors wrote him about "shocking conditions" in San Francisco.

After two weeks of hearings, the subcommittee reported that the Internal Revenue Bureau was run poorly because control of the office had fallen into the hands of incompetent political appointees who cared more about loyalty than competent management. "It is apparent that the inefficient, politically dictated administration of the collector's office has been well-known for many years, but nothing done about it," the report concluded. "Mr. O'Gara and Mr. Doolan can in good part share the credit for bringing the situation to light. It is to their discredit that their conduct in some instances and particularly in the case of Mr. O'Gara was impetuous and ill advised."

At about the same time, visiting district court judge James Alger Fee of Oregon ruled that the second grand jury had a right to investigate and indict James Smyth and that O'Gara had every right to present information to the grand jury. As an assistant US Attorney, O'Gara could do anything that the US Attorney could do—until he was discharged. The ruling was a bitter lashing of Judge Goodman, who in a heavy-handed manner had circumscribed the jury on Wild Wednesday.

Congress was not finished with the judges. In 1953, a more formal hearing was held by a house judiciary subcommittee, headed by Representative Kenneth B. Keating, a Republican from New York, at City Hall. Before the hearings, Judge Goodman criticized legislative investigations that forced witnesses to incriminate themselves. He told the *San Francisco Chronicle* that these hearings ran counter to the Fifth Amendment, which guarantees witnesses in criminal cases the right not to be compelled to testify against themselves. "It is beyond dispute that effort should be made and encouraged both by investigating and prosecuting officials and by lawmakers to expose, prevent, and punish crime—to make our people safe and secure in their persons, home, and property," Goodman said. "But in so doing, there is never any need to depart from orderly process or to weaken the fundamental protective Constitutional device."

Several former grand jurors told the subcommittee their version of what had happened at the courthouse. "Their stories were long: they spoke of vexing delays in grand jury investigations, of harassment and abuse by federal lawyers, and of crimes allegedly covered up in a welter of confusing legal maneuvers," reported one newspaper. The members of the subcommittee continued undaunted. They issued a subpoena for Judge Goodman to testify, a move that was considered unprecedented. Robert A. Collier, chief counsel for the subcommittee, said that Goodman was opposed to grand jurors being questioned by the subcommittee, the *Chronicle* reported. "He also commented he was interested in protecting the dignity of the court and the sanctity of the grand jury, and he was not interested in any of this other hogwash going on," Collier told the committee.

"What?" asked an astonished Keating.

"Hogwash," said Collier.

"Did he use that word?"

"He did. I wrote it down."

"It is at the very least startling to hear a member of the bench refer to the work of a duly authorized congressional committee as hogwash," said Representative Hillings. "I suggest the committee consider inviting him before us." The committee huddled and asked Collier to issue a subpoena, which was then served on the judge.

Goodman, after much reluctance, appeared before the subcommittee. His appearance was filled with drama. Photographers popped flashes as the judge arrived. US Attorney Tramutolo, who was on the stand, was asked if he would step aside. After Goodman took a seat, the congressmen huddled together to consider going into executive session.

"Before you do that," Goodman announced, "let me tell you that the statements I am to present on the part of the court will not be presented in executive session."

Applause rang out—but for just a moment.

"I'm not going to answer your question," Goodman said. "I will not be subservient to the legislative branch of government and give an opinion with respect to the rules of the court. I will send you a copy of the rules governing grand juries."

"Specifically then," Keating asked, "any matter passed upon in open court by you or any other judge is not a matter or subject of inquiry for us?"

"That is correct," Goodman declared.

The judge then delivered a written statement that clarified his use of the term "hogwash." It stated that Goodman told attorney Collier that grand jury matters could be made public only in judicial proceedings. Collier asked if the committee hearings were a judicial proceeding, and the judge replied, "Mr. Collier, that is just plain hogwash. Of course the committee is not conducting a judicial proceeding."

Keating accepted the explanation.

Goodman also released a statement signed by six federal judges stating that the legislative branch can't compel members of the judicial branch to testify about court matters. The subcommittee failed to gather any information from Goodman about why he made his decisions on Wild Wednesday.

Two other district court judges, Michael Roche and Edward Murphy, also appeared. Roche spoke briefly and in general terms, saying that the subcommittee had been misled. Murphy was more specific: "I'm not going to stand on legalistic formulas. Ask me any question you want and you'll get a truthful answer."

He told the congressmen that he dismissed the original grand jury because the jurors' oath of secrecy "had not only been breached but had actually been flouted." Murphy said some jurors had contacted newspaper reporters and had tarnished the reputations of men who had not been indicted. "It is a dangerous and grave thing for any body of laymen, however well intentioned, to appoint themselves a band of vigilantes," Murphy told the subcommittee. "It is doubly dangerous when that body acts under the color of the law, yet itself does not respect the curbs and restrictions imposed by the law. From such license flows black tyranny, trial by newspaper and destruction of democratic safeguards."

Congressman Keating eventually released a report to the House Committee on the Judiciary criticizing US Attorneys Frank Hennessy and Chauncey Tramutolo for their handling of the tax scandals. The nineteen-page report—supported by Republicans Keating and Hillings and repudiated by Democrat Byron G. Rogers of Colorado—determined that assistant US Attorney Charles O'Gara should not have been stopped from presenting the tax fraud allegations on Wild Wednesday. "The San Francisco grand juries encountered obstructionist tactics from the United States attorney and his staff, the Department (of Justice) in Washington, and, to some extent, from the local federal judges as well," the report concluded. "The jurors' efforts to clean out inefficiency and corruption among local federal officials in San Francisco were fully merited by the conditions with which they were confronted." The report says that Tramutolo should not have prevented O'Gara from leading the jurors: "The grand juries to whom the charges were presented were fully within the prerogatives traditionally accorded to federal grand juries when they sought to inquire into conditions within the collector's office." The judges were "less than vigorous" in guiding and protecting the grand juries.

But the report did criticize O'Gara, who resigned in early 1952: "He was young and inexperienced. He received support from members of the local press, and it would be unrealistic to rule out an element of personal publicity among the motivations for his actions." Representative Rogers, who called the report slanted and filled with half-truths, said that news stories at the time proved that the grand jury had violated its rule of secrecy.

Smyth was acquitted by a jury in 1952 of backdating his own tax return to defraud the government. The trial was held by a visiting judge. Harris dismissed additional charges against Smyth in 1954. Smyth's deputy was convicted of backdating three delinquent estate tax returns and defrauding the government. Another deputy was convicted of conspiracy to fix tax liability, but the Board of Appeals overruled the conviction. The office was reorganized. Harris, in a 1980 oral interview, said the runaway grand jury was "a classic illustration of the process of the law becoming unbridled and completely out of hand."

A New Courthouse

Almost since the day the Post Office and Courthouse was dedicated in 1905, judges complained about the court facilities. Judge William Van Fleet, who began his term at the courthouse in 1907, considered the building "altogether inadequate." His successor, Maurice Dooling, called the courthouse "greatly overcrowded." The building was remodeled several times to accommodate the growing court, but complaints from judges grew more common and more pointed as the building aged. By the 1950s, district court judges had started to campaign for a new court building by talking to reporters. "San Francisco is the worst area in the whole country as far as federal judicial facilities are concerned," Goodman told the *Chronicle* in 1954. "We have the odious distinction of having the only courthouse in the US where the main entrance is on an alley."

Later that year, seven San Francisco federal judges wrote a memo to local officials and congressmen that outlined their criticism of the courthouse at Seventh and Mission Streets. The three trial courts, they wrote, were too noisy. The single Court of Appeals courtroom used by the district court is "totally inadequate," they wrote, because of poor lighting and bad ventilation. "The present building is located in a congested area with poor accessibility and practically no parking facilities," they stated. "The site provides no approach to the area and entirely lacks the traditional courthouse setting. There are insufficient facilities in the building for juries, for witnesses, or for the press. The library is inadequately and poorly lighted."

The *Chronicle* soon joined the push for a new courthouse. The paper cited many of the judges' concerns in a 1954 editorial: the courthouse was "overcrowded, poorly ventilated, ill lighted, constantly beset by disturbing street noises, lacking in facilities for lawyers, witnesses, and juries. Three of its district courtrooms are made-over offices, low-ceilinged, cramped, uncomfortable for judges, lawyers, juries, and spectators." The paper wrote that the courthouse did not have adequate space for the US Attorney, the marshal, probation officers, or grand jurors. "The dignity and importance of the law suggest, good business advises, and the rapid increase in federal court business (more than 50 percent in the last two years) insists that a new federal courthouse be provided as quickly as possible."

Congress received a formal request in 1956 for a new nine-story federal building that would house the district court. The request, forwarded to the House and Senate public works committees, was for a skyscraper that would cost $40 million to build, plus an additional $5.4 million for land costs and architectural and engineering fees. The plan called for a private firm to build the structure and lease it to the government for twenty-five years.

In 1956, the House and the Senate approved the project, and a team was dispatched to find a site. Two were favored: the Civic Center area and the old Crystal Palace Market at Eighth and Market Streets. Several San Francisco officials worried that a thirteen- or fourteen-story skyscraper built in the Civic Center would dwarf the city's landmark City Hall. The San Francisco planning department favored the Crystal Palace site, but federal officials worried that the ground was soft and watery and could not support a skyscraper. The *Examiner* reported that the Government Services Administration (GSA) had chosen a block bounded by Golden Gate Avenue and Polk, Turk, and Larkin Streets, but then the project suddenly came to a standstill. As city and federal officials mulled a decision, Oakland leaders suggested the new federal office tower be built there. All of a sudden, Oakland and San Francisco were fighting over the new courthouse. But the battle was brief. In December 1956, the *Chronicle* headlined an article with "Federal Building Stalled; Mayor Will Fly to East." That same day, the Oakland City Council voted unanimously to send officials to Washington to try to land the building. But when San Francisco mayor George Christopher returned from Washington, he announced that he had saved the building for the city as long as San Francisco officials would support the GSA's site.

The following year, judges on the Court of Appeals voted not to move to the new building. The appellate judges were satisfied with their elegant chambers and courtrooms in the main post office. In 1958, designs for the new $45 million structure were completed, but by 1959, momentum for the new courthouse had faded. The *Chronicle* reported in June that it had received reports that the building had been shelved. The *Examiner* confirmed, reporting "Hopes Fade For Federal Building" because President Eisenhower opposed new public works projects.

In the early 1960s, plans for a new courthouse were again revived. San Francisco architect John Carl Warnecke was hired to design a federal

FIG. 6-5
The Phillip Burton Federal Building and United States Courthouse on Golden Gate Avenue, designed by John Carl Warnecke, 1964. Courtesy of the Historical Society and Archives, US District Court for the Northern District of California.

FIG. 6-6
San Francisco mayor John F. Shelley (left) and Governor Edmund G. Brown flank President Lyndon Johnson at the June 19, 1964, dedication ceremony for the new federal building and courthouse on Golden Gate Avenue in San Francisco. Courtesy of the San Francisco History Center, San Francisco Public Library.

building and courthouse on the block previously chosen by the GSA. The design of the plain, twenty-one-story modernist box—composed of granite, aluminum, and glass framed in steel—was questioned even before the building opened. The *Chronicle*'s Allan Temko expressed "fervid distaste" for the new building, which he wrote was built to fit as many government officials as possible. He found it "insensate, cold, vulgar, pompous, depressing, dehumanizing, and not at all admirable." His paper agreed, editorializing, "The structure is so oafish in concept and execution that it properly merits no more than the passing contempt accorded the Jack Tar Hotel."

But the newspaper, in an editorial, was careful not to blame the architect. Federal bureaucrats were not concerned with aesthetics or human amenities, the paper wrote: "They demand only that each building house as many bureaus and as many bureaucrats, complete with multigraphing machines and files cases, as the appropriation can buy." Warnecke had to go along with the government's bland design ideas, according to the paper: "After all, an architect has to eat just like everybody else, doesn't he?"

On June 19, 1964, President Johnson came to dedicate the $38.5 million federal building, one of the largest ever built at that time. That same day, he also broke ground for the Bay Area Rapid Transit system. The next month, the district court judges moved from the old courthouse at Seventh and Mission Streets to the new federal building, about four blocks northwest. "I hate to move," said Judge Lloyd Burke, "but I know we have to accommodate ourselves to the special needs of the court." Chief clerk James P. Welsh, one of the last to leave, said, "I'm leaving the Queen of Seventh Street for a new bride."

On the opening day of the new court building, all seven district judges gathered for a group photo. Almost two decades later, in 1983, the courthouse was renamed the Phillip R. Burton Federal Building and United States Courthouse. Burton, a congressman from San Francisco who served in the House from 1964 to 1983, was an influential politician known nationwide for the progressive laws he shepherded through Congress, including the creation of the Golden Gate National Recreation Area.

Earl Warren's Boys

President Eisenhower named five judges to the district court during his two terms in office. Most were connected in some way or another with Earl Warren, the former California governor Eisenhower had appointed as chief justice of the Supreme Court.

Oliver D. Hamlin Jr. was nominated to the court in 1953 to the seat briefly occupied by Monroe Friedman. Hamlin served on the district court for almost five years, until Eisenhower appointed him to the Court of Appeals. Born in Oakland in 1892, Hamlin, the son of a surgeon, considered medical school but chose law school because he would graduate one year sooner. He received a bachelor of law degree from the University of California in 1914, was appointed a deputy district attorney in Alameda County the following year, and worked in private practice in Oakland from 1920 to 1947, when he took a seat as a judge on the Alameda County Superior Court.

During his five years in the Northern District, Hamlin presided over two major criminal trials. In 1953, he oversaw the trial of Arthur H. "Artie" Samish, a prominent lobbyist who wielded control over the state legislature by commanding a political slush fund that he used to make political contributions. His power was cast in the limelight by a magazine article that quoted Governor Warren saying, "Artie unquestionably has more power than the governor." His power days ended in the district court, where Samish was convicted of dodging $72,000 in income tax. Hamlin sentenced Samish to three years in prison and fined him $40,000. "That case was a shame, and a lot of people that took a great deal of credit for winning it should have been ashamed of themselves," said Samish's attorney, Harold Faulkner, in his 1981 oral history. Samish fought hard to appeal the conviction but ended up spending twenty-six months in the McNeil Island penitentiary. It was the end of his political career.

In 1958, Hamlin oversaw over the trial of George K. Jue, a powerful leader of the Chinese community and former president of the Chinese Chamber of Commerce. Jue was sentenced to a year and a day in prison for illegally transporting thirty-five Chinese aliens into the country by making fraudulent passports and visas. Fourteen of the aliens turned against him after he shook them down for money upon their arrival in San Francisco. At the end of the trial, Hamlin recommended that Jue, who turned out to be an illegal alien himself, not be deported. That got the judge into political quicksand because he was viewed as soft on communism. Representative Francis E. Walter, head of the House Un-American Activities Committee, called for Hamlin's impeachment. Hamlin went on to serve fifteen years on the Court of Appeals before his death in 1973. Jue was eventually deported.

Eisenhower nominated Sherrill Halbert to the seat vacated by Dal Lemmon in 1954. Halbert, born in Terra Bella, California, in 1901, served on the district court through 1966, when he was assigned to California's new Eastern District Court. He received his undergraduate degree and law degree from the University of California and began working in private practice in Porterville, about 250 miles southeast of San Francisco. He served as the Tulare County chief deputy district attorney from 1927 to 1936. He left private practice in 1941 to serve as California deputy state attorney general under Earl Warren, who imbued in Halbert a desire to improve the world through law. During the war, Halbert moved to San Francisco to open a private practice and worked under Lieutenant General DeWitt to help round up residents of Japanese ancestry for internment. "I feel very sympathetic towards the Japanese, but it's just the luck of war," he said years later. "I make no apology for what we did, and I'm just disappointed that these people are now making it a big civil rights issue."

Halbert found that San Francisco was not the place for him. "After I'd been around there a couple of years, it was pretty obvious that there are two ways that you can be a partner in a big firm: you either married one of the partner's daughters, or you bring in Standard Oil as an account," Halbert said. He was already married and had no oil prospects, so he left for Modesto in 1944 to work in private practice and serve as chief deputy district attorney and later as district attorney for Stanislaus County. Halbert aspired to be a first-rate trial lawyer, and prosecuted five hundred cases during his five years in Stanislaus. In 1949, Governor Warren named Halbert to a judgeship on the superior court. When he was sworn into office, he declared that "no one coming into my court as a stranger shall go away with anything less than he's entitled to, and no friend coming into my court shall go away with more than he's entitled to." That became his axiom for his life on the bench.

In 1954, when Dal Lemmon was elevated to the Court of Appeals, Halbert was approached about seeking Lemmon's district court job in Sacramento. "I went around and got some of my friends, and they started a little campaign," he said. They started corresponding with Republican senators William Knowland and Thomas Kuchel, but there were a dozen applicants for the job. Eventually Halbert was called into Knowland's office in Sacramento, where the senator said, "Will you tell these guys to stop sending all these letters and telegrams? I haven't got the space for any more." Knowland told Halbert he would get the appointment. Weeks later, Halbert got a call from a reporter at the *Modesto Bee* informing

---

Identity Theft

"For years, Frank J. Hennessy, the former U.S. Attorney here, and Frank J. Hennessy, a former manager for Ernie's Liquor Stores, had been plagued by their identical names. Although they never met face-to-face, they got each other's phone calls, mail, messages and so on. The final great coincidence took place on Monday, March 18. That day, both Frank J. Hennessys died."

—Herb Caen's *Examiner* column, March 27, 1957

---

him he was to be a federal judge. Not fully believing him, Halbert went to the local radio station, KTRB. "Sure enough, there it was on the UP wire. 'Sherrill Halbert from California has been confirmed as US District Judge for the Northern District of California,'" he recalled. The next day, he got his certificate from the president.

As in San Francisco, the district court in Sacramento eventually outgrew its facilities. In 1961, the General Services Administration finished construction on a new federal building at 650 Capitol Mall to accommodate the expanding court. Halbert balked at the change, announcing that he would not move from his lavish courtroom in the Sacramento post office building unless major design changes were made. Most everything about the new utilitarian courtroom bothered him. His bench was not elevated and court watchers had a direct view into the prisoners' toilet. Halbert declared that the GSA had botched the job, and predicted that the building would "stand as a monument to their stupidity for all time."

Although the Sacramento court was growing, it was still considered something of an outpost of the Northern District. Like Martin Welsh and Dal Lemmon, Halbert was the only district court judge assigned to work in Sacramento. Occasionally, Judge Carter came to reduce a backlog of cases, but as the caseload increased it became apparent that Halbert needed more help. Judge Thomas McBride was appointed in 1961 as the second full-time Sacramento judge. But his appointment was still not enough. Halbert later recalled:

> I remember on one occasion that I had a firm commitment from a judge in San Francisco, who would come up and help Tom and me with some work. And I had a jury trial, a criminal jury trial, set. And I had a trial involving—it was patents—set, where lawyers were already there from New York. And the clerk called me on the morning that the case was to go to trial and said they didn't have any judges to spare, that all their judges were busy down in San Francisco. And I kind of blew my stack, I must confess. But nevertheless, that was the straw that broke the camel's back, and we kept on until we were able to get the new district created.

Halbert helped start a campaign that resulted in the establishment of another district court in 1966: the United States District Court for the Eastern District of California, which encompasses the eastern part of the state from the Oregon border on the north to Kern County in the south and includes Sacramento, Redding, South Lake Tahoe, Yosemite, Fresno, and Bakersfield.

Eisenhower's next choice for the district court was Albert C. Wollenberg Sr., nominated in 1958 to the seat vacated by Michael Roche. Wollenberg, born in 1900 in San Francisco, was the son of Charles M. Wollenberg, a prominent San Francisco social service administrator who served as the director of city and county institutions as well as the state welfare system. Young Wollenberg attended Lowell High School, received a bachelor's degree from UC Berkeley, and earned a law degree from Boalt Hall in 1924. He went into private practice for three years, then served as an assistant US Attorney from 1927 to 1934, mostly prosecuting bank cases. In 1939, he won a seat in the California legislature as a Republican, defeating future district court judge George Harris. In Sacramento, Wollenberg became a close friend of Earl Warren, who appointed him to the Superior Court of California in San Francisco in 1947.

During the mid-1950s, Wollenberg applied for a judgeship on the district court. He said he had been interested in becoming a federal judge since his days in the US Attorney's office, but he took a serious interest when two vacancies became available. He contacted Senators William Knowland and Thomas Kuchel, both of whom he had known for decades, and made a strong push for the job. Kuchel, a former colleague from the state legislature, offered his support but said the decision would be made by Knowland, the senior senator. Wollenberg, who had been instrumental in Knowland's 1946 campaign, approached the senator with confidence. Wollenberg, in his oral history, recounted:

> He told me I was awfully late in getting started. A lot of other people had applied and so forth. I remember a remark he made, something about, "Why, there's a line clear from here to Baltimore, from my desk to Baltimore," some statement of that kind, "all of whom want consideration."
>
> I said, "That's great. The more the merrier. You'll get a good man. I'm at the head of that line right now, in front of your desk. It's up to you to give me an answer. I'm not late. I'm in the front of the line, not in the back of the line."
>
> He said, "Okay, Al, we'll think about it."
>
> The next day he phoned me and told me he'd send my name into the president. That's all I had to do. I didn't talk to any people. I didn't bring in any political people or have anyone else talk to Knowland. I talked to him myself. No one else at my request did, and I never heard of anyone that did.

The process went quickly. Eisenhower nominated Wollenberg in April 1958. He was called to Washington for a Senate hearing that lasted only ten or fifteen minutes and received word of his appointment while on his way back to San Francisco.

Wollenberg must have felt right at home with the judges when he started on the district court. He lived next door to Judge Harris and had served on the superior court with Murphy, worked in the legislature with Carter, and campaigned for years with Hamlin. Wollenberg had known Chief Judge Goodman since their days in private practice decades before. Wollenberg's district court tenure ran from 1958 to 1981. A salt-of-the-earth kind of a man, Wollenberg was sweet and gentle on the bench. Modest and wise, he gave the impression that he was everybody's grandfather with a lot of common sense. In 1970, Wollenberg ruled that unemployed California residents were entitled to a hearing before their unemployment benefits could be stopped. The state's Department of Human Resources routinely cut off payment if officials received information that recipients were not seeking work. Wollenberg ruled that those charged must have a chance to confront their witnesses. Later that year, he ruled that a commune is not a family under the law after commune residents filed suit against Palo Alto charging that the city's zoning laws prohibited their way of living in single-family districts. And in 1971, the judge ruled that a candidate could run for public office in San Francisco without paying the filing fee if he or she could not afford it.

Two months after Wollenberg's nomination, President Eisenhower nominated Lloyd Hudson Burke to the district court seat vacated by Oliver Hamlin. Burke was born in Oakland, the son of fire chief James H. Burke. Lloyd received an undergraduate degree from St. Mary's College, just east of Berkeley, and a law degree from Boalt Hall. He served as deputy district attorney in Alameda County before World War II, and then served in the army's counterintelligence unit.

After the war, Burke returned to his job as deputy district attorney and was then appointed US Attorney for the Northern District of California in 1953. He was the youngest US Attorney in the district's history when he was sworn in at age thirty-seven. During his five-year tenure, Burke made a name for himself by successfully prosecuting Arthur Samish. Burke's stiffest challenge as US Attorney came later, when Judge Carter quashed his attempt to subpoena and examine all the historical records of twenty-four Chinese American family associations. Carter stopped Burke's probe into immigration fraud, calling it a "mass inquisition."

Burke was the first US Attorney ever appointed to the district court. As with Wollenberg, Kuchel and Knowland recommended Burke. He was also supported by Warren Olney III, the assistant US attorney general who had backed the Samish prosecution. Burke served on the district court for almost thirty years, until his death in 1988. Strong-willed and opinionated, Burke had a reputation among lawyers as a heavy drinker, but he did not let his drinking get in the way of his decisions. The judge also developed a reputation for his determination both on and off the bench. "Burke seldom eats lunch, occasionally using the time to walk as far as the Ferry Building and back," one reporter wrote. "When he doesn't take the walk, it's not uncommon for him to run a hearing right through the lunch period, sometimes an upsetting experience for those involved."

Burke was conservative—once telling a reporter that he had never been "accused of being a liberal"—but he made some surprisingly liberal decisions and took tough stances on a number of cases. In 1968, Palo Alto attorney James R. Hagan and three others filed a lawsuit challenging the constitutionality of the Electoral College. Hagan argued that the process denies due process and equal protection of the law to voters. Burke did not dismiss the lawsuit. "The suit, in my opinion, is certainly not frivolous and does present a substantial constitutional question," he wrote. He called for a three-judge federal panel to convene and hear the case. That same year, he tossed out a lawsuit by Stefan Ray Aronow challenging the printing of "In God We Trust" on US currency. The Court of Appeals agreed with him in 1970, writing, "It is quite obvious that the national motto and the slogan on coinage and currency 'In God We Trust' has nothing whatsoever to do with the establishment of religion."

In 1969, Alameda County spent $170,000 to remodel one of its rooms in the County Administration Building for use by the district court. Oakland, the county seat, was officially designated as the location of a federal court by President Johnson in September 1969. Burke, an Oakland native, was assigned to take the first case. During the early 1970s, Burke found himself in the center of several hot-button education cases. In 1970, he rejected a request that the San Francisco Board of Education provide bilingual instruction for Chinese-speaking students. Two years later, he upheld the strict grooming rules of El Camino High School. The school's policy forbid boys from coming to school with hair covering their ears or reaching below their shirt collars and girls from wearing jeans, cutoffs, or hot pants. "We won't even register a kid who moves here from San Francisco if he looks like a fugitive from the Haight-Ashbury," said the school principal. The school rules were okay, Burke ruled, because they reflected community values.

The most important case that Burke ruled on was the City of Petaluma's plan to limit new growth. Petaluma, about forty miles north of San Francisco, issued an anti-growth zoning plan after its population increased from 10,000 residents in 1950 to 24,500 in 1970. The case was viewed around the country as a test of a municipality's ability to limit growth. Burke ruled that the Petaluma Plan, an innovative scheme that banned the construction of more than five hundred new homes in subdivisions each year, was unconstitutional. Burke's decision sent shock waves out to planners and government officials around the nation. But he was overruled by the Court of Appeals, which called the Petaluma Plan constitutional.

Upon Burke's death in 1988, the *San Francisco Chronicle* wrote, "Judge Burke was noted for his sharp humor, for ruling from the bench and then making the winning attorney prepare the written ruling, and for starting his court an hour later than any other judge."

Eisenhower's final appointment, William Thomas Sweigert, was nominated in April 1959 to replace Judge Murphy. Sweigert, the only Democrat named by Eisenhower, took the federal bench at age fifty-eight after five months as a municipal judge in San Francisco and nearly a decade on the Superior Court of the State of California. A local paper dubbed him the "fastest rising jurist in California." Born in San Jose in 1900, Sweigert spent his life in the Bay Area. He obtained a law degree from University of San Francisco in 1923 and went on to private practice, during which time he also lectured at his alma mater. Sweigert served as assistant state attorney general under Earl Warren, and served as Warren's executive secretary. "If anybody did anything to convert Earl Warren to the liberal that he eventually became, I would say it was Judge Sweigert," commented Judge Alfonso Zirpoli, a colleague on the federal bench and a friend of Sweigert's for nearly sixty years.

Zirpoli also credited Sweigert with updating and standardizing the district court's procedures. "His rules are the basis for everything we have today," Zirpoli noted in his oral history. In 1962, Chief Judge Harris set up a committee to update the Northern District's rules for civil cases. Sweigert did the bulk of the work, Zirpoli recalled, most of which focused on pretrial hearings and discovery. He created time limits for case development to keep attorneys moving, and he streamlined the process of trying a case by ensuring that witness lists were revealed in advance, all exhibits were prepared before trial, and all facts not in dispute were stipulated—updates that proved invaluable when the court's caseload exploded in response to the escalation of the Vietnam War. Sweigert and Zirpoli completed another revision of federal rules in 1968. Three years later, Sweigert investigated the effects of reducing jury size in civil cases, and as of December 1971, civil juries included six, rather than twelve, members.

Sweigert's attention to proper procedure and organization carried over into his own courtroom as well. As a young attorney, William Schwarzer (who later became a district court judge) recalls trying cases before Judge Sweigert. "He would make me restate and restate a question until it was absolutely tight and clear, with no extra words and no ambiguities, before he would let the witness answer," Schwarzer recalled. "It was just his way of bringing young lawyers along....It was a little intimidating at the time. But when I think back now of what I learned in that court about asking questions…it was invaluable."

Sweigert's notable rulings included his 1970 jab at the Supreme Court for failing to consider the constitutionality of the Vietnam War and his 1974 decision that altered the rules of the NFL draft. He denied Black Panther activist Angela Davis bail while she awaited trial for her part in a 1970 murder-kidnapping-conspiracy at the Marin County Civic Center. Six people, including superior court judge Harold Haley, were killed that day. Davis was accused of having supplied the weapons.

Sweigert assumed senior status in 1973. Two years later, more than five hundred members of the San Francisco bar gathered to honor him. "At the time, Judge Sweigert remembered being told by Public Defender James Hewitt that lawyers referred to the Judge as 'S.O.B.'—and that the initials stood for Sweet Old Bill," reported the court historical society's *Historical Bulletin*. "If they meant that, I am deeply moved," Sweigert said. "But if they meant the other, as I suspect they did, I can only plead that in the best tradition of judicial fairness I have been equally one to both sides."

CHAPTER 7
CONSCIENTIOUS
OBJECTION

AS THE 1960S BEGAN, the lazy, folk music–infused lifestyle of San Francisco's Haight-Ashbury neighborhood began gathering the speed and energy that would propel its artists and free spirits into psychedelic celebration of 1967's Summer of Love. But their jubilation would be short lived, as the drugs they used became illegal and the specter of war in Vietnam made life's cares all too clear. This shifting culture of the late sixties would soon envelop the district court along with the rest of the city. And despite the liberal, activist label that would soon descend over a portion of the bench, the district court proved itself perfectly willing to follow signals sent from Washington as the decade opened.

In 1959, the Landrum-Griffin Act served as yet another example of the extent to which the fear of communism had crept into American life. The act barred any member of the Communist Party from holding union office. Shortly after the law was enacted, police arrested Archie Brown. His crime: Brown was an executive board member of the local San Francisco branch of the International Longshore and Warehouse Union and an admitted communist. A district court jury convicted Brown of violating the new act. He took his case to the Court of Appeals, which reversed the verdict. The Supreme Court concurred in a landmark 1965 decision.

Originally from Iowa, Brown had come to California to seek his fortune as a young man in the 1920s. He soon found a job as a longshoreman at San Francisco's bustling piers and took an active role in organizing dockworkers into labor unions, first as a member and then as an officer of the longshoremen's union. Brown interrupted his waterfront career in 1938 to fight fascism with the Abraham Lincoln Brigade during the Spanish Civil War and again during World War II when he was sent to Europe with the US Army. After his return, Brown was elected to the executive committee of the longshoremen's union, of which Harry Bridges—a man with his own set of legal troubles—was president. As a member of the Communist Party, Brown ran (unsuccessfully) for several public offices, but his ultimate misstep may have been his vocal campaign to end the House Un-American Activities Committee's drive to root out communists within the United States.

During Brown's six-day trial in 1962, Judge Albert Wollenberg accepted the parameters of the Landrum-Griffin Act and limited the jury to consider only whether Brown was a member of the Communist Party. "There was no question he was admittedly the secretary of the union," Wollenberg explained in a 1980 interview. After Brown took the stand and testified that he was a member of the Communist Party, the jury had little to deliberate. They took only twenty minutes to reach a guilty verdict. Wollenberg sentenced Brown to six months in jail, but Brown vowed to appeal. "I anticipate the courts will find that unions have a right to elect to office those people they want to serve," he told a crowd of reporters after his sentencing. He was correct.

At about the same time, another Eisenhower appointee, Judge William Sweigert, found himself presiding over a case that foreshadowed many cases to come. In 1962, US Attorney Cecil Poole and Assistant US Attorney Jerold Ladar filed civil and criminal actions against protesters who sought to sail their thirty-foot boat, the *Everyman*, into an American nuclear testing zone near Christmas Island in the Indian Ocean. The federal government requested a temporary restraining order to stop them, which Sweigert granted. The case brought waves of demonstrators to the San Francisco federal courthouse. At one point, an exasperated Sweigert declared their "demonstrating and parading around" to be a "criminal offense," but no major arrests were made. Sweigert eventually ruled that the Atomic Energy Commission's restrictions were reasonable and made permanent the restraining order excluding protesters from the nuclear testing area. The San Francisco demonstrators, claiming to be controlled by their consciences, declared they were unable to comply with the judge's ruling.

The media attention this generated compelled Sweigert to elaborate on his ruling. He said he believed the demonstrators' actions to be sincere and "entitled to respect, and in a certain sense laudable," wrote court historian Joseph Franaszek. Sweigert then went as far as to admit that he likely agreed with much of their cause. But the judge maintained a clear sense of duty. He noted the difference between this situation—in which demonstrators chose "without any particular necessity" to violate the law—and situations in which the government compelled a citizen to act against his conscience with no alternative, and sentenced the protesters to thirty days in jail.

The judge seems to have struggled with this decision, Franaszek writes. Sweigert admitted that any solution left much to be desired. He felt that within a democracy, an individual maintains the right to protest or disobey the law, whatever the circumstances, but must be willing to accept the consequences. Presciently, Sweigert imagined the exact situation he and his Northern District colleagues would face over the next few years. When someone disobeyed a law that he or she argued violated the supreme law of the land, Sweigert contended, "The violation is more apparent than real, and the issue must be resolved through the judiciary." In Sweigert's view, the judiciary should not decline to examine whether state actions are within the "higher good." Small wonder it was Sweigert who, years later, urged the higher courts to look not just at the technicalities of the draft law but at the legality and constitutionality of the Vietnam War itself.

As Sweigert wrestled with the *Everyman* case, Judge Alfonso Zirpoli joined the Northern District bench with a lively political and legal career already behind him. Zirpoli once told writer Donald Dale Jackson that he considered himself "moderately activist" as a judge. Zirpoli insisted he was not out to impose his personal views. "I'm just making constitutional interpretations. They may be new interpretations," he continued, "but not a complete change. I interpret the Constitution and the statutes in the light of changing times."

Like a number of others who served in the courtrooms of the Northern District, Zirpoli spent most of his life in and around San Francisco. The son of Italian immigrants, Zirpoli was born in Denver. His father worked for the Italian consulate there but was transferred to San Francisco when Alfonso was twelve. The boy became a noted debate team member at Lowell High School, where future federal judge Stanley Weigel joined him in the graduating class of 1922, and worked for years as a messenger for A. P. Giannini, head of the Bank of Italy, predecessor to the Bank of America.

Zirpoli commuted by ferry to UC Berkeley and graduated with a law degree from Boalt Hall in 1928. He then opened a private practice that was enhanced by his Italian language skills and contacts. Giannini, who maintained a close relationship with Zirpoli, was instrumental in getting him a meeting with the San Francisco district attorney, which won him a job in 1932. The following year, Zirpoli was appointed an assistant US Attorney for the Northern District and, as was acceptable at the time, continued to be active in Democratic politics. Working with the FBI, Zirpoli went undercover as "Tony Damico" to help locate Baby Face Nelson, a gangster and notorious bank robber, through his associate Fatso Negri. The break in the case came when Zirpoli helped convince Negri to become a government witness. Zirpoli and Negri became so friendly that Negri asked him to serve as his best man.

Zirpoli returned to private practice in 1944 and continued his political work. He served as the Northern California manager for Adlai Stevenson's presidential campaigns in 1952 and 1956, and was elected to the San Francisco Board of Supervisors in 1958. There he was instrumental in convincing the city to participate in the Bay Area Rapid Transit system and to enlarge San Francisco International Airport. A contingent of the local population had begun lobbying Zirpoli to run for mayor when, in 1961, President John F. Kennedy appointed him to a newly created position on the district court. Zirpoli had recently co-chaired the John F. Kennedy Volunteers campaign organization in San Francisco. At his September 1961 confirmation, there were only two senators and just one question: "Do you understand you may no longer engage in politics?" Zirpoli said he did—and was confirmed.

Shortly before his induction, Judge Louis Goodman's widow presented Zirpoli with all of the judge's robes. Zirpoli wore them throughout his thirty-four-year tenure, never purchasing any of his own. But not all aspects of Zirpoli's new judicial career were so easily managed. His first case was a criminal matter, and the defendant expressed a desire to plead guilty. Zirpoli explained that it wasn't his usual practice to accept a guilty plea on first appearance. "Do you appreciate that if you plead guilty, I can sentence you to as many as ten years imprisonment and a fine not to exceed $10,000?" Zirpoli asked.

"I don't appreciate it, your honor, but I do understand," the defendant replied.

Zirpoli made a note to phrase his comments more appropriately in the future. Then, at the end of the day, "The crier again rapped with his gavel and everyone stood up to await the departure of the judge," Zirpoli recalled. "I, too, stood there for several seconds until it suddenly occurred to me that I was the judge."

Zirpoli became much more comfortable with courtroom procedure, but "unlike many judges, Zirpoli never reins in his humanity on the bench," Donald Jackson wrote in his 1974 book *Judges*. After hippies placed daffodils on his desk at the beginning of a draft-evasion hearing, Zirpoli left them there all day. And when a long-haired, barefoot, clearly intoxicated defendant addressed Zirpoli as "Love," he simply went with it. "You've made my morning much brighter," the judge responded.

Martin Glick, an attorney serving California's rural poor in the 1970s, told Jackson that "Zirpoli has a sense of justice in the true, old-fashioned sense of the word....He wants to get to the root of things." Glick recalled watching Zirpoli sentence a young man convicted of opening letters while he worked at the post office. He hadn't stolen anything, which clearly intrigued the judge. Zirpoli asked lots of questions and discovered something the prosecutors hadn't: the man was afraid of being drafted, so he had committed a felony—tampering with the mail—to disqualify himself. Zirpoli treated the incident as a juvenile case and had the man's record expunged.

Although Zirpoli pledged to give up politics when he joined the federal bench, he reveled in cases with a political tinge. In 1964, Zirpoli ruled, as part of a three-judge panel, that the Postal Service's practice of intercepting "communist propaganda" sent through the mail violated the First Amendment. Six years later, Zirpoli ordered an increase in California's Aid to Families with Dependent Children to keep up with the rising cost of living. At first, the state did not comply, and Governor Ronald Reagan denounced the order. But when the Ninth Circuit Court of Appeals affirmed Zirpoli's ruling, Zirpoli announced he would cut off $700 million in federal welfare funds if the state did not act. This time, California officials responded. (Reagan later took credit for having increased California's welfare payments when he ran for president in 1980.)

Zirpoli turned down an opportunity to move to the Ninth Circuit Court of Appeals in 1968, saying his position as a district court judge fulfilled his greatest ambition. He added that "he thought he could do more for 'my country, my court, the administration of justice and myself' by remaining a district judge," reported the *San Francisco Examiner*. Zirpoli later noted that he might have been interested in the position with the appeals court if it could have led to the Supreme Court, which he described as the "greatest achievement for anyone in the law," but at age sixty-three, he felt he was already too old.

Judge Zirpoli assumed senior status in 1975 and took his annual month-long vacation to France and Italy with his wife, Giselda. He continued to hear cases, with a reduced workload, until his death in 1995.

Free Love

It was not long before the forces shaping the culture and lifestyle of many young people in Northern California found their way into federal court. In fact, steps to curtail the free love and psychedelia of the sixties were well underway before the movement had even reached its peak. Lysergic acid diethylamide (better known as LSD) was outlawed by the federal government as a dangerous substance in 1966, with the Summer of Love yet to occur, but Augustus Owsley Stanley III—grandson of a former Kentucky governor and senator, early promoter of the Grateful Dead, and a highly skilled chemist—had already earned himself a reputation as "the Henry Ford of Acid" as he made and distributed some ten million LSD tablets, known as Owsleys, which sold for anywhere between two and ten dollars each.

After LSD was outlawed, Owsley (as he was most often known) went from wealthy hippie hero to closely watched man. In 1967, federal agents raided his three-story suburban residence in Orinda and found 67.5 grams of pure LSD—enough to make seven hundred thousand tablets—as well as a sophisticated laboratory. Federal drug supervisor Emmitt Warner seemed a bit in awe of Owsley after the raid, saying, "He's a psychedelic missionary [who]...gives the impression that he feels the average person can never actually know himself without turning on with LSD."

Owsley was charged with unlawful manufacture of drugs and conspiracy, but his trial was delayed for almost two years by legal maneuvers. When it finally began in 1969, a captivated press gave it full attention, as the Tune In, Turn On, Drop Out movement was now in full swing. Assistant US Attorney Paul Sloan read the charges against Owsley, but New York–based defense attorney Henry Rothblatt noted that the charges were not in dispute. Instead, he argued, the issue was whether the LSD and STP (another hallucinogenic drug) in Owsley's home had been seized legally. Gordon White, the narcotics agent who had led the raid, demonstrated for Judge Sweigert how he had shouted, "Federal agents! Have search warrant for these premises! Open the door!" But under cross-examination he admitted that he couldn't be sure the agents who

FIG. 7-2
"LSD King" Augustus Owsley Stanley III attends a hearing in Oakland on charges of conspiracy and manufacturing drugs, circa 1967. During the 1960s, Stanley produced popular varieties of the hallucinogen, which was outlawed in California in 1966. Courtesy of The Bancroft Library, University of California, Berkeley.

came in through the two rear entrances announced themselves the same way. Nevertheless, Owsley was convicted and Judge Sweigert sentenced him to the maximum, three years in prison and a $3,000 fine. Owsley's incarceration did little to slow the trafficking of LSD in California. By this time, he had a number of protégés.

As the 1960s wound down, law enforcement officials in Northern California cracked down further on alternative lifestyles and political activism. As an unpopular war demanded more and more young male participants, the idea of evading the draft gained momentum. However, when speaking to members of the California State Bar in 1965, Judge Stanley Weigel urged attorneys to "unmask the clamor for law and order as a demand for order at the expense of law." Throughout his legal career, Weigel—who joined the district court in 1962—worked to find a moderate path to justice. "The priceless values of our American society—including most importantly the freedoms spelled out in the Bill of Rights—require all thoughtful Americans to reject the extremes," he told the 1968 graduating class of Pennsylvania's Lincoln University.

Born in Helena, Montana, Weigel moved to San Francisco after his father's clothing store failed. He arrived in time to finish grammar school, graduated from Lowell High School in 1922, and worked his way through Stanford University as a correspondent for the *Call-Bulletin*. He recalled how, armed with a ruler, he would run down to get the paper and measure how much he'd be getting paid, for he was paid by the published inches of copy that he produced. From there, he moved to the *Oakland Post Enquirer*, a now-defunct paper owned by William Randolph Hearst, working in the summers while he went to law school at Stanford. After graduation in 1928, Weigel approached *Post Enquirer* publisher Carl Hoffman to say that he planned to stay in the newspaper business. "You've got your law degree," Hoffman told him. "You're a good newspaper man, but look at all the drunks and so on that are on the newspaper. You get out of here and go practice law." So Weigel did.

Appalled by Hitler's treatment of Jews during World War II (Weigel described himself as an agnostic Jew), Weigel applied to every branch of the armed services, despite a busy private law practice. He was turned down because of his age (he was in his mid-thirties), but eventually he was accepted into the Naval Reserves, and after being frustrated with a desk job, he pulled strings to receive active duty. Weigel attended gunnery school and was dispatched to a ship in the Philippines. At Weigel's installation to the district court, Court of Appeals judge Ben C. Duniway joked that Weigel fired one shot during the war. He thought it was at an enemy submarine, but it turned out to be a whale.

Perhaps Weigel's most famous case as an attorney was his defense, during the McCarthy Era of the early 1950s, of thirty-one professors fired from the University of California for refusing to sign an anti-communist oath. The professors had trouble finding an attorney. The California Supreme Court eventually ruled the oath unconstitutional and ordered the professors reinstated. Sixteen returned to their jobs and received back pay. The case received national attention and affirmed for Weigel that he had chosen the right career. "Perhaps it's self-aggrandizing," he stated in a 1989 oral history, "but my feeling is that these decisions helped turn the tide against McCarthyism."

A registered Republican, Weigel served on the national committee of the American Civil Liberties Union and long dreamed of being a federal judge. In the early 1960s, President Kennedy had begun to take criticism for appointing so many Democrats to the federal bench, Weigel recalled. He had come to know Pierre Salinger, Kennedy's press secretary, who arranged for Weigel to meet with Attorney General Robert Kennedy. Weigel walked through the door of Kennedy's office just as he threw a football. Weigel grabbed it, and for years thereafter joked that he became a federal judge by making the catch.

Although he had no criminal trial experience, Weigel was confirmed on the same day as his Senate hearing in 1962. A week later, he took the bench, and soon came to be known as a stickler for court protocol. Tough-minded, independent, and plenty smart, Weigel was also a difficult, irascible man who made life nearly impossible for lawyers. He prided himself on having been a well-prepared attorney and showed little patience for lawyers who appeared unprepared. Although he never held an attorney in contempt, Weigel did confess in his oral history that he was far harsher than necessary on lawyers and colleagues. He demanded that some of his law clerks arrive early and turn on the lights in his chambers. If he arrived before them, Weigel would wait, sitting in the dark. He demanded that clerks robe him. In court, he made exorbitant demands on lawyers, exploding if they did not respond. "We just tried to keep our head down," said one attorney, "and hope that we went unnoticed." Weigel's eccentricities were plentiful, and the stories about his irascibility are legion.

Automatic Justice

"Justice cannot be dispensed casually or automatically in the same way as a candy bar from a vending machine. Justice is not so cheap nor so easy a product. It is not mass-produced. It cannot be prepackaged. It is—in the nature of things it can only be—the product of care, diligence, and hard work by all involved in the judicial process. This applies especially to attorneys in acquitting their duties to their clients and to the courts."

—Stanley Weigel, as quoted by the *San Francisco Chronicle* in 1970

Weigel considered himself to be a judge who spent a career on the bench deciding cases exactly how he saw them "There's something to be said for the idea that the punishment should not so much fit the crime as...fit the criminal," he said in 1989. "My sentencing philosophy has been [that] whenever there's a real prospect, probability that a convicted criminal would make good on probation, then I give probation....By and large one reason I've been able to sleep at night is that I do not recall an instance...in all the years I've had on the bench and the hundreds of people that I've had to pass judgment on, that I've ever been unfair or excessive."

Weigel was an enigma. Despite his eccentricities, few judges were more precise, determined, and thoughtful. During the late 1960s, Weigel joined judges Zirpoli and Robert Peckham in sentencing Vietnam draft resisters who appeared before them to community service rather than jail time. And he worked for years trying to find the most humane outcomes in complex and sprawling cases, including the battle over the displacement of low-income residents in the neighborhood south of Market Street, the fight to improve conditions for inmates in Northern California's prisons, and the quest to desegregate San Francisco's public schools.

Weigel took his most courageous stand in 1970, when he issued a sweeping injunction against the demolition of the blighted neighborhood south of Market and east of Powell Street. The suit, known as *Tenants and Owners in Opposition to Redevelopment ("TOOR") v. United States Department of Housing and Urban Development,* became Weigel's defining moment. He halted a huge city redevelopment project to build a convention center because more than one thousand poor, elderly men who lived in the area were not being offered safe, affordable housing in return for their displacement. Weigel ruled that the American Housing Act of 1949—a law long ignored—made it clear that residents living in blighted neighborhoods should benefit rather than suffer from urban renewal. He defied Mayor Joseph Alioto, who said the city's future hung in the balance of the project and declared that no federal judge had the ability to stop construction. Weigel ignored resolutions passed by labor unions that railed against his decision and resisted pressure to step down. Weigel held strong until the Redevelopment Agency signed a consent decree agreeing to build or rehabilitate up to eighteen hundred low-rent housing units. When the agency balked, he added more units.

Weigel assumed senior status in 1982, but he continued to hear cases until failing health forced his retirement in 1997. He died in 1999 at age ninety-three.

The Man for San Jose

The Northern District of California added one judge in 1966. Robert Peckham's office would be in San Francisco for the next twenty-two years, but his heart was always in San Jose.

Peckham was born at San Francisco's Mount Zion Hospital on November 3, 1920—the day after Warren Harding and Calvin Coolidge were elected to the White House, he liked to recall. His mother, Evelyn, was from Ireland and his father was from France, but John La Fargue died when Peckham was a baby. In 1928, the boy's mother met and married attorney Robert F. Peckham. Young Robert came to know this man as his father, although he referred to him as Peck.

Peckham spent his early life in Palo Alto. He attended elementary school on the campus of Stanford University and skipped two grades to enter Palo Alto High School at age twelve. He graduated at sixteen in 1937. Peckham's uncle, I. M. Peckham, was a San Jose attorney who represented a number of Japanese clients during World War II. He kept their Santa Clara County property safe during their internment and returned it upon their release. Although his family was largely Republican and Peckham was head of his high school's Young Republicans club, he recalled growing less conservative during high school. "I began to have a very general curiosity about issues, political and socioeconomic issues," he said. While a freshman at Stanford he switched allegiance to the Democratic Party. As his graduation grew near and he considered what to do next, "law seemed most appropriate," he recalled in a 1992 oral history. " I looked upon law as a way to be active in politics, to be in public life, to be in government, and to do public interest work....I chose it because I thought it was the way I could do what I thought I wanted to do with my life," he said. And despite a lack of certainty in the beginning, he said, "It worked out that way."

Peckham started at Yale Law School in the fall of 1941, which was his first experience of life outside California. The Japanese bombed Pearl Harbor that December, and while at home during the summer of 1942, Peckham announced that he planned to join the military. His father forbade it,

but in August 1942 Peck died of a heart attack. Young Peckham's eyesight
kept him out of the service after all, but he began working with the Office
of Price Administration, which regulated prices and rationed goods for the
wartime economy. And because he was now back home and his mother
was alone, he decided to finish his legal training at Stanford.

After passing the California bar, Peckham set up a private practice in
Santa Clara County. In 1944 and 1945, he served as state president of
the Young Democrats—a position that gave him the opportunity to meet
Senator Harry Truman, the vice presidential nominee, and to attend the
founding of the United Nations in San Francisco on June 26, 1945.
Peckham spent five years as an assistant US Attorney for the Northern
District of California and served as chief assistant for the criminal divi-
sion in 1952 and 1953.

"Once you've been an assistant United States Attorney, I think you
do tend to aspire to be a judge," Peckham said in a 1992 oral history.
After a time in private practice, Peckham served as US commissioner

in San Jose from 1957 to 1959, and after another short stint in private practice, he jumped at the opportunity to become a Santa Clara County Superior Court judge when appointed by Governor Edmund G. Brown. He jumped again when appointed in 1966, at age forty-five, as the first federal district court judge for Santa Clara County. Peckham was sworn in at San Jose. He would sit in San Francisco until business justified establishing a San Jose federal court.

By 1969, Peckham was averaging one week per month in San Jose, and he told the *San Francisco Examiner* that number would only increase as the population of Santa Clara, Monterey, San Benito, and Santa Cruz Counties increased. He was known as a patient, evenhanded, courteous judge, who "rarely displays irritation," noted the *Examiner*. Alfred T. Goodwin, an Oregon federal judge who met Peckham at the regional annual meeting for the federal bench and bar in the early 1970s, described him as "a master at settlement, because he could bring parties together when they were spitting at each other, just fighting mad. And he could settle them down and get them to…talk reasonably because he was so reasonable."

During the Vietnam War, Peckham was assigned all the Northern District draft evader cases in which the defendant was to plead guilty. "His attitude toward sentencing probably…reflected his attitude toward the war," said Robert W. Peterson, Peckham's law clerk. "I don't think he agreed with it, and he certainly thought that given the bank robbers and tax cheats and people that are the normal grist of the criminal system there, that by and large these were people of conscience and worth." However, Peckham did not believe this made them above the law. "He typically sentenced a draft defendant to probation and two years of alternative service, typically at the Los Angeles Department of Charities," Peterson said. "He wanted them to suffer some inconvenience, because they weren't doing something a good deal more inconvenient, so he wanted them to move away from where they were."

Many of Peckham's major cases involved government. In 1972, he ordered the state to pay legal bills after losing environmental lawsuits. In 1979, he required the largely white male–dominated San Francisco Police Department to make 50 percent of their hires minorities and 20 percent women for the next ten years. A decade later, he extended the order, expressing "disappointment and sadness" at the department's lack of progress. And for years Peckham oversaw the desegregation plan for the San Jose Unified School District and changed the way IQ tests could be used in assessing minority students.

Peckham became chief judge in 1976 upon the death of Oliver Carter, and he immediately began making administrative changes. Until that point, the court had no real formal meetings. During Peckham's tenure, meetings were held in the dining room and had formal agendas. "He had always enjoyed very much attending meetings of other judges, where he would learn a good deal, and he always shared his new-found knowledge with the rest of us when he returned," Judge William Orrick Jr. said. "He did a great deal toward bringing the court together just through the simple process of holding regular judges' meetings once a month in the dining room and encouraging judges to come down and eat. We were then, and are now, a very collegial court." In 1977, Peckham started the United States District Court, Northern District of California Historical Society, and during the 1980s, he joined an effort to prevent the National Archives and Records Administration from trashing the records of many old court cases. History and innovation were always on his mind.

Peckham also began taking the district court to the forefront of new judicial ideas and programs. "He pioneered alternative dispute resolution, that much used and often maligned method for settling controversies among litigious citizens," Orrick said in a 1993 interview. Under

---

A Watchful Eye

In a 1995 interview, San Francisco attorney Edward Steinman recounted his days as clerk to Judge Peckham in 1969:

> He didn't write his own decisions....His law clerks wrote [them]....He didn't like to write. But he would do tremendous editing....As he got to know you, he'd trust you. And many times, we were thinking he wouldn't touch or change our draft. He'd read it and wouldn't touch it. We sometimes felt that he wasn't spending enough time looking at our stuff. So one time, I can't remember whether it was Bob [another law clerk] or myself, we put a footnote in a case saying, "And Bob Peterson and Ed Steinman are awarded $2 billion," and he caught it....This is pre-computer days...and he was really mad at us that we were fooling around. We would not pull that one again.

Peckham's leadership, the district court became one of three courts that attempted a pilot program to explore alternative dispute resolution. The process of nonbinding mandatory arbitration initially applied only to civil cases involving less than $100,000, but over time the program began to show results. Cases terminated in arbitration rather than going to trial, and in the early 1980s, Congress authorized funding for an administrator to run the program in ten districts, including the Northern District of California. What began as arbitration soon blossomed into mediation, and then into early neutral evaluation—a process by which attorneys or litigants can present their dispute to another attorney shortly after filing the case, but before any proceedings have begun. This evaluating attorney then provides a report on the merits of the case (or lack thereof). The idea, also created by Peckham, "was to cut down the exorbitant costs inherent in discovery these days," said Orrick. "A trial is just too expensive for almost everybody, except for the very rich and the very poor." The court soon had, on file in the clerk's office, a roster of lawyers willing to act as third-party evaluators. These alternative dispute resolution proceedings "brought the bench and the bar much closer together than they had been previously," Orrick observed.

Today, the frequent and effective use of these ADR procedures in civil cases is "what characterizes our district and makes it stand apart," said district court clerk Richard Wieking in a 2005 interview. "ADR and Northern District are heavily associated in the minds of court administrators and judges around the country." Wieking credits this current status to Peckham:

> Peckham wrote a groundbreaking article in 1981—"The Federal Judge as a Case Manager"—in the *California Law Review*. It was quite eye opening to federal judges around the nation, as it was a well thought out manifesto that judges should remain aggressive in managing the cases before them. Out of that grew the notion that we need a broader array of approaches to the resolution of cases, not just litigation. Peckham and Wayne Brazil (then a professor at Hastings College of Law) started working this idea. Then Brazil became a magistrate judge in the late 1970s and was here to shepherd the program, which he did single-handedly until the 1990 Civil Justice Reform Act, which commanded courts to experiment with handling cases.... This court's ADR program is most robust, and now also includes settlement conferences with a magistrate

judge or with a private sector organization as an option, so about three full-time attorneys are devoted to it now and about four or five staff members. It's a very aggressive program.

Of the six thousand civil cases filed each year in the Northern District, thirty-three hundred are sent directly to one of the ADR programs: arbitration, early neutral evaluation, mediation, or settlement conferences. One thousand of these cases are resolved quickly, and another thousand use some form of ADR—so Peckham's program has had a substantial impact on the district court and other courts around the nation.

An additional court activity that can be traced back to Peckham is the trial advocacy program, which began in 1982. It provides lawyers with lectures and training from judges over two or three Saturdays on topics including local and federal rules. Unique in its early days, the program was an instant success and is now known as the Federal Practice Program. More than two thousand lawyers have participated in it.

Peckham assumed senior status in 1988 and relinquished his post as chief judge. This afforded him the chance to sit full time in San Jose rather than commuting back and forth to San Francisco. A permanent courthouse was established there in 1984, with district court judges William Ingram and Spencer Williams sitting full time in that location and Peckham sitting part time.

Peckham died in 1993. At a memorial service held two days after his death, district court judge Thelton Henderson remembered Peckham as wise and compassionate almost to a fault. But Peckham's most memorable trait was his unflagging support for programs that supplied legal assistance for indigent defendants, Henderson said. "It is virtually impossible to exaggerate how important a judicial leader he was," said Wayne Brazil, who worked closely with Peckham for more than a decade. Barry Portman, a federal public defender, added, "There are a lot of defendants who never heard of Bob Peckham whose defense came because he was a good politician and a generous man."

A New Generation

Robert Peckham's intellectual foil was lifelong San Franciscan Robert H. Schnacke, who was elevated to the federal bench in 1970 after two years on the Santa Clara County Superior Court. President Richard Nixon nominated Schnacke to replace retiring district court judge George Harris. The appointment was a return to the federal courts for Schnacke, who had served as assistant US Attorney and chief of the criminal division for the Northern District from 1953 to 1958. From there, he was promoted to US Attorney after his friend and mentor, Lloyd Burke, was made a district court judge. Burke and Schnacke had previously served together in the Army Counter-Intelligence Corps from 1942 to 1946.

A Republican, Schnacke graduated from Hastings College of Law in 1938, worked in private practice, and served as deputy commissioner for California's Division of Corporations from 1947 to 1951. After being confirmed to the district court at age fifty-six, Schnacke told the *San Francisco Chronicle* he had "no intention of being a tough judge." Despite his stated intentions, however, many attorneys who appeared before him found Schnacke tough. A bright, no-nonsense man with a rapier wit, Schnacke was all business in court and adept at keeping a trial going. But he did have personal eccentricities. "A stickler for proper court behavior, Schnacke at one time had taped his court rules to the counsel tables," reported the *San Francisco Daily Journal*. Controlling in court, Schnacke was known for his unusual propensity to pepper his own questions at witnesses, which sometimes had a devastating effect on a carefully crafted case. "His aim was to make sure the jury got it all," defense attorney Jerold Ladar told the *Daily Journal* in 1994.

Despite their occasional exasperation or trepidation, most attorneys ultimately seemed to find Schnacke a fair judge. "He was certainly master of all he surveyed, but I don't think he was a tyrant," noted former US Attorney Joseph Russoniello. Attorneys often referred to Schnacke affectionately as "the Schnack," and when he returned to court in 1993 after being hospitalized for bronchitis, he announced to the room, "The Schnack is back."

Judge Schnacke preferred to deliver his opinions orally. These included a rejection of San Francisco public television station KQED's request to televise the 1991 execution of Robert Alton Harris, and a decision in 1988 to bar the National Weather Service from requiring meteorologists to submit to drug tests. The Schnack presided over the 1989 trial of Steve Psinakis, a Greek-born American citizen accused of plotting to ship explosives to the Philippines in the hopes of overthrowing the government led by Ferdinand and Imelda Marcos. More important than the case itself, the trial encouraged whistleblower Frederic Whitehurst to come forward.

John F. Kelly and Phillip K. Wearne summarized Whitehurst's role in their 1998 book, *Tainting Evidence: Inside the Scandals at the FBI Crime Lab*. Whitehurst revealed the shoddy work and recordkeeping he had observed at the FBI crime laboratory; these lab irregularities later raised questions about a number of prominent cases.

Judge Schnacke assumed senior status at the end of 1983, but he continued to hear a reduced load of cases for another decade. For many court watchers, he will be remembered for being caught in a vice squad raid in 1985 at the X-rated Market Street Cinema. The seventy-one-year-old judge was found sitting in the front row of the adult theater. He was not arrested, but a dozen women in the theater were charged during the raid with lewd conduct, and police officers deemed the theater a house of prostitution. Schnacke was listed as a witness. "I was questioned and released," the judge told an *Examiner* reporter months after the incident. "I was never held. The cops came in. I talked to them and I went home."

Schnacke passed away in 1994 at age eighty, after twenty-four years in the federal court.

Another Republican, Samuel Conti, also joined the district court in 1970. Nominated by President Nixon, Conti filled one of two newly authorized positions to expand the Northern District federal bench. Conti, born in Los Angeles in 1922, always wanted to be a lawyer. "My father knew some and they were held in high esteem, and I admired them and so I always knew that was what I wanted to do," he said. Conti's father was a baker who immigrated to the United States from Italy. Conti joined the army in World War II, then graduated from Santa Clara University in 1945 and from Stanford Law School in 1948. He worked as a trial lawyer for eighteen years. One of his first jobs was working in San Francisco for famed criminal defense and divorce trial lawyer J. W. "Jake" Ehrlich, the model for TV lawyer Perry Mason. Conti also served as city attorney for the city of Concord from 1960 to 1967, when Governor Reagan named him to the Contra Costa County Superior Court, where he presided over the juvenile court.

Conti said that some of the most interesting and rewarding work of his career came from this era: "I wanted the job—the other judges didn't want it, and I thought a judge could do more good there than anywhere." He said he treasured a letter from a woman who said his brief imprisonment of her son had turned his life around. He admits that he was always heavy-handed with sentencing, leading to nicknames such as Maximum Sam and Slammin' Sam. A superior court bailiff told the *Oakland Tribune*, "A lot of the older youth prefer adult court to Judge Conti's. They think they'll get off easier."

Conti was not a disciplinarian without reason. "Before you start considering rehabilitation and probation, which so many bleeding hearts advocate today, you have to punish the offender," he explained in 1972. But until a verdict is delivered, Conti said he sides with defendants. "I'll give every break that I can to a defendant to see that he gets a fair trial, but if you're found guilty, then that's a whole different ball game," Conti said in 2006. "If you're found guilty then I feel you should pay something for the crime you've committed....Most people think that a compassionate judge is someone who is compassionate for the defendant[;] my idea of a compassionate judge is one that, after a defendant is found guilty,

FIG. 7-4
In a drawing by journalist and courtroom artist Rosalie Ritz, Sara Jane Moore appears before Judge Samuel Conti on January 15, 1976, following her 1975 assassination attempt of President Gerald Ford. Courtesy of the family of Rosalie Ritz.

is compassionate to the victims and to the crime that he's committed against society."

As a jurist, Conti waged a personal war against permissiveness. "Freedom is all right and a wonderful thing," he told the *Examiner* in 1979. "But the end result of complete freedom is anarchy. People must also face up to their responsibilities...to their neighbors and fellow men." Conti applied this firm hand in the cases of numerous draft evaders and drug offenders, plus a whole slew of Hells Angels (from behind a Plexiglas partition specially constructed for the trial), as well as in the sentencing of Sara Jane Moore, who attempted to assassinate President Ford in 1975. His first case for the court turned out to be his longest, *United States v. Standard Oil Company of California*, an antitrust case in which the US government accused the oil company of monopolizing the sale and distribution of fuel in American Samoa. It finally settled in 2004.

Conti also presided over one of the court's early technology cases, *Memorex v. IBM*, a 1979 a behemoth of an antitrust case that sought to decide if IBM had monopolized various markets. Even choosing a jury for a case that might last a year was extremely challenging, Conti said. "If you're trying an ordinary criminal case, people find that easy to understand, but when you're talking about a highly technical case....It was not the best jury," he said. Conti recalled how one juror had a unique excuse to be excluded from jury duty. "He said it would be detrimental to his health so I asked him why since he looked pretty good to me. And he said that if he had to sit on a jury for ten to twelve months, 'My wife would kill me.'...I let him off." Jurors needed to understand the nuances of complex aspects of reverse engineering, "subordinated debentures," and confusing accounting practices. In fact, the jury was unable to arrive at a unanimous verdict after nineteen days of deliberations. Conti declared a mistrial, stating "the magnitude and complexity of the present lawsuit render it as a whole beyond the ability and competency of any jury to understand and decide rationally." He ruled that if the case was retried that a judge should decide it, not a jury.

In 1981, Conti heard a case involving a secret germ warfare experiment in San Francisco. The family of Edwin J. Nevin accused the government of causing his death when it released bacteria into the air for three days in 1950. A navy minesweeper sprayed clouds of airborne *Serratia marcescens*, common bacteria then thought to be harmless, to see where airborne contaminants might go if released during a germ warfare attack.

The Korean War had just begun and the West Coast was considered vulnerable to attack. A month after the experiment, seventy-five-year-old Nevin died of a bacterial heart infection at a San Francisco hospital following prostate surgery. Several other patients at the hospital developed similar infections but survived. Conti found the government not liable for the man's death.

The most mail Conti said he ever received was about a case involving whales and other marine mammals possibly affected by sonar testing off the coast of California. A number of environmental groups filed suit to stop the testing of a low-frequency sonar. When Conti issued an injunction against the National Marine Fisheries Service permit in 2003, he was briefly hailed as a hero. He received even more letters when he denied a permanent injunction against the practice in 2004.

More than a conservative or a Republican, which he is, Conti says that he is a strict adherent to the law. Former law clerk Michael Page described Conti's courtroom as "a crap shoot...anything can happen." Conti holds everyone in his courtroom to the same standards of behavior. In 1979, he sentenced Charles Kirk, a deputy attorney general, to ten days in federal prison for lying about the whereabouts of records pertaining to the case of Black Panther Geronimo Pratt. Kirk had told Conti he had the files in his Sacramento office, when in fact he did not. Pratt's lawyer had filed a motion to review some of the state's files, which Conti had granted. When the lawyer went for a second day to review the files, they had disappeared, and the state claimed it did not know where they were. Conti said he told Kirk and his team, "If you can't find the files, I'll hold you all in contempt—somebody will go to jail." Kirk's sentence was suspended and within two days the files reappeared.

In 1988, Conti held Secretary of Agriculture Richard E. Lyng in contempt and imposed stiff penalties on the Forest Service for failing to comply with a 1981 consent decree to comply with equal opportunity laws for female employees. A Berkeley Forest Service employee sued the agency in 1973 claiming she hadn't been promoted because of her gender. Fifteen years later, Conti said he "finally got so annoyed I said unless you start integrating women I will take over personnel and do the hiring and firing." In 1992, the Forest Service agreed to increase the number of women and minorities employed in California—including those working in management. While the case technically only applied to California forestry employees, it caused the agency to overhaul its hiring and personnel management practices nationwide.

In an unusual 1988 copyright suit, Conti permitted singer-songwriter John Fogerty to play his guitar in court to demonstrate how he composes songs. Fogerty was sued by a Berkeley record company for allegedly copying one of his own songs, the Creedence Clearwater Rival hit "Run Through the Jungle," in a new song he composed for another record company. "Everybody had a good time and enjoyed it and Fogerty proved his point," said Conti. Fogerty won in district court, but the case went all the way to the Supreme Court, which decided that defendants as well as plaintiffs in copyright cases should also be able to recover attorney's fees. In 1995, Conti awarded Fogerty $1.35 million in legal fees, a record at the time.

Conti presided over the first of the district court's two espionage cases during the 1980s, and he made it known he had no qualms about imposing the death penalty for a man who pled guilty in 1984 to selling US missile research data to Poland, then part of the communist Eastern Bloc controlled by the Soviet Union. James D. Harper Jr. and his wife had worked at high-tech firms in Palo Alto where documents had been stolen. He sold more than one hundred documents to Polish agents in return for $250,000. The Ninth Circuit Court of Appeals ruled that the death penalty (in its 1984 incarnation) did not apply to cases related to the Espionage Act—a ruling that must have offered comfort to Jerry Whitworth, the next Soviet spy on the district court's docket—so Conti sentenced Harper to the maximum of life in prison. "You are a traitor to your country who committed the crime not for any political reason but for greed," said Conti at the sentencing. "There can be no crime more serious than selling our defense secrets."

"I've never thought of it as work," said Conti, who served as acting chief judge of the district court in 1974 and assumed senior status in 1987, about the same time the federal government introduced sentencing guidelines that removed much of a judge's discretionary power. Soon after, Conti stopped hearing criminal cases. He said judges today really don't have control over sentencing anymore: "I like to try criminal trials[;] I find them very interesting but you can't put people into a grid.... Everybody is different." He said while an appellate court only "sees a piece of paper," a trial court judge sees the defendant and can learn much about them from their mannerisms and comportment. "When I got on the bench you could either give a person probation or twenty years, that was up to you," said Conti. "In the early days we had a very good provision of the law where you would sentence somebody...for five to ten years but then you would suspend it all except for six months or three months and let them know what jail is like. That was for first-time offenders. And then if you violate the law after you get out, you know who's sending you to jail—you're sending yourself to jail. You can't do that anymore," said Conti. "I had great results with that."

Conti says the Northern District Court has changed dramatically during his tenure. "When I got here there was one court, eight judges, and two magistrates; now there are eighteen judges, twelve magistrates, and courthouses in San Francisco, San Jose, Oakland, and Eureka. It's a bigger court." Conti sounded wistful for the days when it was a more cohesive court. "But maybe that satisfied us but not the public," he said. In those days, court started at ten o'clock, recessed at noon for lunch, and returned at two o'clock. "There were no cell phones, which was wonderful. At least when you were going to court you had some time to think. And there were no emails. And the rules of court, it was probably about three pages long. Now our rules of court look like the internal revenue code. I feel sorry for the lawyers today."

Another major change is that judges' salaries have not kept up with the standard of living, Conti said. "You don't take the job for the money," he said in 2006, "but if you've got kids you can't afford it today. In 1970 my salary was $40,000, and you could buy a whole house, paid in full. Today my salary is $165,000, and you can't even make a down payment on a house in San Francisco....My law clerk just left me to work for a firm here in town and he's making more money than I am."

Conti has written notes on every case he's had and keeps them in white leather-bound books in his office. His memory remains strong, and he recalls a vacation in Paris when he saw President Nixon. The judge introduced himself and thanked him for the judicial appointment. He says Nixon told him, "Don't retire. If you retire, you're dead." Conti continues to follow this advice and in 2013 surpassed Ogden Hoffman's previous record of forty years on the court.

The Court and Vietnam

Among the more widely known bits of Northern District Court history is the active role judges played during the later years of American involvement in Vietnam. President Kennedy sent one hundred Special Forces troops to aid in the South Vietnamese fight against communist North

Vietnam in 1961. As the decade progressed, the federal government sent more and more GIs to Vietnam. Many of those men had been drafted. Yet many draft-eligible men resisted the call to serve by filing for conscientious objector status, burning their draft cards, or moving to Canada. In the late 1960s and early 1970s, tales of the Northern District judges' lenience toward conscientious objectors swirled throughout the country via underground channels and mainstream media. But this perspective tells only part of the story. Historian John T. McGreevy, writing in *Western Legal History* in 1989, noted that the Northern District of California was "viewed by both resistance activists and government attorneys as the national focal point for legal issues concerning the draft."

For the first years of the conflict, little distinguished Northern California from other parts of the country. In 1966, one assistant US Attorney, Paul Sloan, managed all the Northern District draft cases: thirty-nine criminal cases and only one trial. In 1967, sixty-four draft-related

FIG. 7-5
Anti-draft demonstrators block the entrance to the Oakland Armed Forces Induction Center during Stop the Draft Week in October 1967. A federal law enforcement officer peers out behind them. Courtesy of the Oakland Public Library, Oakland History Room.

criminal cases came to trial in the Northern District. Yet by the end of that year, the winds of dissent had begun to blow. By that point, 485,000 American troops, including many draftees, had landed in the muck and mayhem of Vietnam, and Stop the Draft protests at the Oakland Induction Center had begun to make national news. Bay Area draft violations were on the rise. During the next twelve months, 140 criminal draft cases were filed in the Northern District, and 1,696 Selective Service–related complaints were registered.

By 1970, almost 40 percent of all Americans who refused the draft did so at the Oakland Induction Center. Their cases went to the Northern District Court. Why the sudden rise? San Francisco had long been a haven for hippies and other flavors of peaceniks, and the district court bench included several judges with a penchant for probationary sentences in conscientious objector cases. But there were other factors as well. Attorney Aubrey Grossman approached Chief Judge Oliver Carter in 1967, requesting that a stable of willing attorneys be gathered to provide counsel for those appearing before the court on Selective Service charges. Carter agreed, and Grossman formed the Lawyers' Selective Service Panel. To Grossman's surprise, Carter also instructed the public defender's office to prepare lawyers for draft cases. Eventually, two hundred lawyers were affiliated with the lawyers' panel, and the information they compiled and shared gave them an edge in navigating the highly technical and somewhat archaic draft statutes. The laws governing who was selected for military service, in what order, and when had not been revised since the World War II draft, although the government had maintained a standing draft order since 1948 that permitted the armed services to call eligible (and registered) young men into service to cover vacancies. "The government didn't know [much]," explained attorney Michael Weiss. "[They were] far less prepared for technicalities and sheer number [of cases]."

The training of attorneys in the Northern District did not guarantee that a draft resister would prevail in court. In 1968, Judge George Harris issued a preliminary injunction to postpone Charles Gabriel's induction into the military until his request for conscientious objector status, denied numerous times by the Selective Service, was given judicial review. Gabriel, twenty-three, was the son of a white father and black mother who asserted that his moral upbringing and opposition to violence as well as his beliefs about the government's failure to protect the rights of African Americans rendered him a conscientious objector. However, in a 1968 ruling on *Clark v. Gabriel*, the Supreme Court put an end to the district court's injunction and declined any change in Gabriel's draft status.

Despite Gabriel's misfortune, many others seeking conscientious objector status—or at least an alternative to military service—found success in the Northern District. The January 2, 1969, issue of the *Chicago Tribune* reported that "word is spreading in anti-draft circles across the country that San Francisco is a good place to avoid entry into the armed services." The article reported a national average sentence of three years for draft evasion and noted that federal court records showed much lighter sentences in the Northern District. "Most of those convicted do not go to jail at all," the paper stated. The Los Angeles–based anti-draft newsletter *Counterdraft* urged its readers to establish residency in Northern California so they might refuse induction in Oakland and have their cases heard in the Northern District Court. The instructions also encouraged readers not to be too specific about the reasons for their cross-country move. Grossman told the paper he thought local judges were "enlightened" about the draft and gave more lenient sentences because they felt it was the call of conscience that led many men to resist induction and because they suspected the draft laws might be improper.

By this point, many Americans had begun to have questions and misgivings about Vietnam. The 1968 My Lai Massacre, which resulted in more than one hundred Vietnamese civilian deaths, sparked protests around the country, including the Bay Area. "Some of the judges' children now have friends who have refused induction," noted Paul Harris, law clerk to Judge Zirpoli. The judge's daughter was active in the Berkeley Free Speech movement, and Judge Lloyd Burke's son served a tour of duty in Vietnam.

But the Northern District judges were hardly of one mind. In 1969, Judge Zirpoli—who led the charge toward sentences of probation and alternative service—ruled that at least three members of the draft board must live in the district they represent for a draft to be considered legal. Judge Peckham issued a similar ruling, and for a moment it looked as if the Selective Service might be thrown into disarray. State draft officials began polling members of California's 144 draft boards to see where they lived. Two months later, Judge Sweigert countered slightly when he ruled that draft board members ought to live in the same county, but not necessarily "within the geographical confines" of a draftee's neighborhood, which effectively overruled the previous decisions. Further settling the matter, President Nixon issued an executive order in 1970 that waived draft board residency requirements altogether.

Two decisions related to conscientious objection, described as landmarks and among the most significant Northern District rulings, were issued by Judge Weigel and Judge Zirpoli in 1969 and 1970. On Christmas Eve 1969, Weigel acquitted twenty-four-year-old Leslie Charles Bowen of refusing induction into the army. Bowen, a Catholic, opposed the Vietnam War because it was unjust, although he did not necessarily object to war in general. Weigel's opinion noted that draft boards had discriminated against Catholics like Bowen in favor of Quakers and Jehovah's Witnesses, who are opposed to all war on religious grounds. "In denying conscientious objector status to Bowen, based upon his religious opposition to the Vietnam War but permitting it to one whose religious opposition is to all war, the effect...is to breach the neutrality between state and religion required by the mandate of the First Amendment," Weigel wrote. A few months later, Zirpoli continued Weigel's line of reasoning in *McFadden v. Selective Service System, Local Board 40*, and struck down the portion of the Selective Service Act that required conscientious objectors to be opposed to "war in any form." Catholic doctrine differentiates between "just" and "unjust" wars, so Zirpoli concluded that this portion of the act "violates equal protection and due process of the law."

But again, the Supreme Court saw things differently. Although the high court justices declined to rule specifically on either of these cases, their combined ruling on two cases in 1971 made their views clear. Justice Thurgood Marshall, writing the opinion, agreed that there was an obvious difference between opposing all wars and opposing one war, but said the law recognized only one valid type of conscientious objector, regardless of the many religions practiced in the United States.

"I worked pretty hard on that case," Zirpoli recalled in a 1983 interview. "I thought I did a pretty fair job." But for the Supreme Court, "the test was that you had to be opposed to all war....This is denial of recognition of Catholic teachings in my view....Just about every religious faith filed some kind of brief as a friend of the court....That's the irony of the whole thing, that the fellow [James McFadden] who wouldn't budge an inch, who wouldn't do anything conditional, whose convictions were so strong, he probably had greater justification as an objector than anyone else, and he's the one that went to jail every time." McFadden declined any sort of alternative service, so he was sentenced to two years in prison.

Throughout the Vietnam conflict, rulings from the Northern District earned the ire of Selective Service officials, and controversial decisions by Zirpoli and Peckham made them the named recipients of an angry 1970 missive from Selective Service headquarters. When the letter failed to affect the judges' rulings, President Nixon used his power to appoint judges who might alter San Francisco's status as the promised land for draft evaders. Nixon's appointees, Judges Schnacke and Conti, soon separated themselves from their colleagues by imposing much more forceful sentences on those who refused to go to war. Conti in particular preferred to send convicted draft evaders directly to jail, without bail.

Draft resisters feared drawing Conti as a judge. "My philosophy was if there was some poor American kid who had to go to Vietnam and come back either dead or maimed, then the least some other guy could do who is found guilty of evading the draft law is to spend two years in jail, same as a tour of duty, and come back whole-bodied," Conti said in 2006. "Everyone would come to this court and say 'I'm a conscientious objector' and get probation…but no one looked at the cases. I was up first so I got a lot of flak, but you do what you think is right and that's it."

Four attorneys pled for probation for their clients in a February 1971 appearance before Judge Conti, using a full range of arguments and approaches. The first attorney, Richard Wertheimer, described his client's draft evasion as "a crime of conscience, a crime with no person as a victim," but Conti disagreed. "He chose not to go, so someone else had to go and, perhaps, today that person is maimed or dead," the judge countered. He sentenced the man to two years.

The next lawyer, Michael Weiss, argued that probation would be rehabilitative, and noted that tax evaders are also eligible for five-year sentences but are frequently given probation. "Judge Conti took off his glasses, leaned forward and said, 'Not in this court,'" reported the *San Francisco Chronicle*. Conti added that probation for rehabilitation purposes is fine, "but in most cases where that fits, the defendant comes in, says he's sorry and won't do it again. But in these cases, these people aren't sorry, and I believe they would do it again." Weiss's client got two years.

The next attorney, Bert Green, said, "Today is Ash Wednesday. My client is a man of conscience and on this day of conscience, I ask he be given probation." Green's client also got two years. Attorney John Hansen, the last to approach the bench, said he saw no reason to ask for probation, in light of the other sentences. True to form, Judge Conti gave the final defendant two years as well.

Although adding Conti and Schnacke to the judicial mix made getting probation a slightly more risky gamble in the Northern District, the odds remained appealing for those faced with fighting for a cause they couldn't support. As the war dragged on, Selective Service cases threatened to overwhelm the Northern District. Staff member Joseph Franaszek compiled astounding statistics: in 1971, nearly 60 percent of the criminal cases in the district were related to the draft—511 out of 868 criminal actions, not to mention a backlog of 275 indicted draft law violators awaiting trial. While the US Attorney's office slogged through the FBI investigations and Selective Service administrative procedures, an average of twenty-four new people refused induction in Oakland each week.

In 1970, Judge Sweigert gave three Berkeley law students who were members of the armed forces reserves the right to sue the United States on the grounds that the war in Vietnam was unconstitutional. In his twenty-eight-page opinion in *Mottola v. Nixon*, Sweigert wrote he had taken "judicial notice of the fact that the armed forces of the United States are now committed and have been for nearly five years, to a full scale war in Vietnam; that this war has never been declared by the Congress and that the President of the United States, through the incumbent and his predecessor in office, has continued, nevertheless, to conduct the war without receiving or even requesting a congressional declaration."

He listed the government's usual justifications for the continued fighting and proceeded to pick them off, one by one, focusing in particular on Article I of the Constitution, which gives Congress the power to declare war:

> It will be noted that none of the foregoing arguments make any pretense that Article I, Section 8 (II) has been complied with in the case of Vietnam; they merely purport to explain why, for various reasons of expediency, the Constitution has *not* been complied with. They are, therefore, of doubtful relevance in a court whose duty it is to see that the Constitution *is* complied with.

Sweigert then asked why the Supreme Court had not issued a ruling on the legality of the war. He attributed the lack of an appropriate case to the fact that federal courts have chosen to rule on assorted "technical, jurisdictional, procedural grounds" rather than the main issue. Previous excuses cited included that the war is a political issue that should not be decided by the courts; that the government has not consented to be sued; and that the person challenging the war did not have standing to sue. But he added that the Supreme Court had also denied petitions seeking review of the question. Sweigert noted that the Supreme Court had intervened when President Truman sought to take over steel mills where workers were striking during wartime: "It seems to this court that to strike down as unconstitutional a President's wartime seizure of a few private steel mills but to shy away on 'political question' grounds from interfering with a presidential war itself, would be to strain at a gnat and swallow a camel."

Here was a district court judge taking the Supreme Court to task—and standing up alone in his questioning of the entire war. When discussing the merits of the case, Sweigert said that "to say these three plaintiffs must wait until they are called up, perhaps suddenly, and ordered to the Vietnam area, perhaps quickly, and then file a court suit, perhaps with too little time to properly do so, borders, we think, on the absurd."

Judges at the Ninth Circuit Court of Appeals overturned Sweigert's ruling in 1972. Not surprisingly, the appeals judges declined to tackle the constitutional issues raised by the case and instead dismissed the appeal because those who sought to sue were "not under military orders to report to the Indochina theatre of hostilities" and therefore did not have the personal stake in the outcome they would need to file a lawsuit. As a side note, the Ninth Circuit panel also included with their ruling a list of the many cases in which the Supreme Court had declined to consider the legality of the Vietnam War (over Justice William Douglas's dissent). Sweigert's gauntlet remained on the ground.

Despite the fact that the rulings of Northern District judges regarding the draft were reported in both the mainstream and the underground press, the Northern District's influence on the overall war effort should not be overstated. By the end of 1972, Nixon was reducing the number of American troops in Vietnam, and 1973 saw both the end of the draft and the withdrawal of many US soldiers from the war zone. None of these events occurred because of the Northern District Court. But "judges and attorneys in the Northern District made it much more difficult to raise an army," noted McGreevy in *Western Legal History*. "They did not make it impossible.…Essentially, attacks on the draft in the Northern District remained local attacks, dependent upon either the approval of the higher courts"—which was rarely received—"or the willingness of other districts to follow Northern California's lead"—also not a common occurrence. What this era did demonstrate was a willingness among the Northern District judges to break new legal ground, make unpopular decisions, or try something new. But these attributes were not unique to this time period.

Tensions between the federal government and the district court were not restricted to draft-related issues. In 1969, President Nixon nominated San Francisco County Superior Court judge Gerald S. Levin to a new federal judgeship. President Lyndon Johnson had twice nominated US Attorney Cecil Poole for this position, which was authorized in 1966. The first time, in 1968, the Senate adjourned without taking action on the nomination. Johnson resubmitted it in January 1969, but Nixon, who took office later that month, withdrew Poole's nomination. Newspapers reported that Democrats blamed California Republican senator George Murphy for blocking Poole's confirmation, a charge Murphy denied.

It was Murphy who introduced Levin, also a Republican, at a San Francisco press conference. Born in Danville, Illinois, in 1906, Levin moved to San Francisco four years later. He attended UC Berkeley and worked full time at the school's law library to pay his way. He graduated from Boalt Hall in 1930 and began a private practice. Levin was named to the municipal court in 1956 and to the superior court in 1958. He was elected presiding judge in 1966.

Levin was well known for his work ethic and dedication to charitable causes. "Everyone asks me how I find the time for all these things," he said in a 1962 interview. "If you work eighteen to twenty hours a day, you find time to do what you want to do." He described taking the oath of office as a district court judge as "one of the sublime moments of my life." Shortly thereafter, Levin found himself presiding over the contentious libel lawsuit filed by San Francisco mayor Joseph Alioto against *Look* magazine. Alioto claimed that a story published in the magazine, which included a juicy detail about him having ties to the mafia, was untrue and had harmed his political career. The case dragged on for eleven years, and Alioto finally prevailed, though he received only a fraction of the damages he'd requested. But by the time it was settled, Levin was no longer presiding. In early 1971, Levin underwent surgery for a brain tumor. He never left the hospital. He passed away in June 1971, at age sixty-five.

President Nixon nominated Charles B. Renfrew to fill Levin's seat and Spencer Williams to fill a newly created seat. Unlike many of their fellow judges, who were products of the Bay Area, Renfrew was born in Detroit in 1928 and educated at Princeton University and the University of Michigan Law School. After stints in the army and the navy, he moved to San Francisco in 1956, and joined Pillsbury, Madison, and Sutro, the city's largest law firm at the time. He was made a partner in 1965. Williams, born in Reading, Massachusetts, in 1922, graduated from UCLA and served in the navy before attending Boalt Hall, which he graduated from in 1948. Williams's law career included stints in private practice in San Jose and Sacramento as well as service as Santa Clara County's deputy county counsel and county counsel from 1949 to 1966. He was secretary of the California State Human Relations Agency from 1967 to 1970 before returning to private practice in San Jose, where he was working when nominated to the district court.

At age forty-three, Renfrew became the youngest judge on the San Francisco federal bench, and he was perhaps also the earliest riser. A self-described "morning man," Renfrew "sent shock waves through the legal community" when he responded to a request for the soonest available court date by scheduling a hearing on a preliminary injunction for 7:30 a.m. on an upcoming weekday, reported the *San Francisco Chronicle*. "And they have to bring in their own court reporter," he told the paper.

Renfrew's tenure on the bench was only a few years longer than Levin's. In early 1980, he retired to serve as deputy US attorney general in the Jimmy Carter administration. "Who would have ever thought he would only last one term," Renfrew later said. He was the first judge on the court to voluntarily retire, and was given a special farewell as he left for Washington, DC. Admired for his hard work, Renfrew surprised even himself when he took the political appointment. Reflecting on his eight-year tenure, Renfrew told his colleagues as he left, "I thought then that there would be nothing in the world that could entice me to leave the federal judiciary." After Carter's term ended in 1981, Renfrew returned to San Francisco to go into private practice. He was appointed legal counsel for Chevron in 1983 and became a vice president of the oil company in 1984. During his tenure, Chevron named a 784-foot oil tanker after him. He remained with the company through 1993 and then returned to private practice, focusing on dispute resolution for businesses.

In contrast, Spencer Williams stayed on the court for the rest of his professional life. He retired in 2002 and died in 2008. During one of the most notable cases of his career, he presided over IBM's 1993 lawsuit against National Semiconductor Corp., which claimed that NSC conspired with Hitachi Ltd. of Japan to steal computer secrets. The defendants pled no contest, but even though there would be no trial,

Williams ordered that the video and audio evidence collected by the FBI be released for public access. IBM later settled out of court with Hitachi, which paid $300 million for their use of stolen computer software information. The companies agreed to arbitration for all future trade secret disputes between them.

Black Power

Despite the overwhelming presence on Northern District dockets of those conscientiously objecting to the war in Vietnam, that conflict was far from the only one being protested at the time. The founding of the Black Panther Party in Oakland in 1966 led to more than a decade of community activism, rising political awareness among young, urban African Americans, and violent clashes with police and government officials. In a 1969 annual report, FBI leader J. Edgar Hoover announced that, of any black extremist group, "The Black Panther Party, without question, represents the greatest threat to the internal security of the country." The Black Panther Party, in its militant Black Power incarnation, was created by twenty-four-year-old Huey P. Newton, who moved with his family from Louisiana to Oakland as a child. With help from friends Bobby Seale and David Hilliard, Newton created the Ten-Point Program to articulate the group's goals, which centered on gaining freedom and equality for the "Black and oppressed." Their manifesto called for full control over "all institutions which exist in our communities," "decent housing and education," as well as free health care, an end to police brutality, and the equivalent of forty acres and two mules for each black person in the United States. Intrinsic in this series of statements was a demand that these needs be met by the federal government, and a pledge to use "self-defense" to promote this agenda. The Panthers sponsored sickle cell anemia research and provided free breakfasts to needy children, but the group first gained national attention when party chairman Bobby Seale led a group of weapon-toting Panthers into the California legislature to protest a pending gun control law. The Mulford Act passed and made it a crime to carry a gun in public.

At the height of their popularity, the Black Panthers boasted of chapters in forty-eight states, but by the early 1980s, criminal convictions, infighting, and FBI intervention led to the party's demise. Throughout the group's existence, Panther members moved constantly in and out of California's state and federal courts and incarceration facilities, as

FIG. 7-6
Founders of the Black Panther Party for Self-Defense (later the Black Panther Party) Bobby Seale (left) and Huey P. Newton pose with a Colt .45 and a shotgun in Oakland on April 25, 1967. Shortly afterward, the party staged a protest at the California State Assembly that helped establish their presence in national politics. Courtesy of The Bancroft Library, University of California, Berkeley.

the party made little effort to separate its legal and illegal activities. The same people responsible for feeding hungry children—first at Bay Area churches and then at party chapters across the nation—were cited repeatedly for having (and using) illegal firearms.

At one point, the incarceration of party founder Huey Newton led to a popular movement almost larger than the party itself. In October 1967, Newton and other Panthers took part in a shoot-out with Oakland police after being stopped for questioning. The incident left police officer John Frey dead and Newton wounded and arrested. In 1968, an Alameda

County judge convicted Newton of voluntary manslaughter in Frey's death and sent him to the California Men's Colony in San Luis Obispo for a term of two to fifteen years. Anger over the mounting conflict in Vietnam and a general sense of social unrest drove many young whites to join with the Panthers to cry "Free Huey!" After exhausting their appeals at the state level, Newton's attorneys appeared before Judge Zirpoli in 1969. They argued that Newton had been deprived of bail while awaiting appeal on "arbitrary and discriminatory" grounds that were "based upon the assumption that black leaders are violent and a menace to the community," rather than focusing on whether Newton would appear at his next court date. Zirpoli granted them a hearing.

The Black Panther propaganda machine cranked into action. Seizing on the coincidence of a hearing on May Day, a traditional labor holiday, the Party summoned protesters to San Francisco's Federal Building. In his heavily guarded seventeenth-floor courtroom, Judge Zirpoli listened to ninety minutes of arguments and noted that his research revealed no case in which a federal judge had granted bail to a state felony prisoner. However, he added that the law continues to change "and there is always the element of setting precedent."

Outside, plainclothes police officers patrolled the crowd of two thousand protesters. A red flag with the Black Panther emblem was briefly run up the flagpole, and later a group of young whites attempted to lower the US flag. A week later, Zirpoli denied Newton's request for bail, explaining that without evidence of abuse of discretion, a federal judge was not permitted to substitute his ruling for that of a state judge. However, based on a separate appeal (*People v. Newton*, 1970) in state court, Newton's manslaughter conviction was soon overturned, and a new trial ordered. In July 1970, Newton was released from custody on $50,000 bail. By that point, other party-related lawsuits and legal entanglements had garnered national attention.

Earl Caldwell, an African American reporter for the *New York Times*, had written a series of articles on the Black Panther Party and in the process developed a number of confidential sources within the group. In 1970, Caldwell received a subpoena to appear before a San Francisco federal grand jury investigating the party. Two weeks later, he appeared before Judge Zirpoli requesting that the subpoena be quashed. Caldwell told the judge he would not reveal his sources. Zirpoli determined that Caldwell should honor the summons to appear, but added to the ruling that the reporter would not be required to divulge his contacts. He noted that the courts had never before ruled on a reporter's constitutional right to keep sources confidential and stayed his order pending appeal, which meant Caldwell could not be called before the jury until a higher court had ruled.

In the ensuing months, Caldwell was repeatedly issued subpoenas, which he repeatedly declined to obey. Zirpoli continued to maintain that Caldwell was required to appear before the jury, although he had a journalist's right to keep his sources confidential. Yet Caldwell would not cooperate, as he believed that his presence before the jury would damage his credibility in the black community. Zirpoli found Caldwell in contempt. He remained free pending his appeal.

Later that year, two young journalists entered the fray. Brenda Presley, twenty-two, and Sherrie Bursey, eighteen, both writers for the Black Panther Party newsletter, were also called before the Panther-probing grand jury. When they refused to appear, Judge Zirpoli was again called to rule. He maintained that the women, like Caldwell, would need to appear, but he added that his ruling in "no way intimates that the court has any views as to any alleged subversive or criminal activities of the Black Panther Party, its central committee, or any members of its newspaper staff." Zirpoli, after a final attempt to get the two women to answer the grand jury's questions, held them in contempt and ordered them into custody. Presley, who was nine months pregnant, remained free, but on the day Bursey went to jail, Huey Newton called on women's liberationists to rise up in support of a revolutionary.

Meanwhile, judges on the Ninth Circuit Court of Appeals reversed Zirpoli's ruling on Caldwell, stating that he did not have to appear before the grand jury. The three-judge panel, with an opinion written by Judge Charles Merrill, noted that when the public's right to be informed could be infringed upon, the government must make a compelling argument about why the witness is needed. They cited the First Amendment protection designed to "provide the public with a wide range of information about the nature of protest and heterodoxy." The government's argument had not been compelling enough. But in 1972, the Supreme Court, combining the Caldwell case with a number of similar cases from other states, reversed the Ninth Circuit's ruling, declaring that reporters, like all citizens, have a constitutional requirement to appear before a grand jury.

This ruling was a factor in the 2005 standoff between *New York Times* reporter Judith Miller and the federal government over the outing of covert CIA agent Valerie Plame. Miller went to jail for more than twelve weeks on contempt charges for refusing to testify before the grand jury. She was released after obtaining a waiver of confidentiality from her source, I. Lewis Libby, Vice President Dick Cheney's chief of staff, and agreeing to testify. In 2006, district court judge William Alsup sent journalist-videographer Josh Wolf to prison for more than seven months for defying a grand jury subpoena to provide video footage of a protest in San Francisco's Mission District. Alsup rejected Wolf's claims that the Constitution upheld his rights as a journalist to withhold unpublished material. "Every person, from the President of the United States down to you and me, has to give information to the grand jury if the grand jury wants it," Alsup told Wolf. His imprisonment was the longest of a reporter over journalists' rights in United States history.

With controversy and disobedience in the air, it soon seemed that nothing in the Bay Area was above sparking protest—including what, for the majority of the population, was simply a local landmark. Alcatraz Island, about one mile north of San Francisco in the middle of San Francisco Bay, had served as a military fortress and prison (1859 to 1934) and a federal penitentiary (1934 to 1963), but the government was not the first to use Alcatraz Island for incarceration. Native American oral histories say that indigenous tribes had used Alcatraz as a place of isolation for members who had broken tribal laws—as well as for hunting and gathering food—for perhaps hundreds of years. With this history in mind, Richard Oakes, a Mohawk Indian, led a group of Native Americans to a symbolic occupation of the nearly vacant island in late 1969. His initial goal was to raise awareness about the Native American claim to the land, but as he scouted the terrain and noted the abandoned buildings, Oakes began thinking that long-term occupation of the island might be possible. He soon recruited other American Indians, many of them students at UCLA's American Indian Studies Center, to his cause.

On November 20, 1969, eighty Native Americans took possession of Alcatraz Island, and forty more joined the next day. They announced that the island was reclaimed in the name of all Indian peoples and demanded the deed to the land so they could establish an Indian university, cultural center, and museum. These demands mirrored, almost exactly, those put forth during the first Indian occupation of Alcatraz—a brief four-hour standoff conducted by five Sioux in 1964.

The federal government ordered the Indians to vacate the island (which is federal property, despite falling within the city limits of San

Francisco) in 1969. Instead, they organized for long-term residence at Alcatraz. They elected a governing council and gave each person on the island a job. The Department of Justice agreed to formal negotiations and adopted a policy of non-interference. For several months, the FBI, Coast Guard, and Government Services Administration were all restricted from interacting with or removing the island's new occupants.

As the year waned, the organization began to collapse. Rival factions competed for power with Oakes—and then tragedy struck. Oakes's thirteen-year-old stepdaughter fell down three flights of stairs in an abandoned building on the island in January 1970. She did not receive outside medical treatment and died three days later. Oakes left the island, leaving its leadership in disarray. As classes resumed at UCLA, many of the student occupiers exchanged radicalism for academia. They were replaced by Native American newcomers as well as an assortment of hippies and drifters unrelated to the cause.

Negotiations continued, often in secret and at times including US Attorney James L. Browning. Electrical power to Alcatraz was shut off, and a barge that provided fresh water was removed. At one point, the occupiers were offered a segment of Fort Miley, near Ocean Beach in San Francisco, instead of Alcatraz, but the offer was rejected. Shortly after the water barge was removed, a bonfire accidentally spread to several historic buildings, including the 1853 lighthouse. The buildings burned all night and into the morning of June 2, 1970, as the Coast Guard was restricted from Alcatraz without a formal request.

The fire sparked a shift in perception, and public support for the occupiers declined. Shortly thereafter, news that people were stripping copper wiring and tubing from Alcatraz buildings and selling it for scrap prompted outrage. Three people from the island were arrested while on a covert trip to the mainland, charged with selling six hundred pounds of copper. The government cut off talks, claiming there was no longer any recognizable leadership.

The collision of two oil tankers at the entrance to San Francisco Bay in January 1971 led to the end of the occupation. Some blamed the accident on the darkened Alcatraz lighthouse. Though it was eventually determined that the lighthouse played no part in the accident, the incident was enough to spur the government to action. President Nixon approved a removal plan that called for as little force as possible.

On June 10, 1971—nineteen months after the occupation began— federal marshals, special operations forces, and FBI agents raided the island and removed five women, four children, and six men, none of whom were armed. The occupation ended. A statement from the US Attorney's office explained that negotiations had been non-productive and that "public safety and community welfare would not permit a continuance of this intolerable situation." It was also noted that three people were charged with stealing federal government property in conjunction with the evacuation.

Eventually, three Native Americans were convicted of stealing and selling more than sixteen hundred pounds of copper from government buildings on Alcatraz Island. Visiting district court judge Ronald N. Davies, of Fargo, North Dakota, presided over the trial. Before the jury left for deliberation, he criticized the government's handling of the case. "There is a very great possibility these men may have thought they had a right to this copper," he said. The men were convicted, and Davies sentenced them to three years of probation. The government appealed, but the appeal backfired. In 1973, the Ninth Circuit reversed the convictions on the grounds of "erroneous jury instructions by the visiting trial judge."

CHAPTER 8

RISE AGAINST THE ESTABLISHMENT

THE END OF THE VIETNAM WAR heralded a new era for the Northern District as the government began to crack down on drugs and organized crime, and residents found they could successfully challenge established practices such as the death penalty, school segregation, and even the pace of development in cities and towns. Northern California and the country in general were becoming less trusting of government and established powers and more activist in nature, an evolution fueled in part by the federal government's growing intervention in the redevelopment of American cities, including San Francisco.

As military industry transformed to civil industry in the wake of World War II, San Francisco was at a crossroads. Some residents envisioned a city transformed into a high rise–filled center for commerce like Chicago or New York City. Others wanted to preserve its small-town atmosphere. But the war had raised the city's profile on the international stage and provided a base for big business to expand. The 1950s brought freeways all over California, including San Francisco, and with them came the dream of an expanded downtown commercial area that would rival New York's.

Developers were aided by the San Francisco Redevelopment Agency, an organization created by a state law in 1948 to "better urban living conditions through the removal of blight." Although the agency was an independent entity, the mayor appointed its members and the city's Board of Supervisors approved its decisions. The following year, President Truman signed the American Housing Act of 1949 to provide federal funding for

FIG. 8-1 A (PREVIOUS PAGE)
Talks of redeveloping areas south of Market Street, including this lonely stretch of Howard Street between Third and Fourth Streets, prompted the *San Francisco News-Call Bulletin* to publish this photo in January 1960. Courtesy of the San Francisco History Center, San Francisco Public Library.

FIG. 8-1 B
Hotel owner and financier Benjamin H. Swig (seated) and associates reveal a plan for the redevelopment of three city blocks south of Market Street, an area the *San Francisco News-Call Bulletin* called "Skid Row Ghost Town" in January 1960. Courtesy of the San Francisco History Center, San Francisco Public Library.

rebuilding American cities, encouraging demolition and reconstruction of blighted urban areas.

Widened streets, tunnels, skyscrapers, and modernization of San Francisco's run-down Victorian neighborhoods were at the heart of the San Francisco Redevelopment Agency's aggressive plan, steered by Justin Herman, the agency head appointed by Mayor George Christopher. As San Francisco's downtown district grew, developers yearned for a convention center, hotel, and sports arena to complement it. They eyed the area south of Market Street, a run-down neighborhood of warehouses, small factories, businesses, apartment buildings, and single-room-occupancy (SRO) hotels populated mostly by poor single men and immigrants.

South of Market, commonly referred to as SoMa, had been a working-class neighborhood since the 1860s, when the former marshland was filled. Over the years it had accommodated miners, sailors, longshoremen, factory workers, and immigrants of all kinds. Novelist Jack London was born there, at Third and Brannan Streets, in 1876. By the 1950s, the majority of SRO rooms were rented to a rather stable community of men who clung to one of the last low-rent areas in the city.

Armed with the Housing Act, the redevelopment agency turned its attention to SoMa. In 1953, the San Francisco Board of Supervisors designated nineteen blocks of SoMa as the home of their redevelopment plan. In 1955, Fairmont Hotel owner Benjamin Swig produced the San Francisco Prosperity Plan, which called for a major redevelopment program to boost downtown. While Swig's plan was not adopted, his ideas planted the seeds for redevelopment to come. Meanwhile, urban renewal began in earnest in the Western Addition, west of Van Ness Avenue, where Herman used eminent domain to demolish existing housing in this working-class, non-white neighborhood, which had been home to immigrant Irish, Jews, Japanese (most of whom had been sent to internment camps during World War II), and African Americans.

In 1964, John Shelley became the first Democrat elected mayor of San Francisco in fifty years. He had represented the city in Congress for fifteen years and pledged to "plan San Francisco's future with a heart as well as a bulldozer," according to the *National Trust Guide to San Francisco*. Shortly after becoming mayor, Shelley's South of Market Development Committee, packed with North of Market businessmen, announced a Yerba Buena Center proposal similar to the old Swig plan.

The proposal was submitted to the Department of Housing and Urban Development in the hopes of receiving federal funding, and was also sent for review to San Francisco Planning and Urban Research (SPUR), a group formed to satisfy the Housing Act requirement that residents be represented during plans for urban renewal. SPUR, which included no residents living south of Market Street, found fault only with the replacement housing planned for the elderly men who were being displaced by the proposed project. SPUR deemed it "utterly incompatible" with the planned upscale shopping, office, and hotel facilities.

The San Francisco Labor Council soon weighed in on the Yerba Buena Center plan. A labor leader asked whether policy makers had considered "the social and economic effect on over three thousand single persons, a third of them aged, who will be displaced in the area without realistic provision for relocation." Redeveloping SoMa would eliminate blue-collar jobs as warehouses and factories were cleared out. In light of labor opposition as well as protest from SoMa residents, Mayor Shelley put a temporary stop to the project.

But when $19.6 million in federal funds arrived to support the Yerba Buena Center plan, Herman began public hearings. Despite residents' protests, the plan approved by the Board of Supervisors in 1966 covered eighty-seven acres of land and included only 176 units of replacement housing.

Land acquisition began in 1967, an election year. By then, those in favor of expansion had grown tired of Shelley's delays and stopped supporting him for mayor. Shelley dropped his re-election bid and Joseph Alioto Jr., the redevelopment agency's first chairman, became the new, well-financed front-runner for mayor. In just forty-five minutes, Swig raised $203,000 for Alioto during a meeting at his Fairmont Hotel.

Once in office, Mayor Alioto moved forward rapidly: he traveled to Washington and secured more federal funds (eventually reaching $49 million) and won over the San Francisco Labor Council with promises of union jobs on redevelopment projects and seats on assorted city commissions. In the meantime, the redevelopment agency condemned and demolished empty SoMa buildings.

In 1969, the redevelopment agency unveiled the final design for the Yerba Buena Center: a 22-acre complex with a 350,000-square-foot exhibition hall, a 14,000-seat sports arena, an 800-room hotel, a 2,200-seat theater, office buildings, shops, parking for 4,000 cars, and landscaped plazas. This prompted the remaining residents of SoMa to organize. They formed Tenants and Owners in Opposition to Redevelopment (TOOR) and elected George Woolf, an eighty-year-old hotel resident and longtime union organizer, as their leader. Their goal was to end the redevelopment agency's bullying and ensure access to adequate replacement housing.

Using the Housing Act to its advantage, TOOR filed a lawsuit in the district court against the redevelopment agency and HUD in 1969 and demanded "decent, safe, and sanitary" replacement housing, at comparable rents, for any residents displaced, as required for a revitalization project using federal funds. They also charged that developers had failed to consult minority groups about their plans (as HUD required) and had shut out area residents from hearings before the plan was approved. They asked for fifteen hundred units of replacement housing and demanded the renovation of four existing SRO hotels. In April 1970, after hours of testimony and myriad exhibits, district court judge Stanley Weigel found for TOOR and issued a preliminary injunction against development of the Yerba Buena Center, stopping demolition and resident displacement until a revised plan was approved.

After four lengthy meetings and one plan accepted by attorneys but rejected by SoMa residents, Weigel replaced the injunction with a court order. He ruled that the developers must build fifteen hundred to eighteen hundred units of replacement housing within the next three years, and not demolish any of the five existing residential hotels until the new units were complete. Although four thousand units were being destroyed, and TOOR believed that two thousand was the minimum number of new units required, the group's leaders signed the agreement in 1970.

Time passed, but no new housing materialized. Herman figured the longer the city waited, the more of SoMa's elderly residents would pass away or move on, and fewer new housing units would be needed, wrote sociologist Chester Hartman in his 1984 book *City for Sale: The Transformation of San Francisco*. But in the meantime, support for the project began to erode. Roger Boas, the city's chief administrative officer, raised

"A Labor Man All My Life"

My name is George Woolf, I'm eighty-three years old, and have lived in and around San Francisco for the last seventy years. I have been a labor man all my life, working on the waterfront and organizing the Cannery Workers union in the thirties. I live in the Milner Hotel, which is situated on Fourth and Mission, just one block south of the Main stem, Market Street. I came down to the Milner because I liked the neighborhood. It was close to business, banks, groceries and restaurants. Nobody invited me down here and nobody is going to invite me out. I don't want anyone to come in and tell me that I have to move to some undesirable place where I wouldn't have the facilities that I enjoy, or did enjoy, here. Today I can sit in my room looking out the window and for four city blocks all I can see is where demolition has taken place, nothing but vacant lots with fences around them to protect people from falling in. Thousands of automobiles are parked where buildings and business formerly prospered.

—George Woolf, Milner Hotel, San Francisco, 1971

concerns about financing and cited potential conflicts of interest; even Swig's son, Richard, and other hotel investors began to criticize the plan. In 1971, Mayor Alioto decided to scrap the design and start over. Herman is rumored to have been drafting a letter of protest to Alioto when he died of a heart attack at age sixty-two in his apartment at the Golden Gateway, a complex built by the redevelopment agency after it cleared San Francisco's old produce market from the waterfront in the 1960s.

Herman's death did not silence the city's demand for progress and expansion. "How much longer must the city of San Francisco put up with the dictatorial decisions on community affairs of US District Judge Stanley Weigel?" lamented a 1972 *San Francisco Examiner* editorial. "What now? How long, oh lord?" Shortly thereafter, the redevelopment agency's attorneys entered a motion to disqualify Weigel from the Yerba Buena case on the grounds that he was biased and too emotionally involved. Weigel temporarily disqualified himself while Chief Judge Oliver Carter reviewed the matter. Carter's opinion, issued in February 1972, reflected careful consideration—as well as a sense of humor:

> In paragraph 16 of the affidavit it is alleged that Judge Weigel accused the local agency of "shenanigans." I would think that if that is the worst that persons could ever be accused of the world would be a much improved place. Dictionaries variously define the word to mean prankishness, mischief, trickery, foolery, evasion, or deceit. I do not believe that such a puckish word is sufficiently condemnatory to reveal bias and prejudice. In fact as a contemporary of Judge Weigel I believe its use reveals a judge's age more than his state of mind.

Carter declared Weigel to be objective and fit for the Yerba Buena case. A few weeks later, appellate court judges denied without comment the redevelopment agency's request for an additional hearing.

The lawsuits multiplied as opposition grew to the project. Six environmental groups, including the Sierra Club and San Francisco Tomorrow (a local urban environmental group), filed suit in 1972, alleging that the project failed to meet the requirements of both the California Environmental Quality Act and the National Environmental Policy Act. To settle this, the city agreed to conduct environmental impact studies.

In an attempt to keep things moving, city supervisors approved a $225 million bond issue to fund public facilities at the Yerba Buena Center. This only prompted further legal action, as residents opposed to the project argued that such a bond required voter approval. Noting that the redevelopment agency had made little progress in addressing replacement housing, Weigel revised the previous settlement and in 1973 ordered that four hundred more units be built, to be funded by a new city hotel tax. The court-supervised agreement between the city and TOOR was signed in 1973 in the well-worn lobby of the Milner Hotel. The settlement gave TOOR—which had become the nonprofit development company Tenants and Owners Development Corporation (TODC)—three lots to build on. In 1979, TODC opened Woolf House as their first affordable housing building. It was named for George Woolf, who passed away shortly before the 1973 agreement was signed.

Term limits sent Mayor Alioto out of office in 1975. George Moscone took office next and revised the Yerba Buena Center plan again, this time adding public gardens and cultural facilities as well as affordable housing. Construction began on the convention center in 1979, but builders found water just below the soil, which slowed underground construction. The convention center was named in honor of Mayor Moscone, who was assassinated at City Hall in 1978 by Supervisor Dan White. The building opened in 1981 to the realization that it was not big enough for any major convention. Meeting rooms were added on top in 1993, as well as a second convention hall under Yerba Buena Gardens. This public garden complex, touted as the crown jewel of San Francisco, is now home to a number of museums, as well as a skating rink, playground, art galleries, movie theaters, and performing arts spaces.

TODC opened new housing developments about every two years during the 1980s. By 1989, the units of housing required by Weigel's 1973 ruling were finally complete, but the nonprofit developer continued working and remodeled or built five more housing buildings to the west of the Moscone Center. They are populated with low-income tenants—many of them elderly, handicapped, or minorities—and offer social services from counseling and medical care to art workshops.

While the Yerba Buena case might not have curtailed "the effort to make money in real estate," as Judge Weigel observed in a 1989 interview, it did result in less "willingness for some to break the law in a pursuit of avarice."

"Judge Weigel enjoined demolition and relocation despite the fact that the decision was principally responsible for holding up a $400 million project for four years," wrote Joseph T. Henke in the *San Francisco Law Review*. "Few judges in the country have had the temerity to block these huge clearance projects."

All of Northern California developed rapidly in the 1960s and 1970s, leading to battles between residents and developers over growth as well as redevelopment. While the bitter fight over South of Market raged in San Francisco, another fight for community preservation gathered momentum to the north.

The city of Petaluma, incorporated in 1858 about forty miles north of San Francisco in Sonoma County, proudly proclaimed itself as the Egg Capital of the World. Once populated largely by farmers and chicken ranchers, the town maintained a charming historic downtown that had escaped damage in the 1906 earthquake. The widening of the US 101 freeway in the 1950s made a daily commute from Petaluma to San Francisco or San Rafael conceivable. Housing needed for the newcomers soon began to replace chicken coops with sprawling subdivisions.

In 1962, Petaluma had just 17,000 residents. By 1970 it had 24,870. Mayor Helen Putnam and the city council worried that if the city kept growing at this rate, by 1985 there might be 77,000 people packed into Petaluma. Not only was the small-town way of life in danger, but the city's water and sewer facilities weren't capable of handling such growth. Residents received a questionnaire with their water bills in 1971 asking what kind of city they would like Petaluma to become. The majority of those who responded wanted the city to stay small. The city council created the Petaluma Plan, which capped growth at five hundred new housing units a year (with a few exceptions for public housing) for five years, starting in 1972. It required developers who wanted to build multiple units to submit plans for review to a committee that would score them based on criteria including aesthetic quality, furtherance of the city's social goals, and environmental impact. The higher-scoring proposals would be placed at the top of the list, and the top five hundred units would be authorized. The plan also preserved green space around the town by limiting urban expansion.

Petaluma's residents approved the plan in 1973 by a vote of 4,181 to 906. Developers, and some business people, were not pleased, but city officials were. "All of a sudden we've had an impressive array of builders competing for the (available) allocations," Mayor Putnam told the *San Francisco Examiner*. Petaluma city planner Frank Gray reported that instead of tract homes and subdivisions filled with cookie-cutter copies, builders were branching out into clusters of homes surrounded by green space. Builders fought back by filing a lawsuit in the district court that claimed the Petaluma Plan was unconstitutional because it inhibited the right to travel and settle freely, violated federal interstate commerce regulations, and denied them due process and equal protection under the Constitution.

Mayor Putnam, a local first-grade teacher who was described as grandmotherly, sent letters to every city and county in California asking for financial support in Petaluma's legal fight. The letter asked for $250 or whatever the community could afford. By the fall of 1973, when the *San Francisco Examiner* caught wind of the campaign, twenty-three local agencies had sent $250, and one hundred cities had sent letters of support or pledged money, including Fort Bragg in Mendocino County and Beverly Hills, for a fund totaling more than $6,000.

The trial of *Construction Industry Association of Sonoma County v. City of Petaluma* began in district court in San Francisco before Judge Lloyd Burke in January 1974. "The issue is relatively simple," Burke explained to those gathered in the courtroom for the bench (non-jury) trial. "It is the use of zoning by people who live there versus those who want to live there. Is this program to limit growth a legitimate exercise of the city's police and public welfare powers? If it is not legal…it is unconstitutional."

David A. Young, a Petaluma city engineer, testified that the city was already using more than its share of state-allotted water and that new sewage facilities would not be available for several years. Attorney Malcolm Misuraca, representing the builders, asserted that if Petaluma were allowed to close its borders or limit its population, other cities in California—or even the state itself—might do the same. After just four days, Judge Burke ruled the Petaluma Plan unconstitutional. "No city may regulate its population growth numerically so residents of other cities cannot enter and establish residency there," he said. The Petaluma Plan violated the part of the Constitution that guarantees the "right to travel and enter any city, temporarily or on a permanent basis." Burke retained jurisdiction over the matter and declared that he would review any building permit rejected by the city at the developer's request. Misuraca hailed Burke's decision as landmark in that it expanded the constitutional right to travel to cover land use, a concept that had previously been subject to debate.

In May 1974, Burke denied the city of Petaluma a stay on his order, pending an appeal. "The rights involved in this case, if I'm correct, are so fundamental in nature [that] a stay order would lose for these people entitled to relief irretrievably their constitutional rights," he explained. In July 1974, the Ninth Circuit also denied the city a stay but agreed to hear the case. The Ninth Circuit reversed Burke's decision in 1975, finding that the developers "did not have standing to bring a challenge on the grounds that the plan interfered with the right to travel." The court also found the Petaluma Plan to be "rationally related to a legitimate state interest" and held that "the zoning ordinance fell within the broad concept of public welfare." Overall, the Petaluma Plan "was a legitimate exercise of appellant's police power and did not burden interstate commerce." Despite additional appeals from the builders, the Ninth Circuit and Supreme Court both denied further review of the matter.

In 2000, Petaluma's population was 54,549. Whether these results are due to the city's innovative growth-control plan or simply to the naturally fickle nature of those fleeing to the suburbs remains open to discussion.

Challenging Death

Legal execution in California is nearly as old as the state itself, having been authorized by the state's Criminal Practices Act of 1851. Individual counties carried out the death sentences, usually by hanging, until 1891, when the state legislature required that executions take place inside a state prison.

For the next forty years or so, convicts sentenced to death—307 in all—were sent to San Quentin or Folsom State Prison to be hanged. In 1937, the gas chamber replaced hanging, which was ruled to be cruel and unusual and therefore unconstitutional. The state's only gas chamber was constructed at San Quentin. From its first use in 1938 through 1967 (when executions were halted until 1992), 194 prisoners were executed in the San Quentin gas chamber.

In April 1967, Aaron Mitchell, who had killed a police officer during a 1963 robbery, was the last man to lose his request for a stay of execution in the Northern District Court and the last man executed by the State of California for twenty-five years. In June of 1967, fifty-eight men awaited execution in San Quentin, nine of them scheduled to die within the next two months. A number of them did not have lawyers, so the American Friends Service Committee, a Quaker organization, found lawyers for them. Young attorneys Jerome Falk Jr. and Roy Eisenhardt took on the case of Frederick Saterfield, who was scheduled for execution on July 20.

Falk and Eisenhardt, along with lawyers for other death row inmates, held a meeting in San Francisco to work out a legal strategy against the death penalty as a whole. Lawyers for death row inmates in Florida had recently filed a class action habeas corpus petition and secured a statewide

FIG. 8-2
Picketers confront Governor Edmund G. Brown in Los Angeles in May 1960, demanding
that he halt executions at San Quentin State Prison. Courtesy of the San Francisco History
Center, San Francisco Public Library.

stay of execution. The group in San Francisco decided to try something
similar. On June 28, 1967, the group filed *Hill v. Nelson* in the Northern
District Court. The named petitioners sued San Quentin's warden on
behalf of all condemned California inmates on the grounds that capital punishment was unconstitutional. On June 29, Falk made his first
appearance in federal court—ever—before Judge Robert Peckham to
request that all executions in the state of California be stayed.

Specifically, the plaintiffs argued that the death penalty, as administered in California, was unconstitutional for four main reasons: those
opposed to the death penalty were excluded from criminal juries; juries
were given no guidance in making death penalty decisions; it constituted
cruel and unusual punishment, especially when administered in a stan-
dard-less sentencing system; and the state did not provide lawyers for
those on death row after their sentences and convictions were upheld by
the California Supreme Court.

On July 5, Judge Peckham issued a temporary stay and planned procedural briefings. Other than in Florida, nothing like this had ever been tried before. After weeks of hearings, Peckham issued a second order in August 1967, ordering each case to be treated as an individual petition with common questions of law and fact to be consolidated later. One of the death row plaintiffs, Robert Massie, suddenly decided he no longer wished to fight his death sentence. Peckham dispatched Falk to San Quentin to meet with Massie. The prisoner would not change his mind. But the California Supreme Court ordered a temporary stay of all executions.

The state court ruled in 1968 against all four of the constitutional attacks in *Hill*, but agreed to appoint counsel for death row inmates to handle any appeals arising after the automatic appeals had been exhausted. Meanwhile, two Supreme Court rulings changed the death penalty landscape. *Witherspoon v. Illinois* (1968) said people opposed to the death penalty could not legally be excluded from juries and *McGautha v. California* (1971) established that juries needed standards as to how to apply the death penalty. All this meant that new trials were needed for a number of California's condemned inmates. The *Hill* cases were assigned to Judge Alfonso Zirpoli in the district court. At the same time, the high court remanded *Furman v. Georgia*, a case that asked the same question as those pending with Zirpoli: Was the death penalty a cruel and unusual punishment as defined by the Eighth Amendment?

In 1972, the California Supreme Court answered that question for itself in *People v. Anderson*. Falk, defending condemned inmate Robert Anderson, convinced the court that the state's death penalty was cruel and unusual punishment. The court declared the death penalty unconstitutional according to the state constitution. Nine months later, California voters amended the state constitution to allow for death sentences. The Supreme Court countered, ruling that a death sentence imposed by a jury at its own discretion, which was the practice in a number of states, including California, violated the Eighth Amendment. All of a sudden, the death penalty cases pending before Zirpoli were moot and 107 inmates had their sentences changed to something other than death.

Death penalty proponents, who included a majority of California residents, continued to tinker with the state law over the next twenty-five years in order to bring executions back to San Quentin. In 1973, the state legislature made the death penalty a mandatory sentence under certain conditions. This legislation provided the standards and jury instructions required under the *McGautha* ruling. However, in late 1976, the Supreme Court declared the California death penalty statute unconstitutional because the accused was not allowed to present any mitigating evidence. This ruling changed the sentences for another seventy death row inmates. A year later the state legislature reinstated the death penalty, this time allowing mitigation and introducing a new list of crimes for which the death penalty could be considered.

The California Penal Code was also revised to include life without the possibility of parole, which became the required punishment for some crimes and a sentencing choice, along with the death penalty, in others. In 1978, California voters passed Proposition 7, which became the death penalty standard by which California still operates. This constitutional amendment ensured that convicts sentenced to death receive an automatic appeal to the California Supreme Court. In addition, even if the state supreme court affirms the death sentence, the condemned prisoner may file other state and federal appeals on separate constitutional issues.

It would be fourteen years before this statute was exercised. Robert Alton Harris, convicted of the 1978 murder of two teenage boys that he and his brother abducted from a San Diego fast food restaurant, would be the first death row inmate to be executed under the 1978 law. Harris was scheduled to die in San Quentin's gas chamber in 1992. Barely eighty hours before his execution, he and two other death row inmates filed a class action lawsuit on behalf of the 323 condemned prisoners in California. In *Fierro v. Gomez*, they alleged that the state's use of cyanide gas for gas chamber executions constituted cruel and unusual punishment, in violation of the Eighth Amendment. They sought a temporary restraining order for Harris's execution, as well as a permanent injunction against this method of execution. Judge Marilyn Hall Patel, who had joined the district court in 1980, issued a ten-day restraining order to weigh the merits of the plaintiffs' arguments.

Cyanide gas induces hypoxia—a lack of oxygen in the body—which produces pain similar to that of a heart attack. The seizures and vomiting that follow can last as long as ten minutes before death finally occurs. Patel noted that recent evidence of cyanide executions "suggests that lethal gas may be slow, painful, and torturous." She added that the effects of a gas chamber execution were "comparable to descriptions of hanging," a method of execution already declared unconstitutional in California. Only three states used the gas chamber for executions, and only Arizona had done so in the last twenty-five years. "The clearest and most reliable evidence of contemporary values is the legislation enacted by the country's legislatures," Patel wrote. She granted Harris and the other death row inmates the stay of execution they requested.

The state immediately appealed, and two days later judges at the Ninth Circuit Court of Appeals vacated Patel's stay and ordered the execution to proceed as scheduled. But then the Ninth Circuit ordered its own stay so the court could review its decision en banc. Late on the evening of Monday, April 20, 1992, the Supreme Court vacated this stay. The high court focused more on timing. Harris could have—and should have—filed his case a decade before he did. "There is no good reason for this abusive delay, which has been compounded by last-minute attempts to manipulate the judicial process," the opinion concluded. However, Justices John Paul Stevens and Harry Blackmun dissented, asserting that a court, given the opportunity, would likely find death by gas chamber to be unconstitutional.

Will the Execution Be Televised?

With Robert Alton Harris poised to become the first California prisoner executed in twenty-five years, one TV station requested permission to film it. In early 1990, San Francisco public broadcast television station KQED asked to film Harris's execution for a planned documentary on the death penalty. San Quentin warden Daniel Vasquez denied the request. While sixteen of the fifty seats in the execution viewing room had been set aside for the press, no tape recorders or cameras would be allowed due to security regulations. The station filed a lawsuit in the district court in 1990 arguing that the right to televise the execution was guaranteed by the First Amendment. Judge Robert Schnacke disagreed in 1991. "I'm quite satisfied that neither the press nor the public has a First Amendment right to be [at an execution]," he stated. "The death chamber witness area is not a public area by statute."

During the trial, the state attorney general declared the media had no right to attend executions. KQED maintained that videotape would be the most objective medium for reporting an execution; Vasquez said a camera in the viewing area was a security risk and that televised executions might incite violence among other inmates.

In the first hours of Tuesday, April 21, Harris was taken to the gas chamber. Judge Harry Pregerson of the Ninth Circuit entered one last stay, literally moments before Harris's execution, arguing that the state court had not yet ruled on the whether the gas chamber was unconstitutional. Within two hours the Supreme Court overturned this stay. "No further stays of Robert Alton Harris's execution shall be entered by the federal courts except upon order of this Court," the justices wrote. The execution began at 6 a.m. and at 6:21 Harris was pronounced dead in San Quentin's gas chamber.

In 1993, district court judge Ronald Whyte heard the death row case of *Mason v. Vasquez*, in which the plaintiff, convicted serial killer David Mason, sought to stop his habeas corpus appeal process and be executed. "I had to appoint two attorneys—one to represent his desire to die and another to represent his right to appeal. It was very unusual," said Whyte in a 2006 interview. "I remember the hearing extremely well. Despite his despicable crimes, he was in some ways likable and had done extremely well in prison in recent years. He had apparently become a model prisoner. It troubled me; does it make sense to execute this guy at this place in time? And yet I was convinced that he was mentally competent to make a decision."

When asked if he had a choice between getting the death penalty or not, Mason replied, "I'd take life in a minute, but I did the crimes, I got the death penalty. I have a brother who's starting to get into trouble and I just don't want him to feel that you can get away with things." Mason said he had always believed in the death penalty and that his view shouldn't change just because his life was at stake. "I ruled that he was mentally competent, which subsequently led to his execution," Whyte later said. David Mason would be the last inmate to be executed in San Quentin's gas chamber.

Meanwhile Judge Patel forged ahead with *Fierro v. Gomez* (known as *Fierro* II). In 1994, Patel issued an opinion that California's use of the gas chamber violated the Eighth and Fourteenth Amendments. She enjoined the state from using lethal gas to execute any of the remaining plaintiffs or other prisoners on death row. Once again, the state appealed, but the Ninth Circuit unanimously affirmed the district court's decision. Days later, serial killer William Bonin became the first California prisoner to be executed by lethal injection in San Quentin's former gas chamber.

In the last ten years, public and medical opinion about lethal injection has continued to evolve as the widely used three-step drug protocol has come under growing scrutiny. Judge Jeremy Fogel made national headlines in 2006 when he declared California's procedure for death by lethal injection to be unconstitutional in *Morales v. Tilton*. Just six days before Michael A. Morales's scheduled execution, Judge Fogel denied his stay but found that his claim raised substantial questions about the state's lethal injection procedures. He ordered the state to review them before any further executions and ruled that doctors must be present at the execution or that a medical professional administer the lethal injection of sodium thiopental. The Ninth Circuit affirmed Fogel's decision and reiterated that any doctors present would have to intervene if something went wrong at any stage of the execution. Just hours before Morales's scheduled execution, two anesthesiologists walked off when told they were not merely observers. Participation would violate their medical oath to do no harm. The state was unable to find any replacements.

Fogel was criticized for virtually banning executions in California. In March 2006, he began the first hearings on California's lethal injection protocol. He visited San Quentin's death chamber and examined equipment and records from previous executions. He heard from members of the execution team, a veterinary euthanasia expert who works with gorillas, and other experts. The visit to the death chamber was "very sobering," he said in an interview that same year. "I had a kind of delayed reaction to it. The next day I really felt a sort of emotional after-effect realizing what happens in that chamber and just how weighty the debate is."

Judge Fogel learned that the execution team had no doctors and that its members had been arrested for drunk driving, been reprimanded for smuggling drugs into the prison, and taken leave for depression and post-traumatic stress disorder. He also found that no meaningful training, supervision, or oversight was provided for such a procedure, and that the death chamber was poorly designed for lethal injection. In December 2006, Fogel issued his formal seventeen-page ruling in the case. The case, Fogel wrote, presented a very narrow question: Does California's current protocol, "as actually administered in practice…create an undue and unnecessary risk that an inmate will suffer pain so extreme that it offends the Eighth Amendment?"

Fogel found the answer to be yes. "Given that the state is taking a human life, the pervasive lack of professionalism…is at the very least disturbing," Fogel wrote. He ordered Governor Arnold Schwarzenegger to oversee a complete review of the lethal injection protocol and report to the court with planned changes to the procedure before any further executions. The state began constructing a new death chamber at San Quentin State Prison in March 2007.

Later that year, the Supreme Court agreed to review a Kentucky case similar to the *Morales* lethal injection challenge and in 2008 found that the three-drug protocol in that case did not constitute cruel and unusual punishment. The moratorium in *Morales* has been lifted and the case remains pending awaiting the adoption of new regulations by the state and the resolution of a related state court action.

The New World of Antitrust

In the 1970s, antitrust statutes, designed to prevent monopolies, were tested in court by an ever-broader assortment of industries. Battles that began nearly a century ago over oil and steel, manufacturing and banking, now encompassed the nation's newspapers and leisure activities.

The counterculture movement and antiwar protests had produced a wealth of alternative press publications, including the *Berkeley Barb* and the *San Francisco Oracle*. Yet overall, the number of newspapers in the United States had been diminishing since the 1940s, a result of shrinking audiences as the public migrated to radio, television, and eventually the Internet. In the early 1960s, *New Yorker* writer A. J. Liebling declared, "Freedom of the press is for those who own one." In 1961, he reported that the United States had competing daily newspapers in only sixty-one cities and was advancing toward "a monovocal, monopolistic, monocular press."

In an attempt to combat this, or to keep their businesses in the black and bring in advertising revenue, competing newspapers in a number of cities, including San Francisco, began to negotiate joint operating agreements. Under JOAs, newspapers could combine their business and printing operations while keeping their editorial departments separate. According to the *Daily Commercial News*, mechanical operations for the de Young family's *San Francisco Chronicle* and the Hearst Corporation's *San Francisco Examiner* joined together in 1965 with "somewhat reluctant" Justice Department approval, making San Francisco one of twenty-two cities in the country at the time with an active JOA. This concluded a fierce ten-year circulation war between the two morning dailies. At the time, the *Chronicle* had a circulation of 363,000 and the *Examiner* 300,000. As part of the agreement, the *Examiner* published in the afternoons and produced most of the Sunday paper while the *Chronicle* published in the morning. Although touted as a means of keeping competition alive, the merger looked more like a consolidation of power. As part of the JOA, the *News Call-Bulletin*, another local Hearst-owned paper, had to cease publication, silencing a distinctive media voice. Further, after combining their printing operations, the newspapers went on to combine their advertising and circulation departments, an act that displeased many advertisers and competitors, and which had not been part of the initially approved JOA.

Antitrust accusations against JOAs emerged first in Arizona, where a federal judge ordered the *Tucson Citizen* and *Tucson Star* to sever their JOA and separate, and the sentiment spread to San Francisco. After the Supreme Court affirmed that JOAs could be prosecuted under antitrust laws, San Francisco resident Guy McCauliff sued the Hearst Corporation, the Chronicle Publishing Company, and the San Francisco Newspaper Printing Company—the actual printing press operation—for violating the Clayton Antitrust Act. McCauliff, owner of an agency that provided part-time secretarial help, sued on behalf of himself and fifty thousand other advertisers in the two papers. The suit alleged that after the merger, ad rates at the papers were fixed and substantially raised without any increase in circulation. McCauliff requested that the printing company be dissolved, the two papers resume their independent status, and that he be awarded triple damages of approximately $30 million.

By May 1975, five lawsuits with seventeen plaintiffs, including the publishers of the biweekly *San Francisco Bay Guardian,* were pending. Four days before the combined trial was to begin, *Chronicle* attorney James J. Brosnahan announced a settlement: $1.35 million would be divided, not necessarily equally, among the seventeen plaintiffs, and the three defendants would divide the court costs.

In 1999, the San Francisco JOA came to an end. The de Young family decided to sell the Chronicle Publishing Company. The Hearst Corporation announced it would buy the *Chronicle* and put the *Examiner* up for sale or close it. In 2000, local real estate investor Clint Reilly filed an antitrust lawsuit in the district court to block the sale of the *Chronicle* to Hearst, which he claimed planned to shut down the *Examiner* and create a monopoly. District court judge Vaughn Walker finally ruled that the sale didn't violate antitrust law, although he described it as malodorous and fraught with political cronyism. He said he was "astonished and disappointed that the Department of Justice would allow itself to be put in a position where the inference can be so easily drawn that its action or inaction in the case was political favoritism masquerading as law enforcement." Within hours, Hearst announced it had purchased the *Chronicle* for $660 million and sold the *Examiner* to the Fang family, who owned several printing presses and a number of English- and Chinese-language publications, including the *San Francisco Independent* and *AsianWeek*. As part of the Justice Department–approved sale, the Fangs also got the paper's archives, delivery trucks, editorial computer system, news racks, and a $66 million subsidy from Hearst to run the paper. After struggling for four years, the Fangs sold the *Examiner* to Denver billionaire Philip Anschutz in 2004. It is now a free daily paper with a conservative bent.

Is Nothing Sacred?

The National Football League's draft also became the subject of a protracted antitrust lawsuit in the district court when quarterback Joe Kapp charged that the league's draft and free agency rules violated the Sherman Antitrust Act.

Kapp did not have the classic style of Green Bay Packers quarterback Bart Starr or Baltimore Colts quarterback Johnny Unitas, but he knew how to get the job done. "Playing with Kapp was like playing in the sandlot," former Minnesota Vikings safety Dale Hackbart once said; "bloody-nose stuff." Kapp hurled the ball javelin-style and his wobbly passes, called "ruptured ducks," challenged convention. "Classics are for Greeks," he once said. "I'm a winner." And Kapp usually did find success. He had been a high school football star in Santa Fe, New Mexico, which earned him a scholarship to UC Berkeley. As both quarterback and kickoff returner, Kapp earned All-American status and helped the Golden Bears earn a trip to the 1959 Rose Bowl. In 2004, Kapp was elected to the College Football Hall of Fame, and he remains the only quarterback to have played in the Rose Bowl, the Super Bowl, and Canada's Grey Cup.

Kapp's federal lawsuit was intended to address an injustice he believed had deprived him of much of his football career. This time he did not come out a winner. When Kapp entered the NFL draft in 1959, the league's rules contained a reserve clause, which dictated that a college player could negotiate only with the team that drafted him. Even if the team and player failed to reach an agreement, the team could keep the player on its reserve list, which made it impossible for other teams to make an offer without violating the NFL's tampering rules. The Washington Redskins tapped Kapp in the twelfth round, but he didn't like the team's offer, so he opted to play in Canada. There he earned a starting quarterback position, beating out Jack Kemp, who would go on to be an American Football League star (and eventual Republican presidential candidate). Kapp was the Canadian Football League's Most Valuable Player in 1963 and took Vancouver to the Grey Cup in 1964.

Despite these achievements, Kapp still longed to play in the United States. In 1966, when the Redskins finally removed him from their reserve list and his Canadian contract was about to expire, he began secret negotiations with the Houston Oilers (then of the American Football League). The Canadian team chose to retain Kapp for his 1967 option year but then it suspended him when it learned of his dealings with the Oilers. By this time, however, Kapp and the Oilers had reached an agreement, and Kapp prepared to join them for the 1968 season. At the time, the NFL and the AFL were in the midst of a merger that had received an exemption from federal antitrust sanctions. NFL Commissioner Pete Rozelle, along with the AFL's leader, ruled Kapp's agreement with Houston invalid because it had been finalized while Kapp remained under contract with the Canadian Football League.

Again forced to forgo his first choice, Kapp eventually signed a two-year, $300,000 contract with the Minnesota Vikings. According to the Rozelle Rule, after a player had fulfilled his contract and played out the option year, he could sign with a new team. However, this new team must compensate the player's previous team for the loss. In compliance, the Vikings paid the Vancouver team $50,000 for Kapp's release. Then, with his rough-and-tumble style, Kapp led the Vikings to their first and only league championship, in 1969.

After the Super Bowl, the Vikings offered to renew Kapp's contract, but he declined. The Houston Oilers again expressed interest in him, as did the Philadelphia Eagles, but neither made an offer, which Kapp believed was because they feared the amount that the Rozelle Rule would require them to pay the Vikings for his release. When Kapp was approached by the Boston Patriots, he signed a memorandum of agreement, not a standard contract, for the remainder of the 1970 season, to continue on through 1972. In return, the Patriots gave the Vikings the player who had been their first-choice draft pick from 1967 and their future first-choice draft pick for 1972. They gave Kapp a contract worth approximately $600,000, making him the highest paid player in the NFL. But after the 1970 season—when Kapp had played eleven games and been paid $154,000, according to the *Oakland Tribune*—Rozelle announced that "no player could play, or even practice, with an NFL team unless he had signed a contract." Rozelle refused to honor Kapp's agreement. Kapp refused to sign the standard contract and left the Patriots training camp before the 1971 season began.

In 1972, Kapp filed a lawsuit against the NFL in district court, asserting that the NFL's Rozelle Rule, tampering rule, draft rules, and standard player contract procedures "constitute a combination among defendants to refuse to deal with players except under the above stated conditions—in effect a boycott or blacklist." Kapp asked for damages from each team, as well as from the NFL, in an amount that totaled $11.8 million.

"I didn't quit," Kapp told the *Oakland Tribune*. "I reported to Boston to play football and they threw me out. What else could I do? I was forced into legal proceedings because they wouldn't let me play….I don't know if it will ever be worth missing out on the prime of my pro football career, but I thought the fight was worthwhile." The NFL responded that Kapp was a member of the Players Association, the union for professional football players, and had therefore agreed to the standard contract and was in breach of contract.

Judge William Sweigert issued a partial summary judgment in Kapp's favor in 1974. The judge ruled the NFL draft system was "patently illegal and unreasonable" as related to rookie players "insofar as it enables the NFL to exert control over a player's employment even though the drafting club fails to sign him." He said the Rozelle Rule can "perpetually restrain a player's employment choice [by establishing a compensation arrangement between two clubs] even after he has otherwise become a free agent by fulfilling his contract." Sweigert also declared Rozelle's "one-man rule" policy, which made Rozelle himself the final arbiter of all disputes, illegal. Damages for Kapp would be determined by a separate jury trial.

"Judge Shocks Pro Football" and "Verdict for Kapp Jolts the NFL" were some of the headlines of the day as the NFL's stricken coaches weighed in. George Allen of the Washington Redskins told the Associated Press the Rozelle Rule was necessary to avoid bidding wars. "The team with the money will go after the best players," he explained. "I hated to see that decision because it won't help football. It could hurt football."

In contrast, Ed Garvey, executive director of the Players Association, said, "Assuming this decision holds up, pro football players will be the first players to be free when their contracts come to an end. We are very excited and simply delighted. We think this will redress the balance [between players' shares and owners' shares of revenue]. This is what we think Congress should have done when the two leagues merged."

An assortment of football greats took the stand to testify about Kapp's quality as a player during the four-week trial to award damages. But some also noted that Kapp probably only had two or three seasons of peak playing left in him. Commissioner Rozelle said Kapp was the only player ever to refuse signing the standard contract, which, far from anything sinister, was intended to prevent the "administrative nightmare" of keeping track of the myriad customized agreements that would likely be created without it. In 1976, after six hours of deliberation, a jury declined to award Kapp any damages.

During his 1978 appeal to the Ninth Circuit Court of Appeals, Kapp's attorney Moses Lasky insisted "the NFL action was to bring Kapp to his knees and make him an object lesson to all the other players." Although the court upheld Sweigert's decision, it didn't change Kapp's financial situation. Kapp "failed to prove that he was injured by reason of one of [the NFL's] unlawful practices, because he chose to discontinue playing professional football and did not demonstrate that his decision was the result of the antitrust violations," the court stated.

The Plight of Migrant Workers

Since the gold rush, Northern California—and the Bay Area in particular—has been home to a diverse racial and ethnic population while remaining predominantly white. Several minority groups—from Chinese immigrants in the nineteenth century to Hispanic farm workers in the 1960s—used the district court in their quest for civil rights. These included Cesar Chavez, who would become an icon in his push for decent working conditions for migrant workers.

Chavez grew up in Yuma, Arizona. His father farmed, operated a general store, and was elected postmaster. When Cesar was ten, in 1937, his father lost everything in a bad business deal. Still recovering from the Depression, the Southwest had little to offer, so the family, including six children, became migrant workers. They moved from location to location within California, traveling according to the harvest season. Cesar managed to attend school until he finished eighth grade, then he worked the fields full time. He chose to pick grapes whenever possible because those workers stayed in one place longer than other harvesters. Migrant laborers were expected to work long hours in the hot sun but were given little pay and no benefits. Chavez began to ask farm owners for better pay and working conditions and urged other workers to join him, but the need to earn a living—even a meager one under grueling conditions—kept most of the Mexican and Mexican American workers from speaking out.

In 1944, Chavez joined the navy and served in the Pacific. By 1948 he had returned to the fields. He and his new wife, Helen, taught workers how to read and write so they could pass the American citizenship test. Chavez thought that as citizens the workers might feel more secure and be willing to fight for better treatment. In the early 1950s, Chavez began work with California's Community Service Organization, helping at night to register migrant workers to vote. Eventually Chavez went to work for the CSO full time as an organizer and advocate, advising workers of their rights, enrolling their children in school, and encouraging them to vote. He left the CSO in 1962 to form a migrant workers union. He traveled from labor camp to labor camp, gradually recruiting followers. After six months, the National Farm Workers Union had three hundred members and held its first meeting in Fresno. The goal was more than just money—it was a quest for a better life. They called it La Causa.

But growers were not receptive to their demands. The union began staging strikes, boycotts, and protests against grape growers in 1965, often leaving grapes rotting on the vine. Chavez and other union members were replaced by illegal workers, beaten by strikebreakers, and frequently sent to jail. Eventually, their cause earned national attention and Chavez's union convinced fourteen million Americans to not buy grapes until conditions improved for migrant workers.

Negotiations with grape growers began in 1969, and by 1970 Chavez and the United Farm Workers Organizing Committee (as they were now known) signed their first union contracts with wine and table grape growers in Southern California's Coachella Valley. Next, Chavez called for a national boycott of lettuce after growers in Salinas had the Teamsters union take over harvest contracts. In 1972, the United Farm Workers Organizing Committee was accepted as a full member of the AFL-CIO, an extensive labor union representing workers in a variety of trades. It

FIG. 8-3
Striking grape pickers lead with the flag of the National Farmworkers Association—
founded by Cesar Chavez in 1962—on a three-hundred-mile pilgrimage from Delano,
California, to Sacramento. Courtesy of the California Historical Society, FN-28722/
CHS2013.1141.

changed its name a final time to the United Farm Workers Union. With
this much larger organization, Chavez and the workers looked forward
to making further progress. But in 1973, when their contracts with the
Coachella Valley grape growers began to expire, the Teamsters were ready.
In no time the Teamsters had contracts with 85 percent of the farms in
the valley.

Chavez denounced the Teamsters' actions as attempts to bust his union.
With the support of George Meany, president of the AFL-CIO, Chavez
called for a congressional investigation into the Teamsters' relationships
with lettuce, grape, and other produce growers. "For the nation's largest union to seek to destroy this smaller union representing some of the
most exploited workers in the nation is intolerable," Meany said, according to the *Oakland Tribune*. Teamsters president Frank Fitzsimmons
fought back, calling the conspiracy charges ridiculous and unfounded.

Meanwhile, tensions continued to mount. UFW supporters picketed vineyards across California and tangled frequently with law enforcement and Teamsters organizers.

A federal grand jury indicted two Salinas vegetable packers and one former Teamster in 1973, charging them with misdemeanor violations of the Taft-Hartley Act, formally known as the Labor Management Relations Act. More specifically, they were charged with multiple counts of conspiracy and bribery. The Teamsters used an arsenal of tactics to delay the trial. "US District Judge Robert F. Peckham ordered a special medical examination of an ousted Teamster official's illness that has delayed a much-postponed bribery trial," reported the *San Francisco Examiner* in 1974. The Teamster pleaded no contest to five misdemeanor charges related to his attempts to ruin a UFW organization drive in Salinas Valley. A jury acquitted the two vegetable executives, but their trial showed the seamy side of the dispute. One government witness, Frank Cunha, a member of the Teamsters Local 860 in San Francisco and a self-described kung fu master, testified that he hired about three hundred men in 1970 to pressure the San Francisco Wholesale Produce Market into refusing fruit and vegetables picked by UFW members. The plan failed; UFW-picked lettuce was accepted at the market as soon as Cunha's men left.

Chavez and the UFW continued to work for migrant workers. The California Agricultural Labor Relations Act of 1975 guaranteed workers the right to hold secret-ballot elections to choose a labor union and required growers to negotiate with that union. The UFW won hundreds of these elections between 1975 and 1980, but few of them ever resulted in contracts. In time, the UFW's efforts were further hampered by a shift in California politics. Pro-labor governor Jerry Brown gave way to pro-grower governor George Deukmejian in 1982, and the union declined in size and significance throughout the 1980s. Cesar Chavez died in 1993, but the union remains active in California today.

Nixon-Era Judges: Washed Out?

The Nixon administration's Watergate scandal affected a number of judicial appointments, including that of William H. Orrick, who was sworn in just before the president resigned. Orrick, a lifelong San Franciscan, was nominated to the district court in 1974 by President Nixon to fill the spot of retiring judge William Sweigert. Orrick was confirmed

The Magistrates Act: Welcome Relief

In 1968, the Federal Magistrates Act was passed, abolishing the post of US commissioner and creating US magistrates, who were authorized to handle misdemeanors, habeas corpus proceedings, and much of the pre-trial and discovery work for civil cases. This freed district court judges to spend more time on criminal and complicated securities and intellectual property cases. Judge Zirpoli said the magistrates were a welcome relief as cases became more complicated and the jurisdiction of the federal courts continued to expand. The role of the magistrate has expanded, too, as the Northern District Court has been at the forefront of broadly interpreting their duties. Magistrate judges now hear civil cases, if all parties involved agree, and can handle many aspects of criminal cases, apart from ruling on felony matters.

This was not an instantaneous transition. "When I first came on, magistrate judges couldn't eat in the judges' lunchroom...[or] ride the judges' elevator," Judge Thelton Henderson, who joined the court in 1980, said in a 2006 interview. "There was really a caste system." In the early days, Henderson recalled, magistrate judges mostly got what judges didn't want to do: discovery. "They still get some of that, but they have a caseload now, they get quality stuff. That's changed the nature of the court."

The Northern District Court has a number of magistrate judges who were respected partners at major San Francisco law firms. "The only difference between the magistrate judge and me is I'm Article III," Henderson said. "I lucked out to be an Article III judge. But they're as smart as we are and as capable and everybody knows it."

---

unanimously by the Senate in June and received his commission less than three weeks before the Supreme Court ordered Nixon to turn over taped conversations that revealed his involvement in the scandal.

Orrick and his family were on vacation in the mountains when his mother-in-law called at breakfast on August 8 to tell him that Nixon had announced he would resign the next day. Orrick phoned best friend Potter Stewart, a Supreme Court justice, and the two decided that although technically Orrick's judgeship was in the clear since he had already been confirmed and commissioned, it might be wise to do the swearing in before the president left office. Orrick packed up his family and drove three and a half hours back to San Francisco, picked up his father, and went to the federal courthouse, where Chief Judge Carter quickly swore him in.

Orrick was no stranger to political drama of this sort. He already had a colorful career behind him when he joined the federal bench. The son of a prominent San Francisco attorney, Orrick attended Yale University and considered a career in journalism before returning to San Francisco and Berkeley's Boalt Hall. The day after Pearl Harbor, Orrick tried to enlist, but poor eyesight prevented him from joining. Instead, he served as a community air raid warden and spent four years in the army's counterintelligence unit. After the war, he joined his family's law firm—Orrick, Herrington, Rowley, and Sutcliffe—and became active in Democratic politics.

Fig. 8-4
District court judge William H. Orrick (far left) at the Press and Union League Club of San Francisco in 1956, with (left to right) Roger Kent, former president Harry S. Truman (speaker), Henry F. Grady, host Richard Reinhardt, and William M. Malone. Courtesy of The Bancroft Library, University of Berkeley, California.

Orrick was introduced to John F. Kennedy in 1956, and in 1960 he worked for the Kennedy campaign. He became assistant attorney general for the Civil Division in 1961. He moved his family to Washington, DC, and managed three hundred lawyers. Orrick was deeply involved in the Kennedy administration's reactions to the civil rights movement of the early 1960s, sparked by Rosa Parks's 1955 refusal to give up her seat on a public bus in Montgomery, Alabama. Orrick recalled being sent south, along with other Department of Justice officials, to help prevent violence, integrate schools, negotiate with the segregationist Alabama National Guard, and protect Freedom Riders, who rode interstate buses into segregated Southern states to test the 1960 Supreme Court decision that outlawed segregation at interstate bus and train stations.

In 1962, Orrick became deputy undersecretary of state. He was in the State Department during the Cuban Missile Crisis, a confrontation that began with the discovery of Soviet nuclear missiles in Cuba and concluded twelve tense days later with Soviet leader Nikita Khrushchev's agreement to have them dismantled. In 1963, he returned to the Department of Justice, this time as assistant attorney general for the Antitrust Division. He remained there until 1965, when he returned to San Francisco and resumed a private practice focused on antitrust law. He remained active in politics and public life, and was appointed to the State Commission on Public Education as well as Mayor Alioto's San Francisco Crime Commission. He also served as president of the board of the San Francisco Opera for three years.

A friend, federal judge Charles Renfrew, asked Orrick if he'd be interested in a position on the district court. "I love the law," he said in a 1986 interview for UC Berkeley's Bancroft Library. "And the law without clients is a particularly good way to live."

After joining the district court in 1974, Orrick presided largely over civil cases, including many civil rights cases. Orrick did not enjoy his role in the numerous wrongful termination suits (usually due to alleged sexual discrimination) that came before him. The cases rendered "the role of the judge forever as the last word in a particular industry," he explained. "The judge becomes personnel manager." He felt strongly that judges should not be put in those sorts of positions. "To keep the country running, the federal court has to step out of what should be its main role," he said, and act on occasion as administrator, rather than interpreter, of the law. "In my view, the federal judiciary is the most important branch of the government in many ways," he said in 1986. "And, like all of our institutions, it is fragile. It demands, much as a church demands, a certain amount of dignity." Because of his respect for the institution, Orrick received a reputation as a stickler in the courtroom, showing no mercy to unprepared attorneys. "If they're late, I [sanction] them the amount it cost the other fellow to come and wait," he told the *Los Angeles Daily Journal*.

In his courtroom, Orrick weighed in on an ongoing battle between California and local Native American tribes over salmon fishing rights and has found San Francisco in contempt for its county prison conditions. He issued a consent decree and fined the city, despite protests of budget constraints, $300 a day for each inmate housed beyond the legal limit. The city eventually constructed a new jail. In 1992, he ruled that San Francisco's enforcement of a California law against begging for money was unconstitutional, as peaceful panhandling was protected speech.

Orrick assumed senior status in 1985 and gave up his criminal caseload. He retired in 2002, and died in his sleep the next year at age eighty-seven. "He really was a kind-hearted man," fellow judge Vaughn Walker told the *Record* shortly after Orrick's death. "He told stories exceedingly well. He could be a little testy on the bench, but he was never so without a reason."

San Francisco Schools: The Desegregation Cases

Orrick was also one of several Northern District judges who have played a role in the ongoing litigation regarding the desegregation of San Francisco public schools. As a magnet city, San Francisco has had its share of residents from a variety of ethnicities since its founding. And each ethnicity, from Native Americans to Californios to Chinese to African Americans, has faced both subtle and overt racism from the white majority. While California and the Bay Area have a reputation for tolerance, San Francisco residents have, until recent years, been for the most part intolerant of other cultures, countenancing the ghettoization of Chinatown at the turn of the century, Japanese internment during World War II, and segregation of city schools, which was only reversed through forced integration. Thus the San Francisco Unified School District has had a forty-year relationship with the Northern District Court.

Since the early 1960s, groups of parents have sought both forced segregation and civil rights protections for students in city schools. In 1962, the parents of nine San Francisco Central Junior High School students sought to prevent the school from opening rather than accept its 60 percent African American student body. Attorneys for the parents estimated the city's school-aged population to be only about 20 percent African American and asked that the school's enrollment be adjusted accordingly. The Board of Education defended their neighborhood schools policy and insisted that because the population of students in the community surrounding Central Junior High was 60 percent African American, that percentage should be allowed to attend the local school.

From the beginning, Judge Zirpoli urged the parties to settle the issue without court intervention:

Fig. 8-5
In August 1965 , picketers marched in front of the Board of Education, protesting San Francisco's segregated schooling. Courtesy of The Bancroft Library, University of Berkeley, California.

The very first question I would propound to all concerned is whether the intervention of this court is necessary. San Francisco has prided itself as one of the great cosmopolitan centers of America and a community in which people of all races and creeds and cultures have learned to live together in peace and in brotherhood, with such an acceptance of ethnic differences as to be a source of hope and a model for the entire country. I had hoped that because of this great tradition in San Francisco, and because of the pride that the city has in this reputation that it enjoys, it would find an avenue by which to resolve problems of this character.

Zirpoli scheduled a hearing, but the night before, the Board of Education voted to close Central Junior High, as it "had become a symbol of racial strife." Zirpoli said, "Thus, by voluntary action, the board has made court intervention unnecessary; and this is as it should be." However, he added, "The major problem presented still remains....If all concerned will approach the problem with an even greater desire to understand than to be understood, this problem can be resolved honorably and with dignity commensurate to San Francisco's great tradition as one of the finest cosmopolitan cities of the world."

But the issue of appropriate "racial balance"—as the *San Francisco Examiner* referred to it—was as far from resolved in San Francisco as it was across the country. San Francisco had seen an influx of African Americans during World War II, when many families migrated from the south to the Bay Area to work in the booming ship building and military industries. Racial tensions between blacks and whites had been rising ever since.

In 1970, six black elementary school students in San Francisco, assisted by the National Association for the Advancement of Colored People, sued the San Francisco Unified School District, the Board of Education, and the Superintendent of Schools because "in the following school year they would be forced to attend schools racially segregated as to student composition, faculty, and staff," explained Judge Weigel, who was assigned the case. They asked for a court order to desegregate the schools.

The public outcry was immediate and featured prominently in the local newspapers. "San Francisco's position historically has been that segregation here is *de facto*, resulting from residential neighborhood patterns; that it is undesirable but not unlawful[;] and that quality education can be achieved only by a careful, step-by-step program of integration," said an *Examiner* editorial. The case "stirred up almost an unbelievable amount of not only public interest but public controversy," Weigel recalled in a 1989 interview. His April 1971 ruling only added fuel to the fire:

> More than seventeen years ago, a unanimous decision of the United States Supreme Court [1954's *Brown v. Board of Education*] made it clear that racial discrimination in public education violates the Constitution of the United States. Today it is established beyond all question that any law, ordinance, or regulation of any governmental agency (whether federal, state, county, or city) requiring or furthering such discrimination violates the Constitution of the United States.... The law is settled that school authorities violate the constitutional rights of children by establishing school attendance boundary lines knowing that the result is to continue or increase substantial racial imbalance. The law is settled that school authorities violate the Constitution by providing for the construction of new schools or enlargement of existing ones in a manner that continues or increases substantial racial imbalance. The law is settled that school authorities violate the Constitution by assigning black teachers and teachers of limited experience to "black" schools while assigning few, if any, such teachers to "white" schools.

Based on *Brown*'s precedent, Weigel found that the current boundaries and policies of the San Francisco School District promoted segregation. He ordered parents and school officials to develop plans for desegregation of both students and teachers. The plans were to be submitted to the court for approval within two months, by June 1971.

Weigel found that the school district's Horseshoe Plan and the parents' Freedom Plan both solved the segregation problem in a satisfactory manner. Both plans required significant busing of San Francisco elementary school students in order to achieve better racial balance at the schools. The school district chose its own plan, which required less busing. Beginning in September, forty-eight thousand students attending one hundred elementary schools would be integrated by busing half the children to schools outside their neighborhoods.

Mandatory busing was met with anger by San Francisco parents, particularly those of Chinese descent, many of whose children were in special bilingual programs designed for their learning needs. The desegregation plan also required that no ethnic group in any particular school should constitute more than 15 percent more or less than its proportion in the overall San Francisco population. The Board of Education appealed Weigel's decision to the Ninth Circuit and asked for a stay. The appellate court denied the stay but agreed to review the case. Thousands of students were bused to new schools out of their neighborhoods and complaints exploded.

When the school district announced plans in 1972 to build a new elementary school in Hunters Point, a neighborhood that had been predominantly African American since World War II, the debate turned ugly. "We may be sacrificing other families to this infernal busing," warned city supervisor Quentin Kopp, who also served as attorney for a group of Chinese parents opposed to the desegregation plan. Kopp (now a San Mateo County Superior Court judge) called Hunters Point a ghetto and lamented the court's decision, which forced students to be bused into and out of bad neighborhoods to achieve racial balance.

In 1974, the Ninth Circuit upheld the busing but determined that Weigel had applied the wrong legal standard in determining a constitutional violation. He should have determined that the "school authorities had intentionally discriminated against minority students by practicing a deliberate policy of racial segregation." They ordered him to reopen the case and to allow the Chinese parents represented by Supervisor Kopp to join the suit.

The case lay dormant for three years, Weigel recalled. "The plaintiffs seemed to lack interest in enforcement through court action," he said. Instead, they assured the judge they were attempting a settlement out of court and requested that a trial date not be set. Finally, in 1978, Weigel dismissed the case and ended the seven-year-old desegregation order (and the busing it required). None of the six original black plaintiffs were elementary students anymore, and the racial mix of San Francisco's elementary school population had become "decidedly different," Weigel explained in a 1981 speech. By then, San Francisco public school enrollment had shrunk to under fifty-seven thousand, a nearly 40 percent drop in twenty years. The percentage of white students enrolled dropped from 41 percent to 18 percent.

The end of Weigel's order cleared the way for the Board of Education to move forward with its new redesign plan, under which a school would be deemed racially balanced so long as no ethnic group composed more than 45 percent of the student body, and as long as at least four ethnic groups were represented. Many of the city's elementary schools already met this requirement. The plan was immediately criticized as a step backward by the NAACP and the American Civil Liberties Union.

The desegregation case was re-filed about a week later as *San Francisco NAACP v. San Francisco Unified School District*, a class action lawsuit sponsored by nine students on behalf of black students throughout the city. This time the call for desegregation applied not only to elementary schools but junior high and high schools as well. Those bringing the suit claimed black students were unfairly stuck in low-performing schools on the city's east side. Weigel recused himself from the case because his son-in-law had professional dealings with the NAACP. Judge Orrick heard the new case.

In 1983, the school district settled the case by agreeing that no racial group could comprise more than 45 percent of a particular school's population, or 40 percent at highly selective schools. But in 1994, Chinese parents on the west side of the city sued the Board of Education on the grounds that these racial caps were keeping their children out of San Francisco's best schools, particularly top-performing Lowell High School.

Again Judge Orrick heard the case, which was settled in 1998 when the school district created a diversity index that uses a variety of socioeconomic indicators, as well as race, to assign students to schools each year. But after a contrary Supreme Court ruling in 1999, Orrick ruled "the use of race in the index violated both the equal protection requirement of the Constitution and a settlement of a lawsuit by Chinese American families that had challenged racial enrollments," according to *AsianWeek*. The San Francisco school district still uses six socioeconomic factors, but not race, to assign students to schools. Dissatisfaction with public school assignment, coupled with rising housing costs and expensive private schools, has forced even more families with school-aged children to leave San Francisco.

A related school district lawsuit, *Lau v. Nichols*, would go all the way to the Supreme Court and affect bilingual education across the country. When busing began after Judge Weigel's 1971 desegregation order, more than twenty-eight hundred Chinese students who did not speak English found themselves not at neighborhood schools sensitive to their language needs but instead scattered to elementary schools across the city. Most of these reassigned students did not have remedial English help. Former Peckham law clerk Edward Steinman of the San Francisco Neighborhood Legal Assistance Office represented the parents of these Chinese students in their 1971 class action claim that the desegregation plan created a situation of "unequal educational opportunities" in violation of the Fourteenth Amendment.

Although both the district court and Ninth Circuit Court of Appeals ruled against the students, the Supreme Court ruled in their favor in 1974. The high court found that because San Francisco public schools receive federal money, they are subject to compliance with the Civil Rights Act of 1964, which bans discrimination based on race, color, or national origin. Further, the Supreme Court opinion, written by Justice William Douglas, contended that basic English skills are at the core of what these public schools teach. "Imposition of a requirement that, before a child can effectively participate in the educational program, he must already have acquired those basic skills is to make a mockery of public education," he wrote. "We know that those who do not understand English are certain to find their classroom experiences wholly incomprehensible and in no way meaningful."

As a result, the school district devised a system of bilingual education that allowed students who speak little or no English to be taught lessons in subjects including math, science, and social studies in their primary language while they also received special instruction in English. This system prevailed until 1998, when—after another emotional and divisive campaign—California voters passed Proposition 227, which asserted that current bilingual education programs in California schools were too expensive and were failing. The new law dictated that children "shall be taught English by being taught in English."

In another 1971 case, the parents of six African American children challenged the use of IQ tests by the San Francisco Unified School District to determine class placement by evaluating whether students had the appropriate learning ability for mainstream classes. The six children had been placed in classes for the educable mentally retarded (EMR) or for "slow learners" when they scored below the required 75 IQ score. The parents believed that the tests were biased toward a white, middle-class cultural background and led to a disproportionate number of minority students being placed in special classes, often without the knowledge of their parents. "I was not told [my son] was mentally retarded," parent Lucile Lester testified. The suit alleged that placement in EMR classes damaged the children's self-esteem and educational prospects.

In 1972, after reviewing their claims and a weighty collection of expert affidavits, Judge Peckham issued a preliminary injunction against the use of IQ tests by the San Francisco Unified School District. In 1974, the California school superintendent voluntarily issued a statewide order against the use of IQ tests "that do not properly account for the cultural background or experience" of the students taking them. Peckham began a non-jury trial on the case in 1977. Eventually yielding more than ten thousand pages of testimony, psychologists, sociologists, and testing experts spoke of the effects of IQ testing on education. Princeton University professor and psychologist Leon Kamin testified that "it is impossible to measure innate capacity [to learn] with IQ tests." Instead, he asserted, these tests measure only the extent to which someone has been exposed to particular topics and experiences.

California Superintendent of Public Instruction Wilson Riles testified that he believed that IQ tests were biased culturally, not racially, and asserted that poor and underprivileged students always have difficulty with the tests, regardless of race. But when asked if he wanted schools to continue using the tests, knowing that they were biased, Riles said yes, deeming them an instrument that helps properly place students. "Every instrument you use in schools is biased," he said. "If you want to throw out everything that's biased, we'll have nothing left."

In 1979, Peckham found that the use of IQ tests for placement in EMR classes "violated equal protection, and the tests violated Title VI of the Civil Rights Act of 1964, the Rehabilitation Act, and the Education for All Handicapped Children Act." Peckham left California's ban on IQ testing in place. His decision also broadened parents' rights, requiring that they be notified if their child was placed in an alternate classroom and providing them the opportunity to participate in developing an educational plan for their child, as well as to convene a hearing if they disagreed with the school's assessment. This ruling formed the foundation for the Individual Education Plan (IEP) that public schools all over the nation currently use.

Peckham had to modify the ruling in 1986 after an appeals court decision. He established timelines for schools to follow in implementing the means to gather and report on enrollment data and expanded his initial ruling to state that there are no special education–related purposes for which IQ tests are appropriate to assess African American students. But in 1992, a different group of African American parents sued for the right to have IQ tests used to assess their children's learning disabilities. Peckham withdrew the expanded order so that IQ tests could be used when merited by a student's IEP.

Radical Femmes

On the night of February 4, 1974, three members of a violent, radical brigade known as the Symbionese Liberation Army abducted at gunpoint from her Berkeley apartment Patty Hearst, the nineteen-year-old granddaughter of newspaper magnate William Randolph Hearst. Wearing only a blue bathrobe, the University of California art major was tossed screaming into a waiting car, which sped away following a struggle in which her fiancé, Steven Weed, was beaten.

Three days later, the kidnappers released a tape stating that Hearst was a prisoner of war who could be exchanged for two SLA members charged with the 1973 murder of Oakland Superintendent of Schools Marcus Foster. This was the first of several "communiqués" issued by SLA leader Donald DeFreeze, an escaped convict who called himself General Field Marshal Cinque. Almost two months later, the SLA released another tape from Hearst calling Weed an "ageist, sexist pig" and her father, billionaire Randolph A. Hearst, a "corporate liar." Randolph and his wife, Catherine, dismissed the tape, saying that their daughter had joined the SLA under duress. "I have been given the choice of being released in a safe area or of joining the forces of the Symbionese Liberation Army and fighting for my freedom and the freedom of all oppressed people," Patty Hearst declared on tape. "I have chosen to stay and fight."

The fight began twelve days later as Hearst, holding an assault rifle, took part in the SLA's robbery of the Hibernia Bank in San Francisco's Sunset District. After fleeing to Los Angeles with the SLA, Hearst surfaced again a month later when she sprayed thirty bullets from an automatic weapon to free SLA members William and Emily Harris, who were robbing a Mel's Sporting Goods store. The following day, hundreds of law enforcement agents firebombed an SLA safe house at 1466 East Fifty-fourth Street in Los Angeles, killing DeFreeze and five other SLA members. Hearst, not in the house, watched the battle on TV and went into hiding for the next sixteen months, crisscrossing the country with SLA members and sympathizers until she was arrested in San Francisco in September 1975. Taken to the Federal Building, Hearst was asked her occupation, to which she replied, "Urban guerilla."

Drew McKillips and Maitland Lane of the *San Francisco Chronicle* described Hearst in her first court appearance as having "long, auburn hair and the pale-peach complexion of a young woman who hasn't been out in the sunshine." She was arraigned on armed bank robbery and firearms charges before Magistrate Owen E. Woodruff Jr. She was represented by Terence "Kayo" Hallinan, who was working with his father, Vincent Hallinan. The following week, Hearst appeared before Judge Carter. A few days later, Hearst's parents replaced her first attorneys with star Boston attorney F. Lee Bailey, who had won fame by defending Dr. Sam Sheppard and the Boston Strangler, Albert DeSalvo.

The trial in *United States v. Patricia Campbell Hearst* was held in the Ceremonial Courtroom on the nineteenth floor of the Federal Building. Jury selection began in January 1976. US Attorney James L. Browning Jr. personally prosecuted the case, assisted by F. Steele Langford and D. Michael Nerney. Bailey was assisted for the defense by Albert Johnson and E. John Kleines. Opening arguments started on February 4, 1976, exactly two years to the day after Hearst was abducted. Many called it the trial of the century. From the start, Judge Carter took control. He decided who would sit in the sixty-three permanent press seats, assigned Randolph Hearst a private parking space, and ordered federal marshals to accompany the Hearsts after their arrival. "What [Carter] has done and said has provoked ire on some days and endearment on others," wrote Lacey Fosburgh in the *New York Times*. "It has certainly caused talk and some small controversy. The judge himself, however, is clearly having a good time and has obviously not been at all intimidated by the circumspections of a ticklish legal case."

The trial was filled with drama. Early on, the government played surveillance film of the Hibernia robbery that was meant to show Hearst as a convert to terrorism who threatened customers and smiled when guns were fired, but the movie was difficult to make out. On another day, Hearst gave the jurors and Judge Carter a tour of two SLA safe houses where she was held—at 37 Northridge Drive in Daly City and a third-floor apartment at 1827 Golden Gate Avenue in San Francisco—as well as the Hibernia Bank's Sunset branch at Twenty-second Avenue and Noriega Street in San Francisco.

Bailey called three experts who related Hearst's brainwashing to the experience of US soldiers during the Korean War, arguing that her behavior was consistent with the trauma she experienced. Government experts countered, saying she participated willingly because she liked the notoriety. The most damning information was provided by William and Emily Harris, who refused to cooperate with the prosecution but sought revenge against Hearst, whom they considered a turncoat. In an interview with *New Times* magazine, the Harrises contradicted Hearst's testimony that SLA member Willie Wolfe had raped her. In fact, they said Hearst had fallen in love with Wolfe, who was killed in the Los Angeles shootout, and that she wore or carried a Mexican figurine charm that Wolfe had given to her as a token of their love. One of the last items entered into evidence was the charm, which Browning told the jury was found among Hearst's belongings when she was arrested. "She couldn't stand him, and yet there is the little stone face that can't say anything, but, I submit to you, can tell us a lot," Browning said.

Bailey argued in court that statements and actions by Hearst were made under duress and should not be admissible, but Browning successfully argued against him. Carter denied Bailey's motion to suppress government evidence and ruled "statements made by the defendant after the happening of the bank robbery, whether by tape recording, or oral communication, or in writing, were made voluntarily." The tapes introduced by the prosecution included some in which Hearst spoke of joining the SLA and denied that she had been brainwashed.

Against her objections, Bailey put Patty Hearst on the stand. She described in detail the abduction and the months spent in a closet being sexually abused and brainwashed by her captors. She said the SLA wrote the text of the tapes that were released, and said she believed the SLA when they told her that her parents had abandoned her and that the FBI would kill her if she was found. When asked why she didn't escape, she said she feared both the SLA and FBI. She said she would have been killed by the SLA if she didn't use the gun to defend the Harrises at Mel's Sporting Goods.

During Hearst's cross-examination, Bailey again attempted to cut Browning off when he asked about the "lost year" following the Hibernia bank robbery. Bailey told the judge that Browning was trying to get Hearst to incriminate herself and open prosecution in another case (in which Hearst was accused of having taken part in an SLA bank robbery in Carmichael, California, in 1975), leaving only the Fifth Amendment option, which would imply guilt. But Carter ruled that he would allow Browning to ask about the year because Hearst had waived her right not to testify when she took the stand. Browning asked forty-two questions about the lost year. Bailey stood next to her and ordered her not to answer each one. Carter instructed jurors to draw inferences from her silence.

In his closing argument, Browning listed every action by Hearst that could indicate her sympathy to the SLA cause, from the shooting at Mel's to keeping the charm from Wolfe. The question jurors faced was whether Hearst was a willing participant or a brainwashing victim who sympathized with her captors due to psychological scarring. Hearst later wrote that she believed that Bailey flubbed the case in his closing argument. He appeared slightly drunk, she wrote, and made a rambling, irrelevant final plea to the jury. To compound matters, he spilled a glass of water, which made it look to jurors that he had wet his pants. "It was," she wrote, "to say the least, distracting."

After twelve hours of deliberation, a jury found Hearst guilty of the bank robbery. At least six of the jurors said the most convincing evidence was the monkey charm love token, which indicated that Hearst had lied about her true feelings in her testimony. Judge Carter initially sentenced Hearst to thirty-five years in prison, but said he would reduce her sentence by at least ten years if she underwent ninety days of psychological study. Carter suffered a fatal heart attack at his home before final sentencing.

Sentencing was then assigned by lottery to Judge Orrick, who read the transcript of the case and asked for advice from colleagues. Judge William Ingram remembered when Orrick approached the judges at lunch: three wanted to give Hearst probation, and two wanted to give her the maximum, he wrote. The rest suggested five to seven years. Orrick also received letters from hundreds of people around the country who suggested a wide range of sentencing terms. In his 1986 oral history, Orrick said it wasn't clear whether she had actually pulled the trigger in the Hibernia robbery. But he decided that morning to sentence her to seven years. "I was punishing her as I would any other person, male or female, who was convicted of armed robbery and in which a gun was fired," he stated. But he knew it was a no-win situation. "For days and weeks and months I got letters, not from local people so much, but from people

Fig. 8-6
F. Lee Bailey and district court judge Oliver Carter hear Patty Hearst's testimony at a preliminary hearing in 1975. Hearst, an heiress to the Hearst family fortune, was tried and found guilty the following year in the district court of armed robbery and the use of a firearm to commit a felony. Bailey was Hearst's defense attorney. Courtesy of the family of Rosalie Ritz.

all over the world, people in little towns in Louisiana," he said. "I got a weekly death threat from a fellow in New Jersey. I got a number of death threats. I just turned those over to the FBI. I got letters from Belgium, from Australia, from Tonga, the Midwest, but very few from California."

Orrick released Hearst on $1 million bail as she appealed the decision. In a separate proceeding, she pleaded no contest to weapons charges in the Mel's Sporting Goods robbery and was given probation by a Los Angeles judge. After Hearst served almost two years in prison, President Jimmy Carter commuted her sentence. The White House argued that Hearst would have not participated in criminal acts had she not been abused by the SLA. In 2001, President Bill Clinton gave Hearst a presidential pardon.

The Assassin

Before she found herself trapped in a crowd of people outside San Francisco's St. Francis Hotel on September 22, 1975, Sara Jane Moore had been married and divorced five times, dropped out of nursing school, joined the Women's Army Corps, and trained to be a certified public accountant. She had also been evaluated for mental illness. In 1972, at age forty-two, she had left all this behind and embraced underground radical politics. Once established among the militants and subversives, Moore was recruited as an informant by the FBI to provide them with information on the Patty Hearst kidnapping. But her cover was blown after only a short time, leaving her ostracized from the underground community.

Desperate and now completely alone, Moore concocted a way to regain her radical friends' respect, which is what brought her to the sidewalk outside the St. Francis. President Gerald Ford was inside, and when he came out, Moore planned to shoot him. For a moment her courage wavered, but the crowd was too thick for her to leave. Ford emerged and Moore raised her .38 Smith and Wesson revolver. Rather than striking the president, Moore's bullet ricocheted off the wall a foot away and wounded a nearby cab driver. The prosecution would later point out that she would have succeeded if she had ever test-fired the gun, as it fired one foot off at forty feet.

After her arrest, "she came in and wanted to plead guilty," said Samuel Conti, the judge in Moore's case. "I told her how serious the crime was, and I said, 'I want you to be sure of what you're doing.'" Conti had Moore evaluated by several psychiatrists for mental competency to enter a plea. Months later, he listened to the reports of four court-appointed psychiatrists and two psychologists and determined Moore to be capable of standing trial.

When Moore came back to court, she said again that she wanted to plead guilty, and Conti reminded her that most people who plead guilty have second thoughts later, after they're in jail. He said he still wouldn't take her plea. "I want you to know exactly what you're doing, and I want you to be happy with your lawyer." Conti gave her five days to think about it. She came back and again said she wanted to plead guilty. Conti said he wouldn't take her plea yet and asked if she had a priest or a rabbi to talk to first. Moore then went through a series of spiritual consultations.

When she returned for her hearing, she assured Conti that she had thought it over and had no intention of changing her mind. During the hearing she also stated that she had acted alone, although her cryptic language raised questions in Conti's mind.

"Were you acting alone?" Conti asked.

"All I can speak of is for that day. No one assisted me in doing this act," Moore replied.

"Did anyone encourage you?"

"As to this particular time and place, no sir."

Further questioning revealed that Moore had formed her intention to assassinate Ford prior to September 22, and she had chosen that day on her own. However, when asked if she had worked with others to form a plan for assassinating the president on some other day, Moore refused to answer. Many have speculated that the assassination was originally conceived in league with others in the underground community, and Moore sought to complete it on her own to gain their admiration.

Moore's attorney cited her mysterious testimony as evidence that a jury trial was necessary, but Conti overruled him. US Attorney Browning said his office would look into Moore's statements, but also said he believed the questions raised were "a matter of semantics," rather than an indication that others might have conspired with Moore.

A friend of Moore's testified that he felt her guilty plea was motivated by her desire to avoid having her psychiatric records revealed in open court. Conti did have Moore's evaluations sealed after the proceedings, but he concluded that her plea was acceptable and sentenced her to life in prison. She is serving her time at Alderson Federal Prison Camp, a minimum-security facility in West Virginia where Martha Stewart would be an inmate thirty years later.

One Philosophy

"There comes a point when the only way
you can make a statement is to pick up a gun."

—Sara Jane Moore

Fig. 8-7
Secret Service agents, police, and bystanders react to Sara Jane Moore's attempted assassination of President Gerald Ford on September 22, 1975, outside San Francisco's St. Francis Hotel. Courtesy of the Gerald R. Ford Presidential Library.

Conti said in a 2006 interview that he received a letter from Moore from prison once, and that she had written him that "she liked Ford but not the president."

Sara Jane Moore's 1975 attempt on President Ford's life came just seventeen days after Lynette "Squeaky" Fromme, a member of Charles Manson's cult, pointed a .45-caliber gun at the president from two feet away as he shook hands in Sacramento's Capitol Park. She later claimed she knew the gun contained no bullets, but witnesses reported that at the time, she had seemed quite dismayed when it did not fire. Fromme's trial was held in Sacramento before Judge Thomas MacBride of the Eastern District, who was nominated to the bench by President Kennedy and began his career as a federal judge in the Northern District in 1961 and sat with Sherrill Halbert in Sacramento. When new legislation divided California into four districts in 1966, MacBride and Halbert became the senior members of the new three-judge United States District Court for the Eastern District of California. MacBride served as chief judge of this court from 1967 to 1979, when he assumed senior status.

Fromme refused to participate in her defense, and was convicted of attempted assassination. During her sentencing, she threw an apple at one of the prosecutors and was removed from the courtroom by federal marshals. Like Moore, she received life in prison as mandated by a 1965 law, prompted by President Kennedy's assassination, that made life in prison the maximum sentence for someone convicted of the attempted murder of a president. "Had John Kennedy, Robert Kennedy, or Martin Luther King been allowed to live out their lives rather than having fallen at the hands of a person like yourself," MacBride told her, "they could have accomplished more for our environment and for all mankind than all the terrorists in the history of the world, you and Charles Manson included."

Three New Judges

At the same time the Patty Hearst trial focused national attention on the district court, three new judges joined the federal bench in the summer of 1976: William A. Ingram, William Schwarzer, and Cecil Poole, all nominated by President Ford.

Ingram was born in Indiana in 1924 and attended Culver Military Academy there before traveling to California in the early 1940s to take classes at Stanford University and UC Berkeley. He served as a drill instructor in the Marine Corps Reserves, and after the war moved to Kentucky, where he earned his law degree at the University of Louisville. In a 1993 interview, Ingram said he was drawn to a career in law because he was "interested in...the varieties of human conduct and misconduct....I think I saw it more as a people-related discipline than anything else."

Ingram returned to California in 1950, and joined the firm Littler, Coakley, Lauritzen, and Ferdon. Not many of his cases made it to trial, and he had little criminal work, so Ingram volunteered as a public defender through a federal court program run by Judge Zirpoli, the man whose seat he eventually took on the district court. In 1955, Ingram moved his law practice to San Jose, where he also served as deputy district attorney for Santa Clara County. He became a municipal court judge in 1969 and a Santa Clara County Superior Court judge in 1971, where he remained until joining the district court five years later.

Once on the federal bench, Ingram joined Judge Peckham's effort to reestablish a full-time branch of the Northern District Court in San Jose. Judge Hoffman had first convened the district court in San Jose in 1852, but, according to Peckham, after a half-hour of hearing land grant cases, he returned to San Francisco and wrote the attorney general that holding court in such an "inconsiderable town" was useless.

Ingram heard a portion of his cases in San Jose, even though the temporary courthouse, a Quonset hut off the Guadalupe Expressway, "looked like a Greyhound bus station in a small town," Paul Meltzer, a former federal public defender, told the *San Francisco Daily Journal* in 2002. "It was a trick to impart great dignity to the federal court, but [Ingram] did it." Ingram was chief judge from 1988 to 1990, and by that time he was sitting full-time in San Jose, which made him the first chief judge to preside from there.

Ingram was also instrumental in developing the court's leading position in the field of intellectual property law. San Jose's location within Silicon Valley brought a variety of complex cases into his courtroom, including a copyright infringement suit involving Intel and NEC. In 1998, Ingram presided over a whistleblower case that revealed defense contractor FMC defrauded the government during construction of Bradley Fighting Vehicles. The case was eventually settled.

"I would like to be remembered as a person who had at least a modicum of human sympathy and who understood the problems of his fellow men and women and who never let anybody be distressed or embarrassed in court," he said in 1993. "I would like to be remembered by trial lawyers in a favorable way. I think that's the most one can hope for."

Ingram got his wish. In 2000, he received the American Inns of Court Professionalism Award for the Ninth Circuit, given to a "senior practicing judge or lawyer whose life and practice display sterling character and unquestioned integrity, coupled with ongoing dedication to the highest standards of the legal profession." Ingram retired from the federal bench in early 2002 and passed away the following year at age seventy-seven due to complications from pneumonia. Following his death, the Santa Clara American Inn of Court, which he helped found, was renamed the William A. Ingram Inn of Court. It hosts monthly discussions on professionalism, ethics, and legal skills.

Judge William Schwarzer became a lawyer because "I got out of the army and finished college and had no particular idea of what I should do," he said in a 2006 interview. Born in Berlin, Germany, in 1925, Schwarzer came to Los Angeles at age thirteen. He returned to Germany during World War II as an army intelligence officer, interrogating German prisoners and investigating technology. After the war, he returned to California and graduated with honors from the University of Southern California. His father encouraged him to consider law, so he did. "In those days it was pretty easy to get into law school. You didn't have to take an LSAT, and I was admitted to Harvard Law School at the last minute. I never could understand how that came to be, but I was," he recalled. After graduating, he settled in San Francisco as a private attorney. In 1975, he served as a senior counsel on President Ford's Commission on CIA Activities.

Equally uncalculated, he said, was his joining the federal bench. "There were three vacancies on this court in 1975, and without giving it much thought I indicated some interest in it. There were a lot of people who were interested, all of whom had better political connections than I did, but in the end I was the only survivor," he explained. In 1976, the court was composed of "what you would call now old white men," Schwarzer said:

> They were elderly, and their experience was somewhat narrow. Most
> of them had been either assistant US attorneys or otherwise involved
> in state or federal government. What can I say about them? They were
> typical of the federal bench in those days. They had all been appointed
> through some political connection. It was a well-regarded bench, but
> very disparate, with quite a difference among judges and their approach
> to things. That all changed with the Carter administration, when the first
> new appointees were an Hispanic [Robert Aguilar] and a woman [Marilyn Hall Patel] and a black judge [Thelton Henderson].

Schwarzer presided over *Alioto v. Cowles Communications,* a libel case that received a fair amount of press and three or four hung juries. A Cowles publication, *Look* magazine, had published an article with the headline "The Web That Links San Francisco's Mayor Alioto And The Mafia," which suggested that Joseph Alioto consorted with at least six mafia members. "By manipulating bits of information and pictures, they had made this story," Schwarzer said. "Alioto at the time was a potential candidate for vice president with Humphrey in the 1968 election, so he took that very seriously. There was no question that *Look* was liable," but because Alioto was a public figure, "to state a claim for defamation you had to prove the publication was made with malice. I certainly found malice, but then the question was how to determine damages. The damages I gave him were the amount he paid in legal fees to clear his name, probably $600,000." The judgment was actually $350,000 plus costs.

In 1989, Schwarzer was in line to become the chief judge. He looked forward to it, but then changed his mind after being offered a job as the new director of the Federal Judicial Center, an education and training agency in Washington, DC. Schwarzer had strong views on how to improve the operation of the federal court system. "I guess they liked what I had been doing in terms of writing on case management and other legal issues, and participating in a lot of educational programs while I was a district court judge," he said. Schwarzer spent five years as head of the FJC.

As of 2006, Schwarzer spent a good deal of his time sitting by designation with the Ninth Circuit Court of Appeals, as well as the Sixth and First Circuits. The appellate courts are "considerably more intellectual and isolated," said Schwarzer, who has written dozens of law review articles and law books. "You spend your time reading briefs and writing opinions and then a relatively small amount of time hearing arguments. It's intellectually more rewarding than trying cases. On the other hand, doing the work at the district court level, which a lot of it does not involve trying cases, you deal with people—lawyers and witnesses. And you're on the firing line. You have to make decisions, so to many judges that's more interesting and rewarding. They both have their attractions and their downsides."

Schwarzer also had no plans to retire. "The wonderful thing of this job is you can work as long as you're physically able, and you can carry a reduced load," he said. True to his word, he remained on the court until April 2009, when he retired at age eighty-three.

Completing the summer of '76 trio was Cecil Poole, who, at age sixty-one, added another first to his long list of accomplishments. Poole had been the first black US Attorney in San Francisco (and anywhere else other than the US Virgin Islands) from 1961 to 1970, and his years in that post likely contributed to the difficulty he had being confirmed as a federal judge.

In 1968, five demonstrators were arrested for sedition during a war protest at the Oakland Induction Center. Poole, furious to learn that the federal marshal had not requested a warrant, released the demonstrators.

During his tenure in the US Attorney's office, Poole, a moderate Democrat according to the *San Francisco Examiner*, also declined to prosecute numerous draft evaders and denounced a plan to prosecute Black Panther leader David Hilliard for "an implied threat to kill president Richard M. Nixon" made during a rally in Golden Gate Park.

President Johnson had twice nominated Poole for a federal judgeship. When President Ford revived Poole's nomination, Poole was in private practice and found himself unsure if he wanted the position. "I enjoyed my work at the firm and made more money than the judges, so I was not really thinking about it," he explained in a 1993 interview. "I don't know what to do," he confessed to his wife, Charlotte, while on vacation in Hawaii. "The hell you don't," she responded. The decision was made: go for it.

Born in Birmingham, Alabama, in 1914, Poole moved to Pittsburgh, Pennsylvania, when he was four years old. In the ninth grade, he informed his teacher that he would be a trial lawyer when he grew up. He subsequently attended the University of Michigan and Harvard Law School, graduating in 1939. He began his career with a private practice in Pittsburgh but was drafted into a segregated unit of the army in 1942. When he left the service in 1945, Poole set his sights on California. He was disappointed when he arrived. "This was January and it was cold as hell in San Francisco. I had always thought it was going to be dancing girls and palm trees on the sandy beaches," he recalled years later.

Nevertheless, Poole began work with the Office of Price Administration and eventually became its chief. Meanwhile, no realtor would show the Pooles a house in the new Ingleside Terraces, so he purchased their home on Cedro Avenue directly from its owner. Poole became San Francisco's first black assistant district attorney and chief superior court deputy in 1951. He left that post in 1958 to serve as secretary and legal counsel to Governor Edmund G. Brown. One day in June of that year, Poole and his six-year-old daughter, Patti, came home to find a cross burning in their front yard.

After a stint as US Attorney for the Northern District of California, Poole returned to private practice with a focus on entertainment law. His clients included Carlos Santana, Jefferson Airplane, Janis Joplin, and the Doobie Brothers. One of the Doobie Brothers' platinum albums "later hung on the wall in his judge's chamber next to photographs of him with

Poole on "Activist Judges"

I remember when I was in my confirmation hearing, one of the senators asked if I recognized that it was the function of Congress to make the laws, and the judges should not, by their decisions, attempt to enact legislation that Congress hadn't intended. I think he was a little bit surprised at my response....I said there are comparatively few judges who really believe it is their function to enact or to change the law. Their function is to decide what it is and to do the best they can with the compromise that you've given them. Very often the matter that is of crucial importance is a matter that legislators stayed away from, and they left it up there to be thrashed out as litigation might do it....It may well be that the person who, in fact, introduced the law never intended to give federal sanction to what the court decides. But, how do you know that? When you're sitting on the bench, you know that in a particular case, this may have very large implications.

—Cecil Poole, from a 1993 interview for the Bancroft Library

presidents Kennedy and Johnson," noted the *New York Times*. He also served on the board of directors of Levi Strauss & Co.

From his first moments on the federal bench, Poole grasped and later clearly articulated the importance of the decisions being made. "Federal judges do get a sense of both the importance of cases before them and of the need and desire to decide them properly," Poole said in 1993. "Just because a president may have appointed a particular judge doesn't mean that when [he] come[s] to a situation in which the president has enunciated some particular position or bias that [he] is going to go right with him because he's the president. I guess some of them do, but, by and large, you have to try to decide the law based upon all of the criteria, all of your knowledge, and all of the feeling you have that this is what the Congress was trying to get to."

Poole's tenure on the Northern District Court was brief, as President Jimmy Carter elevated him to the Ninth Circuit Court of Appeals in

1979. He spent seventeen years on that bench and took part in a number of influential decisions, including a 1994 ruling on voter representation for Mexican Americans and a 1990 decision upholding limits on political campaign contributions. Poole was also part of the three-judge panel that reviewed and confirmed the 365-year sentence given to convicted spy Jerry Whitworth. Poole assumed senior status in 1996. Until his health failed, he continued to go to court every day, daughter Patti told the *San Francisco Examiner*. Poole died in 1997 at age eighty-three due to complications from pneumonia. In an obituary in the *San Francisco Daily Journal*, Henderson said, "Judge Poole was a true pioneer with a career full of 'firsts,' as well as a great jurist."

Before his nomination to the Court of Appeals, Judge Poole weighed in on the fate of California's old-growth redwood trees. A National Geographic Society study conducted in 1963 revealed that only three hundred thousand acres of the original two-million-acre spread of primeval redwoods remained. A few years later, the tallest trees in the world were discovered in a Redwood Creek canyon, unfurling their branches more than 350 feet in the air. Under pressure from the Sierra Club, the National Geographic Society, and the Save the Redwoods League, the government took possession of fifty-eight thousand forested acres in far Northern California, near Crescent City, and created Redwood National Park in 1968. For a short while, this solution satisfied those who would save the trees, but outside the boundaries of the park, machinery rumbled and redwoods continued to be turned into logs.

In 1977, Judge Orrick convicted Patricia Gillum Hay, who signed her letters "Misty," of having sent death threats by mail to both the president of the Sierra Club and to a lumber company executive. Hay felt neither side of the logging dispute was doing its part to protect the trees. In her handwritten notes, she threatened to chop the men if they didn't stop chopping trees. For her efforts (and because she used the Postal Service), Hay, an admitted follower of Charles Manson, received three years in federal prison.

A plan to expand the national park by acquiring an additional forty-eight thousand acres of redwood forest by powers of condemnation gained ground, and in 1977 President Jimmy Carter sent a personal message endorsing the plan to Congress. His memo noted that logging and road-building on privately owned land near the national park had created severe erosion problems and explained that acquiring additional land would not only expand the park but would also protect the existing trees from further damage. Knowing that logging employees and area residents were likely to protest (as they had in the past) that selling the land and ending logging would cost their local economy vital jobs, President Carter and Secretary of the Interior Cecil Andrus included in their recommendation instructions for the labor secretary and commerce secretary to develop a compensation program to "cushion the effects of temporary unemployment in the Redwood National Park area."

That same week, the government formally filed its plans in district court to seek condemnation of land to expand the park. "It is now a literal race between the lumber companies' chainsaws and Congress with the fate of old-growth redwoods adjoining the park being in the balance," John Dewitt, director of the Save the Redwoods League, told the *Oakland Tribune*. The battle began in earnest.

"In a dramatic escalation of the 'war of the redwoods,' the US government obtained a court order yesterday giving it immediate possession of a privately owned timber parcel near Redwood National Park in Humboldt County," reported the *San Francisco Chronicle* in 1977. Arcata National Lumber Company refused to obey the order to refrain from logging a 36.8-acre area that was part of the segment proposed for addition to the national park, so Judge Poole authorized seizure of the land. A payment of $1 million, raised by the Save the Redwoods League, was deposited to cover the estimated value of the land.

Poole scheduled a subsequent hearing, where Arcata attorneys insisted that the timber alone on the land in question was worth $3.3 million. Activist Dewitt countered that Arcata had never paid more than $25,000 an acre for old-growth redwoods, making the parcel of land currently in question worth about $800,000. Poole concluded by saying he didn't think the government had acted unreasonably, but added, "it's a question which leaves room for argument and different reasonable opinions."

In1978, Congress approved the Redwood National Park Expansion Act, which validated the seizure of land by law and brought the total area of protected land to 106,000 acres. In 1994, three nearby state parks entered a joint operating agreement with the national park and have added more acreage since then. The Redwood National and State Parks are now unified into a 130,000-acre preserve of forest and rivers. This land, approximately one-sixth the size of Yosemite National Park, contains half of all the earth's old-growth redwoods.

Because of its abundant forests, Northern California has long been an area of particular focus for the Forest Service. As early as 1963, the Forest Service began planning a road to connect the towns of Gasquet, in Del Norte County, and Orleans, in Humboldt County, to provide timber workers, firefighters, and campers access to the more remote areas of the Six Rivers National Forest. Two separate draft environmental impact statements prepared and circulated during the mid-1970s stated that construction of the G-O Road, as it came to be known, would have "no adverse impact." But forty-five hundred members of the Tolowa, Karuk, Yurok, and Hoopa tribes, including their leaders, begged to differ. The tribes considered this land their Sacred High Country. Lush, pristine forests and rock formations covered most of the 13,500 acres, which were essential to their religion. It was "Indian heaven," according to Chris Peters of the Seventh Generation Fund. It is "an area that is so sacred that there is no mitigation of any disturbance—you can't mitigate a disruption to heaven," he said.

The passage of the American Indian Religious Freedom Act in 1978 led to another study of the potential effects of the G-O Road, and this one advised against the road project. Three years later, in 1981, the Sacred High Country was made eligible for the National Register of Historic Places. The Advisory Council on Historic Preservation, an independent federal government agency, formally criticized the Forest Service's G-O Road plan and recommended finding another location. Nevertheless, in 1982 the Forest Service issued their final environmental impact statement and pledged to move forward with the G-O Road. Logging would be allowed, but the Sacred High Country would not be disturbed because the road would be located away from specific religious areas and archaeological sites. Yet it was the area as a whole that was sacred to Native Americans. "The Sacred High Country is literally the center of the universe to northwest California Indians. Destroying it means destroying the world," explained Michael Pfeffer, executive director of California Indian Legal Services, in 2002.

Construction on the G-O Road began in segments, working inward from both Gasquet and Orleans. Each section of road was authorized by its own environmental assessment under the National Environmental Protection Act. When the Forest Service formally announced construction of the last six-mile portion of the G-O Road, the tribes and their attorneys headed to federal court. Judge Weigel denied their request for a temporary restraining order but scheduled a trial on the road, to begin just six weeks later. This meant that the verdict would be rendered before the winter snows melted and construction could begin again. From the first day of the hearings, Weigel's San Francisco courtroom was packed with environmentalists, logging officials, US Attorneys, the press, and Indians in full tribal regalia. Weigel recalled, in a 1989 interview, having to ask them each day to remove their headdresses in deference to the court. They always politely complied.

The Native Americans built their case on the constitutional right to freedom of religion. Marilyn Miles, now a judge on the California Superior Court, was then working at California Indian Legal Services and represented the plaintiffs. She introduced a slide show illustrating the beauty and unique environment of the Sacred High Country. One by one, Indians took the stand to explain how their religion worked and what the High Country meant to them. Yurok elder Sam Jones told the

Fig. 8-8
G-O Road opponents at the Six Rivers National Forest Headquarters in Eureka in May 1988. Left to right: Lyn Risling (Karuk/Yarok/Hupa), Byron Nelson (Hupa), Jimmy James (Yurok), Donna Martin (Yurok, in background), Junie Mattice (Tolowa), Julian Lang (Karuk/Wiyot), and medicine woman Elizabeth Case (Karuk). Courtesy of Heyday.

judge how his mother, a medicine woman, had sent him to the High Country for blessings and protection before he left for service in World War II. Lowana Brantner of the Yurok tribe invited Weigel to close his eyes and accompany her to the High Country. For minutes, the room was silent, until Brantner opened her eyes and commanded Weigel to return. "Now do you know what I mean?" she asked him.

"Yes, I do," he said.

Weigel later stated that the evidence seemed overwhelming in establishing the importance of the High Country. He said, "There just wasn't any rational basis for holding that the federal rights in the land prevailed....While it may have entailed some engineering difficulty to build a road connecting those two communities...in a manner and in locations which would not have interfered with the religious freedom of the Indians, it wouldn't have been all that expensive."

In 1983, Weigel enjoined the Forest Service from any further construction on the G-O Road. Indians rejoiced, and the Ninth Circuit Court of Appeals upheld Weigel's ruling. However, in 1988, the Supreme Court overturned the decision in a five-to-three ruling. The opinion, written by Justice Sandra Day O'Connor, stated, "Even assuming that the Government's action here will virtually destroy the Indians' ability to practice their religion, the Constitution simply does not provide a principle that could justify upholding the Indians' legal claims." Because the Forest Service was not acting to literally outlaw the Indians' religion, she wrote, construction of the road was legal.

After more than a year of protest by Native Americans and environmentalists, Congress passed the Smith River National Recreation Area Act, which formally closed the G-O Road corridor and left the last incomplete section relatively undisturbed. However, in 1997, citing forest health concerns, the Forest Service reopened the area around Little Medicine Mountain for salvage logging.

A Hell of a Trial

The Hells Angels Motorcycle Club started in Fontana, just west of San Bernardino, around 1948. From the start, club members developed a reputation for being wild and aggressive as they cruised astride their Harley-Davidson bikes. As the 1960s waned, federal authorities kept a close eye on the Angels. Although club members claimed to be nothing more than fun-loving motorcycle riders, the Angels came to be viewed by the government as an extensive drug ring and a crime organization akin to the mafia.

In 1979, federal agents in San Francisco carried out a series of raids against the club. Firearms, drugs, and documents yielded indictments against thirty-three Hells Angels and associates. It was one of the first cases in which the government used the RICO (Racketeer Influenced and Corrupt Organizations) anti-racketeering statute to prosecute. Some of those indicted could not be found and some charges were dropped, but when the case went to trial in the district court in 1979, there were still eighteen defendants—fifteen burly, bearded men and three women. Judge Conti provided jurors with notebooks containing pictures of the accused to help them keep track. In a 2006 interview, he said he decided to take on all eighteen defendants at once because, "I wasn't going to take a trial that lasts nine months and the other fellas have to sit in jail waiting to try their case. I said no, I can handle the trial. I was young, I thought I could handle it."

Conti's courtroom was transformed: tables and chairs were bolted down, and a bulletproof Plexiglas partition separated the audience and the participants. Between defendants, prosecutors, and lawyers, nearly sixty people needed to be present for the trial to proceed. Conti and the courtroom received extra protection from federal marshals. "The US Attorney spoke of 'Angel crank' and machine guns and silencers and plastic explosives that make your hands glow. But the real drama at the Hells Angels conspiracy trial is the cast, not the plot," noted *San Francisco Examiner* reporter Jim Wood. As the trial began in October 1979, Wood listed a litany of disruptions: attorneys threatened with contempt; defendant Sonny Barger threatened with hearing the rest of the trial from a holding cell if he couldn't refrain from comment; government witnesses granted immunity who suddenly declined to testify; and mouthy family members who wanted the judge to "kick some of the cops out" to make room for more audience members. "Between Conti and the Angels," Wood concluded, "there has been, clearly, a clash of styles."

Despite all this, assistant US Attorney Robert Dondero proceeded systematically as he laid out the government's case in his opening presentation. The Hells Angels Motorcycle Club was a criminal enterprise under federal RICO statutes and therefore subject to amplified punishment for their crimes, he told the jury. Since 1966, members had conspired to sell heroin, cocaine, LSD, and methamphetamines (known as speed or crank) in a drug network that had spread through Northern California and across the United States. Because of this criminal undertaking, Dondero argued, Angels had become involved in trading drugs for weapons and explosives as well as in murder and attempted murder.

Court concluded for the day after Dondero's two-hour opening. That afternoon, Barger's lawyer, Frank Mangan, assembled the press to deny that the Hells Angels were a criminal conspiracy. "Instead, he maintained, they are a social club built around the enjoyment of motorcycles," Wood reported in the *Examiner*. If perchance a club member committed a crime, that was an individual's choice, not a Hells Angels policy.

By February 1980, it was clear that the trial was a strain on nearly everyone. On February 27, Judge Conti, then fifty-seven, collapsed twice while hearing the case and was taken to the University of California Medical Center. The diagnosis was exhaustion. He was hospitalized for a few days. "Low potassium," Conti recalled with a chuckle in 2006. "They pumped me full of potassium at the emergency room."

The trial was tedious, Conti said. "When you have eighteen lawyers representing defendants…it took a lot of attention to what was going on to handle eighteen people and keep the trial moving. And we had a lot of problems too." Problems like a witness who was found dead along with her two children, all with their throats slit. Two other witnesses had their throats slit but survived. They refused to take the witness stand. Conti and his family were also threatened. Arsonists torched a house in his neighborhood. Rumors spread that the house was mistaken for his. His mother's house was burglarized by a man who was caught with newspaper articles about the Hells Angels trial in his wallet. "There were a lot of strange things going on then," said the judge, who never feared for his own safety but did worry about his family. "People don't like to go to jail and they always blame you," he said. "It is part of the action."

In mid-June, after eight months of testimony and an estimated $5 million in court costs, the jury was sequestered and placed under armed guard as members began deliberations on the forty-four charges. More than two weeks later, they returned with decisions on only twelve charges, including an acquittal for Barger on racketeering charges. In fact, only one of the twenty-nine racketeering counts—the focus of the government's case—resulted in a conviction. The remaining convictions related to lesser firearms and narcotics charges, and Conti declared a mistrial. Shortly thereafter, the government prepared to begin again.

When it was time for the retrial, in October 1980, Judge Orrick drew the lot to preside. "I want to emphasize that my case was very different from Judge Conti's case," Orrick said. Because the Hells Angels had gotten a mistrial the first time around, they "thought that they would get the same again and maybe even be acquitted, if they behaved themselves." At one point, the twelve Angels still on trial even took to disciplining themselves. After one defendant spent the morning making faces and giving Orrick the finger when he wasn't looking, several of his co-defendants beat him severely during a recess. Orrick returned to the bench to find him sitting calmly with a large bandage on his head.

With the exception of a few federal agents, the government's witnesses "were nothing more nor less than thugs," Orrick said. "One had even been given immunity from prosecution for murder. I thought that was outrageous, but the government all over the country was anxious to put an end to these motorcycle gangs." Many of the prosecution's witnesses had once been Angels themselves. "You could just feel the hate between the defendants and the witness on the stand," Orrick recalled. Each day, he said, "we had at least a dozen of these smelly, rowdy hulks in the courtroom staring at the witness. Even with the metal detector there, the marshals told me they picked up big belt buckles and tire chains and all that before they even came into my courtroom." During the course of his opening statement, defense attorney Tony Serra shouted, "Ladies and gentlemen of the jury, you will find these witnesses are nothing but SCUMBUCKETS!" Orrick chastised him for yelling, but as the trial moved forward, "I looked at [each] witness and wondered whether the marshal was close enough to pull him back. I thought, well, Serra was right. That is a scumbucket—witness after witness after witness."

Adding to the outrage, two months into the trial Orrick learned that one of the government's witnesses had been paid for his testimony. Thomas Bryant, a former Hells Angel who had also testified in the first conspiracy trial, acknowledged under oath that federal law enforcement officers provided him $30,000 in cash. "I was shocked to pieces," Orrick recalled, and the defense moved for a mistrial due to misconduct on the part of the prosecution. Orrick spoke with a judge in Philadelphia who had declared a mistrial after learning a witness had been paid, but after weighing the money and effort already put into the trial, Orrick decided to continue. Nevertheless, the result was again a hung jury and a mistrial.

Rather than attempting a third major trial, US Attorneys brought an assortment of smaller drug and weapons cases against a few core Hells Angels. The government has never accomplished its goal of eliminating motorcycle gangs, and the Angels are still riding today.

CHAPTER 9
A BROADER SCOPE

THE RISE OF SILICON VALLEY and the subsequent evolution of intellectual property law, as well as new interpretations of civil rights and environmental responsibilities, continued to broaden the jurisdiction of the Northern District Court. In response, the court itself began to expand, both tangibly—as new court buildings were constructed around the Bay Area and more judges were added to handle an ever-increasing caseload—and intangibly, as the court's perspective grew more fully representative of the community at large. In addition to younger judges who replaced many of the retiring old guard, the district court welcomed to the bench in 1980 its first Latino judge, its first female judge, and a second African American judge—Robert Aguilar, Marilyn Hall Patel, and Thelton Henderson, respectively. Judge Patel filled the seat vacated by Lloyd Burke and Judge Henderson the seat left by Cecil Poole when Poole moved to the appellate court.

A prime example of this added depth is the relationship that has developed between the district court and California's federal prisons. The court's jurisdiction over death penalty cases has forged a link between the courtroom and the prison cell—and California prisoners have always been an active bunch. Jailhouse lawyers in the 1970s started this trend, as more prisoners demanded their civil rights; now many California death row prisoners are more acquainted with their legal rights than their counterparts in other states. A part of the clerk's office in the Northern District of California is dedicated solely to receiving, evaluating, and processing inmate complaints. Court clerk Richard Wieking estimated that prisoners generate 25 percent of the court's civil caseload; the office includes six

FIG. 9-1 (PREVIOUS PAGE)
A model of a solitary cell and a photograph of the San Quentin State Prison tier were used as evidence in a class action lawsuit against the California Department of Corrections. The case was filed in 1973 by prisoners confined in administrative segregation in four California state prisons. © Eric Luse/San Francisco Chronicle/Corbis.

FIG. 9-2
John Clutchette
(left), Fleeta Drumgo
(center), and George
Jackson (right), of
the Soledad Brothers,
walk in shackles.
© JACKSON2-b-
24JUL01-MG-HO/San
Francisco Chronicle/
Corbis.

law clerks dedicated to handling pro se prisoner petitions. Many of these complaints are related to civil rights.

Prisoners mail in petitions that, Wieking said in a 2005 interview, range from "strange complaints on weird pieces of paper" to legitimate pleas for relief from overcrowded or decrepit facilities. "Virtually everything—unless it's really crazy—is filed," Wieking said. And although at times this may seem futile, it's worth the effort when systemic wrongs are identified and corrected. "Certain districts have a history [with prison cases], but few have more of a history than the Northern District," said John Hagar, a veteran civil rights litigator and now court-appointed special master overseeing the Pelican Bay maximum-security prison.

Although prisoner suits increased substantially in the 1970s, this history stretches back further. In 1966, Robert O. Gilmore Jr., a San Quentin prisoner, sued to protest a new California law that prohibited prison law libraries from containing any legal materials other than twelve specific books and barred inmates from owning their own law books. A Folsom inmate filed a similar suit, the two cases were combined, and in 1970 a three-judge panel found the law unconstitutional, as it deprived convicts of equal protection by giving greater legal protection to prisoners with attorneys. The state appealed to the Supreme Court, saying that access to an assortment of legal resources would encourage convicts to fill their petitions with "voluminous, irrelevant, and confusing citations." In 1971, the high court denied the appeal. California prisons contain legal libraries with more than twelve books as a result, and prisoners in good standing may use their free time to study law.

In 1973, in response to another case filed by San Quentin prisoners, the same three-judge panel ruled that California prisons could not censor an inmate's personal correspondence. The judges instructed the Department of Corrections to restructure regulations so that only obscenity or security risks could be censored. "Statements critical of prison life and personnel cannot be subject to censorship by the very people who are being criticized simply to stifle such criticism," the opinion stated.

Other civil rights cases filed by prisoners had a more life-and-death bent. On January 14, 1970, a guard shot and killed three African American Muslims at Soledad State Prison. Three days later, guard John Mills was pushed from a prison tier and fell to his death. Charged with the murder were Fleeta Drumgo, John Clutchette, and Black Panther and political activist George Jackson (then in his ninth year of incarceration for an armed robbery that netted seventy-one dollars; he had received an indeterminate sentence and never made parole). They came to be known as the Soledad Brothers, and their cause called attention to the treatment of African American inmates, especially those who expressed strong political views. Jackson published *Soledad Brother* in 1970, which explained, among other things, his belief that capitalism led to the oppression of people of color.

Shortly after Mills's death, the Soledad Brothers were moved to San Quentin to await trial. Rumors circulated that they had been victims of a prison conspiracy, and in August 1970, Jackson's brother Jonathan burst into a Marin County courtroom and took three hostages—two inmates and superior court judge Harold Haley, whom he planned to exchange for George's release. But as they attempted their getaway, Jonathan Jackson and all three hostages were killed. In November 1970, while awaiting transfer to San Francisco for their trial, Clutchette and George Jackson had a fight with prison guards that left one guard dead. The two men were charged with yet another murder and, according to prison rules, sentenced to sixty days of lost privileges and thirty-six days in isolation. Clutchette filed a class action civil rights case on behalf of all prisoners, asserting that the prison disciplinary procedures denied them due process and any opportunity to mount a defense.

In June 1971, Judge Alfonso Zirpoli declared the prison's disciplinary procedures unconstitutional, because they did not provide adequate notice of charges and counsel for the accused, did not allow favorable witnesses to testify or provide for cross-examination of accusing witnesses, and did not provide a fact-finder uninvolved with the incident to make the final decision. Zirpoli noted that the courts normally avoid telling prison authorities how to run their facilities, but in this case there involved unusual circumstances. He ordered that the procedures be rewritten, and he barred any additional hearings under the old rules. Zirpoli's ruling also ordered that Jackson and Clutchette be removed from isolation and returned to normal confinement until their hearings. He ruled that indefinite solitary confinement, potential increase in a prisoner's sentence, or forfeiture of a prisoner's earnings were unlawful punishments.

In April 1974 the Ninth Circuit Court of Appeals denied the state's appeal and affirmed Zirpoli's ruling on disciplinary action. The Supreme Court in 1976 modified the ruling to allow prison officials to decide whether prisoners involved in an incident could have counsel, except when the prisoner was not competent enough to handle the matter on his own. The case went back to the district court, where a 1979 summary judgment hearing finalized the parameters and conditions under which staff members or other counsel substitutes could assist prisoners. But the matter that had begun at Soledad in 1970 was far from over.

On August 21, 1971, George Jackson, still being held at San Quentin, pulled a semiautomatic pistol from his Afro, ordered guards to open the doors, and called his fellow prisoners to arms. "We got to do it now or never," Jackson shouted as twenty-six inmates, some armed with razors wedged into toothbrush handles, swarmed out of their cells in an attempt to escape. But minutes later, three guards and three prisoners, including Jackson, were dead. The six inmates accused of having participated in the escape attempt with Jackson—Drumgo, Johnny Spain, Hugo Pinell, Willie Tate, David Johnson, and Louis Talamantes—were soon placed in San Quentin's Adjustment Center (known as the AC), a maximum-security isolation area for the most dangerous prisoners. In a sixteen-month state court trial, three of the "San Quentin Six" were convicted of murder, assault, and conspiracy; the other three were acquitted. Simultaneously, the six filed a civil rights case claiming that imprisonment in the AC constituted cruel and unusual punishment and had a psychologically debilitating effect. They wanted the AC closed.

In 1974, *Spain et al. v. Procunier* began in Judge Zirpoli's courtroom. Security at the Federal Building was significantly increased. Before the trial, attorneys agreed that the prisoners would not be chained or handcuffed in court, but Zirpoli stipulated that only one inmate could appear at a time. When twenty-four-year-old Spain took the stand on the second day of the trial, ten federal marshals kept watch as he gave an account of the more than three years he had spent in a six-by-eight AC isolation cell. Spain described suspending his food from the ceiling to keep it away from mice and explained how he ran hot water in the winter and cold water in the summer to make the temperature tolerable, as well as to muffle noise. Spain said he left his cell about three times a week for an hour of exercise.

When Spain returned to the stand the following day, he had spots of blood on his orange jumpsuit. When questioned by his lawyer, he explained that his mustache and goatee had been forcibly shaved by a group of prison guards after he refused their orders to do it himself. In the process he had been cut. Zirpoli declined to bar guards from forcibly shaving inmates. "I am not going to act as a warden issuing day-to-day orders in the case," he said.

Drumgo was the second of the San Quentin Six to take the stand. His testimony revealed his communist political leanings and his loyalty to George Jackson. "If I feel the rules are unjust, I'm not going to abide by them," he testified. Drumgo also testified to frequent abuse from prison guards. He said he had been beaten by a guard as soon as he returned to San Quentin after his acquittal in the Soledad Brothers trial. (Clutchette was also acquitted in that trial and was paroled in 1972.)

Pinell, infamous as a dangerous and combative prisoner, told Zirpoli that in almost every fight he'd had in prison, the guards had caused the problem. "I don't look for justice anymore," he said. As his time on the stand came to a close, the twenty-nine-year-old convicted rapist looked Judge Zirpoli in the eye and said, "I have something to say." The *San Francisco Examiner* reported that, "For the next 44 minutes, Pinell held Zirpoli, his own lawyers, and a half-full courtroom spellbound with a sometimes eloquent, sometimes emotional, and always bitter soliloquy about the sordid conditions of prison life"—particularly his five years in the AC and other prison segregation areas, known by prisoners as holes.

A San Quentin guard who had been fired after twenty-one months on the job also testified. Cedric B. Jackson said guards often revised their incident reports to conform to the administration's version of events, even when it meant overlooking brutality. White prison officials favored white inmates, he said. And "the rest of the inmates are treated like animals."

As the evidentiary hearing came to a close, Stanford University psychologist Philip G. Zimbardo testified that he could not imagine a more cruel and unusual punishment than the Adjustment Center at San Quentin. Even extreme physical punishment would be more tolerable than complete isolation, Zimbardo said. "Fundamental human rights and basic constitutional rights are being denied, distorted, and degraded by the conditions" in the AC, he concluded.

After a two-week recess, state prison director Raymond K. Procunier was one of the first to take the stand. "If I was to close the San Quentin Adjustment Center and put these guys out with the general population, the state of California would have a new director of corrections the next day," he said, threatening to quit. Procunier said that he might be willing to break up the six, sending them to an assortment of prisons, but he would not approve of returning them to the general prison population. Because guards and inmates who were present during the George Jackson escape attempt were still at San Quentin, he said, trouble could arise if these six were reintroduced. "And whatever happened to them, we would be accused of setting them up," Procunier said. "I'm just not going to allow us to be put in that position."

Yet in December 1975, after months of testimony and a visit to the AC, Judge Zirpoli's ruling put the Department of Corrections in precisely that position. "It is evident that the continued segregated confinement of plaintiffs to the first tier of the Adjustment Center not only militates against reform and rehabilitation of the plaintiffs, but is so counterproductive that it instills in them a deeper hatred for and alienation from the society that initially and justly put them there," Zirpoli wrote. He declared several practices related to San Quentin's Adjustment Center, including the use of tear gas and ankle, neck, and waist chains, to be cruel and unusual punishment in violation of the Eighth and Fourteenth Amendments, except when used in relation to prison riots or violent prisoners. Zirpoli also ordered the state to give the five remaining incarcerated inmates involved with the case (Willie Tate had been paroled) a due process disciplinary hearing. Although cheered by the inmates' lawyers, Zirpoli's narrow ruling fell short of the prisoners' original intent to shut down the AC.

The *San Francisco Examiner* hailed Zirpoli's ruling as an unprecedented "breakthrough in penal jurisprudence." The California Correctional Officers Association (now the California Correctional Peace Officers Association) was not pleased. Arnold Thompson, president of the organization, accused Zirpoli of having ignored the deaths of the three guards and three inmates that led to the San Quentin Six's incarceration. Ken Brown, spokesman for the Sacramento correctional officers' union, said, "I'm quite certain that the morale of our officers will be at an absolute all-time low. I can't imagine anything that would affect a correctional officer any more personally than this type of decision." Procunier, who was now head of the state parole board, was saved from having to resign as prison director.

By the end of 1975, neck chains were no longer used on California prisoners being transported to court, in compliance with Zirpoli's ruling. The judge issued a formal order finalizing his ruling in February 1976, but the state appealed to the Supreme Court for a stay in enforcing the provisions. In March 1976 the Supreme Court stayed the sections of Zirpoli's ruling that required due process hearings for the prisoners and limited the use of tear gas and mechanical restraints. The ban on neck chains and the daily exercise requirement were left in place.

In 1979, the Ninth Circuit Court of Appeals ruled on the case a final time, leaving the right to outdoor exercise and ban on neck chains in place but allowing for other types of mechanical restraint beyond handcuffs. The Ninth Circuit judges also reversed the district court on the matter of tear gas, ruling that safe quantities could be used in circumstances other than riots. The case was remanded to the district court, where the final parameters for the use of tear gas were determined.

In addition to these details, the Ninth Circuit commented on the larger issues involved with this case and others like it:

> The principal position taken by the state…is that federal judicial interference in prison management is not justified on the facts of this case. The federal courts should use great restraint before issuing orders based on the finding that the state has followed unlawful procedures in discharging the unenviable task of keeping dangerous men in safe custody under humane conditions. This said, it must also be remembered that enforcement of the Eighth Amendment is not always consistent with allowing complete deference to all administrative determinations by prison officials. Whatever rights one may lose at the prison gates (prisoners have no right to unionize), the full protections of the Eighth Amendment most certainly remain in force.

"The court's role is an unfortunate one," Judge Zirpoli said in a 1983 interview about this case. "The court should not be running the prisons, but if you can't get the legislature to appropriate the money, and you can't get the executive office to invoke the proper administrative procedures, then the courts have to come in." Zirpoli also noted that in the end prison officials complied with the bulk of his ruling and that conditions for inmates were better because of it.

"The first cases were about basic things, political struggles," said John Hagar, Pelican Bay special master. "These were different types of cases than what we deal with today." These earlier cases helped establish humane conditions for those in California's prisons, but as time passed, there were more and more inmates. California's prison system held 22,500 at the beginning of the 1980s, and by 1991 more than 100,000 people were behind bars.

Almost before the San Quentin Six case was resolved, another prisoners' rights case began in the federal courtroom of Judge Stanley Weigel. This class action case, filed by inmates at four California prisons (Folsom, San Quentin, Soledad, and Deuel Vocational Institute), again alleged cruel and unusual punishment. Again those suing alleged that solitary confinement caused them psychological damage, but an added injustice in this case was severe overcrowding. Prisoners were often double-celled, with two inmates crammed into a cell space designed for one.

"[The state's] position was that practically nothing constituted improper treatment or unconstitutional treatment of prisoners and that no conditions were of a nature of which violated Eighth Amendment rights of prisoners," Weigel recalled in a 1989 interview. "Indeed, I have the impression now—although it may not be accurate—that the position of the defendant…was basically the idea that prisoners had virtually no rights at all."

After ten years of legal maneuvering between inmates' attorneys and the Department of Corrections, Weigel issued a preliminary injunction in 1980 mandating improvements at San Quentin, Soledad, and Deuel. Weigel considered testimony from inmates, psychiatrists, and prison staff, depositions of the defendants, and photographs of the prisons, and his opinion reviewed the physical conditions, sanitary conditions, food services, educational practices, medical services, placement and retention procedures, and the psychological impact of confinement in the administrative segregation units, or solitary confinement areas, of the prisons. "The court did not conclude that any one condition amounted to cruel and unusual punishment. Instead…the court concluded that the totality of conditions under which the plaintiffs are confined warranted the issuance of a preliminary injunction," the opinion from a 1981 appeal explained.

Ninth Circuit judges threw out Weigel's injunction, saying he should have ruled on each specific complaint instead of using the totality approach. In 1983, Weigel issued a revised injunction that specifically ordered an end to double-celling in isolation units and again ordered improvement in overall prison conditions. The trial to determine whether the injunction should be lifted or made permanent began in November 1983. In addition to testimony from thirty inmates, as well as a slew of sociologists, psychologists, sanitation and noise experts, prison counselors, and correctional officers, evidence in the case included a life-sized replica of a solitary cell constructed in Weigel's courtroom and an actual-size photograph of the view down a prison tier. Judge Weigel also paid a surprise visit to San Quentin to examine the facilities for himself.

In October 1984, Weigel ordered that the injunction be made permanent for San Quentin and Folsom. They were ordered to stop double-celling isolated prisoners, and the court appointed a special master to monitor their compliance. In 1986, the Ninth Circuit Court of Appeals ruled that "the district court had assumed too much control over the day-to-day affairs of the prisons." That ruling reduced the due process and evidentiary requirements for placing a prisoner in isolation, rejected the district court's view that denial of contact visits and the available medical facilities violated constitutional rights, and deemed that prison authorities, not the court, would determine when a prisoner should be released from segregated confinement. With these modifications, the injunction remained active, and Weigel continued to hold hearings and issue orders related to the prisons until the order was vacated in 1997, after more than twenty years of litigation.

Although Weigel's injunction related to only two of the state's prisons, it had broader effects. Essentially, Hagar said, this ruling caused the Department of Corrections to design a new type of prison. The new units at Folsom, built in a cloverleaf pattern so guards could monitor more prisoners at a time, and the more restricted Pelican Bay Prison, which opened in 1989 near the Oregon border in Del Norte County as a high-tech, super-maximum-security facility and received many of the most hardcore inmates from Folsom and San Quentin, are direct descendants of this decision.

But the construction of new prisons has not solved the problem of inappropriate conditions for inmates. Thelton Henderson, chief judge of the district court, ruled in 1995 (*Madrid v. Gomez*) that the rights of inmates housed in a separate, high-security part of Pelican Bay Prison (the Security Housing Unit, or SHU) were violated by conditions including excessive force, inadequate medical and mental health care, the placement of mentally ill prisoners in isolation, and a lack of due process in the procedures used to declare prisoners gang members, which led to their placement in the SHU. His 345-page opinion was for many a scandalizing and lurid look into the inner workings of a maximum-security segregation unit, a separate facility designed to hold "the worst of the worst," as the state called them. "Dry words on paper cannot adequately capture the senseless suffering and sometimes wretched misery that defendants' unconstitutional practices leave in their wake," Henderson noted.

Since this decision, Hagar has monitored the progress being made toward Henderson's required improvements, first as assistant special master and now as special master. The state did not appeal Henderson's ruling, and just over a year later, in February 1996, the Department of Corrections issued a press release touting its progress.

Henderson was also pleased. "One of the things I'm proudest of about *Madrid* was that after a lot of resistance, the warden at Pelican Bay was brought to Sacramento to be part of the senior management of the California Department of Corrections, and many of the things I had sort of forced upon him he began to like and instituted them at other prisons around the state," Henderson said in 2006. "So the ramifications of *Madrid* are much greater than just Pelican Bay."

But problems remain. In June 2004, Hagar reported that incidents of prisoner abuse by guards were not isolated occurrences and that the guards' union had used its power to limit investigations into these incidents and to prevent officers from being disciplined. But with Hagar and the district court's oversight in place, some things have gradually improved. "Over the years things are monitored, and once they're fixed and stay fixed for a couple of years, I stop monitoring them," Hagar said.

In 2001, the Prison Law Office, a prisoner advocacy group based at San Quentin that has been involved in many of the cases mentioned here, filed *Plata v. Davis*, the largest prisoner class action suit in US history. Heard by district court judge Maxine M. Chesney, the case sought adequate medical care for the 160,000 prisoners in California's thirty-four state prisons. In 2002, the state settled the case and agreed to revamp the prison health-care system and phase in improvements by 2008. However, on June 30, 2005, Judge Henderson had had enough. Citing little progress despite the good intentions of some state officials, Henderson removed the prison health-care system from state control and placed it in the hands of a receiver who would be responsible for all related decisions and report directly to the court. Henderson reasoned that extreme measures were required to, as the *Los Angeles Times* reported, "fix a system that kills one inmate each week through medical incompetence or neglect." In 2006, Henderson appointed a health official to act as the state prison health-care system's receiver.

"I still get letters" about these prison cases, Henderson said. "People say, 'I don't understand this. You're advocating for these murderers, killers, and rapists, and you want them to have better medical treatment than I have.' That's the general complaint. People who have borderline kinds of jobs don't have good [health care]. They have to go to the county hospital or wherever, and they think we're coddling [the criminals]," he said. "But they don't understand what I understand, that the Constitution demands that people walking along the street, they're not entitled to any medical treatment from the government, but when you take them off the street and incarcerate them, a constitutional duty attaches to give them a certain level of medical treatment if they need it. And that's all I'm doing."

The Prison Litigation Reform Act of 1996

Buried in the 1996 budget signed by President Bill Clinton, the Prison Litigation Reform Act had two major provisions: it limited judicial control over prisons and prisoners' access to the courts. "The new law requires all court orders governing prison conditions to end after two years if prison authorities demand it," wrote the *San Francisco Recorder*. "To keep an order in force, inmates would have to prove their cases again." The new legislation discouraged class action suits related to prisons, as well as individual suits challenging prison conditions.

This legislation led to the end of a number of longstanding consent decrees in the Northern District. In 1997, Judge Charles Legge, who had taken over the case when Judge Weigel assumed senior status and reduced his caseload, ended the eighteen-year-old consent decree governing *Thompson v. Gomez*, which had ensured prisoners the right to gather for religious services, read law books, and seek relief from excessive noise. Shortly thereafter, Judge Susan Illston struck down the thirty-two-year-old consent decree governing *Gilmore v. State of California*. This order had guaranteed prisoners throughout California access to a fully equipped law library. Contributing to Illston's decision was a 1996 Supreme Court decision, *Lewis v. Casey*, which changed the requirements for prison law libraries. After the high court's ruling, prisons had only to provide inmates the tools needed to challenge their sentences or to protest the conditions of their incarceration.

The prisoners affected by the dissolution of these consent decrees filed a combined appeal, and in August 2000, the Ninth Circuit ruled that while the Prison Litigation Reform Act was constitutional and legal, the district court had erred in its application. The appellate court said the district court should not have placed "the burden on plaintiffs to establish a current and ongoing violation of a Federal right rather than requiring the defendants, warden, and state prison officials to prove compliance with the consent decree." The ruling ordered that the portion of the Prison Litigation Reform Act that had resulted in dissolved consent decrees not be applied in those cases until prison officials had proved that the original conditions of the consent decrees had been met.

The district court also has a longstanding relationship with county jails in Northern California. In 1973, Judge Robert Schnacke declared the San Francisco jail system in violation of the Eighth and Fourteenth Amendments (as well as the minimum jail standards defined by California law) because it didn't provide adequate medical care and appropriate bedding, clothing, and food; classify pretrial prisoners according to security risk; or adopt appropriate rules and procedures for disciplinary hearings. In 1978, civil rights attorney Morton Cohen asked Judge William Schwarzer to shut down the four isolation cells in the San Francisco jail, saying they amounted to little more than a "human zoo" on the Hall of Justice's sixth floor. Built in the 1950s, the Hall of Justice at 850 Bryant Street houses law enforcement offices, two jails, and several superior court courtrooms. Rather than close the isolation cells, Schwarzer proposed that Cohen and Deputy City Attorney John Etchevers work together on guidelines to govern their use. But their efforts had little effect.

Ten years later, Cohen was still fighting to improve the jail conditions caused by deteriorating buildings and gross overcrowding. San Francisco's County Jail No. 3, then located in San Bruno, was built in 1934, and from 1985 to 1995 it housed two inmates per twenty-four square feet of living space, when the state standard was one inmate per eighty square feet. It was Cohen who brought the case that would finally change the jail system: *Jones v. City and County of San Francisco*, which Judge William Orrick heard from 1991 through a final ruling in 1997. In 1989, Cohen set out to find the inmate who had had the most horrific experience from jail overcrowding, he told the *New York Times* in 2004. The person he found was Billy Besk.

Besk left his home in New Hampshire at age eighteen for a visit to San Francisco. Along the way he found marijuana growing by the side of the road. He filled his duffel bag with about twenty ounces, planning to sell it to offset the cost of his travels. When he got to San Francisco, local police stopped him because he looked like a car thief they were hunting. When they found the marijuana, Besk was arrested and sent to County Jail No. 3 in San Bruno, near San Francisco International Airport. "That is where [Besk's] 1989 journey took a terrible turn," wrote Carol Pogash of the *New York Times*. "Because at County Jail No. 3, a cavernous, crumbling, overcrowded place, Mr. Besk was so brutalized by other inmates that his case became a symbol of the jail system's failings." After repeated beatings and abuse at the hands of other inmates, Besk was raped by a prisoner with a history of sexual abuse.

In 1991 Cohen filed *Besk v. City and County of San Francisco*, a class action lawsuit seeking relief from the jail's conditions. After hours of hearings and negotiations, in 1993 Besk and Cohen agreed to dismiss their action if the jail would comply with thirty-three requirements to improve prisoner safety and living conditions, known as the Besk Stipulation. The agreement included additional guards, an end to double-celling, and an agreement that younger, more vulnerable inmates would be housed separately from veteran prisoners, particularly those in jail for sexual or violent crimes. Besk also received $145,000 in damages.

Less than a year later they were back in court. Cohen filed an amended complaint that focused on the situation of inmate Arnold Jones, charging the jail with failing to implement and adhere to the Besk Stipulation. Overcrowding continued, and jail administrators had not separated mentally ill prisoners. Jones's cellmate had AIDS and frequently threatened to bite him. A court investigation revealed that Jail No. 3 had improved some conditions but had not even tried to comply with other parts of the Besk Stipulation. Judge Orrick reopened the case to examine continued problems relating to guaranteeing prisoners' safety, air quality, and confidentiality of legal visitation. He eventually ordered jail officials to develop a plan for improved conditions.

Jail No. 3 remained the oldest operating county jail in the state. San Francisco sheriff Michael Hennessey lobbied the city for money for a new jail; after bond issues failed in 1994 and 1996, a Supreme Court ruling in the Besk case finally cleared the way. "In sixteen pods of forty-eight inmates each in the new jail, deputies are positioned above twenty-four glass cells. An incident in any of the well-lighted cells could be spotted immediately," wrote the *San Mateo Daily Journal* in 2005. The new Jail No. 3 (now known as Jail No. 5), which can house 768 inmates, opened in 2006. The old jail was demolished in 2012.

The Peoples Temple

Jim Jones rose to public prominence in Indiana during the late 1950s as his Peoples Temple, an interracial congregation focused on aiding the sick, homeless, and jobless, grew to more than nine hundred members. Jones disliked the racism he perceived in Indiana and eventually looked for a more welcoming place to move his church. In 1965, he settled on Ukiah, California, where he felt the group's brand of social justice would flourish.

The Peoples Temple expanded into San Francisco in 1972, opening a church in the Fillmore District, which was then a low-income area populated largely by African Americans. The temple offered services that included testing for sickle cell anemia, free child care, and help collecting Social Security payments. In 1974, Jones, increasingly paranoid about government interference with his church and IRS investigations into his finances, moved again—this time to four thousand acres of jungle he leased from the government of Guyana in South America for the Peoples

FIG. 9-3A
The Peoples Temple was headquartered at 1859 Geary Boulevard in San Francisco from the early to mid-1970s, when the temple relocated to northwestern Guyana. Nine hundred and twenty congregants died in a mass suicide and killing there on November 18, 1978. Courtesy of the California Historical Society, MSP 3800.28.0691.

Temple Agricultural Project. In early 1977, just fifty members were living there, along with Jones and his wife, Marceline. But calls for an investigation of the group by former members, known as the Concerned Relatives, and an audit by the IRS led Jones to urge more members to move to the compound he called Jonestown. By the fall of 1977, about one thousand people, mostly African Americans from San Francisco, had heeded his call.

An article in the November 13, 1977, *San Francisco Examiner* then caught the attention of Representative Leo J. Ryan of San Bruno. "Headlined 'Scared Too Long,' the story recounted the death of Bob [Houston] beneath the wheels of a train on October 5, 1976, one day after he had announced his decision to leave the Peoples Temple," said an official report later submitted to the House Committee on Foreign Relations. Houston's father, Sam Houston, was an old friend and constituent of Ryan's. As Ryan's interest in the subject became known, letters from relatives of temple members began to arrive, and he met with a group of them. He began to investigate potential violations of federal and California laws.

Ryan left for Guyana on November 14, 1978, with nine reporters and eighteen Jonestown relatives. He had sent Jim Jones a telegram about the impending visit and immediately encountered suspicion and resistance. The delegation arrived at the Port Kaituma airstrip after dark on November 17. After traveling to Jonestown, Ryan's party was treated to a dinner and musical performance. Reporters casually interviewed members of the group throughout the evening, and Ryan briefly addressed the audience of about nine hundred. During his speech, he said, "For some of you, for a lot of you that I talked to, Jonestown is the best thing that ever happened to you in your lives." He received a standing ovation. But one member of the temple passed a note to NBC reporter Don Harris indicating his desire to leave immediately. Harris passed the note to Ryan, and the next morning, another member approached them, indicating covertly that she and her family desired to leave Jonestown.

That afternoon, on November 18, the delegation and fifteen Peoples Temple members began boarding trucks to return to the airfield and on to the United States. Jones was apparently not pleased to learn that members of the Peoples Temple were leaving, and, according to court documents, offered to pay at least one of them $5,000 to stay. After being seen in conversation with Jones and Peoples Temple security officers, group member Larry Layton suddenly announced his desire to leave Jonestown and boarded a truck. "Layton's announced defection surprised and concerned some of those who were leaving because they did not trust him, and believed he was feigning defection from Jonestown," court records said.

A six-seat Cessna and nineteen-seat Otter airplane had been arranged to take the group to nearby Georgetown, and the smaller plane arrived first. Layton insisted he be on the first plane. Although he tried to avoid being frisked, he was eventually deemed to be without a weapon and allowed to take a seat on the Cessna. After the Cessna was loaded, the Otter arrived, and the remaining passengers began to board. The Cessna taxied down the runway and was prepared to take off when a tractor-trailer burst onto the runway, crossed in front of the Cessna, and moved alongside the Otter. Peoples Temple members inside the truck opened fire. Several people in the Otter were wounded. Ryan, who was outside the plane, was killed, as were four others.

Those on the Cessna heard the gunfire, and Dale Parks, one of the Peoples Temple members leaving Jonestown, urged the pilot to stop. Another defecting member, Monica Bagby, suggested everyone leave the plane. But Layton insisted the plane take off. He pulled out a revolver and shot Bagby and Vern Gosney, another Temple member, wounding them both. The gun failed before he could shoot Parks. After a struggle, Gosney and Parks took Layton's gun. By this time, many people had escaped into the jungle, and Guyanese civilians were on the scene. They took Layton to local authorities, and he said, "I'm glad I shot [them]."

Meanwhile, Jim Jones put into action a plan for group suicide that Peoples Temple members had practiced many times before. By the time it was over, Jones and more than nine hundred followers were dead. Many had swallowed a cyanide-and-sedative-laced grape drink, while others appeared to have been injected with the drugs. A few were shot. Photographs of hundreds of swollen bodies in the intense jungle sun covered the front pages of newspapers and magazines around the world.

A few days later, in a voluntary written confession, Layton took responsibility for the deaths and injuries at the Port Kaituma airstrip. "I had begged the Bishop Jim Jones that I be allowed to bring down the plane, but he disapproved," Layton wrote. "I felt that these people were working in conjunction with the CIA to smear the Peoples Temple and to smear Guyana. I got a gun from a friend of mine, one Poncho, and I went to the airstrip intending to bring down the plane. But when the shooting started, I also started shooting as I thought it was all too late. I don't know why I did it."

FIG. 9-3B
Jim Jones staged this 1976 promotional photograph using market-bought fruit to show abundance and prosperity at the Peoples Temple Agricultural Project in Guyana, known as the Jonestown compound. Courtesy of the California Historical Society, MSP 3800.39.0883.

Layton was eventually returned to the United States, where he stood trial in district court in 1981 on four counts of conspiracy to commit murder and aiding and abetting in the killing of Leo Ryan and the injury of Richard Dwyer, the deputy chief of the mission. The proceedings resulted in a hung jury—eleven to one for acquittal—and Judge Robert Peckham declared a mistrial.

The government vowed to try the case again, and at the second trial, it asked that certain evidence that had been ruled inadmissible in the first trial be allowed. Peckham again ruled that the evidence—which included statements made by Jim Jones to Peoples Temple members that Ryan came to Guyana at his own risk and that temple members had taken weapons to the airport on November 18, 1978—was still not admissible, because the government had not adequately presented a case for conspiracy and some of the statements were hearsay. However, in 1983, a trio of judges at the Ninth Circuit Court of Appeals overturned Peckham's ruling, affirmed the government's case for conspiracy, and required the district court to admit the bulk of the evidence in dispute.

Due to evidentiary delays, Layton's second trial did not begin until November 18, 1986, the eighth anniversary of the Jonestown killings. The government's theory in the first trial had been that Layton "knew of the plot to kill Ryan and that he was involved in it," wrote Frank Bell, one of Layton's attorneys in the first trial, in a 2003 essay. Because that approach had not resulted in conviction, in the second trial the government "argued that there was an overarching conspiracy in the works at Jonestown, a conspiracy that was designed to keep the world from knowing about the conditions at the compound," Bell wrote. Because Layton had tried to kill people at the airstrip, he was part of the same conspiracy as those who had killed Ryan and was therefore equally guilty. "The system wanted to hold someone accountable," Bell wrote. "The system decided it should be Larry Layton, because everyone else who could have been held accountable was dead."

Layton, a former Quaker and pacifist who joined the Peoples Temple along with his mother and sister in 1968, "is not a man of violence," said defense attorney Tony Tamburello in his closing statement at the second trial. "November 18…was unique, bizarre, crazy." Nevertheless, in December 1986, a jury convicted Layton on all counts, and Peckham sentenced him to life in prison, as required by law. However, the judge ordered that Layton be considered for parole in five years, half the usual amount, and also gave him a year off for time already served, making his prison time possibly as little as four years. Peckham did not believe Layton had been a major member of the conspiracy, he explained at the sentencing hearing.

Layton went to prison but was released on $250,000 bail in March 1987 after filing an appeal. He requested a new trial, asserting that he had been denied effective counsel because "his trial lawyers failed to learn he faced a mandatory life sentence if convicted and decided not to put on an insanity defense," reported the Associated Press. This statement, made by Layton at an April hearing, represented the first time he had been willing to speak on his own behalf. He had not testified at either trial. Two months later, Peckham revoked Layton's bail and returned him to incarceration. In 1988, the Ninth Circuit Court of Appeals affirmed Peckham's ruling that Layton did not need a third trial.

"Five years later, Judge Peckham himself wrote letters to the parole authorities asking for Larry's release," noted Bell. "[Peckham] died before he could see those efforts through." In 2001, one of those shot by Layton in 1978, Vern Gosney, who had become a police officer in Hawaii, flew to California to testify in favor of Layton's release. Bell credits Gosney's statement with finally securing Layton's freedom. He was released in 2002, after eighteen years in prison.

Robert Aguilar's Legal Troubles

While the Layton case captured headlines, a district court judge faced troubles of his own. Much has been written about the FBI inquiry, wiretap controversy, and ensuing federal case that resulted in Judge Aguilar's departure from the federal bench in 1996, but he had raised eyebrows throughout his judicial career.

Appointed by President Jimmy Carter in 1980 to fill a new seat on the bench, Robert Aguilar came from the Santa Clara County Superior Court. He immediately shocked many by opting to run for his state seat again after being sworn in as a federal judge. Aguilar told the *National Law Journal* that he would make more money as a state judge and that he didn't think anyone running for his old seat was qualified. However, others speculated that Aguilar wanted to win the state seat again and then reject it to give Governor Jerry Brown, a Democrat, a vacancy to fill by appointment. Aguilar won enough votes to force a runoff election, but he was ultimately defeated at the polls.

Aguilar continued to make headlines during his first years on the federal bench. In 1982, Jose Robert Gomez-Soto and his son Peter were charged with plotting to kill Aguilar after he sentenced the elder Gomez-Soto to twenty years in prison for cocaine smuggling and tax evasion. That same year, Aguilar ruled that immigration officials could not prevent gay people from entering the country, and that authorities could not search for illegal immigrants on private property without a warrant. He also dismissed charges against three people accused of industrial espionage against IBM after the prosecution refused to provide FBI records that would have indicated IBM's involvement in the sting operation. But the attorneys appearing before him generally perceived the judge as fair. "He's got a lot of guts, and is not a tool of the prosecution," a veteran defense attorney told the *San Francisco Examiner* in 1983. "He follows the dictates of his own conscience and integrity and does what he thinks is right."

Born in 1931 to Mexican parents in Madera, California, Aguilar was the fifth of eleven children. His father taught himself to speak seven languages but never learned to read and write, and the family was on welfare until World War II, when Aguilar's father first got steady work. Aguilar attended UC Berkeley and Hastings College of Law, but he took frequent time off to earn money to pay for school. He completed his law degree in 1958.

Aguilar took the federal judgeship, he later said, partly because he wanted to pay back the nation for the opportunities it had provided his family. "After I became a judge, I sort of was sorry because the cut in pay was tremendous," he said. "As a judge I was making 25 percent of what I was making as a lawyer, and I had kids to send to college."

Starting in the late 1980s, Aguilar was the focus of a federal investigation that resulted in his 1989 indictment on four counts of obstruction of justice, two counts of illegal disclosure of wiretap information, one count of racketeering, and one count of influence peddling. Aguilar spent the next seven years in a legal fight to stay on the bench and out of jail.

The events that led to Aguilar's legal woes had their roots in 1980, when Teamsters official Rudy Tham was convicted in a San Francisco federal courtroom of embezzling $2,000 in union funds. Tham filed a motion in 1987 to have his conviction set aside. When he learned that the motion was assigned to Judge Weigel, Tham contacted Aguilar through Abe Chapman, a former mafia hit man and distant relative of Aguilar's. Soon after, Aguilar spoke with Weigel about the case, according to court records.

Meanwhile, federal investigators had become interested in Tham and Chapman as they looked into labor racketeering. Judge Peckham authorized a wiretap of Tham in April 1987. Four months later, agents noted meetings between Chapman and Aguilar and informed Peckham, who told Aguilar at a cocktail party that Chapman's name had appeared on a wiretap authorization. Shortly thereafter, Aguilar alerted Chapman to the possible presence of a wiretap. The FBI noted several more meetings between the two and in January 1988 received authorization to tap

Aguilar's phones at home and in his chambers. The next month, Aguilar sent his nephew to remind Chapman that his phones might be tapped.

A federal grand jury began investigating Aguilar in 1988 to determine whether he had participated in the alleged conspiracy to influence the outcome of Tham's embezzlement case. In 1989, Bay Area newspapers reported that the Department of Justice was preparing a racketeering indictment based on the findings of the grand jury. Aguilar hired attorneys, but he continued to hear cases until his indictment on June 13, 1989. Aguilar became the first federal judge to be indicted in California and the first in the nation to be indicted on racketeering charges.

In a 2006 interview, Aguilar said he thinks the problems started when he made a series of rulings against government police power that upset Joseph Russoniello, the Reagan-appointed US Attorney for the Northern District from 1982 to 1990. Aguilar issued a temporary injunction in 1989 to stop the Immigration and Naturalization Service from raiding factories and warehouses in search of illegal aliens. "Next thing I know, I get indicted…all of these counts," Aguilar said. "I was shocked that they came after me. Ridiculous." However, federal agents actually started investigating Aguilar well before the 1989 injunction. "The only thing that had any substance to it was that I revealed the existence of a wiretap to another person," Aguilar said in 2006. "Well, the wiretap, when I found out about it, no longer existed."

Russoniello, who served as US Attorney from 1982 to 1990 and again from 2008 to 2010, said that Aguilar is "revising history." He said that the US attorney's office recused itself from the investigation and prosecution of Aguilar from the first notice that the FBI and the Justice Department's Public Integrity Section were investigating Aguilar. Russoniello said he was careful to protect the integrity of the dozens of cases his office had before Aguilar during the pending criminal investigation.

"We played no role," Russoniello said in 2013. "We didn't interview witnesses; our entire office was recused," he said. "The Department of Justice created a team that came to San Francisco, and set up their own operation."

The day after his indictment, Aguilar recused himself from the thirty criminal cases before him in San Jose and 350 of his civil cases. He continued work on one hundred civil cases. Chief Justice William H. Rehnquist selected district court judge Louis Bechtle, who normally sat in

FIG. 9-4
Robert Aguilar, the district court's first Latino judge, was appointed in 1980 and was convicted of unlawfully disclosing a government wiretap and obstructing justice in 1990. The convictions were overturned by the Ninth Circuit in 1994, but the Supreme Court later remanded the case back to the Ninth Circuit, which again reversed the conviction. Aguilar took senior status and retired from the bench in 1996. Reproduced courtesy of the Historical Society and Archives, US District Court for the Northern District of California; photograph by Ira Nowinksi.

Philadelphia, to preside over the Aguilar trial in San Francisco. Proceedings began in February 1990. Tham and Chapman were co-defendants with Aguilar, but Aguilar was the only witness for the defense. Three district court judges testified for the prosecution. Judge Samuel Conti told the court that Aguilar called him in 1987 to talk about a former casino operator who was about to be tried by Conti for bank fraud. Conti said he changed the subject when Aguilar mentioned that the defendant was a friend. Conti told the court that he thought Aguilar's action was inappropriate but not criminal. Judge Weigel testified that Aguilar approached him several times before he heard the Tham case. Weigel said he did not think Aguilar was trying to pressure him and testified the inquiries seemed innocuous. Weigel refused an FBI request that he secretly tape Aguilar. Judge Peckham testified about telling Aguilar of the FBI investigation of Chapman.

Aguilar took the stand in the fifth week of his trial and on cross-examination denied every accusation. "I would never attempt to extort a United States district judge that I considered a judicial brother," Aguilar said. After 38 witnesses and 110 wiretap tapes, the case went to the jury. "There are things that were said and done that were foolish," Aguilar's attorney Patrick Hallinan summed up. "There were things that were said and done that were improper. But, ladies and gentlemen, we are not in church. We are in a court."

After more than a week of deliberation, the jury acquitted Aguilar on the count of obstruction of justice involving Conti but deadlocked on the other seven. Judge Bechtle declared a mistrial. Less than two hours later, district court judge William Ingram stated that Aguilar had the right to return to the bench full time, although he would not likely be able to hear criminal cases given the government's desire to retry him on the remaining charges.

After the first trial, the court granted a motion by prosecutors to dismiss two of the remaining seven counts. Aguilar was retried in August 1990. This time, a jury found him guilty of two charges—disclosing

Weigel v. the FBI

As it gathered information for the case against Judge Robert Aguilar, the Federal Bureau of Investigation sent two agents to call on Judge Stanley Weigel in 1989. Their plan was to interview Weigel about his relationship with Aguilar, but Weigel threw the agents off by recording their conversation. Excerpts from their barbed discussions (which never entered the court record) were published by the *San Francisco Recorder* a week after Weigel's death, in 1999.

FBI Agent Thomas Carlon: We came here to allay your fears that, uh—as to why some inquiry has been made of your whereabouts.

Weigel: You know, Mr. Carlon. I don't like that language. I don't have any fears. I have a certain amount of anger at the two-on-one approach. Do you understand that, sir?

Carlon: I can understand that. I appreciate that.

Weigel: Do you have any reason to believe I have been guilty of any wrongdoing of any kind whatsoever?

Carlon: Absolutely not.

Weigel: Well, you stop referring, if you will, please, to my fears or my concerns and mind your own business in that regard. Do you understand me?

Carlon: Yes, sir. But I perceived that that was a fear. Just by the way you acted, sir.

Weigel: Well, you thought I showed fear yesterday?

Carlon: I thought that you were—showed some form of anxiety as to why we made an inquiry.

Weigel: Do you think I'm showing it now?

Carlon: Absolutely not. Your Honor, please let me explain.

Weigel: You, please. You brought this on; you asked to see me.

FBI Agent Gordon Gibler: That's correct.

Carlon: Can I explain—

Weigel: I'll let you speak in a moment. But Mr. Carlon, I think you should mind your manners. I'm a federal judge and I'm entitled to be treated with respect and concern.

[Carlon assures the judge of their respect for him and explains that they did not mean to upset him.]

Weigel: All right, well, that clears that up. Now the next thing is, are you afraid, Mr. Carlon? You look a little nervous to me.

Carlon: Afraid?

Weigel: You look a little nervous. Are you nervous about something?

Carlon: I'm not nervous about anything.

Weigel: You look nervous to me.

Carlon: Well, have you seen me before? Do you know what I look like when I'm nervous?

Weigel: Well, I can generally—

Carlon: I'm not nervous.

Weigel: No, I'm just—I'm just using your tactics on me. You see, you ask me if I was nervous. I'm playing that back. You have to be careful about what you say. Would you agree?

A month later, the agents returned to ask Weigel if he would wear a microphone to secretly tape his conversations with Judge Aguilar.

Gibler: We need to ask you one more thing.

Weigel: All right.

Gibler: Along those lines.

Weigel: Yes.

Gibler: Because we're required to. Would you consider recording a conversation with him?

Weigel: Absolutely not.

Gibler: OK.

Weigel: That's a ridiculous request to make of a judge.

Gibler: Well—

Weigel: I really feel that was out of line. You may be required to do it, but to ask a judge to wear a voice recorder to entrap another judge I think is absolutely an outrageous suggestion.

Gibler: Your honor, believe me, I wasn't asking you to do something to entrap him. I wouldn't do that.

Weigel: Well, there's no purpose to it otherwise.

Gibler: OK.

Weigel: No, no—

Gibler: Again, like I said—

Weigel: No, no, I don't think you meant any offense.

Gibler: I didn't.

Weigel: But, uh, go ask Judge Peckham to wear a tape recorder. He'll be there tomorrow. There will be a lot of other judges there. Ask them to wear tape recorders.

Gibler: Again, your honor, I wasn't trying to be offensive to you in that regard.

Weigel: No, I don't think you were.

Gibler: I wasn't.

---

a wiretap and obstruction of justice—and acquitted him on the other three. The Ninth Circuit reversed both convictions in 1994. But in 1995, the Supreme Court reinstated the conviction related to Chapman's wiretap. On an eight-to-one vote, the justices disagreed with the Ninth Circuit's conclusion that Aguilar violated no law because the wiretap had expired by the time he disclosed it. The Supreme Court remanded the wiretap charge to the Ninth Circuit, which reviewed the case in January 1996 and again reversed the conviction.

While the Justice Department contemplated a third trial, prosecutors and Aguilar settled. Aguilar admitted disclosing the wiretap but denied breaking the law and acknowledged no other criminal wrongdoing. The charge against him was dismissed in exchange for his immediate retirement from the federal bench. He was allowed to retain his salary as part of this agreement.

More than a decade later, Aguilar still believes that the US Attorney was behind the charges and that he was targeted by the Reagan administration because he was a liberal Hispanic judge. "He didn't like me," Aguilar said of Russoniello. "I didn't take his crap; I didn't fit the mold that he had for a United States district judge."

Said Russoniello in 2013: "There is absolutely no truth to the proposition." As it turns out, Russoniello thinks that Aguilar benefited from the fact that the case was prosecuted by the DC-based public corruption unit rather than the US attorney's office in San Francisco.

"It's just unconscionable that he still harbors this animus," Russoniello said of Aguilar, who made rulings that were "outlandish, contrary to law, and arrogant" during his years as a district court judge. "He should re-examine what he did from the moment he was nominated to the bench until the day he resigned," Russoniello said.

Aguilar was asked what he learned from the experience. "Not to trust the government," he replied. "What they should have done, and it's what they do and I know as a fact that they do this, they come and visit you and say, 'Judge, we notice you hang around with this guy here. We want to warn you, as a word to the wise, disassociate yourself. You need not say another damn word.'... They've done that to other guys."

The other question that bedevils Aguilar is why the federal government went after him and not Judge Peckham, who testified in court that he told Aguilar about the wiretap. Aguilar said in 2006 that he agreed to step down because he was tired of the financial and physical drain of fighting. If convicted, he couldn't practice law and would not qualify for his pension and salary. "I had all these problems, I figured, why fight these bastards?" he said. "I've been here long enough to retire; I get my pension. Adios."

Aguilar also faced the prospect of impeachment if he returned to the bench, but he believes he would have prevailed. "I doubt very much that I would have been impeached," he said. "Congressman Don Edwards, a very good friend of mine to this day, told me not to worry about any impeachment process. He was on the Judiciary Committee, a longstanding congressman, highly respected by both sides of the aisle. 'It won't happen,' he said."

Aguilar has quietly continued his law work in San Jose. His troubles are not often discussed among the sitting Northern District judges, but his term remains a fresh wound. "It's almost twenty years ago, but I think it's still a black mark on the court," Judge Schwarzer said in an interview. "The judges who have come on, who were not there at the time, probably don't think much about it, but whatever the legal outcome, it was to me a very offensive episode."

A New Diversity

Born in 1938 near Amsterdam, New York, in the Mohawk Valley, Marilyn Hall Patel graduated in 1959 from Wheaton College, an evangelical Protestant liberal arts college whose motto is "For Christ and His Kingdom." "I was sixteen years old," she said in an interview. "My parents were religious. I wanted to go to school, and that's where I had to go." Patel, who is not proud of her conservative undergraduate education, had to sign a pledge that she wouldn't dance, drink, smoke, play cards, or go to the movies during her four years at Wheaton. Decades later, sitting in her district court office, Patel smiled at the thought. "I had a problem with not questioning and not doubting," she said.

From Wheaton, she returned to New York to attend Fordham University School of Law. Her choice of law was based on the Kuder Preference Tests aptitude survey. "I took them, and I believed them, because I didn't have any direction otherwise," Patel said. "My parents were not well educated. My father was very bright, but he had to drop out of school. My mother had not graduated from high school yet. I always came out high on being a lawyer."

She started at Fordham at age twenty and took four years to graduate because she worked during the day and attended school at night. She worked in private practice in New York City during her first four years out of law school, then moved to San Francisco in 1967 to work for the Immigration and Naturalization Service. She left in 1971 to return to private practice, becoming the legal vice president and counsel for the National Organization for Women, handling discrimination, employment, and immigration cases. Patel taught as an adjunct professor at Hastings College of Law for several years before Governor Jerry Brown appointed her to the Oakland-Piedmont Municipal Court in 1976. She was serving there when President Carter nominated her to the federal bench in 1980, a move that ended the Northern District Court's 129 years as an all-male institution.

"I would never make it now," Patel told a reporter in 1997. She said she would have been tripped up in the Republican-controlled Senate Judiciary Committee for her liberal connections—serving on the boards of the American Civil Liberties Union and Planned Parenthood as well as working for NOW. But at her confirmation hearing, "[Senator] Strom Thurmond never said a word to me," she told Howard Mintz of the *San Jose Mercury News*. "I got a couple of softball question and that's it." She sailed through the judicial hearings.

Judge Peckham noted at Patel's induction ceremony in 1980 that this was a "joyous and historical time" in the court's history. When she spoke, Patel gave the first hint at how much her presence would change the court. "Each of us brings to this position a variety of legal skills, backgrounds, and life experiences," she told the audience. "While there are some who, in a spirit of equanimity, would say it makes no difference whether the person is a man or woman, I would respectfully dissent. For the life experiences of women in this society are different from those of men. Those very experiences affect our perceptions and our judgment. No one's experiences are more valid than any other. Each is significant, and our exposure to each other can only enhance and enrich our collegial body."

In 1983, Judge Patel became the first federal judge to denounce the United States' internment of Japanese Americans during World War II when she formally corrected the Supreme Court decision in the 1944 conviction of Fred Korematsu. This is perhaps her favorite case, she said in 2006, because how often does a district court judge have a chance to overrule the Supreme Court? "The government wanted me to grant a motion that essentially would dismiss the charges against Mr. Korematsu, and that would be the end of it," she said. "And I said you can't do that. The law says that someone who has served some period of incarceration and was out on parole or probation, you might still have the power, but you lost that power years ago, you cannot do it." So Patel overturned Korematsu's conviction for violating a military order because she determined that the government had lied by telling the Supreme Court it was a military necessity to intern Japanese Americans.

The word most often used to describe Patel on the court is *fearless*. In 1991, Patel took on US Attorney General Richard Thornburgh for allowing prosecutors to interview defendants without their lawyers present. He made a "mockery of the court's constitutionally granted judicial powers," she wrote. For ten years she supervised the desegregation of the San

FIG. 9-5
Napster founder Shawn Fanning, flanked by attorney Jonathan Schiller (left) and company CEO Hank Barry, at a 2001 press conference in San Francisco, after district court judge Marilyn Hall Patel ordered the pioneering online music sharing service to halt the trading of copyrighted material. © Reuters/Corbis.

Francisco Fire Department. In 1988, she declared that the department was out of control and told top officials they would face fines and jail if they did not end the harassment of women and blacks in the department. Within days, Fire Chief Edward Phipps resigned.

"She saw the historic and persistent inequities in that troubled department and resolutely set about to right the wrongs brought to her by the plaintiffs," said Judge Henderson. She approved a settlement for hiring and promoting women and blacks and monitored a consent decree for several years. "Now the chief of the fire department is a woman," she said in 2006. "I take some measure of pride in that."

"Tough, Fearless Judge Marches to Own Drummer" headlined the *Recorder* in a 2002 profile. But that fearlessness sometimes led to charges of arrogance. Her nickname around the courthouse was La Supremacia, meaning "Your Supremacy," a name given to her by an immigrant in a pre-sentencing letter addressed to the judge. In 2003, the *San*

Francisco Daily Journal ran its own headline about Patel: "Fearless—and a Bit Scary."

Patel was considered the court's liberal standard bearer, but that description doesn't characterize many of her key decisions. She imposed stern sentences, especially against drug dealers. She sided with big business in the Napster case, ruling in 2001 that the Internet file-sharing service was violating copyright law. Patel will be known as "the judge who killed Napster" to many around America. "I raised the ire of all the teenagers in the country," she said.

"I really feel if you have lifetime tenure, that doesn't mean you just thumb your nose at society. You can't just go off on every issue you think you have something to say on and not follow the law," Patel said. "You have to follow the law, but there a lot of areas where there's discretion, and you shouldn't be afraid to exercise that discretion. After all, legislative officials have to run for office. They are concerned about their backs. I think they should be more courageous than they are. There are many courageous state court judges, but that's a tough job, they have to stand for election." Patel was not afraid to take an active role in controversial issues. She told colleagues at a judicial conference, "You have life tenure. If you don't have guts now, you are never going to have them."

From 1997 to 2004, Patel served as the Northern District's first female chief judge, helping establish electronic court filing, revising the way criminal defense lawyers are paid when representing indigent defendants, and helping give more responsibility to magistrate judges. "I've just been very lucky, a woman in the right place at the right time," Patel said in 2006. "My time has been very fortunate." She retired from the bench in 2012.

Judge Thelton Henderson was nominated to the district court on the same day as Marilyn Patel, was confirmed by the Senate on the same day, and received his commission on the same day. Born in Shreveport, Louisiana, in 1933, Henderson grew up in Los Angeles. "Back then if you grew up in South Central LA and you were going to be successful through education, you would go to college—generally state college—and you'd be a schoolteacher, a probation officer, a social worker, or some sort of government job," he said in a 2006 interview. "My mother said those weren't good enough for her son. 'You're going to be a doctor or a lawyer,' she told me. She had an eighth-grade education. She didn't know about science and other things didn't occur to her, so that was a successful person in her mind. So after looking at science and chemistry, which I hated and was not good at, law was the only thing left."

Henderson was primarily raised by his grandmother, Estelle Herring. "During those early years, I saw my mother only on weekends, because she was out living with other families and cleaning their houses, and my grandmother took care of me," he recounted at his 1980 induction ceremony. He attended all-black Jefferson High School and never would have considered college if his high school counselor, Isaac McClelland, had not called him off the high school football field in 1950 and asked about his plans. "Mr. McClelland personally sent for the forms and filled them out and sent them in, something I could not and probably would not have done on my own. So I went to college," he said.

Henderson attended UC Berkeley on a football scholarship (although a knee injury cut his sports career short) and graduated from Boalt Hall School of Law in 1962. He was soon working for the Civil Rights Division of the Department of Justice and frequently monitored voting in Alabama. Because Jim Crow laws were still in force, he often found himself in the same hotels as civil rights leaders, including Martin Luther King Jr., and over time they became friendly. When King's car turned up with a bad tire one night in a rough rural area, Henderson agreed to lend him his rental car—and inadvertently caused a scandal. Governor George Wallace cited the incident as evidence that the federal government supported King, and Alabama newspapers plastered this all over their front pages. Henderson resigned from his job and returned to California to practice law.

He practiced in Oakland until 1966, when he became directing attorney of the East Bayshore Neighborhood Legal Center in East Palo Alto. He served as assistant dean of Stanford Law School from 1968 to 1977, then returned to private practice, this time as a founding partner of Rosen, Remcho, and Henderson in San Francisco.

Henderson credits his law partners, Sandy Rosen and Joe Remcho, with badgering him to fill out the application for the federal judiciary that arrived in his mailbox from Senator Alan Cranston's office in 1978. They reasoned that with so few black attorneys practicing in federal court, Henderson might have an advantage. "Based on that shaky premise, I very reluctantly filled out the papers and turned them in on the last day they were due," Henderson recalled. "Miracle of miracles, a year and a half later—it was a very slow and painful process—I got the judgeship."

Since joining the court in 1980, Henderson has watched it change in many ways. "It's certainly much more diverse," he said. "I can remember when Marilyn and I first came on the court, the judges went down for lunch, and the hallway from the elevator to the lunch room wasn't carpeted like it is now. [She and I would] go together, because we were buddies. She was my best friend, and we sort of felt like outsiders so we hung out together—and I clearly remember the click-click of her heels, which you [could] clearly hear before we appeared, and the conversation would stop. We'd all say, 'I wonder what they were talking about?'"

When asked in 2006 about his most important cases, Henderson chose *Plata v. Schwarzenegger*, a current lawsuit against the state Department of Corrections that follows on from *Plata v. Davis*, alleging failure to provide sufficient health care to prisoners. Henderson noted that this is a key case because even the state has tacitly acknowledged that the system is broken. During one evidentiary hearing, Henderson found that on average a prisoner dies every six to seven days because of inadequate medical care. As he wrestles with this case, Henderson has also begun looking at the end of his career; he assumed senior status in 1998. "That's a massive case, it's a critically important case, and probably at this point is going to be, I hope, my last big case," he said. "I think I'll probably retire on this one if we're able to bring the system around and make it work."

Henderson also cited the Earth Island dolphin case as important in his career. Because they often swim above schools of tuna, hundreds of thousands of dolphins were being slaughtered as fishermen caught tuna in their nets. In 1990, Henderson ordered a ban on imported tuna unless the exporting country could prove it was not killing more dolphins than allowed by US law. "This led, I believe, to the dolphin-safe label and [to] the United States and other countries actually changing the way they go after tuna and the way they treat the dolphins that swim over the tuna," he later said. Subsequent rulings in 2000 and 2004 have ensured that the requirements for a dolphin-safe tuna label are not relaxed.

Henderson said one of his biggest cases had been a class action brought against State Farm Insurance over employment discrimination and gender discrimination: 1985's *Kraszewski v. State Farm*. Would-be agents were told that they needed a college degree or to put up a $10,000 investment in the office. Henderson ruled that this was illegal. Now, after years of regular reporting to the court, nearly 50 percent of the company's agents are women. "I think they saw the other shoe dropping, and they also now have many more minority agents," Henderson said. "One of the more gratifying things about [the case] is that eight or ten years ago I went to dinner with some of the boys in the 'hood where I grew up, and one of them came over while we were having cocktails and said, 'You know, I really owe you a lot,'" Henderson recalled. "This was a guy who [had been] a big athletic hero at the high school. I didn't know him that well, but knew who he was. It turned out that he was a struggling insurance agent, independent, and as result of *Kraszewski*, he got a job and was doing quite well."

A Court for Northern California

For much of the Northern District's history, the court has been rather San Francisco–centric. Those in the city often seemed to forget that a working federal courtroom had existed for decades 270 miles north in Eureka. Housed on the second floor of the federal building at Fifth and H Streets, the courtroom is full of antique oak furniture and Works Progress Administration murals that detail scenes of farm life and gold mining. Presiding over a case there in 1946, Judge Adolphus F. St. Sure told the Humboldt County Bar Association that the artworks belonged in a "cow palace," not a courtroom, and recommended that they be removed, so "they won't continue to frighten judges who come here," reported the *Humboldt Times*.

But for much of the twentieth century, few district court judges were faced with that possibility. Bankruptcy judges have long heard cases in the Eureka courtroom, and Social Security matters and National Labor Relations Board hearings are held there, but it was not until 1971 that Larry B. Nord was appointed to serve in Eureka as a magistrate judge. For more than twenty years Nord maintained a private practice in addition to his part-time work hearing Indian rights cases, fish and game violations, and Forest Service and Bureau of Land Management citations. Nord estimated in 1997 that only 25 percent of his time was spent hearing federal cases that originated in his jurisdiction, which includes Humboldt and Del Norte Counties and half of Mendocino and Trinity Counties.

However, in 1997, at the request of Chief Judge Henderson, Nord developed new procedures to handle the three hundred grievances filed each year by inmates at Pelican Bay State Prison. Nord would hear the matters in the Eureka courtroom or at the prison itself, greatly enhancing the likelihood that they would be processed in a timely manner. Nord remained the Eureka magistrate judge for more than thirty years before he retired in 2003. Magistrate Judge Nandor J. Vadas now sits in Eureka.

While Eureka was largely ignored, the 1966 authorization of federal court proceedings in San Jose and Oakland yielded cantankerous outbursts from a variety of sitting judges (and wild enthusiasm from others), although the debate over locations was hardly something new. Judge Ogden Hoffman held district court proceedings in San Jose for the first time in 1852. He was not impressed and famously described the experience to the *Recorder* as "a useless and almost ridiculous formality." In 1854 he convinced Congress that the district court for the Northern District of California could function in San Francisco alone, and it did so for the next 113 years. But eventually agriculture in the Santa Clara

FIG. 9-6
The courthouse view of the United States Courthouse and Federal Building complex along South First Street in San Jose. Courtesy of the Historical Society and Archives, US District Court for the Northern District of California; photograph by Ira Nowinksi.

Valley, south of San Francisco, gave way to urban settlements and a more educated population that was also more inclined to sue. Settling federal legal disputes involved a sixty-mile trip to San Francisco.

After much lobbying from judges who lived in Santa Clara County, as well as local attorneys acting as the Federal Court Advisory Committee, Representative Don Edwards introduced legislation that in 1966 allowed Northern District judges to hear cases in San Jose, Oakland, or Eureka, if the parties involved agreed. Having joined the district court with the specific goal of sitting in San Jose, Judge Peckham began lobbying to have cases originating in the San Jose area heard in San Jose, and in 1967 he held the first session there in more than a century, in a courtroom borrowed from the Santa Clara County Superior Court.

Although many, including a number of Peckham's fellow judges, hoped the San Jose experiment would fail, local attorneys soon warmed to the idea of trying cases closer to home, and the San Jose court received more and more business. In 1970, Peckham appealed to the Ninth Circuit and was granted a change in court rules that required all federal criminal cases originating in Santa Clara, San Benito, Santa Cruz, and Monterey Counties to be heard in San Jose. But Peckham still worked largely alone to keep the court alive. "We would periodically pack everything up and drive down here with the files and do San Jose business," former Peckham law clerk Robert Peterson said in a 1995 interview.

As the community grew more and more accustomed to having a federal court close by, local support swelled for the construction of a new federal building to house the district court as well as other government agencies that were renting offices around the city. The new building was approved around 1973, amid a federal spending crunch and an estimated six years before construction would begin. In the meantime, a temporary district court complex was dedicated in San Jose in 1973. It consisted of trailer-type buildings that Judges Peckham and Spencer Williams, another Santa Clara County resident, had found in San Diego and moved to Guadalupe Parkway and West Taylor Street. Edwards assured the crowd gathered for the dedication that this would be a temporary solution and that the Nixon administration considered a permanent federal building a high priority.

Some progress was made toward a full-fledged presence when Judge Ingram began sitting part time in San Jose shortly after he joined the court in 1976, but holding proceedings in the shacks, as the judges called them, introduced a number of problems, including security. "I think once they lost a prisoner who broke out of the trailer and took off," Judge Schwarzer said in a 1997 interview. Another time, an inexperienced court reporter and an extremely noisy furnace combined to produce a woefully inadequate record of proceedings, which eventually required the appeals court to set aside a guilty verdict.

The San Jose judges continued to fight for better accommodations and to make San Jose an equal partner in the Northern District Court. Ingram was hearing about half his cases in each location by 1980, and, in an attempt to show San Francisco attorneys what it felt like to travel to court, he began calling San Francisco cases at San Jose. Finally, in 1983, the rules for civil cases were changed so that those from the central coast counties could be filed and heard in San Jose. The rule change also provided for a full-time judge there, and Judge Aguilar moved his chambers to the shacks and became the first sitting San Jose judge. He tried the first criminal cases in a trailer before the actual courthouse was built, and later presided over the first jury trial in the new court facility.

During the early years of the San Jose court, only two trailers were available as courtrooms. So when Peckham and Ingram were hearing cases, Aguilar and Williams would occasionally have to hold court outside, underneath the walnut trees in front. "That's what would happen— justice outdoors, alfresco," Aguilar said. At least a dozen times, they set up a little table and conducted law and motion matters.

The courthouse that was built during the 1980s was inadequate from the start, Aguilar said. "The GSA [General Services Administration] will tell you it was the worst courthouse in the United States," he said. "It was built on the cheap—doesn't look like a courthouse. It was overcrowded when we got there." As the orchards surrounding San Jose disappeared and new companies opened, the court quickly matured, taking on the most securities fraud cases in the United States and the most patent infringement cases outside Washington. San Jose, with its mild climate, good transportation, and great universities, was an ideal center for the technology boom, and the district court responded quickly.

Even in cumbersome quarters, the San Jose court heard important cases, including the IBM theft scandal, in which employees of Hitachi and of Mitsubishi Electric were convicted of paying for confidential blueprints of an IBM computer processor. "The indictment of the two Japanese electronics giants drew worldwide attention to San Jose, and a horde of Japanese reporters to the makeshift temporary courthouse," reported the *Recorder.*

The temporary court was also the site of mafia boss Joe Bonanno's trial in 1981. Born in Sicily in 1905, Joseph "Joe Bananas" Bonanno was head of one of New York City's five mafia families for more than thirty years. He had been accused of running guns with Al Capone in the 1930s, "but was never found guilty of anything more serious than a misdemeanor violation of a New York wage and hours act in 1945," wrote the *San Francisco Chronicle.* Bonanno moved his business endeavors west in the 1960s and, with his health failing, eventually retired to Arizona. After fifty years on his trail—and four years of sorting through his garbage for evidence—federal authorities finally convicted Bonanno of a felony in 1981. He was seventy-five years old.

FIG. 9-7
Joseph Bonanno Sr. and his lawyer, Albert J. Kreiger, leave the San Jose courthouse after sentencing in 1981. © Fred Larson/San Francisco Chronicle/Corbis.

The trial lasted almost four months in Judge Ingram's courtroom, but Bonanno watched the proceedings from the judge's chambers via closed-circuit television because he was prone to heart attacks. Bonanno was charged with attempting, in league with his nephew, to obstruct a 1978 San Francisco grand jury investigating his two sons' business dealings. Ingram found Bonanno guilty and sentenced him to five years in prison and a $10,000 fine, the maximum, but reduced the sentence because of Bonanno's complaints of failing health in prison. Bonanno left prison in 1984 after serving less than eight months. He returned to prison in 1985 on a civil contempt charge after refusing to testify about the mafia. This time he served fourteen months. He died in 2002—a free man at age ninety-seven.

The long-promised San Jose federal courthouse, at 280 South First Street, was finally dedicated on May 3, 1985. When Judge Peckham died in 1993, the San Jose court facility was serving two million people in the four-county area. The next year, the San Jose Federal Building and United States Courthouse was dedicated again, this time in Peckham's honor.

Judge Schwarzer, among others on the Northern District bench, had not been in favor of a San Jose court. "I was never happy about the idea of dividing up the court, because I think it resulted in a loss of the collegial quality of the court, and we basically lost contact with the judges down there," he said in a 1997 interview. Yet even he was eventually won over. Nine years later, he said, "The San Jose branch of our court is [now] the leading court in the United States for intellectual property litigation. So retrospectively, it made a lot of sense."

The Bench Gets Bigger

New trial venues and a continually increasing caseload did increase the size of the bench in the Northern District, although according to the judges, the arrival of more jurists usually lagged behind the influx of new cases. In the early 1980s, the court replaced three retiring members with younger judges, but it would be some years before the bench would actually expand.

Eugene F. Lynch, a San Francisco native, joined the Northern District Court in 1982. Lynch, fifty-one years old, took over from retiring judge Charles Renfrew. Lynch received a bachelor's degree from the University of Santa Clara in 1953 and then served two years in the army. He graduated from Hastings College of Law in 1958 and began private practice in San Francisco. He was appointed to San Francisco's municipal court in 1971 and was elevated to the city's superior court in 1974. He was serving there when President Reagan tapped him for the federal judiciary.

In 1984, Judge Lynch began hearings in a case that would last for most of his remaining federal career. In December 1983, the *New Yorker* had published a two-part article by Janet Malcolm about psychoanalyst Jeffrey M. Masson that was later published as a book, *In the Freud Archives.* Malcolm had based her story on recorded interviews with Masson, but when the piece was published, Masson sued her for libel, saying she had fabricated quotes attributed to him that "falsely portray him as egotistical, vain, and lacking in personal honesty and moral integrity," court documents said. Malcolm's story quoted Masson referring to himself as an "intellectual gigolo" and claiming he would one day be hailed as "the greatest analyst that ever lived," except for Freud himself.

Proceedings began with Judge Lynch requiring Masson to amend his complaint to specifically identify the passages he deemed libelous. Eventually Masson settled on twelve offending passages. In a 1986 hearing, four of them were thrown out as essentially factual, and a battle began as to whether the remaining eight statements had been altered with malicious intent. Lynch gave an initial summary judgment in Malcolm's favor, which the Ninth Circuit Court of Appeals affirmed in 1989.

Masson refiled his lawsuit. In the subsequent trial, the jury found that Malcolm had defamed Masson with two of the story's quotations, but it could not come to a consensus on damages. Lynch ordered a new trial and also dismissed the *New Yorker* from the case because Malcolm had been a freelancer when she produced the story. The second trial yielded the same results: Masson "failed to prove reckless and deliberate alteration of his words to materially change their meaning," court documents noted. The Ninth Circuit affirmed this decision and barred Masson from pursuing further claims in the matter.

As an expert in and proponent of alternative dispute resolution methods, Lynch served as the court's designated settlement judge. He retired in 1997 to pursue a career in private mediation.

About a year after Judge Lynch joined the court, President Reagan nominated John P. Vukasin Jr. to fill the seat vacated by Stanley Weigel. Reagan and Vukasin were friends throughout their adult lives, and this was the third post in which Reagan had installed Vukasin. Born in Oakland in 1928 to Serbian immigrants, Vukasin attended UC Berkeley and served three years in the army between graduating in 1950 and receiving his law degree in 1956. He worked as a trial attorney for the Highway Division of the California Department of Public Works in 1956 and 1957, then opened a private practice in San Francisco. He transferred his practice to his native Oakland the following year and maintained it for nearly a decade before being appointed to the California Public Utilities Commission (by then governor Reagan). In 1974, four months after an unsuccessful attempt to place Vukasin on the First District Appeals Court of San Francisco, Reagan appointed Vukasin to the Alameda County Superior Court. Vukasin had worked on Richard Nixon's 1960 presidential campaign and served as vice chairman of Senator Barry Goldwater's presidential campaign committee, where he first came to know Reagan, the committee chairman. When a local paper endorsed Lyndon Johnson rather than Goldwater, "Vukasin issued a statement calling the endorsement 'an endorsement of street riots, of smut, the fast buck, and of ninety-mile-an-hour beer-drinking limousine drivers,'" reported the *Examiner*.

Despite some controversy, the Senate confirmed Vukasin, and he joined the district court in 1983. But the controversy did not go away. "Since his appointment...Vukasin has been called everything from homophobic to lazy, criticisms that date back to his days as an Alameda County Superior Court judge," wrote the *Recorder*. Members of the bar had labeled him "Judge Vacation" during his Superior Court days. "If I'm so tardy, how come I find myself, so often, waiting for attorneys to show up for scheduled appearances?" the judge responded in a letter to the *Recorder* in 1989.

In 1984, Vukasin alienated the local gay community by ruling that a Bay Area organization could not call its upcoming event the Gay Olympics, because the US Olympic Committee maintained exclusive rights to the word "Olympics." The Ninth Circuit Court of Appeals affirmed his decision. Vukasin's most famous case was the 1986 Jerry Whitworth spy trial, which resulted in a gargantuan sentence of 365 years. Such tough sentences were typical of Vukasin. He sentenced a member of the Hells Angels to forty years for selling two pounds of methamphetamine, rather than the ten years the man's probation officer suggested. When two former Oakland police officers were convicted in his courtroom of lying under oath about improperly using their sick leave, Vukasin sentenced them to publishing apologies in the Oakland newspapers and police newsletter, as well as reading their apologies three times each at department briefings. The two officers also received three years' probation and 150 hours of community service.

Despite the criticisms that seemed to follow Vukasin wherever he went, several attorneys praised his humanity on the bench and credited him with being an excellent listener. "To depreciate the value of his contribution to the community and the legal profession because he reached politically unpopular results in a handful of cases does injustice to Vukasin and undermines the integrity of the judiciary," wrote San Francisco attorney Daniel Girard in "Remembering a Judge," an article reflecting on Vukasin's career.

Vukasin also dedicated himself to the process of obtaining an official district court presence in Oakland. Beginning in 1987, he headed the Oakland courthouse committee. The 1966 legislation that allowed Northern District judges to hear cases in San Jose allowed the same in Oakland for cases from Alameda and Contra Costa Counties. However, as with San Jose, the process of making this a regular and eventually permanent occurrence was long and challenging.

The battle to create a district court in Oakland began in 1969 in a courtroom leased from the Alameda County Superior Court. Judge Lloyd Burke was assigned there, and in the ensuing years a few civil cases were heard there, although Burke continued to conduct most of his trials in San Francisco. The first criminal jury trial was not held in Oakland until 1974, after the superior court had reclaimed its space and new federal court facilities had been built in the old post office building at Thirteenth and Alice Streets. The case, drawn by Judge Peckham, involved a convicted felon charged with possession of an unregistered fire grenade, which had been transported over state lines.

In 1987, the General Services Administration and the city of Oakland began discussing construction of a new downtown federal building. In 1990, plans for twin eighteen-story towers were drawn up, and construction began at 1301 Clay Street. The $191 million Oakland federal building, now called the Ronald V. Dellums Federal Building and Courthouse (after the congressman—later Oakland's mayor—who was instrumental in acquiring federal money for it), was completed in 1993. The Internal Revenue Service, Department of Veterans Affairs, Department of Energy, and other federal agencies quickly moved in, but at the building's dedication the district court facilities were not ready. The district court had come to realize a need for more space than it had estimated, and funding constraints left the court without the money for the five-floor complex it needed.

Judge Vukasin died of cancer at age sixty-five on September 20, 1993. His funeral was held on the day the Oakland Federal Building was dedicated. Just over a year later, the actual United States Courthouse in Oakland was dedicated, and Judges Lowell Jensen, Claudia Wilken, and Saundra Armstrong moved their chambers there. Vukasin was not forgotten. Said Jensen, "He put in countless hours and trained his critical and constructive eye on virtually everything that took place here, from the crises that we had to the refinements that make this such a wonderful court."

The United States District Court for the Northern District now had four courts—in San Francisco, San Jose, Oakland, and Eureka—and was split into three divisions. The San Francisco Division included the counties of San Francisco, San Mateo, Marin, Sonoma, Napa, Lake, Mendocino, Humboldt, and Del Norte; the San Jose Division included Santa Cruz, Santa Clara, San Benito, and Monterey Counties; and the Oakland Division included Contra Costa and Alameda Counties.

A year after Judge Vukasin's appointment, yet another San Francisco native arrived on the bench; Judge Charles A. Legge replaced Judge Schnacke in 1984. Legge graduated from Stanford University and Stanford Law School, and he opened a private practice in San Francisco in 1956 after two years in the army. He specialized in complex commercial litigation.

While sitting in the Northern District of California, Legge issued a consent decree in one of the broadest-reaching decisions ever made in relation to the Americans with Disabilities Act of 1990, which required accessibility to public buildings, services, and employment for those with mental or physical impairments. Legge's national consent decree outlined the terms by which Equilon Enterprises and Shell Oil Products—the corporations that owned, leased, or operated some three thousand Shell stations in the United States—would conduct accessibility surveys at the gas stations and make improvements to meet the needs of customers with disabilities. Legge seemed to relish his role as mediator in many cases, and he retired in 2001 to pursue a career in private alternative dispute resolution. He remains in the San Francisco area.

National Security

Many remember the 1980s for rising interest rates and real estate speculation. The 1980s also inevitably saw an assortment of real estate fraud cases, but few were as bold as the one attempted by George Benny. In the 1940s and 1950s, Benny was struggling to make a life for himself in war-torn Budapest, Hungary. Trained as a civil engineer, he immigrated to New York in 1957. In 1965, Benny became a US citizen and made his way to San Francisco, where he found a job with Kennedy-Jenks Engineers designing sewer systems. His salary was about $36,000 a year when he left the firm in 1977 to try real estate. Less than five years later, he claimed to be worth nearly $200 million and presided over a property empire that included the largest condominium complex in San Francisco, property in Las Vegas, a Reno hotel and casino in need of renovation, a mansion once coveted by John F. Kennedy, and two buildings in downtown San Francisco—not to mention seventeen Mercedes Benzes. But then it began to fall apart.

Benny began his real estate career with the 1977 purchase of Diamond Heights Village, a 396-unit apartment complex near the Twin Peaks area of San Francisco that he quickly converted to condominiums. With the real estate market on a roll, the units sold quickly, particularly since many of them were transferred to Benny's friends and associates through special straw buyer arrangements. From 1979 to 1981, more than two hundred units were "sold" to buyers with good credit who made no down payment, paid no taxes, and made no monthly payments. They simply obtained the loan, kept their properties for a few months, and then deeded them back to Benny, who now had a low-interest loan for himself and a unit ready for resale. He hardly noticed the few thousand dollars he gave the "buyers" as thanks. This and related schemes netted Benny $40 million over four years, which he invested in other properties.

When a federal grand jury began investigating Benny in late 1982, six San Francisco deputy district attorneys, including two who specialized in white-collar fraud, were found to be among those who had temporarily owned Diamond Heights Village properties. Their degree of involvement with the scam was not immediately clear, and ultimately they were not indicted, although one attorney involved in the Benny litigation suggested to the *San Francisco Examiner* that, at the very least, they might be guilty of "felony stupidity." If so, they were not the only ones. Benny's charms were legendary. Robert Fitzpatrick, co-founder of Robert Dean Financial, recalled being so in awe of Benny when they met that he wrote him a check for $200,000 on the spot.

Even Judge Peckham was a bit amazed by all that Benny had accomplished. In 1983, when Peckham sentenced Benny to thirty years in prison for twenty-two federal counts of mail fraud and racketeering, he deemed the proceedings "one of the most extraordinary cases I've presided over in my judicial career" before sentencing Benny to twenty-eight years more than the two his attorney had hoped for. Benny showed no remorse, Peckham explained, and he had repeatedly perjured himself as he tried to justify his convoluted business. By this time, a number of other lawsuits—including a suit filed by the Chicago Title Insurance Company alleging that Benny had bilked it out of $17.6 million in a check-kiting scheme—had forced Benny into bankruptcy, and his vast fortune was collapsing. Benny served ten years in Leavenworth, Kansas, before being released on parole.

Also doing time at Leavenworth is Jerry Alfred Whitworth, convicted in the Northern District Court in 1986 of participating in one of this country's most devastating spy operations. And it wasn't even his idea.

Navy sailor John Walker Jr. met Barbara Crowley at a Boston roller skating rink in 1957. Their first date was a tour of the USS *Johnnie Hutchins*, on which Walker was stationed. After Barbara became pregnant, the two married in Durham, North Carolina, but their marriage was difficult from the beginning because of Walker's dedication to advancing his naval career and his long absences for duty. After years of yearning to be stationed on a submarine, Walker finally achieved his dream when the navy lowered its eyesight requirements in 1960. Soon Walker was off to submarine school in New London, Connecticut, once again leaving Barbara, and now their four children, behind.

By 1965, Walker was running the radio room as a communications officer on the USS *Simon Bolivar*, a nuclear submarine. Once, while Walker was on duty, another submarine had mechanical troubles at sea. Until she could be repaired, the *Bolivar* had to cover some of her targets. These were found in a thick book with a bright red binder and TOP SECRET-SPECAT (special category) printed on the cover, meaning even those with top-secret clearance needed special permission to look inside. The captain of the *Bolivar* gave Walker this permission. The book contained the Pentagon's playbook in the event of war with the Soviet

Union. Walker didn't need long to copy over the new assignments for the *Bolivar*, but, fascinated, he took his time looking through the book. He read as much as possible before locking it back in the safe. He later told Pete Earley, a *Washington Post* reporter and author of *Family of Spies: Inside the John Walker Spy Ring*, that he remembers wondering what the Soviets would pay for something like that, but he insisted this thought was merely idle curiosity.

Walker's career (and security clearance) continued to advance, while his marriage and financial situation deteriorated. In 1967, Walker became a watch officer in the message room at the Norfolk, Virginia, headquarters of the Atlantic Fleet. When on duty, all messages to and from submarines, naval stations, spy satellites, and warships in the sector came through him.

In late 1967, Walker stole his first document. He later described this as an impulsive act brought about by his depression over his finances and marriage. It was a KL-47 keylist, which contained the codes for the oldest cryptographic machine still in use. Walker later told journalist Earley he stole it because it was impressive-looking (stamped Top Secret), not because of its content. While Walker had the document on the photocopier, another officer walked by and chastised him for making a personal copy but didn't stop to investigate. Walker says this was the closest he ever came to getting caught. At the end of his shift, Walker smuggled the document off the base, but he couldn't sleep when he got home, so he drove to Washington. There, he took a cab to within a block of the Soviet embassy, slipped inside the gate just as a car was leaving, and announced, "I am interested in pursuing the possibilities of selling classified United States government documents to the Soviet Union."

The Soviets were skeptical but eventually determined Walker might be useful to them. The navy was just switching to nuclear submarine technology, and having a man on the inside would prove invaluable. Walker left with $1,000 and instructions for his first meeting, which would be in two weeks in Alexandria, Virginia. In the meantime he was to compose a list of the documents he could acquire.

At the Alexandria meeting, Walker received instructions for the elaborate dead-drop protocol for turning over documents (which involved leaving a soda can by the side of the road and disguising anything he had to turn over as trash), as well as his $4,000 weekly salary (he earned $725 a month as a warrant officer), plus a $1,000 bonus. In early 1968,

Walker delivered the keylist for a KW-7 cryptography machine, which the Soviets had specifically requested. His career in espionage was off and running, and it would eventually earn him more than $1 million.

In 1970, Walker had a post as commanding officer to instructors at a radio training school in San Diego, and soon Jerry Alfred Whitworth arrived as one of those instructors. Although their personalities were quite different, the two spent a lot of time together for the year they were both in San Diego. In the summer of 1971, Walker volunteered for sea duty off the coast of Vietnam, and in November he was named the system custodian of classified material for the USS *Niagara Falls*, a position that gave him prime spying opportunities once again. Although the United States had soldiers in Vietnam, Walker rationalized himself out of any responsibility for compromising their positions. The Soviets simply wanted a steady supply of keylists, he explained to authorities after his arrest: "If the KGB started giving the North Vietnamese information that I provided, word would have leaked out."

But other reports from that era belie Walker's theory. Vietnamese adversaries "usually had forewarning of the B-52 strikes," Theodore Shackley, a retired Central Intelligence Agency officer who was Saigon station chief from 1968 to 1973, told John Barron, author of *Breaking the Ring*. "Even when the B-52s diverted to secondary targets because of weather, they knew in advance which targets would be hit. Naturally, the foreknowledge diminished the effectiveness of the strikes because they were ready. It was uncanny. We never figured it out."

Back in California in 1974, Walker took Whitworth to lunch at a San Diego restaurant and introduced the idea of spying. Promising huge payoffs and little risk, Walker carefully couched his proposal in the most positive terms. He neglected to mention he was spying for the Soviets, and instead allowed Whitworth to believe the Israelis, allies of the United States, were interested in the information. This appealed to Whitworth's political sensibilities (he later told Earley he'd felt heroic at the time, and hadn't even been interested in the money), and he agreed.

However, Whitworth's time in the navy was up, and in early 1975 it took some convincing from Walker to get him to re-enlist and attend satellite communications school. The navy was in the midst of a communications overhaul and preparing to launch the first of four communications satellites. Just as Walker had provided valuable insight into emerging nuclear submarine technology, Whitworth now positioned himself to supply the details of cutting-edge satellite communication.

When he finished school, Whitworth requested and received a commission to Diego Garcia, an island hub for naval communications and a center for cryptography. In December 1978, Walker and Whitworth met at a hotel in Manila. For four months, Whitworth had been systematically copying the technical manuals for five new cryptographic machines, as well as the necessary keylists. He passed these documents to Walker, who in turn delivered them to his Soviet handlers in Vienna. After receiving these materials, the Soviets had a diagram of nearly every coding and decoding machine in the US arsenal. Federal prosecutors later characterized this as Whitworth's most damaging delivery, and intelligence experts estimated that the military eventually spent millions of dollars altering their coding machines or speeding new ones into production to counteract this espionage.

Walker left the navy for a career in private investigation in 1979, and by 1983 Whitworth was also thinking of leaving the navy and the spy business. However, he had by now become accustomed to the money and intended to turn over his remaining documents as slowly as possible. Walker remained Whitworth's liaison to their contact, whom Whitworth by now knew to be Soviet, but in early 1984, after a batch of information supplied by Whitworth contained a roll of fogged film, both Walker and the KGB became angry. Whitworth's payments were delayed for a while, and he and Walker argued in April. A few days later, Whitworth wrote to Walker that he was through being a spy. But this was not the only letter Whitworth had typed and sent.

On May 11, 1984, Janet Fournier, an investigative assistant in the San Francisco FBI office, opened a letter addressed to "Agent in Charge." Signed "RUS," the letter appeared to be from a spy. It outlined what he had been doing, identified his receiver as the Soviet Union, and provided a means to contact him through a personal ad in the *Los Angeles Times*.

While the San Francisco FBI played cat and mouse with Whitworth, agents in the Norfolk, Virginia, office got a much more straightforward contact: Barbara Walker. By now the Walkers had been divorced for ten years, and Barbara had been an alcoholic longer than that. She had known of Walker's spying since 1968, when she stumbled upon the tiny Minox camera he used to photograph documents. Over the years, Walker had learned to ignore her threats and demands for money. She had no better luck with the FBI. The Boston office referred her to a small office in Hyannis, Massachusetts. An agent spoke with Barbara and her daughter Laura but believed their story to have little merit. "I decided that no one really cared," Barbara later told Earley. "John had gotten away with it, and there wasn't anyone who was going to stop him."

In 1985, the Hyannis office presented Barbara Walker's story, and agents in Norfolk, where Walker was living, took notice. Special Agent Joseph R. Wolfinger, trained in Soviet espionage techniques, recognized the elaborate procedures Barbara described right away. They were textbook descriptions of Soviet spy practices. Soon the agents had wiretaps on Walker's phone and began monitoring his movements. In a follow-up interview, Barbara mentioned that a friend of her ex-husband's named Jerry Wentworth might also be involved in the spy scheme.

Meanwhile, the San Francisco FBI had been trying for eight months to contact RUS, but to no avail. Whitworth had changed his mind about terminating his spy career. He had failed the stockbroker's exam and had no success as a computer salesman, so he wrote another letter to Walker to try to patch things up. But the FBI was putting the pieces together. At the end of April 1985, the FBI's counterintelligence unit surveyed all ongoing investigations. Both RUS and John Walker seemed to have been involved in espionage for nearly twenty years—could their cases be related? Further conversation with Walker's daughter Laura gave agents the correct name of his potential co-conspirator. Rather than Wentworth, agents in California now began searching for Whitworth.

Phone taps on Walker soon paid off, and the FBI learned of an important meeting set for May 18. Agents trailed him to rural Maryland and watched him deposit items at the side of the road. Unfortunately, an unwitting agent collected the 7UP can Walker placed as a signal to the Soviets, so the drop was aborted. Nevertheless, the documents were recovered, and Walker was arrested. Included in the batch of materials he had intended to deliver were a study of problems with the Tomahawk missile, schematics of the missile defense system aboard the USS *Nimitz*, and the codes needed to launch the United States' nuclear missiles.

On May 20, hours after Walker's arrest, FBI agents knocked on the door of Jerry Whitworth's trailer in Davis, California. Invited inside, agents told Whitworth they believed he was John Walker's accomplice. Whitworth took this in for a moment and then said he needed some water. He got up from the dining room, where the three were seated, and walked into the kitchen. But instead of getting a drink, he kept going and headed into the den. The agents dashed after him and got there just in time to see him hide a floppy disk under the computer's keyboard.

Whitworth then said he would like to explain his relationship with Walker. After agents read him his rights, he spent two hours reviewing his naval career and explaining that he didn't much like or trust John Walker. Toward the end of the interview, the agents showed Whitworth a copy of the first RUS letter. When asked if he recognized it, Whitworth simply stared at it for more than a minute. He then said he would like to speak to an attorney. One of the agents asked Whitworth if they could search the trailer, and he agreed. One of the first items found was the floppy disk under the computer. It contained a letter to John Walker in which Whitworth asked if he could rejoin the spy ring.

Whitworth was put under constant surveillance because the FBI's case against him remained circumstantial. Despite all they had, they lacked proof that Whitworth had passed a confidential document to Walker. Weeks went by. Walker's arrest, as well as the arrests of his son Michael and brother Arthur (whom he had also recruited as spies), became international news. Agents found both Walker's and Whitworth's fingerprints on stolen documents in Walker's home, conclusively linking the two. The Justice Department then issued an arrest warrant for Whitworth, who drove to San Francisco to turn himself in.

Each member of the spy ring was given a separate trial, beginning with Arthur, who had spoken to a Baltimore grand jury in May and virtually sealed his own fate. He was convicted and sentenced to life in prison and a $250,000 fine. The severity of the sentence unnerved Walker, and he ordered his attorneys to make a deal. When the FBI showed Walker the RUS letters that Whitworth had allegedly written, Walker gave him up. Despite this, Whitworth maintained his innocence, and it seemed Walker's testimony would be the only thing that could prove Whitworth was a spy. The Justice Department was reluctant to make a deal with Walker, but when the case against Whitworth began to look shaky, the FBI agreed. Walker would testify against Whitworth in return for consideration during his own sentencing, as well as leniency in sentencing his son.

In an assortment of pretrial hearings, Judge Vukasin ordered that Whitworth be provided a public attorney. Despite allegedly having received $332,000 from the Soviets, Whitworth maintained he could not afford an adequate defense. Whitworth faced a maximum sentence of life in prison for each of the espionage charges against him.

The trial began, and both sides focused on Walker. "John Walker was the consummate trickster for almost twenty years," said defense attorney Tony Tamburello. "There will be no evidence that Whitworth conspired with the Russians. It was all John Walker." US Attorney William Farmer agreed that Walker had started the spy ring and recruited Whitworth but said Walker's testimony and a "diary of evidence" would show Whitworth was equally complicit.

The prosecution began its case by giving everyone in the courtroom a course in American security systems. Expert after expert testified, and a coding and decoding machine was demonstrated for the jury. The real drama began a month into the proceedings, in April 1986, when John Walker himself took the stand. "It seemed to me that he had enough larceny in his heart that he would be willing to commit espionage," Walker said of Whitworth. Walker described how he had recruited his brother Arthur as a spy in an attempt to help him. "Being the good-hearted person that I am, and if he could get access to classified material, I figured I would get him on the gravy train as well," William Carlsen of the *Chronicle* reported him as saying. Walker also explained his failed efforts to recruit his daughter Laura as an attempted remedy to her dire financial situation.

Emotional testimony from Laura and from Walker's ex-wife Barbara followed. Because her contact with the FBI had led to Walker's arrest, Barbara was granted immunity from prosecution. In May, Walker's twenty-three-year-old son Michael became the last member of the family to testify. "I did it for the money and to please my father," he confessed.

"With its soap opera–like labyrinth of intimate details, the story of the Walker Family Spy Ring, as it has come to be known, continues to be the main focus of a trial in which forty-six-year-old Whitworth sometimes appears as an almost subsidiary figure," reported Gene Ayres of the *Oakland Tribune*. But prosecutors eventually turned their attention to Whitworth, focusing first on tax evasion and then on spying. Whitworth himself did not take the stand. "Mr. Whitworth has no defense to the income tax evasion charges, and for him to admit that on the stand would affect his credibility as to the other charges," attorney James Larson said. After three months of testimony from 141 witnesses, the prosecution concluded its case against Whitworth.

FIG. 9-8
Jerry A. Whitworth, a former navy radioman, received a 365-year sentence in 1986 and was fined $410,000 for supplying cutting-edge communications to the Walker Family Spy Ring. © Bettmann/Corbis.

The defense got a boost when Judge Vukasin ruled that he "would instruct the jury that the government is bound to prove that Whitworth passed navy secrets to confessed spy John Anthony Walker Jr. with the intent or reason to believe that it would aid the Soviet Union or injure the United States," reported the *Washington Post*. "Vukasin's ruling could be of critical importance for Whitworth's defense, which hopes to convince the jury that Whitworth did not know the material was going to the Soviets." Whitworth's defense then decided to stake their whole case on this point. "The issue here isn't whether or not the material was passed but whether or not Mr. Whitworth knew he was spying for the Soviet Union," Larson said in his closing statement for the defense.

After ten days, the jury found Whitworth guilty of twelve of the thirteen charges. After his conviction, Whitworth did admit to being a spy, and professed to being extremely sorry during a pre-sentencing evaluation. Yet he maintained he had not stolen all the documents that Walker said he had. Vukasin, who described Whitworth as "one of the most spectacular spies of the century," sentenced Whitworth, then forty-seven, to 365 years in prison—with no possibility of parole for sixty years—as well as a $410,000 fine. "Jerry Whitworth is zero at the bone," the judge said. "He believes in nothing. His life is devoted to determining the wind direction and how he can make a profit from the coming storm." A few months later, Walker received two life sentences plus one hundred years, to be served concurrently. He would be eligible for parole in 2015.

A Republican Tilt

Three new judges joined the Northern District in the late 1980s to replace judges assuming senior status. President Reagan nominated Delwen Lowell Jensen in 1986 and Fern M. Smith in 1988, and President George H. W. Bush nominated Vaughn Walker in 1989.

Judge Jensen was born in Brigham City, Utah, in 1928 and came to UC Berkeley to attend college. He graduated from Boalt Hall in 1952 and spent two years in the army. After a year of private practice in Oakland, Jensen began working his way up the hierarchy in the Alameda County District Attorney's Office. He served first as a deputy, then an assistant, and finally as district attorney for Alameda County from 1969 to 1981.

"I tried a Black Panther case where Huey Newton was accused of killing an Oakland police officer," he recalled. "I tried the sit-in at [the University of California's] Sproul Hall, where some 780 people were arrested. We had a trial in Berkeley with fifty-five defendants that we'd collected. They were convicted of trespass and in some instances of resisting arrest because they went limp, which was an issue at the time." Retired superior court judge Richard Hodge, who was then the attorney opposite Jensen in defense of another group of protesters, told the *San Francisco Daily Journal* in 2003 that Jensen never gave in to the conservative backlash against Black Panthers and war protesters.

As district attorney, Jensen personally brought one of the first cases against the Symbionese Liberation Army when Joseph Remiro and Russell Little were prosecuted for the murder of Oakland school superintendent Marcus Foster. Both were convicted, although one later had his sentence overturned because of improper jury instructions. Jensen also later prosecuted William and Emily Harris for kidnapping Patty Hearst.

Starting in 1981, Jensen took three appointments in the Reagan administration: assistant attorney general for the criminal division of the Department of Justice from 1981 to 1983, associate attorney general from 1983 to 1985, and deputy attorney general from 1985 to 1986. He then joined the Northern District court, filling the seat vacated by Judge Orrick. At his induction in 1986, Jensen explained that his role as a prosecutor included special responsibilities: "You not only represent the people of California, or the people of the United States, but you have a positive duty and a responsibility to protect the rights of the accused. And now we even recognize that prosecutors have critical responsibilities to victims and witnesses." Attorney Leo Sullivan said at the ceremony, "Lowell, you are a prosecutor with a great deal of compassion. I have seen your heart swell up to the size of buckshot. I hope it is a little larger than that."

In a 2006 interview, Jensen said he knew little about federal law when he was appointed—"The first federal trial I ever really went to, I was the judge." Jensen doesn't know exactly when he first became interested in law, but he was majoring in pre-law when he started at Berkeley as an undergraduate. "It was just something that grew over a period of time," he said. "I don't have any role models in my family who are lawyers. It just came about that I thought the law would be an interesting thing to do."

Jensen, long a resident of Alameda County, began his federal judgeship in San Francisco. After years of commuting across the bay, "I watched with interest when they decided maybe they'd open up a court over here," he said. "Ultimately they did, and I volunteered to stay on this side of the bay." During the establishment of the Oakland court, district court judges decided to combine civil venues for Oakland and San Francisco. "So if you filed a case in Oakland, you could get assigned to Oakland or San Francisco, and vice versa," he said. On the criminal side, however, the venues are separate. "The question was, are the lawyers going to be unhappy about that?" Jensen said. "The answer has been, the lawyers don't mind. You can get to Oakland probably faster from downtown Market Street, where a lot of law firms are, than you can get to the courthouse in San Francisco."

Jensen balks at discussing "important" cases. "I don't know that the cases could be described as important contributions to the law," he said.

"I'm in a trial court on purpose. I didn't want to be in an appellate court. The important things I've done are to resolve civil and criminal actions. I think that's the whole purpose of being in a trial court, and I think that's my contribution—to actually resolve disputes."

His best-known decision was the 1995 case of George Franklin Sr., who became the first person in the United States to be convicted of murder based solely on repressed memory. Jensen overturned the conviction after Franklin served six years in prison. He was convicted in 1990 in state court of the murder of eight-year-old Susan Kay Nason after his daughter, Eileen, said she had witnessed the killing of her best friend. That memory, she said, was recovered twenty years after the incident. The California Supreme Court affirmed Franklin's murder conviction, and the case then came to federal court on habeas corpus grounds. It was one of the first high-profile cases where key testimony was based on repressed memory. The question became whether this sort of memory should be admissible.

FIG. 9-9
George Franklin Sr. is greeted by investigator Leslie Harrison (left) and attorney Kristine Burk as he leaves the San Mateo County Jail in 1996. © Lea Suzuki/San Francisco Chronicle/Corbis.

Jensen's examination of the case focused on how the state trial had been conducted. He determined that after Franklin's daughter testified as to her recovered memory,

> the defense was not allowed to put on evidence that some of her testimony had appeared in the public papers. The argument was made that she must be telling the truth because the only way she could know the truth was by being there. But when you don't allow the papers to be introduced that could be a source of the information other than her own observation, I found that to be an error of constitutional proportions. The other error was that the daughter had gone to visit her father [in prison] and had asked him some question about why he did it....He had pointed to a sign that said 'These conversations are being monitored,' and he said nothing. That was allowed as evidence of his guilt on the basis that he had failed to answer when she asked that question. That was a constitutional error. The state court had said it's a harmless error. I said it couldn't conceivably be harmless.

Those two mistakes were sufficient for Jensen to reverse Franklin's conviction.

Fern Smith, a native San Franciscan born in 1933, was at home raising her two daughters, six-year-old Julie and ten-year-old Susan, when she decided to return to school full time and finish college. Her daughters and husband, Bob Burrows, didn't always agree with the decision, Smith later recounted, but she graduated from Foothill Community College in 1970, Stanford University in 1972, and Stanford Law School in 1975. After eleven years in private practice in San Francisco, she became a judge for the San Francisco County Superior Court. Two years later she was elevated to the federal court and took the seat of Judge Conti, who had assumed senior status.

One of her first law clerks, Peter Jakab, recalled his job interview with Smith at the Boston home of Smith's elder daughter. Smith was visiting her family, including her seven-month-old granddaughter Julia Morgan. They sat in the living room, the new judge asking questions about federal securities law, antitrust statutes, federal rules, and civil procedure. "The judge greeted me at the door with Julia in her arms, introductions were done, and we retired over to the living room where the three of us sat down," Jakab said years later. "Judge Smith and I sat in chairs and Julia sat in the judge's lap." For the next half hour, Judge Smith tended to the baby's every need. She held the baby close, coaxed smiles from the baby, laughed with the baby, and fed the baby—while conducting the interview. "Ever since, I've always thought that in those thirty minutes I learned more about life than I did in my entire twenty years of formal education," the law clerk said.

In 1991, Smith helped define the emerging gaming industry by ruling that the Game Genie Video Game Enhancer did not infringe on Nintendo of America's copyright, even though it temporarily altered their games. She awarded the enhancer's maker, Galoob, $15 million for profits lost during litigation. In 1993's *United States v. Reese*, Smith presided over the criminal prosecution of four housing authority police officers accused of using excessive force. She instructed the jury specifically about how to weigh their decision, noting that they needed to find that the officers had intended to use more force than necessary in the situation. The Ninth Circuit Court of Appeals upheld her instructions (and the resulting conviction) over the defendant's claim that specific intent requires that the officers knew the amount of force in question was illegal.

Smith was also not afraid to tackle the war on drugs. Her preliminary injunction in 1997 prevented the Clinton administration from implementing a plan to punish doctors who recommend marijuana to their patients under California law. Smith said prosecuting doctors because of the recommendations they offer patients would infringe their right to free speech.

In 1999 Smith became the Northern District's second delegate to serve as director of the Federal Judicial Center in Washington, DC, a post Judge Schwarzer had held during the early 1990s. Smith returned to the Northern District and assumed senior status in 2003. She retired two years later and joined JAMS, the nation's largest private provider of alternative dispute resolution services. Smith is based at JAMS San Francisco Resolution Center, but she works to resolve cases throughout the world.

Vaughn Walker was one of President Reagan's final choices for the district court and President George H. W. Bush's first choice. Walker's first nomination to the court, by Reagan, was stalled in the Senate Judiciary Committee because he had represented a slew of controversial clients and because he was a member of San Francisco's all-male Olympic Club, which didn't admit a black member until 1988 and still excludes women. Walker balked at resigning from the club, saying he preferred staying and working on reform, and continued his daily swim there for almost a year. But when Bush re-nominated Walker in 1989, Walker gave up his membership and was eventually confirmed by the Senate. That was the first hint of Walker's independence and unpredictability.

"Unpredictable?" he asked during a 2006 interview. "Where did you get that?" He smiled, and said, "I would certainly prefer that reputation to being considered a judge who always came down on the side of the prosecution, or was a weeping, bleeding heart for the criminal defendant or somebody who comes in with a sob story." But more seriously, Walker said, "To the extent that it applies that you are erratic, or that you are guided by flip-of-the-coin considerations, obviously it is pejorative."

Born in 1944 in Watseka, Illinois, Walker was a young man when he first became interested in how to work out problems through debating and argumentation. His high school did not have a debate team, but Walker entered speech and oratory contests and later joined the varsity debate team at the University of Michigan, where he majored in economics. After college, he briefly studied economics. "With some reluctance, I went to Berkeley," he said. "I thought California was a strange place with odd people and weird lifestyles and so forth (all of which is completely correct). When I got out here, after about six weeks, I realized that I liked it."

But he also figured out he wasn't cut out to be a professional economist. He tried combining economics and law at the University of Chicago but hated the weather and missed California. He returned when he was accepted at Stanford Law School, from which he graduated in 1970. He clerked for Judge Robert J. Kelleher, a district court judge for the Central District of California, from 1971 to 1972, after which he worked as a business lawyer with Pillsbury Madison & Sutro in San Francisco, where he specialized in antitrust work and became a partner in 1978. He won high marks as a lawyer but got tripped up on his nomination because he represented the National Rifle Association as well as the US Olympic Committee in its effort to stop Gay Olympics organizers from using the word "Olympics." He told the *New York Times* in 1989 that his representation of clients did not reflect his own philosophy: "A lawyer acting in a professional way must divorce himself from personal views. The effective representation of a client requires that you do that."

His years on the court contradict the dominant view of Walker as narrowly conservative. He publicly called for the decriminalization and regulation of drugs, but said, "I hope no one has got the impression that I believe using narcotics is good or helpful." In 2003, Walker sentenced a man for stealing letters from mailboxes to two months in jail—and ordered him to stand outside the San Francisco post office for one hundred hours wearing a sign that read "I have stolen mail. This is my punishment."

Walker has gotten more than his share of major cases. In 1992, he found that Apple's licensing agreement with Microsoft covered most of the distinctive elements of the screen design in dispute, and ruled that other appropriated features were not copyrightable. A dozen years later, Walker ruled that antitrust laws did not prohibit Oracle from purchasing PeopleSoft; he judged that the $7.7 billion hostile takeover would still leave substantial competition in the market. In 1998 and again in 1999, Walker threw out a $30 million lawsuit filed by Golden State Warriors basketball player Latrell Sprewell against the Warriors and the National Basketball Association. Sprewell, suspended for six months for assaulting coach P. J. Carlesimo, argued that the suspension violated his rights and restricted his ability to play. Walker, who had never heard of Sprewell, said the lawsuit was a "wasteful diversion of this court's resources."

In 2010, Walker ruled that California's ban on same-sex marriage, known as Proposition 8, was unconstitutional under the due process and equal protection clauses. "Proposition 8 fails to advance any rational basis in singling out gay men and lesbians for denial of a marriage license," he wrote in his 136-page opinion. "Indeed, the evidence shows Proposition 8 does nothing more than enshrine in the California Constitution the notion that opposite-sex couples are superior to same-sex couples."

Walker said that one of his biggest decisions was his 2001 ruling not to allow former American prisoners of war who were held in Japan during World War II to sue for reparations against Japanese firms. Walker ruled that the peace treaty signed in 1951 settled all forced labor claims by American soldiers, and he wrote that a lawsuit seeking to bring such claims "infringes on the federal government's exclusive power over foreign affairs."

His most enjoyable case, he said, was *Reilly v. Hearst*, in which millionaire Clint Reilly sued to stop the sale of the *San Francisco Chronicle* to the Hearst Corporation and the sale of the *San Francisco Examiner* to the Fang family. Reilly, who had run for mayor of San Francisco, charged that the deal violated antitrust law. From the first day of testimony, when *Examiner* publisher Timothy White told the court he promised San

Francisco mayor Willie Brown favorable coverage if Brown supported the sales, the trial opened the lid on the newspaper industry. "It was great fun," Walker said. "I don't think I ever enjoyed a case that much. There was a lot of San Francisco lore in the case."

Walker ruled that the Hearst takeover of the *Chronicle* from the de Young family did not violate antitrust law, and that Hearst could then rid itself of the unprofitable *Examiner* to the Fang family, who at the time published the *San Francisco Independent*. Hearst bought the *Chronicle* for $660 million, merged the staffs of the *Chronicle* and *Examiner*, and promised to make it a world-class newspaper. Walker expected the *Examiner*—given to the Fangs with a $66 million subsidy—to survive, but after it was remodeled into a free daily newspaper, Walker was not so sure: "It is a functioning newspaper—but altogether different, with a new business model." Later he acknowledged, "None of the experts envisioned this."

In 2006, Walker bucked the Bush administration by refusing government efforts to dismiss a lawsuit over its terrorist surveillance program. The suit argued that AT&T and other phone companies illegally shared information on millions of phone calls and e-mails with the National Security Agency after the September 11, 2001, attacks. The Department of Justice argued that the lawsuits would endanger national security, but Walker ruled that there was no risk because the administration had already acknowledged that it authorized wiretaps without a warrant. The lawsuit involves "ongoing, widespread violations of individual constitutional rights," wrote Walker, concluding, "Dismissing this case at the outset would sacrifice liberty for no apparent enhancement of security."

Because of his tenure, Walker was named chief judge of the court in 2004, a position he held until his retirement in 2011. Although he said he had no agenda, economics was never far from Walker's thoughts. "The cost-benefit calculus that economists have given us is implicit in many legal decisions, particularly common law," said Walker, a libertarian. District courts, he said, were established primarily to encourage commerce across states. The court's jurisdiction—patent and trademark disputes, job discrimination, lawsuits filed by a person in one state against a person in another state, even civil rights cases—all center on business. "The importance in deciding commercial disputes is key to what we do," he said. "I think that's the real service that we perform."

Although Walker dismissed the idea that the court's primary function is to make a better world, he saw the district court model as the key for building progressive nations. "When you see countries moving away from a centralized economic region, what they are struggling to develop is some kind of dispute resolution mechanism analogous to our court system," he said. "They are actually following our model fairly close in many respects."

District courts, Walker said, do go beyond settling business disputes. "One of the most interesting things about being a judge and seeing things from the judge's perspective is we don't have a beacon that shines a light on the path that we should go on," he said.

> All we can do is kind of light a little flickery match or a ray. And consequently everything is somewhat tentative. At least at this level we engage in balancing multifactor tests, weighing this factor and that factor and so forth. It's different from a court that deals with constitutional issues, looking at principles. It's trying to solve these problems that are narrower, and don't necessarily admit clear-cut answers.
>
> There is no doubt that judicial decisions are informed and biased by the times in which they occur, as well, of course, as by the poor souls who are making those decisions. Those poor souls have all the frailties of human beings.

CHAPTER 10

MODERN TIMES

THREE DISTRICT COURT LUMINARIES—Robert Peckham, William Ingram, and William Schwarzer—assumed senior status during the first years of the 1990s. James Ware, the third African American judge, replaced Peckham in 1990. The following year, Saundra Brown Armstrong, the third woman and first African American woman, replaced Ingram, and Barbara A. Caulfield, the fourth woman, replaced Schwarzer. All of a sudden, this was a new court.

Born in 1946 in Birmingham, Alabama, James Ware became interested in the law as a boy. His father, a coal miner, used to tell him inspiring stories about black lawyers. "When you are in the South and growing up, you are either going to be a preacher, or a teacher, or in my case a lawyer," Ware said. "That was his wish for me, and that kind of guided my own development." Ware participated in debate and oratorical contests in high school. He moved to California and joined the debate team at Compton Junior College. A professor at California Lutheran University in Thousand Oaks noticed Ware and suggested that he apply to the school. Ware majored in speech and debate and graduated in 1969. Then a Stanford University alum recruited Ware for law school. He traveled to Palo Alto without an appointment and walked into the office of Thelton Henderson, the admissions dean. "I got into a conversation that day, and it has continued until this very moment," Ware said in a 2006 interview.

Ware prospered in law school because every day was a debate, both within the classes and with fellow students. Before graduating in 1972,

FIG. 10-1 (PREVIOUS PAGE)
Northern California Federal District Court judges in 1994. Top, left to right: Hon. Charles Legge, Hon D. Lowell Jensen, Hon. Ronald Whyte, Hon. Vaughn Walker, Hon. Saundra Brown Armstrong, Hon. Spencer Williams. Bottom, left to right: Hon. William Orrick Jr., Hon. Marilyn Hall Patel, Hon. Thelton Henderson, Hon. Eugene Lynch, Hon. Fern Smith, Hon. James Ware, Hon. Stanley Weigel, Hon. Barbara Caulfied, Hon. Robert Aguilar, Hon. Claudia Wilken. Courtesy of the Historical Society and Archives, US District Court for the Northern District of California; photograph by Ira Nowinski.

he was appointed to the Stanford Judicial Council, which adjudicated student disciplinary cases. The council interested young Ware in life as a judge. After law school, he joined a private Palo Alto law firm and specialized in criminal defense and civil trial work. His pro bono activities included fighting racial discrimination in housing under the auspices of the Stanford Mid-Peninsula Urban Coalition and assisting indigent litigants at the East Palo Alto Community Law Project. By the 1980s, he worked primarily as a business lawyer, taking professional negligence, intellectual property, and trade secret cases to state and federal courts.

Ware was named to the California Superior Court in 1988 and was nominated to the district court two years later. At his induction ceremony, on Martin Luther King Jr. Day in 1991, Ware talked about King's credo that injustice anywhere is a threat to justice everywhere. "As you've heard, I grew up in Alabama and I've suffered the injustice of segregated schools, the pain of racial violence, the indignity of separate drinking fountains, but more importantly, I was there to see for myself the wonderful transformation to society which takes place when the dark desolate valley of injustice is replaced by the sunlit path of justice," Ware said. "I was there to see the federal judges, the United States marshals, the outside agitators from the North and East and the West moving toward trying to restore constitutional life in the face of life-threatening opposition. Those federal judges became my heroes."

Ware's first assignment was to fill the void left in San Jose by Robert Aguilar, who kept a greatly reduced caseload as he battled legal troubles. Ware sat much of his career in San Jose, where the district court has played a key role in making Silicon Valley the world's high-tech center by resolving cutting-edge technology and intellectual property cases. "I think there is a little bit of security that comes out of knowing that if you have a problem there is a place to get it solved," Ware said. "Lots of companies will go to different places to practice, and they prefer to get even further away. But they are fearful if there is a problem, they are not going to get the problem solved in a commercially reasonable manner. I think that despite labor costs being far cheaper elsewhere, many companies place their intellectual property trust in the Valley. That's where their headquarters are because they want to have a competent place to get their problems resolved."

Ware won praise for his work on the bench. "My philosophy quite frankly is that every case is an important and major case," he said in

2006. "I try to treat every litigant in that way. I know that the principles that we hold dear in our society were developed out of cases that no one would have cared to talk about at the time. The case of the Scottsboro boys established our right to a jury of one's peers. The case of *Miranda v. Arizona* was just some person arrested on the streets of Arizona. So basic problems, basic protections of our constitutional and most important rights, come out of regular cases."

Ware's reputation was tarnished in 1997 when he was caught in a scandal that threatened his career. For several years, Ware had delivered inspiring speeches in which he told a story of Virgil Ware, a thirteen-year-old boy shot to death by white supremacists in 1963 while the boy was riding on the handlebars of his brother's bike down a Birmingham road. Ware said he was pedaling the bike, which landed in a ditch, and that Virgil was his brother. "I came out of that ditch with a hunger for justice," Ware would say. "Since that day, I dedicated my life toward equal justice and a life where everyone can be proud."

President Clinton nominated Ware to the Ninth Circuit in 1997, and it was then that the press learned that the story was untrue—that another young Birmingham boy named James Ware had been the brother of the murdered Virgil Ware. When the press reported the story of the misrepresentation, Ware asked that his name be withdrawn from consideration. He wrote President Clinton, "I am deeply committed to the cause of civil rights and do not wish to be seen, as is being suggested, as using the unfortunate tragedy which befell Virgil Ware as trying to better myself at someone else's expense." Ware explained that "initially he had told the story of Virgil Ware's death not as a personal recounting, but later had improperly placed himself into the story in what became a misguided effort to make audiences feel the tragedy which is caused by racial discrimination. I regret my lack of honesty."

Ware traveled to Birmingham to apologize to the James Ware whose brother was killed. One week later, the judge returned to the bench.

When asked about the experience in 2006, Ware said that his zeal to educate people about discrimination had led him to tell the story in the way that he had. Although he was publicly reprimanded by the Ninth Circuit Court of Appeals in 1998 for his misstatements, the circuit court also concluded that Ware's off-the-bench conduct had no effect on his "highly regarded abilities as a judge," and the Ninth Circuit invited Ware the following year to sit by designation on six appellate panels.

Ware anchored the San Jose Court for years, presiding over a heavy trial court docket laden with complex technology cases and epic patent battles—including cases involving industry giants such as Google and Microsoft. On the political front, he sided with the federal government in 2008 when he dismissed a lawsuit filed by five detainees who accused the CIA of transporting them to foreign prisons for interrogation and possible torture as part of their "extraordinary rendition" program. Ware said the district court could not take on the case because of the risk of exposing state secrets.

Due to his seniority, Ware served as the court's chief judge from 2010 to 2012, when he retired.

The Expanding Court

Saundra Brown Armstrong was born in 1947 in Oakland, attended Oakland public schools, and graduated from Castlemont High School. She then went to Merritt College in Oakland, where she received an associate's degree in 1967, and to California State University, Fresno, where she received a bachelor's degree two years later.

Armstrong has had many firsts in her varied career: she was the first African American policewoman in the Oakland Police Department, the first African American woman to serve as a deputy district attorney for Alameda County, and the first African American woman to serve on the Alameda County Superior Court. Armstrong's experience as a policewoman prompted her to enroll in law school. What spurred her decision was the fact that the Oakland Police Department required men to possess a high school diploma and women to possess a college degree. What's more, women were not allowed to compete for promotion.

Armstrong worked full-time as a policewoman throughout law school. She graduated magna cum laude from the University of San Francisco School of Law in 1977. Following law school, she joined the Alameda County District Attorney's Office as a deputy district attorney. In 1982, she moved to Washington, DC, where she worked in the Department of Justice's Public Integrity Section. In 1984, President Reagan appointed her to the Consumer Product Safety Commission. She returned to California in 1986 after being appointed by Reagan to serve on the US Parole Commission. Governor George Deukmejian appointed her in 1989 to the Alameda County Superior Court, where she worked in the criminal and juvenile divisions. Two years later, Senator Pete Wilson recommended Armstrong to fill the district judgeship vacated by Judge Ingram. President Bush nominated her in April 1991, and she was confirmed and sworn in two months later. She started in the San Francisco division, but moved her chambers to the Oakland division in 1994.

In 1996, Armstrong was handed a case that challenged the Clinton administration's "don't ask, don't tell" (DADT) policy on gay people in the military. Former lieutenant Andrew Holmes, who claimed he was dismissed from the California National Guard because he was gay, filed the suit. Armstrong found the policy unconstitutional and ordered Holmes reinstated. In a split decision, the Ninth Circuit Court of Appeals reversed Armstrong and upheld the constitutionality of DADT.

Armstrong is active in judicial and community service organizations. For many years, she has served as chairwoman of the Northern District's CARE Committee, organizing annual Law Day programs for high school students, and holding annual "Fireside Chats" in her home for new law students. She also volunteers at Oakland's Hunger Relief program and, for several years, volunteered as a crisis hotline operator.

Her interest in community service and her work as a judge converged in a class action lawsuit for which she had the opportunity to distribute more than $12 million in unclaimed settlement funds to charity. With the assistance of attorneys, she invited charities to submit proposals and appear in court to explain how they would ues a share of the settlement money. She conducted extensive hearings in 2004 and eventually distributed money to seventy-eight charities and children's hospitals.

In 2010, Armstrong presided over a class action suit that resulted in an agreement by the California Department of Transportation to commit $1.1 billion over thirty years to improving access to Caltrans facilities. It was the nation's largest single settlement to improve access for persons with disabilities.

Barbara A. Caulfield was born in Oak Park, Illinois, in 1947. Unlike many of those on the Northern District Court, she did not make her way to the Bay Area until well into her career. Caulfield attended Northwestern University, just north of Chicago, and graduated from Northwestern's law school in 1972. She worked at the university, first with the Chicago Law Enforcement Study Group and then with the legal aid clinic, until joining the faculty at the University of Oregon School of Law in 1974. After four years, she moved to San Francisco to teach at Hastings College of Law, where she served as academic dean in 1980 and 1981.

Caulfield left the academic world for private law in San Francisco in 1983, and then was appointed senior counsel for Pacific Bell in 1990. She returned to private practice in 1991, when she was nominated to the federal judiciary. Caulfield was confirmed, filling the seat vacated by Judge Schwarzer, who would be spending five years as head of the Federal Judicial Center in Washington, DC. Judge Caulfield continued to teach as she worked with Judge Peckham on the Trial Advocacy Program, a series of training sessions designed to better prepare attorneys for trying cases in district court.

In 1992, Jimmy Smyth, who had escaped from prison in Northern Ireland in 1983, was arrested in San Francisco after working there as a house painter for eight years. The British government sought his extradition, but Caulfield denied the request. She ruled that Smyth's professed status as a Sinn Féin activist would put him in danger if he returned to his home country.

FIG. 10-2
Irish fugitive Jimmy Smythe in front of the district court in San Francisco after district court judge Charles Legge revoked his bail in 1996. © Vince Maggiora/San Francisco Chronicle/Corbis.

The Ninth Circuit Court of Appeals reversed Caulfield's ruling, and in 1995 the Supreme Court declined to hear Smyth's request for asylum. Smyth's extradition hearing again brought him to a San Francisco federal court, but Caulfield had retired. Instead, Judge Charles Legge denied a petition from Smyth's attorney for a restraining order against extradition. Despite protests in San Francisco and Washington, DC, federal agents returned Smyth to Northern Ireland.

Caulfield returned to private practice, where her clients included Microsoft, Apple, and Affymetrix, a biotech company. In 2001, she joined Affymetrix as executive vice president and general counsel. Caulfield's departure for the tech industry illustrates the ways the law and technology were beginning to intersect in uncharted territory.

One of the earliest and most publicized cases in this new genre was titled simply *Apple v. Microsoft*, business rivals then and now.

"Yes, well, that's kind of a sad chapter," said Judge Schwarzer, the second of the case's three Northern District judges, in a 1997 interview. "This is one case where one's sympathies were likely with the plaintiff, but all the facts were the other way."

In the early 1980s, computer engineers at Cupertino, California–based Apple Computer developed a graphical user interface (what a person sees on the screen and the procedures they use to make the computer work) that included the mouse, the cursor, desktop icons, and drop-down menus, among other things—in short, the bulk of the tools taken for granted in computer use today. But Apple was primarily in the hardware business then, and the company was not equipped to create its own software. So it entered into a partnership with Microsoft, which began creating programs that would run on Apple's Macintosh and Lisa models.

Soon Microsoft released a new type of graphical user interface for other (non-Apple) types of personal computers. Up to this point, those computers had used a complicated language known as DOS, which required some expertise to operate. Microsoft's new system, known as Windows 1.0, included many of the same sorts of user-friendly features that Apple had created.

Apple complained. The two companies resolved their dispute by entering into a licensing agreement. Microsoft gained "the right to use and sublicense derivative works generated by Windows 1.0 in present and future products," according to court documents. Microsoft then went on to release a second and third improved version of Windows and licensed Hewlett-Packard to create NewWave, a program that ran along with Windows and made IBM-compatible computers simpler to use. But Apple complained again. Microsoft's changes to Windows had made it too "Mac-like," the company argued. No longer just using similar ideas, Microsoft had exceeded the parameters of its license and was now infringing upon Apple's copyright, the company alleged. But Microsoft was less inclined to negotiate this time, and Apple filed suit at the Northern District's San Jose courthouse in 1988.

"The case came before me," Judge Schwarzer recalled, "and I looked at the contract that Apple and Microsoft had entered a few years earlier, and it seemed to me that it pretty much eliminated any claim that Apple had." After a series of hearings, Schwarzer granted a summary judgment on the issues related to Windows 2.0, ruling that this software was covered by the licensing agreement. Then in 1990, when Schwarzer took a five-year leave of absence from the court, he sent all of his cases, including *Apple v. Microsoft*, to newly appointed judge Vaughn Walker.

Walker hit the ground running as the new face of the lawsuit. "Last fall, *Computer Reseller News* voted him one of the twenty-five 'most influential' figures in the computer industry, though he had to spend a day getting some basic lessons on how the products in the Apple case operate," the *Wall Street Journal* wrote in 1992. The next year, Walker ruled that the legal standard for copyright infringement to be used in this case (and subsequently in the computer industry, making this a landmark ruling) was "virtually identical" rather than just "substantially similar." This sounded the death knell for Apple's case.

In a May 1993 hearing, the judge parsed and compared features of the Windows operating system and Apple's Finder interface down to the last icon, overlapping window, and dialog box. Walker scheduled a trial for June, but when Apple did not oppose the remaining motions, judgments were entered in favor of Microsoft and the secondary defendant, Hewlett-Packard. It was true that Windows had icons, menus, and a cursor just like Apple's interface, but those features were not visually identical, so they did not infringe Apple's copyright, Walker ruled, and Apple had not patented these features.

"The Apple-Microsoft case was difficult because law was scanty and in flux at the time," Walker said in 2006. "The approach I took was against the grain of where the law had been, but where the law eventually moved." Appeals court judges affirmed Walker's decision in 1994.

During Judge Caulfield's brief tenure, the court added two new judges—Ronald M. Whyte, nominated by President Bush in 1992, and Claudia Wilken, nominated by President Clinton in 1993—to fill the thirteenth and fourteenth seats of the court. They, too, would soon find themselves in the midst of the court's struggle to keep up with technology's rapid evolution and our country's changing culture.

The Challenge of Technology

Ronald Whyte was born in Pomona, in Los Angeles County, in 1942. His father, James G. Whyte, was a Los Angeles County Superior Court judge, and his uncle, Ronald M. Crookshank, was an Orange County judge. His mother, Eleanor, died of cancer when Whyte was in high school. The young Whyte went to law school because he didn't know what he wanted to do after he graduated in 1964 from Wesleyan University, in Connecticut, with a math degree. Whyte enjoyed his years at the University of California Law Center. After graduating, he was drafted and served from 1968 to 1971 as a lieutenant in the navy's law firm, the Judge Advocate General's Corps. He was stationed at Great Lakes Naval Base in North Chicago, Illinois. After leaving the navy, he moved to San Jose, where he entered private practice and was made a partner in 1977. He was appointed to Santa Clara County Superior Court by Governor Deukmejian in 1989. Whyte and his wife, Ann, raised their two children in Los Gatos, in Santa Clara County. In 1991, Senator Wilson, who was soon to become governor of California, recommended Whyte for a vacancy in the San Jose court.

President Bush nominated him in July 1991, but Whyte's Senate confirmation hearing was not held until early 1992. Whyte had virtually no experience in criminal law or intellectual property, but he said he has worked hard to catch up.

Although Judge Whyte made headlines in 1993 when he heard the unusual death row case *Mason v. Vasquez*, in which David Mason sought to stop his habeas corpus appeal process and be executed, he is best known for his rulings in technology and patent cases. Whyte has been likened to a sheriff in cyberspace, as his San Jose courtroom has seen an extraordinary number of groundbreaking cases that have changed how technology is used and litigated. The soft-spoken, intense Whyte, who confesses he never even learned how to program a VCR, made some of

FIG. 10-3
The new "gold rush" of Silicon Valley has generated technology cases for the district court and at a national level. Here Microsoft chairman Bill Gates (left) testifies at an antitrust hearing in 1998, before the Senate Judiciary Committee in Washington, DC, as Sun Microsystems chairman Scott McNealy (center) and Netscape Communications chairman James Barksdale look on. © Jessica Persson/AFP/Getty Images.

the Northern District's earliest rulings regarding high-tech patents and copyrights on the Internet, including *Religious Technology Center v. Netcom On-Line Communications.*

The *Netcom* case was the first in which an Internet service provider (ISP) was found not liable for the copyright infringement of documents posted on the Internet by its subscribers. In this case, Dennis Erlich, a former Scientology minister, had posted secret church documents to a Usenet newsgroup, including confidential lectures by church founder L. Ron Hubbard. The church's Religious Technology Center asserted that many of its literary works were trade secrets that it controlled through copyright. Judge Whyte found that Netcom could not be held liable for a subscriber's possible copyright violations. He likened ISPs and message boards to bookstores rather than publishers. Only if an ISP knew that copyrighted material was being posted could it be liable, and that would involve screening millions of Internet posts, something Netcom said was impractical if not impossible. First Amendment enthusiasts applauded Whyte when he further ruled that the former minister's posts were noncommercial protected criticism. His 1995 decision was eventually incorporated into the Communications Decency Act of 1996.

Whyte ruled for Sun Microsystems in its 1997 case against Microsoft over standards for its Java programming language. Microsoft had adapted Java to make it work better with Windows than with other operating systems. Whyte's 1998 injunction delayed Microsoft's shipping of its Windows 98 operating system until it added a version of Java that was compatible with Sun's testing programs.

Whyte was also the first judge in the country to rule, in 1998, that typefaces can be patented. In addition, Whyte presided over the first legal challenge to the 1998 Digital Millennium Copyright Act (DMCA). A Russian software maker, Elcomsoft, was accused of selling a program that hacked Adobe's electronic book software. A twenty-six-year-old Russian programmer had been arrested by federal agents and charged with violating the DMCA in 2001. The following year, a San Jose jury found the programmer and the company not guilty. Whyte said the case was an example of how often courts have to interpret technology laws. "That was an act that perhaps the legislature didn't realize the ambiguity of it and how far it went," said Whyte in a 2006 interview. "Too often the hard decisions are left to the courts rather than being handled by the legislature."

Whyte is considered one of the best patent judges in the country and speaks regularly at conferences, particularly regarding jury instruction in complex cases. He worked with a nationwide network of legal scholars and lawyers to develop guidelines for juries in patent cases. He said the need for clear instructions, not technical jargon, is essential with the growing number and complexity of patent cases. In an unusual practice among district court judges, Whyte sometimes issues tentative rulings to allow the losing side another chance to plead its case once it has seen his reasoning.

After 9/11, Whyte ruled on a case involving antiwar banners hung on California freeways. The state Department of Transportation had allowed American flags and other patriotic symbols to be hung from freeway overpasses after the attacks and during the American invasion of Afghanistan in 2001. In October, two women from Santa Cruz hung an antiwar banner that said "At What Cost?" over Highway 17 in Scotts Valley. It was removed twice while a nearby US flag was left hanging. Amy Courtney and Cassandra Brown filed suit on free speech grounds. Judge Whyte agreed with them that Caltrans needed to apply a uniform policy to banners and flags. The agency issued a new regulation in 2002 banning all banners from freeway overpasses. Whyte was roasted by conservatives for forcing the agency to take down American flags. "Sometimes we have to make unpopular decisions," said Whyte. "It's part of our jobs to protect the minority when their rights are being overridden by the majority."

One of his favorite cases involved a man who had been charged with assaulting a forest ranger. "He was kind of a character. One day he would have a British accent, the next day a French accent, and sometimes he thought he was Jesus Christ," recalled Whyte. The defendant had been sleeping in his car in a federal national park and got into a fight with the ranger when asked to move. The prosecutor was getting frustrated during the trial because the man refused to give yes or no answers, so Whyte stepped in and asked the man to only answer with yeses or nos. "So the next question, the defendant said, 'Well, the answer to that question is sixty percent yes and forty percent no.' And the next was seventy-five percent yes and twenty-five percent no. And I was sitting there saying, 'I'm not interfering with this, this is too fun.'" The man was convicted.

In 2007, Whyte found that a California law banning the sale of violent video games to minors was unconstitutional. The law would have added additional warning label requirements for violent games and made it illegal for retailers to rent or sell them to minors. Game makers sued on First Amendment grounds. Whyte concluded that the defense had not shown that violent video games are any more dangerous to minors than violent television shows, movies, Internet sites, or speech.

Judge Whyte helped round out the San Jose court, and Judge Claudia Wilken arrived to round out the Oakland court. A Minnesota native, Wilken graduated from Stanford University as a psychology major. "I thought of going to grad school for psychology, but I didn't," she recalled in a 2006 interview. Instead, she got a job as a social worker in East Palo Alto next to the Legal Aid Society and became interested in the legal aspects of welfare. She decided to go to law school and become a Legal Aid attorney. She enrolled at Boalt Hall but never made it to the Legal Aid Society. After her first year of law school, she took a summer public defender job in Santa Clara County. The second summer she worked in the federal public defender's office, and she returned there upon graduation. "At that time, there had not ever been any women in the federal public defender's office," she said. "Pat Trumbull and I started at about the same time. We argue about who was first." (Patricia Trumbull became the chief magistrate judge in the district.)

Women were scarce across the federal legal landscape at that time, Wilken recalled. Only a handful practiced private federal criminal law, and only a few more handled federal civil cases. There were none on the federal bench. But during Wilken's tenure as an assistant federal public defender from 1975 to 1978, she began to notice a change. "Women were starting to go to law school at that time in significant numbers," she said. "Judge Patel was on the municipal court then, and Shirley Hufstedler was on the Ninth Circuit." As to her interactions with the Northern District Court as a federal defender, Wilken will only say there were some "characters on the bench."

Wilken left the public defender's office in 1978 to set up a private practice with a friend from law school. Wilken also returned to her alma mater as an adjunct professor, but she kept an eye on the federal landscape as well. "I applied for one magistrate opening, but Joan Brennan got it," she said. Then a part-time magistrate opening in Oakland came up in 1983, and Wilken was hired. The magistrate position became full time the following year. "This court, even when I started, had a better utilization of magistrates than many other districts," she recalled. "In other courts, magistrates do mostly prisoner and Social Security work. In this court they could do settlement conferences and some trials. We have tried to get more trial work to magistrates, and at this point they do more."

After nearly a decade, Wilken applied for a district court judgeship and was appointed in 1993. She was the first of eight judges nominated in the Northern District of California by President Clinton, the most by any president. As she expected, Wilken noted substantial differences between her two jobs on the court: "District court judges have all the civil cases and felony trials, and magistrates have the misdemeanors. I have five hundred civil cases, and a magistrate might have fifty. I have one hundred felonies, and a magistrate might have one hundred misdemeanors. They do settlement conferences, and they're appointed to eight-year terms."

Wilken says one of her most important cases was her 1997 hearing of the first challenge to San Francisco's 1996 ordinance requiring local businesses to provide health benefits to their employees' domestic partners. Well before the 2004 directive from Mayor Gavin Newsom to issue county marriage licenses for gay couples, San Francisco was a pioneer in recognizing domestic partnerships in order to extend benefits to the partners of gay men and lesbians. The suit, brought by airline companies, resulted in only a slight revision to the ordinance. Wilken's decision was affirmed on appeal by the Ninth Circuit. In 1996, Wilken was the first to rule that the Americans with Disabilities Act applies to state prisoners and parolees. A similar case was affirmed at the Supreme Court in 1998.

Since she joined the bench, Wilken says, the greatest change is that there are now more women and minorities on the bench. The Oakland division has also changed dramatically. When she started there as a magistrate judge, she was the only judge working in Oakland. Now Oakland has four judges and two magistrate judges. San Jose has five judges and two magistrate judges. San Francisco has ten judges and six magistrate judges. One magistrate judge works in Eureka. Wilken meets other judges at monthly meetings and goes on a retreat once a year. "Now that we have videoconferencing, it's tempting to stay here," she said. "But I try to make an effort. I feel like that's important. There probably is some loss of collegiality with multiple locations, but it's more important to serve the public."

In 2012, Wilken became the chief judge of the district court, replacing James Ware. She is the first chief judge to work out of the Oakland courthouse.

After Judge Caulfield's retirement in 1994, President Clinton nominated Susan Illston to replace her and Maxine Chesney to fill the seat that had been vacated by Judge Vukasin upon his death.

"Nobody in my family was ever a lawyer. I didn't know any lawyers," Illston said in a 2006 interview. She became interested in law while attending Duke University in the late 1960s, a time of rampant racial discrimination and segregation. "I wanted to fix that, so I thought I would become a lawyer," she said. "There was a sign on the bus that I rode every day that said something like 'Racial discrimination in housing isn't just wrong, it's also illegal.' So I'd stare at that and I thought, 'Well, that's something I could do.'"

After a somewhat nomadic childhood following her father's army career (Illston was born in Tokyo in 1948) and four years at Duke, Illston was determined to strike out for the West Coast. She was accepted at Stanford Law School and got a part-time job with a small law firm near the school doing civil work during the summers. "I enjoyed them, and I enjoyed the kind of law they practiced, so when I graduated from law school, then I stayed there, and I stayed there for twenty-some years," she said. Only an appointment to the district court in 1994 could persuade her to leave Cotchett, Illston & Pitre, where she had become a partner in 1977 after only four years on the job.

Since joining the district court, Illston has been no stranger to out-of-the-ordinary cases. "Early in my judgeship I had a death penalty case, which was the first death penalty case in this district—ever, or at least in anyone's memory," Illston said. While the district court frequently makes decisions regarding death penalty sentences via habeas corpus cases, what made this case unusual was that the death penalty was sought as punishment in a murder case that had originated in federal court. In the end, the defendant received a term of imprisonment.

Illston is reluctant to claim any particular legal significance for her own cases, but she is quick to outline the types of cases that most frequently make their way through the Northern District Court: "We have a lot of environmental cases—Endangered Species Act, critical habitat cases. They're particularly significant on the West Coast because we have so much park land and other open spaces out here. I've had a lot of fish cases—salmon cases, steelhead cases. The intersection between fish and water and farming has historically been very, very complex in California, and that remains true today. Clean Water Act cases, also, have been significant."

She said the court receives a large number of employment cases—racial discrimination, sexual discrimination—and intellectual property and patent cases. "Those take up a huge amount of our time and are a significant portion of the legal work we do," said Illston. "We have a fair number of securities fraud class action cases. I think both with respect to the intellectual property cases, the patent cases, and to a slightly lesser degree the securities litigation, [the court] does impact the rest of the country because we have so much of it, and the way we handle those cases tends to be a model for other districts."

One of the most interesting cases Illston said she has heard concerned a methadone clinic. The owner bought a building that already had a medical clinic in it and was zoned for the kind of medical treatment he was providing, namely drug rehabilitation. Neighbors, who were worried that the clinic's clientele would make the residential neighborhood unsafe, passed an emergency zoning ordinance that outlawed methadone treatment. "So it was an issue of first impression, at least in the Ninth Circuit, concerning whether the Americans with Disabilities Act covered zoning," said Illston. "That's a tough question because zoning is by its nature an exclusionary process, and the ADA prohibits that." As the trial progressed, the issue came to be whether the clinic could operate safely in a residential neighborhood, Illston said. In the end, she allowed the methadone clinic to move in. "I get reports from time to time letting me know how things are going over there," she said. "And they're by all accounts going just fine, so I'm relieved about that."

BALCO and Starbucks

The most publicized case ever to enter Illston's court involved drugs and sports. In February 2004, after a long federal investigation and grand jury testimony into the use of anabolic steroids by dozens of elite and professional athletes, four men connected with the Bay Area Laboratory Co-operative (BALCO) were indicted on forty-two drug-related charges, including possession of anabolic steroids with intent to distribute, money laundering, and fraud relating to mislabeled drugs.

"The BALCO drug cases were interesting to me situationally," said Illston. "Legally they were not complex, but [they] did seem to prompt a national dialogue that's proved to be significant." A front-page story in the *San Francisco Chronicle* called the BALCO legal proceedings a "simple case turned catalyst." Reporters Lance Williams and Mark Fainaru-Wada noted that facts surrounding the case forced the public, as well as the federal government and professional sports leagues, to confront a dirty secret of American sports: high-caliber athletes of all kinds have used steroids, growth hormones, and other illegal substances to perform better. The authors credited the BALCO legal proceedings with prompting an unprecedented crackdown on illegal drug use among US Olympians, spurring a March 2004 congressional investigation into illegal drug use among professional athletes and motivating Major League Baseball to ramp up its drug-testing program for players.

In 2003, federal investigators raided the BALCO headquarters in Burlingame, south of San Francisco International Airport, and took a statement from BALCO founder Victor Conte that he provided steroids to twenty-seven athletes—including Olympic medalist Marion Jones, San Francisco Giants star Barry Bonds, and major-leaguers Jason Giambi and Gary Sheffield. "The drugs that the [indicted] were accused of providing were designer steroids designed to avoid detection by the then-extant testing mechanisms that the athletes were subjected to," explained Illston. "So [the drugs] were not on many of the controlled substance lists that other traditional drugs might be on."

In the end, forty of the forty-two charges were dropped after all four of the indicted BALCO men pled guilty to lesser charges. Conte was

FIG. 10-4
BALCO lab owner Victor Conte in his Burlingame, California, office in March 2007, with bottles of his nutritional supplements and the book *Game of Shadows: Barry Bonds, BALCO, and the Steroids Scandal That Rocked Professional Sports* by Mark Fainaru-Wada and Lance Williams. © Kimberly White/ Corbis.

sentenced to four months in prison and four months of house arrest for conspiring to distribute the drugs. Greg Anderson, a personal trainer whose clients included Bonds, received three months in prison and three months of house arrest for conspiracy. Two other defendants were put on probation. "They received very inconsequential sentences because of the nature of the charges and the way that the sentencing guidelines worked with respect to them," Illston said. "Any sentence of imprisonment is significant to the person to whom it happens, but compared with what would have happened if they'd sold marijuana or cocaine or something, their penalties were very light."

Bonds, who broke baseball's all-time home run record, was indicted in 2007 on four counts of perjury and one count of obstruction of justice stemming from the BALCO investigation. In 2011, a jury convicted him of the obstruction charge for lying to a federal grand jury that was investigating doping in sports. Illston declared a mistrial on the three remaining perjury charges after the jury was unable to come to a unanimous verdict. Later that year, Illston sentenced Bonds to thirty days of house arrest, two years of probation, 250 hours of community service, and a $4,000 fine for the obstruction conviction.

Judge Maxine M. Chesney was born in San Francisco and raised in the Peninsula towns of San Mateo and Hillsborough, where she attended Burlingame High School. She majored in psychology and graduated from UC Berkeley in 1964. After attending Boalt Hall, where she received her law degree in 1967, she worked for eleven years in the San Francisco District Attorney's Office. During the 1970s, Chesney was the first female district attorney to prosecute sexual assaults. She eventually created the country's first special unit to handle sexual assaults.

In 1979, Governor Jerry Brown appointed her to the San Francisco Municipal Court, where she presided over the 1982 trial of attorney F. Lee Bailey on drunk driving charges. He was acquitted. In 1983, she was elevated to the San Francisco County Superior Court. There she served in the juvenile, civil, and law and motion divisions, deciding on a number of high-profile cases. Among the most notable was *American Academy of Pediatrics v. Lungren*, a 1992 case that challenged a new California law that required minors to get written parental consent before obtaining an abortion. Chesney found that the patients' right to privacy under the state constitution had been violated, a decision upheld on appeal in state courts.

Senator Dianne Feinstein recommended Chesney for the Northern District Court in 1994. President Clinton nominated her in May 1995, and she was confirmed and sworn in that month. Chesney was surprised she was not questioned about her ruling in the abortion case. "I was ready to explain my decision," she said in a 2006 interview. "To me it seemed like a hot topic. But they didn't ask me about it."

In 1998, Chesney issued a last-minute stay of execution for death row prisoner Jaturun Siripongs, a Thai national and former Buddhist monk convicted and condemned to death in 1983 for killing two people during a robbery in Southern California in 1981. Siripongs admitted taking part in the robbery but maintained that an unnamed accomplice committed the murders. Chesney found "serious questions" were raised as to Governor Wilson's clemency process and ordered a stay until a hearing could be held on the process. "[This] presented a new legal issue[;] someone felt they had not been treated fairly in regard to their clemency petition and [the court had to decide] how it should be handled procedurally," Chesney said. "I felt that if I was going to err, I was going to err on the

BUY MORE NOW

Consumer Whore Parody Logo ©2000 Kieron Dwyer   www.LCDcomic.com

FIG. 10-5
Kieron Dwyer's reimagined Starbucks logo led to legal actions from the corporation in 2000 for copyright and trademark infringement. The logo appeared on the first cover of Dwyer's creator-owned series *LCD: Lowest Comic Denominator* in 1999. Courtesy of Kieron Dwyer; kierondwyer.com.

side of not having the man executed." Chesney halted the execution, but incoming governor Gray Davis denied clemency. Siripongs was executed by lethal injection less than three months later.

In 1999, Starbucks Coffee sued San Francisco comic book artist Kieron Dwyer for copyright and trademark infringement to stop him from poking fun at the company. Dwyer took the Starbucks logo and gave the siren a cell phone and cup of coffee to hold. He then changed the Starbucks Coffee name on the logo to Consumer Whore and sold the new emblem on merchandise. According to Chesney, Dwyer "had taken the little Starbucks mermaid and put dollar signs on her and made sure she was fully unclothed from the waist up." The cartoonist argued that his art was a legitimate parody protected by the First Amendment.

Dwyer, who has drawn for Marvel and DC Comics and received help from the Comic Book Defense Fund, said the lawsuit was like "carpet-bombing an anthill." In a Solomonesque ruling, Chesney found that Dwyer had tarnished the logo by using the word "whore" but that his parody didn't infringe on Starbuck's trademark. He was barred from selling the image for profit. "I never looked at the Starbucks logo the same way," Chesney said in a 2006 interview. "I'm more of a tea drinker, so I don't slurp Frappuccinos, and felt I could hear the case without having to recuse myself as a customer."

Another Chesney case involved a transsexual woman, Victoria Schneider, who sued San Francisco for civil rights violations. "She was very shabbily treated after having been arrested—was gratuitously, humiliatingly strip-searched, body-cavity searched, all, she felt, with a goal towards demeaning her and also perhaps some curiosity as to just what was there after a surgery of this nature," Chesney recalled. "[The city] was not going to pay any money for that case in terms of settlement and felt that no jury would have any sympathy for the plaintiff." The attorneys misjudged the jury's response, Chesney said: "The plaintiff made a very good witness. She was a sad person, and they reacted to that and awarded a very high sum of money." Schneider won a $750,000 verdict against the city. She eventually settled for close to $500,000.

In 2004, Chesney ruled against San Francisco retailer Sharper Image when she tossed out its suit against the Consumers Union's *Consumer Reports* magazine. The Ionic Breeze was one of the company's top-selling products, but the magazine's reviews in 2002 and 2003 found that the product produced "almost no measurable reduction in airborne particles." Sharper Image attorneys said the reviews were false and malicious, but the magazine countered by showing that its testing methods were evaluated by outside experts at two universities who found them to be sound. Chesney ruled that Sharper Image "has not demonstrated a reasonable probability that any of the challenged statements were false." She dismissed the lawsuit. "That case I think may have some repercussions, because people may think twice if they've gotten a bad review and feel they may be able to get some recompense by suing Consumers Union," said Chesney. Sharper Image filed for Chapter 11 bankruptcy in 2008 and closed all of its retail outlets.

Just six months into her tenure on the district court bench in 1995, Chesney took a medical leave of absence and endured two rounds of harsh media conjecture in San Francisco's two legal newspapers, the *Recorder* and the *Daily Journal,* for that absence and a second one in 2001. The papers reported that her condition was "stress-related medical problems including abrupt weight loss," attributed to unnamed sources who described her as being "overwhelmed with her new job as a federal judge." Chesney, who declined to be interviewed by the papers or explain her illness, later said she did not want to reveal at the time that she had ovarian cancer. "I didn't really want to put it in the paper....It wouldn't have been such a big deal, but, you know, you like to keep some aspects of your life private."

In 2000, Chesney ruled on a San Francisco landmark that was the subject of a pitched court battle that lasted a decade. Mount Davidson, at 938 feet, is the highest point in San Francisco. In 1934, the nation's tallest cross was erected at the top of the hill. President Franklin D. Roosevelt lit the cross by telegraph from DC, while as many as fifty thousand people looked on. But by 1990, not everyone felt so positively about the structure.

That is when the American Civil Liberties Union, the American Jewish Congress, and Americans United for Separation of Church and State filed suit on behalf of seven individuals, claiming "city ownership and maintenance of the 103-foot-high cross violates state and federal guarantees for the separation of church and state." Deputy city attorney Mara Rosales countered that the cross was a cultural symbol, like other San Francisco landmarks, and was no more an endorsement of Christianity than the city itself, which was named for Saint Francis. "If the Mount Davidson cross has nothing to do with Christianity," countered Marty Kassman, vice president of the San Francisco chapter of Americans United for Separation of Church and State, "why are Easter Sunday services held there every year?"

Both sides had their day in district court in 1992 before Judge Vukasin. Rosales, representing the city, again characterized the cross as part of San Francisco's history and a popular local attraction—just one of twenty-five hundred works of public art around the city, including an enormous statue of Buddha in Golden Gate Park, she explained. "History alone cannot justify this cross," stated Thomas Steel, an attorney representing the seven people of assorted faiths who brought the lawsuit. "[It] broadcasts the message to people of minority faiths that they are…less powerful than people of the majority faith." Vukasin did not agree. He ruled:

> The Mount Davidson Cross is not situated within, on top of, adjacent to, or near City Hall or any other governmental buildings, nor can it be viewed with governmental buildings as the primary backdrop. Instead, it stands silently, often obstructed by darkness, fog, and trees, in the same location where it has stood for fifty-seven years as part of the rich history and culture of San Francisco. The park is not even identified as belonging to the city. It appears ironic that San Francisco, which not only tolerates but appears to embrace literally almost any activity, conduct

or philosophy, regardless of how strange or unusual, would somehow be deemed to be making law establishing or preferring any particular religion. Therefore, the display of the Mount Davidson Cross, in this context, need not be permanently enjoined.

But the battle was not over. A panel of Ninth Circuit appellate judges reversed Vukasin's decision. "The Mount Davidson cross carries great religious significance," wrote Judge Diarmuid O'Scannlain. "Indeed, to suggest otherwise would demean this powerful religious symbol. Thus, we conclude [its] presence on public land violates the No Preference clause of the California Constitution." The Supreme Court declined to hear a further appeal.

Rather than remove the structure, the Mount Davidson cross and the land around it was sold at a public auction in 1997. Under terms of the sale, the winning bidder was not allowed to build a fence or anything else to prevent public access to the area, and the city maintained the right to refuse any bid. The Council of Armenian American Organizations of Northern California outbid two other organizations and won the auction at $26,500. The group said it would preserve the cross and use it as a war memorial honoring Armenians killed by Turks during World War I.

Once the sale was approved, two opponents of the cross filed suit. They alleged that San Francisco remained in violation of the California Constitution's No Preference clause because the land had been sold solely for the purpose of keeping the cross standing. Judge Chesney heard their case and ruled in 2000 that the sale was legal. The next year, judges on the Court of Appeals concurred. So the Mount Davidson cross still stands on the western side of San Francisco, a privatized war monument atop a public hill—and a testament to the imperfect compromise and diverse points of view that compose the Northern District of California.

Different Backgrounds

Charles R. Breyer, confirmed by the Senate as a district court judge in November 1997, and Martin J. Jenkins, confirmed the following day, were both raised in San Francisco but came to the court from very different backgrounds.

Breyer grew up near the University of San Francisco and attended Lowell High School. His father, Irving, was a legal adviser who worked more than forty years for the San Francisco Board of Education; his mother, Anne Roberts, was an active volunteer in civic and political causes. They had two children: Stephen, who was interested in law and would eventually join the US Supreme Court, and Charles, who wanted to be an actor. After receiving an undergraduate degree from Harvard University, Charles moved to New York City at the urging of Sesame Street composer Joel Raposo, a Harvard alum, to start a career on the stage. But from the first auditions for summer stock, young Breyer could see what a difficult career he was choosing. He chose to return to San Francisco instead.

Breyer applied to Boalt Hall School of Law on the advice of his father. At first, Breyer disliked the competitive atmosphere of the school, but a summer internship with flamboyant attorney Marvin E. Lewis made Breyer realize how he could combine his love of the stage with law. He returned to school with renewed vigor. Upon graduation, he clerked at the district court for Judge Oliver Carter, where, he later said, "I joined in as a member of a judicial family, an extraordinary court, where I saw the wit of Bill Sweigert, the brilliance of Al Zirpoli, the enormous political judgment of Robert Peckham, and the warmth and the compassion of Al Wollenberg." He next worked for the San Francisco Legal Aid Society and served as an assistant district attorney. During the Watergate crisis, Breyer worked for Archibald Cox as assistant special prosecutor investigating the Nixon administration. Breyer distinctly recalls the Saturday Night Massacre in 1973 when Nixon fired Cox. "The president has made a serious mistake," Cox told his staff. "He fired me, but he didn't fire you." Breyer stayed on and worked with Leon Jaworski until Nixon resigned the following year. Then Breyer returned to San Francisco and began working in private practice, specializing in complex commercial litigation and white-collar defense. He also served on the juvenile probation commission, a job he said at his induction ceremony was the most worthwhile he ever did.

In the late 1990s, Breyer started campaigning to be a district court judge. He met with Senator Feinstein, whom he had known for years, and began gathering support: "My brother said, 'If you want to be federal judge, lots of friends will go to bat for you, so you better really want it, and stay there.'" Breyer did—and still does.

"The issues in federal court are more interesting than in state court," said Breyer in a 2006 interview. Many state court judges are mired in "endless asbestos cases" and serving as traffic cops in personal injury litigation, he says. District court judges have on average two hundred fifty to three hundred cases, which gives them enough time to thoughtfully prepare and consider arguments. Federal judges are generalists, he says: "You come with what you think is a wide range of experience, and you realize how narrow it was." The only downside for him is hearing patent cases, which Breyer says requires a great deal of expertise that he finds difficult to acquire.

In 1997, Breyer ordered the National Park Service to stop building roads and lodges near historic Yosemite Lodge after it was severely damaged by a flood. Breyer ruled that park officials had not done enough planning before construction began and that the work threatened the sanctity of the park. The government abandoned its plan. "That gave me some personal satisfaction," he said. "Perhaps it was almost personal because I grew up in San Francisco, I worked at Yosemite. There was a camp called Camp Mather, which was the San Francisco–run camp, a family camp. I worked there and developed a tremendous love for Yosemite and the Sierras, and it would break my heart to see anything happen to that gift."

Almost a decade later, Breyer faced a more difficult case when he ruled against the federal government's plan to allow increased logging in the Giant Sequoia National Monument in the southern Sierra Nevada. "Environmental cases are not all black and white," he said. The Forest Service developed a plan in 2004 that allowed for the logging of smaller trees near the sequoias to reduce the risk of fire. So Breyer had to try to figure out whether the logging would benefit or hinder the world's largest trees. In 2007, the Forest Service said it would not appeal Breyer's decision but would come up with new plans.

Breyer has had at least two major rulings on immigrant rights. In 2002, he ruled that Macan Singh, an undocumented worker from India, could sue his uncle for not paying him. Singh's uncle reported the thirty-three-year-old to immigration officials after he demanded to be paid for three years of work. "The question, as he waited for deportation for months, was what rights he had," said Breyer, who allowed Singh to sue for emotional distress and punitive damages despite his status as an undocumented worker. A jury awarded Singh $200,000. He settled with his uncle before the case was appealed.

In 2007, Breyer slowed the government's effort to crack down on illegal aliens when he stopped a federal rule that would require employers to fire employees within ninety days if their employees' Social Security numbers and W-2 tax forms did not match. The rule was aimed at illegal immigrants. Breyer approved a temporary injunction against the Department of Homeland Security. He said the administration's plan might result in the firing of thousands of legal workers and "would result in irreparable harm to innocent workers and employers."

The cases that are perhaps Breyer's most famous involved medicinal marijuana. In 1998, Breyer barred an Oakland pot club from distributing marijuana for medical use. That ruling was affirmed by the Supreme Court. (Stephen Breyer always recuses himself from cases his brother ruled on.) In 2003, a jury in Breyer's court convicted Ed Rosenthal of manufacturing and distributing marijuana. Rosenthal had been designated by the city of Oakland to grow and dispense medical marijuana, but Breyer refused to allow the jury to know the drug was for medical use. The judge eventually sentenced Rosenthal to one day in jail. The case was re-tried in 2007 with similar results. The federal government banned the growth and distribution of marijuana for any reason, and despite Breyer's opinions on marijuana, he felt the law was clear:

> It was my belief that a local municipality can't simply designate or delegate authority to an individual to go out and do something contrary to the federal law. There are arguments about legalization of all sorts of drugs. I'm sure if you went from municipality to municipality, you would find a majority, especially in California, who would think it's a very good idea, a more sensible approach to legalize it. Whether it is or not, I don't know, but it's their view. Some people would say that's a good idea, but that's not my role. That is the role of the executive branch. My role is to apply the law impartially.

In contrast to Breyer's middle-class childhood, Martin J. Jenkins grew up on Holloway Avenue in the Ingleside District near San Francisco State University. He attended St. Michael's Grammar School and Lincoln High School. He remembers his first visit to the San Francisco district courthouse well:

> I came here when I was twelve years old because my father was a janitor at Coit Tower, and one of his best friends was a janitor who worked in the Federal Building. And I came with my dad to visit his friend. It was before the remodeling. I walked around here and looked into the courtrooms, and said, "My God, what kind of place is this? What happens here?" My dad told me they are courtrooms. That was about all he could

say because he knew nothing about what transpired there. The gentleman we came to visit didn't know much either. You could not have told me that twenty to thirty years later, I'd be working here. It just wasn't on my radar.

Jenkins also remembers being inspired by neighborhood speeches given by California assemblyman (and later mayor) Willie Brown, San Francisco judge Joseph Kennedy, San Francisco supervisor Terry Francois, and Judge Cecil Poole. But it wasn't until his senior year at Santa Clara University that he gave law a second thought. It was there that his football coach, George "Pat" Malley, asked Jenkins what he planned to do after college. Jenkins, who was a top student and All-American captain of the Broncos football team, told his coach that he was thinking about working as a teacher and football coach. Malley suggested law, and he brought three Santa Clara law students to meet Jenkins. Soon after, Malley brought another friend, district court judge Eugene Lynch, to meet the young football star.

Jenkins left Santa Clara and tried to catch on with the Seattle Seahawks as a free-agent cornerback. He was with the team through the second preseason game, but when it became clear he would have trouble making the team, Jenkins decided to try law school. He returned home and enrolled at the University of San Francisco. Jenkins rose quickly through the legal profession. He worked three years as a deputy district attorney in Alameda County, traveled the country for two years as a civil rights lawyer with the Department of Justice, then returned home to be near his ailing mother and worked for four years as a corporate attorney with Pacific Bell. He sat on the Alameda County Municipal Court from 1989 to 1992 and on the Alameda County Superior Court from 1992 to 1997. During his last eighteen months on the superior court, Jenkins took over as presiding judge of the Alameda County Juvenile Court. "It was the hardest job I ever had," he said.

Jenkins was nominated in 1997 to fill the seat vacated by Eugene Lynch, the judge who had helped convince him to go to law school. At Jenkins's induction ceremony, his friend Sherwin Bailey talked about a day he and Jenkins had volunteered to pass out lunches and blankets to the homeless at an Oakland bus terminal. One man refused lunch or a blanket, so they asked him if there was anything they could do for him.

"I need a pair of shoes," the man replied. "Marty asked the man what size shoe he wore, and he told us," Bailey recounted. "And it was the same size that Marty wore. Right then and there on the spot Marty took off his shoes and gave them to that man. And the man said, 'These look brand new.' Marty said, 'They are. I just bought them yesterday. Well, today they are yours.'"

As with Breyer, one of Jenkins's most difficult judicial decisions concerned marijuana. In 2002, two seriously ill women—Angel Raich and Diane Monson—sued to stop the government from interfering with their growing and using marijuana for pain relief. They argued that California's Proposition 215, which legalized the medical use of marijuana, allowed them to make and use marijuana despite federal laws. Jenkins ruled against them. "I thought those women were really helped through the use of marijuana, and there were medical practitioners steeped in the art who said the same thing," Jenkins said in a 2007 interview. "It was pretty clear that Western medicine had failed these women. But I didn't think that the case law allowed me to grant the remedy they requested."

He ruled that the federal Controlled Substances Act was not unconstitutional. "I felt terrible about that," he said. "I tried to write an order that reflected that from a human perspective there may be one resolution of this, but my job is to follow the law." The Ninth Circuit disagreed with Jenkins's decision, but the Supreme Court sided with him.

In 2004, Jenkins presided over the jury trial of former Ukrainian prime minister Pavel Lazarenko, the first foreign official tried in the United States since Panamanian general Manuel Noriega. Lazarenko, who had stepped down in 1997 and fled to the United States two years later, was found guilty of money laundering, extortion, and wire fraud. Jenkins sentenced him to nine years in prison and fined him $10 million.

That year Jenkins approved class action status for a suit filed by six women (on behalf of more than a million women who have worked for the retailer since 2001) who accused Wal-Mart of discrimination in pay and promotions. "While the size of the proposed class is unique, the issues are not novel, and plaintiffs' claims are relatively narrow," Jenkins wrote. The Ninth Circuit later approved Jenkins's certification of the case, the largest gender discrimination case in American history, but the Supreme Court granted certiorari and reversed the Ninth Circuit in June of 2011. The case was remanded to the district court, has been reassigned to another judge, and a further attempt at class certification in view of the Supreme Court's decision is now proceeding.

Jenkins left the district court in 2008 to serve as an associate justice in the First District of the California Court of Appeals. Giving up the life-time appointment for the state court was unusual. "I'm interested in the appellate function," he told *San Francisco Chronicle* reporter Bob Egelko. "I've been a trial judge for seventeen years, and the opportunity came to look at the law from a different perspective."

Filling Seats

The year after Breyer and Jenkins joined the district court, Jeremy Fogel was appointed to the seat vacated by Judge Aguilar. President Clinton nominated him in 1997, and the Senate confirmed him in early 1998. Born in San Francisco in 1949, Fogel grew up in Los Angeles, where his father, Daniel Fogel, was a personal injury lawyer. He returned north to attend Stanford University, where he majored in religious studies and graduated in 1971. He received his law degree from Harvard Law School in 1974, and then settled in San Jose, where he went into private practice. Negative trial experiences as a young lawyer inspired Fogel to become a judge. "I was appearing with clients who had a lot of problems, and I saw a number of judges who I thought really didn't treat people well," Fogel said in a 2006 interview. "They were good on being firm and everything, but they weren't very thoughtful about the people who appeared before them. I thought that one day I'd like to try and do better just at that piece of it, at respecting people and treating them well."

In 1978, Fogel joined the Mental Health Advocacy Project as direct-ing attorney and later worked as its executive director. This public interest law program serves Santa Clara residents with developmental or mental disabilities. The project is part of the Law Foundation of Silicon Valley, a nonprofit legal aid group founded in the mid-1970s. Fogel left the project in 1981 when Governor Brown appointed him to Santa Clara County Municipal Court. Five years later, he was elected to the Santa Clara County Superior Court, where he worked in family court and saw a number of early high-tech and securities cases as the once-agrarian Santa Clara Valley turned into Silicon Valley. He also handled the law and motion calendar, which he said was excellent preparation for being a federal judge.

"I learned just about every area of the general law, and I've also learned a lot about people—that people will disappoint you, people will fail,"

Fogel said as he left the state court system. "Sometimes things don't work out. Sometimes you have to make some very, very hard calls as a judge. Sometimes you have to do things you really don't want to do. You really don't want to do them, but you've got to do them because the law requires that they be done and that's your job."

Fogel was voted the county's best judge by the state bar association for the two years before his nomination and was known statewide as an expert on judicial ethics. He was forty-seven when Senator Feinstein recommended him to President Clinton for the district court. Fogel said the process was sort of a whirlwind. His appointment meant the San Jose office of the district court was fully staffed for the first time in nearly a decade. After he was given his share of discarded lawsuits from judges, Fogel recalled, Judge Spencer Williams walked in with a can of dog food and said, "Take good care of my cases."

Fogel, who currently serves as the director of the Federal Judicial Center while on leave from the court, has been one of the Northern District's main champions of alternative dispute resolution. Besides being dedicated to the practice in his own courtroom, he teaches mediation at the Federal Judicial Center and is a lecturer at Stanford Law School. "My hope is that as these students become lawyers, they will think more broadly instead of trying just to issue-spot…and try to find out what their clients really need as opposed to what really fits into a nice legal pigeon, hole and be more effective problem-solvers and not just warriors for their clients," Fogel said.

One case he said he was particularly proud of having mediated involved day workers in San Jose who sued to block a broad city ordinance that made it illegal to solicit work from sidewalks. Fogel issued a preliminary injunction and then suggested that they all mediate a new ordinance together. "The day workers, the city council, and the administration were all sitting here at this table, on equal footing, talking to each other, and it was a very empowering thing," said Fogel. "Something happened in a social sense that wouldn't have happened if they had been opponents in court."

Issues like abortion, the definition of marriage, and the death penalty are a no-win for the legislative branch, Fogel told the *New York Times Magazine* in 2007: "Cases like this do tend to end up in the courts because the legislature is having difficulty reaching consensus that reflects all the interests involved." Fogel nearly held up the 2003 election to recall

Governor Davis after a Monterey County resident argued that the election would violate the Voting Rights Act. And in 2006, Fogel ruled that California execution procedures violated the Eighth Amendment ban against cruel and unusual punishment, just ten months after granting a last-minute stay in the execution of Michael Morales.

If civil rights cases are the meat of the Northern District caseload, then technology cases are the potatoes. Fogel has ruled in a number of precedent-setting cases involving Google, PayPal, Netscape, Yahoo, Hewlett-Packard, and Microsoft. Now, he said, San Jose is "the hottest venue in the country" for high-tech cases. In *Online Policy Group v. Diebold*, Fogel ruled against the country's largest electronic voting machine maker in the first legal test of a key provision of the Digital Millennium Copyright Act. In 2003, students at Swarthmore College in Pennsylvania posted to the Internet internal Diebold documents that mentioned weaknesses in the company's voting machines. Diebold sent cease-and-desist letters to the students and asked that the documents be removed. Many students refused to comply. Diebold eventually withdrew its demands, but two students sued Diebold. Fogel found that Diebold had misused the copyright act and ordered the company to pay $125,000 in damages and legal fees. California decertified Diebold as a voting machine vendor in 2007. It has since changed its name to Premier Election Systems and been sold to a third party. The Diebold case was "a combination of technology and First Amendment issues," said Fogel. "I thought [it] was really fun, apart from being really interesting and important."

In 1999, President Clinton nominated William Alsup to the district court. Alsup had thought he would follow in the steps of his father, a self-taught civil engineer, when he began college at Mississippi State University in the mid-1960s. Once there, Alsup joined the debate team and learned to construct an effective argument. Almost immediately, he found himself in the midst of the civil rights movement. As president of the student YMCA, which was at the center of the student movement for equal rights, Alsup led fellow students in inviting Aaron Henry, the state NAACP president, to speak on the college campus. University officials threatened to ban the speech, the first at the school by an African American, but the students threatened to go to court. "We are concerned that those in this state who lustily demand the rights of states are often the same who would deny the rights of men," Alsup wrote. Henry gave a powerful speech to a huge crowd in 1967, and Alsup was hooked on the law. "It was a critical point in our campus history," said Alsup. "I was proud of myself that I was on the right side of the issue. And that plus the debating convinced me that I was better off being a lawyer as opposed to being an engineer."

Alsup went to Harvard Law School, then clerked for Supreme Court justice William O. Douglas in the early 1970s. He assisted Douglas in *Roe v. Wade* and the landmark environmental law case *Sierra Club v. Morton,* in which Douglas ruled that inanimate objects have standing to sue in court. At Alsup's induction ceremony in 1999, Douglas's wife, Catherine Douglas Stone, recalled how impressed her husband was with Alsup's modesty, his work ethic, and his love of nature.

Alsup returned to Mississippi and practiced law for six months. He did civil rights work and quickly went broke. He moved to San Francisco to work as a civil litigator for the Morrison and Foerster firm. Alsup was happy being a trial lawyer for the first twenty years he practiced in San Francisco, but he was distressed that the legal profession was shifting from a profession to a business. He applied for a seat on the district court three times. On the third attempt, he said he elicited support from fellow lawyers and an unusual source, Senator Trent Lott, the Republican majority leader from Mississippi, who sent Senator Barbara Boxer a message that Alsup was confirmable in the Republican-controlled Senate. "I don't know what was on his mind," Alsup said. "Maybe he thought it would be kind of cool to have a guy from Mississippi serve on a federal court in San Francisco."

Like Justice Douglas, Alsup has long been attracted to the mountains. Douglas was called to the Appalachian Trail, Alsup to the High Sierra. He has written two works on the Sierra: *Such a Landscape!,* about the 1864 expedition of the California Geological Survey, and *Missing in the Minarets,* about the 1933 search for mountaineer Walter A. "Pete" Starr. Alsup has led more than one hundred Sierra expeditions and spent, all told, more than a year sleeping in the mountains.

In 2005, Alsup ruled that the government must better protect the endangered North Pacific right whale in the only case that has generated him a lot of fan mail, he says. That year, Alsup rejected the federal government's attempt to reduce endangered species protection to the California tiger salamander in Sonoma and Santa Barbara Counties. They were declared endangered in 2003 but reclassified as threatened the following year after a group of developers sued the government. Alsup rejected the reclassification because, he said, it was not based on science. "I can imagine that there are developers and rangers who roll their eyes," Alsup said. "What I say to them is what I say in court. We are here to do what Congress told us to do. If a rancher loses because of the Endangered Species Act, don't blame the judge. Go to Congress and get them to repeal or modify."

In 2005, Alsup put an end to the district court's supervision of the San Francisco public school desegregation plan. Alsup, who took the case after Judge Orrick retired in 2002, questioned whether the consent decree, signed in 1983 and modified in 2001, was still working. He ruled that elected school board officials and administrators could better desegregate the schools. "What is best for the children of San Francisco should be left to the professionals in the district, subject to the voices of all in the community," he wrote.

That year, Alsup sentenced Greg Anderson, the trainer of Barry Bonds, to prison for contempt for refusing to cooperate with a grand jury investigation in the BALCO steroid case. After Anderson was released briefly in 2006, Alsup sent him back to prison again with a warning: "Maybe in sixteen months he will change his mind." Anderson was released in November 2007 but is still not talking.

Alsup and his family received a scare in 2004 when FBI agents told him they suspected that Amr Mohsen, founder and former CEO of the Sunnyvale-based Aptix Corporation, was plotting to kill him. Alsup had ruled against Mohsen in a patent case and had referred criminal charges against him to the US Attorney's office. News of the plot was sobering, the judge said in 2006. "My wife, now that this trial is going on, has had nightmare after nightmare," the judge said. "I haven't had any nightmares. I am pretty fatalistic about things like this, but it has caused me to become more practical in some ways. When I start my car in the morning, I actually glance slightly to see if it looks like anything is askew, like they were trying to put a bomb under my hood. In the old days, we never locked our back door at night. Now we do."

Mohsen was later acquitted of plotting to kill Alsup, but he was convicted of perjury, soliciting arson, and tampering with witnesses. He was sentenced to seventeen years in prison in 2007.

Despite all the drama, Alsup wants to remain in trial court. "This is where ninety percent of the action is; ninety percent of the decisions are actually made in the district court," he said. "They never go up on appeal, and when they do they are almost always affirmed. This is where records are made, witnesses are sworn, jurors are sworn. Blood is on the floor here. So we as judges are like the frontline generals or colonels in a war. We are the ones making the records. After all the shooting is over, it goes up on appeal on that record."

Serendipity

Phyllis Jean Hamilton's career has been "fairly serendipitous," she said in 2006. "I certainly lucked into this position," she said, "because I wasn't projected into it by some preordained game plan."

Hamilton, born in 1952, is from a typical small Midwestern town—Jacksonville, Illinois—about thirty-five miles east of Springfield. Her mother died when she was quite young, and a maternal aunt raised her. Although her aunt had only a ninth-grade education, she worked hard to ensure that Hamilton obtained a good education. Beginning in elementary school, she was placed in advanced classes. "When you are treated as though people think you have some vision, leadership ability, et cetera, you respond to that as a young person," she said. Hamilton had excellent grades and a good rapport with teachers and always knew that she would go to college, even though the majority of graduates of the one high school in town went directly to work at factories or farms or entered the military. In addition to her studies, she worked after school at various jobs, including her favorite as a carhop at Tops Big Boy Hamburgers.

While a foreign exchange student in Switzerland during her junior year of high school, Hamilton met an American student from California who suggested that she apply to Stanford. She was accepted and awarded a scholarship, becoming the first in her family to attend college. Although she had thought about a number of professions, she went to college thinking she wanted to be a veterinarian, but the math was too challenging. She switched to communications and graduated in 1974, and then did what many people who aren't good at math or science do—she went to law school.

She enjoyed studying the law and reveled in the supportive environment of Santa Clara University's law school. Learning the law was like learning a foreign language—sometimes incomprehensible, but satisfying when it clicked. Hamilton took a job in 1976 as a deputy public defender with the Office of the State Public Defender, a new office in California established to handle the appeals of those convicted of felonies. She was trained in writing appeals and making appellate arguments, but decided she was not suited for the work. She left in 1980 and took a non-legal job at a telecommunications company, where she quickly learned she preferred working in a legal environment. Six months later, she was hired as an administrative judge with the Merit Systems Protection Board, an agency that provides employment hearings for federal employees. Work as a quasi-judge appealed to her, and she enjoyed traveling throughout the region's wide jurisdiction, but layoffs changed the feel of the office.

Because of her interest in a non-advocacy role, she volunteered as a temporary judge for the night court at Oakland's municipal court. She was hired in 1985 as the court's first commissioner. She assisted judges by hearing traffic, small claims, and misdemeanor cases. The state trial courts, she learned, were where all the world's problems seemed to end up, and it was a challenge to deal with the tension, animosity, and hostility against the system. "We had two hundred fifty to three hundred on the traffic calendar. Courtrooms were filled; we had x amount of time, and all these people," she said. The challenge was not intellectual. It was managing the huge numbers of people and cases, and the judge represented to them all that was bad about the criminal justice system. "It felt like a public relations job," she said. Hamilton worked for the municipal court for six years before applying for a magistrate judge position on the district court. She was one of five recommended by the merit selection panel, and was chosen by the judges in 1991.

She worked as a magistrate judge for nine years, and then she applied for the district judgeship. What drove her? "Ego. I thought I could do it," she said. "I am who I am because of the experiences that I've had." She was nominated by President Clinton in 2000 to fill Judge Fern Smith's seat on the district court, becoming the second magistrate judge, after Claudia Wilken, to ascend to the Northern District bench.

The most dramatic case in Hamilton's courtroom was probably *United States v. Ngoc-Hanh Thi Dang Nguyen*, involving a Vietnamese refugee who tried to immolate herself in 2001 at the San Francisco Marriott Hotel as a protest against communist rule in Vietnam. Nguyen was accused of taking a container of gasoline into the hotel and trying to light it during a trade conference attended by Vietnamese officials. She was charged with attempted arson, terrorism, and assault on federal agents, who subdued her. Nguyen's 2002 trial attracted packed crowds of Vietnamese refugees who came to lend moral support. Nguyen saw herself as a political prisoner. She argued that she intended to set herself on fire rather than the building. "She gave incredible testimony," said Hamilton, who allowed Nguyen to speak despite the fact that her testimony had little to do with the relevance of the charges. A jury acquitted Nguyen of two counts of terrorism but found her guilty of attempted arson and assault. Hamilton sentenced Nguyen to five years, the mandatory jail term for arson.

The most-watched case to cross Hamilton's court was *Planned Parenthood v. John Ashcroft*. In 2004, Hamilton ruled that the Partial-Birth Abortion Ban Act of 2003, signed by President George W. Bush, was unconstitutional. It was the federal government's first attempt to outlaw an abortion procedure and was seen as a step toward banning abortion entirely. The law would stop abortions performed during the second trimester in which the fetus is removed partially intact. Hamilton signed a temporary restraining order the day after the act was signed in 2003 and held a three-week trial on the case. She wrote that the law would endanger women's health and would violate their right to an abortion.

Similar cases were soon filed in two other states, but Hamilton was determined to decide first. "I didn't want to be influenced by what other judges decided," she said. Hamilton felt on top of her game during the trial. "In sports, you play down or up to your competition," she said. "Here the lawyering was so good, the topic was so interesting, it was easy."

Immediately after her ruling, she received hate mail, e-mails, and phone calls. She knew people would disagree, but she didn't think her name would run across a CNN banner and her photograph would be in newspapers across the country. "It was scary," she said. But she received support from her colleagues, which was a turning point in her career as a district court judge. She had felt buried with work during her first years as a judge and wondered why she had left her magistrate position. Now she felt the decision was worthwhile. As added confirmation, her decision in the case was affirmed by the Ninth Circuit, although that decision was reversed by the Supreme Court.

For much of her time as a district judge, one set of cases has dominated Hamilton's docket. She has presided over the multi-district litigation titled *In Re Dynamic Random Access Memory (DRAM) Antitrust Litigation* since its filing in 2002. The litigation involves allegations of price fixing among many manufacturers in the semiconductor industry.

Dozens of class action lawsuits filed nationally were consolidated before Hamilton. In 2006 and 2007, Hamilton approved antitrust settlements of more than $300 million for direct purchasers of DRAM. Claims by indirect purchasers were still pending as of 2013. Criminal indictments were handed down against six corporations and sixteen executives charged in the price-fixing scandal. All indictments except one resulted in guilty pleas. Corporations paid about $730 million in fines. "Everything that I know about antitrust law I learned on these cases," said Hamilton. "The work has been voluminous, resource intensive, and challenging."

Jeffrey White, who joined the district court in 2002, has always been something of a wild card. Raised in a Democratic family, White grew up somewhat apolitical but found that he voted more frequently for Republicans because he favored the party's approaches to crime and business. So he was considered a Republican when nominated by President Bush. At the end of White's Senate confirmation hearings, his father sat nearby filled with pride, but then confided to Senator Patrick Leahy, the ranking Democrat, about his son: "I didn't even know he was a Republican until he told me he was selected. I don't know what I did wrong."

White laughs at the story, aware that he has always played his politics close to his vest. He believes he was a "stealth candidate" when he applied for the job. He was the first Northern District candidate to make it through the screening process of the California Judicial Advisory Committee, a bipartisan group set up to recommend judicial candidates that can be approved by the Senate. The process took eighteen months. White's not certain how he won the nomination, but he thinks that he may have made it because his politics were not clear to the committee members. "When I look back, it's almost like walking through a minefield blind and drunk, and saying, 'How did I ever get through this?'" he said in a 2006 interview. "Retrospectively, if somebody asked me for a strategy on how to do it, I couldn't tell them. I didn't know what I did that was successful."

Born in New York City in 1945, Jeffrey Steven White received a bachelor's degree from Queens College in 1967. He entered college taking premed courses, but a D in biology and a C in chemistry made him consider other careers. He attended the University at Buffalo Law School, part of the State University of New York, graduating in 1970. He served as a federal prosecutor for his first eight years, doing two stints in the criminal division of the Department of Justice sandwiched around six years as an assistant US Attorney in Maryland. He moved to California in 1978 and worked in private practice until his nomination to fill the seat vacated by Charles Legge.

White's decision-making has been difficult to predict. In 2005, he approved a preliminary injunction that ordered officials at the Contra Costa County Library in Antioch to allow the Faith Center Church Evangelistic Ministries to use the library's public meeting room for discussion, reflection, and prayer. "I struggled with it in terms of my intuitive response, which is typical of judges and me," White said. "Without knowing anything about it, how could this be; we can't allow public libraries to become synagogues, temples, mosques, places of prayer they're not. As I got more into the law it struck me more that that was the right result—the one I reached." The Court of Appeals overturned his decision. Also that year, White ruled that the California red-legged frog—made famous in Mark Twain's story "The Celebrated Jumping Frog of Calaveras County"—was at risk because the federal government was not enforcing sanctions against pesticides. "The government, by its own papers, showed that pesticides are a threat to the frog," he said. "I required them to come up with a plan to address those impacts."

In 2006, Judge White stepped into the BALCO steroids scandal when he found *San Francisco Chronicle* reporters Mark Fainaru-Wada and Lance Williams in contempt of court and ordered them sent to prison for up to eighteen months after they vowed never to reveal how they had gained access to grand jury transcripts that provided content for their newspaper stories and book, *Game of Shadows: Barry Bonds, BALCO, and the Steroids Scandal That Rocked Professional Sports.* The two journalists were waiting on an appeal when former BALCO attorney Troy Ellerman said that he had leaked grand jury transcripts, so they avoided jail time.

White was presiding in Ellerman's case when, in 2007, the judge rejected a plea agreement between prosecutors and defense attorneys. After Ellerman admitted that he was the source of the leaks, his defense attorneys made a deal with the US Attorney stipulating that Ellerman would serve two years in prison and pay a $250,000 fine. White told both sides to work out a harsher sentence or get ready for a full trial.

White's decision did not surprise those familiar with his court, for it was far from the first time the judge had rejected a plea agreement. White believes judges should make independent decisions on sentencing and not simply rubber-stamp plea deals. "Some judges feel that when

FIG. 10-6
San Francisco Chronicle writers Mark Fainaru-Wada (left) and Lance Williams refused to name the source of leaked grand jury testimony quoted in their stories about professional athletes using steroids. © Darryl Bush/San Francisco Chronicle/Corbis.

the parties make an agreement in an adversary proceeding, the court generally should go along with it," White said. "I have a different view that I have an obligation to take into account what they say." So when a prosecutor moves to reduce a defendant's sentenced based on substantial assistance, White looks the deal over carefully. "I believe I owe an obligation to society to determine whether that person has earned a downward departure," he said. "So yes, I am viewed as more of a wild card."

A month after Ellerman's first plea deal, attorneys brought a new one to White. Ironically, in the meantime, President Bush had commuted the sentence of administration official Lewis "Scooter" Libby for his role in leaking grand jury information about a CIA informant. Ellerman's attorney pointed out that Libby was not going to jail for a leak involving national security and his client was going to jail for leaking information about a sports scandal. Judge White would have none of it. The Constitution gave Bush the power to commute sentences, White said, but he was bound to abide by sentencing guidelines. White then criticized Bush, the man who nominated him to the district court: "Under the president's reasoning, any white-collar defendant should receive no jail time, regardless of the reprehensibility of the crime." The judge accepted the new plea agreement and sentenced Ellerman to two and a half years in prison. He did not fine Ellerman but ordered him to talk to law students at ten California schools about being "a fair and honest advocate" within three years after his release.

White said he has been surprised that the quality of lawyering—filing papers on time, being prepared in court, knowing how to try a case—has not been as high as he expected. He's also been surprised at the amount of work. "If you don't act aggressively and affirmatively, and play what I call offense, the job can quickly overwhelm you and become undoable," he said. But perhaps what has surprised him most is how difficult it is to put his personal mark on cases. "I had a view that you can pretty much have some decision-making ability to do the right thing," White said. "But the parameters, the wiggle room, is very small. Every decision must be consistent with the law."

In 2006, a defendant appeared in White's court on the verge of being sentenced to prison for illegal entry into the United States. The man, who had dozens of relatives in the courtroom, now wanted to move back to Mexico and stay there forever. He had come into the country three times illegally, and prosecutors and defense attorneys were seeking a forty-one-month prison sentence.

White asked the defendant how the court could be assured that he would never return to the United States.

"Because I'm now married, have a child," the man replied. "My wife is going to move to Mexico; my sister will move temporarily."

White called the man's wife to the bench, and she confirmed that her new husband was telling the truth. Judge White sentenced the man to time served and released him.

"I told him if you come back into country, you will let me and your family down," said White. "They gave me a standing ovation when I left."

Epilogue

Rome wasn't built in a day, but California nearly was. Taken from Mexico in 1846 and fed by the gold rush of 1849, the isolated coastal colony became a state within only a few years and soon evolved into one of the most important in the union. The first federal court arrived in San Francisco in the spring of 1851 and hasn't caught its breath since.

From physical property in the nineteenth century to intellectual property in the twenty-first, the United States District Court for Northern

California continues to resolve disputes and influence the course of California's economic, agricultural, and cultural development. Fifty-nine men and women have served on the court with lifetime appointments from almost every president since Millard Fillmore. When established, the court encompassed the northern half of the state of California. More than 150 years later, the court's jurisdiction has been reduced to a narrow northern coastal strip of fifteen counties bounded by Oregon to the north and San Luis Obispo County to the south—but the court's caseload and workload continue to grow as California has become the sixth largest economy in the world.

In the 1850s, the gold rush brought hundreds of thousands of immigrants to San Francisco. By 1852, San Francisco was the second busiest port in America. Most who came west never found gold, but they settled in California anyway and made a buck however they could. While the rest of the country was being ripped apart by the Civil War, California's pioneers were busy prospecting for new fortunes, building towns and cities—and suing each other. San Francisco was the hub of the litigious new world being cobbled together from gold dust and sand dunes. The Northern District's early decisions set the tone for the burgeoning state. From deciding the fate of the valuable Spanish and Mexican land grants to establishing civil rights for sailors and Chinese immigrants, the judges of the Northern District court literally tamed California's Wild West, bringing order to the chaos of land allocation, shipping disputes, and immigration hysteria.

And ever since, the court has continued to shape and reflect each generation of Californian history. It was the district court that sorted out conflicting claims after the earthquake and fire of 1906 and made it possible for San Francisco to rebound. It was the district court that rooted out a conspiracy meant to undermine American neutrality at the start of World War I. And it was the court that questioned the legality of the Vietnam War. Chocolate maker Domenico Ghirardelli, boxer Jack Dempsey, longshoreman Harry Bridges, heiress Patty Hearst, author Henry Miller, union organizer Cesar Chavez, spies John Walker and Jerry Whitworth, and assassin Sara Jane Moore as well as the Hells Angels, Apple, Microsoft, Starbucks, and Napster have all had their day in court. The decisions made in the court—not all correct in the light of history—have helped shape San Francisco, Northern California, and the nation. And the cases that spawned those decisions provide a glimpse into the passion and psyche of the American people.

ADDENDUM

John Briscoe

SINCE THE AUTHORS completed their work on the manuscript for this book, five judges have been appointed to the bench of the Northern District of California.

RICHARD SEEBORG earned a degree in history from Yale University in 1978 and graduated from Columbia Law School in 1981, where he was a Harlan Fiske Stone Scholar. He then served as a law clerk to Judge John H. Pratt of the District Court for the District of Columbia.

After his clerkship, Seeborg entered private practice and became a partner at Morrison and Foerster, where he not only acted as a mentor to young associates but also headed up the Christmas toy drive for disadvantaged children and served on the college scholarship committee.

In 1991, Seeborg left the firm to become an assistant US Attorney for the Northern District of California, where he prosecuted a wide variety of complex white-collar and other federal crimes, and became deputy chief of the San Jose US Attorney's office. Renowned for his intellect and integrity, Seeborg was well respected by colleagues and adversaries alike. In an act unprecedented in the history of prosecutors, after one sentencing was over, a defendant's mother came over to hug him. Seeborg also served as adjunct faculty at Santa Clara Law School, where he taught federal criminal practice.

In 1998, Seeborg returned to private practice, but, as he said, "It's a badly kept secret that I wanted to be a judge." Like Claudia Wilken and Phyllis Jean Hamilton, Seeborg began his career on the bench as a magistrate. In 2001, he became a magistrate judge for the district court; in 2009 President Barack Obama nominated Seeborg to the seat vacated by Maxine Chesney. He was confirmed by the Senate and assumed office early in 2010.

Born in Washington, DC, **LUCY KOH** moved as a child with her family to Mississippi, where her mother taught at Alcorn State University, the nation's first historically black land grant college. During this time, Koh was bused to a predominantly African American public school. Many of her classmates lived in poverty. These indelible childhood experiences, she said, led her to work for the NAACP Legal Defense Fund in law school.

One day, upset by teasing she received from classmates in first grade for being Asian, Koh decided to head home from school. Her father said little and let her watch cartoons all that morning. He took her for a cheeseburger lunch, and then dropped her back at school. The two never spoke then or later about the incident, but her father's gentle handling of the situation still serves as his legacy to her, she says.

Koh attended Harvard-Radcliffe Colleges and Harvard Law School, after which she worked for a subcommittee of the Senate Judiciary Committee and for the Justice Department in several positions, including special assistant to the deputy attorney general. In 1997, Koh became an assistant US Attorney for the Central District of California; in 2000 she went into private practice in Silicon Valley.

In 2008, California governor Arnold Schwarzenegger appointed Koh to the Superior Court of California for Santa Clara County, a position she held until becoming a district judge in 2010. Nominated by President Obama to fill the vacant seat left when Ronald Whyte assumed senior status, she is the first federal district court judge of Korean descent and the first Asian American judge in the Northern District.

Judge Koh joined the federal bench in a period of great turnover, and in her few years on the court she has become the most senior of the full-time district judges in San Jose. She presided over the patent infringement case *Samsung v. Apple*, which after a lengthy and contentious trial resulted in a jury verdict awarding Apple $1.05 billion dollars in damages. Her other high-profile cases include a class action lawsuit over iPhone privacy, a series of class action antitrust cases aimed at tech companies, and *Fraley v. Facebook*, a privacy class action case.

At his induction to the federal bench, **EDWARD DAVILA**'s wife, Mary Greenwood, described him as one who inspires the best in people.

Davila graduated from San Diego State University and Hastings College of the Law. In 2001, California governor Gray Davis appointed

Davila to serve as a judge on the Santa Clara County Superior Court. While a superior court judge, he presided over the high-profile case of a Las Vegas couple who had planted a severed human finger in a bowl of chili from a Wendy's fast food restaurant.

Judge Davila is a former president of the Santa Clara County Bar Association and was twice president of the La Raza Lawyers Association of Santa Clara County. In 2006, Davila received the Justice Baryl Salsman Award from the Santa Clara County Bar Association for his contributions to the legal community.

In 2010, President Obama nominated Davila to the Northern District bench to fill the seat vacated when Marilyn Hall Patel assumed senior status, but the Senate recessed without confirming him. Obama re-nominated Davila in January 2011, and he was unanimously confirmed by the Senate the following month.

Born and raised in Oakland, **EDWARD CHEN** earned a bachelor's degree from UC Berkeley, where he had considered majoring in astronomy before becoming enthralled with the civil rights movement. This interest led him to study economics and later to attend law school at Boalt Hall.

After law school, Chen clerked for district judge Charles Renfrew and circuit judge James R. Browning. Chen then entered private practice in San Francisco at Coblentz, Cahen, McCabe and Breyer, and later became a staff attorney for the American Civil Liberties Union. There he was part of the legal team that successfully overturned Fred Korematsu's World War II–era conviction for failing to comply with the Japanese internment order.

In 2001, Chen was chosen as a magistrate judge for the Northern District bench. Eight years later, President Obama nominated him to a federal judgeship, a process that dragged on for nearly two more years due to Republican objections to his work with the ACLU. During the confirmation process, however, he had the unequivocal support of the legal community and of California senator Dianne Feinstein—a Democrat and San Francisco resident—who administered the oath of office at his 2011 induction ceremony. He is the first Chinese American federal judge in the Bay Area.

Judge Chen credits some of his problem-solving skills to his family's habit of giving him math problems starting when he was eight years old.

He has brought these skills to bear on a variety of cases during his tenure on the Northern District bench, from disputes over the ownership rights of a new cancer drug, to the limits on arbitration, to how competing companies acquire supermarket shelf space.

President Obama nominated **YVONNE GONZALEZ ROGERS** to the Northern District Court in 2011. Like Judge Koh and Judge Davila, she served on the California Superior Court prior to her appointment, presiding over about fifty trials. She says that the recent crop of judges with state court experience may have a cross-pollinating effect, as those judges bring prior judicial experience to bear on issues such as voir dire, where federal practice is significantly different from state court practice. Gonzalez Rogers said she is willing to experiment with innovations from other districts, including the practice of requiring pre-motion conferences for summary judgment motions, which she finds helps focus the later briefings and arguments on those motions.

Gonzalez Rogers was raised in San Antonio, Texas. Her father managed properties for the Veterans Administration, and from a young age she spent afternoons and weekends mowing lawns and painting houses. She always assumed she would attend the University of Texas, but she came to the attention of Princeton University through participation in statewide student leadership activities. Following the advice of her favorite seventh-grade teacher, she applied to Princeton and was accepted. It was the only school she applied to besides UT. The Princeton acceptance came as an unwelcome surprise for her parents, who were not eager to see her leave Texas. The day she moved into her Princeton dorm was the first time she'd seen the college.

Though she attended law school at UT, she left Texas again upon graduating and started her career in law in the Bay Area. After practicing at Cooley Godward, she took a mid-career break only to find herself appointed to the Alameda County Civil Grand Jury, a watchdog group that investigates the county and local government. Work there brought her to the attention of local judicial officers and the district attorney, which in turn led to her appointment to the state bench.

Judge **JON S. TIGAR** joined the Northern District Court bench in January 2013. He previously served as a judge on the Alameda County Superior Court for eleven years.

Judge Tigar received degrees in economics and English from Williams College and a law degree from Boalt Hall School of Law (now Berkeley Law School), where he was a member of the Order of the Coif and an articles editor for the *California Law Review*. After graduating from law school, Judge Tigar clerked for Judge Robert S. Vance, a judge of the Eleventh Circuit. During that clerkship, Judge Vance's life was tragically cut short by a mail bomb sent to his home by someone angry with his civil rights decisions. Both Judge Vance's life, during which he was renowned for standing up for the oppressed, and the circumstances of his death made an indelible mark on Judge Tigar, who to this day keeps a picture of Judge Vance in his chambers.

After his clerkship, Judge Tigar practiced law in the litigation department of Morrison and Foerster; in the San Francisco Public Defender's Office as a trial lawyer; and at the law firm of Keker and Van Nest in San Francisco, where he litigated complex commercial cases and became a partner in the firm. Judge Tigar has a distinguished record of public service. He is a member of the American Law Institute, and an adviser to the forthcoming *Restatement (Third) of Torts: Liability for Economic Loss*. From 2006 until 2012 he served as a member of the California Judicial Council's Advisory Committee on Civil Jury Instructions. He has served on the board of directors of the Volunteer Legal Services Corporation, and as a judicial mentor for the Alameda County Bar Association's Judicial Diversity Mentor Project and Centro Legal de la Raza's Youth Law Project. He is frequently asked to speak to both lawyers and judges on a wide variety of topics, including trial practice, evidence, civil discovery, punitive damages, and judicial ethics. He also taught pretrial litigation at Berkeley Law School.

As a judge on the Alameda County Superior Court, Tigar served as the presiding judge of the court's appellate division. In his tenure at the state court, he presided over a variety of complex litigation matters, including the implementation of the statewide consent decree in *Farrell v. Cate,* which concerned reform of California's juvenile justice system. He also presided over a family law department for two and a half years, which he says is the most important assignment he has ever had in his development as a judge. While sitting on the bench, he developed the habit of taping small pieces of paper with quotes on them to the back of the bench. These quotes, which are visible only to the judge himself, remind him to make sure that the litigants who appear before him are—and feel—heard.

WILLIAM H. ORRICK III is the newest judge to join the Northern District bench. Orrick was born in San Francisco. He attended Yale University and Boston College Law School, where he received the Susan Grant Desmarais Award for public service. After graduating, he began his legal career by working for the Georgia Legal Services Program from 1979 to 1984. He joined the San Francisco law firm of Coblentz, Patch, Duffy and Bass in 1984 and continued there for twenty-five years, becoming a partner in 1988.

While in private practice, Orrick served for sixteen years as outside general counsel to the Episcopal Diocese of California, for which he was chancellor. Orrick co-chaired his firm's pro bono committee for many years and was the founding chairman of the firm's diversity committee.

Orrick was recognized as an "outstanding lawyer in public service" by the San Francisco Bar Association. His nonprofit service has also included work as president of the board of trustees of the Good Samaritan Family Resource Center, the North Fork Association, and the Katherine Delmar Burke School.

Orrick's more recent career has hewn more closely to the path forged by his father, William H. Orrick Jr., who served as assistant attorney general for the Civil Division in the Kennedy administration. From 2010 to 2012, William Orrick III served as a deputy assistant attorney general in the Civil Division, returning to an office he had played in as a child. Orrick was in charge of the Office of Immigration Litigation, where he oversaw the work of the more than three hundred lawyers who defend the United States in civil immigration proceedings in federal district and appellate courts.

Judge William Orrick III has now taken the seat on the Northern District bench once held by his father. While he demonstrates the same great intellect and integrity as his father, early litigants appearing before Judge Orrick suggest that, compared to his father, he is "less tremble-inducing."

ACKNOWLEDGMENTS

The Northern District Court Historical Society, who originally commissioned this work, wishes to gratefully acknowledge the following law firms and individuals without whose generous support this book would not have been possible: Altshuler Berzon; Arnold & Porter LLP; Berman DeValerio; Briscoe Ivester & Bazel LLP; Cotchett, Pitre, Simon & McCarthy; Cooley LLP; Covington & Burling LLP; Farella Braun & Martel; Gibson Dunn & Crutcher LLP; Howard Rice, Nemerovski, Canady, Falk & Rabkin; Keker & Van Nest; Latham & Watkins LLP; Lief Cabraser Heimann & Bernstein; Morrison & Foerster; Orrick, Herrington & Sutcliffe, LLP; Pearson Simon Warshaw & Penny; Pillsbury Winthrop Shaw & Pitman; Stoel Rives, LLP; Wilson Sonsini Goodrich & Rosati Foundation; Ashlie Beringer; Rachel Brass; Frederick Brown; Elizabeth Cabraser; Frederick Chung; Paul Collins; Ethan Dettmer; Scott Fink; Frederick Furth; Daniel Kolkey; George Nicoud; Denis Salmon; Joel Sanders; Michael Sitzman; and Michael Wong.

The NDCHS also wishes to express its gratitude to the members of the Book Committee, whose tireless efforts have brought this work to its successful conclusion: Hon. Marilyn Hall Patel, Hon. William Alsup, John Briscoe, William Edlund, Mel Goldman, Richard Odgers, Clara Shin, and Ragesh Tangri.

The NDCHS also extends its appreciation to the Court's exceptional librarians Susan Wong Caulder and John Milton Hendricks.

APPENDIX A

Court Chronology

1850 On September 28, Congress organized California as two judicial districts and authorized one judgeship each for the US district courts in the Northern and Southern Districts. The district courts in California were granted the same civil jurisdiction as US circuit courts, except in appeals and writs of error, which were the jurisdiction of the Supreme Court.

1852 An act directs the sitting judge for the Northern District of California to also serve as the judge for the Southern District.

1855 An act establishes the US Circuit Court for the Districts of California and repeals the authority of the California district courts to exercise the trial jurisdiction of a US circuit court. District courts continues to exercise appellate jurisdiction in certain cases involving land claims.

1866 California is reorganized as a single judicial district with one judgeship authorized for the district court.

1886 California is again divided into the Northern and Southern Districts, with one judgeship authorized for each district.

1907 One additional judgeship is authorized for the Northern District.

1922 One temporary judgeship is authorized for the Northern District.

1927 The temporary judgeship in the Northern District is made permanent.

1938 One additional judgeship is authorized for the Northern District.

1946 One additional judgeship is authorized for the Northern District.

1949 Two additional judgeships are authorized for the Northern District.

1961 Two additional judgeships are authorized for the Northern District.

1966 An act establishes the Eastern and Central Districts of California. It transfers two judgeships from the Northern District to the Eastern District. Two new judgeships are authorized for the Northern District.

1970 Two additional judgeships are authorized for the Northern District.

1978 One additional judgeship is authorized for the Northern District.

1990 Two additional judgeships are authorized for the Northern District. Under the terms of the act, a new judge is to be appointed to any court from which an active judge assumes the duties of a full-time office in federal judicial administration. If the judge returns as an active judge of the court, the first vacancy occurring thereafter will not be filled. This act provided for the appointment of an additional judge to the district court in both 1999 and 2011, when sitting judges Fern Smith and Jeremy Fogel, respectively, became directors of the Federal Judicial Center.

(Source: Federal Judicial Center)

APPENDIX B

While attemps have been made to ensure the accuracy of this information, not all of the historical records were complete, and therefore this data is provided for informational purposes only.

Judges of the Northern District of California

Ogden Hoffman Jr. (1851-1866) (1886-1891)

William W. Morrow (1892-1897)

John Jefferson DeHaven (1897-1913)

William Cary Van Fleet (1907-1923)

Maurice Timothy Dooling (1913-1924)

John Slater Partridge(1923-1926)

Frank Henry Kerrigan (1924-1935)

Adolphus Frederic St. Sure (1925-1949)

Harold Louderback (1928-1941)

Michael Joseph Roche (1935-1964)

Martin Ignatius Welsh (1939-1953)

Louis Earl Goodman(1942-1961)

George Bernard Harris (1946-1983)

Dal Millington Lemmon (1947-1954)

Herbert Wilson Erskine (1949-1951)

Oliver Jesse Carter (1950-1976)

Edward Preston Murphy (1950-1958)

Monroe Mark Friedman (1952-1953)

Oliver Deveta Hamlin Jr. (1953-1958)

Sherrill Halbert (1954-1966)

Albert Charles Wollenberg (1958-1981)

Lloyd Hudson Burke (1958-1988)

William Thomas Sweigert (1959-1983)

Thomas Jamison MacBride (1961-1966)

Alfonso Joseph Zirpoli (1961-1995)

Stanley Alexander Weigel (1962-1997)

Robert Francis Peckham (1966-1993)

Gerald Sanford Levin (1969-1971)

Robert Howard Schnacke (1970-1994)

Samuel Conti (1970-present)

Spencer Mortimer Williams (1971-2008)
Charles Byron Renfrew (1971-1980)
William Horsley Orrick Jr. (1974-2003)
William Austin Ingram (1976-2002)
Cecil F. Poole (1976-1980)
William W. Schwarzer (1976-2009)
Robert Peter Aguilar (1980-1996)
Thelton Eugene Henderson (1980-present)
Marilyn Hall Patel (1980-2012)
Eugene F. Lynch (1982-1997)
John P. Vukasin Jr. (1983-1993)
Charles A. Legge (1984-2001)
Delwen Lowell Jensen (1986-present)
Fern M. Smith (1988-2005)
Vaughn R. Walker (1989-2011)
James Ware (1990-2012)
Saundra Brown Armstrong (1991-present)
Barbara A. Caulfield (1991-1994)
Ronald M. Whyte (1992-present)
Claudia Ann Wilken (1993-present)
Maxine M. Chesney (1995-present)
Susan Yvonne Illston (1995-present)
Charles R. Breyer (1997-present)
Martin J. Jenkins (1997-2008)
Jeremy D. Fogel (1998-present)
William Haskell Alsup (1999-present)
Phyllis Jean Hamilton (2000-present)
Jeffrey Steven White (2002-present)
Richard G. Seeborg (2010-present)
Lucy Haeran Koh (2010-present)
Edward John Davila (2011-present)
Edward Milton Chen (2011-present)
Yvonne Gonzalez Rogers (2011-present)
Jon Steven Tigar (2013-present)
William H. Orrick III (2013-present)
(Source: Federal Judicial Center)

Chief District Judges

Michael Joseph Roche (1948-1958)
Louis Earl Goodman (1958-1961)
George Bernard Harris (1961-1970)
Oliver Jesse Carter (1970-1976)
Robert Francis Peckham (1976-1988)
William Austin Ingram (1988-1990)
Thelton Eugene Henderson (1990-1997)
Marilyn Hall Patel (1997-2004)
Vaughn Richard Walker (2004-2010)
James Ware (2011-2012)
Claudia Ann Wilken (2012-present)

Magistrates and Magistrate Judges

Richard S. Goldsmith (1971-1984)
Owen E. Woodruff Jr. (1971-1984)
David Richard Urdan (1971-1978)
Cameron W. Wolfe (1971-1975)
Larry B. Nord (1971-2003)
Nordin F. Blacker (1971-1986)
Francis J. Carr (1971-1976)
Thomas Henry Rothwell (1975-1983)
Arthur Charles Atteridge (1977-1985)
Frederick J. Woelflen (1977-1991)
F. Steele Langford (1979-1997)
Joan Stevenson Brennan (1982-1998)
Claudia Wilken (1983-1993)
Wayne D. Brazil (1984-1996)
Edward A. Infante (1986-2001)
Patricia V. Trumbull (1987-2010)
William Lee Garrett (1988-2002)
Phyllis J. Hamilton (1991-2000)
Maria-Elena James (1994-present)
Bernard Zimmerman (1995-2012)
James L. Larson (1997-2011)
Elizabeth D. Laporte (1998-present)
Joseph C. Spero (1999-present)
Richard G. Seeborg (2001-2009)

Edward M. Chen (2001–2011)
Howard R. Lloyd (2002–present)
Nandor J. Vadas (2004–present)
Laurel Daniels Beeler (2009–present)
Donna M. Ryu (2010–present)
Paul S. Grewal (2010–present)
Jacqueline Scott Corley (2011–present)
Nathanael M. Cousins (2011–present)
Kandis A. Westmore (2012–present)

Bankruptcy Court Judges

Evan J. Hughes (1926–1964)
Thomas J. Ledwich (1936–1949)
Burton J. Wyman (1936–1960)
Bernard J. Abrott (1949–1968)
Conley S. Brown (1959–1987)
Daniel R. Cowans (1959–1974)
Lynn James Gillard (1960–1975)
Sheridan Downey Jr. (1961–1975)
Robert Elmer Woodward (1964–1966)
Warren C. Moore (1965–1987)
Robert Louis Hughes (1968–1984)
Seymour Jack Abrahams (1975–1986)
Cameron W. Wolfe (1975–1987)
Lloyd King (1975–1992)
Jack James Rainville (1981–1986)
Thomas E. Carlson (1985–present)
Jack James Rainville (1986–1987)
Edward D. Jellen (1987–2012)
Alan Jaroslovsky (1987–present)
Leslie J. Tchaikovsky (1988–2010)
Marilyn Morgan (1988–2010)
Randall J. Newsome (1988–2011)
James Grube (1988–2006)
Arthur S. Weissbrodt (1989–present)
Dennis J. Montali (1993–present)
Roger L. Efremsky (2006–present)
Charles Daniel Novack (2009–present)
Stephen L. Johnson (2010–present)

William J. Lafferty (2011-present)

Mary Elaine Hammond (2012-present)

Hannah L. Blumenstiel (2013-present)

United States Attorneys

(Note: Incomplete records were kept on the appointments of US attorneys, US marshals, and clerks of the court during the early years of the district court. In some cases, the appointment dates are estimated.)

Calhoun Benham (appointed 1850)

Samuel W. Inge (1853)

Caleb Cushing (1853)

William Blanding (1856)

Peter Della Torre (1857)

Calhoun Benham (1860)

William H. Sharp (1861)

Delos Lake (1864)

Frank M. Pixley (1868)

Lorenzo D. Latimer (1869)

Walter Van Dyke (1873)

John M. Coghlan (1876)

Philip Teare (1878)

Samuel G. Hilborn (1883)

John T. Carey (c. 1888)

Charles A. Garter (1890)

Samuel Knight (1894)

Harry S. Foote (1895)

Frank L. Coombe (1899)

Marshall B. Woodworth (1901)

Robert T. Devlin (1905)

John L. McNab (1912)

John W. Preston (1913)

Annette Abbott Adams (1918)

Frank M. Silva (1920)

J. T. Williams (1921)

Sterling Carr (1924)

George J. Hatfield (1925)

I. M. Peckham (1933)

Henry H. McPike (1933)

Frank J. Hennessy (1937)

Chauncey F. Tramutolo (1951)

Lloyd H. Burke (1953)

Robert H. Schnacke (1958)

Lynn J. Gillard (1959)

Lawrence E. Dayton (1960)

Cecil F. Poole (1961)

James L. Browning Jr. (1969)

G. William Hunter (1977)

Rodney H. Hamblin (1981)

Joseph P. Russoniello (1982)

William T. McGivern Jr. (1990)

Joseph A. Mendez (1992)

Michael Joseph Yamaguchi (1993)

Robert S. Mueller III (1998)

David W. Shapiro (2001)

Kevin Vincent Ryan (2002)

Scott N. Schools (interim 2007)

Joseph P. Russoniello (2008)

Melinda L. Haag (2010)

US Marshals

William H. Richardson (appointed 1855)

P. L. Solomon (1858)

William Rabe (1861)

C. W. Rand (1862 or 1866)

William Gouverneur Morris (1869)

E. P. Marcellus (1873)

A. W. Poole (1878)

Moses M. Drew (1882)

John Christian Franks (1886)

William G. Long (1890)

Barry Baldwin (1894)

John H. Shine (1898)

James B. Holohan (1914)

Frederick L. Esola (1924)

George Vice (1933)

John A. Roseen (1949)

Edward J. Carrigan (1950)

John A. Roseen (1952)

Frank O. Bell (1953)

Edward A. Heslep (1961)

George C. Heeg Jr. (interim 1968)

Louis H. Martin (1968)

George E. Tobin (1969)

Frank X. Klien (1974)

Glen E. Robinson (1978)

Reginald Boyd (1990)

James M. Sullivan (1994)

James J. Molinari (1994)

Thomas A. Klenieski (acting 2001)

Federico Lawrence Rocha (2003)

Donald M. O'Keefe (2010)

Clerks of Court

(Note: Some of the early clerks may have been working in the US circuit court for the districts of California.)

John A. Monroe (appointed 1852)

George Pen Johnston (1855)

William H. Chevers (1859)

Henry L. Hyde (1862)

George C. Gorham (1863)

George E. Whitney (1867)

Edward B. Cotter (1871)

Southard Hoffman (1876)

George E. Morse (1897)

John P. Brown (1905)

Walter B. Maling (1912)

Carl W. Calbreath (1943)

James P. Welsh (1961)

Chris C. Evensen (1969)

Charles J. Ulfers (1972)

Fergus R. Pettigrew (interim 1973)

William L. Whittaker (1974)

Richard Wieking (1989)

(Source: US District Court for the Northern District of California Library)

A NOTE ON SOURCES

The authors depended on firsthand information whenever possible in recreating the history of the United States District Court for the Northern District of California. Our major source of information about cases came from the National Archives in San Bruno, keeper of district court papers. The staff in San Bruno was infinitely helpful as we searched hundreds of case files, exam motions and opinions, official records, and exhibits, dating back to Mexican and Spanish California.

At the National Archives in College Park, Maryland, we looked through correspondence about the appointment of district court judges, marshals, clerks, and US attorneys dating back to the 1800s.

Crucial to our research were newspaper articles about the district court. Northern California is blessed with fine journalists who have covered the courts assiduously since Ogden Hoffman Jr. stepped forward as the first district court judge. Reporters from the *San Francisco Chronicle, San Francisco Examiner,* and their daily newspaper predecessors, as well as the from the *San Francisco Daily Journal* and the *San Francisco Recorder* legal publications are the true historians of the court. This story could not have been gathered without their work.

We also had the unique and wonderful opportunity to interview twenty district court judges and court officials. Their look back at their careers and their insight into the significance of the court was crucial in helping us understand the impact of the court in contemporary times.

To get a sense of the court decades ago, we depended on a mountain of books by authors who brought the court and the issues surrounding the court alive in a treasury of San Francisco history. Many of our most worthwhile guides are mentioned in the text. The many collections at the Bancroft Library—especially at the library's Regional Oral History Office, which has interviewed a dozen district court judges—and the archives at the district court itself, some produced by the Northern District Historical Society, the impetus for this book, were also invaluable sources. We thank the society for its vision in seeking journalists, not legal historians, to tell the vital story of the court.

All of this information would not be helpful if it were not made available. For years, we scoured the Bay Area's best and most inviting libraries to find books and periodicals that would allow us to travel back in time. Most helpful were the San Francisco History Room at the San Francisco Public Library, the Ninth Circuit Library in the Phillip Burton Federal Building and United States Courthouse in San Francisco, the Bancroft Library at the University of California in Berkeley, the San Francisco Maritime Museum Library, the Dr. Martin Luther King Jr. Library in San Jose, and the University of California Hastings Law Library in San Francisco.

Hundreds of people assisted us in our trek. One person, attorney John Briscoe, was with us from the start. We dedicate this book to him and to his remarkable love for life and learning.

—Richard Cahan, Pia Hinckle, and Jessica Royer Ocken

INDEX

Johnson, Walter Perry, 191
Johnson, William Penn, 80
Johnston, James A., 207
Jones v. City and County of San Francisco, 392
Jones, Arnold, 393
Jones, James McHall, 6, 7
Jones, Jim, 393-399
Jones, Marion, 457
Jones, Sam, 373
Jones, William Carey, 61
Jonestown, 394-399, *397*
Jordan, Frederick W., 146-148
Jouan, Augustus, 84
Jue, George K., 271
Jung, Ah Lung, 122-123
jury selection process, 213-215
Kapp, Joe, 338-341
Karesh, Joseph, 246
Kassman, Marty, 462
Kearney, Dennis, 96, 114, 115
Keating, Kenneth B., 263-265
Kefauver Committee, 259
Kelleher, Robert J., 437
Keller, G. Frederick, *104*
Kelley, John, 212, 215
Kennedy, John F., 283, 288, 302, 347, 363, 364
Kennedy, Robert, 288
Kent, Roger, *346*
Kerrigan, Frank Henry, 174, 186-188, 191, 192, 196
King, Martin Luther Jr., 411
Kirk, Charles, 300
Knight, H. L., 115
Knowland, Joseph R., 191
Knowland, William F., 253, 272, 274-276
Knowles, Elijah E., 34-35
Koh, Lucy, 484
Kopp, Quentin, 352
Korematsu v. United States, 226-230; see also Korematsu, Fred Toyosaburo
Korematsu, Fred Toyosaburo, 221-224, 226-230, *231,* 240, 408, 485
Kraszewski v. State Farm, 412-413
Kreiger, Albert J., *417*
Kuchel, Thomas, 272, 274, 276
Kuwabara, Masaaki, 233-234
Ladar, Jerold, 281, 296

LaGuardia, Fiorello H., 196-197
Lake, Delos, 3, 86
Land, John, 26, 31
Landrum-Griffin Act (1959), 280-281
Lang, Julian, *373*
Langford, F. Steele, 357
Larkin, Thomas O., 69
Larson, James, 430, 431
Lasky, Moses, 341
Lau v. Nichols, 353
Laurie, Annie, 188
Law and Order Party, 38, 41, 43
Layton, Larry, 395-399
Lazarenko, Pavel, 468
Leach, Frank A., 143
Leake, W. S. "Sam," 197-198
Lee, Archy, 80
Leese, Jacob P., 66
Legge, Charles A., 391, 422, *441, 447,* 448, 478
Lemmon, Dal Millington, 252, 271, 272, 273
Leon Willard and Company, 156
Lessing, George, 26, 29-30
Levi Strauss Realty Company, 156-157
Levin, Gerald S., 310, 311
Lewis v. Casey, 391
Lewis, Marvin E., 464
Libby, I. Lewis "Scooter," 316, 479
Limantour, José Yves, 83-84, *85*
Lincoln, Abraham, 72, 77, 87, 90, 101
Lippmann, Walter, 217
Little, Russell, 432
longshoremen's strike, 209-212, 247-251
Louderback, Davis, 194
Louderback, Frances Caroline Smith, 194
Louderback, Harold, 194-201, *195,* 231
LSD, 285-286,
Lundeberg, Harry, 210
Lynch, Eugene F., 418-419, *441,* 467
MacBride, Thomas, 363-364
MacInnis, James M., 207, 248-250, *251*
Madrid v. Gomez, 389-390
mafia, 257, 259, 310, 366, 400, 417-418
Magistrates Act, 345
Majus, John George, 234
Malcolm, Janet, 419
Malley, George "Pat," 467
Malone, William M., *346*
Maloney, James Reuben, 40-41

ABOUT THE AUTHORS

RICHARD CAHAN is the author or coauthor of more than a dozen books on a variety of topics, ranging from baseball to newspapers, snapshots, art, and law. His most recent book is *Vivian Maier: Out of the Shadows* (CityFiles Press, 2012). He worked as the picture editor of the *Chicago Sun-Times* from 1983 to 1999 but left to direct CITY 2000, a project that documented Chicago in the year 2000. Since then, he has served as an independent scholar at the Newberry Library in Chicago and as a program officer at the Richard H. Driehaus Foundation. He is the author of an acclaimed history of the US District Court for the Northern District of Illinois, *A Court That Shaped America* (Northwestern University Press, 2002).

PIA HINCKLE is a San Francisco–based writer and editor. She is the publisher of *The FruitGuys Almanac*, a web magazine focused on healthy living, cooking, and sustainable farming. She was a Knight-Bagehot Fellow at the Columbia University Graduate School of Journalism and has written for a number of publications, including the *Columbia Journalism Review*, the *San Francisco Chronicle*, *Fairness and Accuracy in Reporting*, the *San Francisco Business Times*, and *Newsweek*, as well as the *San Francisco Bay Guardian*, where she was managing editor, and the *San Francisco Examiner*, where she was the business editor.

JESSICA ROYER OCKEN is a freelance writer and editor based in Chicago. Her clients have included the *Chicago Tribune*, Content That Works, and Omnific Publishing, and she's written on topics from technology to teenagers, health and wellness, and fashion and design. She contributed an essay chapter to *Fantasy Girls: Gender in the New Universe of Science Fiction and Fantasy Television* (Rowman and Littlefield, 2000), as well as to *McDonald's @ 50* (Imagination, 2005), and she served as staff writer for CITY 2000. She holds a master's degree with an emphasis in magazine writing from the Missouri School of Journalism at the University of Missouri and is a 1998 graduate of the National Critics Institute in Waterford, Connecticut.

HEYDAY
into California

About Heyday

Heyday is an independent, nonprofit publisher and unique cultural institution. We promote widespread awareness and celebration of California's many cultures, landscapes, and boundary-breaking ideas. Through our well-crafted books, public events, and innovative outreach programs we are building a vibrant community of readers, writers, and thinkers.

Thank You

It takes the collective effort of many to create a thriving literary culture. We are thankful to all the thoughtful people we have the privilege to engage with. Cheers to our writers, artists, editors, storytellers, designers, printers, bookstores, critics, cultural organizations, readers, and book lovers everywhere!

We are especially grateful for the generous funding we've received for our publications and programs during the past year from foundations and hundreds of individual donors. Major supporters include:

Anonymous (4); Alliance for California Traditional Arts; Arkay Foundation; Judy Avery; James J. Baechle; Paul Bancroft III; BayTree Fund; S. D. Bechtel, Jr. Foundation; Barbara Jean and Fred Berensmeier; Berkeley Civic Arts Program and Civic Arts Commission; Joan Berman; John Briscoe; Lewis and Sheana Butler; California Civil Liberties Public Education Program; Cal Humanities; California Indian Heritage Center Foundation; California State Parks Foundation; Keith Campbell Foundation; Candelaria Fund; John and Nancy Cassidy Family Foundation, through Silicon Valley Community Foundation; Charles Edwin Chase; Graham Chisholm; The Christensen Fund; Jon Christensen; Community Futures Collective; Compton Foundation; Creative Work Fund;

Board of Directors

Getting Involved

To learn more about our publications, events, membership club, and other ways you can participate, please visit www.heydaybooks.com.